POLITICS AND SOCIETY
IN THE USSR

Also by David Lane

The Roots of Russian Communism (1969)

Politics and Society in the USSR

David Lane
Lecturer in Sociology
University of Essex

Random House
New York

ISBN: 0–394–31547–2

Library of Congress Catalog Card Number: 70–141442

Manufactured in the United States of America by
The Book Press, Inc., Brattleboro, Vermont.

First American Edition

1 3 5 7 9 8 6 4 2

Contents

List of Tables

A *

List of Diagrams

List of Maps

List of Charts

Acknowledgements

The author and publisher would like to thank the following for permission to quote from copyright sources: Novosti Press Agency for 'Basic Principles of Legislation in the USSR' and 'Union's Report on Marriage and the Family'; Frederick A. Praeger, Inc. for diagram from Z. Brzezinski, *Ideology and Power in Soviet Politics*; Office Statistique des Communautes Europeennes for 'Basic Statistiques; Collins Publishers for material from N. Struve, *Christians in Contemporary Russia*; Workers' Press for material from *The Twentieth Congress and World Trotskyism;* Routledge and Kegan Paul for material from R. Schlesinger, ed., *Changing Attitudes in Soviet Russia* ('The Family in the USSR'); Soviet Booklets for 'Rules of the CPSU'; Basil Blackwell Publisher for J. R. Boyd, 'The Origin of Order No. 1' from *Soviet Studies*; Houghton-Mifflin for 'Code of Moral Education Recommended by Soviet Academy of Pedagogic Sciences' from *The Changing Soviet School*.

Preface

Some justification is perhaps needed to add one more book to the enormous volume of writing on Bolshevism and Soviet Russia. While there are many excellent books on certain aspects of the USSR, particularly its history and politics, there is nothing which for university students gives an overview including history, politics and sociology. In the study of Soviet Russia, a knowledge of one is crucial to the understanding of another. Though it has been recognised that politics has played an important role in shaping the structure of social institutions such as the family and the school, the more social aspects have generally been neglected at the expense of the political. But they are important and should be studied in their own right and in the way they have developed through time. I have, therefore, tried to provide a text-book which is wider in scope than most others used by students of Soviet society: there is, for example, a discussion of the problems of class and status, the functions of the family, the structure of nationalities and the role of pressure groups in the political process. These topics are included in addition to the traditional study of the Communist Party, the Soviets, the economy, the ideology of Marxism–Leninism and the historical background. I have sought to bring together the fruits of research, conducted both in the west and in the USSR, to give a synoptic view of Soviet society studied from the viewpoint of the social sciences. While the political process is examined as a political 'system', other more traditional ways of study, such as the description of political 'institutions', have not been excluded. All methods have their merits.

Among the most crucial problems of writing an introductory book about the USSR are those of selection and emphasis. Here the Soviet Union is depicted as a modernising industrial society and those past events and policies have been selected which elucidate the present. I have concentrated more on structures than on personalities and, as political history is well covered in other books, I have minimised it in favour of economic and social history. Though conflict between political elites is studied, the details of personal intrigue between Soviet leaders have been kept to a minimum to the advantage of the study of the social composition of the Communist Party and parliamentary bodies. The particulars of the administrative structure of

local government have had to be ignored and more space is given to the role
of groups in the political process. As the USSR sees itself as a competitor
to the political systems and social order of the west, much writing about it is
infused with political bias. I have tried to describe Soviet society in its own, as
it were 'official', terms while also taking into account the major criticisms
made by non-Soviet commentators. My own viewpoint is to regard the modern
USSR as a particular species of industrial society which in many ways is
similar to that of advanced western societies but which in other respects has
peculiar and unique features.

It is hoped that the book will contribute to a more comparative study of
society: not only to bring home to Soviet 'area specialists' the fact that
Soviet society is in many ways like other industrial societies, but also to
awaken the interests of sociologists and others in the problems of 'directed'
social change and in the structure of a command or state socialist society.
As well as for students of comparative politics, political sociology and
comparative sociology, the book is intended for those who study Soviet society
as a component in language and literature and regional studies courses; it is
also my hope that it might be useful to other readers, not necessarily studying
at universities, who have an interest in the development and structure of the
Soviet Union.

The book has the following plan. In the first chapter the main tenets of
Marxist–Leninist ideology are considered. It might be emphasised that there
are many kinds of Marxism and I have taken as a point of departure the Soviet
variety, for this is what is most relevant to the understanding of Soviet
society. Next, in Chapter 2, I summarise the social and economic characteristics of the Tsarist empire, from the Emancipation of the Serfs in 1861 to the
Revolution of 1917 and I bring out the attitude of the Bolsheviks to social
and political change. Here are described not only the events of 1917 but also
the main reasons for the successful seizure of power by the Bolsheviks. In
Chapters 3 and 4, the historical development of Soviet Russia is outlined.
First, I consider the major policy decisions which were taken between 1917
and the beginning of the Second World War, then go on to evaluate their
chief effects (industrialisation, centralisation and collectivisation). This is
followed by a summary of the USSR's changing role in the international
arena. These chapters are not intended to be full-blooded histories but are
designed to give the reader an understanding of the development of the
Soviet Union and some of the dilemmas which her leaders have had to face.
Here again both the perspective of the ruling Bolsheviks and some of the
views of their critics are noted.

In the next four Chapters (5 to 8), we turn from historical narrative to the
political aspects of contemporary Soviet society. In Chapter 5, are described
the main political institutions – the structure of the Communist Party of the

Soviet Union and the Soviets (or parliaments). Chapter 6 deals with theories about power and society in Soviet Russia which non-Soviet writers have developed; for example, the bureaucratic, state capitalist, industrial society and totalitarian models. In Chapters 7 and 8 we focus on political processes, the functions of the Communist Party and pressure groups. Finally, roughly the second half of the book is devoted to the economic and social aspects of Soviet society. In Chapters 9 and 10 are outlined the structure of the economy, the nature of management and labour relations and the level of living standards. Chapters 11 to 14 are concerned with the social system: the family, social classes and strata, nationalities and religions, and the structure and function of educational institutions. In these chapters, an historical introduction shows how such aspects of Soviet life have changed since the October Revolution under the impact of Marxist ideology and other factors.

A feature of the book is the addition of adaptations or readings from original sources which illustrate or expand points made in the text. Longer pieces, such as the constitution, and statistics are placed in appendices. Wherever possible, I have referred to English language sources so that the widest possible range of readers may use them. Reference to place and date of publication is made in footnotes. Unless otherwise stated, books originate in London. The bibliographies at the end of each chapter contain full details of books cited.

Authors are indebted to many people. I am grateful to many students at Essex and Birmingham Universities and to members of University Extension classes in Coventry and London who have provided critical audiences to many of the chapters in this book which originated as lectures. Ron Amann, Bob Davies, Peter Frank, Geoff Hoskings, Mary McAulay and Alan Ryan were kind enough to comment on and suggest improvements to parts of the manuscript. I am particularly grateful to Jan Maher and my wife who have read the whole book and have made numerous suggestions.

Department of Sociology   David Lane
University of Essex
August 1969

THE UNION OF SOVIET SOCIALIST REPUBLICS

1 Lithuania S.S.R.
2 Latvia S.S.R.
3 Estonia S.S.R.
4 Moldavia A.S.S.R.
5 Mordvinia A.S.S.R.
6 Chuvash A.S.S.R.
7 Mari A.S.S.R.
8 Tatar A.S.S.R.
9 Udmurt A.S.S.R.
10 Bashkir A.S.S.R.
11 Abkhaz A.S.S.R.
12 Adzhar A.S.S.R.
13 Kabardin A.S.S.R.
14 North Osetia A.S.S.R.
15 Georgia S.S.R.
16 Dagestan A.S.S.R.
17 Armenia A.S.S.R.
18 Nakhicheva A.S.S.R.
19 Azerbaidzhan S.S.R.
20 Kalmyt A.S.S.R.

ICELAND
SCOTLAND
ARCTIC OCEAN
WRANGEL I.
Kamchatka Peninsula
JAPAN
SAKHALIN
SEA OF JAPAN
Vladivostok
Khabarovsk
Okhotsk
CHINA
NEW SIBERIAN IS.
Verkhoyansk
Yakutsk
YAKUTSK A. S. S. R.
Vilyuisk
SEVERNAYA ZEMLYA
Igarka
BURYAT A.S.S.R.
Ulan-Ude
Lake Baikal
Irkutsk
MONGOLIA
TUVIN A.S.S.R.
Krasnoyarsk
NOVAYA ZEMLYA
Salekhard
Tomsk
Novosibirsk
Omsk
Tobolsk
R. S. F. S. R.
KOMI A.S.S.R.
Syktyvkar
Sverdlovsk
Perm
Karaganda
Lake Balkash
Alma Ata
CHINA
KHIRGIZ S.S.R.
TADZHIK S.S.R.
Tashkent
UZBEKISTAN S.S.R.
AFGHANISTAN
FINLAND
KARELIA A.S.S.R.
Lake Onega
Lake Ladoga
WHITE SEA
Archangel
Ufa
Kazan
Gorky
MOSCOW
Kuibyshev
ARAL SEA
Karsakpai
KAZAKHSTAN S. S. R.
Ashkabad
TURKMENISTAN S.S.R.
Leningrad
R.S.F.S.R.
Riga
Minsk
BYELORUSSIA S.S.R.
Kiev
UKRAINE S.S.R.
Odessa
POLAND
ROMANIA
BLACK SEA
Kharkov
Rostov
Volgograd
Astrakhan
Guryev
CASPIAN SEA
Baku
Tbilisi
TURKEY
PERSIA

PERSIA

Miles
0
500

THE UNION OF SOVIET SOCIALIST REPUBLICS

1

THE IDEOLOGY OF MARXISM-LENINISM

The Soviet Union is a country which, at least ostensibly, is devoted to the achievement of a particular goal – the building of a communist society. To achieve this goal, the Soviet rulers have employed different methods of gaining compliance of the population. Amitai Etzioni has suggested that there are three means by which such compliance may be attained. These are coercion, remuneration and persuasion or normative power[1] and we shall see that in Soviet society combinations of all methods have been used. *Coercion*, including the application of threats and the infliction of pain or death, was important in the terror after the revolution and during Stalin's rule. *Remunerative or utilitarian power* (the allocation of rewards, financial or in kind) has been utilised in the economy during the whole of the Soviet period, but especially in more recent times. *Normative power*, or persuasion, entails the allocation and manipulation of values and symbols; ideology is a form of normative power for it may inculcate certain responses in the individual towards his environment – towards the legitimacy of the rulers, or the powerful, and towards the legitimacy of the rewards and privileges enjoyed by certain groups.

Ideology, the subject of this chapter is in Mannheim's terms a pattern of beliefs which justifies the social order and which explains to man 'his historical and social setting'.[2] But it is not simply an instrument used by the political rulers to ensure compliance, ideology also acts as a constraint on their own activity, for it gives rise to expectations on the part of the governed which the rulers must try to fulfil.

The dominant political institution in the USSR is the Communist Party of the Soviet Union, and its ideology is based on Marxism-Leninism. The kind of Marxism embodied in the Soviet *weltanschauung* (world view) and official policy is of a simplified and often dogmatic type but it provides a unifying and integrating set of values both for the description of the present and for the

---

[1] Amitai Etzioni, *A Comparative Analysis of Complex Organisations* (1961), Chapter 1. These are similar to C. Wright Mills's distinction between coercion (the use of force), authority (power justified by the beliefs of the voluntarily obedient) and manipulation (power wielded unbeknown to the powerless). C. Wright Mills, 'The Structure of Power in American Society', *British Journal of Sociology* No. 3 (1958).

[2] Karl Mannheim, *Ideology and Utopia* (1936), p. 239.

prescription of the future. It provides a vocabulary in which Soviet politics are discussed. Here we are not primarily concerned with whether Marxism-Leninism offers a true or false analysis of society nor with whether the Soviet rulers present a correct interpretation of Marx. Our main task is to describe briefly the ideology of the Communist Party and the ways it has adapted the original ideas of Marx. As an introduction, we need to become acquainted with the Soviet version of the underlying theory and with the chief criticisms of it.

Marxism as social and political theory seeks to explain the course of human history and the structure of past, present and future societies: it postulates a model of society and an explanation of the nature of social change. There are many interpretations of Marxism as a doctrine or theory of society. In this book we are primarily interested in the Soviet version, the authoritative statement of which may be studied in *Fundamentals of Marxism-Leninism*.[1] But Soviet and non-Soviet Marxists alike share certain common views about the nature of societies and the process of social change. These basic tenets of Soviet Marxism may be explained under three main headings: the materialist conception of history, the political economy of capitalism, the nature of socialism and communism. It is over whether the USSR fulfils sufficient conditions to qualify as a 'socialist' society that there is much disagreement between Soviet and non-Soviet Marxists.

The Materialist Conception of History

Marxists hold that the 'primary component' of the life of a society is labour which provides the material means to control nature, and which makes tools and creates cultural life.

> . . . We must begin by stating the first presupposition of all human existence, and therefore of all history, namely, that men must be in a position to live in order to be able to 'make history'. But life involves before everything else eating and drinking, a habitation, clothing, and many other things. The first historical act is, therefore, production of material life itself. This is indeed a historical act, a fundamental condition of all history, which today, as thousands of years ago, must be accomplished every day and every hour merely in order to sustain human life.[2]

The 'productive forces' of a society are on the one hand, the instruments of production (tools) and, on the other, labour. Production is social and derived from interdependent human activity, based on the division of labour. Save in very simple societies, the ownership of the productive forces is separated

---

[1] Foreign Languages Publishing House (Moscow, 1963). See also H. Fleischer, *Short Handbook of Communist Ideology* (Dordrecht, 1965).

[2] 'The German Ideology', cited by T. B. Bottomore and M. Rubel, *Karl Marx, Selected Writings in Sociology and Social Philosophy* (1963), p. 75.

from those who use them. This phenomenon, the ownership of the means of production separated from labour, gives rise to social classes. At the capitalist stage of society, the two main classes determined by the ownership of capital goods (the ruling class), or non-ownership (the exploited class) are the bourgeoisie and the proletariat. Class in the Soviet Marxist sense is not concerned with gradations of status or honour as it is sometimes used in non-Marxist literature; it is a general concept bringing together into one category those who are 'employed' and those who own and live off property: the proletariat, the bourgeoisie.

The course of human history is explained by Marx in terms of such class relationships: 'The history of all hitherto existing society is the history of class struggles.'[1] The causes of social change are not to be found in ideas, but in material processes: 'The ultimate causes of all social changes and political revolutions are to be sought, not in the minds of men, in their increasing insight into eternal truth and justice but in changes in the mode of production and exchange. They are not to be sought in the philosophy but in the economics of the epoch concerned.'[2] The ruling classes and, therefore, the forms of economic and social relations, are not identical in all societies which are classified into five 'ideal types':[3] primitive-communal, slave, feudal, capitalist and communist.[4]

In primitive-communal society there were no social classes. Classes were first formed because some individuals had control over weapons, stocks of materials and other human beings – slaves. This form of 'slave society', however, could not continue indefinitely. Within it another class developed based on ownership of land and knowledge of agricultural techniques. By a revolutionary process the landowners defeated the slave-owning classes and created feudal society. Feudal society[5] again developed productive forces in the form of manufacture and international trade and the groups of traders, merchants and industrialists who needed to meet demands for trade and commerce generated by feudal society, formed the basis of a new capitalist class which overthrew feudalism and set up the capitalist form of society in its place. Capitalism in turn is to dig its own grave, the working class fulfilling its class interest by the abolition of capitalism and the establishment of communist society.

Each class, therefore, goes through three functional relationships to society.

[1] 'Communist Manifesto', in K. Marx and F. Engels, *Selected Works* (Moscow, 1958), vol. 1, p. 34.

[2] F. Engels, *Anti-Dühring* (Moscow, 1954), p. 369.

[3] By 'ideal type' we mean an idealization of a pure form. In practice, societies are much more fluid and may contain elements of many of these types.

[4] *Fundamentals of Marxism-Leninism* (Moscow, 1961), p. 154. An alternative formulation is Asiatic, ancient, feudal, bourgeois, and communist. K. Marx, 'Preface to the Critique of Political Economy', in *Selected Works* (Moscow, 1958), vol. 1, p. 363.

[5] For further discussion see George Lichtheim, *Marxism* (1961), part 4.

First, it is a revolutionary class struggling to assert its own power. Second, it is dominant, being necessary for and promoting economic development. Third, it is in decline being a parasitical social group no longer essential for the further growth of society.

The theoretical underpinning of Marxism-Leninism is the dialectic which explains the relationships between all forms of matter and all processes of change. Matter (or unity) is divided into opposing elements which interact one with another.

A developing thing has within it the embryo of something else. It contains within itself its own antithesis, a 'negating' element which prevents it from remaining inert and immutable. It contains an objective contradiction; opposite tendencies operate within it and a mutual counteraction or 'struggle' of opposite forces or sides takes place leading eventually to the resolution of the contradiction to a radical qualitative change of the thing.[1]

In other words, matter may be divided into 'thesis' and 'antithesis'. The two elements react on each other to form a new state, 'synthesis'. An example from history was given above when it was pointed out that medieval society was composed of two elements: the landowning gentry (thesis) and the bourgeoisie (antithesis). Through the struggle of these two social groups, the contradiction is resolved in the synthesis of capitalism. Capitalism itself is subject to the same laws and within it, the embryo of socialism is to be found. This interacts with the thesis of capitalism to form a new synthesis, communism. The dialectic is concerned with the processes or logic of change, with the ways in which in nature one thing is transformed into another. It does not provide us with a knowledge of the structure of nature. The anatomy of human society is described by Marxists in terms of basis and superstructure. We may explain these concepts by considering the Marxist interpretation of capitalism.

Capitalism

Capitalism is important not only because it is the form of society in contemporary Britain and the United States, but because it is the last class society. Its fundamental features are explained by the Marxist notions of basis (or base) and superstructure.

The economics of society, or the nature of its productive forces, form the basis, which is made up of two elements: the forces of production (the tools, or technology, or the stock of capital goods) and the relations to the means of production – the property relationships. The kind of technology or tools (the power-press or automated production line) together with its ruling class (fac-

---

[1] *Fundamentals of Marxism-Leninism* (Moscow, 1961 ed.), pp. 94-95. Other Marxists distinguish between what Marx and Engels said. Marx saw the dialectic only in the process of history, whereas Engels also applied it to nature. See G. Lichtheim, *Marxism* (1961), pp. 245-6.

tory directors or bankers) shape the remaining social institutions of the society, which are called the superstructure.[1] 'The sum total of these relations of production constitutes the economic structure of society – the real foundation, on which rise legal and political superstructures and to which correspond definite forms of social consciousness.'[2] In capitalist society, the superstructure includes, for example, such institutions as the government, political parties, religious bodies, voluntary associations, the educational system, the press and mass media. The superstructure is made up of human associations of these groups and the ideas and processes which are part of them. The 'dominant institutions' (such as the government, judiciary and mass media) promote the interests and share the values of the ruling class.

The relationship between basis and superstructure is often regarded as a weak link in Marxist theory. It is often seen as a monistic interpretarion of society: changes in the superstructure being determined by the basis. But Engels in one passage recognised that the superstructure could influence the basis:

> . . . Because we denied that the different ideological spheres, which play a part in history, have an independent historical development, we were supposed therewith to have denied that they have any *historical efficacy* . . . a historical factor, once it has been brought into the world by another – ultimately economic factor – is able to re-act upon its surroundings and even affect its own causes.[3]

The superstructure also includes the institutions of the exploited – in capitalist societies, the working class has its own values expressed in political organisations, such as trade unions and socialist parties. Such groups cannot live co-operatively with the capitalist class: conflict is inherent in the exploiting relationship and when capitalist society has reached its zenith, a revolutionary transformation takes place, bringing to power the working class. In terms of dialectics, the thesis is the capitalist class, its opposite (or antithesis) the working class, the revolutionary transformation creates the synthesis, in this case communist society.

Revolutionary change comes about because the class interests of the worker and capitalist do not allow for reconciliation. The capitalist is driven by inexorable economic laws to make profit. Competition forces him to keep his costs as low as possible. Increases in productivity are limited and therefore reductions in the total wage bill must be made. Technological advance giving economies of scale to large firms forces the small ones out of production through price competition. Prices fall, however, not only because of changes

---

[1] There is a basis and superstructure in all forms of society. Here examples are given from the capitalist stage.

[2] K. Marx, 'Preface to The Critique of Political Economy', *Selected Works* (Moscow, 1958), vol. 1, p. 363.

[3] Engels, 'Letter to Mehring' 14.7.1893, cited by S. Hook, *Towards the Understanding of Karl Marx* (1933), pp. 282-3.

in supply conditions but also because of insufficiency of demand. Demand falls because wages of the employed are forced down by firms seeking to reduce prices, because technological innovation results in redundancy, and because a part of the 'surplus' received from labour (in the form of profits) remains unspent. These economic forces provide the objective conditions for revolution.

Now we may turn to another component of Marxist theory, the theory of value. By value, Marx means the amount of labour which is expended on the production of a good.[1] The worker does not receive the full reward for his labour: a part is alienated from him and goes to the capitalist: this is 'surplus value'. The extent to which the worker is exploited is measured by the ratio of surplus value to the value embodied in a commodity. As labour is purchased by the capitalist he is able to pay the worker an amount less than his labour value. This is because the bargaining process is weighted against the worker: there are many workers chasing few jobs and there is a tendency for real wages to fall. The theory has important social and political implications. The profit of the capitalist is not a reward: capital is not a scarce factor of production which justifies a reward, but profit represents a political relationship in which the capitalist is able to extract from the worker part of his labour. In the Marxist schema there can be no economic or moral justification for profit. This economic relationship forms the antagonistic character of class relations. At the same time it provides the legitimacy for the expropriation of the capitalist: his private property is theft; only the working class has a right to the produce of property, for the working class alone is the producing class.

The ideology of capitalism, argues Marx, seeks to deceive the worker, to persuade him that profit is justified as a payment for risk or the consumption foregone by the investor, that capitalist and worker have a common not a conflicting interest. To accept such views is to show one's 'false consciousness': that is, to be unaware of one's real class interest. Marx believed that the proletariat would become class conscious. The education necessary to operate a highly developed economy together with the growing intensity of the class struggle, of the increasing 'immiseration of the proletariat' would transform it from a class 'in itself' to a class 'for itself'.[2] In this way the subjective psychological and political condition of the proletariat coincides with the objective forces described above.

Along with the constantly diminishing number of the magnates of capital, who usurp and monopolise all advantages of this process of transformation, grows the mass of misery, oppression, slavery, degradation, exploitation; but with this too

---

[1] Unlike in modern economic theory where value and price are identical.

[2] A class 'in itself' may be identified simply by the fact of class position (workers, capitalists), a class 'for itself' is one highly aware of its political aims and the antagonistic nature of its class opponent; it is dynamic, seeking to change the *status quo*.

grows the revolt of the working-class, a class always increasing in numbers, and disciplined, united and organised by the very mechanism of the process of capitalist production itself. The monopoly of capital becomes a fetter upon the mode of production, which has sprung up and flourished with, and under it. Centralisation of the means of production and socialisation of labour at last reach a point where they become incompatible with their capitalist integument. Thus integument is burst asunder. The knell of capitalist private property sounds. The expropriators are expropriated.[1]

Revolution would usher in socialism, then communism. Let us now turn to discuss what Marx and the Soviets mean by these concepts in Russian history.

Communism and Socialism

According to Soviet theory, until the February 1917 Revolution, Russia was a feudal power in which capitalism was rapidly developing.[2] The February Revolution, with the abdication of the Tsar and the assumption of power by the Duma, ushered in a short period of capitalism. The October Revolution brought proletarian power. At the outset, even in Soviet political theory it did not bring socialism but 'the dictatorship of the proletariat'. The proletariat defended its class position against the hostile and counter-revolutionary bourgeoisie and aristocracy. Whether in fact the October Revolution was proletarian and could usher in a socialist order is a matter of dispute and I shall return to this problem in Chapter 6.

It was not until 1936 that the country was proclaimed to be 'socialist' and the remnants of the old social order were completely routed. The capitalist class being abolished, there could be no ruling exploiting class in the USSR.[3] Socialism by definition means that no social classes exist based on property and that, therefore, human relationships are harmonious. This does not mean that there is complete harmony: there remain certain contradictions or opposing forces: but *antagonistic* contradictions which are based on class have been obliterated. The Soviet view of Socialism gives the worker control over the means of production and does not make him alienated from his work. That is, the fruits of his labour are owned by him, not by entrepreneurs, and are controlled by him. Under socialism wages are paid 'according to one's work', incentives for skilled or arduous work are still necessary for there are insufficient goods to satisfy all needs. Commodities, therefore, usually have prices reflecting their relative scarcities. In both socialist and communist society, no hostile 'antagonistic' social groupings are said to exist and harmony prevails between social strata.

[1] *Capital*, vol. 1 (Moscow, 1958), p. 763.
[2] See historical background, Chapter 2.
[3] We consider criticisms of this by non-Soviet Marxists later, see Chapter 6. The social stratification of socialism is considered in more detail in Chapter 12.

Socialism, however, is but the first stage of communism, which is the highest form of society. Marx defined its features only in general terms.[1] This can be seen by examining Marx's own definition of a communist society:

In the higher phase of communist society after the enslaving subordination of individuals under division of labour, and therewith also the antithesis between mental and physical labour, has vanished; after labour has become not merely a means to live, but has become itself the primary necessity of life; after the productive forces have also increased with the all-round development of the individual, and all the springs of co-operative wealth flow more abundantly – only then can the narrow horizon of bourgeois right be fully left behind, and society inscribe on its banners 'From each according to his ability, to each according to his needs'.[2]

As there are no classes in communist society, there can no longer be any coercive state or government apparatus which, by Marxist definition, is the executive of the ruling class. Economically too, communism differs from socialism. Under communism an abundance of goods is produced, money and prices are otiose: for money is only a means to ration goods. There is no division of labour. Men work according to their ability and receive according to their needs.

This view has been reiterated as a social and political goal in the *Programme of the Communist Party of the Soviet Union* as follows:

Communism is a classless social system with one form of public ownership of the means of production and full social equality of all members of society; under it, the all-round development of people will be accompanied by the growth of the productive forces through continuous progress in science and technology; all the springs of co-operative wealth will flow more abundantly, and the great principle 'From each according to his ability, to each according to his needs' will be implemented. Communism is a highly organised society of free, socially conscious working people in which public self-government will be established, a society in which labour for the good of the society will become the prime vital requirement of everyone, a necessity recognised by one and all, and the ability of each person will be employed to the greatest benefit of the people.[3]

Later we shall examine in more detail the Soviet plans for the building of communism. Here we may recapitulate the main points. Communism is based on public ownership and self-government, there are no hostile social classes, no antagonistic contradictions, and economically it entails a state of abundance.

Criticisms of Marxism

Many criticisms are made in the west of the Marxist and Soviet views of

[1] See Reading No. 1, 'The Manifesto of the Communist Party', *Selected Works* (Moscow, 1958), pp. 27-9.

[2] 'Critique of the Gotha Programme', *Selected Works*, vol. 2, p. 23.

[3] *The Programme of the Communist Party of the Soviet Union*, Soviet Booklet, No. 83 (1961), p. 44.

socialism and communism. Non-Marxists deny that economic class is a fundamental determinant of social relations, therefore they conclude that the abolition of economic classes does not entail 'full social equality'. Some, it is argued, will always be taking decisions and others, the majority, will be subject to them. This is a consequence of the division of labour, not of ownership relations. The obvious Marxist retort to this is that under communism, there will be no division of labour either. The notions of 'ability' and 'needs' are ambiguous. It is not clear by what mechanism individual ability will be employed to 'the greatest benefit of the people'. Again, critics say that it cannot be assumed that human needs may not conflict; and it may be that human needs may be satisfied at the expense of equality or individual freedom. Benevolent utopias such as Huxley's *Brave New World*, and malevolent ones such as Orwell's *1984* have both been considered as possible and undesirable developments of man's control over man. It is claimed that 'abundance' in the Marxist sense is a pipe-dream, for abundance is only relative, there will always be shortages of some goods relative to others. Another criticism of the Marxist view of a communist society is that social hierarchy will always persist, because some men are inherently superior to others – by intelligence, physical dexterity, or some men will have occupational roles which give them status – the scientist, the politician, the doctor, the creative writer. At the root of all objections to the communist Utopia is a pessimistic view of human nature: that man seeks power and desires inequality, that conflict is endemic, that police will always be necessary to maintain order and control. There is no authority to which one may appeal to resolve this disagreement; it is a matter of belief.

It is not relevant here to discuss at length how 'true' Soviet Marxist concepts are of the nature of matter, of the course of history or of the dynamics of capitalist society, or even of how valid an interpretation they are of classical Marxism. Many objections may be made to Marx's prognosis. Let us again note them briefly. Non-Marxists reject the notion that the dialectic can explain history, because the historical process is a continuous stream of events and processes which are not reducible to thesis, antithesis and synthesis. The Marxist view of social change, of progressive changes from one stage to another, does not adequately explain decay or stagnation. The relationship between the basis and superstructure is often unclear, and the impact of superstructure (say ideas, or science) on the basis is often ignored; if one admits that the superstructure can play an important role in social change, then the power of economic factors is reduced. Consequently, critics of Marxism have pointed out that the role of 'great men' as agents of social change is belittled and that the theory ignores chance. Non-Marxists maintain that social analysis cannot be reduced to class terms; other factors, such as bureaucracy, play an important part in shaping the power structure of modern society.

Social relations too may be determined by racial, national or status factors; and these may outweigh purely class considerations. One of the most important criticisms is that Marx's view of industrial relations has been falsified. It is sometimes claimed that workers have been able to improve their position *vis-à-vis* capitalists through the stronger bargaining power afforded by trade unions. Therefore, proletarian immiseration and degradation and polarised class relations have not occurred. Indeed, it is argued that the links between class, class consciousness and revolution do not exist in modern capitalist society which is characterised by conflicts of 'interests'. The modern state is an institution which has mitigated many of the ills foreseen by Marx: it acts to redistribute wealth, to prevent structural unemployment and to provide social welfare. Other Marxists, not the Soviet kind, have sought to develop the early writings of Marx where he describes alienation or estrangement as being particularly relevant to the human condition. (This is discussed below, pp. 326–32.) In so doing, the emphasis on economic factors and class consciousness is minimised. Later in the book we shall examine, in more detail, the inadequacy of Marxist interpretations of the USSR.[1]

In criticising rather dogmatic Soviet interpretations of Marx, it is easy to become dogmatic oneself; to see Marx's writings as a doctrine or as a prophecy which can be either true or false. Soviet writers utilise Marxism as an ideological tool, to justify the structure and process of their own society and to declare illegitimate that of the class enemy. Many of the above criticisms must be accepted as accurate. Marx has been superseded by history, by events, by the writings of others. In a sociological sense, Marx's writings provide only certain insights which in practice are only partly accurate or inaccurate: his work is a contribution to the study of society in which no one person can have the last word.

Here we are concerned with the ideological determinants of the Soviet government's action and its impact on the citizens. As it is often pointed out: 'If men define situations as real, they are real in their consequences.'[2] The ideology of a society defines the situations which men regard as real. Marx expressed this as 'the ideas of the ruling class are in every epoch the ruling ideas'. The Soviet Communist Party, therefore, consciously attempts to adapt Marxist ideas to its own interests, for it regards itself as articulating the ideology of the working class.

[1] For further accounts and criticisms see C. W. Mills, *The Marxists* (New York, 1962), R. N. Carew Hunt, *The Theory and Practice of Communism* (1963), K. R. Popper, *The Open Society and its Enemies* (1945), R. C. Tucker, *Philosophy and Myth in Karl Marx* (1961), R. Dahrendorf, *Class and Class Conflict in an Industrial Society* (1959), George Lichtheim, *Marxism* (1961), R. Aron, *Main Currents in Sociological Thought*, vol. 1, (1965).

[2] W. I. Thomas, cited in R. K. Merton, *Social Theory and Social Structure* (Glencoe, Ill., 1947), p. 421.

Lenin's Theory of Party Organisation

We have already seen in our discussion of Marxism that the dominance of the bourgeoisie, in conditions of capitalism, would be subverted by the proletariat. Lenin devised tactics for the Russian working class to achieve and maintain political power. Leninism, after Marxism, provides a second major ingredient of Soviet political ideology. It has three main elements: the theory of the party, the theory of revolution and the theory of imperialism. The theory of the party is the classical statement of Communist Party organisation and it will briefly be outlined here.[1]

According to Lenin, under Russian conditions in the early twentieth century, the Russian working class would not spontaneously develop into a revolutionary body. Many workers, not seeing their long-term interests, would concentrate on short-term trade-union 'economistic' activity confined to marginal improvements in wages and conditions. Those convinced of the need for revolutionary action should be organised in a revolutionary party, with disciplined and dedicated leaders and members, to lead the working class.[2]

The need for firm leadership and the desirability of democratic participation were to be reconciled in the doctrine of 'democratic centralism'. Resolute action against the proletariat's class enemies called for a party based on 'absolute centralism' and the 'strictest discipline'. To provide decisive political leadership the party had to be monolithic: that is, unified and centralised in its organisational structure, its members bound by strict discipline, its pronouncements being definitive representing, in theory if not in practice, the unanimous voice of the party.

> Marxism . . . teaches that only the political party of the working class, i.e. the Communist Party, is capable of uniting, training and organising a vanguard of the proletariat and of the whole mass of the working people, a vanguard that alone will be capable of withstanding the inevitable petty-bourgeois vacillations of this mass and the inevitable traditions and relapses of narrow craft unionism or craft prejudices among the proletariat, and of guiding all the united activities of the whole proletariat, i.e. of leading it politically, and through it, the whole mass of the working people.[3]

Originally, the main reasons for firm leadership and strict discipline and a limited party membership were the conditions in which the social-democrats had to operate in pre-revolutionary Russia. As political parties and trade-unions were illegal, 'open' forms of workers' organisation, as found in Western Europe, led to their penetration by the police and to subsequent downfall.

---

[1] The theory of revolution is considered later in Chapter 2, and the theory of imperialism in Chapter 4.

[2] See Reading No. 2, V. I. Lenin, 'Organisations of Workers and Organisations of Revolutionaries', *What is to be Done?*

[3] V. I. Lenin, 'Tenth Congress of the RCP. (B)', *Collected Works*, vol. 32 (1965), p. 246.

Lenin's form of party organisation, therefore, was specifically devised to promote the interests of the working class under autocratic conditions. As Lenin put it: 'Only an incorrigible utopian would have a *broad* organisation of workers, with elections, reports, universal suffrage etc. under the autocracy.'[1]

Though central control of day-to-day policy and strict discipline were important, democratic participation was also an ingredient in the party's organisational form. All party members in theory were to have an equal voice over the general policy and the party leadership was to be elected and answerable to the party congress.[2]

Lenin's justification for the hegemony of one party over the working class was based on Marx's sociological theory of class, or rather his own interpretation of it. The working class, being unified socially and having a homogeneous political interest in the abolition of the capitalists, needed a single united party devoted to the promotion of the revolution. A politically fragmented working class organised in separate trade-unions and numerous socialist parties (often based on nationalist sentiment) could only weaken and might even thwart its revolutionary potential. Therefore, one party composed of workers from all trades and nationalities was essential, though membership, of course, had to be restricted to ardent Marxist revolutionaries.

Lenin distinguished between the social composition of a party and its political goals. The fact that a party is composed of, and led by, workers does not ensure its Marxist nature. On the contrary: 'The history of all countries shows that the working class, solely by its own forces, is able to work out merely trade-union consciousness i.e. the conviction of the need for combining in unions, for fighting against the employers and for trying to prevail upon the government to pass laws necessary for the workers and so on'.[3] The theory of Marxism and revolutionary tactics developed by some of the revolutionary bourgeois intelligentsia had to be transmitted to the workers. It was necessary that the awareness of the 'irreconcilable contradiction of their interests with the whole modern political and social system . . . be brought to them from the outside'.[4] This was the task of the revolutionary intelligentsia and, of course, revolutionary working men organised in a revolutionary Marxist party. Here Lenin was opposing the more orthodox social-democratic parties of western Europe, based on wide trade-union organisations. Lenin argued that such Balkanised movements would weaken the proletariat as a class; it would define its social interest in specific 'trade-union' terms, be more concerned with short-term gains, which would be ephemeral, at the expense of

---

[1] 'What is to be Done?' *Collected Works*, vol. 5 (Moscow, 1961), p. 459.

[2] The organisational forms of the modern CPSU are described in detail in Chapter 5. Here we are concerned only with the fundamental elements of Lenin's theory.

[3] V. I. Lenin, 'What is to be Done?', *Collected Works*, vol. 5, p. 375.

[4] *Ibid.*

workers' power. One group of workers (say the skilled) would be turned against another (the unskilled) and the capitalists having a divided enemy, would remain supreme. Lenin considered Marxism to be a doctrine which emphasised the historic role of the proletariat to build a socialist society; his own contribution was to devise, as it were, the organisational weapon.

The main additions to Marxism made by Lenin's theory of party organisation may be summarised as follows: first, that ideas had to be brought to the proletariat by the intelligentsia; second, that a political party should be formed to lead the proletariat to revolution; third, that the party should be based on an organisational pattern of 'democratic centralism'.

Marxist critics of such views have argued that if the workers by themselves would not develop a revolutionary class consciousness, then Marx's analysis of class (particularly the realisation by the proletariat of its own class interest) is undermined and that Lenin's theory of the party, therefore, contradicts Marx's theory of class. Marx, obviously, was concerned with the more economically advanced countries of the West having a relatively large proletariat and a more open liberal-democratic political life. More orthodox Marxists, dubbed 'revisionists' by Lenin, opposed this form of party organisation and advocated trade-union activity to ameliorate the pressing problems of the workers. This argument, even if relevant to Western Europe, had little support in Russia, where unions and other forms of workers' associations were illegal. Under the Russia autocracy political organisation was more important. Leninism is compatible with Marxism in that it stresses the revolutionary role of the proletariat and the revolutionary nature of social and political change. On the other hand, Marx had much more faith in the spontaneous growth of the proletariat's class consciousness. Lenin's emphasis on the role of the intelligentsia bringing ideas to the proletariat and helping to create a revolutionary consciousness is alien to Marx. This has led to the charge that the intelligentsia takes on a directing role *over* the proletariat. Whether Lenin's theory of the party contradicts Marx's theory of class very much depends on the way one interprets the role of basis and superstructure in social change. Classical Marxists tend to stress the determinism of the former, whereas Lenin, by emphasising the role of ideas and organisation regarded Marxism as a more voluntaristic doctrine. When Lenin spoke of the 'unity' of the working class, he referred to what the working class would be if it were imbued with Marxist philosophy and aware of its objective class position. He assumed that there was such a thing as an 'objective' class consciousness, which only the party could properly articulate. Lenin fully realised that, in fact, the subjective feelings of the workers did not coincide with their objective class position and, as we have seen, led to non-Marxist political leanings which his form of organisation sought to combat. Lenin, probably sincerely, believed that the working class as a whole would, with time and education, readily accept party leadership.

Lenin, however, left himself open to the criticism of self-interest. The centralisation of decision-making in the party and the absence of adequate democratic controls over the leadership, left effective power with the Central Committee of the party and particularly with the leader. In practice, the 'democratic' elements of democratic-centralism were outweighed by the centralism: the Party Congress met only infrequently, and initiative, information and day-to-day activity were in the hands of the centre. Lenin, it is argued by his adversaries, was concerned with maximising his own personal power, therefore, he was ruthlessly revolutionary and 'centralist' to suit his own desires. Rosa Luxembourg raised this point just after *What is to be Done?* was published. She wrote: 'The ultra-centralism asked by Lenin is full of the sterile spirit of the overseer. It is not a positive and creative spirit. *Lenin's concern is not so much to make the activity of the party more fruitful as to control the party – to narrow the movement rather than to develop it, to bind rather than to unify it.*'[1] While it is true that Lenin – like all political leaders – was motivated by a desire for power, this view overlooks the purposes for which Lenin wanted power and the socio-political goals of the Bolsheviks. Furthermore, it is unfair only to single out Lenin for adverse comment in this respect. Organised political parties have certain built-in characteristics tending to create oligarchical leadership forms resulting in something like a 'Leninist' structure even in theoretically open social-democratic parties.[2] Lenin not only argued that a large amount of central direction was necessary, but also made it a virtue.

A more strident criticism of Leninism stems from many involved in the contemporary student revolutionary movement. Opposing organisation and centralisation on the grounds that it is by definition anti-democratic, they stress the spontaneity of the masses, and advocate grass roots democracy based on workers' control. This is an anarchist criticism both of Marxism and Leninism: it sees government, hierarchy, authority and bureaucracy as the opponents of freedom and democracy. Marxist-Leninists would retort that property is more important than authority and that in practice both 'spontaneity' and workers' control are irrelevant and even harmful to the revolutionary struggle under capitalism.

Before considering Lenin's theory of revolution and imperialism we must consider the Russian background against which his views were developing.

---

[1] R. Luxembourg, *Leninism or Marxism?* (Ann Arbor, 1961), p. 94 (italics in original).

[2] See R. Michels, *Political Parties* (New York, 1959), especially Part 6, and R. T. McKenzie, *British Political Parties* (1958), esp. Chapter 10. It is sometimes objected that these writers have underestimated the degree of democratic control in social-democratic parties.

Reading No. 1
'The Manifesto of the Communist Party'
Source:
Marx-Engels, *Selected Works* (Foreign Languages Publishing House, Moscow, 1958), vol. 1, pp. 53-4.

. . . [T]he first step in the revolution by the working class, is to raise the proletariat to the position of ruling class, to win the battle of democracy.

The proletariat will use its political supremacy to wrest, by degrees, all capital from the bourgeoisie, to centralise all instruments of production in the hands of the State, i.e., of the proletariat organised as the ruling class; and to increase the total of productive forces as rapidly as possible.

Of course in the beginning, this cannot be effected except by means of despotic inroads on the rights of property, and on the conditions of bourgeois production; by means of measures, therefore, which appear economically insufficient and untenable, by which, in the course of the movement, outstrip themselves, necessitate further inroads upon the old social order, and are unavoidable as a means of entirely revolutionising the mode of production.

These measures will of course be different in different countries.

Nevertheless in the most advanced countries, the following will be pretty generally applicable.

1. Abolition of property in land and application of all rents of land to public purposes.
2. A heavy progressive or graduated income tax.
3. Abolition of all right of inheritance.
4. Confiscation of the property of all emigrants and rebels.
5. Centralisation of credit in the hands of the State, by means of a national bank with State capital and an exclusive monopoly.
6. Centralisation of the means of communication and transport in the hands of the State.
7. Extension of factories and instruments of production owned by the State; the bringing into cultivation of waste-lands, and the improvement of the soil generally in accordance with a common plan.
8. Equal liability of all to labour. Establishment of industrial armies, especially for agriculture.
9. Combination of agriculture with manufacturing industries; gradual abolition of the distinction between town and country, by a more equable distribution of the population over the country.
10. Free education for all children in public schools. Abolition of children's factory labour in its present form. Combination of education with industrial production, etc., etc.

When, in the course of development, class distinctions have disappeared, and all production has been concentrated in the hands of a vast association of the whole nation, the public power will lose its political character. Political power, properly so called, is merely the organised power of one class for oppressing another. If the proletariat during its contest with the bourgeoisie is compelled, by the force of circumstances, to organise itself as a class, if, by means of a revolution, it makes itself the ruling class, and, as such, sweeps away by force the old conditions of production, then it will, along with these conditions, have swept away the conditions for the existence of class antagonism and of classes generally, and will thereby have abolished its own supremacy as a class.

In place of the old bourgeois society, with its classes and class antagonism, we shall have an association, in which the free development of each is the condition for the free development of all.

Reading No. 2
'Organisation of Workers and Organisation of Revolutionaries'
Source:
What is to be Done? V. I. Lenin, *Collected Works* (English ed., Moscow, 1961), vol. 5, pp. 451-67.

. . . if we begin with the solid foundation of a strong organisation of revolutionaries, we can guarantee the stability of the movement as a whole and carry out the aims of both Social-Democracy and of trade unions proper. If, however, we begin with a broad workers' organisation, supposed to be most 'accessible' to the masses (but as a matter of fact most accessible to the gendarmes and making the revolutionaries most accessible to the police), we shall achieve neither one nor the other of these aims; we shall not eliminate our amateurishness, and because we remain scattered and our forces are constantly broken up by the police, we shall only make the trade unions of the Zubatov and Ozerov type most accessible to the masses.

I assert: 1) that no revolutionary movement can endure without a stable organisation of leaders that maintains continuity; 2) that the wider the masses spontaneously drawn into the struggle, forming the basis of the movement and participating in it, the more urgent the need of such an organisation, and the more solid this organisation must be (for it is much easier for demagogues to sidetrack the more backward sections of the masses); 3) that such an organisation must consist chiefly of people professionally engaged in revolutionary activity; 4) that in an autocratic state, the more we *confine* the membership of such an organisation to people who are professionally engaged in revolutionary activity and who have been professionally trained in the art of combating the political police, the more difficult will it be to wipe out such an organisation, and 5) the *greater* will be the number of people of the working class and of the other classes of society who will be able to join the movement and perform active work in it.

Our chief sin with regard to organisation is that *by our amateurishness we have lowered the prestige of revolutionaries in Russia.* A person who is flabby and shaky in questions of theory, who has a narrow outlook, who pleads the spontaneity of the masses as an excuse for his own sluggishness, who resembles a trade union secretary more than a people's tribune, who is unable to conceive of a broad and bold plan that would command the respect even of opponents, and who is inexperienced and clumsy in his own professional art – the art of combating the political police – why, such a man is not a revolutionary but a wretched amateur!

Let no active worker take offence at these frank remarks, for as far as insufficient training is concerned, I apply them first and foremost to myself. I used to work in a circle that set itself very wide, all-embracing tasks; and all of us, members of that circle, suffered painfully, acutely from the realisation that we were proving ourselves to be amateurs at a moment in history when we might have been able to say, paraphrasing a well-known epigram: 'Give us an organisation of revolutionaries, and we shall over-turn Russia!' And the more I recall the burning sense of shame I then experienced, the more bitter are my feelings towards those pseudo Social-Democrats whose teachings 'bring disgrace on the calling of a revolutionary', who fail to understand that our task is not to champion the degrading of the revolutionary to the level of an amateur, but to *raise* the amateurs to the level of revolutionaries.

FOR FURTHER STUDY

INTRODUCTORY

Aron, Raymond. *Main Currents in Sociological Thought*, Vol. 1. London: Weidenfeld and Nicolson, 1965.

Bottomore, T. B., and M. Rubel (eds.). *Karl Marx, Selected Writing in Sociology and Social Philosophy*. London: Penguin, 1963.

Dahrendorf, Ralf. *Class and Class Conflict in Industrial Society*. London: Routledge, 1959.

Hook, S. *Towards the Understanding of Karl Marx*. London: Gollanz, 1933.

Hunt, Carew R. N. *The Theory and Practice of Communism*. London: Penguin, 1963.

Lichtheim, George. *Marxism*. London: Routledge, 1961.

Meyer, Alfred G. *Leninism*. Cambridge, Mass.: Harvard University Press, 1957.

Mills, C. W. *The Marxists*. New York: Dell Publishing Co., 1962.

BASIC

Engels, F. *Anti-Dühring: Herr Eugen Dühring's revolution in science*. Moscow: Foreign Languages Publishing House, 1954.

Fainsod, Merle. *How Russia is Ruled*. Cambridge, Mass.: Harvard University Press, 1963.

Kuusinen, O. (ed.). *Fundamentals of Marxism-Leninism*. Moscow: Foreign Languages Publishing House, 1961.

Lenin, V. I. *What is to be Done?*, in *Collected Works*, Vol. 5. Moscow: Foreign Languages Publishing House, 1961.
See also the edition translated and edited by S. V. and P. Utechin. Oxford: Clarendon Press, 1963.

Marx, K. 'Preface to the Critique of Political Economy', in *Selected Works*, Vol. 1. Moscow: Foreign Languages Publishing House, 1958, pp. 361-5.

Marx, K., and F. Engels. 'The Manifesto of the Communist Party', *Selected Works*, Vol. 1. Moscow: Foreign Languages Publishing House, 1958, pp. 21-65.

Meyer, Alfred G. *Marxism*. Cambridge, Mass.: Harvard University Press, 1954.

The Programme of the CPSU (Adopted at the 22nd Congress, 1961). Reprinted in *Soviet Booklet No. 83*. London, 1961.

SPECIALISED

Etzioni, Amitai. *A Comparative Analysis of Complex Organisations: On Power, Involvement, and Their Correlates*. New York: Free Press of Glencoe, 1964.

Fleischer, Helmut. *Short Handbook of Communist Ideology: Synopsis of the* Osnovy Marksizma – Leninizma. Dordrecht: Reidel, 1965.

Huxley, A. *Brave New World*. London: Chatto and Windus, 1947.

Lenin, V. I. 'Tenth Congress of the RCP (B)', *Collected Works*, Vol. 32. Moscow: 1965, pp. 165-271.

Luxembourg, Rosa. *Leninism or Marxism?* Ann Arbor: University of Michigan Press, 1961.

McKenzie, R. T. *British Political Parties*. London: Heinemann, 1958.

Mannheim, Karl. *Ideology and Utopia*. London: Routledge, 1936.

Marcuse, Herbert. *Soviet Marxism: A Critical Analysis*. New York: Columbia University Press, 1958.

Marx, K., and F. Engels. 'Critique of the Gotha Programme', *Selected Works*, Vol. 2. Moscow: Foreign Languages Publishing House, 1959, pp. 13-45.

Marx, Karl. *Capital*, 3 Vols. Moscow: Foreign Languages Publishing House, Vol. 1, 1958; Vol. 2, 1957; Vol. 3, 1959.

Merton, R. K., 'The Self-Fulfilling Prophecy', in R. K. Merton, *Social Theory and Social Structure*. Glencoe, Ill.: Free Press, 1947, pp. 421-36.

Michels, R. *Political Parties*. New York: Dover Publications, 1959.

Orwell, G. *1984*. London: Secker and Warburg, 1949.

Parsons, Talcott. *The Social System*. Glencoe, Ill.: Free Press, 1961.

Popper, K. R. *The Open Society and its Enemies*. London: Routledge, 1945.

Schapiro, Leonard. *The Communist Party of the Soviet Union*. London: Eyre and Spottiswoode, 1960.

Tucker, R. C. *Philosophy and Myth in Karl Marx*. Cambridge: University Press, 1961.

2

RUSSIA
BEFORE SOVIET POWER

How can Russia before 1917 be related to the general theory of development outlined by Marx? At what 'stage' of economic development was she? In what direction would technological change lead her? Let us look at Russia in terms of the five 'ideal type' societies defined in the model of historical materialism. Unlike the countries of western Europe where the bourgeoisie had already abolished feudalism, in Russia wealth and power was based on an agrarian aristocratic ruling class. Before 1861, the conditions for rapid economic growth did not exist: there was an archaic agricultural framework, there was no influential elite either materially or ideally interested in economic change, there was no value system favouring entrepreneurial activity. Western advanced societies had little economic influence on Russia. Geographically, she was relatively isolated, cut off by her land mass and poor communications. But, even before the emancipation of the serfs in 1861, Russia was stirring. Her population was growing rapidly, the market and money relations were replacing barter; following her defeat in the Crimean War, modern communications and armaments were seen to be necessary for security thus providing a stimulus for industrialisation. In this chapter we shall become acquainted with the structure of the Russian Empire before 1917 by considering the economy, the main social groups, and the political scene, then we shall turn to consider the nature and causes of the revolution which took place in 1917.

The Economy

A convenient point at which to begin our analysis is the emancipation of the serfs in 1861. Until the emancipation, Russian peasants had been bound to the land. As it was owned by the Tsar, Church or lord, this meant that a peasant was largely dependent on the landowner. Politically, he was deprived of rights; socially, he was regarded as inferior; economically, he was restricted to working the land: he could neither change his occupation nor his place of residence. The peasant was required to work on the landowner's land (or in some cases pay money instead) for about half his working time, after which he could farm his own allotment.

The main provisions of the emancipation were to allow the peasants to use the lands they had previously farmed; they were no longer bound to their masters and were able, subject to the permission of the village assembly or commune, to move to the towns. The details and implementation of the settlement varied from one region to another. Generally, the landlord kept the land he had farmed; to the serfs went their cottages and garden patches. The communal fields previously worked by the serfs were made over to the village commune for peasant use. In fact, the peasants often received less land than they had before the reform, and Lyashchenko has shown that in the black earth average land holdings declined, though in other poorer areas they increased.[1]

The peasants did not own the 'emancipated' land as private property. Its control was vested in the village assembly which was responsible for paying, over a period of 49 years, an indemnity to the government as compensation to the previous landowners. After 1861, the peasant became dependent on the commune. He could not leave his place of residence without its permission and was 'tied' to the commune in a similar way as before he was 'tied' to the feudal lord, though in practice many peasants left to work in the towns. The commune periodically redistributed the land, which was held in unconsolidated strips, according to the size of the peasant household.

The effects of the emancipation of the serfs were five-fold. Firstly, dues in kind were abolished, furthering the growth of a money economy. Secondly, labour mobility between occupations and between town and country was improved, though many restrictions remained. Thirdly, the subsequent sale by the aristocracy of parts of the land enabled differentiation to take place among the peasantry. Fourthly, though there were some exceptions, the technologically backward open field and strip farming was perpetuated. Fifthly, the functions of the village commune, elected by the heads of families, were extended. It collected taxes, distributed land, issued passports and resolved disputes.

The process of differentiation among the peasantry was speeded up by the establishment of a Peasants' Bank in 1882 and by the Stolypin reform of 1906. The former assisted groups of peasants to buy land from large estate owners – or garden plots from inefficient peasants. The Stolypin reform pinned its hopes on the creation of a group of property-owning farmers which would act as a political prop to the regime. Peasants were allowed to 'enclose' or to consolidate commune land into private holdings. The process of peasant differentiation, however, was slow. In 1877, the peasantry owned only 6.3 per cent of

[1] P. I. Lyashchenko, *History of the National Economy of Russia* (New York: Macmillan, 1949), p. 382.

the land, whereas by 1900 the share under their private ownership was 15.4 per cent.[1] Between 1907 and 1915 only two million peasant land holdings came onto the market, and some of these had been given up by migrants to Siberia.

On the eve of the First World War, the 'peasant problem' had not been solved. Adequate land *ownership* was still largely the perogative of relatively few large-scale estate owners. The majority of the peasantry either subsisted on small private plots or utilised commune land. As these latter units were inefficient they absorbed much of their own agricultural produce. The large estates, located in southern Russia and to the east of the lower Volga, catered for the market.

To satisfy the peasants' demand for land, the large estates would have to be redivided among some fifteen million peasant households. Such a redivision would have met the peasants' political demands, but would have been disastrous for the urban population – for the supply of marketable grain would rapidly have fallen. The effects would also have harmed Russia's balance of payments, for she was chiefly an agricultural exporter and an industrial-goods importer: at the beginning of the twentieth century, a third of world wheat imports originated from Russia. The destruction of the large estates, therefore, would seriously threaten the town population and would have prevented Russia paying for industrial imports. From the 1890s, American grain coming on to the world market caused world prices to fall. Russia increased her grain exports by squeezing the peasants, for example by forcing them to pay taxes soon after the harvest when grain prices were low.[2]

The agrarian changes discussed above were only one aspect of the developments taking place in nineteenth century Russia. In addition, the population was rapidly growing: from an estimated 42.5 millions in 1815 to 125.6 millions in 1897.[3] In the early nineteenth century, the issue of money increased as did production for the market; for example, trade in the Nizhenovgorod market increased four to five-fold between 1817 and 1861.[4] After the ignominious defeat of the Russians in the Crimean War (1853–56), Tsar Alexander II encouraged industrial development. 'The tariff was lowered, foreign capital and know-how invited. As Russians hurried again to Western Europe, western books, ideas, experts and standards of doing things flowed into Russia'.[5] A modern system of communications was built. The railways had only some thousand miles of line in 1860, but this increased to forty-eight thousand miles by 1914: a network linking Warsaw to the Pacific coast and St Petersburg

[1] P. A. Khromov, *Ekonomicheskoe razvitie Rossii v XIX-XX vekakh* (Moscow, 1950), pp. 156-7.
[2] Theodore H. Von Laue, *Sergei Witte and the Industrialisation of Russia* (New York, 1963), pp. 26, 30-1.
[3] See below, p. 28 *et seq.*
[4] P. A. Khromov, *Ekonomicheskoe razvitie Rossii v XIX-XX vekakh* (Moscow, 1950), p. 91. See this book for a discussion of the growth of an internal market in Russia.
[5] Von Laue, *op. cit.*, p. 6.

to the Volga and Tashkent. Improved rail communications were paralleled by
the growth of a network of telegraph and telephone lines.

At the time of the emancipation of the serfs, Russia's industrial capacity
rested on a traditional iron industry founded on the ore of the Urals, a crafts-
man kind of textile industry in the area to the north-east of Moscow, and
handicraft industries in the western territories, the Caucasus and Volga areas.
During the latter half of the nineteenth century, however, large-scale investment and factory production of a more advanced type based on the western
European model was introduced. The Donbass quickly outstripped the Urals
areas in output of metal, and large textile enterprises were set up in Poland,
Ivanovo-Voznesensk and St Petersburg. For example, coal output in the
Donbass increased from 15.6 million *puds*[1] in 1870 to 671.1 million in 1900;
iron smelting rose from 2 million *puds* in 1885 to 50.6 million in 1900 when it
accounted for over half of Russian iron-smelting.[2]

The late nineteenth century industrialisation was carried out with the aid
of West European skill and capital. British, French, German and Belgian
money was invested in Russia, and western engineers supervised the erection
and operation of the new industrial plants. To take the Donbass, only one of
the nine blast furnaces was wholly Russian-owned[3] and more than half the
mines were under Franco-Belgian ownership. British interests were well
represented in textiles and oil.[4] Even oil production had increased so rapidly
that in 1901, Russian production surpassed the total American output. The
newer industrial areas were characterised by western capital, and modern
capital-intensive production, while in the older traditional regions, in the
Urals particularly, and to some degree around Moscow, almost pre-industrial
methods continued, and ownership and control were largely in Russian
hands.

The activity of the state was one of the most important factors in encouraging
this economic growth. Protective tariffs supported the new industry: foreign
investors were often guaranteed a fixed rate of return on capital, the government was a large purchaser of Russian industrial produce. The state itself
directly owned and managed many factories, particularly in brewing and
armaments and by 1900 most of the railway system had been nationalised.

During the late nineteenth century and particularly between 1890 and 1899
and between 1907 and 1913, Russia experienced a rapid rate of growth. The
growth rates are shown in the second column of Table 1. (p. 25). Industrial
production increased five-fold between 1885 and 1913, an annual growth rate

---

[1] A Russian *pud* equals 36.1 British pounds.
[2] S. I. Potolov, *Rabochie Donbassa v XIX veke* (Moscow, 1963), pp. 80-1.
[3] Potolov, pp. 88-9.
[4] The *Cotton Factory Times* of 20 July 1899, even carried an article on cricket in Sepwchoff – a
pattern of genteel rules which was not to be followed in the socio-political order.

of 5.72 per cent from 1861 to 1913.[1] The Table shows growth rates larger than in the USA, the United Kingdom and Germany in similar periods.

Table 1.Average Annual Rates of Growth of Industrial Output (per cent) 1885–1913

Period	Russia	USA	UK	Germany
1870–1884	—	4.65	1.98	4.22
1885–1889	6.10	8.75	4.56	5.15
1890–1899	8.03	5.47	1.80	5.44
1907–1913	6.25	3.52	2.72	3.90
1885–1913	5.83	5.26	2.11	4.49

Source: A. Gerschenkron, 'The Rate of Growth in Russia', The Journal of Economic History, vol. 7 (Supplement), p. 156.

Of course, despite these large strides forward in the direction of industrialisation, Russia was very backward compared with the industrialised states of the West. A Soviet estimate is that the value of Russian industrial large-scale output was only 6.9 per cent of American gross industrial output,[2] and Russian per capita production in 1913 was only 4.8 per cent of American.[3]

A corollary to this industrial development was the growth of the working class. Its exact size is a matter of some dispute. One of the most widely accepted estimates is that of A. G. Rashin who has said that the number of factory and mining workers increased from eight hundred thousand in 1861–70 to some two million five hundred thousand in 1913.[4] This figure of course, excludes workers in service industries (like railways), agricultural labourers, and men in handicraft industries. It serves to show a more than three-fold rate of growth.

The introduction of modern industry led to a high concentration of workers in Russian industry. In 1910, the proportion of workers in factories with over five hundred employed was 53.5 per cent compared with only 33 per cent in the USA.[5] While this fact may have been important from a social point of view, from an economic one it is misleading, for Russian industry was more labour-intensive and less efficient than American at this time. In terms of horsepower per industrial worker in large scale industry, the Russian figures were much lower: three-fifths of the English figure and only a third of the American.[6] More striking figures illustrating Russia's industrial backwardness are the horsepower used in production as a proportion of the population:

[1] Alexander Gerschenkron, 'The Rate of Growth in Russia', The Journal of Economic History, vol. 7 (Supplement), pp. 146, 155.
[2] Cited by Gerschenkron, p. 155.
[3] Gerschenkron, ibid.
[4] A. G. Rashin, Formirovanie rabochego klassa Rossii (Moscow, 1958), p. 192.
[5] P. I. Lyashchenko, op. cit., pp. 669-70.
[6] Figures for Russia in 1908, USA 1910, England 1907: Lyashchenko, op cit., p. 673.

Russia had only 1.6 (per hundred of the population), the USA 25, Germany 13 and England 24.[1]

The Russian economy then under the Tsars at the beginning of the twentieth century had the following salient features. Under the impetus of state control and encouragement, the economy was growing swiftly; a network of communications had been established, as had a base for heavy industry, textiles, chemicals and oil. But compared to western European states, Russia was economically backward. Her industrial development had features which were quite different from the western states. A modern economic system was largely 'imported' by the government, it did not grow out of an indigenous capitalist class.

The political formations did not conform to a classical Marxist situation. The state, not the bourgeoisie, played the dominant role in industrial development which in its turn promoted the growth of the proletariat. On the basis of this, it would hardly be fair to reject the Marxist prognosis of history. The fact that the Russian bourgeoisie played a small part in economic development does not refute the hypothesis that the bourgeoisie *as a whole* had a major role in the transformation of Russia after 1861. Russia, Marxists would argue, was part and parcel of the world capitalist economic system and cannot be understood independently of it. The underlying need for security, the finance and organisation of Russian industry, the technological innovation all stemmed from the western bourgeoisie. To be viable and realistic, Marxist analysis has to take into account the effects on the internal political and social structure of a country, of economic development largely performed by a foreign bourgeoisie. Whereas in the West, such development could take place in a stable, more or less liberal political structure, in Russia both bourgeois and proletarian groups found themselves constrained by an autocratic straitjacket.

Social Groups

The Russian social structure in the late nineteenth and early twentieth century was under stress from the changes that were taking place in the economy. These changes in social structure in turn affected the political and economic order. Here we shall consider the demographic data on Russia before the revolution and some of the more important social and national divisions of the population.

The official social classification of Russia's population was based on estate: the gentry (or nobility), townsman and peasant. One's estate gave certain legal rights but it also had social significance. The system of 'estates' signified a stratified but mutually interdependent and harmonious social order. Theoretically, membership of an estate was fixed at birth, though some social move-

[1] Lyashchenko, *ibid.*

ment was possible. The Russian *nobility* (*dvoryanstvo*) or gentry included the hereditary owners of large estates, senior government officials and officers of state. The nobility was stratified into 14 different ranks ranging from Chancellor (or Field-Marshall in the army) to a College Registrar: some intermediary ranks, for instance, were of an army Colonel in sixth position, and a Second-Lieutenant in the twelfth, (there were corresponding civilian categories too). The first of the three main divisions of the nobility was the *potomstvennoe* (hereditary) whose members until 1861 had enjoyed the privilege of owning serfs; secondly, the *lichnoe* (personal), who held their title for life only; and thirdly, the *kupechestvo* (merchants), who held office in the two highest guilds (members needed a certain minimum capital and had to pay fees).[1] The *townsman's* estate (*meshchanstvo*) was composed of men living in the town who had certain property or professional qualifications. The *peasantry* consisted of men who worked the soil and came under the jurisdiction of a village court. In addition to these three main strata there was the clergy who held office in the Orthodox Church. These then were the formal legal divisions of the population.

The estates in Russia were not rigid in structure. The nobility strata were relatively open to new members irrespective of birth. In addition to honours conferred by the Tsar, the attainment of positions in state service automatically brought ennoblement. One could, by having sufficient wealth, join one of the merchant guilds which gave *dvoryanin* status. A university degree was also a sufficient condition to give entry to the nobility. The relative ease of entry to the Russian nobility compared with that of Western Europe is sometimes recognised by giving it the wider social term, 'gentry'.

After 1861, the legal and actual position of the estates was undermined. The emancipation denied the right to the hereditary nobility to own serfs, and from 1874 all estates had to perform military service. Internal passports were issued by the police and not the estate offices. The growth of industry resulted in the appearance of managerial and commercial occupations. The development of education and health services increased the numbers of professional groups which could not be easily assimilated into the estate structure. Factory workers, recruited from all estates, albeit disproportionately from the peasantry, appeared on the social scene. The 'peasantry' was heterogeneous: some were substantial landowners – 'rich peasants', others were agricultural labourers, or factory workers. The only thing 'the peasants' had in common was their common subjection to the village *mir* (or community) to which they had to apply for passports and which had civil jurisdiction over them. In short, the 'estate' of an individual indicated social origin which should not be ignored, but did not connote any collective norms. One of the main reasons

[1] Robert A. Feldmesser, 'Social Classes and Political Structure', in Cyril E. Black, *The Transformation of Russian Society* (Cambridge, Mass. 1960) p., 238.

for the break-up of the old social structure was population growth, to which
we may now turn.

Population

The population of Russia was growing well before the nineteenth century.
Between 1722 and 1796 the Russian population had increased from 14 to 36
millions.[1] In the nineteenth century the population rose even more rapidly
reaching a total of 94 millions in 1897.[2] The growth was due to changes in the
birth and death rate: the former rising from 43.7[3] in the years 1801 to 1810
to 52.4 in 1851 to 1860. The birth rate in other countries in 1851 to 1860 was:
France 26, Prussia 38, England 34, Sweden 36. In 1801 to 1810,[4] the death
rate in Russia was 27.1 – higher than in other European countries and
between 1891 and 1900 it rose to 32.8: in England in the latter period it was
18.2, in France 21.5, Germany 22.2 and Sweden 16.4 (per 1000 of the population).[5] The enormous growth is illustrated by the fact that the population
trebled between 1815 and 1900. The national increase was 1.66 per cent in
1801–1810 and 1.3 per cent between 1851 and 1860.

The 1897 census for the whole Empire showed the main divisions as follows:

Nobility (all ranks and including chinovniki[6])	2,193,000
Clergy	588,900
Merchants	281,100
Townsmen	13,386,300
Peasants	96,896,500
Cossacks	2,928,700

(Pervaya vseobshchaya perepis' naseleniya (Obshchi svod), vol. 1 (Spb. 1905), pp. 160-1).

Obviously, the figures are only a very rough guide to the actual configuration
of social groups. Notable, as one would expect, is the large number of peasants
(97 million) and townsmen (13 million); many of the latter were Jews. The
official classification ignores those engaged in industry and commerce.
Industrial workers, therefore, would be in all the above groups, though most
were in the peasant bracket. Khromov, using Lenin's estimates, says that 21.7
million[7] were engaged in industry and trade.[8] More detailed figures have been

---

[1] P. A. Khromov, Ekonomicheskoe razvitie Rossii v XIX-XX vekakh (Moscow, 1950), p. 79.
[2] Here we refer to the Russian population; the total population in 1897 was 125.6 millions.
See F. Lorimer, The Population of the Soviet Union (Geneva, United Nations, 1946), p. 10.
[3] Per thousand of the total population.
[4] Figures cited in Khromov, op. cit., p. 81.
[5] Khromov, op. cit., pp. 240-1.
[6] State officials not having noble status.
[7] Including members of families.
[8] P. A. Khromov, Ekonomicheskoe razvitie Rossii v XIX-XX vekakh (Moscow, 1950), pp. 228-9.

worked out by Eason. Of a total population of 139 million in 1913, he estimates that 16.7 per cent (or 23 million) were wage and salary earners, excluding another 7.2 per cent who were handicraftsmen (cobblers, watch-
makers and so on).[1]

As I have mentioned above, by the beginning of the twentieth century, the
working class was still small in size. It had grown from about 0.4 per cent of
the population in 1815 to 1.41 per cent in 1913. The detailed statistics are
shown on Table 2. The comparable figure in the United States in 1910
was 11.6 per cent.

Table 2. The Number and Proportion of Industrial Workers in Russia
1815–1913 (selected years)

Year	Estimated Total Population (000s)	Industrial Workers (000s)	Industrial Workers as per cent of total population
1815	42,510	173	0.4
1835	60,185	288	0.48
1860	74,120	565	0.76
1900	131,710	1,692	1.28
1913	161,723	2,282	1.41

Source: Frank Lorimer, The Population of the Soviet Union (Geneva,
1946).

According to Rashin of the some 2.5 million industrial workers in 1913,
under half (918,000) were employed in textiles, in the metal industry were just
over a third of a million (385,000) and in mining 215,000.[2] The industrial
working class was concentrated in certain areas of the Empire, particularly in
Moscow and Vladimir provinces (over half a million in 1913) and St Petersburg (218,000). The southern metal and mining area, though it had sustained
a very high growth rate, only encompassed about ten per cent of all industrial
workers in the same year. In Siberia and Central Asia, industrialisation had
made hardly any headway. In Siberia there were about 37,000 industrial
workers in 1908 – only 0.4 per 100 of the total population. In Central Asia
and the Asiatic Steppe there were some 21,000 workers of whom about a third
were employed in cotton-ginning and another fifth was engaged in the
petroleum and silk industries. The Caucasus was little touched by industrial
activity, except in the oilfields of Baku where there were about 55,000 workers
employed.[3]

The growth in population and the changes in production methods led to a
shift in balance between town and country. In 1850 the urban population has

[1] Warren W. Eason, 'Population Changes', in Cyril E. Black, The Transformation of Russian
Society (Camb., Mass., 1960), p. 88. The figures include dependents.
[2] A. G. Rashin, Formirovanie rabochego klassa Rossii (Moscow, 1958), p. 48.
[3] Lorimer, op cit., p. 23.

been estimated at 5.5 per cent or only some 3 million.[1] By 1870 the figure had risen to 12.3 per cent and on the eve of the First World War it was 14.6 per cent, when the total living in towns was over 20 million (*ibid.*). The degree of urbanisation varied considerably between different areas of Russia: whereas in Poland 23 per cent of the population was urban, in the rest of European Russia it was half this figure (12.9 per cent) and in Siberia it was only 9 per cent.[2]

In the recruitment of labour, Russian industrialisation followed a similar process to that in other countries developing today. Surplus population moved from the village to the town. In a survey of 31 provinces of Russia before 1917, 31.3 per cent of the factory workers (or their families) had land; and 20.9 per cent, with the aid of their families, continued to work on it.[3] Land-working varied between regions and kinds of industries. The textile workers in the central and northern provinces had relatively stronger links with the country-side than the metal-workers; in the Ukraine only 5.7 per cent of the latter had any land.[4] A survey of 5,723 factory workers in Shuya[5] in 1899 showed that over half were of the farming peasantry: of the married, 27 per cent and of the single, 41 per cent were of families which continued to work the land.[6]

The attitudes of the migrants to town life and the degree to which they considered themselves as 'workers' rather than peasants are extremely complex and difficult questions. Some, in areas with close links between town and country, no doubt were 'anxious to find a way to return to the peasant villages whence they had recently come',[7] others, however, quickly adapted to town life. The following quotation from the memoirs of a worker in the northern textile industry was probably typical of many such uprooted men. 'At first . . . all seemed better than in the village. Although there was no cow's milk, on holidays there was white bread and despite the tiring factory work, urban life seemed more interesting and attractive.'[8] In this area of Russia, the Soviet writers Varentsova and Bagaev have argued that village life had little attraction because of the small amount and poor quality of land available.[9] The notion that the new urban workers idealised a peasant world of staunch yeoman values is a proposition which had been much exaggerated.

---

[1] Warren W. Eason, 'Population Changes', in Cyril E. Black, *op. cit.*, p. 83.
[2] Figures for 1897, *Pervaya vseobshchaya perepis' naseleniya* (Obshchi svod), vol. 1 (Spb. 1905), p. 6.
[3] A. G. Rashin, *Formirovanie . . .*, p. 575.
[4] Figures for 1914-17, Rashin, *op cit.*, p. 576.
[5] Situated to the northeast of Moscow.
[6] A. V. Shipulina, 'Ivanovo-voznesenskie rabochie nakanune pervoy russkoy revolyutsii', *Doklady i soobshcheniya instituta istorii*, No. 8 (Moscow, 1955), p. 48,
[7] R A. Feldmesser, 'Social Classes and Political Structure', C. Black, *op cit.*, p. 244.
[8] F. N. Samoylov, *Vospominaniya ob Ivanovo-Voznesenskom rabochem dvizhenii*, Part I (Moscow, 1922), p. 9.
[9] O. A. Varentsova and M. A. Bagaev, *Za 10 let* (Ivanovo 1930), p. 18.

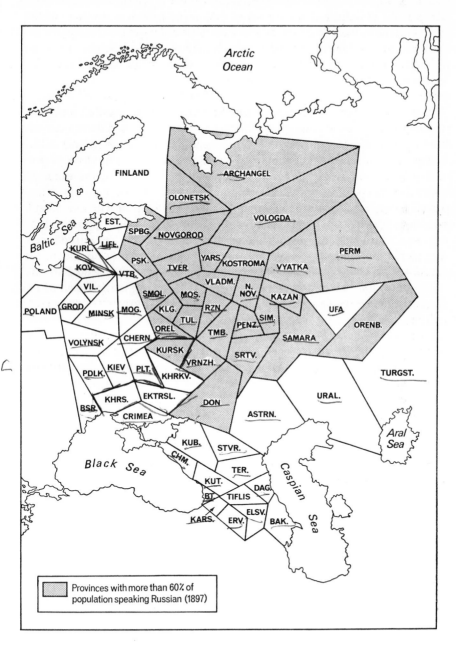

MAP 1 Great Russian Areas of Russia 1897

The break-up of the old social structure and the development of classes on the pattern of industrial society was a feature of Russia at the turn of the century. The categories of estate and class grouped together the population horizontally. In addition, however, the various national, religious and linguistic groups united vertically the various occupational, estate and class divisions.

Several groupings may be distinguished. The largest was a 'Great Russian' area in which some two-thirds of the population spoke Russian and were Orthodox by religion. This area is shown on Map 1. In the Polish areas the Catholics predominated. In the southern and western areas the main languages spoken were Ukrainian and White Russian, though in some provinces in the south-west (Minsk, Kherson, Vilna and Grodno, for example) more than ten per cent of the population were Jews. The Baltic provinces and Finland were again racially and linguistically apart. Central Asia and Siberia had been penetrated by Russian settlers, but were mainly populated by diverse and small indigenous Asiatic groups. The Caucasus had mixed racial, linguistic, and religious stock, ranging from the Christian Georgians to the small groups of Muslims making up the population of Azerbaidzhan. We shall return later to consider in more detail the national composition of the population as it is today.[1]

Here we may conclude that social divisions in the pre-revolutionary Russian Empire were great. The population was extremely heterogeneous with regard to occupation, religious belief, language, national and racial background. Many of the problems which later faced the Bolshevik government were concerned with welding together into a communal state these disparate groups.

The Polity

Before 1905, complete political authority was vested in the Tsar. Article 1 of the Fundamental Laws (1892) decreed: 'The all-Russian Emperor is an autocrat and unlimited monarch – God himself commands his supreme power be obeyed out of conscience as well as fear.' In fact, given the complexity of government, the Tsar was advised by a number of committees and individuals. While we cannot study here the complex structure of the Tsarist administration, it is important to note that the main holders of political influence were the ministers (especially of Finance, of the Interior and of the Army) and the governors of each province. Nicholas II who reigned from 1894 to 1917, faced with the difficult problems of ruling the Russian Empire, vacillated between the advice offered him by his many advisers, among whom figured the mystic Rasputin, and remained a weak and ineffectual ruler. It should not be thought, however, that the dynasty eventually fell simply because of a

[1] See Chapter 13.

weak ruler. A radical change was required in the social, economic and political structure.

The Tsarist system as it was in the early twentieth century may illustrate the difficulties which are inherent in an autocratic system having no representation of the interests which an industrial order creates and which, to a greater or lesser extent, are ensured by parliamentary representation. The possible reaction of important social groups could not be well gauged by the government. Furthermore, a social harmony of interests could only be achieved after a fundamental alteration of the autocracy's powers.

While, until 1905, no representation prevailed at the national all-Russian level, this was not the case in local government. The Zemstva had been set up from 1864 and were concerned with the administration of the post office, education, public health, works and sanitation; they provided services for agriculture and collected statistics. In addition to providing accommodation for police and other officials, in some areas the Zemstva were required to pay the salaries of local priests.[1] Their social composition, however, was hopelessly unrepresentative. Of deputies elected to the Zemstva between 1865 and 1867, 74.2 per cent were of the gentry, 10.9 per cent from the merchant strata, and 10.6 per cent peasants (4.3 per cent were unclassified).[2]

In the sphere of political liberty Russia lagged behind the advanced countries of Western Europe. Until 1905, political parties and trade unions were illegal – for they sought to 'represent' particular interests and were, therefore, inimical to autocratic Tsarist rule. There were, however, associations of industrialists who met to discuss their common industrial interests, and friendly and benevolent societies, such as the Red Cross. Among the working class, mutual aid associations flourished to provide for sickness, unemployment and funerals. In an attempt to keep the workers' organisations under control, the police had organised workers' unions which sometimes discussed problems with the factory administration. It is not true to say that there were *no* organised groups in Russia before 1905. But as the groups were illegal, the political system was under no compulsion to come to terms with them, hence they functioned weakly as political inputs. Political parties, whose *raison d'être* is to influence the government, only existed in the underground. In 1905, they came into the open and contested elections. These groups had a complex history going back into the nineteenth century. Here we may consider only the general background.

Before 1861, the emancipation of the peasant dominated Russian politics. Alexander Herzen, in the 1850s, had postulated a new social order based on a self-sufficient and self-governing village commune. Influenced by these ideas,

---

[1] Alexander Vucinich, 'The State and the Local Community', in C. E. Black, *The Transformation of Russian Society* (Cambridge, Mass., 1960), p. 199.

[2] 'Zemskaya reforma 1864', *Bol'shaya Sovetskaya entsiklopediya*, vol. 17 (Moscow, 1952), p. 37.

Populist (or Narodnik) groups in the 1880s conducted revolutionary activity with the aim of establishing a form of peasant socialism. Most of these groups opposed the centralised autocratic state and advocated populism or a form of decentralised agrarian socialism with small-scale handicraft industry – but not the capitalist industrial order of Germany and Great Britain. Particularly noteworthy are the groups following Tkachev and Nachaev, which advocated a revolutionary seizure of power, developed terrorism as a means of change and set up a secret centralised organisation to accomplish the revolution. But these groups, which idealised the peasant and saw salvation in a socialist but mainly agrarian social order, failed and were superseded by the Marxists. Probably the most important reason for failure was that the Narodniks did not penetrate the peasantry, and remained essentially a movement of intellectuals.[1]

From the middle of the 1880s, Marxism began to make an impact in Russia, and numerous circles were organised. In these it was argued by the Marxists that large-scale industrialisation was not only inevitable in the unfolding of history, but was also desirable, for capitalism brought with it progress – a higher level of economic and social development. We cannot study these groups here, they were the forerunners of the political parties which came into the open in 1905. A description of the latter will give a good idea of the political alternatives suggested for Russia's future development.

The main peasants' party was formed by the *Socialist Revolutionaries* (S.R.s) the heir to the populist tradition. Its main characteristics were as follows. It was revolutionary: many supported terrorist tactics (assassination and bomb-throwing) and the seizure of the land by the peasants (some wanted to compensate the landlords, but others did not). The party advocated a decentralised economy with small-scale industrial manufacture. While many Utopian Socialist Revolutionaries wanted a form of cooperative socialist agriculture based on the old Russian commune (the *obshchina*), many others, probably the majority, wanted an independent yeomanry with small holdings. The numerous national minorities were to be given the right of self-determination. Though the leaders of the Socialist Revolutionaries were intellectuals, their popular support lay with the peasantry.

The *Constitutional Democratic Party* (*Cadets*) or the Russian liberal party was supported by the professional classes – the leading academic, legal and journalistic groups. Its policy was the adoption of parliamentary democracy based on the Duma.[2] It wanted the peasants' land area to be increased, but the landlords were to be indemnified. It advocated labour legislation for the protection of child and female labour and wanted to set up a sort of labour relations board to resolve industrial conflicts. It was, in other words, a 'progressive' liberal party. Though persuasion and peaceful change were

---

[1] See Franco Venturi, *The Roots of Revolution* (London 1960).
[2] The Duma was an advisory body to the Tsar.

preferred to abolish the autocracy, the party conceded that revolution might be necessary.

The *Octobrist Party* was a centre party. It supported civil liberties and representative government but firmly believed in a constitutional monarchy rather than the republic wanted by the liberal groups. The party believed that labour legislation should protect workers from exploitation and that they should also have the right to strike and form unions. Based on the promise of a constitutional regime in the October Manifesto[1], from which the party took its name, it was strongly anti-revolutionary and advocated change by peaceful means.

The *Union of the Russian People* was an extreme right wing party. Its policy was based on 'Orthodoxy, Autocracy and Nationalism'. 'Orthodoxy' represented the values and the religious outlook of the Russian Orthodox Church. 'Autocracy' was support for the ruling Tsar. The nationalism of the party was grounded on the Great Russian nation. It is sometimes said that the ideas of the Union were one of the earliest manifestations of Fascist ideology: belief in a personal figurehead (the Tsar), Great Russian folk supremacy (they were particularly hostile to Jews), and opposition to parliamentary institutions and socialist ideas.

The chief Marxist party was the *Russian Social-Democratic Labour Party* (RSDLP). As this was the forerunner of the Communist Party of the Soviet Union we shall study it more closely than its rivals. It was formed in 1903. At its formation, however, the party split into two parts: the Bolsheviks, led by Lenin, and Mensheviks, headed by Martov and others. As Marxists, the social-democrats of both factions believed that capitalism had to develop in Russia. It was impossible to build a form of socialism on the basis of the peasant commune, as advocated by the socialist-revolutionaries. Both factions of the party, Bolsheviks and Mensheviks, agreed that the next stage in the evolution of Russia was the bourgeois-democratic. But they disagreed on the role that the social-democrats should play during and after the bourgeois-democratic revolution. Though we shall dwell on this later, it might be pointed out here that the Mensheviks felt that the bourgeoisie could and should complete the revolution. The Bolsheviks, however, argued that the social-democratic party had a more dynamic part to play. Another difference between the factions was on the question of the form of party organisation relevant to Russian conditions. Lenin and the Bolsheviks wanted a centralised conspiratorial party of Marxist revolutionaries (see discussion above p. 11 *et. seq.*), whereas the Mensheviks advocated a more widely based party with a strong trade-union wing, rather like the German Social-Democratic Party (and the British Labour Party today). If one bears in mind that the Mensheviks antici-

[1] A Manifesto put out by the Tsar in October 1905, promising a constitutional form of government. See below, pp. 41–2.

pated a liberal-democratic society after the abolition of the autocracy, their party organisational theory follows quite logically from this assumption.

The social-democrats of both factions were mainly led by intellectuals. The Mensheviks tended to be supported by the more highly skilled workers and the Bolsheviks drew more support from the unskilled. Another difference was that the Bolsheviks were largely Great Russian, whereas the Mensheviks were composed of the non-Russian national groups (particularly Georgians and Jews),[1] though they too had some support among the Great Russians.

The Russian political scene in 1905 had a different set of main actors compared to either England or America one hundred years earlier. The 'bourgeois' interests with a base in manufacturing were very weak. The largest party, the socialist-revolutionaries, had no English counterpart, based as it was on the agrarian demands of the peasantry. The well-organised urban social-democrats had no analogous grouping in America during its revolution when a large industrial working class had yet to be formed and the Marxist conception of class struggle remained to be formulated. Yet Russia was a divided nation in terms of both class and nationality. Among the Poles, Ukrainians, Georgians and other national groups hostility existed to the politically dominant Russians. Though important regional differences were felt in western states, no comparable dissensus could be found at this time.

Against this political background the social-democrats of various shades of opinion, grouped into the Bolshevik and Menshevik factions sought to apply Marxist theory. We have already discussed Lenin's theory of political organisation, we shall now turn to the second defined ingredient in Leninism: the theory of socialist revolution.

Socialist Theories of Revolution

In our discussion of Marxism, we saw that in theory social change was the result of a dialectic process; that capitalist society developed out of feudalism, from the class conflict of the nobility and bourgeoisie. Socialist society is the synthesis arising from the clash of the dominant social forces of bourgeoisie and proletariat. How was this theory related to Russia at the beginning of the twentieth century? How did Russian Marxists perceive the course of change?

Russia did not fit very easily into either of the ideal types of feudal or bourgeois society. Political power was held by the autocracy and based, in the Marxist analysis, on land ownership. The ruling class was the landed gentry whose values and interests were defended by the Tsar. We have seen that its power was on the wane: the serfs had been emancipated, landowners' estates were being sold, capitalist enterprises were being set up. At first sight, it would

---

[1] For a detailed analysis of the social composition of both factions see: David Lane, *The Roots of Russian Communism* (Assen, Holland, 1969).

seem that the classical antithesis between aristocracy and bourgeoisie was taking place. But we have seen that much of the entrepreneurial activity was carried out at the behest of the Tsar, much of the ownership was foreign. Russia lacked a strong indigenous bourgeoisie. On the other hand, we have seen that the factory proletariat had grown rapidly and was highly concentrated in large factories. In terms of their own theory, the Marxists had to account for a trinity, rather than a duality, of social interests: nobility, bourgeoisie and proletariat. We should note here that the peasantry was *not* regarded as a social class: it was divided roughly into poor landless peasants (the 'rural proletariat') and the richer land-owning peasantry (the rural petty bourgeoisie). What role should the proletariat play in a country where a feudal rather than a capitalist ruling class existed? All Marxists agreed that they could not live in harmony. All three had antagonistic class interests. But what combination of interests could promote the advance of the proletariat?

Martov and the Mensheviks adopted a traditional Marxist position. In the struggle with nobility, the social-democrats should not play a decisive or even a leading role, for this was the responsibility of the bourgeoisie which would bring about a revolution. The revolution would legalise trade unions and political parties and create conditions for a social-democratic party on the model of German social-democracy. The party, recommended Martov, was to prepare for the time when it would be in opposition to (or the antithesis of) the bourgeoisie. In practical terms this meant the widening of the base of the party and grafting on to it where possible the emerging trade unions. After the successful bourgeois revolution, the party should not participate in the provisional government as this would entail identification with the actions of the bourgeoisie.

Trotsky (with Parvus) differed by suggesting the thesis of 'permanent revolution' or the 'law of combined development'. They argued that in Russia the bourgeoisie was too weak to carry through the bourgeois-democratic revolution. In support of their argument were used some of the facts already known to us: the Russian state had played a leading role in industrialisation, foreign capital predominated, a politically weak indigenous bourgeoisie relied on the Tsarist government for support. Under these conditions the bourgeoisie would not play a role as a revolutionary vanguard. The Russian proletariat, on the other hand, was a more potent revolutionary force. Russian industry had borrowed the most advanced techniques of production from the west. The total number of men in very large factories was the same as in the United States. The Russian proletariat had assimilated socialist (Marxist) doctrine and was highly class conscious. The proletariat, therefore, argued Trotsky, could play a dominant role in a revolutionary upheaval. The impending Russian revolution would not stop at the bourgeois stage but would pass on into the proletarian.

'Once the revolution is victorious political power necessarily passes over into the hands of the class that has played the leading role in the struggle, the working class'.[1] It 'necessarily passes over' to the working class because the bourgeoisie would resist the workers demands (say, for the eight hour day). They argued further that a proletarian dictatorship, under the leadership of the social-democrats, would be supported by the poor peasantry. While the poor peasantry's political interest was similar to the proletariat's, it did not have the political organisation or the political consciousness to lead a revolution.

Lenin and the Bolsheviks

Lenin combined elements of both the Menshevik and Trotskyite prognosis. He agreed with Trotsky that the bourgeoisie alone would not carry out the bourgeois-democratic revolution. It was too weakly formed in Russia and part of it, while opposing the autocracy, would shrink from revolution which, if carried out, would put it at the mercy of the proletariat. Lenin argued that as the revolution would not be carried out by the bourgeoisie, then the party should not prepare itself for a period of opposition in a liberal-democratic republic, as thought by the Mensheviks.

But Lenin in 1905 agreed that the country was not sufficiently mature to support a socialist revolution: social-democracy representing the proletariat could not introduce 'the dictatorship of the proletariat.' Lenin objected to Parvus's view that the 'revolutionary provisional government of Russia will be a government of labour democracy . . will be an integral government with a Social-Democratic majority'. This could not be so, 'because only a revolutionary dictatorship relying on the overwhelming majority of the people can be at all durable. . . . The proletariat, however, at present constitutes a minority of the population in Russia. . . . It would be harmful to it if any illusions were entertained on this score. . . . The objective logic of historical development confronts [the masses] at the present time, not with the task of making a socialist revolution, but with the task of making a democratic revolution'.[2]

Lenin's recommendations for action were based on his analysis of the political stratification of Russia. He saw the bourgeoisie as divided into two parts: the large-scale urban capitalist magnates and the petty-bourgeoisie. The large-scale capitalist elements were closely linked to, and dependent on, the Tsarist government. The small-scale capitalists or petty bourgeoisie comprising the middle and richer peasants and some elements of the urban professional classes, were truly revolutionary; they would be prepared to consummate the

---

[1] L. Trotsky, *The Permanent Revolution*; see B. Wolfe, *Three Who Made a Revolution* (1956), p. 290.

[2] V. I. Lenin, 'Two Tactics of Social Democracy in the Democratic Revolution', *Selected Works* (1936), vol. 3, pp. 35-6. See also David Lane, *The Roots of Russian Communism* (Assen, 1969), Chapter 3, part 6.

revolution. The social-democrats (composed of both rural and urban proletariat), therefore, should join an alliance with the petty bourgeoisie to
destroy the autocracy and set up a revolutionary provisional government.
The Bolsheviks should play the leading role in the seizure of power; for the
class consciousness of the proletariat and the organisation of the Bolsheviks
was superior to that of the petty bourgeoisie. The proletariat would have to
partner the petty bourgeoisie in the provisional revolutionary government.
This was necessary for three reasons: firstly, to ensure that the revolution
went its full course; secondly, to prevent counter revolution from the deposed
ruling groups; and thirdly, to secure the minimum programme of Russian
social-democracy – the eight hour day, freedom of the press, trade unions and
political parties. But the revolution would *not* make a socialist society. Its
class character would be bourgeois.

Marxists are absolutely convinced of the bourgeois character of the Russian
revolution. What does this mean? It means that the democratic changes in the
political regime and the social and economic changes which have become necessary
for Russia do not in themselves imply the undermining of capitalism, the undermining of bourgeois domination; on the contrary, they will, for the first time,
properly clear the ground for a wide and rapid European, and not Asiatic, development of capitalism, they will, for the first time, make it possible for the bourgeoisie
to rule as a class.[1]

The socialist revolution would only be achieved after the increased development of productive forces and the growth of the proletariat.

Let us now turn to consider what happened in Russia from 1905 to 1917 and
to examine how these theories were applied in practice.

Political Activity 1905

We have seen that at the beginning of the twentieth century, the Tsar was
under pressure: from the growing entrepreneurial, managerial and professional
groups for liberal conditions as in West Europe, from the working classes for
better living conditions and higher pay, from the peasantry to reduce their
land repayments and taxes. The general discontent erupted in a series of
revolts known as the 1905 Revolution which Lenin later regarded as a 'dress
rehearsal' for October 1917. It will be instructive to study the events of 1905
before turning to the more decisive happenings of 1917.

Strikes and disturbances were not new phenomena to the Russian scene.
But nothing quite like the demonstration of 9 January 1905 had taken place
before. On that day, Father Gapon, a celebrated Orthodox priest, organised a
petition to the Tsar calling upon him to help the people. The petitioners, some

[1] V. I. Lenin, 'The Two Tactics of Social-Democracy in the Democratic Revolution', *Selected
Works*, vol. 3 (1936), p. 73.

thousands strong, with banners proclaiming their needs, converged on the Royal Palace. These were loyal subjects who regarded the Tsar as a protector, their message was one of despair, not revolt, and their Ikons held high showed their patriotic and religious zeal. The demonstrators, however, were forcibly dispersed and reports claimed that several hundreds were killed or wounded. The event has become known as the 'Bloody Sunday' massacre.

Gapon was later murdered by a socialist-revolutionary. He had been a police agent 'planted' among the workers both to inform on them and to lead them along a peaceful, non-revolutionary, path of change, though he was probably sincere and had a genuine concern for the workers. It is significant too, that the workers in the Gapon demonstrations revered the Tsar and looked to him, over the heads of the officials and industrialist strata to ameliorate their position. The firing on the crowd severely weakened this belief and had the effect of strengthening support for the revolutionary elements. In the spring and summer, strikes and uprisings continued to be directed against factory administrations, landlords and the Tsar. The government, worried by the continuing outbreaks, made concessions: a limited consultative assembly was promised.[1] Self-government was also granted to the universities, an act which gave the revolutionaries a sanctuary, later in the year. These actions did not assuage the rebellious clamour and by the end of October the country was locked in a general strike, which included students and even ballerinas, showing the width of feeling against the Tsarist order.

In the course of the strikes, meetings took place between the leaders who had formed quite spontaneously Councils (or Soviets) of Workers' Deputies. The first was formed in the textile town of Ivanovo-Voznesensk in May and was followed by others, the best known of which were in Moscow and St Petersburg. The Soviets were composed of workers' representatives and frequently led by social-democrats of both factions (Bolsheviks and Mensheviks). They agitated for improvements in working conditions (especially for the eight hour day) and democratic rights. In December the police dissolved the St Petersburg Soviet, led by Trotsky, and its leaders were arrested and put on trial. No armed resistance was offered in the capital. In other areas, armed uprisings took place. In Moscow, the insurgents led by the Soviet erected barricades and controlled parts of the town. At the end of December, troops put down the revolt at the cost of some thousand casualties. In Moscow, as in other places where armed conflict took place, Bolshevik organisations and, to a lesser extent, socialist revolutionaries were at the head of popular revolts. The Mensheviks supported and participated in the revolutionary activities.

In the armed forces some insubordination occurred. The famous Battleship Potemkin had mutinied in the spring. In the winter, a few troops fraternised with strikers, and those returning from the Far East through Siberia

[1] The Bulygin Duma envisaged was a consultative assembly formed mainly from landowners.

were particularly militant. But, on the whole, the armed forces remained disciplined and loyal to their commanders. With the crushing of the Moscow uprising, the Revolution was over.

What was the significance of the revolution? It must be said that it did not achieve a rapid and decisive change in the social, political or economic order. But the constitutional position of the Tsar was undermined and after October he was in a much weaker position. On 17 October 1905, the October Manifesto was published. This was not a constitution, but a promise of civil freedoms by the Tsar: inviolability of the person, freedom of conscience, speech, assembly and association; an elected Duma, with legislative powers and participation in the supervision of officers of state. It was promised to admit all classes to participate in the affairs of the Duma. Consequently, in 1906, the First Duma was elected. It was part of a two-chamber legislature, the upper-house appointed by the Tsar having equal power with the lower which was indirectly elected through electoral colleges based on social class. It was thought by the government that the peasantry was pro-Tsarist: it chose the largest proportion of deputies, 43.4 per cent (the landlords chose 31.8 per cent, the townsmen 22.4 per cent and the workers 2.4 per cent).[1]

Because of the biased representation, the left-wing parties did not fully participate in the election. Despite this, the radicals emerged with a majority many of whom were elected by the peasantry. The Cadets (Constitutional Democrats) were the largest party with 177 members out of 524. But political power was firmly left in the hands of the Tsar. He appointed ministers who were responsible to him and not to the Duma which could show its displeasure but could not remove a minister. The control of the budget was ineffective and military expenditure was outside the Duma's competence. The Tsar could veto acts passed by both chambers. In practice the Tsar by-passed the Duma. Legislation was carried out by decree which was quite legal when the Duma was not in session. After 1906, the Duma was made even less representative by an increase in the proportion of deputies with landowning qualifications.

The chief effects of the 1905 Revolution were that some concessions were made to liberal and democratic forces. In the Duma, freedom of speech was ensured and public criticism was made of the government. But a wider degree of civil liberty was not attained: people were still liable to arbitrary arrest, correspondence was examined by the police, censorship continued and political parties and trade unions remained underground, though the representatives of the political parties participated in the Duma. Perhaps the greatest change was that the legitimacy of the autocracy had been undermined. The Tsar had admitted the rights of society to participate in the government of the

[1] F. Dan, 'Vtoraya Duma', in Martov, Maslov, and Potresov, *Obshchestvennoe dvizhenie v Rossii v nachale XX-go veke* (Spb. 1909-14), vol. 4, part ii.

country. Thereafter, he was arguing from a theoretically insecure base: he was no longer 'the supreme power to be obeyed out of conscience'.

The events of 1905–1907 resulted in the failure of the revolutionaries to seize power. The October Manifesto, with its promise of a liberal constitution was a turning point: following its publication, many elements of the bourgeoisie called off the revolutionary struggle. The Mensheviks' view of the revolution proved erroneous: the bourgeoisie did not seize power. The Bolsheviks were wrong too: the uprisings of workers and others were crushed, the attempted seizure of power was premature. In fact, the Tsar still remained supreme ruler and a liberal-democratic regime was not set up.

After 1907, revolutionary activity declined. The membership and morale of the social-democrats was at a low ebb. Many left the party. Economic growth, which received a set-back in 1905–7, picked up and averaged 6.25 per cent between 1907 and 1913. It seemed that the autocracy, having come through the storm of 1905, might be able to continue indefinitely. The hindsight of history tells us that this was an incorrect view.

From 1905 to 1914 the main social problems remained still unsolved. The Duma became less representative and had little effective control over the government. The social strata seeking a liberal-democratic regime were not politically satisfied and could not be expected to support the autocracy. An alternative was the development of a yeoman peasantry, a free small-holder class of moderately prosperous land-owning farmers, who would politically uphold the Tsarist order in the same way that the old nobility had done. Stolypin encouraged the peasants to leave the commune and to buy land through the Peasants' Land Bank and he gave assistance to them to settle in Siberia and Central Asia. But by the beginning of the First World War his policy had not succeeded in breaking down the communal pattern of owner-ship. The Russian countryside was still farmed mainly in the traditional man-ner: three-field rotation based on strip farming. Plots were uneconomic and too small, ranging from a half to two-and-a-half acres in size. By 1915, less than one tenth of peasant holdings had been consolidated into small farms. Unlike the farmers of the West who were individual landowners, or at least tenant farmers, the Russian peasants remained largely members of a com-munity (the village commune). In the towns, the workers' demands for better conditions had not been satisfied. The liberal bourgeoisie was excluded from the apex of political power. The Tsar had admitted the right of the people to participate in government, but had not subsequently acted on it. Russia had fared badly in the international arena: she had suffered an ignominious defeat in the war with Japan[1] to whom she had ceded some of her eastern territories.

---

[1] The Russo-Japanese War took place in 1904-5. The Russians were defeated at the battle of Tsushima in May 1905. A peace treaty was signed in September 1905 when Russia ceded to Japan territories in Asiatic Russia.

Public confidence in the Tsar was low. These factors, which precipitated political and social change, were aggravated by the First World War, which Russia had entered on the side of the allies.

During the war fifteen and a half million men had been drafted into the armed forces. They were poorly armed and incompetently led: during the war six to eight million men were killed, wounded or captured. The mobilization withdrew approximately a third of the male labour force from industry and agriculture. Agricultural and industrial production declined between 1915 and 1917. By the end of 1916, the amount of grain marketed dropped by at least a third and the amount transported by rail dwindled by as much as sixty per cent.[1] The value of money fell; by the summer of 1917, bread prices had increased three times, and meat prices seven times. Peasants refused to market grain and supplies were requisitioned by the government. In 1915 and 1916 the Russian army was badly defeated; morale was low, and in 1916 some million and a half men deserted. The court had no consistent policy, ministers were dismissed and replaced, but no improvement in policy occurred. The Tsar fell largely under the influence of the Tsarina and the mystic Rasputin. Such a system could not endure. By the beginning of 1917 all social groups – military, intelligentsia, entrepreneurs, civil service, peasantry and working class – were ready for a radical change. In February and October 1917 two sudden changes in government were to take place: in the first, the autocracy collapsed and the Provisional Government was formed; in the second, the Bolsheviks came to power. These two events have come to be regarded as the Russian Revolution[2] of 1917.

The Russian Revolution of 1917

A 'revolution' has been defined as 'a popular movement whereby a significant change in the structure of a nation or society is effected. Usually an overthrow of the existing government and the substitution by another comes early in such a movement and significant social and economic changes follow.'[3] In terms of this definition the February 'Revolution' was only partial, involving a change of government but not carrying out 'significant social and economic changes'. Let us describe what happened.

In February 1917 strikes and riots had taken place in the capital. The government's conduct of the war and of internal policy was under strong criticism by the Duma. On 28 February, the Petrograd garrison mutinied. It became impossible for loyal Tsarist officers to find troops to maintain public order.

[1] M. Dobb, *Soviet Economic Development Since 1917* (1966), p. 71.
[2] Sometimes they are regarded as separate revolutions: the February and the October.
[3] Louis Gottschalk, 'Causes of Revolution', *American Journal of Sociology* vol, 50 (no. 1), July, 1944, p. 4.

Soldiers and workers were in revolt against the government, which became
powerless. On 1 March, the Duma Committee reluctantly assumed responsibility for maintaining public order. The Tsar abdicated. Rule by autocracy
was ended. But what form of government was to replace it?

The Duma, the 'official' forum of public criticism of the autocracy, was not
the only alternative organ of government. The Soviets, which had sprung up
in 1905, began to assert their authority. Above, we saw that in 1905 the St
Petersburg Soviet had been arrested, though in Moscow it organised a seizure
of power. In 1917, Soviets were to a much greater extent composed of soldiers
and took more radical and concerted action.

Between February and October 1917, political power was divided between
the Provisional Government and the Soviets. The Tsar having abdicated in
March 1917, the Duma Committee was the legal government. Formally, the
provisional government replaced the Duma after the abdication of the Tsar;
it was headed by Prince Lvov and then Kerensky. Effective power, however,
lay with the Soviets which had control over the army, communications and
the streets. The Soviets independently issued directives: in March the eight
hour day was proclaimed. Soviet Order No. 1 decreed that:

1. All units were to elect men to the Soviets,
2. All military units were to obey the Soviet,
3. All units were to execute orders of the military commission of the Duma
   unless they conflicted with the Soviet,
4. Company committees were to control arms, which were not to be given to
   officers,
5. Soldiers were to have the same political rights as other citizens.[1]

From the time it assumed power, the Provisional Government's authority
crumbled. As we have seen, it was in no way representative of the nation as a
whole: the peasantry and working class had little participation. The activity
of the government ensured its downfall. Its policy was to continue the war
with the allies and to postpone economic and social change until the end of
hostilities with the Germans. This policy only aggravated a situation which
had dislodged the autocracy in the first place. The armed forces would not continue the struggle against the Germans and therefore became hostile to the new
government. Both the peasantry's demand for land and the working classes'
demands for better conditions went unfulfilled. With the abdication of the
Tsar, claims for autonomy were asserted by the non-Russian peoples.

As for the organised political parties, only the Bolsheviks, some Left
Socialist-Revolutionaries (S.R.s) and the anarchists completely rejected the
Provisional Government's policy. The Mensheviks and S.R.s supported the
government with reservations. Russia had to continue the war of self-defence
against the Germans. The international working class, however, was called on

[1] Full text printed in *Izvestiya*, 2 March 1917. See Reading No. 3.

by the Mensheviks to renounce all imperialistic aims. Fundamental social change had to wait until the end of the war. The Cadet, Socialist Revolutionary and Menshevik leaders all identified themselves with the Provisional government's policies. The Bolsheviks and Left S.R.s campaigned against the war and advocated the immediate confiscation of the large estates.

It would be wrong, however, to represent the political parties and groups as having a clear and consistent policy. Many leaders were abroad and confusion was paramount. The Bolsheviks in Russia were inclined to compromise with other groups and until the summer of 1917 had no intention of seizing power. In April 1917, Lenin arrived in Russia. He had a clear analysis of the situation and extreme recommendations to make. On arrival he said '. . . The robbers' imperialistic war is the beginning of civil war in Europe . . . Any day may come the crash of European imperialism. The Russian Revolution, which you have carried out, has laid the foundation for it and opened a new epoch. Long live the world-wide socialist revolution!'

The Bolsheviks and 1917

Lenin's views in the summer of 1917 were more radical than his analysis of 1905. There were now stronger preconditions for a socialist revolution. Important in Lenin's thinking was the role of the proletariat abroad. If the proletariat in the advanced European states could overthrow the bourgeoisie, then help would be forthcoming for the Russian proletariat. 'We stand on the threshold of a world-wide proletarian revolution . . . If we come out now, we shall have on our side all proletarian Europe.'[1] As Russia was part of the world capitalist system and the 'weakest link' in its chain, it was necessary for the Russian proletariat to take the initiative, to overthrow the bourgeois Provisional government and thereby set off a chain reaction in Western Europe. The first task was to seize power.

Lenin's policy was set out in his April Theses. (Reading no. 4). It called for a boycott of the Provisional Government and the installation of a 'Republic of Workers, Agricultural Labourers and Peasants' Deputies'. Lenin advocated the confiscation of all landlords' estates, the establishment of a single national bank and the elimination of the army, police and official class. He said that the Bolsheviks should adopt the name of Communist Party. Finally he called for the nationalisation of the land and the *control* of production by a government made up of the Soviets of Workers' Deputies.

From April, the Bolsheviks began to mobilise support for revolution. The party's slogans were 'Bread, Peace and War' and later 'All Power to the Soviets'. Bolshevik strength was growing, particularly among the workers in

---

[1] V. I. Lenin, cited by E. H. Carr, *The Bolshevik Revolution* (1950), vol. 1, pp. 94-5.

Petrograd and Moscow, among the soldiers of the garrison and among the sailors of the Baltic Fleet. At the end of May, three-quarters of the delegates to the Conference of Petrograd Factory Committees were Bolshevik. But Lenin did not yet control the Soviets. Of some eight hundred delegates to the First Congress of Soviets early in June, only one-eighth were Bolsheviks.

The reaction of the Provisional Government was to ban the Bolshevik party, to destroy its press and to imprison many of its leaders (Kamenev and Lunacharsky). Others (Lenin and Zinoviev) went into hiding. The Bolsheviks of course were not unused to organising illegally and party organisation remained intact and membership even grew. In August, at the Sixth Congress a total membership of 200,000 was claimed.

At the end of August 1917, General Kornilov, commander-in-chief of the armed forces, sought to destroy the Soviets and reorganise the Provisional Government. He marched troops on Petrograd. His venture dismally failed. Resistance was put up by the Soviets and the General was unable to find troops loyal to his command: trains were sabotaged, agitators persuaded his men not to fight against the government. The failure of Kornilov showed the weakness of the Right and of the army officers to organise an alternative government. After the Kornilov offensive, the tide turned for the Bolsheviks: on 31 August and 5 September they gained majorities in the Petrograd and Moscow Soviets respectively.

In September, Lenin felt that the time was ripe for insurrection. The Central Committee of the party, however, was not in agreement. Kamenev and Zinoviev, for example, believed that though a *coup* might succeed in Moscow and Petrograd, a social revolution could not yet be carried through. They maintained that the majority of the Russian population and the international proletariat were not with the Bolsheviks. On 9 October, by 10 votes to 2 (Kamenev and Zinoviev opposing), the Central Committee decided to prepare for an armed insurrection. Armed detachments were mobilized.

On 25 October the Bolsheviks seized the Winter Palace. The Provisional Government was overthrown. Kerensky fled. The Military Revolutionary Committee proclaimed: 'All railway stations and the telephone, post and telegraph offices are occupied. The telephones of the Winter Palace and the Staff Headquarters are disconnected. The State Bank is in our hands. The Winter Palace and the Staff have surrendered ... The Provisional Government is deposed. Power is in the hands of the Revolutionary Committee of the Petrograd Soviet of Workers' and Soldiers' Deputies'.[1]

On 26 October, the Government of People's Commissars was established. The first decree nationalised the land; peace was offered to the Germans. The Bolsheviks had taken power.

[1] Cited in James Bunyan and H. H. Fisher, *The Bolshevik Revolution 1917-18* (Stanford, 1934), p. 100.

Causes of the Revolution

Why were the Bolsheviks successful in seizing political power? What were the causes of the Revolution? In discussing the revolutionary process, Lawrence Stone has distinguished between the long-run causes (the preconditions) and the immediate factors (the precipitants).[1] It is useful to discuss the revolution in these terms. The long-run causes have already been discussed: the forces of population growth and industrialisation created social classes which could not be absorbed into the autocratic system of government. The Tsars were unable to adapt the political system to the new demands put on it. The precipitants were the war and its ensuing chaos. Russia's allies, who might have injected sufficient economic aid to save the government, were locked in the grave struggle with the Germans. The legal government, instead of being insulated from direct stresses by political parties and groups which articulate and modify interests, was directly exposed to mass activity, and organs of direct rule, the Soviets, were organised.

This led to a social situation described by William Kornhauser as a 'mass society'[2] which in his theory is one of four different kinds of society: communal, totalitarian, pluralist and mass. They are distinguished by the availability of non-elites on the one hand and by the accessibility of elites on the other.[3]

Availability of Non-Elites

		Low	High
	Low	Communal	Totalitarian
Accessibility of Elites			
	High	Pluralist	Mass

The availability of non-elites may be high or low and the accessibility of elites may also be high or low. The four types of society are characterised by their relative high and low accessibility of elites and availability of non-elite, as shown above. Only 'mass' society concerns us here.[4] A mass society exists when elite positions are accessible to organised political groups: in other words, it is relatively easy for a revolutionary group to seize the reins of government to control communications and organise the economy. The mediating role of other political groups is absent. At the same time, the masses are easily mobilised: they can be whipped up to support radical policies and activists. Given these conditions (highly accessible elites and highly available masses) radical political groups may seize power.

[1] Lawrence Stone, 'Theories of Revolution', *World Politics* (vol. 18), Jan. 1966, no. 2, p. 164.
[2] *The Politics of Mass Society* (1960).
[3] Kornhauser, *op. cit.*, p. 40.
[4] We return to discuss the 'totalitarian' notion below, Chapter 6, pp. 188–90.

In the Russian context, from February to October 1917, Kornhauser's typology fits the facts. The elite positions were not firmly structured and there was no heritage of democratic participation. With the abdication of the Tsar, a political vacuum existed. The masses were available: firm democratic political groupings (such as trade unions) had been forbidden under the autocracy; individuals under the upheaval of the war were prone to involvement in radical behaviour.

The inadequacy of Kornhauser's theory lies in its inability to explain why the *Bolsheviks* should have assumed power. The conditions were equal for Bolsheviks, Anarchists or Left Socialist-Revolutionaries who were all radical, revolutionary groups. Here the ideology and organisational theory of the Bolsheviks are important, for they enabled the Bolsheviks to capitalise on a mass situation.

Kornhauser too ignores the social nature of the October Revolution. The smallness of the urban working class has led other commentators such as Barrington Moore to attribute the revolutionary impetus to the peasantry.[1]

This however, seems an exaggeration. Even though the peasant was not an individual landowner, but dependent on the commune, this does not necessarily involve a high degree of 'peasant' consciousness, for even the commune could be highly differentiated. It is also extremely difficult to isolate 'peasant' behaviour from the influence of the towns and to speak of peasant 'mass support' for a revolution as does Moore.[2] The peasantry was differentiated not only between poor and rich but also in terms of its access to and connexion with the town. The movement of peasants to urban areas and their subsequent transfer of money to the village community is well known. This had the effect of undermining the structure of the traditional village community. As Moore scorns quantitative approaches he provides no evidence for his assertion that 'the peasantry' was a prime factor behind the Revolution. The fact that a revolution takes place in a mainly peasant society is again not proof that the peasantry plays a determining role in the revolution. It is germane to point out that much of the action towards change in 1917 came not from the peasant village, but from the army where the peasant was exposed to urban values and ideas. It is also true that in purely economic terms the real income of the peasant family rose during the First World War.[3] But Moore's conclusion that the leadership of the revolution was non-peasant is certainly correct. The peasants, if they did share social norms as a collective group (a debatable proposition), had insufficient *political* consciousness to act collectively. Their outbursts were largely spontaneous uncoordinated local insurrections or riots. They

[1] Barrington Moore, *Social Origins of Dictatorship and Democracy* (1967), p. 427.
[2] *Ibid.*
[3] M. T. Florinsky estimates that it rose by 18 per cent. *The End of the Russian Empire* (New York, 1961), p. 190.

were incapable of leading a revolution. Trotsky so rightly has pointed out: 'as all modern history attests – especially the Russian experience of the last twenty-five years – an insurmountable obstacle on the road to the creation of a peasants' party is the petty bourgeoisie's lack of economic and political independence and its deep internal differentiation'.[1] To determine the social character of the Revolution one must turn to the social support of the Bolsheviks.

The Bolsheviks had their strength in the urban areas of the Russian speaking parts of the Empire, where their support lay among the proletarian strata. Even ten years before the October Revolution, the Bolsheviks were entrenched in the older industrial areas of Moscow, St Petersburg and the Urals. It is true that they only had nine million or 25 per cent of the votes in the election to the Constituent Assembly conducted in November 1917. A careful examination of the voting statistics, however, shows that in the industrial centres of Petrograd and Moscow they also had over half the votes (an average of 53 per cent), in Vladimir province 56 per cent. In the armed forces in the key northern and western fronts they had over half the votes. But more than half of the peasants' party's votes (the S.R.s) were from non-Russian nationalities.[2] The national complexion of the Bolsheviks is important: they were drawn from relatively homogeneous areas socially, which were Russian and Orthodox. Their support coincided with the areas shaded on Map 1. (p. 31.) Their location was important strategically: it gave them control of Petrograd and Moscow.

Finally, to return to Stone's 'precipitants' of revolution, no explanation can exclude Lenin's leadership of the Bolshevik faction. His charisma over his Bolshevik followers, his analysis of the situation, the timing of the *coup*, all contributed to the victory of the Bolshevik Party. These factors, given the general mass society situation, enabled the seizure of power by a socialist party in a backward agrarian country. The 'dictatorship of the proletariat' paradoxically for Marxists took place in the country where the working class was in a minority. The Constituent Assembly which met in the winter of 1917 had a majority of Socialist Revolutionaries (410 delegates) compared to the Bolsheviks 175 (the nationalist minority parties had 86, the Cadets 17 and the Mensheviks 16).[3]

Whatever interpretation one may put on the Bolshevik strategy of revolu-

[1] L. Trotsky, *The Permanent Revolution* (1930 edition, republished by New Park, 1962), p. 154.

[2] V. I. Lenin, 'The Constituent Assembly Elections and the Dictatorship of the Proletariat, *Collected Works*, vol. 30 (Moscow, 1965), pp. 253-74.

[3] These figures do not coincide with voting strength: the Bolsheviks had some 25 per cent of the votes compared to the Socialist Revolutionaries' 38 per cent; the Mensheviks had only 3 per cent.

tion in October 1917, there can be no doubt that Russia had not reached the
peak of bourgeois social and economic development. Despite considerable
industrial growth before the revolution, the country was still backward. As
we have seen, economic take-off had occurred, but the country had a small
industrial capacity, a small working class, and the greatest part of the peasantry
was illiterate. Can it be said that the Bolshevik Revolution proves Marxism to
be a false doctrine? Such writers as Raymond Aron and George Lichtheim
argue that it does. First they argue that rather than the revolutionary proletariat destroying capitalism, in fact the 'bourgeois revolution' was about to be
carried out by a movement hostile to the traditional aims of the middle class.[1]
Second, it is said that the Marxian interpretation of history has been falsified
by the historical process itself: feudalism does not lead to socialism via
capitalism. 'One conclusion at least must be drawn from the Soviet experiment and this is that history can bypass the phase of capitalism. The main
task of the Soviet regime has been the growth of the economy, the building of
heavy industry, which were the tasks which Marx allocated to capitalism.'[2] To
be sure, what Aron and Lichtheim say is true, or rather, half-true. Their interpretation of Marxist doctrine is formal; it assumes Marxism is a 'doctrine'.
Rather like Stalin's conception of the USSR as a 'socialist' society (see Chapter
5), it is mechanical and scholastic in approach. Marxism is a method of
analysing society, and as a method it may be modified and amended in the
light of experience; otherwise, it is a dogma. The question of whether a
revolution fulfills Marxist prophecy is a pointless one, because Marx was not
a prophet. The Bolshevik Revolution was not an inevitable event in history
for there are no inevitable events. The social and economic changes once
started in the nineteenth century continued under their own momentum and
undermined the autocracy. The administrative machinery could not cope. The
war aggravated the economic and political problems. Russian society became
a mass society. The lack of leadership by the Provisional Government perpetuated the stresses in the social system. The Bolshevik Party capitalised on
this situation. Its leaders were the only ones who were capable of seizing power
and keeping it. Any adequate analysis of the revolutionary process must take
into account both long-run and precipitating elements: they include chance
and economic, military, ideological, and individual factors.

---

[1] G. Lichtheim, 'On the Interpretation of Marx's Thought', *Survey*, No. 62 (1967), p. 14.
[2] Raymond Aron, *Democracy and Totalitarianism* (1968), p. 206.

Reading No. 3
Order No. 1 of the Petrograd Soviet
Source:
Izvestiya, 2 March 1917. Translated by J. R. Boyd in *Soviet Studies*, Vol. 19 (January 1968).

1 March 1917

To the garrison of the Petrograd Military District, to all soldiers of the guard, army, artillery and fleet for immediate and exact execution, and to the workers of Petrograd for their information.[1]

The Soviet of Workers' and Soldiers' Deputies has decreed:

(1) Committees are to be elected immediately in all companies, battalions, regiments, parks, batteries, squadrons, and in individual units of the different forms of military directorates, and in all naval vessels, from elected representatives of the rank and file of the above-mentioned units.

(2) All troop units which have not yet elected their representatives to the Soviet of Workers' Deputies are to elect one representative per company. Such representatives are to appear, with written certification, at the State Duma building at 10 a.m. on 2 March.

(3) In all political actions, troop units are subordinate to the Soviet of Workers' and Soldiers' Deputies, and to the committees thereof.

(4) The orders of the Military Commission of the State Duma are to be obeyed with the exception of those instances in which they are in contradiction to the orders and decrees[2] of the Soviet of Workers' and Soldiers' Deputies.

(5) All types of arms, such as rifles, machine guns, armoured cars, and others, must be put at the disposal of company and battalion committees, and under their control, and are not, in any case, to be issued to officers, even upon demand.

(6) On duty and in the performance of service responsibilities, soldiers must observe the strictest military discipline, but when off duty, in their political, civil and private lives, soldiers shall enjoy fully and completely the same rights as all citizens.

In particular, standing at attention and compulsory saluting when off duty are abolished.

(7) In the same way, addressing officers by honorary titles ('Your Excellency',

---

[1] The order is addressed solely to the garrison of the Petrograd Military District. The words 'to all soldiers of the guard, army, artillery and fleet' is by way of amplification and definition of the term 'garrison'.

[2] This passage was amended slightly in the text of Order No. 1 as published in *Pravda* on 8 March. In the *Pravda* version, the passage read 'only in such instances when they do not contradict the orders and decrees of the Soviet'.

'Your Honour', etc.) is abolished and is replaced by the following form of address, 'Mr General', 'Mr Colonel', etc.

Coarse address to soldiers by anyone of higher rank, and in particular, addressing soldiers by *ty* is prohibited, and any breach of this provision, as well as any misunderstandings between officers and soldiers, are to be reported by the latter to the company committees.

The order is to be read to all companies, battalions, regiments, ships' crews, batteries and other combatant and non-combatant units.

Petrograd Soviet of Workers' and Soldiers' Deputies.

Reading No. 4
'The Tasks of the Proletariat in the Present Revolution'
Source:
V. I. Lenin, *Collected Works* (Moscow, 1964), Vol. 24.

THESES

1) In our attitude towards the war, which under the new government of Lvov and Co. unquestionably remains on Russia's part a predatory imperialist war owing to the capitalist nature of that government, not the slightest concession to 'revolutionary defencism' is permissible.

The class-conscious proletariat can give its consent to a revolutionary war, which would really justify revolutionary defencism, only on condition: (a) that the power pass to the proletariat and the poorest sections of the peasants aligned with the proletariat; (b) that all annexations to be renounced in deed and not in word; (c) that a complete break be effected in actual fact with all capitalist interests.

In view of the undoubted honesty of those broad sections of the mass believers in revolutionary defencism who accept the war only as a necessity, and not as a means of conquest, in view of the fact that they are being deceived by the bourgeoisie, it is necessary with particular thoroughness, persistence and patience to explain their error to them, to explain the inseparable connection existing between capital and the imperialist war, and to prove that without overthrowing capital *it is impossible* to end the war by a truly democratic peace, a peace not imposed by violence.

The most widespread campaign for this view must be organised in the army at the front.

Fraternisation.

2) The specific feature of the present situation in Russia is that the country is *passing* from the first stage of the revolution – which, owing to the insufficient class-consciousness and organisation of the proletariat, placed power in the hands of the bourgeoisie – to its *second* stage, which must place power in the hands of the proletariat and the poorest sections of the peasants.

This transition is characterised, on the one hand, by a maximum of legally recognised rights (Russia is *now* the freest of all the belligerent countries in the world); on the other, by the absence of violence towards the masses, and, finally, by their unreasoning trust in the government of capitalists, those worst enemies of peace and socialism.

This peculiar situation demands of us an ability to adapt ourselves to the *special* conditions of Party work among unprecedentedly large masses of proletarians who have just awakened to political life.

3) No support for the Provisional Government; the utter falsity of all its promises should be made clear, particularly of those relating to the renunciation of annexations. Exposure in place of the impermissible, illusion-breeding 'demand' that *this* government, a government of capitalists, should *cease* to be an imperialist government.

4) Recognition of the fact that in most of the Soviets of Workers' Deputies our Party is in a minority, so far a small minority, as against *a bloc of all* the petty-bourgeois opportunist elements, from the Popular Socialists and the Socialist-Revolutionaries down to the Organising Committee (Chkheidze, Tsereteli, etc.), Steklov, etc., etc., who have yielded to the influence of the bourgeoisie and spread that influence among the proletariat.

The masses must be made to see that the Soviets of Workers' Deputies are the *only possible* form of revolutionary government, and that therefore our task is, as long as *this* government yields to the influence of the bourgeoisie, to present a patient, systematic, and persistent *explanation* of the errors of their tactics, an explanation especially adapted to the practical needs of the masses.

As long as we are in the minority we carry on the work of criticising and exposing errors and at the same time we preach the necessity of transferring the entire state power to the Soviets of Workers' Deputies, so that the people may overcome their mistakes by experience.

5) Not a parliamentary republic – to return to a parliamentary republic from the Soviets of Workers' Deputies would be a retrograde step – but a republic of Soviets of Workers', Agricultural Labourers' and Peasants' Deputies throughout the country, from top to bottom.

Abolition of the police, the army and the bureaucracy.[1]

The salaries of all officials, all of whom are elective and displaceable at any time, not to exceed the average wage of a competent worker.

6) The weight of emphasis in the agrarian programme to be shifted to the Soviets of Agricultural Labourers' Deputies.

Confiscation of all landed estates.

Nationalisation of *all* lands in the country, the land to be disposed of by the local Soviets of Agricultural Labourers' and Peasants' Deputies. The organisation of separate Soviets of Deputies of Poor Peasants. The setting up of a model farm on each of the large estates (ranging in size from 100 to 300 desyatinas according to local and other conditions, and to the decisions of the local bodies) under the control of the Soviets of Agricultural Labourers' Deputies and for the public account.

7) The immediate amalgamation of all banks in the country into a single national bank, and the institution of control over it by the Soviet of Workers' Deputies.

8) It is not our *immediate* task to 'introduce' socialism, but only to bring social

---

[1] i.e., the standing army to be replaced by the arming of the whole people.

C*

production and the distribution of products at once under the *control* of the Soviets of Workers' Deputies.

 9) Party tasks:
    (a) Immediate convocation of a party congress;
    (b) Alteration of the Party Programme, mainly:
        (i) On the question of imperialism and the imperialist war;
        (ii) On our attitude towards the state and *our* demand for a 'commune state'[1];
        (iii) Amendment of our out-of-date minimum programme.
    (c) Change of the Party's name.[2]
 10) A new International.

We must take the initiative in creating a revolutionary International, an International against the *social-chauvinists* and against the 'Centre'.[3]

---

[1] i.e., a state of which the Paris Commune was the prototype.

[2] Instead of 'Social-Democracy', whose official leaders *throughout* the world have betrayed socialism and deserted to the bourgeoisie (the 'defencists' and the vacillating 'Kautskyites'), we must call ourselves the *Communist Party*.

[3] The 'Centre' in the international Social-Democratic movement is the trend which vacillates between the chauvinists (='defencists') and internationalists, i.e., Kautsky and Co. in Germany, Longuet and Co. in France, Chkheidze and Co. in Russia, Turati and Co. in Italy, MacDonald and Co. in Britain, etc.

INTRODUCTORY

Carr, E. H. *A History of Soviet Russia*, Vol. 1. London: Macmillan, 1950.

Dobb, Maurice. *Soviet Economic Development Since 1917*. London: Routledge, 1966.

Florinsky, M. T. *The End of the Russian Empire*. New York: 1961; New Haven Connecticut: Yale University Press, 1931.
Russia. New York: Macmillan, 1955.

Kochan, Lionel B. *The Making of Modern Russia*. London: Jonathan Cape, 1962.

Seton Watson, Hugh. *The Decline of Imperial Russia*. New York: Praeger, 1952.

Sumner, Benedict H. *A Short History of Russia*. New York: Harcourt and Brace, 1949.

Wolfe, Bertram. *Three Who Made a Revolution*. London: Thames and Hudson, 1956.

BASIC

Bunyan, James, and H. H. Fisher. *The Bolshevik Revolution, 1917-18: Documents and Materials*. Stanford, California: Hoover Institute, 1934.

Carr, E. H. *The Bolshevik Revolution, 1917-1923*. 3 Vols. London: Macmillan, 1950-1953.

Chamberlin, William H. *The Russian Revolution, 1917-1921*. New York: Macmillan, 1952.

Eason, Warren W. 'Population Changes', in Cyril E. Black (ed.). *The Transformation of Russian Society*. Cambridge, Mass.: Harvard University Press, 1960, pp. 72-90.

Feldmesser, Robert A. 'Social Classes and Political Structure', in Cyril E. Black (ed.). *The Transformation of Russian Society*. Cambridge, Mass.: Harvard University Press, 1960, pp. 235-52.

Haimson, Leopold. *The Russian Marxists and the Origins of Bolshevism*. Cambridge, Mass.: Harvard University Press, 1965.

Khromov, P. A. *Ekonomicheskoe razvitie Rossii v XIX-XX vekakh, 1800-1917*. Moscow: Gospolitizdat, 1950.

Lenin, V. I. 'The Tasks of the Proletariat in the Present Revolution', *Collected Works*, Vol. 24. Moscow, 1964, pp. 19-26.

Lorimer, Frank. *The Population of the Soviet Union*. Geneva: League of Nations, 1946.

Lyashchenko, P. I. *History of the National Economy of Russia*. New York: Macmillan, 1949.

Pipes, Richard (ed.). *The Russian Intelligentsia*. New York: Columbia University Press, 1961.

Rashin, A. G. *Formirovanie rabochego klassa Rossii*. Moscow: Sotsekgiz, 1958.

Schapiro, Leonard. *The Communist Party of the Soviet Union*. London: Constable, 1960.

Trotsky, Leon. *The History of the Russian Revolution*. New York: Simon and Schuster, 1936.

SPECIALISED

Aron, Raymond. *Democracy and Totalitarianism*. London: Weidenfeld and Nicolson, 1968.

Dan, F. 'Vtoraya Duma', in Martov, Maslov, and Potresov, *Obshchestvennoe dvizhenie v Rossii v nachale XX- go veke*, Vol. 4, Part ii. Spb., 1909-14.

Gerschenkron, Alexander. 'The Rate of Industrial Growth in Russia since 1805', in *The Journal of Economic History*, Vol. 7 (Supplement), pp. 144-74.

Gottschalk, Louis. 'Causes of Revolution', in *American Journal of Sociology*, Vol. 50, No. 1, 1944, pp. 1-8.

Kornhauser, William. *The Politics of Mass Society*. London: Routledge, 1960.

Lane, David. *The Roots of Russian Communism*. Assen: Van Gorcum, 1969.

Lenin, V. I. 'The Two Tactics of Social Democracy in the Democratic Revolution', in *Selected Works* (1936), Vol. 3. Moscow, 1936, pp. 39-138.

   'The Constituent Assembly Elections and the Dictatorship of the Proletariat', *Collected Works* (1965), Vol. 30, pp. 253-75.

Lichtheim, George. 'On the Interpretation of Marx's Thought', in *Survey*, No. 62, 1967, pp. 3-14.

Moore, Barrington, Jr. *Social Origins of Dictatorship and Democracy*. London: Allen Lane, 1967.

Potolov, S. I. *Rabochie Donbassa v XIX veka*. Moscow, 1963.

Reed, John. *Ten Days that Shook the World*. New York: Vintage Books, 1960.

Samoylov, F. N. *Vospominaniya ob Ivanovo-Voznesenskom rabochem dvizhenii*, Part I. Moscow, 1922.

Shipulina, A. V. 'Ivanovo-voznesenskie rabochie nakanune pervoy russkoy revolyutsii', *Doklady i soobshcheniya instituta istorii*, Nol 8. Moscow, 1955.

   'Soviet Order No. 1', *Izvestiya*, 2 March 1917.

Stone, Lawrence. 'Theories of Revolution', in *World Politics*, Vol. 18, No. 2, January 1966, pp. 159-76.

Trotsky, L. *The Permanent Revolution*, translated by Max Schactman. New York: Pioneer Publishers, 1931.

Varentsova, O. A., and M. A. Bagaev. *Za 10 let*. Ivanovo, 1930.

Venturi, Franco. *The Roots of Revolution: A History of the Populist and Socialist Movements in 19th Century Russia*, translated by Francis Haskell. London: Weidenfeld and Nicolson, 1960.

Von Laue, Theodore H. *Sergei Witte and the Industrialisation of Russia*. New York: Columbia University Press, 1963.

Vucinich, Alexander. 'The State and the Local Community', in C. E. Black (ed.). *The Transformation of Russian Society*. Cambridge, Mass.: Harvard University Press, 1960, pp. 191-208.

'Zemskaya reforma 1864', *Bol'shaya sovetskaya entsiklopediya*, Vol. 17. Moscow, 1952, p. 37.

3

BOLSHEVIK
CONSOLIDATION OF POWER
AND RECONSTRUCTION

After the Revolution, Soviet Russia's leaders were faced with the problem of reconstruction. As Marxists, they believed in the establishment of a new form of society previously unknown to history. But what form should this society take? In theory it was to be socialist: the polity was to be democratic, the economy was to be governed by the principle of production for use, not for profit, and social relations were to be equalitarian. The needs of the people were to be fulfilled by a rational plan and not the whims of the market. In the Communist Manifesto, Marx had said: 'When in the course of development class distinctions have disappeared and all production has been concentrated in the hands of a vast association of the whole nation, the public power will lose its political character.'[1]

Marx and Engels, however, had formulated no plans for the actual organisation of a socialist society. The immediate post-revolutionary period was regarded by the Bolshevik government as a transitional one. The 'dictatorship of the proletariat' rather than democracy would be necessary to prevent the revival of counter-revolutionary groups. It was expected that socialist revolutions would occur in the advanced industrial countries of the West. The 'building of socialism' would not be Russia's task alone: as Lenin pointed out in the summer of 1918:

We do not close our eyes to the fact that we cannot achieve a socialist revolution in one country alone, even if that country were less backward than Russia and even if we lived under easier conditions than those created by four years of hard, distressing war . . . We are deeply convinced that in the near future historical events will bring the West European proletariat to supreme power, and in this respect we shall not be alone in the world arena as we are now. Through this, the road to Socialism and its embodiment in life will be made easier.[2]

The period from October 1917 to the summer of 1918, did not see 'the intro-

---

[1] 'Communist Manifesto', *Selected Works*, vol. 2 (Moscow, 1958), p. 54.
[2] Cited in A. Baykov, *The Development of the Soviet Economic System* (1946), pp. 47-8.

duction of socialism' in Russia. Politically, the Bolsheviks consolidated their
power: from July 1918 other opposing 'bourgeois' parties were banned; a one-
party state was set up. The freedom of the press was curtailed. The enemies
of the regime were harassed. Trotsky, who was Commissar for War between
1918 and 1925 declared, 'You protest against the mild terror which we
are directing against our class enemies. But you should know that not later
than a month from now the terror will assume very violent forms after
the example of the great French revolutionaries. The guillotine will be
ready for our enemies and not merely the jail.'[1] The Bolshevik secret police
organisation, the Cheka, was soon formed. In 1918, the Red Terror took
place against the enemies of the regime. The Tsar and his family were
murdered. Others, either connected with the old order or opposed to the
new, such as the anarchists, were shot. The Cheka was the instrument of class
justice. 'The Cheka is the defence of the Revolution as the Red Army is.
And just as in the civil war the Red Army cannot stop to ask whether or not
it may harm individuals . . . the Cheka is obliged to defend the Revolution and
conquer the enemy, even if its sword does by chance sometimes fall upon the
heads of the innocent.'[2] An estimated 50,000 were shot by the Cheka during
the Civil War.[3]

On 3 March 1918, a peace treaty with Germany was signed at Brest-
Litovsk. The most important terms of the treaty entailed that Russia lost
considerable territories including much of Poland, the Baltic Provinces and
some of the Ukraine. The imperialist war was not turned into a civil war.
Lenin sued for peace when he realised that the army was exhausted.

During the first six months of Soviet rule, spontaneous seizures of power
took place, workers introduced 'workers' control'. Some left-wing socialists,
rather naively, held that such elemental activity was the introduction of
proletarian democracy and many workers' committees regarded their factories
as 'their own'.

The main objective for the Bolshevik leadership was to secure the 'commanding heights' of the economy. The first steps of the new government were to
nationalise the land and to take measures to give the proletariat 'control'
over capitalist industry. It was not until June 1918 that a decree was published
nationalising the key industries of the economy: coal, oil, iron and steel,
chemicals and textiles. In December 1920, nationalisation extended to all
enterprises employing more than five workers using any kind of mechanical
power or more than ten workers without mechanical power. Nationalisation
went further than the Bolsheviks had intended in October 1917 for two main
reasons: firstly, the workers, like the peasants, had carried out a *de facto*

---

[1] Cited by E. H. Carr, *The Bolshevik Revolution 1917-1923*, vol. 1 (1950), pp. 157-8.
[2] Dzerzhinsky, cited by Robert Conquest, *The Soviet Police System* (1968), p. 15.
[3] *Ibid.*

seizure of property; secondly, legal nationalisation, it was thought, would thwart intervention by foreign governments to protect their nationals' property. In industrial organisation, ideas current immediately before October were not implemented. The April Theses[1] declared the Soviets sovereign, but special organs of central and local administration were set up. One-man control of factories and industrial discipline were introduced. Syndicalism and workers' control were repudiated.

The role of the state was clearly defined in Marxist thought and Lenin in August/September 1917 had attempted to apply Marxist doctrine to what he believed was the impending revolution in Russia. In *The State and Revolution* (sections are reprinted in Reading No. 5) he argued that under capitalism the state was the instrument of the bankers and industrialists for the exploitation of the oppressed class. The bourgeois state machine, therefore, had to be smashed. The police, the standing army and the bureaucracy had to be 'abolished'. The salaries of all officials, who were to be elected and be subject to recall at any time, were 'not to exceed the average wage of a competent worker'.[2]

With the abolition of the capitalist state, it would be necessary, argued Lenin, to replace it with government institutions controlled by the proletariat. In the short run, the state would not begin to 'wither away' but the *dictatorship of the proletariat* or the *proletariat organised as the ruling class* would be dominant. This was necessary 'to abolish completely all exploitation', to defend the proletariat against a possible counter-revolution and to organise a socialist economy. The dictatorship of the proletariat was essential during the transitional period from capitalism to communism. 'Revolution consists not in the new class commanding, governing with the aid of the *old* state machine, but in this class *smashing* this machine and commanding, governing with the the aid of a *new* machine.' (*State and Revolution*). Lenin pointed out that only under *communism*, when no exploiting class would exist, would no 'special apparatus of suppression' be necessary and that with the development of society from capitalism to communism, would the state begin to 'wither away'. Let us now turn to consider what happened in Russia after the revolution.

War Communism

From 1918 to 1921 the country was enveloped in the chaos of civil war and foreign intervention: it was a period known as 'War Communism'. For much of the time the Bolsheviks ruled only one-seventh of Russian territory, mainly the Great Russian areas of the country, the remainder being occupied by other governments. The Whites had the support of foreign powers whose troops

[1] See Reading No. 4.
[2] 'The Tasks of the Proletariat in the Present Revolution', *Selected Works*, vol. 6, p. 23.

symbolically fought at their side.[1] The decisive factor in this struggle was the allegiance of the peasantry. While the Red Army confiscated the farms' produce, they defended the rights of the peasants to the land they possessed. Although it is not true to say that the peasantry 'supported' the Bolsheviks, they were even more opposed to the White Armies who it was believed did not recognise their rights to the land which had been seized. This fundamental social factor probably gave victory to the Red Army.

In the sphere of industry, the Soviet government in these early years tried to set up a centralised system of production and exchange. This was facilitated by the role the state had played in the past and by the extra wartime controls over the private sector which had been imposed by the Tsarist government. During War Communism an attempt was made to organise supply and output in a centralised manner though due to the general chaos, this was not particularly effective. The central powers had insufficient information to plan properly and, in short, could not enforce their decisions. In fact, only war industries and some other large industrial units were amenable to control, the majority of enterprises produced what they could barter best locally.

In the countryside, the 'friendly alliance' between worker and peasant was disrupted. To meet the needs of the Red Army and the town population, the Bolsheviks sent armed detachments to the countryside to confiscate agricultural produce, which led to the claim that 'little short of war had been declared by the town on the country'.[2] Lenin's *April Theses* had recommended the creation of large farms on confiscated estates. These were set up only where technical organisation of production was required, such as in sugar-beet and flax. The elemental land seizure and division of the larger units resulted in an equalisation of the size of land holdings. Whereas in 1917, 58 per cent of arable land was farmed in units of under four *desyatinas*[3] in size, by 1920 the proportion was 86 per cent.[4] Lenin's pre-revolutionary policy was not implemented: large-scale socialist collective production was not introduced, private small holdings proliferated and flourished.

The economic and administrative chaos cannot simply be attributed to the Bolsheviks' intention of destroying the bourgeois state, though this added to the confusion. The breakdown was caused by the after-effects of the First World War, by the seizure of the land and by the stress of the civil war. Money lost its value and exchange was conducted through barter. Rationing of necessaries was introduced: in 1918 there were four rationing categories depending on the recipient's contribution to the economy, by 1920 these had increased to thirty, finally the number was reduced to five. By 1921, money

[1] David Footman, *Civil War in Russia* (1961). John Bradley, *Allied Intervention in Russia* (1968).
[2] A Left S.R., cited by E. H. Carr, *The Bolshevik Revolution* (1963), vol. 2, p. 147.
[3] 1 *desyatina* is equivalent to 2.7 acres (4 *desyatinas* are 10.8 acres).
[4] L. Kritsman, *Geroicheski period velikoy Russkoy revolyutsii* (n.d.), p. 68, cited by E. H. Carr, *The Bolshevik Revolution*, vol. 2, p. 168.

payment for rations, fuel, lodgings, newspapers, medical supplies and post and telegraph services was abolished. Under War Communism, output fell considerably. By 1920 total industrial output was only twenty per cent of the 1913 figures.[1] The decline of output, the inflation and the almost complete paralysis of trade did not bode well for the government. In 1921 the Soviet leadership introduced the New Economic Policy which involved a return to private enterprise.

The New Economic Policy

In the West, the abolition of War Communism was regarded by many as *proving* the failure of planning and communism in general. This view was based on the assumption that War Communism was an attempt to introduce a communist system. Of course, it was nothing of the kind. 'War Communism' signified the complete breakdown of market production and exchange; it was an expeditious attempt by the Soviet government to shore up the economy. The 'abolition' of money was no more the introduction of communism than was the use of cigarettes for currency in Germany after the Second World War. Other proposals, such as those for 'free love',[2] were also a reflection of the breakdown of social norms rather than of the introduction of 'communism'. In Lenin's words: 'War Communism was thrust upon us by war and ruin. It was not, nor could it be, a policy that corresponded to the economic tasks of the proletariat. It was a temporary measure.'[3] The New Economic Policy (NEP) was introduced primarily to get the economy back on its feet. It was a controversial policy. To the control of the commanding heights of the economy (through the nationalisation of banking and large scale enterprises) was grafted a market mechanism similar to those in capitalist societies. Soviet Russia moved from *de jure* administrative control to a mixed economy, in which large industrial units were nationalised, but small industrial units and almost the whole of agriculture were privately owned. Prices were determined by the market through the operation of supply and demand. Other policies moved away from the immediate post-revolutionary administrative system. Gradually wage differentials were increased and higher payments to 'specialists' were justified. In this respect Lenin before the revolution had overestimated both the degree to which a modern economy could be run on egalitarian lines and the ability of the proletariat to perform the functions of bourgeois technical staff. NEP, in Etzioni's terms,[4] added utilitarian stimuli to gain the public's acceptance of the Bolshevik rulers.

---

[1] Figures cited by A. Baykov, p. 8.

[2] See Chapter 11.

[3] Cited by M. Dobb, *Soviet Economic Development since 1917* (Routledge, London, sixth edition 1966), p. 123.

[4] See Chapter 1, p. 1.

The economic aims of the government were to restore the value of money, to induce the peasants to give up grain to feed the towns, and to bring up industrial production to the pre-war level. The arbitrary requisitioning of peasants' produce was stopped. In its place, the peasant had to hand over to the state by way of a 'tax in kind', a certain proportion of his produce, the remainder of which he could trade on the market. While large industrial enterprises and banks continued nationalised, other enterprises were de-nationalised. With the exception of war industries, municipal enterprises, locomotive works and enterprises concerned with major government projects, state institutions were allowed to trade with each other in the same way that free trade took place between town and country. In order to encourage efficiency, 'profit and loss' criteria were introduced and all undertakings were to be managed on a commercial basis.

By 1926 industrial production was roughly back to the pre-war (1913) level. By 1927 the gross value output of large-scale industry was 123.6 compared with a base of 100 in 1913, by 1928 the index had risen to 154.3.[1] The immediate economic objectives of the NEP had been realised. In the political and social spheres the Bolsheviks were now established as a government and were no longer an illegal political party. The powers of tradition, of day-to-day administration were beginning to assert themselves over the more revolutionary aspects of Bolshevik policy. But the position of the new government was still insecure, many of the policies adopted were determined by expediency and long-term policies had still to be worked out.

On the political side, the existence of private agriculture and trade provided a basis on which a political counter-revolution could arise. As we have seen, Russia's Bolshevik rulers believed that economic class determined political behaviour. As classes could not live harmoniously, Russia's political structure of the late 1920s could not endure. The Bolshevik leaders had always lived in the hope that revolution would occur in the West and that the victorious European proletariat would come to their aid. As the years passed, this hope faded. The Soviet Union was the only state socialist society, situated in a hostile world environment. A greater rate of increase in industrial development was essential. Such an increase would enlarge the proletariat, strengthen the Communist Party's hold internally and it would provide the means for greater military security from the capitalist states. The questions arose, therefore, of how such industrialisation could take place and at what pace it should proceed.

Before considering the changes brought about in such respects under Stalin, it is necessary to outline the discussions of doctrine which were taking place in

[1] A. Gerschenkron, 'The Rate of Growth in Russia', *The Journal of Economic History*, vol. 7 (Supplement), p. 161.

the Communist Party and which later provided an ideological basis for the formulation and execution of the Five-Year Plans.

Socialism in One Country

We have seen that one of the justifications for the Bolshevik seizure of power in 1917 was the belief that help would come from the proletariat of advanced European states. But in the absence of a proletarian revolution abroad and the apparent 'stabilisation of the capitalist world', the problem of the course of development for the USSR was sharply posed. At the crux of the matter was the interpretation of historical materialism. Earlier, we saw that Russia under the Tsars was regarded by Marxists as being in the feudal stage of development and that the Mensheviks regarded the creation of a capitalist bourgeois society to be the next principal development. Trotsky, on the other hand, it will be recalled, argued for passing straight through the capitalist to the socialist stage. This argument was taken up again during the period of the New Economic Policy and afterwards. In this post-revolutionary situation, the argument shifted from the problem of carrying out a socialist revolution to that of the building of a socialist society after the revolution had been achieved. The chief antagonists were now Trotsky and Stalin.

The core of Trotsky's argument was that a socialist social system could not be completed by the proletariat in one country alone. Capitalism was seen as international in character and could only be destroyed by an international revolution. Trotsky pointed out that Lenin in the earliest days of the infant Soviet republic made it a 'fundamental task' to establish a 'socialist organisation of society and the victory of socialism in all countries'.[1] The building of socialism, argued Trotsky, was dependent on the victory of the proletariat abroad: 'The real rise of a socialist economy in Russia will become possible only after the victory of the proletariat in the most important countries of Europe.'[2] He therefore emphasised the international character of socialism and the international role the USSR should play in supporting workers' revolutions abroad.

Stalin writing in *Foundations of Leninism* (April 1924) had taken a similar theoretical position to Trotsky:[3]

. . . overthrowing the power of the bourgeoisie and establishing the power of the proletariat in a single country does not yet guarantee the complete victory of socialism. After entrenching itself in power and leading the peasantry after it, the

[1] V. I. Lenin, 'The Declaration of the Rights of the Toiling and Exploited People', cited by L. Trotsky, *The Revolution Betrayed* (Plough Press ed., 1957), p. 291.

[2] L. Trotsky, cited by E. H. Carr, *Socialism in One Country* (1959), vol. 2, p. 42.

[3] Trotsky cites the following passage from the same work: 'For the final victory of Socialism, for the organisation of socialist production, the efforts of one country, especially a peasant country like ours, are not enough – for this we must have the efforts of the proletarians of several advanced countries' (*The Revolution Betrayed*, p. 291).

proletariat of the victorious country can and must build up socialist society. But does that mean that in this way the proletariat will secure a complete and final victory for socialism, i.e. does it mean that with the forces of a single country it can finally consolidate socialism and fully guarantee that country against intervention, which means against restoration? Certainly not. That requires the victory for the revolution in several countries.[1]

Stalin's views, however, changed between April 1924 and January 1926, when, in *Problems of Leninism*, he wrote that the above quoted formulation was 'inadequate' and 'inaccurate'.[2] In the same article Stalin says that the victory of socialism 'means the possibility of the proletariat seizing power and using that power for the construction of a complete socialist society in our country, with the sympathy and support of the workers of other countries, but without the preliminary victory of the proletarian revolution in other countries . . . To deny such a possibility is to display lack of faith in the task of building socialism, is to abandon Leninism.'[3] Stalin too found references in the works of Lenin to support his view that socialism could be built in one country: '. . . the victory of socialism is possible in the first instance in a few capitalist countries or even in one single capitalist country.'[4]

 It is somewhat fruitless to pursue the question of who was right. Stalin was in command and his analysis became enshrined as official doctrine. The credo that socialism could be achieved by the efforts of Soviet Russia alone became a belief system which acted as a stimulus for the population to carry out the later rapid industrialisation. It harnessed traditional national and patriotic values and it directed them to definite economic tasks. Politically, it was a positive policy involving independent social action by the Soviet Republic. 'Stalinism' as an ideology contained many of the values specific to Russia's peasant past, it reified the official ideology of the Tsars: *samoderzhavie* (autocracy) became embodied in Stalin the leader, *pravoslavie* (orthodoxy) became the rigidified dogma of the Communist Party, *narodnost'* (national community) became the peculiar Soviet Russian concept of socialism. On the other hand, as Trotskyists have argued, Stalin lay himself open to charges of neglecting the world proletariat. In terms of Marxist theory, Trotsky had the better case: 'contradictions' would continue to exist in the USSR as long as there was a state apparatus which would be necessary to defend the USSR from the capitalist world. In terms of practical policy, there was much to be said from a Soviet point of view for Stalin's policy: from the Kremlin of the late 1920s the forces of world capitalism looked formidably strong and those of socialism extremely weak.

 [1] *Foundations of Leninism* (Moscow, 1934), p. 36.

 [2] *Problems of Leninism* (Moscow, 1934), p. 138.

 [3] J. Stalin *loc. cit.*, p. 140.

 [4] Cited in E. H. Carr, *Socialism in One Country* (Part Two), pp. 40-1. A full discussion of this point is given here.

The doctrine of 'socialism in one country' was the basis of Soviet policy and it entailed the postponement of the final victory of world communism. The supporters of the Communist International were pledged to give priority to the development of socialism in the USSR. Stalinism was an ideology which adapted Marxism to Soviet conditions of the late-1920s. In a nutshell it provided both a political and a spiritual framework for industrialisation. It was a Soviet atheistic version of the Protestant Ethic.

To build socialism in Soviet Russia, Stalin embarked on three interrelated courses; rapid industrialisation, collectivisation and centralised political control. Let us discuss each in turn.[1]

Industrialisation and Economic Change

What were the possible courses for industrialisation open to the Soviet leaders? There were four main economic alternatives. The first was one of the policies adopted by the Tsarist government: investment in agriculture to promote the export of grain which could be used to import industrial capital goods. As Russia had a greater comparative advantage in agriculture than in industry, it followed from the theory of international trade that she could gain by exchanging agricultural produce for industrial goods. This course was rejected by the Soviet government, mainly on political grounds. Internally, it would have entailed (at least at the time the scheme was put forward) the growth of an independent free farming community which might have politically undermined the Bolshevik regime. It would also have left the Soviet Union dependent on a 'hostile capitalist world' for strategic imports.

A second possible course was to invite foreign investments and loans, or to give concessions to foreign firms to build factories in the USSR, in a similar fashion to the agreement with the Fiat motor company in 1966-7. The difficulties here were two-fold: such agreements would again have made the USSR dependent on capitalist states and foreign firms, and governments for their part were highly suspicious of the new Bolshevik order which had renounced the debts of the Tsarist government. Thus loans and help from this direction were not a practical proposition.

If industrialisation could not be financed with outside capital, either earned with exports or borrowed from foreigners, then capital had to be found internally. Trotsky and his followers, the 'left-wing opposition', argued that this 'saving' should be achieved by squeezing the peasantry. This was the third alternative. In this way 'primitive socialist accummulation' could take place. Very simply, this meant that the peasantry would give more in value to the industrial sector than it would receive back, at least in the short run, and the difference could be used for investment. When this plan was put forward, it

[1] For a detailed economic history, see Alec Nove, *An Economic History of the USSR* (1969).

was rejected principally because it was felt that political stability depended on the *smychka* (or alliance) between the proletariat and the peasantry.

The fourth alternative was to make real savings in industry itself. If production could rise and real wages were kept constant then a surplus would be available for investment. Obviously, if some of this surplus could also be used for raising the standard of living, then the population would be better off and also the rate of growth could increase. The net investment of the NEP period came mainly from this source. The chief drawback here was that the margin for such saving was small and a substantial growth-rate for very long could not be expected from this source.

The political climate altered in the USSR between the death of Lenin in 1924 and the rise to power of Stalin by 1928. The First Five-Year Plan, discussed below, was launched on 1 October of the latter year: it profoundly altered the socio-economic structure. A very high growth rate was set and was based largely on the adoption of the third of the above proposals (squeezing the peasants).

The main feature of Soviet planning from the end of the 1920s was that it aimed to sustain a high industrial growth rate. The First Five-Year Plan (1928–1933) envisaged an annual industrial growth rate of from twenty-two to twenty-five per cent. The bulk of this increase was to go into the capital sector. At the same time, a social infra-structure was to be built up: considerable investment had to be made in health and education.

Rather than increasing production within the parameters of the existing structure of enterprises, the Soviet government attempted to develop new industrial complexes which in the short run might give lower returns than the expansion of existing units. Spurning conventional economic wisdom which recommended adding more labour inputs (labour of course was abundant and capital scarce) to cheaper, less technologically advanced machinery bought 'second-hand', the new industrial enterprises were made capital intensive. The policy was intended to bring up the USSR to the industrial standards of the advanced capitalist powers. A similar policy was advocated for industrial location. While greater short-run returns could be achieved by extending the existing industrial structure in the European parts of Russia, in the long run output would be cheaper if based on the minerals located to the east of the Urals. Another and perhaps overriding factor in this last respect was the importance of the development of Central Asia and Siberia for defence purposes.

Economic Change 1928 to 1955

Having discussed the principles of Soviet economic planning, let us now turn to the results of the years between 1928 and 1955 which are a matter of some

controversy. Here I shall rely mainly on western estimates of Soviet achievement. Gerschenkron has estimated on the basis of Soviet figures that Soviet
average annual growth between 1928 and 1932 was 20.35 per cent for
all industry and between 1928 and 1940 it averaged an annual 17.5 per cent.[1]
The relationship between these increases and the growth of western economies
may be seen by expressing Soviet output as a ratio of the American. This is
shown below:

Industrial Output in Russia as Percentage of
Industrial Output in the United States

Year	Ratio
1913	6.9
1928	6.9
1932	27.3
1938	45.1

(*Source:* Gerschenkron, *op. cit.*, p. 166)

Gerschenkron points out that the Soviet figures cited are too big. He suggests that Soviet large-scale industry increased at an annual rate of between
15 and 17 per cent between 1928 and 1938 rather than the claimed 19 per
cent, and that the all-industry increase is more likely to be nearer 14 or 16 per
cent than the claimed 18 per cent.[1] But these reservations do not change the
general picture.

Other indexes have been calculated by Abram Bergson, who has also
compared the Soviet and American performance. His contrast is made firstly
on the basis of relatively similar stages of development: the USSR in 1928/
1940, the USA 1869/1908, and secondly, at approximately identical year by
year comparisons (see Table 3). These figures are calculated on a *per capita*
basis and show higher Soviet figures for nearly all periods compared; this is
especially so if one compares Soviet statistics of the 1928/55 period with the
American ones for roughly the same time (4.4 per cent against 1.7 per cent).

Such industrial growth resulted in rapid urbanisation. Raymond Aron is
probably correct when he says that this rate of growth 'had no parallel in
any western country': the non-agricultural work force increased from 10 to
45 million between 1926 and 1955, in the USA a similar rate of growth (between 1880 and 1930) took twice as long.[2] According to official Soviet figures,

[1] A Gerschenkron, 'The Rate of Growth in Russia,' *The Journal of Economic History* vol. 7,
(1947), Supplement, pp. 161-5.
[2] *Op. cit.*, p. 167.
[3] Raymond Aron. *18 Lectures on Industrial Society* (1961), p. 150.

the urban population rose from 28.7 millions in 1929 to 63.1 millions in 1940 or from 19 to 33 per cent of the total population (see Table – Appendix F). The social upheaval in Soviet Russia was as great, if not greater than in the USA, for the urban immigrants were nearly all from the countryside whereas American immigrants coming from Europe often brought urban values and skills with them.

Table 3. Rates of Growth of 'Real' Gross National Product per Capita, USSR and USA, Selected Periods

YEAR	USSR Average annual rate of growth (per cent) with output in ruble factor cost of 1937	YEAR	USA Average annual rate of growth (per cent) with output:	
			(a) In 1929 dols.	(b) In 1954 dols.
1928–1937	4.5	1869/78–1879/88	4.1	—
1937–1940	1.0	1879/88–1889/98	1.2	—
1928–1940	3.6	1889/98–1899/1908	2.6	—
		1869/78–1899/1908	2.6	—
1940–1950	2.9	1899/1908–1929	1.7	—
1950–1955	5.8			
1928–1955	3.8	1929–1948	—	1.5
1928–1955*	4.4	1948–1957	—	1.9
		1929–1957	—	1.7
(1)	(2)	(3)	(4)	(5)

Source: Abram Bergson, *The Real National Income of Soviet Russia Since 1928.* (Harvard University Press, Cambridge, 1961), p. 264.
* Excluding War Years.

Household consumption, on the other hand, was a different picture. Table 4 shows that whereas Soviet 'real' household consumption (on average) actually *declined* between 1928 and 1940, at a similar period of development in the USA (between 1869 and 1908) consumption increased. It was not until post 1940 and particularly after 1950 that Soviet consumption actually began to rise – and then at a higher rate than the American. Taking the 1928–1955 period as a whole, Soviet household consumption increased by 1.7 per cent, which is identical to the American rise between 1929 and 1957.

There can be no doubt that Soviet economic growth far exceeded and probably doubled that of Russia before the First World War. By the time of the German invasion of Russia in 1941, the USSR had developed an economic base comparable to other more mature states of Western Europe. But Soviet economic advance was not attained without sacrifice. Let us now turn to other important aspects of the Stalin era by discussing collectivisation and political control.

Table 4. Rates of Growth of 'Real' Household Consumption per Capita, USSR and USA, Selected Periods

| | USSR Average annual rate of growth (per cent) with output in adjusted market prices of 1937 | | USA Average annual rate of growth (per cent) with output | |
YEAR		YEAR	(a) In 1929 dols.	(b) In 1954 dols.
1928–1937	−0.3	1869/78–1879/88	4.1	—
1937–1940	−1.5	1879/88–1889/98	1.2	—
1928–1940	−0.6	1889/98–1899/1908	2.6	—
		1869/78–1899/1908	2.6	—
1940–1950	1.9	1899/1908–1929	1.7	—
1950–1955	6.7			
1928–1955	1.7	1929–1948	—	1.5
1928–1955*	2.0	1948–1957	—	1.9
		1929–1957	—	1.7
(1)	(2)	(3)	(4)	(5)

Source: Abram Bergson, The Real National Income of Soviet Russia Since 1928. (Harvard University Press, Cambridge, 1961), p. 284.
* Excluding War Years.

Collectivisation and Agriculture

We have seen that the land seizure of 1917–1918 resulted both in the dissolution of the large estates and the equalisation of land holdings: the proportion of land in peasant hands increased between 1914 and 1928 from 70 per cent to 96 per cent, and the number of peasant households increased by more than a third. In 1927, holdings of between 15 and 27 acres accounted for approximately half of all peasant land compared to one third before 1914. Bolshevik pre-revolution policy of setting-up large model farms was only implemented on a very small scale: in 1927 they accounted only for two per cent of the total grain crop and covered little more than one per cent of the cultivated area.[1] The scale of peasant farming was too small to allow for intensive agricultural production: productivity was low, and methods were primitive; most sowing, a half of the harvesting and a third of the threshing was still done by hand. While the nationalisation of the land and its subsequent division in 1917 had satisfied the peasants socially and politically, it resulted in an agricultural structure unconducive to increasing the marketable surplus.

[1] Maurice Dobb, Soviet Economic Development Since 1917 (1966), p. 209.

The New Economic Policy, by allowing 'market' relationships to develop in the countryside, increased the differentiation of the peasants. This had important political repercussions. The party saw the peasantry as composed of three main groups: the rich *kulaks* who were the class enemy; the 'middle' peasants, party allies; the 'poor' peasants who were supporters of the government. The rational of the market meant that the rich would prosper. While *economically* this had advantages – the size of landholdings and the amount of marketable produce would increase, *politically* it entailed the growth of the government's class enemies. To alleviate economic pressures caused by the market, the poor peasants received tax rebates, were given credit facilities and were encouraged to develop agricultural co-operatives.

By 1926, NEP succeeded in restoring total agricultural production to roughly the pre-war level; but grain production for the market during this period had seriously declined.[1] In 1925/6, marketed grain was only half of that of the 1913 amount.[2] There were two main reasons for this; first, the increase in the number of agricultural holdings and the abolition of the large estates reduced productivity: the number of peasant households increased from 16 million to 25–26 million. Second, the inducement to sell declined: the exchange rate of agricultural against manufactured goods was worse than it had been before the war. In 1927–8, as a short-run measure, the government confiscated grain which peasants refused to deliver at fixed prices and hoarders were imprisoned. The government was in a quandary. There were no grain reserves. State purchases of agricultural produce (*zagotovki*) were of great concern. As Lewin puts it: '*the very existence of the regime was at stake during this campaign. Inevitably, the Soviet authorities found that the* zagotovki *dominated all other considerations, and they were obliged to strain every nerve merely in order to survive.*'[3] Between October 1927 and October 1928 grain collections declined by 17 per cent.

The winter of 1927–8 witnessed discussions in the party as to what permanent solution should be adopted. There were two clear-cut alternatives. The right wing policy was based on encouraging the middle peasant to produce for the market: the prices of agricultural commodities should be allowed to rise which would allow coercive action to be stopped. If necessary, in the short run, grain could be imported to meet deficiencies. At the same time, the tempo of industrialisation would be slowed down. The right did not attach a great deal of importance to the possibility of an attack on the USSR and believed that internal stability could be achieved by agreements with the peasantry who were not regarded as being counter-revolutionary. The

---

[1] In the North Caucasus the grain harvest in 1928 was only sixty-two per cent of the pre-war figure. See M. Lewin, *Russian Peasants and Soviet Power* (1968), pp. 172–3.

[2] M. Dobb, *op cit.*, p. 214.

[3] *Russian Peasants and Soviet Power*, p. 177. Italics as in original.

left wing policy was to liquidate private farming and to substitute in its place full collectivisation. The left believed that the capitalist encirclement was a real threat and that the time had come to break the *smychka* (union or alliance) with the peasants.

In 1928, official party policy fell between these extremes. Within the framework of private enterprise, the poor and middle peasants were to be aided by greater credits to increase their surplus. The number of state farms were to be increased and more collectivisation was to be introduced. In 1927 Stalin at the Fifteenth Party Congress said: 'The way out is to turn the small and dwarf peasant farms gradually and surely, not by pressure but by example and persuasion, into large farms based on common, co-operative cultivation of the soil, with the use of agricultural machines and tractors and scientific methods of intensive agriculture.'[1] Here Stalin's intentions seemed to favour a more gradual and voluntary development of collective farms. The First Five-Year Plan envisaged only about 15 per cent of the cultivated area being collectivised by 1933.

In 1929, however, the party opened an 'offensive against the *kulaks*'. It was believed that industrialisation could not be achieved without a guaranteed supply of agricultural surpluses. These could only be ensured by administrative control of farms. A market relationship would not maintain the dominance of the town over the country. The collectivisation drive began. The livestock and machinery of private farmers were seized for the use of collective farms. It is sometimes said that around five million peasants who resisted were exterminated or despatched to Siberia. The exact numbers are not known. Stalin, when asked by Churchill about the collective farms and whether collectivisation was as bad as the war, is said to have replied: 'Oh yes, worse. Much worse. It went on for years. Most of them [*kulaks*] were liquidated by the peasantry who hated them. Ten millions of them. But we had to do it to mechanise our agriculture. In the end, production from the land was doubled. What is one generation?'[2] The suffering of the deported was terrible. The railways were unable to cope. Many fled the country. Here is how an eye witness described 'dekulakisation'.

Trainloads of deported peasants left for the icy North, the forests, the steppes, the deserts. These were whole populations, denuded of everything; the old folk starved to death in mid-journey, new born babies were buried on the banks of the roadside, and each wilderness had its crop of little crosses or boughs of wood. Other populations dragging all their possessions on wagons, rushed towards the frontiers of Poland, Rumania, and China, and crossed them – by no means intact to be sure – in spite of the machine-guns.[3]

[1] Cited by M. Dobb, *op. cit.*, p. 222.
[2] Lord Moran, *Churchill, The Struggle for Survival* (1966), p. 63.
[3] Cited by M. Lewin, *Russian Peasants and Soviet Power* (1968), p. 506.

The structure of Soviet agriculture was transformed. Whereas in 1929 only 3.9 per cent of homesteads were collectivised, by 1938 the figure had grown to 93.5 per cent.[1] Collectivisation transformed 25 million individual peasant farms into 250,000 collective units which were headed by a chairman sympathetic to the communist government. The land was to be leased in perpetuity by the collective farm. Collective farmers could farm private plots from one quarter to one half hectare[2] in size; they could also own small livestock. From 1932 surplus *kolkhoz* produce and that from individual gardens could be sold on the free market.

While the collectivisation process was successful in establishing urban and communist control over the countryside, in the short run there were considerable agricultural losses; the agricultural production index of 104.2 in 1930 (1928 = 100) fell to 92.4 in 1931 and to 81.7 in 1932.[3] To prevent expropriation, the peasants destroyed their livestock: by 1932 the head of cattle had declined by more than a third of the 1929 figure, the number of sheep and goats had fallen by half, and horses by a quarter. Even ten years later, in 1939, the numbers of sheep, goats and pigs were still below the 1929 figure. The slaughter affected both the supply of meat and dairy produce to the towns and curtailed the amount of horsepower for the fields. Total agricultural production declined for the period 1930–1938.[4] As a result of this, famine occurred in which many died of starvation. As Peter Nettl has aptly put it: 'the famine of 1932 became a Soviet legend of horror, just as the simultaneous industrial depression in the West is still the cautionary basis of our industrial folklore.'[5]

A more positive result of collectivisation for the government was an increase in marketable produce. Comparing marketable production in 1932–3 to 1926–7, grain and potatoes nearly doubled. The only fall was in the amount of meat marketed, which nearly halved.[6] The figures cited here, based on Soviet sources are of course favourable to the collectivisation campaign. While the collectivisation process is often criticised in the West, it cannot be denied that it enabled the government to extract surplus from the peasant and thereby ensured the continuation of Bolshevik rule. Economically, it enabled methods of large scale production to be introduced in the countryside.

The extent and timing of the collectivisation drive may be criticised. As Lewin has pointed out, no administrative machinery had been devised to take

[1] A. Baykov, *The Development of the Soviet Economic System* (1946), p. 327.

[2] In certain areas they could farm up to 1 hectare. (A hectare is about 2½ acres).

[3] D. G. Johnson and A. Kahan in Joint Economic Committee, US Congress, *Comparisons of the United States and Soviet Economies* (Washington, 1960), Part I, p. 204.

[4] See statistics in R. W. Davies, 'Planning for Rapid Growth in the USSR', *Economics of Planning* (1965), vol. 5, nos. 1–2.

[5] *The Soviet Achievement* (1967), p. 121.

[6] Full data are cited in A. Baykov, *The Development of the Soviet Economic System* (1946), p. 326.

the strain of the new system and the massive slaughter of livestock was a cost Russia had to pay for many years.[1] For the peasant industrialisation brought him no short-term gain. He was regimented into the collective farm. If there were shortages, he bore the brunt of them. The concession of small allotments, the possession of a few farm animals, and the possibility of trading surplus on the free market, went some of the way to appease the peasants politically. Further concessions followed in 1934 when the peasants were allowed to own animals and by 1938, three-quarters of the cows and some two-thirds of the pigs and sheep were private, not collective, property. Stalinist agricultural policy had adopted Trotsky's view: the peasants were squeezed to allow industrialisation to proceed.

From the peasant yeoman's point of view collectivisation was a catastrophe. The whole rhythm of work and life was destroyed. He had no control over decisions concerning planting, his produce was no longer his own but the collective's and he was subject to compulsory food deliveries to the government. The statistical achievements of economic growth and the rise in 'procurement' figures were at the same time a tragedy for the dispossessed peasantry. Not only had some been shot, and others despatched to Siberia, but the expectations of generations had been shattered. Fear, violence and disruption reigned during collectivisation in the countryside. Fainsod describes a report on an area in Smolensk as follows: '. . . the looting in the villages had induced an atmosphere of panic among the well-to-do peasants . . . a wave of suicides was sweeping the richer households; *kulaks* (rich peasants) were killing their wives and children and taking their own lives. In order to prevent complete property confiscation, many *kulaks* and their wives were entering into fictitious divorces, in the hope that at least some property and the lives of women and children would be spared. Sensing their impending doom, *kulaks* in growing numbers were fleeing to the east (Moscow, the Urals, Siberia). They dekulakised themselves by selling out all they owned, or leaving their property with relatives and friends, or simply abandoning their fields and homes.'[2] But collectivised agriculture had features of Tsarist Russia: the peasant householders were bound to the collective farm and the land in a way similar to the *krest'yanin* before the emancipation of the serfs. Though we shall describe the collective farm in more detail in Chapter 9, we may note that as a form of social organisation it was similar in some respects to the old Russian *mir* or village assembly; it was a social and an administrative unit as well as an economic one.

Let us now attempt to evaluate some of the more important achievements and failures of the Soviet economy during the Stalin era. Its main achievement

[1] M. Lewin, *Russian Peasants and Soviet Power*, p. 515.
[2] M. Fainsod *Smolensk under Soviet Rule* (1958), p. 246

was rapid industrialisation between 1928 and 1955: ranging from an estimated twelve-fold rise (Seton) to a six-fold increase (Nutter) in industrial output.[1] For an economy which had almost no economic aid from the outside (though it did have the advantage of being able to copy advanced technology), this is quite striking. The command economy system allowed the government to channel a very large proportion of the Gross National Product to the basic producer-goods industries. Centralisation facilitated the injection of advanced technology on a large scale into the economic system, it made possible a very high rate of utilisation of capital equipment and promoted economies of scale.

I have already mentioned the impact of collectivisation in the countryside. This whole process is seen by many commentators as a complete failure. Not only was there a severe social upheaval, but even in economic terms agricultural output fell and the destruction of livestock was a severe blow. The 'rich peasants' were also good farmers and many for political reasons were annihilated. On the other hand, collectivisation ensured the collection of grain which enabled the towns to be fed, and the countryside was politically contained. Economic and social disruption in the countryside were some of the costs of political control, which became authoritarian and centralised.

Centralised Political Control

We have seen that the Bolsheviks justified the 'dictatorship of the proletariat' as a necessary consequence of revolution. In Marx's view this would be an essentially short-term prospect while counter-revolutionary forces would be mopped up. In Russia, however, in the absence of a proletarian revolution in the West, a minority government developed into a dictatorship mobilising the people, rather than, as in the original Marxist scheme, an expression of the people.

The government, through the police and aided by the Communist Party, used coercive sanctions (see Chapter 1) against the enemies or supposed enemies of Soviet power. Also men in positions of authority, whether they were communists or not, sometimes went in fear of their lives. Even party organisations and the state bureacracy were frequently purged of their leading officials. The party itself became highly centralised. Discussion was minimised to a formality. He who spoke out against terror might become a victim of the terror. Large camps were set up in the east and to these were deported the class enemies of the regime, though in reality many of their inmates were either innocent or had only sinned in thinking evil thoughts about their leaders.

The extent of the arrests and deportations to labour camps has been the subject of much speculation and enquiry in the West. Robert Conquest, for

[1] See figures in R. W. Davies, *loc. cit.*

instance, has argued that about eight million were imprisoned in 1938 alone, a figure which had risen from 30,000 in 1928.[1] As Pasternak poignantly describes the disappearance of Lara:

> One day Lara went out and did not come back. She must have been arrested in the street, as so often happened in those days, and she died or vanished somewhere, forgotten as a nameless number on a list which was afterwards mislaid, in one of the innumerable mixed or women's concentration camps in the north.[2]

The conditions in the camps have caused much indignation in some western circles. In the early days they were built by the prisoners themselves: ' "Here you are. This is your camp" – An open snow-field with a post in the middle and a notice on it saying: "GULAG 92 Y.N. 90" – that's all there was'.[3] Food and accommodation was inadequate. The work was hard and arduous: construction, mining and agriculture were the chief tasks of the prisoners; others were released to work for enterprises. Many died. Political and criminal prisoners were not separated. As in Tsarist Russia, some of the camps were mixed, though women accounted for only about ten per cent of the prisoners. The treatment of women seems to have been similar in Tsarist and Stalinist Russia: rape was common and they were required to work hard. (Compare, for example, the accounts of women prisoners in Tolstoi's *Resurrection* and Solzhenitsyn's *Cancer Ward*.)

The purges also became a means to supply labour. While forced or slave labour is generally recognised as being inefficient, it is possible that for a limited period and in the short run forced labour can be put to effective economic purposes. Though this aspect should not be exaggerated, the secret police became an important supplier of labour and carried out substantial public works. As there was no direction of labour it became an important means of overcoming a labour supply bottleneck, especially in those areas where free labour would never have ventured. It has been estimated that in 1941 some three and a half million men were working under conditions of forced labour,[4] another guess is double that figure.[5] The arrests, of course, increased the labour shortage generally but caused some enterprises (defence) to press the secret police to send them more labour. On a national or macro basis this policy was inefficient because labour was not efficiently deployed; but it acted as a justification for police action.[6] Though the purges were

---

[1] Other figures are: 1930, 600,000; 1931-2, 2 million; 1933-5, 5 million; 1935-7, 6 million R. Conquest, *The Great Terror* (1968), p. 335. During the collectivisation campaign about 3½ million peasants were despatched to the camps (70 per cent of the total) (*ibid.*).

[2] B. Pasternak, *Doctor Zhivago* (1958), p. 491.

[3] *Ibid.*, p. 492.

[4] N. Jasny, *Journal of Political Economy*, vol. 59 (October 1951).

[5] R. Conquest, *The Soviet Police System* (1968), p. 81.

[6] This interpretation is discussed at length in S. Swianiewicz, *Forced Labour and Economic Development* (1965), Chapter 12.

undoubtedly motivated by political factors, once under way they became established and other, though less important, factors (such as labour supply) played a part in perpetuating them.

The deportations to the camps were directed at least initially against 'bourgeois' and 'reactionary' opponents of the regime. In addition, the party itself and the administration were also being purged of communists who were possible opponents to Stalin. But the essence of political centralisation and control which appeared from 1928 onwards was a ruthless application and development of ideas which were already largely accepted by the communist political elite. Organised factions in the Bolshevik party had always been excluded by Lenin's concept of a disciplined party. Stalin in enforcing his will claimed Lenin's authority, 'Whosoever in the least weakens the iron discipline of the party of the proletariat (especially during its dictatorship) actually aids the bourgeoisie against the proletariat.'[1]

The centralisation of party control and the concomitant loss of participation by the rank and file communist must be seen in terms of Bolshevik organisational theory and the political stress affecting the political leaders. We have seen that a one-party state was introduced in Russia under Lenin. It was not Stalin's invention. The doctrine of democratic centralism was one of the tenets of Bolshevik organisation theory from the publication of Lenin's 'What is to be Done'. It would be incorrect, therefore, to describe the political regime under Stalin as something new and foreign to the preceding state. As A. G. Meyer has aptly said: 'Stalinism can and must be defined as a pattern of thought and action that flows directly from Leninism.'[2]

Trotsky, on the other hand, advocated the strengthening of democracy in the party. He believed that members should have the right to communicate with each other and to formulate policies criticising and opposing the leadership. The party, argued Trotsky, was 'living, as it were, on two storeys: the upper where things are decided, and the lower storey where all you do is learn of the decisions'.[3] His view that communists should be able to communicate freely outside official party channels was strictly incompatible with the party rules. Stalin quoted Lenin's demand for the 'complete extermination of all factionalism' and for the 'immediate dissolution of all groups, without exception, that had been formed on the basis of this or that pattern' on pain of 'unconditional and immediate expulsion from the party.[4] Trotsky lost his party membership in 1927, was banished to Central Asia in 1928 and was expelled from Russia in 1929. However, in exile he continued to oppose Stalin's rule: he formed an opposition which advocated the overthrow of the regime by force.

[1] V. I. Lenin, cited by J. Stalin, *Foundations of Leninism* (Moscow, 1934), p. 93.
[2] A. G. Meyer, *Leninism* (Cambridge, Mass., 1957), p. 282.
[3] *The New Course* (1923, Ann Arbor, 1965), p. 13.
[4] *Foundations of Leninism*, p. 94.

It is probably true that Trotsky's organisation and support in the Soviet party was small, the 'opposition' was a 'tiny boat overweighted by a huge sail.'[1] But it is possible, as Deutscher has suggested, that Stalin exaggerated the strength of organised opposition to him in the party.

Not for a moment did Stalin himself slacken, or allow his propagandists and policemen to relax, in the anti-Trotskyist campaign which he carried into every sphere of thought and activity, and which he stepped up from year to year and from month to month. The fear of the Pretender robbed him of his sleep. He was constantly on the look-out for the Pretender's agents, who might be crossing the frontiers stealthily, smuggling the Pretender's messages, inciting, intriguing, and rallying for action. The suspicion that haunted Stalin's mind sought to read the hidden thoughts that the most subservient of his own subjects might have about Trotsky; and he discovered in the most innocuous of their utterances, even in the flatteries of his courtiers, deliberate and sly allusions to the legitimacy of Trotsky's claims.[2]

The point to be made here is that in periods of massive social change, irrational factors and fantasies often play on the minds of political leaders, who take what outsiders consider to be wild, even self-destructive actions.

Stalin systematically purged the party. In 1930, 116,000 party members were expelled, in 1933–4 followed over a million others.[3] Purge commissions were set up, before which accused communists had to appear. The aim of the party leadership was to root out 'double-dealers', 'violators of the iron discipline of the party,' 'careerists, self-seekers, bureaucratic elements' and 'moral degenerates'.[4] The most infamous events were to follow in the years 1936–8 when the majority of the Central Committee were arrested and accused of treason and sabotage. Death or imprisonment in corrective labour camps followed: between 1935 and 1938 all Lenin's Politbureau still in Russia were sentenced to death.[5] Sixty per cent of the Party's 1933 membership were no longer so six years later.[6] There is no doubt that many innocent men met their death at the hands of Stalin's secret police.[7] A letter from the Central Committee to party organisations described the 'terroristic activity' of the 'counter-revolutionary' forces in the following terms:

Now when it has been proved that the Trotskyite-Zinovievite monsters unite in the struggle against the Soviet state all the most hostile and accused enemies of the

---

[1] Heinrich Brandler, cited by I. Deutscher, *The Prophet Outcast* (1963), p. 33.

[2] I. Deutscher, *The Prophet Outcast*, pp. 125-6.

[3] L. Schapiro, *The Communist Party of the Soviet Union* (1960), p. 435.

[4] M. Fainsod, *Smolensk under Soviet Rule* (1958), p. 221. Further accounts may be found here.

[5] For details of the trials between 1936 and 1938 see R. Conquest, *The Soviet Police System* (1968), p. 47.

[6] A. L. Unger, 'Stalin's Renewal of the Leading Stratum', *Soviet Studies*, vol. 20 (Jan., 1969), p. 321.

[7] For a detailed account of the secret police see Simon Wolin and Robert M. Slusser, *The Soviet Secret Police* (1957).

D

toilers of our country – the spies, provocateurs, diversionists, White Guardists, *kulaks* etc. – when all boundary lines have been wiped out between these elements on the one hand, and the Trotskyites and Zinovievites on the other, all Party organisations, all members of the Party, should understand that Communist vigilance is necessary in every sector and in every situation.[1]

The effects of this and similar party instructions were denunciations and repression. Here is how the situation in Leningrad has been described.

> The Leningrad Party organisation suffered particularly large losses . . . For a period of four years there was an uninterrupted wave of repressions in Leningrad against honest and completely innocent people. Promotion to a responsible post often amounted to a step toward the brink of a precipice. Many people were annihilated without a trial and investigation on the basis of false, hastily fabricated charges. Not only officials themselves, but also their families were subjected to repressions, even absolutely innocent children, whose lives were thus broken from the very beginning . . . The repressions . . . were carried either on Stalin's direct instructions or with his knowledge and approval.[2]

Trials of Old Bolsheviks including Zinoviev and Kamenev were notable for the way the accused admitted conspiracy against the regime. Some said they had planned to kill Lenin, and others that they were connected with foreign espionage agencies. The extent to which these communists had been exposed to physical and mental torture is not known. It is superficial to believe that force was the only or even the main factor which accounts for the confessions of guilt. The explanation goes deeper than this. It is related to the ideas individuals have of their relationship to society. In liberal theory, the individual is supreme, even glorified; but in Leninist doctrine, society is paramount. The individual's rights and duties are determined by society: collectivism has the same importance to Leninists as individualism to liberals. If it can be shown then, that a thought or an action is, or may be, harmful to society then an individual may believe himself to be guilty. The point to be made here is that in liberal theory a man's conscience is the final arbiter in his conception of guilt; in Leninist theory the collective conscience is the arbiter. The task of the interrogator is to convince the accused that he has acted objectively against the collective interest. If the interrogator can do this, then a confession may be forthcoming and the subsequent trial becomes a formality, the accused readily admitting the ways he sinned against the community.

The motive of Stalin was to decimate any opposition to his rule, real or potential. It is absurd that members of Lenin's Politbureau could be working for British or German or Japanese intelligence agencies. Clearly, Stalin was strengthening his power against his rivals (and possible rivals). He was creating an atmosphere in which opposition or dissent could not flourish. This he

---

[1] Cited in M. Fainsod, *Smolensk Under Soviet Rule* (1958), p. 233.
[2] I. V. Spiridonov, speech at XXII Congress of CPSU. Cited by Conquest, *op. cit.*, p. 236.

did brutally though, it must be conceded, successfully. Khrushchev's Twentieth Congress 'secret speech' graphically draws attention to the destructive aspects of Stalin's rule:

> ... The negative characteristics of Stalin, which, in Lenin's time, were only incipient, transformed themselves during the last five years into a grave abuse of power by Stalin, which caused untold harm to our party.

We have to consider seriously and analyse correctly this matter in order that we may preclude any possibility of a repetition in any form whatever of what took place during the life of Stalin, who absolutely did not tolerate collegiality in leadership and in work, and who practised brutal violence, not only towards everything which opposed him, but also toward that which seemed, to his capricious and despotic character, contrary to his concepts.[1]

The purges had many detrimental consequences. They dislocated the administration. They deprived the economy of experienced managers. They distorted the distribution of skilled labour. The purging of the armed forces debilitated their leadership, which was forced to suffer the consequences of inexperience during the early Nazi invasion. Human suffering was colossal. While *morally* the purges and terror were reprehensible, they also had important *social* implications. They had integrative effects for the society as a whole. Nothing like the presence of a common enemy makes people unite. The role of the purges in providing a mechanism for the integration of the society is often largely ignored. The emotional outlet provided by the witch hunt is vividly shown in the following statement: 'I love the Central Committee, I love Comrade Stalin, but I think that up to now the Central Committee and Comrade Stalin have taken a conciliatory attitude towards the Trotskyite-Zinoviev group. Now it is necessary to finish them off – the Trotskyites and Zinovievites – and to finish them off for good. We should give them no mercy.'[2] Rapid and violent social and political upheavals require both the destruction of the values of the *ancien régime* and their replacement with a new value system, otherwise society may disintegrate. The purges and terror isolated and frightened men and broke down old values: at the same time for those who did not wish to be purged or terrorised they acted as mechanisms through which they could affirm their loyalty to the new order.[3]

The purges had positive effects in the area of social mobility. They removed incumbents of elite positions and thereby encouraged upward social mobility. The new younger party recruits had rapid promotion prospects and provided a basis of support for Stalin's rule.[4] The renewal of party cadres had impor-

[1] Khrushchev's speech, reprinted in *The 20th Congress and World Trotskyism* (New Park ed., 1957), p. 53. For further extracts see Reading No. 6.

[2] Cited in M. Fainsod, *op cit.*, p. 235.

[3] For a development of this view see: Z. K. Brzezinski, *The Permanent Purge* (Cambridge, Mass., 1956).

[4] See Fainsod, *op cit.*, p. 60.

tant consequences for the social composition of the party. Many of the new recruits were men who had been educated under the new regime. The numbers of 'specialists' (men with higher or middle specialised education) in the party rose 77 times between 1928 and 1940: from 1.2 per cent of party membership to 20.6 per cent.[1] From a social and political point of view these men were as important, if not more so, than the purged; they receive less attention by western writers because their presence is less dramatic and their activity less deplorable.

It is important to bear in mind that the purges and deportations were not carried out by one man alone. A considerable body of opinion supported these policies: many persons, party and non-party alike were involved in the process. Not just passively, but actively, they aided and abetted Stalin. It is a one-sided and inaccurate view of Russian history of the 1930s which sees Stalin's rule based merely on coercion and violence:

> . . . Thus, he lived on earth and ruled
> Holding the reins in his hard hand.
> Just try and find the man who
> Didn't praise and glorify him,
> Just try and find him!
> (Alexander Tvardovsky, *Pravda*, 1 May 1960)

Though Stalin was in no way an inevitable result of Soviet historical development, conditions of acute social stress, economic scarcity and political conflict often throw up a dictatorial leader to whom authority is given. He personified a goal and a future as well as police activity. A recent novel by Evgeniya Ginzburg describes the attitude of people towards Stalin at the time of the purges.

> . . . I looked at him [Stalin] with secret hostility, though this was still unconscious, unmotivated, instinctive.
> But you should have seen the other people! The writer, Fyodor Gladkov, by then an old man, looked at Stalin with a sort of religious ecstasy. And a young woman writer from Vologda whispered, as if in a trance: 'I have seen Stalin. I can now die happily'.[2]

As men were purged, so did new people take their place. All positions were susceptible to the purge, the social structure was in a permanent state of flux. As Deutscher has pointed out: 'The permanent terror' kept 'the whole of the bureaucracy in a state of flux, renewing permanently its composition, and not

---

[1] A. L. Unger, 'Stalin's Renewal of the Leading Stratum', *Soviet Studies* 20 (Jan., 1969), pp. 321, 330.

[2] *Krutoy Marshrut* cited in *Times Literary Supplement*, 27 April 1967.

allowing it to grow out of a protoplasmic or amoeboid condition, to form a compact and articulate body with a socio-political identity of its own . . . The managerial groups would not become a new possessing class even if they wanted to . . . they were hovering between their offices and the concentration camps.'[1] The point to be made here is that the purges removed stress on the political system. They allowed goals to be carried out without opposition and criticism which might have undermined the tasks Stalin and the Party had set in motion. The moving force in Soviet history was ideological – the building of socialism in one country. It was not just a result of Stalin's personal ruthlessness, cruelty and vindictiveness. In liberal-democratic societies, the norms of political life depend on all parties playing the political game, in giving and making concessions. In Soviet society the actors did not play by these rules. In addition to ideological values, Stalin had also to use coercion.

In later chapters we shall discuss other aspects of social change under Stalin (see Chapters 11–14), here we may sum up the main features of the Bolshevik consolidation of power and reconstruction. In an economic sense, Stalin completed the industrialisation of Russia which was started by the Tsars. In doing so he brought havoc to the countryside: the collectivisation of agriculture was a momentous movement, which might be compared to the enclosure of the land in England centuries before. In Russia, it ensured the dominance of the city over the country and the political subjugation of the agricultural small-holder. The Stalinist political system was centralised and authoritarian but it would be wrong to regard this simply as a projection of Stalin's personality. It was created by the interaction of many complex factors: the heritage from the Tsarist past; the legacy of administrative and dictatorial rule, of an unsophisticated and backward peasant population, of the absence of popular participation in government; the organisational structure of the Bolshevik Party which had been shaped during its illegal existence. These facts gave rise to centralised control, to an emphasis on unity in action, to an uncompromising attitude to opponents. It is also erroneous to see Stalinist Russia merely as a projection of Tsarist rule. So much of substance had changed: ownership relations were transformed; private property (with the exception of the peasants' plots) had been abolished; the economic market as a mechanism of resource allocation had been replaced by planning. Stalinism was a dynamic creed. By the beginning of the Second World War, the Soviet Union was an industrial power. Whilst this might have been attained by other alternatives, it seems likely that in the absence of policies like those laid down by Lenin and Stalin, Russia might have disinte-

[1] I. Deutscher, *The Prophet Outcast* (1963), pp. 306-7.

grated. While the purges, the terror and the deportations were destructive of human creativeness, the values of socialism, of eventual abundance, of comradeship, of nationalism, provided an ideological dynamism to Soviet society. Ideology not only helped to create social cohesiveness, but it provided a value system on which the elites could be judged. Once under way, it constrained the actions of Stalin. He was pledged to the building of socialism in Soviet Russia and in doing so, he was ruthless. Economically, he succeeded. It is a more open question as to whether he built a society which was able to outgrow its dictatorial strait-jacket: later we shall consider the extent to which 'socialism' was achieved politically and socially.

In the first Chapter of this book, I noted three methods by which compliance could be achieved: coercion, remuneration and normative power. During the Stalin era all three were used. The terror, the deportations, collectivisation, the regime of the camps were all based on coercion. The New Economic Policy and later the wider wage differentials of the Five-Year Plans (see Chapter 12) introduced an element of utilitarian rewards. But the normative, the ideological, were also important: the manipulation of symbols (Stalin, the hero of socialism), the image of the future ('socialism in one country'), and the propaganda ('the most democratic constitution in the world') all played a role as great, if not greater than terror, in ensuring the active compliance and mobilization of the population.

Reading No. 5
'The State and Revolution'. Written August-September 1917.
Source:
V. I. Lenin, *Collected Works*, Vol. 25 (Moscow, 1964), pp. 381-492.

In *The Poverty of Philosophy*, Marx wrote:

The working class, in the course of development, will substitute for the old bourgeois society an association which will preclude classes and their antagonism, and there will be no more political power proper, since political power is precisely the official expression of class antagonism in bourgeoise society. (p. 182, German edition, 1885.)

It is instructive to compare this general exposition of the idea of the state disappearing after the abolition of classes with the exposition contained in the *Communist Manifesto*, written by Marx and Engels a few months later, in November 1847, to be exact:

. . . In depicting the most general phases of the development of the proletariat, we traced the more or less veiled civil war, raging within existing society up to the point where that war breaks out into open revolution, and where the violent overthrow of the bourgeoisie lays the foundation for the sway of the proletariat . . .
. . . We have seen above that the first step in the revolution by the working class is to raise the proletariat to the position of ruling class, to win the battle of democracy.
The proletariat will use its political supremacy to wrest, by degrees, all capital from the bourgeoisie, to centralise all instruments of production in the hands of the state, i.e., of the proletariat organised as the ruling class; and to increase the total of productive forces as rapidly as possible.[1]

Here we have a formulation of one of the most remarkable and most important ideas of Marxism on the subject of the state, namely, the idea of the 'dictatorship of the proletariat' (as Marx and Engels began to call it after the Paris Commune); and also, a highly interesting definition of the state, which is also one of the 'forgotten words' of Marxism: 'the state, i.e., *the proletariat organised as the ruling class*'.

This definition of the state has never been explained in the prevailing propaganda and agitation literature of the official Social-Democratic parties. More than that, it has been deliberately ignored, for it is absolutely irreconcilable with reformism, and is a slap in the face for the common opportunist prejudices and philistine illusions about the 'peaceful development of democracy'.

The proletariat needs the state – this is repeated by all the opportunists, social-chauvinists and Kautskyites, who assure us that this is what Marx taught. But they '*forget*' to add that, in the first place, according to Marx, the proletariat needs only

[1] pp. 31 and 37, seventh German edition, 1906.

a state which is withering away, i.e., a state so constituted that it begins to wither away immediately, and cannot but wither away. And, secondly, the working people need a 'state, i.e., the proletariat organised as the ruling class'.

The state is a special organisation of force: it is an organisation of violence for the suppression of some class. What class must the proletariat suppress? Naturally, only the exploiting class i.e., the bourgeoisie. The working people need the state only to suppress the resistance of the exploiters, and only the proletariat can direct this suppression, can carry it out. For the proletariat is the only class that is consistently revolutionary, the only class that can unite all the working and exploited people in the struggle against the bourgeoisie, in completely removing it.

The exploiting classes need political rule to maintain exploitation, i.e., in the selfish interests of an insignificant minority against the vast majority of the people. The exploited classes need political rule in order completely to abolish all exploitation, i.e., in the interests of the vast majority of the people and against the insignificant minority consisting of the modern slave-owners, the landowners and capitalists.

The overthrow of bourgeois rule can be accomplished only by the proletariat, the particular class whose economic conditions of existence prepare it for this task and provide it with the possibility and the power to perform it. While the bourgeoisie break up and disintegrate the peasantry and all the petty-bourgeois groups, they weld together, unite and organise the proletariat. Only the proletariat – by virtue of the economic role it plays in large-scale production – is capable of being the leader of *all* the working and exploited people, whom the bourgeoisie exploit, oppress and crush, often not less but more than they do the proletarians, but who are incapable of waging an *independent* struggle for their emancipation.

The theory of the class struggle, applied by Marx to the question of the state and the socialist revolution, leads as a matter of course to the recognition of the *political rule* of the proletariat, of its dictatorship, i.e., of undivided power directly backed by the armed force of the people. The overthrow of the bourgeoisie can be achieved only by the proletariat becoming the *ruling class* capable of crushing the inevitable and desperate resistance of the bourgeoisie, and of organising *all* the working and exploited people for the new economic system.

The proletariat needs state power, a centralised organisation of force, an organisation of violence, both to crush the resistance of the exploiters and to *lead* the enormous mass of the population – the peasants, the petty bourgeoisie, and semi-proletarians – in the work of organising a socialist economy.

By educating the workers' party, Marxism educates the vanguard of the proletariat, capable of assuming power and *leading the whole people* to socialism, of directing and organising the new system, of being the teacher, the guide, the leader of all the working and exploited people in organising their social life without the bourgeoisie and against the bourgeoisie.

Marx's theory of 'the state, i.e., the proletariat organised as the ruling class', is inseparably bound up with the whole of his doctrine of the revolutionary role of the proletariat in history. The culmination of this role is the proletarian dictatorship, the political rule of the proletariat.

In 1907, Mehring, in the magazine *Neue Zeit* (Vol. 25, 2, p. 164), published extracts from Marx's letter to Weydemeyer dated 5 March 1852. This letter, among other things, contains the following remarkable observation:

And now as to myself, no credit is due to me for discovering the existence of classes in modern society or the struggle between them. Long before me bourgeois historians had described the historical development of this class struggle and bourgeois economists, the economic anatomy of the classes. What I did that was new was to prove: (1) that the *existence of classes* is only bound up with *particular, historical phases in the development of production* (*historische Entwicklungsphasen der Produktion*), (2) that the class struggle necessarily leads to the *dictatorship of the proletariat*, (3) that this dictatorship itself only constitutes the transition to the *abolition of all classes and to a classless society.*

In these words, Marx succeeded in expressing with striking clarity, first, the chief and radical difference between his theory and that of the foremost and most profound thinkers of the bourgeoisie; and, secondly, the essence of his theory of the state.

It is often said and written that the main point in Marx's theory is the class struggle. But this is wrong. And this wrong notion very often results in an opportunist distortion of Marxism and its falsification in a spirit acceptable to the bourgeoisie. For the theory of the class struggle was created *not* by Marx, *but* by the bourgeoisie *before* Marx, and, generally speaking, it is *acceptable* to the bourgeoisie. Those who *recognise only* the class struggle are not yet Marxists; they may be found to be still within the bounds of bourgeois thinking and bourgeois politics. To confine Marxism to the theory of the class struggle means curtailing Marxism, distorting it, reducing it to something acceptable to the bourgeoisie. A Marxist is solely someone who *extends* the recognition of the class struggle to the recognition of the *dictatorship of the proletariat.*

The essence of Marx's theory of the state has been mastered only by those who realise that the dictatorship of a *single* class is necessary not only for every class society in general, not only for the *proletariat* which has overthrown the bourgeoisie, but also for the entire *historical period* which separates capitalism from 'classless society', from communism. Bourgeois states are most varied in form, but their essence is the same: all these states, whatever their form, in the final analysis are inevitably the *dictatorship of the bourgeoisie.* The transition from capitalism to communism is certainly bound to yield a tremendous abundance and variety of political forms, but the essence will inevitably be the same: *the dictatorship of the proletariat.*

We set ourselves the ultimate aim of abolishing the state, i.e., all organised and systematic violence, all use of violence against people in general. We do not expect the advent of a system of society in which the principle of subordination of the

D*

minority to the majority will not be observed. In striving for socialism, however, we are convinced that it will develop into communism, and, therefore, that the need for violence against people in general, for the *subordination* of one man to another, and of one section of the population to another, will vanish altogether since people will *become accustomed* to observing the elementary conditions of social life *without violence and without subordination.*

The distinction between the Marxists and the anarchists is this: (1) The former, while aiming at the complete abolition of the state, recognise that this aim can only be achieved after classes have been abolished by the socialist revolution, as the result of the establishment of socialism, which leads to the withering away of the state. The latter want to abolish the state completely overnight, not understanding the conditions under which the state can be abolished. (2) The former recognise that after the proletariat has won political power it must completely destroy the old state machine and replace it by a new one consisting of an organisation of the armed workers, after the type of the Commune. The latter, while insisting on the destruction of the state machine, have a very vague idea of *what* the proletariat will put in its place and how it will use its revolutionary power. The anarchists even deny that the revolutionary proletariat should use the state power, they reject its revolutionary dictatorship. (3) The former demand that the proletariat be trained for revolution by utilising the present state. The anarchists reject this.

The point at issue is neither opposition nor political struggle in general, but *revolution.* Revolution consists in the proletariat *destroying* the 'administrative apparatus' and the *whole* state machine, replacing it by a new one, made up of the armed workers. Kautsky displays a 'superstitious reverence' for 'ministries'; but why can they not be replaced, say, by committees of specialists working under sovereign, all-powerful Soviets of Workers' and Soldiers' Deputies?

The point is not at all whether the 'ministries' will remain, or whether 'committees of specialists' or some other bodies will be set up; that is quite immaterial. The point is whether the old state machine (bound by thousands of threads to the bourgeoisie and permeated through and through with routine and inertia) shall remain or be *destroyed* and replaced by a *new* one. Revolution consists not in the new class commanding, governing with the aid of the *old* state machine, but in this class *smashing* this machine and commanding, governing with the aid of a *new* machine.

Under socialism much of 'primitive' democracy will inevitably be revived, since, for the first time in the history of civilised society, the *mass* of the population will rise to taking an *independent* part, not only in voting and elections, *but also in the everyday administration of the state.* Under socialism *all* will govern in turn and will soon become accustomed to no one governing.

Marx teaches us to act with supreme boldness in destroying the entire old state machine, and at the same time he teaches us to put the question concretely: the Commune was able in the space of a few weeks to *start* building a *new* proletarian state machine by introducing such-and-such measures to provide wider democracy and to uproot bureaucracy. Let us learn revolutionary boldness from Communards; let us see in their practical measures the *outline* of really urgent and immediately possible measures, and then, *following this road*, we shall achieve the complete destruction of bureaucracy.

The possibility of this destruction is guaranteed by the fact that socialism will shorten the working day, will raise the *people* to a new life, will create such conditions for the *majority* of the population as will enable *everybody*, without exception, to perform 'state functions', and this will lead to the *complete withering away* of every form of state in general.

We, however, shall break with the opportunists; and the entire class-conscious proletariat will be with us in the fight – not to 'shift the balance of forces', but to *overthrow the bourgeoisie, to destroy* bourgeois parliamentarism, for a democratic republic after the type of the Commune, or a republic of Soviets of Workers' and Soldiers' Deputies, for the revolutionary dictatorship of the proletariat.

Reading No. 6
Special Report by N. S. Khrushchev, delivered to the Closed Session of the Twentieth Congress of the CPSU (1956).
Source:
The Twentieth Congress and World Trotskyism (London: New Park, 1957).

When we analyse the practice of Stalin in regard to the direction of the party and of the country, when we pause to consider everything which Stalin perpetrated, we must be convinced that Lenin's fears were justified. The negative characteristics of Stalin, which, in Lenin's time, were only incipient, transformed themselves during the last years into a grave abuse of power by Stalin, which caused untold harm to our party.

We have to consider seriously and analyse correctly this matter in order that we may preclude any possibility of a repetition in any form whatever of what took place during the life of Stalin, who absolutely did not tolerate collegiality in leadership and in work, and who practised brutal violence, not only toward everything which opposed him, but also toward that which seemed, to his capricious and despotic character, contrary to his concepts.

Stalin acted not through persuasion, explanation and patient cooperation with people, but by imposing his concepts and demanding absolute submission to his opinion. Whoever opposed this concept or tried to prove his viewpoint and the correctness of his position was doomed to removal from the leading collective and to subsequent moral and physical annihilation. This was especially true during the period following the 17th Party Congress, when many prominent party leaders and rank-and-file party workers, honest and dedicated to the cause of Communism, fell victim to Stalin's despotism.

Worth noting is the fact that, even during the progress of the furious ideological fight against the Trotskyites, the Zinovievites, the Bukharinites and others, extreme repressive measures were not used against them. The fight was on ideological grounds. But some years later, when socialism in our country was fundamentally constructed, when the exploiting classes were generally liquidated, when the Soviet social structure had radically changed, when the social basis for political movements and groups hostile to the party had violently contracted, when the ideological opponents of the party were long since defeated politically – then the repression directed against them began.

It was precisely during this period (1935-8) that the practice of mass repression through the Government apparatus was born, first against the enemies of Leninism – Trotskyites, Zinovievites, Bulkharinites, long since politically defeated by the party – and subsequently also against many honest Communists, against those party cadres who had borne the heavy load of the Civil War and the first and most difficult years of industrialisation and collectivisation, who actively fought against the Trotskyites and the rightists for the Leninist party line.

Stalin originated the concept 'enemy of the people'. This term automatically rendered it unnecessary that the ideological errors of a man or men engaged in a controversy be proven; this term made possible the usage of the most cruel repression, violating all norms of revolutionary legality, against anyone who in any way disagreed with Stalin, against those who were only suspected of hostile intent, against those who had bad reputations. This concept 'enemy of the people' actually eliminated the possibility of any kind of ideological fight or the making of one's views known on this or that issue, even those of a practical character. In the main, and in actuality, the only proof of guilt used, against all norms of current legal science, was the 'confession' of the accused himself; and, as subsequent probing proved, 'confessions' were acquired through physical pressures against the accused. This led to glaring violations of revolutionary legality and to the fact that many entirely innocent persons, who in the past had defended the party line, became victims.

We must assert that, in regard to those persons who in their time had opposed the party line, there were often no sufficiently serious reasons for their physical annihilation. The formula 'enemy of the people' was specifically introduced for the purpose of physically annihilating such individuals.

It is a fact that many persons who were later annihilated as enemies of the party and people had worked with Lenin during his life. Some of these persons had made errors during Lenin's life, but, despite this, Lenin benefited by their work; he corrected them and he did everything possible to retain them in the ranks of the party; he induced them to follow him.

An entirely different relationship with people characterised Stalin. Lenin's traits – patient work with people, stubborn and painstaking education of them, the ability to induce people to follow him without using compulsion, but rather through the ideological influence on them of the whole collective – were entirely foreign to Stalin. He discarded the Leninist method of convincing and educating, he abandoned the method of ideological struggle for that of administrative violence, mass repressions and terror. He acted on an increasingly larger scale and more stubbornly through punitive organs, at the same time often violating all existing norms of morality and of Soviet laws.

Arbitrary behaviour by one person encouraged and permitted arbitrariness in others. Mass arrests and deportations of many thousands of people, execution without trial and without normal investigation created conditions of insecurity, fear and even desperation.

This, of course, did not contribute toward unity of the party ranks and of all strata of working people, but, on the contrary, brought about annihilation and the expulsion from the party of workers who were loyal but inconvenient to Stalin.

Our party fought for the implementation of Lenin's plans for the construction of socialism. This was an ideological fight. Had Leninist principles been observed during the course of this fight, had the party's devotion to principles been skilfully combined with a keen and solicitous concern for people, had they not been repelled and wasted but rather drawn to our side, we certainly would not have had such a brutal violation of revolutionary legality and many thousands of people would not have fallen victim to the method of terror. Extraordinary methods would then have been resorted to only against those people who had in fact committed criminal acts against the Soviet system.

Stalin, on the other hand, used extreme methods and mass repressions at a time when the Revolution was already victorious, when the Soviet state was strengthened, when the exploiting classes were already liquidated and socialist relations were rooted solidly in all phases of national economy, when our party was politically consolidated and had strengthened itself both numerically and ideologically.

It is clear that here Stalin showed in a whole series of cases his intolerance, his brutality and his abuse of power. Instead of proving his political correctness and mobilising the masses, he often chose the path of repression and physical annihilation, not only against actual enemies, but also against individuals who had not committed any crimes against the party and the Soviet Government. Here we see no wisdom but only a demonstration of the brutal force which had once so alarmed V. I. Lenin.

Lately, especially after the unmasking of the Beria gang, the Central Committee looked into a series of matters fabricated by this gang. This revealed a very ugly picture of brutal wilfulness connected with the incorrect behaviour of Stalin. As facts prove, Stalin, using his unlimited power, allowed himself many abuses, acting in the name of the Central Committee, not asking for the opinion of the Committee members nor even of the members of the Central Committee's Political Bureau; often he did not inform them about his personal decisions concerning very important party and governmental matters.

Considering the question of the cult of the individual, we must first of all show everyone what harm this caused to the interests of our party.

In practice, Stalin ignored the norms of party life and trampled on the Leninist principle of collective party leadership.

Stalin's wilfulness *vis-à-vis* the party and its Central Committee became fully evident after the 17th Party Congress which took place in 1934.

Having at its disposal numerous data showing brutal wilfulness toward party cadres, the Central Committee has created a party commission under the control of the Central Committee Presidium; it was charged with investigating what made possible mass repressions against the majority of the Central Committee members and candidates elected at the 17th Congress of the All-Union Communist Party (Bolsheviks).

The commission has become acquainted with a large quantity of materials in the NKVD archives and with other documents and has established many facts pertaining to the fabrication of cases against Communists, to false accusations, to glaring abuses of socialist legality, which resulted in the death of innocent people. It became apparent that many party, Soviet and economic activists, who were branded in 1937-1938 as 'enemies', were actually never enemies, spies, wreckers, etc., but were always honest Communists; they were only so stigmatised and, often, no longer able to bear barbaric tortures, they charged themselves (at the order of the investigative judges – falsifiers) with all kinds of grave and unlikely crimes.

The commission has presented to the Central Committee Presidium lengthy and documented materials pertaining to mass repressions against the delegates to the 17th Party Congress and against members of the Central Committee elected at that Congress. These materials have been studied by the Presidium of the Central Committee.

It was determined that of the 139 members and candidates of the party's Central Committee who were elected at the 17th Congress, 98 persons, i.e., 70 per cent, were arrested and shot (mostly in 1937-1938). (Indignation in the hall.) What was the composition of the delegates to the 17th Congress? It is known that 80 per cent of the voting participants of the 17th Congress joined the party during the years of conspiracy before the Revolution and during the civil war; this means before 1921. By social origin the basic mass of the delegates to the Congress were workers (60 per cent of the voting members).

For this reason, it was inconceivable that a congress so composed would have elected a Central Committee a majority of whom would prove to be enemies of the party. The only reason why 70 per cent of the Central Committee members and candidates elected at the 17th Congress were branded as enemies of the party and of the people was because honest Communists were slandered, accusations against them were fabricated, and revolutionary legality was gravely undermined.

The same fate met not only the Central Committee members but also the majority of the delegates to the 17th Party Congress. Of 1,966 delegates with either voting or advisory rights, 1,108 persons were arrested on charges of anti-revolutionary crimes, i.e., decidedly more than a majority. This very fact shows how absurd, wild and contrary to common sense were the charges of counter-revolutionary crimes made out, as we now see, against a majority of participants at the 17th Party Congress. (Indignation in the hall.)

We should recall that the 17th Party Congress is historically known as the

Congress of Victors. Delegates to the Congress were active participants in the building of our socialist state; many of them suffered and fought for party interests during the pre-Revolutionary years in the conspiracy and at the civil-war fronts; they fought their enemies valiantly and often nervelessly looked into the face of death.

How, then, can we believe that such people could prove to be 'two-faced' and had joined the camps of the enemies of socialism during the era after the political liquidation of Zinovievites, Trotskyites and rightists and after the great accomplishments of socialist construction? This was the result of the abuse of power by Stalin, who began to use mass terror against the party cadres.

What is the reason that mass repressions against activists increased more and more after the 17th Party Congress? It was because at that time Stalin had so elevated himself above the party and above the nation that he ceased to consider either the Central Committee or the party.

After the criminal murder of Sergei M. Kirov, mass repressions and brutal acts of violation of socialist legality began. On the evening of 1 December 1934, on Stalin's initiative (without the approval of the Political Bureau – which was passed two days later, casually), the Secretary of the Presidium of the Central Executive Committee, Yenukidze, signed the following directive:

1. Investigative agencies are directed to speed up the cases of those accused of the preparation or execution of acts of terror.

2. Judicial organs are directed not to hold up the execution of death sentences pertaining to crimes of this category in order to consider the possibility of pardon, because the Presidium of the Central Executive Committee of the USSR does not consider as possible the receiving of petitions of this sort.

3. The organs of the Commissariat of Internal Affairs are directed to execute the death sentences against criminals of the above-mentioned category immediately after the passage of sentences.

This directive became the basis for mass acts of abuse against socialist legality. During many of the fabricated court cases, the accused were charged with 'the preparation' of terrorist acts; this deprived them of any possibility that their cases might be re-examined, even when they stated before the court that their 'confessions' were secured by force, and when, in a convincing manner, they disproved the accusations against them.

The mass repressions at this time were made under the slogan of a fight against the Trotskyites. Did the Trotskyites at this time actually constitute such a danger to our party and to the Soviet state? We should recall that in 1927, on the eve of the 15th Party Congress, only some 4,000 votes were cast for the Trotskyite-Zinovievite opposition while there were 724,000 for the party line. During the 10 years which passed between the 15th Party Congress and the February-March Central Committee plenum, Trotskyism was completely disarmed; many former Trotskyites had

changed their former views and worked in the various sectors building socialism.
It is clear that in the situation of socialist victory there was no basis for mass terror
in the country.

The majority of the Central Committee members and candidates elected at the
17th Congress and arrested in 1937-1938 were expelled from the party illegally
through the brutal abuse of the party statute, because the question of their expulsion
was never studied at the Central Committee plenum.

Now, when the cases of some of these so-called 'spies' and 'saboteurs' were
examined, it was found that all their cases were fabricated. Confessions of guilt of
many arrested and charged with enemy activity were gained with the help of cruel
and inhuman tortures.

At the same time, Stalin, as we have been informed by members of the Political
Bureau of that time, did not show them the statements of many accused political
activists when they retracted their confessions before the military tribunal and asked
for an objective examination of their cases. There were many such declarations, and
Stalin doubtless knew of them.

The Central Committee considers it absolutely necessary to inform the Congress
of many such fabricated 'cases' against the members of the party's Central Committee elected at the 17th Party Congress.

An example of the vile provocation, of odious falsification and of criminal
violation of revolutionary legality is the case of the former candidate for the Central
Committee Political Bureau, one of the most eminent workers of the party and of
the Soviet Government. Comrade Eikhe, who was a party member since 1905.
(Commotion in the hall.)

Comrade Eikhe was arrested on 29 April 1938, on the basis of slanderous
materials, without the sanction of the Prosecutor of the USSR, which was finally
received 15 months after the arrest.

Investigation of Eikhe's case was made in a manner which most brutally violated
Soviet legality and was accompanied by wilfulness and falsification.

Eikhe was forced under torture to sign ahead of time a protocol of his confession
prepared by the investigative judges, in which he and several other eminent party
workers were accused of anti-Soviet activity.

Many thousands of honest and innocent Communists have died as a result of this
monstrous falsification of such 'cases', as a result of the fact that all kinds of
slanderous 'confessions' were accepted, and as a result of the practice of forcing
accusations against oneself and others. In the same manner were fabricated the
'cases' against eminent party and state workers – Kossior, Chubar, Postyshev,
Kosarev and others.

In those years repressions on a mass scale were applied which were based on
nothing tangible and which resulted in heavy cadre losses to the party.

The vicious practice was condoned of having the NKVD prepare lists of persons
whose cases were under the jurisdiction of the Military Collegium and whose
sentences were prepared in advance. Yezhov would send these lists to Stalin personally for his approval of the proposed punishment. In 1937-1938, 383 such lists

containing the names of many thousands of party, Soviet, Komsomol, army and economic workers were sent to Stalin. He approved these lists.

A large part of these cases are being reviewed now and a great part of them are being voided because they were baseless and falsified. Suffice it to say that from 1954 to the present time the Military Collegium of the Supreme Court has rehabilitated 7,679 persons, many of whom were rehabilitated posthumously.

Mass arrests of party, Soviet, economic and military workers caused tremendous harm to our country and to the cause of socialist advancement.

Mass repressions had a negative influence on the moral-political condition of the party, created a situation of uncertainty, contributed to the spreading of unhealthy suspicion and sowed distrust among Communists. All sorts of slanderers and careerists were active.

Resolutions of the January plenum of the Central Committee, All-Union Communist Party (Bolsheviks), in 1938 had brought some measure of improvement to the party organisations. However, widespread repression also existed in 1938.

Only because our party has at its disposal such great moral-political strength was it possible for it to survive the difficult events in 1937-1938 and to educate new cadres. There is, however, no doubt that our march forward toward socialism and toward the preparation of the country's defence would have been much more successful were it not for the tremendous loss in the cadres suffered as a result of the baseless and false mass repression in 1937-1938.

Facts prove that many abuses were made on Stalin's orders without reckoning with any norms of party and Soviet legality. Stalin was a very distrustful man, sickly suspicious; we know this from our work with him. He could look at a man and say: 'Why are your eyes so shifty today?' or 'Why are you turning so much today and avoiding to look me directly in the eyes?' The sickly suspicion created in him a general distrust even toward eminent party workers whom he had known for years. Everywhere and in everything he saw 'enemies', 'two-facers' and 'spies'. Possessing unlimited power, he indulged in great wilfulness and choked a person morally and physically. A situation was created where one could not express one's own will.

When Stalin said that one or another should be arrested, it was necessary to accept on faith that he was an 'enemy of the people'. Meanwhile, Beria's gang, which ran the organs of state security, outdid itself in proving the guilt of the arrested and the truth of materials which it falsified. And what proofs were offered? The confessions of the arrested, and the investigative judges accepted these 'confessions'. And how is it possible that a person confesses to crimes which he has not committed? Only in one way – because of application of physical methods of pressuring him, tortures, bringing him to a state of unconsciousness, deprivation of his judgment, taking away of his human dignity. In this manner were 'confessions' acquired.

During the war and after the war, Stalin put forward the thesis that the tragedy which our nation experienced in the first part of the war was the result of the 'unexpected' attack of the Germans against the Soviet Union. But, comrades, this is completely untrue. As soon as Hitler came to power in Germany he assigned to himself the task of liquidating Communism. The fascists were saying this openly: they did not hide their plans.

In order to attain this aggressive end, all sorts of pacts and blocs were created, such as the famous Berlin-Rome-Tokyo Axis. Many facts from the pre-war period clearly showed that Hitler was going all out to begin a war against the Soviet state, and that he had concentrated large armed units, together with armoured units, near the Soviet borders.

Documents which have now been published show that by 3 April 1941, Churchill, through his Ambassador to the USSR, Cripps, personally warned Stalin that the Germans had begun regrouping their armed units with the intent of attacking the Soviet Union.

It is self-evident that Churchill did not do this at all because of his friendly feeling toward the Soviet nation. He had in this his own imperialistic goals – to bring Germany and the USSR into a bloody war and thereby to strengthen the position of the British Empire.

Just the same, Churchill affirmed in his writings that he sought to 'warn Stalin and call his attention to the danger which threatened him'. Churchill stressed this repeatedly in his dispatches of 18 April and on the following days. However, Stalin took no heed of these warnings. What is more, Stalin ordered that no credence be given to information of this sort, in order not to provoke the initiation of military operations.

We must assert that information of this sort concerning the threat of German armed invasion of Soviet territory was coming in also from our own military and diplomatic sources; however, because the leadership was conditioned against such information, such data was dispatched with fear and assessed with reservation.

Had our industry been mobilised properly and in time to supply the Army with the necessary material, our wartime losses would have been decidedly smaller. Such mobilisation had not been, however, started in time. And already in the first days of the war it became evident that our Army was badly armed, that we did not have enough artillery, tanks and planes to throw the enemy back.

Soviet science and technology produced excellent models of tanks and artillery pieces before the war. But mass production of all this was not organised, and, as a matter of fact, we started to modernise our military equipment only on the eve of the war. As a result, at the time of the enemy's invasion of the Soviet land we did not have sufficient quantities either of old machinery which was no longer used for armament production or of new machinery which we had planned to introduce into armament production.

All the more monstrous are the acts whose initiator was Stalin and which are rude violations of the basic Leninist principles of the nationality policy of the Soviet state. We refer to the mass deportations from their native places of whole nations, together with all Communists and Komsomols without any exception; this deportation action was not dictated by any military considerations.

Thus, already at the end of 1943, when there occurred a permanent break-through at the fronts of the Great Patriotic War benefiting the Soviet Union, a decision was taken and executed concerning the deportation of all the Karachai from the lands on which they lived.

In the same period, at the end of December 1943, the same lot befell the whole population of the Autonomous Kalmyk Republic. In March 1944, all the Chechen and Ingush peoples were deported and the Chechen-Ingush Autonomous Republic was liquidated. In April 1944, all Balkars were deported to faraway places from the territory of the Kabardino-Balkar Autonomous Republic and the Republic itself was renamed the Autonomous Kabardian Republic.

The Ukrainians avoided meeting this fate only because there were too many of them and there was no place to which to deport them. Otherwise, he would have deported them also. (Laughter and animation in the hall.)

Not only a Marxist-Leninist but also no man of common sense can grasp how it is possible to make whole nations responsible for inimical activity, including women, children, old people, Communists and Komsomols, to use mass repression against them, and to expose them to misery and suffering for the hostile acts of individual persons or groups of persons.

After the conclusion of the Patriotic War, the Soviet nation stressed with pride the magnificent victories gained through great sacrifices and tremendous efforts. The country experienced a period of political enthusiasm. The party came out of the war even more united; in the fire of the war, party cadres were tempered and hardened. Under such conditions nobody could have even thought of the possibility of some plot in the party.

Instructive in the same way is the case of the Mingrelian nationalist organisation which supposedly existed in Georgia. As is known, resolutions by the Central Committee, Communist Party of the Soviet Union, were made concerning this case in November 1951 and in March 1952. These resolutions were made without prior discussion with the Political Bureau. Stalin had personally dictated them. They made serious accusations against many loyal Communists. On the basis of falsified documents, it was proven that there existed in Georgia a supposedly nationalistic organisation whose objective was the liquidation of the Soviet power in that republic with the help of imperialist powers.

In this connection, a number of responsible party and Soviet workers were arrested in Georgia. As was later proven, this was a slander directed against the Georgian party organisation.

We know that there have been at times manifestations of local bourgeois nationalism in Georgia as in several other republics. The question arises: Could it be possible that, in the period during which the resolutions referred to above were made, nationalist tendencies grew so much that there was a danger of Georgia's leaving the Soviet Union and joining Turkey? (Animation in the hall, laughter.)

This is, of course, nonsense. It is impossible to imagine how such assumptions could enter anyone's mind. Everyone knows how Georgia has developed economically and culturally under Soviet rule.

Industrial production of the Georgian Republic is 27 times greater than it was before the Revolution. Many new industries have arisen in Georgia which did not exist there before the Revolution: iron smelting, an oil industry, a machine-con-struction industry, etc. Illiteracy has long since been liquidated, which, in pre-Revolution Georgia, included 78 per cent of the population.

Could the Georgians, comparing the situation in their republic with the hard situation of the working masses in Turkey, be aspiring to join Turkey? In 1955, Georgia produced 18 times as much steel per person as Turkey. Georgia produces 9 times as much electrical energy per person as Turkey. According to the available 1950 census, 65 per cent of Turkey's total population are illiterate, and, of the women, 80 per cent are illiterate. Georgia has 19 institutions of higher learning which have about 39,000 students; this is 8 times more than in Turkey (for each 1,000 inhabitants). The prosperity of the working people has grown tremendously in Georgia under Soviet rule.

It is clear that, as the economy and culture develop, and as the socialist conscious-ness of the working masses in Georgia grows, the source from which bourgeois nationalism draws its strength evaporates.

As it developed, there was no nationalistic organisation in Georgia. Thousands of innocent people fell victim to wilfulness and lawlessness. All of this happened under the 'genial' leadership of Stalin, 'the great son of the Georgian nation', as Georgians like to refer to Stalin. (Animation in the hall.)

We should, in all seriousness, consider the question of the cult of the individual. We cannot let this matter get out of the party, especially not to the press. It is for this reason that we are considering it here at a closed Congress session. We should know the limits; we should not give ammunition to the enemy; we should not wash our dirty linen before their eyes. I think that the delegates to the Congress will understand and assess properly all these proposals. (Tumultuous applause.)

Comrades! We must abolish the cult of the individual decisively, once and for all; we must draw the proper conclusions concerning both ideological-theoretical and practical work. It is necessary for this purpose:

First, in a Bolshevik manner to condemn and to eradicate the cult of the indi-vidual as alien to Marxism-Leninism and not consonant with the principles of party leadership and the norms of party life, and to fight inexorably all attempts at bringing back this practice in one form or another.

To return to and actually practice in all our ideological work the most important theses of Marxist-Leninist science about the people as the creator of history and as the creator of all material and spiritual good of humanity, about the decisive role of the Marxist party in the revolutionary fight for the transformation of society, about the victory of communism.

In this connection we will be forced to do much work in order to examine critically from the Marxist-Leninist viewpoint and to correct the widely spread erroneous views connected with the cult of the individual in the sphere of history, philosophy, economy and of other sciences, as well as in literature and the fine arts. It is especially necessary that in the immediate future we compile a serious textbook of the history of our party which will be edited in accordance with scientific Marxist objectivism, a textbook of the history of Soviet society, a book pertaining to the events of the Civil War and the Great Patriotic War.

Secondly, to continue systematically and consistently the work done by the party's Central Committee during the last years, a work characterised by minute observation in all party organisations, from the bottom to the top, of the Leninist principles of party leadership, characterised, above all, by the main principle of collective leadership, characterised by the observance of the norms of party life described in the statutes of our party, and, finally characterised by the wide practice of criticism and self-criticism.

Thirdly, to restore completely the Leninist principles of Soviet socialist democracy, expressed in the Constitution of the Soviet Union, to fight wilfulness of individuals abusing their power. The evil caused by acts violating revolutionary socialist legality which have accumulated during a long time as a result of the negative influence of the cult of the individual has to be completely corrected.

Comrades! The 20th Congress of the Communist Party of the Soviet Union has manifested with a new strength the unshakable unity of our party, its cohesiveness around the Central Committee, its resolute will to accomplish the great task of building communism. (Tumultuous applause.)

And the fact that we present in all their ramifications the basic problems of overcoming the cult of the individual which is alien to Marxism-Leninism, as well as the problem of liquidating its burdensome consequences, is an evidence of the great moral and political strength of our party. (Prolonged applause.)

We are absolutely certain that our party, armed with the historical resolutions of the 20th Congress, will lead the Soviet people along the Leninist path to new successes, to new victories. (Tumultuous, prolonged applause.)

Long live the victorious banner of our party – Leninism! (Tumultuous, prolonged applause ending in ovation. All rise.)

FOR FURTHER STUDY

INTRODUCTORY

Baykov, A. *The Development of the Soviet Economic System: An Essay on the Experience of Planning in the USSR*. London: Cambridge University Press, 1947.
Nettl, John Peter. *The Soviet Achievement*. London: Thames and Hudson, 1967.
Nove, Alec. *An Economic History of the USSR*. London: Allen Lane, 1969.

BASIC

Carr, E. H. *Socialism in one Country*, Vol. 5 of *A History of Soviet Russia*. London: Macmillan, 1959.
Deutscher, Isaac. *The Prophet Outcast. Trotsky, 1929-1940*. London: Oxford University Press, 1963.
Fainsod, Merle. *Smolensk Under Soviet Rule*. London: Macmillan, 1958.
Footman, David. *Civil War in Russia*. London: Faber, 1961.
Lewin, M. *Russian Peasants and Soviet Power. A Study of Collectivisation*, translated by Irene Nove. London: Allen and Unwin, 1968.
Meyer, A. *Leninism*. Cambridge, Mass.: Harvard University Press, 1957.
Schapiro, Leonard. *The Communist Party of the Soviet Union*. London: Eyre and Spottiswoode, 1960.
Stalin, J. V. *Foundations of Leninism*. Lectures delivered at the Sverdlov University at the beginning of April 1924. London: Lawrence and Wishart, 1942.
Problems of Leninism. Moscow: Foreign Languages Publishing House, 1941.
Trotsky, L. *The Revolution Betrayed*. London: Plough Press, 1952.

SPECIALISED

Aron, Raymond. *Eighteen Lectures on Industrial Society*. London: Weidenfeld and Nicolson, 1967.
Bergson, Abram. *The Real National Income of Soviet Russia Since 1928*. Cambridge, Mass.: Harvard University Press, 1961.
Bradley, John. *Allied Intervention in Russia*. London: Weidenfeld and Nicolson, 1968.
Brzezinski, Z. K. *The Permanent Purge*. Cambridge, Mass.: Harvard University Press, 1956.
Conquest, Robert. *The Great Terror, Stalin's Purge of the Thirties*. London: Macmillan, 1968.
Conquest, Robert (ed.). *The Soviet Police System*. London: Bodley Head, 1968.
Davies, R. W. 'Planning for Rapid Growth in the USSR', in *Economics of Planning*, Vol. 5, No. 1-2, 1965, pp. 74-86.

Jasny, Naum. 'Labour and Output in Soviet Concentration Camps', in *Journal of Political Economy*, Vol. 59, Oct. 1951, pp. 405-19.

Johnson, D. G., and A. Kahan. *Comparisons of the United States and Soviet Economics*. Washington: Joint Economic Committee of US Congress, 1960.

Khrushchev, N. A. 'Speech to the Twentieth Congress', reprinted in *The 20th Congress and World Trotskyism*. London: New Park, 1957.

Kritsman, L. *Geroicheski period velikoy Russkoy revolyutsii*. Moscow, n.d.

Lenin, V. I. *The State and Revolution*. Moscow: Foreign Languages Publishing House, 1958.

Nutter, G. W. *Growth of Industrial Production in the Soviet Union*. Princeton, N.J.: Princeton University Press, 1962.

Pasternak, B. *Doctor Zhivago*, translated by Max Hayward and Manya Harari. London: Collins, 1959.

Seton, F. 'Soviet Industrial Expansion', in *Manchester Statistical Society Paper*, Jan. 1957.

Solzhenitsyn, A. *Cancer Ward*. London: Bodley Head, 1968.

Swianiewicz, S. *Forced Labour and Economic Development: An Enquiry into the Experience of Soviet Industrialisation*. London: Oxford University Press, 1965.

Trotsky, L. *The New Course*, translated by Max Schachtman. Ann Arbor, Mich.: University of Michigan Press, 1965.

Tvardovsky, Alexander. *Pravda*, 1 May 1960 (poem on Stalin).

Unger, A. L. 'Stalin's Renewal of the Leading Stratum', *Soviet Studies*, Vol. 20, Jan. 1969, pp. 321-30.

Wolin, Simon and Robert M. Slusser. *The Soviet Secret Police*. London: Methuen, 1957.

4

THE USSR
IN THE INTERNATIONAL
ARENA

Most books concerned with national societies ignore the external influences on their internal structure and behaviour.[1] This is for two main reasons. First, a 'society' is defined as a relatively autonomous behavioural unit, independent of external influences and, therefore, international affairs are regarded as irrelevant. Second, the international system and the nature of international relations are extremely complex and are usually left to specialists. But the international elements in a society's political and social structure should not be ignored. In the case of Russia and the Soviet Union they have played a crucial part in her development. We have noted in earlier chapters the involvement of foreign firms in Russian industrialisation and the importance of an anticipated proletarian revolution in Western Europe as a catalyst of the October Revolution. The USSR has been seen as the focal point of an international political movement, closely connected with communist parties abroad. As Karl Deutsch has put it, some years ago the American Communist Party was said to scratch when Joe Stalin was itching.[2] While the importance of international factors may generally be conceded, the problem of how to describe adequately the Soviet Union's role in the international arena in a short chapter remains difficult to solve. It is clearly impossible to deal with the complicated history of international relations or the complex nature of Soviet attitudes to Eastern Europe, Western Europe, the USA, China and the Third World. Here I can only explain some of the major Soviet value orientations as they affect foreign policy, and note the changing external setting of Soviet decision-making.

Imperialism

At the beginning of the book I defined three main elements in Leninism:

---

[1] For instance, Robin M. Williams, *American Society* (New York, 1966) ignores international aspects of American society. Historians pay more attention to these aspects – see E. H. Carr, *A History of Soviet Russia*, vol. 3, part 5.

[2] K. W. Deutsch, 'External Influences on the Internal Behaviour of States', in R. Barry Farrell, *Approaches to Comparative and International Politics* (Evanston, 1966), p. 5.

the theory of the party, the theory of revolution, the theory of imperialism. Here we shall consider the third element, imperialism, which has helped shape the Soviet attitude to international relations and international conflict.

Imperialism, in its Leninist sense, emphasises the international character of capitalism and the domination of small relatively undeveloped countries by international monopolies, politically linked to the leading state powers. Imperialism, 'the monopoly stage' of capitalism, has five main characteristics:

1. The concentration of production and capital, developed to such a high stage that it has created monopolies which play a decisive role in economic life.
2. The merging of bank capital with industrial capital and the creation, on the basis of this 'finance-capital', of a financial oligarchy.
3. The export of capital, which has become extremely important, as distinguished from the export of commodities.
4. The formation of international capitalist monopolies which share the world among themselves.
5. The territorial division of the whole world among the greatest capitalist powers is completed.[1]

The theory has many interesting implications and is regarded by Soviet Marxists as an adaptation of Marxism to conditions of the twentieth century. What changes to Marxism are implied by Lenin's formulation?

Firstly, the contradictions of the capitalist order are 'exported' to backward nations where class conflict becomes most intense. For example, exploitation of native labour takes place to provide cheap materials for the homeland. The ruling class is not only a capitalist class but a foreign class carrying out its role through intermediaries and backed up by the presence of foreign armies. Undeveloped nations, therefore, become the centre of the class struggle and national liberation movements play a most important role in the international class struggle.[2]

Secondly, in the advanced capitalist states, the proletarian revolution is temporarily staved off. This is for two reasons: the working class is able to get concessions from the bourgeoisie, albeit at the expense of the people of underdeveloped societies abroad, and monopoly capitalism, by encouraging state regulation of the economy, reduces the internal stresses of capitalism in the advanced states. It is interesting to note that Lenin cites Engels's thesis of the *bourgeoisification* of the English working class:

The English proletariat is becoming more and more bourgeois, so that this most bourgeois of all nations is apparently aiming ultimately at the possession of a bourgeois aristocracy, and a bourgeois proletariat as well as a *bourgeoisie*. For a nation which exploits the whole world this is, of course, to a certain extent justifiable.[3]

---

[1] V. I. Lenin, *Imperialism, the Highest Stage of Capitalism* (1948), p. 108.
[2] See A. Meyer, *Leninism* (Cambridge, Mass., 1957), Part IV.
[3] Engels to Marx, Oct. 1858, cited by V. I. Lenin, *Imperialism . . .*, p. 129.

Lenin described this tendency as follows: 'Imperialism . . . creates the economic possibility of corrupting the upper strata of the proletariat, and thereby fosters, gives form to, and strengthens opportunism'.[1] Here then we have a link with the theory of the party (described above pp. 11–13), for 'trade union' activity tended to segment and bind together the more privileged union members to secure their short term interests. On a world scale the improvement of workers' standards in the advanced capitalist nations is at the expense of the impoverished in the underdeveloped countries.

Thirdly, monopolies protected by state powers compete with each other. Such competition takes on a national form, resulting in international conflicts which are resolved by war. The class struggle, therefore, assumes a global pattern: the class contradictions of classical Marxism are resolved in the international arena and are linked to conflict between nations. Lenin in emphasising the role of relatively underdeveloped countries also justified the Russian October Revolution as a first step on the way to a communist world.

The original Marxist prognosis of history, therefore, underwent an important change. For Lenin, the advanced western capitalist states were no longer the *main* scene in which the proletariat would play out the class struggle with the bourgeoisie. Though capitalism was in a 'crisis', it was a crisis on a world scale. Its centre of gravity had moved from the industrialised west to the industrialising east. And the Russian Revolution having failed to ignite the revolutionary gunpowder in Western Europe, became interpreted as a model and as an example to the downtrodden and exploited east.

This change occurred at the ideological or theoretical level, but the government was also faced with the practical conduct of foreign policy. In this respect Marxist theory had relatively little to offer. The government had to decide, for example, what kind of relationship was to exist between the Soviet state and capitalist governments and between the Soviet state and revolutionary forces abroad.

Soviet Foreign Policy 1917–1941

In foreign affairs the first official act of the Soviet government on 8 November 1917, was to issue the Decree on Peace. This proposed 'a just and democratic peace', which entailed the revocation by the leading European nations of their imperial possessions. The Decree appealed over the heads of governments to the exploited classes: 'The Provisional Workers' and Peasants' government of Russia also appeals especially to the class-conscious workers of the three leading nations of humanity and the largest states which are participating in the war, England, France and Germany'.[2] To the masses went the appeal

[1] *Ibid.*, p. 126.
[2] Cited by Adam B. Ulam, *Expansion and Coexistence* (1969), p. 52.

to free themselves from slavery and exploitation. In 1918, the German government expelled the Soviet diplomatic mission for participation in revolutionary
activity, and in 1919, Chicherin recalls, 'we sent fewer notes to governments
but more appeals to the toiling masses'.[1] Here one can see the duality of
Soviet foreign policy. On the one hand, the immediate need was for peace,
for this would ensure Bolshevik power. On the other hand was the aspiration
for world socialism and the Marxist claim for proletarian solidarity against
the bourgeoisie. Trotsky and his followers have always emphasised the
importance of the latter objective. Immediately after the October Revolution,
Trotsky called for a revolutionary war. But Lenin's view prevailed and the
'Indecent Peace' was concluded with the Germans in March 1918. By the
terms of the Treaty of Brest-Litovsk, Russia gave up large territories: Poland,
the Ukraine and the Baltic Provinces.

For reasons we cannot explore here,[2] in 1918 the Allies intervened against
the Soviet government on the side of the Whites. Though allied troops never
numbered more than 10,000,[3] this was interpreted by the Bolsheviks as sure
evidence of the intentions of the capitalists to destroy Soviet power. The
significance of the allied intervention was not so much the military[4] but the
psychological impact. Later it was used as evidence to justify the Soviet's
conception of a hostile capitalist world. But in 1918 and 1919, the Russian
Communists still envisaged a world proletarian revolution and in March 1919,
the Third International (Comintern) was founded in Moscow. Its declared
objective was to spread communism through the united efforts of Marxist
revolutionary parties. Even at this time the importance of the colonial
areas was recognised: 'Colonial slaves of Africa and Asia: the hour of
proletarian dictatorship in Europe will also be the hour of your own liberation.'[5]

As the revolutionary fires were put out in Western Europe, Soviet policy
changed. The new Soviet state began to play the diplomatic game with western
governments, the Comintern became a movement identified with the success
of the *Soviet* state. The East rather than the West was regarded as the centre
of the revolutionary stage. As Trotsky put it:

The road to India may prove at the given moment to be more readily passable and
shorter for us than the road to Soviet Hungary. The sort of army, which, at the
moment, can be of no great significance in the European scales can upset the unstable balance of Asian relationships, of colonial dependence, give a direct push to

[1] Cited by L. Kochan, *The Making of Modern Russia* (1962), p. 299.
[2] See George F. Kennan, *Russia and the West under Lenin and Stalin* (1961).
[3] Ulam, *op. cit.*, p. 91.
[4] Ulam, for instance, argues that intervention prolonged the Civil War, *op. cit.*, p. 105.
[5] Jane Degras (ed.), *The Communist International, 1919-1943: Documents, I: 1919-1922* (London
and New York, 1956), p. 45, cited by Ulam, p. 113.

an uprising on the part of the oppressed masses, and assure the triumph of such a rising in Asia.[1]

From 1920, Soviet foreign policy was based on the assumption that the capitalist powers would, sooner or later, invade her. The immediate task was to make this later in order to allow her to consolidate the position at home.

The Comintern attempted to enlist opinion in support of the Soviet state, while she exploited where she could 'the contradictions' between capitalist states. To this end, she now sought, not revolution based on the toiling masses, but recognition by the international community. Though the communists gave moral support (and sometimes arms) to insurrectionists, official policy recognised the international *status quo* and, at least temporarily, sought to strengthen Soviet Russia's position in relation to it.

To strengthen Russia, the Rapallo Treaty was concluded with Germany in 1922. It granted to Soviet Russia full diplomatic recognition and to Germany, among other things, access to substantial military equipment. Two further treaties of friendship were signed with Germany, in 1926 and 1929. These made more difficult a concerted western move against the USSR's borders. The economic aspects of Soviet-German relations were an important aspect of the pact. In 1931, 37 per cent of the USSR's imports came from Germany, and in 1932, 46 per cent.[2] The Germans were able to circumvent the provisions of Versailles on rearmament, and the Russians had German help both for the rebuilding of their armaments industry and for the training of the Red Army. Soviet policy in Europe then, was to capitalise on the division of the western powers and to enter into agreements with them.

With China the Soviet leaders faced a different problem. While in 1924 the Soviet Union signed a treaty with the official government, in fact China was in turmoil, and a policy had to be worked out with regard to the various political groups struggling for power. In a short account it is impossible to describe adequately the complex situation. The Kuomintang was a nationalist movement intent on modernising China; it might broadly be described as a national liberation movement. But its leaders were not communists, who had their own party. In the early 1920s the Comintern advocated the participation of the Chinese communists in the Kuomintang while keeping their own party identity. As the Bolsheviks in Tsarist Russia had fought the autocracy, so the Chinese communists had to oppose the Chinese equivalent before taking on the bourgeoisie. Their participation in the Kuomintang would put them in a stronger position to steer its policies in an anti-imperialist (pro-Soviet) direction and, of course, would enable the communists later to secure concessions for the working class.

[1] Jan Meijer (ed.), *The Trotsky Papers, 1917–1922*, Vol. I (The Hague, 1964), II, p. 623, cited by Ulam, p. 121.
[2] Max Beloff, *The Foreign Policy of Soviet Russia, 1929-1941*, vol. 1 (1947), p. 40.

In 1926, however, Chiang Kai-shek restricted the number of communists in the leading positions of the Kuomintang. While the Chinese communists sought a more independent role, Moscow still backed the alliance with Chiang. The time was not ripe, it was argued, for a communist bid for power and the initiative was seized by Chiang Kai-shek, who in 1927 after capturing Shanghai, turned on his communist supporters and annihilated them.

In the USSR this policy led to a stormy controversy between Trotsky and Stalin. It paralleled their divergence over the doctrine of socialism in one country. Trotsky believed that the time had come for a communist led uprising based on Soviets; he stressed the international role of the Soviet Communist Party. But Stalin was more concerned with the impact of such a policy at home. In 1927, it was premature to support a communist rising: '. . . the struggle of Canton . . . dispersed the forces of imperialism, weakened and overturned imperialism, and thereby facilitated the development of the home of the world revolution, the development of the USSR.'[1]

If revolutionary strategy had moved to the East, the greatest threat to security lay in the West. Here the rise of Hitler was seen as a great danger and Nazi Germany came to be regarded as the chief external threat to the USSR. Soviet policy was one of collective security: the Comintern was pledged to the formation of popular fronts. Soviet activity had succeeded in arranging diplomatic relations with the major western powers, and she had entered the League of Nations. Even so, the USSR was isolated. She tried unsuccessfully to arrange effective military pacts with the western powers against Germany but she had no 'allies' in the West. In 1936, Germany and Japan made an 'Anti-Comintern Pact'. German rearmament and the the growing strength of Fascism in Europe were the background to the trials and purges in Soviet Russia which have been described above.

The building of socialism in one country entailed a strengthening of Soviet power internally and against the capitalist world. While still subscribing to Lenin's 'imperialist' analysis, another concept had been grafted on to it: the notion of the 'capitalist encirclement'. This posited the isolation of Soviet Russia in a world of hostile capitalist states, all intent on destroying her, not only by internal sabotage instigated by the intelligence arms of foreign powers but also by possible armed intervention.

For Trotsky the USSR had abandoned proletarian internationalism and revolution in favour of the Russian national interest. In the *Revolution Betrayed* he said:

The degeneration of the governing stratum in the Soviet Union could not but be accompanied by a corresponding change of aims and methods in Soviet diplomacy. The 'theory' of socialism in one country, first announced in the autumn of 1924, already signalised an effort to liberate Soviet foreign policy from the programme of

[1] J. Stalin in Degras, *Soviet Documents on Foreign Policy*, II, p. 238, cited by Ulam, p. 180.

international revolution . . . From the theory of socialism in a single country, it is a natural transition to that of revolution in a single country.[1]

Soviet leaders did not of course see their actions in such a light. They argued that a wider proletarian revolution could only take place after the strengthening of socialism in Russia. Here we see an example of the way which Marxist revolutionary theory became an ideology which justified the activity of the Soviet state. It would be wrong, however, to regard Stalin's foreign policy as a *rapprochement* with the capitalist states. It was an unstable peaceful cohabitation rather than, as later under Khrushchev, peaceful coexistence. While Trotskyites have emphasised the absence of revolution in Stalin's policy, others have stressed the 'fundamental, not merely incidental intention to use the Soviet Union as a base for world revolution'.[2] Stalin in *Problems of Leninism* said '. . . the very development of world revolution . . . will be more rapid and more thorough, the more thoroughly Socialism fortifies itself in the first victorious country, the faster this country is transformed into a base for the further unfolding of world revolution, into a lever for the further disintegration of imperialism.'[3]

In terms of practical policy, Stalin sought alliances with the world powers. He played the diplomatic game. He entered into a treaty of mutual assistance with France in 1935. But it is doubtful whether Stalin regarded her as an effective ally in the event of a German attack on Russia. Therefore, he kept open the possibility of improving relations with the latter country. This was essentially a short-term policy designed to give the USSR more time to build up her military potential.

In 1938, Hitler took the offensive. He invaded Austria in March. The Russians proposed a conference with the western powers to deter further German expansion – particularly in Czechoslovakia. But the British and French advised the Czechs to cede the Sudetenland to Germany. Subsequently, the western powers not only backed down against Hitler's pressure at Munich, but also excluded the Russians from the conference.

We cannot deal here with the details of diplomatic history.[4] From the Soviet point of view, it seemed that if the British and French were not prepared to take a stand over Austria and Czechoslovakia, then there would be little likelihood of them preventing a German attack to the east – against the USSR. It is sometimes suggested that the anti-Nazi powers (Poland, Britain and France) risked eventual defeat by the Nazis through their hatred of communism and their reluctance to form an anti-fascist alliance with the

[1] L. Trotsky, *The Revolution Betrayed* (New York, 1945), pp. 186, 203.
[2] George Allen Morgan, 'Stalin on Revolution', in Alex Simirenko, *Soviet Sociology* (1967), p. 187.
[3] Cited by Morgan, *ibid*.
[4] For a good recent account see Ulam.

Russians. But the Germans could not attack the USSR without first going through other states, and the British and French had given guarantees to Poland and Rumania.

In August 1939, Soviet policy took a violent turn when the USSR concluded a non-aggression pact with Nazi Germany.[1] This included a secret protocol in which any geographical rearrangement would give the eastern areas of Poland to Russia. Doubting the good intentions of the western powers and their ability to stand up to Hitler, the Russians believed that the pact would prevent an attack on the Soviet Union, at least in the short run. Subsequently, Germany attacked Poland, and on 3 September, France and Britain declared war on Germany. The Soviet army moved into Poland on 17 September and claimed the eastern territories; later she incorporated Lithuania, Latvia, Estonia, a small part of Finland and Bessarabia.

The changes in Soviet policy shocked communists in the west. From campaigning against the ideology and activity of National Socialism, they were called to justify and support the Molotov-Ribbentrop pact and to advocate peace between the allies and Germany. Germany overran France and the Low Countries. Britain remained undefeated but weak. It could only be a matter of time before Hitler attacked the USSR.

World War II

Hitler unleashed his attack on the Soviet Union on 22 June 1941. Russia was at war. The Red Army was smashed. On the first day the Red Air Force was destroyed. White Russia and the western Ukraine were quickly overrun with the Germans advancing 300 miles in 18 days. The war was to be a nightmare experience, for the USSR lost 20 million souls, three million were disabled and twenty-five million were made homeless. In the occupied areas some two-thirds of the national wealth was destroyed. The Soviet Unions alliances changed: she now had to join with the British and the Americans against the Third Reich. As in 1812 a national war was waged against a formidable opponent.

In the West, the Soviet position was thought to be hopeless. The British Ministry of Information gave the Russians a few weeks or at most a couple of months. But resistance was stubborn. If some Russians regarded communism as bad, the Germans showed that they could expect worse from Hitler's anti-Bolshevik crusade. The Slavs were *Untermenschen* (subhumans), like the Jews they were destined for extermination. As Field-Marshal von Manstein ordered: '. . . *In enemy cities, a large part of the population will have*

[1] For a detailed account of Soviet relations with Poland and Germany and the West in 1939, see Max Beloff, *The Foreign Policy of Soviet Russia, 1929-1941*, vol. 2 (1949).

to go hungry. Nothing out of a misguided sense of humanity, may be given to prisoners-of-war or to the population unless they are in the service of the German Wehrmacht.[1] The German army reached the suburbs of Moscow, to be met by detachments of workers with rifles or hand-made implements.

The war cemented the loyalty of people, state and party. Party membership trebled from two to six million between 1941 and 1944. It was a war not only between Germans and Russians but between capitalists and communists: national survival meant communist survival. But violence was not only to be committed against Soviet citizens by the Germans. Nationalities thought to be disloyal were uprooted and despatched to the east. A million persons were so moved: Volga Germans, Crimean Tartars, Kalmyks and four Caucasian minorities (Chechens, Ingushi, Karachai and Balkars).

After its initial defeats, the Red Army recovered. Stalingrad was successfully defended and Leningrad resisted a three-year siege in which a million died, mainly from hunger.[2] The Reds after a long and heroic struggle reached Warsaw by July 1944 and took Berlin in May 1945. The military war was over. The Nazi campaign to rid Europe of Bolshevism was instrumental in bringing the Red Army and Soviet power to the banks of the Elbe. The spectre of communism indeed was haunting Europe. In the West, the impact of the war on the Soviet Union is generally underestimated. For Soviet people it now is symbolic of national unity and strength, of suffering and destruction, of *Soviet power* over the might of German militarism. Soviet museums are full of the *Great Patriotic War*; public cemeteries and memorials to the dead are on a scale unknown in the West, including the defeated Germany.

The USSR emerged from the Second World War as a major world military power. Though she had been weakened by the war, her aggressive neighbours, Germany and Japan, had been vanquished. She was able, moreover, to make important territorial gains in East Europe and she attempted to secure as large an area of influence as was possible.[3] Soviet policy was to consolidate the gains made in the Second World War. She was now a military power with a physical presence in the heart of Europe.

After the Second World War the international structure had a much different complexion when compared to 1939. The British and French Empires were in the throes of death. Demands for independence in the Third World were gaining in momentum. The USA vied with Britain for the leadership of the capitalist countries. The communist parties of the West emerged strengthened from the war. The communist resistance in France had been armed and well-organised, the party had considerable electoral support both there and in

[1] Italics in the original. Cited by Alexander Werth, *Russia at War 1941-45* (1964), pp. 637-8. See also Harrison E. Salisbury, *The Siege of Leningrad* (1969).

[2] Harrison E. Salisbury, *The Siege of Leningrad* (1969), p. 516.

[3] For a detailed account see Raymond L. Garthoff, *Soviet Military Policy* (1966), Chapter 1.

E

Italy. In Britain a socialist (Labour) government had been swept into power at the expense of Winston Churchill and the Conservatives.

Soviet policy, however, was cautious in exploiting these developments. The USSR was intent on reconstruction at home and on consolidating her gains in Eastern Europe. Her policy was a continuation of promoting world socialism by securing it in the USSR. This involved priority being given to the bloc incorporation of the Eastern European states: Poland, Czechoslovakia, Romania, Bulgaria, Yugoslavia and Albania,[1] and the Soviet Zone of Germany. Such a policy not only safeguarded Russia's western borders but ensured that these countries were within the Soviet military/economic orbit.

Crucial to the success of Soviet plans and to the structure of Europe after the war was the attitude of the Allies to Soviet policy. At Yalta in February 1945, the broad objectives of each side were discussed and general agreement was reached. Germany was to be disarmed, demilitarised and divided – though no agreement was reached on how this was to be done. Stalin insisted that Poland was to be 'amicably disposed' towards the USSR, and that Germany should pay reparations for war damage.

Stalin's policy is summed up in the following passage:

. . . The Germans made their invasion of the USSR through Finland, Poland, Romania, Bulgaria and Hungary. The Germans were able to make their invasion through these countries because, at the time, governments hostile to the Soviet Union existed in these countries. As a result of the German invasion, the Soviet Union has lost irretrievably in the fighting against the Germans, and also through the German occupation and the deportation of Soviet Citizens to German servitude, a total of about seven million people. . . . In other words the Soviet Union's loss of life has been several times greater than that of Britain and the USA put together [subsequently estimated at twenty million]. . . And so what can there be surprising about the fact that the Soviet Union, anxious for its future safety, is trying to see to it that governments loyal in their attitude to the Soviet Union should exist in these countries? How can anyone who has not taken leave of his senses, describe these peaceful aspirations of the Soviet Union as expansionist tendencies on the part of our State?[2]

The Soviet Union set about creating a 'sphere of influence' in Eastern Europe. Regimes based on the Soviet model were formed in Poland, Hungary, Rumania, Bulgaria and later in Czechoslovakia. Germany was partitioned and the East, under the communist Socialist Unity Party, was incorporated as a people's democracy.

Western policy became hostile to the USSR. This was justified in the West

---

[1] For details on each country see Hugh Seton-Watson, *The East European Revolution* (London, 1956). It should be noted here that political action in Yugoslavia and Albania after the Second World War was from the beginning relatively independent of the USSR.

[2] J. V. Stalin, *Post-War International Relations* (London, Soviet Booklet, 1947), p. 5. Cited by L. Churchward, *Contemporary* (1968), *Soviet Politics* pp. 253-4.

by reference to Soviet policy in Eastern Europe and also to Bolshevik ideology. George F. Kennan wrote in 1947:

> Of the original ideology, nothing has been officially junked. Belief is maintained in the basic badness of capitalism, in the inevitability of its destruction, in the obligation of the proletariat to assist in that destruction and to take the power into its own hands. But stress has come to be laid primarily on those concepts which relate most specifically to the Soviet regime itself: to its position as the sole truly Socialist regime in a dark and misguided world, and to the relationships of power within it.
>
> The first of these concepts is that of the innate antagonism between capitalism and Socialism. We have seen how deeply that concept has become imbedded for Russia's conduct as a member of international society. It means that there can never be on Moscow's side any sincere assumption of aims between the Soviet Union and powers which are regarded as capitalist.[1]

The 'cold war' was the result of two tendencies. On the western side, fears of Soviet expansion and the domination of western societies by communism and the consolidation of 'socialism in one country' by Soviet policy in Eastern Europe. The Russians justifiably mistrusted the motives of the Allies. Their aims in defeated Germany, Austria and Italy were not only to restore the capitalist system there but to use these countries as bulwarks, if not springboards, against the USSR.

The new international conditions after the Second World War led to a change in the Soviet Union's view of socialist-capitalist relations: the theory of capitalist encirclement was superseded by the concept of 'two camps'. With communist governments installed in Eastern Europe (and China), the socialist states formed a relatively equal balance against the capitalist. The geography of the two blocs is shown on Map 2. NATO was formed in 1949 but the *formal* alliance between the Eastern European powers and the formation of the Warsaw Treaty Organisation was not made until 1955. During this period the Russians believed that there was a possibility of war being unleashed by the capitalist powers. Soviet policy was to keep the West at bay and to avoid a direct military confrontation, though differences between the western powers were exploited (for example, between colonial and non-colonial powers and between European and American countries). During the early cold war, the Soviet bloc was at a nuclear disadvantage, not being in possession of a nuclear strike potential until the mid-fifties when the USSR acquired a nuclear capacity with jet bomber delivery; more of military strategy later. Soviet policy in Western and Central Europe was cautious, if not conservative: the Russians did not foment revolution in France or Italy, but allowed the communists to be disarmed, nor did they intervene militarily on the side of the communist insurgents in Greece.

[1] George F. Kennan, 'The Sources of Soviet Conduct', *Foreign Affairs*, vol. 25, July 1947, pp. 571-2.

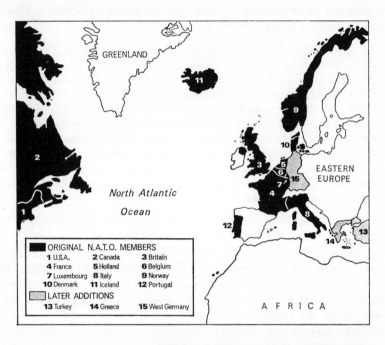

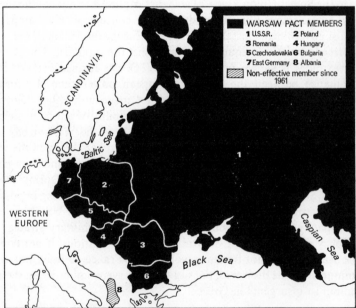

MAP 2 NATO and the Warsaw Pact Countries.

In 1953, Soviet policy took another shift, adopting the doctrine of 'peaceful coexistence', which is the present policy. Here again, we must not be confused between what the Soviet ideology of foreign affairs says is true and what actually is true. The *theory* may be described briefly as follows. State-monopoly capitalism is in decline: unemployment is increasing as a result of technological change and insufficient demand; the exploitation of the underdeveloped part of the world has been limited by colonial independence movements, and by the role of the state socialist countries in their development; military expenditure becomes a means of maintaining profits, and militarism infects bourgeois society. The national liberation movement is the centre of change in the international arena:[1] the 'national democracies' of those liberated from the colonialist yoke are seen as 'an independent force on the world scene' and constitute 'a *progressive revolutionary and anti-colonialist force*'.[2] The alignment of socialist states with those of the national democracies and the international working class can prevent war. The emphasis on the *prevention* of nuclear war is one of the main components of Soviet foreign policy. A nuclear war would not only destroy capitalism but would destroy civilisation. In theoretical statements, peaceful co-existence of the capitalist and socialist systems now takes the place of the inevitable collision of the two systems. Soviet foreign policy 'is based on the principles of peace, the equality and self-determination of nations, and respect for the independence and sovereignty of all countries, as well as the fair, humane methods of socialist diplomacy . . .'[3] Socio-political change in the advanced capitalist states is to take place through internal upheaval. The economic advancement of socialist societies and their more peaceful foreign policies are regarded as beacons as it were for the revolutionary forces of the capitalist world, whose ruling class is under pressure from the internal 'progressive' forces (such as peace movements) of their own society. In colonial areas the struggle for national independence is supported by the Russians – though short of military involvement which might lead to a conflict with the leading capitalist states.

The above, briefly stated, is the Soviet theory. In a later chapter we shall discuss in more detail the role of ideology in Soviet society. What has been discussed above illustrates the malleability of Soviet doctrine. From rejecting the rules of the diplomatic game after the Revolution, the Russians quickly learned to accept them. From regarding the collapse of capitalism as inevitable, the Soviet leaders have been forced to explain its durability. Whereas in the Stalin era, ideology sustained the inevitability of class and international con-

[1] Lloyd Churchward has illustrated the Soviet emphasis by pointing out that the foreign affairs textbook used in Party schools devoted 38 pages to the analysis of intra-bloc relations and 115 pages to Soviet policy in Asia, Africa and Latin America. *Contemporary Soviet Government* (1968), p. 256, n. 23.

[2] *The Programme of the CPSU* (1961), p. 35. Italics in original.

[3] *Ibid.*, p. 40.

flict, under Khrushchev coexistence replaced cohabitation. Soviet ideology of foreign affairs then cannot be regarded as an independent factor which determines practical activity. Rather, it must be conceived of as a doctrine which justifies the political activity of the Soviet political elite given the demands made on it. But ideology does help to shape their view of the external world: the capitalist West is seen with suspicion, economic and political interests are closely related. The USSR supports those movements and groups which she believes will sustain international communism. But when Soviet strategic interest is at stake, radical ideological shifts can be made to suit immediate policy (for example, the Nazi-Soviet Pact) and the self-interest of the USSR is a most important determinant of foreign policy.

The Military Balance

International relations in recent decades have been influenced by the invention of thermo-nuclear weapons. A thermo-nuclear war, it is argued, would result, not in the victory of one side over the other, but in the obliteration of both sides and, possibly, in the extinction of man or at least of the culture which we now know. Nuclear war, from this viewpoint, had to be outlawed as an instrument of Soviet policy. It follows from this, in *Soviet theory*, that all armies and armaments should be abolished. Also, if they were, the economic basis of capitalism would collapse for, as described above, militarism and the arms race are important stabilisers of the capitalist economy. But state socialist countries, having no internal antagonistic contradictions, and no external political objectives, do not need a permanent arms economy.

These views, even if genuinely believed in the USSR, cut no ice in the West. 'General and complete disarmament' is regarded in official circles as unrealistic, mainly because it is not enforceable. Therefore, both sides professing peaceful goals, fervently prepare for war, ostensibly to deter the other side from attack. Herein, however, lies a fundamental instability in international relations. Given mutual distrust and an arms race, one side may find itself, by virtue of a technical discovery, with a comparative advantage over the other side. It may, therefore, rationally decide to use its advantage by declaring war. Otherwise, if it waits, its opponents may at some future time have a military advantage and use it. Khrushchev may have risked the possibility of world war by sending missiles to Cuba in order to reduce the United States' military intercontinental missile superiority, an example of the way an attempt to secure a balance of power may result in armed conflict. Of course, both sides, East and West, profess peace but accuse each other of desiring war: the West for its part holding up the goal of communist world domination, the Soviet bloc predicting it as a possible result of decaying capitalism's internal contradictions.

For the final *deterrent* to be effective, as nuclear armers conceive of it, no side must be in a position to believe it can win in this sense. The crucial factor here is to ensure that the side striking first will nevertheless be obliterated by retaliation (the power of a 'second strike'). The result is peace through nuclear stalemate. Both the USA and USSR pursue such a strategic policy. The Chinese, at least in some official statements, still regard war as a legitimate extension of politics. This does not mean that they 'want war' but that the fear of a nuclear attack should not prevent the communist camp from advancing its own interests.

The Warsaw Pact and NATO must be prepared for yet another strategic contingency: the acceptance of the nuclear stalemate by both sides but the use of conventional forces to impose a conventional military solution, or the utilization of them to 'finish off' the enemy after a nuclear holocaust. The deployment of conventional forces, therefore, must also be considered in the military balance.

At the end of the Second World War, the Soviet Army was made up of fifteen million men. Since that time the USSR has maintained a smaller but still very large land army. By 1947, there were four million men in the armed forces plus 400,000 security troops; these forces were increased during the Korean War, but decreased in 1958. Even so, in the late fifties the Soviet bloc had a numerical superiority over western forces of three to one in both Europe and Asia.[1] The main reason for this large land army was to withstand a possible invasion from the West, either with or without the use of nuclear weapons.[2] In the early period, of course, the USSR had no atomic arms and superiority in conventional forces was believed to redress the balance somewhat. Even after the Soviets had a nuclear strike capacity in 1955, large ground forces were justified in order to combat enemy forces after a nuclear strike:

'It is entirely clear that atomic and hydrogen weapons alone, without *the decisive operations of the ground forces* with their contemporary material, cannot decide the outcome of a war'.[3]

In 1968 the Soviet regular forces comprised 3,220,000 men. The United States had 3,500,000 men in the armed forces.[4] The Warsaw Pact in 1966 had 2,925,000 men in the land army compared with 2,896,000 in NATO but the fire-power at the disposal of NATO countries was much superior.

The defence effort, as shown by the following table, has been both absolutely and relatively greater in the USA than in the USSR. Even in 1963–4, the United States spent absolutely three times as much on defence – 8.9 per cent

[1] Raymond L. Garthoff, *Soviet Strategy in the Nuclear Age* (1958), p. 151.

[2] In addition, troops were needed for internal security purposes in Warsaw Pact countries. But this need does not on its own account for the large size of Russian forces.

[3] Marshal Rotmistrov, cited by R. L. Garthoff, *op. cit.*, p. 154.

[4] *The Military Balance 1968-69* (Institute of Strategic Studies, 1968), p. 57.

of the Gross National Product, compared to 5.7 per cent of the Soviet's. By 1968 Soviet defence expenditure had increased, bringing it only just over the American as a proportion of GNP – though still about half of the total American expenditure (see Table 5).

Table 5. Defence Expenditure, UK, USA, USSR

Defence Expenditure as a Burden on National Economies

	Defence Expenditure (million US $)		As a % of GNP		As a % of total central government expenditure	Per Capita $
	1963/4	*1968*	*1967*	*1968*	*1963/4*	*1968*
United Kingdom	5,140	5,450	5.7	5.3	26	98
USA	52,400	79,576	9.8	9.2	53	396
USSR	15,400	39,780	9.6	9.3	16	169

Source: Institute for Strategic Studies.
   The Military Balance 1955-6. (1965), p. 43.
   The Military Balance 1968-9. (1968), pp. 55-6.
   The Military Balance 1969-70. (1969), p. 57.

The 'Socialist Bloc'

Let us now turn to Soviet relations with other socialist countries. In the decade after the Second World War, the USSR was the dominant power in the communist world. The model of state socialist Russia was copied in the Eastern European states. With the notable exception of Yugoslavia, the communist parties of the world conceded ideological leadership to the CPSU. In the countries of the 'socialist bloc' rigidly centralised regimes were set up which essentially were politically dependent on the Soviet government. But it is important to note that they were *national* communist governments and from the mid-fifties they were to exert greater pressure for independence from the USSR. National communist parties were to define within limits their own roads to socialism and Soviet control over the state socialist countries of Eastern Europe was relaxed.

After the death of Stalin in 1953, 'destalinisation' began to take place in some East European countries. Police control was weakened. Disorders and strikes took place, particularly in East Germany (G.D.R.) and Czechoslovakia. Concessions in the economy were made. Relatively more consumer goods were produced and from 1953 reversions to some forms of private farming were allowed. The government of Imre Nagy in Hungary favoured more liberal policies.[1] But uprisings against the regime, as in East Berlin, were suppressed by troops.

[1] For a description see 'The New Course in Hungary', in R. Pethybridge, *The Development of the Communist Bloc* (Boston, 1965).

The increasing autonomy, the decline in police control, and hostility to the Russians were the background to Khrushchev's famous 'secret speech' of February 1956 in which he abrogated Stalin's policies (see Reading No. 6). This precipitated uprisings in Poland and Hungary. In Poland an imprisoned opponent of Stalin, Gomulka, was elected Secretary of the Party. He promised liberalisation of the regime, but well within the framework of a Soviet style economy and with support for the USSR's foreign policy. In Hungary, on the other hand, the revolution had more extreme aims and ended differently. Many Hungarians not only wanted to end the political monopoly of the Communist Party but also wanted to adopt a foreign policy independent of the USSR by leaving the Warsaw Pact. In November 1956, Soviet armed forces intervened and a pro-Soviet government was installed. There were differences in the strategic position of Hungary and Poland. Poland's western frontier was not officially recognised by the western powers, she had been invaded and plundered by the Germans and she feared German *revanchism*. The international alliance with the USSR was a life line to the country's survival and this limited the demand for autonomy in the international arena. The Hungarians, on the other hand, had no territorial problems. They had been allies of the Germans during the war and there was much pro-western sympathy. They had more to gain from leaving the Warsaw Pact than had the Poles.

The most recent and possibly most interesting case of assertion of independence is given by events in Czechoslovakia. The political reforms of the 1950s largely passed by Czechoslovakia which consequently remained, at least outwardly, one of the most Stalinist countries of Eastern Europe. Changes took place, however, under Novotny, the right-wing leader: foreign travel was more free, culture was less constrained, economic 'stimulation' was introduced in the economy. These changes did not go far enough for the more progressive Czechs who demanded more radical social change. It was advocated that the role of the Communist Party be diminished (see Chapter 12), that the economy be decentralised giving individual enterprises greater autonomy and that trade with foreign countries should be less constrained by administrative control. The economy and polity would, in other words, be more like that of Yugoslavia. In international affairs the Czechs wanted to maintain their alliance with the Russians and to stay in the Warsaw Pact, albeit with greater autonomy. The Russians regarded this policy as essentially incompatible with their conception of socialist internationalism. The reforms, they argued, would weaken the socialist system and make the Czech economy more dependent on the capitalist West. They also asserted that western agents were undermining the Czech state. Soviet troops, aided by those of Poland, Hungary, Bulgaria and East Germany (GDR), occupied Czechoslovakia in August 1968. Since then, the Soviet Union has attempted to undo the progressive reforms.

E*

The Soviet assertion of direct western subversion in Czechoslovakia is probably no more than a pretext for their own intervention which has to be explained in other more general policy terms. Soviet policy to Eastern Europe is based fundamentally on the creation of a buffer zone between the USSR and the western powers. Any attempt to destroy or weaken this is regarded as a threat to Soviet security. The Russians consider these states to be 'in uniformity' with the Soviet system, not only in terms of their foreign policy but also by the nature of their economy. (An analogy may be made with United States policy in Central America.) Hence if there are separate roads to socialism not converging on Moscow, events have shown that these roads must not appear to lead too far away from Moscow. For the states of Eastern Europe, 'independence' and 'autonomy' can only be relative to Soviet strategic interests. Since the Soviet invasion of Czechoslovakia, the Russian government has attempted to justify the intervention in the affairs of other state socialist states by emphasising the 'unity of the socialist camp'. The document published at the International Communist meeting in Moscow (17th June 1969) said that: 'The defence of Socialism is an internationalist duty of communists ... Loyalty to Marxism, Leninism and to proletarian internationalism and dedicated and devoted service in the common cause of socialism was a requisite for the efficacy and correct orientation of united action by the Communist and Workers' Parties and are a guarantee that they will achieve their historic goals'.[1] 'Proletarian internationalism' is interpreted by the Russians to justify their action in Czechoslovakia as 'the fraternal aid of the Soviet Union and other socialist states . . .'[2] In other words, the states of Eastern Europe have limited sovereignty. The greater emphasis placed on the 'unity of the socialist camp' and the limits on the sovereignty of individual countries within it, is sometimes called the Brezhnev doctrine.

While relations between the USSR and China/Albania worsened under Khrushchev, with the Yugoslavs they improved. A joint statement in 1956 by the CPSU and the League of Yugoslav Communists recognised the rights of each side to its own version of socialist development. Since 1958, though Yugoslavia was regarded in a more friendly light, she has not been recognised as a communist bloc power. Until the Soviet intervention in Czechoslovakia, relations were cordial and Yugoslavia was given the right to attend meetings of the permanent commissions of COMECON (Council of Economic Mutual Assistance).[3]

Soviet foreign policy after Stalin involved a movement from a hard to a soft policy in East-West relations – it stressed the containment of capitalism rather

[1] *Soviet News*, No. 5495, 20 June 1969, pp. 161, 167.
[2] *Pravda*, 30 April 1969. *Current Digest of the Soviet Press*, 21, no. 18 (21 May 1969), p. 19.
[3] See Harry Hanak, 'Soviet Foreign Policy since Khrushchev', *The Year Book of World Affairs* (1966), pp. 44-6.

than the eventual world victory of communism and peaceful coexistence rather than temporary peaceful cohabitation. Herein lies one of the main causes of the split between the USSR and People's China which first began in 1957–8 and led to a final rupture in 1960, and the exchange of gunfire in border skirmishes in 1969. Their differences may be summarised as follows. Firstly, the Chinese Communist Party had seized power in an extremely backward country, and the resources channelled to her by the USSR fell short of China's demands.[1] The Soviet policy of increasing consumer welfare at home directly reduced the assistance which could be given to revolutionary forces abroad. Secondly, the maintenance of a world equilibrium through the good offices of the USA and the USSR involved agreement on the use and spread of nuclear arms. Both sides were parties to the non-proliferation of atomic weapons, which meant that Chinese requests for them were refused by the Russians. Soviet national interest for a *détente* with the USA was shown to be detrimental to the interest of the Chinese Communists. Thirdly, the Chinese, being an Oriental and relatively backward though Marxist power, began to assert their own ideological theories on revolutionary tactics and socialist development – the 'Great Leap Forward' and the rejection of peaceful coexistence, for example. Here Russia's leadership of the world communist movement was challenged. In July and August 1960, after bitter ideological polemics, Soviet advisers and technicians were withdrawn from China which was a serious blow to Chinese reconstruction. In the 1960s relations between the two countries could not be considered 'friendly'. The Chinese regarded the Soviet leaders as degenerate and as betraying the cause of the world proletariat. Hereafter, the USSR in the international arena has been faced with continual Chinese criticism.

A fourth area of latent conflict between the USSR and China is given by their relations to the Third World. Until 1955, the Soviet Union's main effort was to consolidate the gains of the Second World War in Europe. The Twentieth Party Congress in 1956 sanctioned the doctrine of peaceful coexistence. While this made explicit the lack of involvement of the USSR in colonial revolutions it also enabled the Soviet Union to enhance its world role by wooing the national bourgeoisie of the Third World. Soviet policy here was to secure friends among the 'uncommitted' nations of the world, whatever their political complexion. If they were 'uncommitted' they were not part of the capitalist bloc, and therefore weakened it. Soviet influence could also be used, it was argued, to keep societies moving from feudalism to capitalism on a progressive path. But the Chinese tended to support the revolutionary underdogs in the developing countries. China was also involved in border incidents with India. She criticised the soft 'reformist' line of the Russians in Iraq and

[1] Even military equipment was inferior, and the Chinese complained that they had to bear the brunt of financing the Korean War – see R. L. Garthoff, *Soviet Military Policy* (1966), pp. 176-7.

Syria when they restrained the communist parties of those countries. Mao argued that local wars were an inevitable result of the contradiction between capitalism and socialism in developing countries. Paradoxically then, Moscow's policy of driving a wedge between the states of the capitalist world by creating a 'third camp' was to sharpen conflict between the leading communist states, the USSR and China.

The impact of Soviet policy in the Third World has been mixed. On the one hand, the USSR has been given recognition as an Asian power and has been accepted as a member of the Bandung conference and the Afro-Asian Peoples' Solidarity Council. This is a significant advance because it gives her direct access to an Asian organisation which is denied to the western powers. She has been seen to act as a peace maker at the Tashkent conference. The economic and military aid to Third World countries has had some military advantages. It has given the Soviet navy a port in the Mediterranean and allies among the Arabs. Cuba is a friendly power in the Americas and provides a base for influence in Latin America. On the other hand, Soviet policy has failed in many ways. Support for India against China has exacerbated Sino-Soviet relations. Economic aid has not always guaranteed political allegiance: the USSR's chosen associates in Indonesia and Ghana, Sukarno and Nkrumah, have fallen from grace. Third World states have not come under Soviet tutelage. Ben Bella has looked for aid both to Russia and China. Soviet support for the Vietcong in its struggle with the Americans has by no means made North Vietnam or the Vietcong more hostile to the Chinese.

In this brief review of Soviet international relations we may highlight a number of general conclusions. First, it must be obvious that Soviet Russia's internal developments have been shaped to a great extent by external factors. Relative economic and military weakness after the Revolution and ideological incompatibility with the leading powers were important factors influencing the industrialisation process of the 1930s, and in no small way created a psychological atmosphere conducive to the purges. One cannot realistically describe the internal social and political system independently of demands generated in the international environment. Second, Marxist ideology has been 'adapted' to serve the Soviet Union's international interests. In the early days of Soviet power it provided a rationalisation of the hostile world which created *internal* dynamism. Leninism subtly shifted the focus of emphasis from the western capitalist powers to the East: the Russian Revolution was thereby given prominence. The world communist movement was subordinated to the immediate aims of Stalin's Russia: to build socialism in one country. In the international arena this entailed peaceful cohabitation. To a Marxist world view of hostile capitalist powers was added the ingredient of Soviet national interest. In the Soviet explanation of the world, Marxism has played an important role in defining the western powers as a class enemy. This has also had a reciprocal effect. The western states have often acted as if the Marxist strategy of world revolution were being put into effect. Though ideology has not inhibited the Soviet Union from changing her alliances and tactics it has had the effect of making the doctrine of 'peaceful coexistence' less credible in the West. Soviet ideology, therefore, has constrained her own actions and those of her ideological opponents in the international arena. Each side has regarded the other's foreign policy in terms of dogmatic unchanging ideological assumptions. But the need to survive has changed the Soviet conception of the inevitability of war between the capitalist and socialist camp. Nuclear strategy has eliminated the possibility of war as a rational policy of external expansion. Peaceful coexistence is a practical policy congruent with Soviet self-interest and is likely to be so until a major technological advance is made. Third, Soviet strategic interest has been shaped by geographical factors. The handicap of a wide western frontier has led to the creation of a buffer zone in Eastern Europe. This has been maintained by a combination of factors: the 'utilitarian' defence of Poland's western borders, by coercion in Hungary and Czechoslovakia. On the other hand, the geographical proximity to India and China has given the USSR the status of an Asian and Oriental power. She has been able, among the uncommitted nations, to bring influence to bear with greater effect than her western antagonists.[1] Fourth, Soviet foreign policy has many aims in common with traditional non-communist states: to secure the Soviet Union's geographical integrity as a separate entity; to enhance her power and influence in the international system. She has espoused the spread of her own ideological values and social system to other parts of the world. In this she is not unique as a study of the late British Empire and American involvement in securing the value of the 'Free World' in other countries would show. But external expansion and support of ideological values have not been at the expense of internal security. Before the Second World War, the Soviet Union was a relatively weak economic and military unit; she maintained her hegemony over other communist parties because a good case could be made for Stalin's view that the interests of the Soviet Union were the interests of the world proletariat. After the Second World War, the Soviet Communist Party's interest and that of other ruling communist parties have been seen to conflict. For underdeveloped China, a greater commitment was demanded from the Soviet Union to fulfil the ideological goal of a communist world over Russia's own desire for internal well being. Czech national demands for greater economic and cultural freedom were seen to conflict with the Soviet Union's own security. Fifth, Soviet foreign policy can best be understood as serving the interests of concrete social and political groups who gain by the preservation of the Soviet order, rather than by promoting the intangible abstract notion

---

[1] See Robert C. Tucker, *The Soviet Political Mind* (New York, 1963), Chapters 9 and 10.

of world communism, for foreign policy objectives have to be balanced against internal claims to resources. At this point we move from the international to the internal political system. In the following chapters we shall describe its structure and the groups which it may preserve.

FOR FURTHER STUDY

INTRODUCTORY

Churchward, Lloyd G. *Contemporary Soviet Government*. London: Routledge and Kegan Paul, 1968.
Kochan, Lionel B. *The Making of Modern Russia*. London: Jonathan Cape, 1962.
Pethybridge, R. *The Development of the Communist Bloc*. Boston: D. C. Heathrow and Co., 1965.
Seton-Watson, Hugh. *The East European Revolution*. London: Methuen, 1956.
Werth, Alexander. *Russia at War, 1941-45*. London: Barrie and Rockliff, 1964.

BASIC

Beloff, Max. *The Foreign Policy of Soviet Russia, 1929-1941*. 2 Vols. London: Oxford University Press, 1947.
Garthoff, Raymond L. *Soviet Military Policy: A Historical Analysis*. New York: Praeger, 1966.
Soviet Strategy in the Nuclear Age. New York: Praeger, 1958.
Lenin, V. I. *Imperialism, The Highest Stage of Capitalism*. London: Lawrence and Wishart, 1948.
Meyer, A. G. *Leninism*. Cambridge, Mass.: Harvard University Press, 1957.
Ulam, Adam B. *Expansion and Coexistence*. London: Secker and Warburg, 1969.

SPECIALISED

Bradley, John. *Allied Intervention in Russia*. London: Weidenfeld and Nicolson, 1968.
Degras, Jane (ed.). *The Communist International, 1919-1943: Documents*, I: 1919-1922. London and New York: Oxford University Press, 1956.
Soviet Documents on Foreign Policy, 3 Vols. London: Oxford University Press, 1951-3.
Hanak, Harry. 'Soviet Foreign Policy Since Khrushchev', in *The Yearbook of World Affairs*. London: Stevens, 1966, pp. 44-6.
Institute of Strategic Studies. *The Military Balance, 1965-66*. London: Institute of Strategic Studies, 1965.
The Military Balance, 1968-69. London: Institute of Strategic Studies, 1968.
The Military Balance, 1969-70. London: Institute of Strategic Studies, 1969.
Kennan, George F. *Russia and the West under Lenin and Stalin*. London: Hutchinson, 1961.
'The Sources of Soviet Conduct', *Foreign Affairs*, Vol. 25, July 1947, pp. 566-82.
Meijer, Jan (ed.). *The Trotsky Papers, 1917-1922*: I. The Hague, 1964.

Morgan, George Allen. 'Stalin on Revolution', in Alex Simirenko (ed.), *Soviet Sociology: Historical Antecedents and Current Appraisals*. London: Routledge, 1967, pp. 168-204.

Salisbury, Harrison E. *The Siege of Leningrad*. London: Secker and Warburg, 1969.

Stalin, J. V. *Post-War International Relations* (Soviet Booklet). London, 1947.

Trotsky, L. *The Revolution Betrayed: The Soviet Union, What It Is and Where It Is Going*. New York: Pioneer Publishers, 1958.

Tucker, Robert C. *The Soviet Political Mind*. New York: Praeger, 1963.

5

SOVIET POLITICAL INSTITUTIONS: STRUCTURE AND PERSONNEL

The Formal Institutions and How They Work Officially

In the foregoing four chapters we have discussed the historical antecedents of the comtemporary USSR. In the next four Chapters we shall turn to consider the political structure and processes of the modern Soviet state. The first chapter considers, from a fairly conventional point of view, the main political institutions – the party, and the structure of the government (the federal system, the Soviets or Parliaments). Here too the social background of party members and elected deputies are described. This Chapter takes as a starting point the 'official' Soviet constitutional point of view. In Chapter 6, theories critical of the Soviet system are outlined. Chapters 7 and 8 are concerned with the process of the Soviet political system, with the articulation and aggregation of interests, with the role of groups and the relationship between the Communist Party of the Soviet Union and other institutions.

Let us begin with a definition of the political system. It has been defined by Gabriel Almond as 'that system of interactions to be found in all independent societies which performs the functions of integration and adaptation (both internally and *vis-à-vis* other societies) by means of the employment, or threat of employment, of more or less legitimate compulsion'.[1] The use of 'legitimate force' is the characteristic which distinguishes the political system from other parts of society. While the bodies (parliaments, parties etc.) and the methods (persuasion, coercion, remuneration) differ from one society to another, in all industrial societies policies must be made which are binding on citizens, and mechanisms are devised to select between alternatives. In this chapter, in a fairly conventional way, we may first describe the theory and the formal institutions, which are mentioned in the Constitution of the USSR and which are known by previous research to play a leading political role. For didactic purposes it is convenient to organise the material under four headings: the *official* view of Soviet political behaviour, the structure and membership of the party, the structure and membership of the Soviets (Parliaments), and finally

---

[1] Gabriel Almond, 'A Functional Approach to Comparative Politics', *The Politics of Developing Areas* (1960), p. 7. See a so David Easton, *A Systems Analysis of Political Life* (1965), p. 21.

in a coda to this chapter is added a brief commentary on the official view. In
the next chapter, we shall describe other models more critical of the Soviet
system. In Chapters 7 and 8 we shall analyse the way they actually do behave –
as far as political scientists are aware. This topic, of course, is what really
matters, but a thorough understanding of Soviet politics must also include a
knowledge of the formal constitutional set-up. The formal statutes, as
defined in a body's rules (such as the constitution of a community), are
important because, in the first instance, they define the activity expected of the
body and its parts. Its role performance, or actual conduct, may be quite
different and is a matter for empirical study.

Socialist Harmony

We have seen that for Marxists, class relations are based on property relations.
What kind of social system did property relations entail in Soviet *theory* for
the USSR? We have seen that after the Revolution, the 'dictatorship of the
proletariat' ensured the rule of the working class over the dispossessed
bourgeoisie and aristocracy, but in 1936, Stalin decreed that socialism had been
achieved and that no 'contradictory' classes existed in the USSR. The nationalisation of property, and planned production guided by the Communist
Party, gave rise to a *socialist* society.

> In socialist society these elements [the main elements of the production process –
> labour power and the means of production] are combined in such a way that those
> taking part in the production process collectively own the instruments of labour
> which they employ. This totally excludes the possibility of the means of production
> being converted by one part of society into a means of exploitation of the other part
> of society. Since they jointly own social property and jointly participate in the social
> production process, all people are equal and their relations are based on principles
> of comradely co-operation and mutual assistance.[1]

The point to be emphasised here is that this consensual view of Soviet society
is based on the Marxist notion, described earlier, that social and political
conflict derives from ownership or class relations. From Stalin's viewpoint
the abolition of property owning classes, therefore, entailed the elimination
of the major forms of socio-political conflict.

In 1936 the 'Stalin' Constitution was decreed. It proclaimed direct election
to the Soviets, secret ballot and the enfranchisement of all social classes. There
was, of course, no freedom for the organisation of political parties: parties
could only rest on a class basis, and, as there were no classes in Soviet Russia,
there could be no basis for them. The state, as an organisation of legitimate
armed force, still existed. This was justified by reference to the encirclement
of the USSR by hostile war-like capitalist states which required a state to

[1] *Fundamentals of Marxism-Leninism* (Moscow, 1961), p. 695.

protect socialist power. According to Stalin's theory there was friendly collaboration between the three main social groups: intelligentsia, working
class and peasantry.[1] This did not mean that there was complete harmony:
there were still some areas of strife. For example, practices and values which
had been learned in previous non-socialist epochs and differences between town
and country gave rise to groups with separate and specific interests. Such
conflicts, however, could be resolved within the parameters of the Soviet
state system: they were 'non-antagonistic' contradictions, rather than the
antagonistic ones of the capitalist system which could only be resolved by a
fundamental change in the social order. While conflict existed on a world scale
between the USSR and the leading capitalist states, internally the social order
and social relations were viewed as basically harmonious. Soviet political
institutions were constructed on these assumptions.

The chief formal bodies are now the Communist Party of the Soviet Union
(CPSU), the ministerial apparatuses (the bureaucracy) and parliaments (the
Soviets). On Chart 1, the main division and organs are shown. At the apex

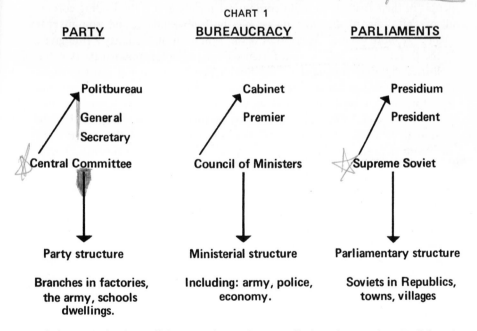

CHART 1

PARTY	BUREAUCRACY	PARLIAMENTS
Politbureau	Cabinet	Presidium
General Secretary	Premier	President
Central Committee	Council of Ministers	Supreme Soviet
Party structure	Ministerial structure	Parliamentary structure
Branches in factories, the army, schools dwellings.	Including: army, police, economy.	Soviets in Republics, towns, villages

of the party is the Politbureau, (sometimes spelled, as in Russian, Politburo)
the General Secretary[2] of the Central Committee in 1969 was Brezhnev; the
Council of Ministers is composed of the heads of ministries and other bodies,

---

[1] For further discussion of the social groups see below, Chapter 12.
[2] The Twenty-Third Congress in March/April 1966 re-established the title General Secretary
which had been dropped after Stalin's death in favour of the term, First Secretary.

led by the Prime Minister who in 1969 was Kosygin; the Presidium is formally elected by the Supreme Soviet (Parliament) and the President at the time of writing is Podgorny. While the party influences the government, and the elites are to some extent overlapping, it is important to emphasise that, as structures, they are separate. They have their own statutes and rules which define the boundaries of their actions, and they possess separate staffs to carry them out. Let us consider each of them in turn.[1]

The Party Structure

In Soviet Russia after the October Revolution of 1917, the Communist Party became the authoritative source of values and now has a monopoly of political organisation. It claims the right to make pronouncements over a wide variety of fields. Its statements on science, education, and the organisation of the economy are more detailed and have more influence than party statements in liberal-democratic states. In theory, the party is the 'vanguard of the working people in their struggle to build communist society and is the leading core of all organisations of the working people, both government and non-government'.[2] A more general description is the definition of the party's role given in the social science text-book for high schools: 'The Communist Party is the well-tried fighting vanguard of the Soviet people occupying the top place among the social-political organisations and joining on a voluntary basis the most [politically] conscious part of the working class, collective farm peasantry and intelligentsia.'[3] The CPSU is the only political party in the Soviet Union. It should be made clear, however, that the CPSU is not the government any more than the British Labour Party or the American Democratic Party, when in office, is the government of Great Britain or the USA. The government is organisationally separate. Here I may anticipate a later chapter by saying that the cohesion of the Communist Party of the Soviet Union is stronger and its influence more direct over the government than that of parties in liberal-democratic societies.

By a monopoly of authoritative political power, it is not meant that every action taken in the USSR is determined by the party. Many decisions taken in social institutions such as the family or in government departments are made without recourse to party authority. What is meant is that the party's values are dominant and solely legitimate: i.e. in Soviet terminology, only the party safeguards the interests of the working class. It decides the social, economic and political *goals* of the society: it fixes the relationship between men and property, shapes the dominant economic and political mores, and

---

[1] The economic ministries are described under the economy, Chapter 9.

[2] Article 126, '*Constitution of the USSR*', See Appendix C.

[3] *Obshchestvovedenie*, Seventh Edition (Moscow, 1969), p. 309.

exercises control over the selection of the leading personnel in the government of the country.

Party Organisation

The notion of democratic centralism as formulated by Lenin has already been discussed in Chapter 1 (see pp. 11–13). The modern party's rules stipulate:

> The guiding principle of the organisational structure of the party is democratic centralism, which signifies:
>
> i. election of all leading party bodies, from the lowest to the highest;
> ii. periodical reports of party bodies to their party organisations and to higher bodies;
> iii. strict party discipline and subordination of the minority to the majority;
> iv. the decisions of higher bodies are obligatory for lower bodies.[1]

The formal structure of the party embodying these formal organisational principles is shown in Diagram 1.

The generic CPSU embraces the Communist Parties of the union republics all of which, except the RSFSR,[2] have their own Republican Communist Party. The single arrows in the diagram show the elective processes within the party; double arrows denote supervision and administration. This diagram, of course, represents what the *rules* define as the proper procedure. We should not imply that the political process actually corresponds to it.

At the bottom of the diagram are the party basic units. They are formed at the place of work of members: in factories, state farms, collective farms, schools, in the armed forces; they may also be formed at the place of residence: in villages or on housing estates. The minimum number required to form a branch is three, though normally basic units are more than three strong. Those fifteen or more in number, elect a bureau (or executive), those with less elect a secretary and deputy secretary. Party branches qualify for a full-time salaried official if branch membership exceeds 150. It must meet at least once a month, unless membership is under 300, when it may meet every two months. Basic units may be sub-divided into branches – in factories, say by shift or workshop.

As shown in the chart (Diagram 1), the basic units elect delegates to area, town or district Conferences which should meet at least once every two years. These in turn elect delegates to Regional Conferences, which (except in the RSFSR) elect to Republican Congresses, which again (together with the Regional Conferences of the RSFSR) elect to the Congress of the CPSU, the party's supreme body.

The formal authoritative bodies elect a secretariat which administers departments concerned with specific questions. These bureaux are of crucial

---

[1] *Rules of the CPSU*, English Edition (London, 1961), Paragraph 19. The complete Rules and the amendments of 1966 are appended, Appendix B.

[2] Russian Soviet Federative Socialist Republic.

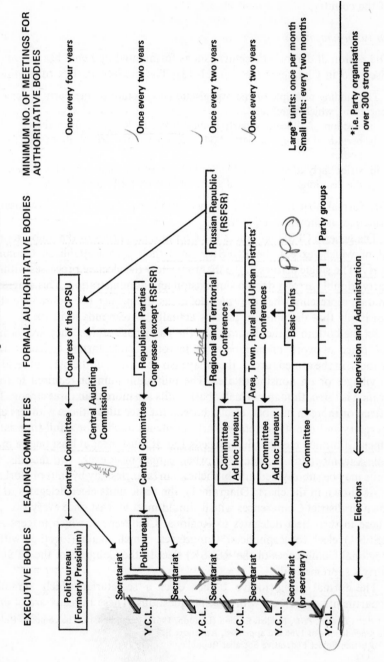

DIAGRAM 1 Organisation Chart of the CPSU

EXECUTIVE BODIES   LEADING COMMITTEES   FORMAL AUTHORITATIVE BODIES   MINIMUM NO. OF MEETINGS FOR AUTHORITATIVE BODIES

Politbureau (Formerly Presidium)

Central Committee

Congress of the CPSU   Once every four years

Central Auditing Commission

Politbureau

Secretariat

Y.C.L.

Central Committee

Republican Parties Congresses (except RSFSR)   Once every two years

Secretariat

Y.C.L.

Russian Republic (RSFSR)

Regional and Territorial Conferences   Once every two years

Committee Ad hoc bureaux

Secretariat

Y.C.L.

Area, Town, Rural and Urban Districts' Conferences   Once every two years

Committee Ad hoc bureaux

Secretariat

Y.C.L.

Basic Units

Committee

Secretariat (or secretary)

Y.C.L.

Party groups   Large* units: once per month
Small units: every two months

Elections   Supervision and Administration

*i.e. Party organisations over 300 strong

importance for they provide information and policy recommendations for the Politbureau and Central Committee of the CPSU. Though they are not now defined in the party rules.[1] Western research has established that there are the following specialised departments: party organs, propaganda and agitation, agriculture, science, higher educational institutes and schools, culture, heavy industry, light industry, machine construction, defence, chemical industry, fuel industry, construction, transportation, trade finance and planning organs, administration, foreign, socialist (bloc) countries, security, chief political administration of Soviet army and navy, special sector, party commission, general department, administration of the Central Committee of the CPSU.[2] An important aspect of the secretariat's work is control of cadres: party membership and recruitment to non-party posts. The All-Union and Republican Party bureaux exercise control of recruitment to all the leading positions: heads of enterprises, editors and government deputies.

A similar structure exists in localities where the secretariat is regularly in contact with the top *apparat*. The secretariat shown in the diagram by arrows pointing leftward, administers policy and provides the full-time party workers. The process of election *formally* takes place at all levels of the organisation. At the Congress, the Central Committee is elected, which in turn elects the Politbureau[3] and the leading secretaries. The Politbureau is the chief deliberating and policy-making body, in 1969 it had 20 members.[4]

The decisions of higher bodies are binding on lower ones. The highest authoritative body is the Congress of the CPSU, which is equivalent to the national conventions of the major American parties, or the British Labour Party or Conservative Party annual conference. Next in order of importance come the congresses of the union republics, the conferences of regions and territories, followed by those of local territorial organisations (towns, rural and urban districts, etc.) and finally, the general meeting of the basic party groups.

The upward pointing arrows illustrate the first condition of the party's organisational structure: the election of all leading bodies. The centralisation of political decision-making and the subordination of the members to the leaders are mainly enforced by the secretariat which is responsible for day-to-day policy. The double lines stand for the processes linking the administration of the party at all levels and ensure that central policy is consistent throughout

---

[1] For Republican and lower bodies see *KPSS, Naglyadnoe posobie po partiynomu stroitel'stvu* (Moscow, 1969), pp. 37-45, and *Obshchestvovedenie*, Second ed. (Moscow, 1964), p. 209.

[2] A. Avtorkhanov, *The Communist Party Apparatus* (Chicago, 1966), pp. 201-5. See below, pp. 209–12. L. Longo, *Problemi e Realtà dell' URSS* (Rome, 1958).

[3] It is sometimes called Political Bureau. This body was called the Presidium between October 1952 and April 1966. It should not now be confused with the Presidium of the Soviet Parliament. (See p. 147.)

[4] For membership, see Appendix E.

the party machine. The double lines pointing down and to the left show the links betwen the party and the youth organisation, the Young Communist League. (*Komsomol*). Here too are links with other bodies, such as the government and trade-unions. As pointed out above, the party is 'the leading core of all organisations of the working people, both government and non-government.'[1] The party and its groups are expected to bring influence to bear over other bodies. This is done through party groups organised in them. (The example of party intervention in the economy is given in Chapter 10.)

In the top left-hand corner of Diagram 1 are the decisive bodies of power within the party. The Central Committee, with a full membership of 360 (1966),

directs the activities of the party, the local party bodies, selects and appoints leading officials, directs the work of central government bodies and public organisations of working people through the party groups in them, sets up various party organs, institutions and enterprises and directs their activities, appoints the editors of the central newspapers and journals operating under its control and distributes the funds of the party budget and controls its execution.[2]

The General Secretary, heading the administration, is in a strong position to influence and guide policy implementation. The secretariat, which he controls, is responsible to the Central Committee for directing 'current work, chiefly the selection of cadres and the verification of the fulfillment of party decisions'.[3] As we shall see later, this gives the secretariat considerable *de facto* power over the party.

Political Recruitment: Party Membership

Like all political parties, the CPSU recruits from the population political activists and trains professional politicians.

Duverger has distinguished between *cadre* and *mass* political parties. A *cadre* party is small, based on quality of members and brings influence to bear on the basis of individual knowledge, prestige, riches or skill. A *mass* party has a large membership, based on quantity: its tactics are to make its influence felt by the strength of numbers of members.[4] Duverger argues that parties 'based on cells . . . are mass parties, but less definitely so'. One must distinguish between different kinds of communist parties: the activity and composition of the Bolshevik party were very different before the October Revolution compared to that of the CPSU to-day. The RSDLP (Russian Social-Democratic Labour Party), the precursor of the CPSU and operating in the Russian underground before the revolution, was more of a cadre party based on mem-

---

[1] Article 126. *Constitution of the USSR.*
[2] Paragraph 35, *Party Rules.*
[3] Paragraph 38, *Party Rules.*
[4] Duverger, *Political Parties* (1964), pp. 62-70.

bers with a strong commitment to Marxism. The modern ruling party, particularly since the end of the Second World War, has had a mass character. The change may be gauged by the growth in membership[1] (excluding the *Komsomol*) from about 115,000 in 1918 to some 13.7 million in 1969, representing about 7.5 per cent of the adult population.

Membership is open to 'any citizen of the Soviet Union who accepts the Programme and Rules of the Party, takes an active part in communist construction, works in one of the party organisations, carries out all party decisions and pays membership dues'.[2] Let us consider how it is recruited socially – by nationality, social position, occupation, age and sex.[3]

The membership of the CPSU is formally made up of Communist Parties of the Union Republics as shown in Table 6. In columns 2 and 4 is shown the

Table 6. Membership of Republican Communist Parties: 1961, 1965*

Republican Party	Col. 1 Republican population (1959) 000s	Col. 2 Membership 1 Jan 1961	Col. 3 Col. 2 Col. 1 %	Col. 4 Membership 1 Jan 1965	Col. 5 Col. 4 Col. 1 %
Ukraine	43,091	1,370,997	3.2	1,829,638	4.2
Byelorussia (White Russia)	8,226	225,541	2.7	319,196	3.9
Uzbekistan	8,665	224,519	2.6	314,279	3.6
Kazakhstan	10,000	345,115	3.5	450,486	4.5
Georgia	4,200	216,866	5.2	248,375	5.9
Azerbaidzhan	3,973	153,221	3.9	198,539	5.0
Lithuania	2,804	60,551	2.2	86,366	3.1
Moldavia	3,040	59,908	2.0	85,379	2.8
Latvia	2,142	72,519	3.4	95,742	4.5
Kirgiziya	2,225	65,866	3.0	84,721	3.8
Tadzhikistan	2,104	52,014	2.5	67,624	3.2
Armenia	1,893	85,062	4.5	104,305	5.5
Turkmenistan	1,626	47,950	2.9	57,206	3.5
Estonia	1,221	37,848	3.1	54,836	4.5
Total	95,210	3,017,977		3,996,692	
Total membership of CPSU		9,275,826		11,758,169	

* Party membership: 'KPSS v tsifrakh', *Partiynaya zhizn*', No. 10, May 1965, p. 8.

party republican membership for 1961 and 1965 respectively. The percentages in columns 3 and 5 are based on the total republican population data for 1959 given in column 1. The table shows that in 1964 nearly four million or a third

[1] See Appendix A for full statistics 1917-1969, p. 515.
[2] Paragraph No. 1, *Party Rules.*
[3] For an historical account and more detailed treatment see T. H. Rigby, *Communist Party Membership in the USSR, 1917-1967* (Princeton, New Jersey, 1968)

of the membership lay outside the Russian Federative Republic and that party membership in these areas increased by nearly a third between 1961 and 1965.

This does not mean, of course, that the republican parties are wholly composed of non-Great Russians. The proportion of Great Russians in each republican party is not available, but a good indication of the participation of

Table 7.Composition of CPSU by Nationality*

Nationality	Col. 1 No. in CPSU 1 Jan 1965 000s	Col. 2 % of party 1965	Col. 3 % of population (1959)	Col. 4 % of republican party membership (1965)
Russians	7,335	62.4	54.5	—
Ukrainians	1,813	15.4	18.0	99.1
Byelorussians (White Russians)	386	3.3	3.8	121.0
Uzbeks	194	1.6	2.9	61.8
Kazaks	181	1.5	1.7	40.2
Georgians	194	1.7	1.3	78.2
Azerbaidzhanies	142	1.2	1.4	71.4
Lithuanians	62	0.5	1.1	72.1
Moldavians	40	0.3	1.1	47.1
Latvians	44	0.4	0.7	45.8
Kirgiz	35	0.3	0.5	41.2
Tadzhiks	42	0.4	0.7	61.8
Armenians	188	1.6	1.4	180.8
Turkmens	32	0.3	0.5	56.1
Estonians	34	0.3	0.5	61.8
Others	1,035	8.8	—	—
Total	11,758	100%		

* Party membership: *Partiynaya zhizn'*, No. 10, May 1965.

the national groups in the CPSU is given in Table 7. Column 1 shows the number of each national group in the CPSU, in column 2 each nationality is expressed as a proportion of total party membership, and column 3 shows each nationality as a percentage of the population as a whole. The differences between columns 2 and 3 bring out the relative dominance of Russians, Georgians and Armenians in the party and the relatively lower participation of Uzbeks, Lithuanians, Moldavians and Latvians. Column 4 shows the number of nationals expressed as a proportion of the republican party membership, given on Table 6, column 4. Byelorussians (White Russians) (121 % of republican party membership) obviously not only predominate in their own republic but also (with Armenians 180.8 %) figure in parties outside; on the other hand, the Kazak (40.2%), Moldavian (47.1%), Latvian (45.8%), and Kirgiz (41.2%) republican parties must be composed to quite a large extent of settlers from other parts of the USSR. (For discussion of the national composition of the elites, see Chapter 13.) Nationality is based on race, language and common culture We may now turn to consider groups formed across racial and geographical lines.

'Social position', in the USSR is based on an individual's relationship to the

Table 8A. Social Background of Party Members and Candidates: 1961, 1964 and 1968[1]

	1961	1964	1968	% of total population[2] (1964)
1. Manual Workers	35.0	37.3	38.8	} 75.1[3]
2. Non-manual or 'Employees'	47.7	46.2	45.4	
3. Peasants on collective farms	17.3	16.5	15.8	24.9
Total	100%	100%	100%	100%

Source:

[1] 'KPSS v tsifrakh', Partiynaya zhizn', No. 10, May 1965, p. 11. 1966 figures, Brezhnev, Pravda, 30 March 1966. 1968 figures, Partiynaya zhizn', No. 7, Apr. 1968, p. 27.

[2] 'Klassovy sostav naseleniya SSSR' SSSR v tsifrakh v 1964g. (Moscow, 1965), p. 12.

[3] Approximately, workers accounted for 55 per cent and 'employees' 20 per cent of the population. Manual workers here include agricultural workers on state farms.

Table 8B. Occupational Composition of CPSU, 1967

Field of Employment	Number	Per cent
1. Government, economic, party etc. bureaucracies	936,000	7.4
2. Science, education, health, culture	1,740,000	13.7
3. Trade and materials-handling	463,000	3.7
4. Housing, civic and personal services	136,000	1.1
5. Communications	109,000	.9
6. Transport	838,000	6.6
7. Industry	3,196,000	25.2
8. Construction	666,000	5.2
9. Kolkhozes	1,330,000	10.5
10. State farms	838,000	6.6
11. Miscellaneous agricultural and related branches	166,000	1.3
12. Other branches of economy	116,000	.9
13. Armed forces (including border guards)	890,000	7.0
14. Pensioners	760,000	6.0
15. Students	200,000	1.6
16. Housewives and miscellaneous	300,000	2.3
Total	12,684,000	100.0

T. H. Rigby, Communist Party Membership in the USSR 1917-1967 (1968). p. 348.

means of production: 'manual workers' are occupied in production, 'peasants' engaged in productive work on collective farms (not state farms), 'employees' (or non-manual workers) are administrative, secretarial and executive personnel.[1] This last group constitutes the largest single group of party members. Official Soviet statistics show the following divisions: (manual) workers, employees and peasants. These are shown on Table 8, together with an estimate made by T. H. Rigby of the party's occupational composition by field of employment. It is claimed that manual workers and collective farmers constitute more than half the total party membership, a correct but misleading statement if one considers that these groups make up about 80 per cent of the total population. The peasantry is under-represented being, in 1964, 16.5 per cent of the party membership but 24.9 per cent of the population.[2] 'Employees' are more than proportional to the population being 46.2 per cent in the party and about 20 per cent of the occupied labour force.[3] Party policy is to increase the share of manual workers. In 1967, of new entrants, 52.2 per cent were manual workers, 33.8 per cent non-manual and 14 per cent, collective farmers. Even so, at the end of 1967, the social background of party members showed that 38.8 per cent were of the manual working class, 15.8 per cent of the collective farm peasantry and 45.4 per cent were of the non-manual stratum.[4]

The above figures are rather general, including many different kinds of workers in the various categories. Rigby's table shows that 10.5 per cent of party members are collective farmers, but not what kind of occupations they follow. This may be discovered by studying Table 9.

In 1964, the largest group of candidate members and a quarter of all communist collective farmworkers were operatives (or mechanics) of farm machinery who might, in a social sense, be more like urban workers than farmhands and should perhaps be included as far as their occupation is concerned under the manual workers classification. The large residual ('others' 17.3 per cent) probably includes officials and other 'non-productive' collective farmers. It must be pointed out that those working on the land on a 'state' farm[5] are not counted with the collective farm hands but divided by occupation between manual workers and non-manual. Of the manual workers joining the party in 1964, 16.1 per cent were on state farms.[6]

---

[1] Social classifications of the population are considered in detail in Chapter 12. The statistics on social background of party members usually refer to social position when joining the party.

[2] i.e., Collective farmers and co-operative handicraftsmen, figures for 1964. *SSSR v tsifrakh v 1964 g.* (Moscow, 1965), p. 12.

[3] *Ibid.*

[4] 'Ob itogakh priema v partiyu i izmeneniyakh v sostave KPSS za 1967 g.,' *Partiynaya zhizn'*, No. 7, Apr. 1968, pp. 26-7.

[5] The difference between 'state' and 'collective' farms is explained later.

[6] The total number of Communists 'engaged in agriculture' on 1 Jan. 1965 was some 2 million 164 thousand. 'KPSS v tsifrakh' (1965), p. 15. 733 thousand being on state farms and 1,285 thousand on collectives. *Ibid.*

Table 9. Social Background of Party 'Collective Farmers'*

Branch of production	Candidate members of the CPSU in 1964		All party members 1 Jan. 1965
	Absolute No.	%	%
Tractor and combine harvester personnel and other mechanics	40,731	40.1	25.1
Field labourers, vegetable farmers and market gardeners	22,729	22.4	30.7
Stockmen	19,514	19.2	17.9
Agronomists, vets and other agricultural specialists	6,491	6.4	5.3
Those working in other production teams and with animals	2,510	2.5	3.7
Others	9,580	9.4	17.3
	101,553	100	100

* Source: 'KPSS v tsifrakh' (1965), loc. cit. pp. 10, 15

Table 10. Employees or Non-Manual Party Members and Candidates on 1 Jan. 1962, 1 Jan. 1965 and 1 Jan. 1967.

	1 Jan. 1962	1 Jan. 1965	1 Jan. 1967
Leaders of organisations, institutions, factories, construction enterprises (stroyki), state farms and their subdivisions	10	7.8	7.9
Technical engineering workers, agricultural specialists	28.2	32.5	34.9
Scientific workers, education, health employees, literary and artistic personnel	21.6	23.3	23.6
Workers in trade institutions, supply, sales and public dining rooms	4.9	5.8	5.5
Inspection workers (rabotnikov kontrolya) accounting and secretarial	11.8	10.8	—
Others	23.5	19.8	28.1
	100%	100%	100%

Source: 'KPSS v tsifrakh' (1965), loc. cit., p. 11 (For 1962 and 1965). 'KPSS v tsifrakh', Kommunist, No. 15, 1967, p. 95 (For 1967).

The various strata of 'employees', or those engaged in mental as distinct from physical labour, are shown on Table 10. Again, some agricultural specialists (from state farms) included here are of similar occupation to others included on the 'collective farmers' table. The two largest categories, the technical specialists (34.9 per cent in 1967) and scientific workers (23.6 per cent), make up over half the total of non-manuals substantiating the party's claim of large membership among the intelligentsia. The 'others' is rather large (19.8 per cent of the total in 1964) and may include government or party functionaries.

Rigby has analysed the occupation and party membership of 2,500 government deputies. He shows that 99 per cent of factory directors, 51 per cent of 'subdirectional management', 38 per cent of foremen and other junior supervisory jobs, and 27 per cent of 'specialists lacking administrative powers' were party members.[1] He estimates that in 1964, 42 per cent of the engineers, 25 per cent of the teachers and 22 per cent of the doctors were party members.[2]

The data cannot be used for a very detailed analysis of the party's stratification – a finer occupational scale would be needed for this. But a few general conclusions may be made. Firstly, that of the non-manual party members, the highest proportion are technical specialists: a striking difference compared to British or American political parties. Secondly, that the manual working class is a large part but does not form a majority of present party membership. Thirdly, that support in the countryside is weak and has a tendency to be recruited from the more technically skilled farm workers. Fourthly, that party membership is changing with the social composition of the population and the number of the technically-trained is rising while the proportion of collective farmers is on the decline.

The figures above are concerned with the *social position* of party members when they joined the party. Their actual work has not been defined and we are unaware, for example, of those working full-time in the party. Rigby, writing in 1957, has argued that Soviet figures underestimate the numbers in the political and administrative hierarchies which he says in 1954 accounted for a million and a half or about 20 per cent of the total membership.[3] Since the late 1950s an attempt has been made to increase the number of voluntary workers in administration and it is most probable that a fall in number of full-time administrators has taken place. In 1967, it is claimed, nearly three-quarters of the membership was in 'productive work', only 8.8 per cent (or under one million) of party members were engaged full-time in the apparatuses, (see Table 11). This is very close to Rigby's latest estimate of 936 thousand or 7.4 per cent of party membership in 1967 – see Table 8 above.

The party's membership is organised in basic units which are shown by size in Table 12. The increase in membership in the 1960s occurred in the very large groups over 50 strong. The party groups in 1966 were, however, still generally rather small: 83 per cent having less than 50 members.

Perhaps surprisingly, the very large groups are to be found in scientific and

---

[1] This was in the period 1950-1961. *Communist Party Membership in the USSR, 1917-67* (Princeton, New Jersey, 1968), p. 433.
[2] *Op cit.*, p. 439.
[3] T. H. Rigby, 'Social Orientation of Recruitment and Distribution of Membership in the Communist Party of the Soviet Union', *The American Slavic and East European Review*, vol. 16 (Oct. 1957), pp. 289-90.

Table 11. Distribution of Employed Communists by Kind of Work: 1961, 1965 and 1968*[1].

	1 July 1961 %	1 Jan. 1965 %	1 Jan. 1968 %
1. In productive work	(71.4)	(72.4)	(73.4)
In: industry and building	33.5	35.9	37.1
transport and communications	9.2	9.2	8.7
agriculture	23.3	22.6	22.1
trade, public dining rooms, supply and marketing	5.4	4.7	4.4
2. Non-productive work	(28.6)	(27.6)	(26.6)
In: science, education, health and culture	15.6	16.5	16.4
government and economic administration, the party apparatus and social organisations	10.8	9.1	8.8
other branches	2.2	2.0	1.4
	100%	100%	100%

* *Source:* 'KPSS v tsifrakh' (1965), p. 14. *KPSS: Naglyadnoe posobie*, p. 69.
[1] Not all the 11.7 million party members in 1965, of course, are employed – some being pensioners or housewives; therefore, if the percentages are related to total party membership a total of (say) 9 million should be used.

Table 12. Size of CPSU Primary Organisations*

Size of group (members and candidates)	1 Jan. 1962 %	1 Jan. 1965 %	1 Jan. 1967 %
to 15	42.5	39.9	40.4
15–49	44.1	43.5	43.0
50–100	8.5	10.5	10.7
over 100	4.9	6.1	5.9

* *Source:* 'KPSS v tsifrakh (1965), *loc. cit.*, p. 16 (For 1962 and 1965). *Kommunist*, No. 15, 1967, p. 101 (For 1967).

academic institutions which were larger in 1964 than in industrial establishments (see Table 13). As one would expect, the membership in collective farms is low, even so, the size of the average basic unit has grown between one and a half and four times between 1946 and 1966.

The rise in party membership has most probably been made up of new members aged between 26 and 40. On 1 January 1965 they constituted 46.8 per cent of all members and those under 25 years accounted for only 7.2 per cent of the membership, compared with 19.3 per cent in 1946.[2] The lower propor-

[2] 1946 figures cited by M. Fainsod, *How Russia is Ruled* (Cambridge, Mass., 1963), p. 280. For 1965 see 'KPSS v tsifrakh' (1965), *loc. cit.*, p. 13. The remaining statistics for 1965 are: members and candidates 41-50 years of age, 24.8 per cent; over 50, 21.2 per cent.

tion of young men under 25 in the party reflects more the official policy of strengthening the *Komsomol* (Young Communist League) than a drastic decline in support among the young,[1] though the wartime generation of young communists was probably more zealous than the post-1960 group.

Table 13. Average Size of Party Basic Unit in Different Kinds of Establishments, 1946, 1962, 1965, 1966

	1946†	1 Jan. 1962*	1 Jan. 1965*	1966†
In industrial undertakings	38	62	78	81
In building and construction	27	37	42	41
On state farms	17	76	78	75
On collective farms	10	34	40	42
In scientific and academic institutions	—	76	86	—

* 'KPSS v tsifrakh' (1965), *loc. cit.*, p. 16
† N. A. Barsukov and I. N. Yudin, *Sotsial'naya baza KPSS* (Moscow, 1967), p. 54.

The proportion of women in the party has nearly doubled between 1927 and 1968, rising from 12.2 to 21.2 per cent of party membership.[2] As women outnumber men in the population, the figures still show a relative under-representation of women in the party's ranks; even so, on a comparative basis, a fifth of party membership, if active, is relatively an extremely high figure. However as we analyse the place of women in higher echelons of the party we see that their share of the membership declines considerably: in 1966 they constituted 2.6 per cent of the full members of the Central Committee and none of the Politbureau.

We may conclude that the CPSU's membership does not include in equal proportion all social groups in Soviet society: most of the minor nationalities, the collective farm peasantry and women are under-represented. More significantly, the educated and scientifically trained strata of the population, which are growing in size and which could possibly provide a challenge to the party's hegemony, if excluded from it, are being absorbed into its ranks, while the traditional base, the urban working class, is still well represented. The increase in size is one of the most important ways in which the party has diversified and strengthened its membership. The participation of different social strata among the party elite is another matter.

It would be most instructive to know the career patterns of the Party elite – the members of the Politbureau and Central Committee. It seems that the party elite has been recruited from men with relatively low social origins. For instance, the ten leading party secretaries in 1957 all came from peasant or worker families. From information available on 148 of the 175 members of the

[1] See 'Izmeneniya v ustave KPSS i vnutripartiynaya zhizn',' *Kommunist*, No. 7 (May 1966), p. 5.
[2] 'KPSS v tsifrakh', in *Kommunist*, No. 15, 1967, p. 97. *KPSS: Naglyadnoe*, p. 23.

Central Committee (1961), 49.3 per cent were of peasant, and a third of worker origin. Only two of the fathers were of higher occupational strata.[1] It seems likely that a party career is now an avenue of social mobility for the children of lower social strata, who may find it more difficult to rise to the top in professional or ministerial sectors of Soviet society. In the earlier years of Soviet power this was not the case. For instance, of 15 members of the Politbureau between 1917 and 1927, 9 had 'middle class' social origins; but of 25 members between the years 1957 to 1967, only 3 hailed from a non-manual background. On the other hand, in the earlier period (1917–27) 8 out of 15 had had higher education, whereas in 1967, the ratio was 9 to 11.[2] A similar improvement in educational level has occurred lower down the party hierarchy. Armstrong found that in 1939 only 40 per cent of county and city party secretaries had even completed *secondary* education,[3] whereas Stewart has calculated that of local first secretaries holding posts between 1950 and 1966 at least 40 per cent had completed a *higher* education.[4]

Important in the training of the leading cadres is the party's own system of schools. These range from modest part-time evening classes to the Academy of Social Sciences which is under the direction of the CPSU's Central Committee. Below this is the Higher Party School. Party members may work their way up the hierarchy until they have received the equivalent of a university education. Such graduates then occupy key positions in the party, government and organs of communication.[5] Here is an avenue, not only for political recruitment, but also for upward social mobility for those to whom other doors have been shut. Of the delegates to the Twenty-Third Party Congress, 24.9 per cent had been educated at party schools; and of a representative sample of party secretaries, Stewart estimates that 31.5 per cent had received such an education.[6] 'Placement' in the political hierarchy is carried out by the party secretariat. The party's schools have also played an important role in training Communist officials both for Eastern Europe and the Third World.

The social position, as distinct from the social origin, of the party elite shows some interesting differences compared with the party membership. Boris Meissner has analysed the composition of the 23rd Party Congress of the CPSU (1966). He shows that while the 'top-level bureaucracy (exclusive of the military)' comprises 2.1 per cent of the total party membership, they

[1] Figures cited by Z. Brzezinski and S. Huntington, *Political Power USA/USSR* (1964), p. 135.
[2] Dan N. Jacobs, 'The Politburo in the First and Fifth Decades of Soviet Power', in Kurt London (ed.), *The Soviet Union: A Half Century of Communism* (Baltimore, Maryland, 1968), pp. 62-3.
[3] John A. Armstrong, *The Soviet Bureaucratic Elite* (New York, 1959), p. 31.
[4] Philip D. Stewart, *Political Power in the Soviet Union* (Indianapolis, 1968), p. 142.
[5] See E. P. Mickiewicz, *Soviet Political Schools* (New Haven, Conn., 1967). p. 143.
[6] Philip D. Stewart, *Political Power in the Soviet Union* (Indianapolis, 1968), p. 143.

F

made up 40 per cent of the Congress delegates, and 81.1 per cent of the full members of the Central Committee. Of full members of the Central Committee (1953–66), 55 per cent were engaged in the party bureaucracy, 18 per cent in the higher government apparatus, 7.6 per cent were military officers and 3.3 per cent were trade union officials. The age structure of the party shows that of the total membership in 1966, 20 per cent were under 30, those over 50 constitute 22.1 per cent. However, the latter group monopolised the Politbureau. In 1966, the average age of the full members of the Politbureau was 58.1 years – Brezhnev was 60, Kosygin 62 and Podgorny 63, and in the same year the heads of Central Committee Departments averaged 56 years.[1]

We may make two fairly obvious points about the social composition of the party elite. It is composed of full-time officials of the state and party bureaucracies; and it is considerably older than the party membership as a whole. The membership figures noted above provide us only with a quantitative index of party support, it is the raw material from which political recruitment may take place. One should bear in mind that the statistical data tell us nothing about what membership means, of the intensity of party allegiance compared to other group allegiance (say to a profession or to a government ministry). But before we consider the political process in the party, we must describe the government apparatus.

The Government Structure

While the Communist Party is an authoritative source of values, the state, or government, has the legal power of enforcement: it has the right to apply physical force and sanctions. The party mobilises the population towards the achievement of particular goals, whereas the state formally arranges the administration and enforcement of policy. In Russian terminology the Soviets are 'working corporations vested with authority both to decide matters and to implement the adopted decisions, i.e. to pass legislation and to administer'.[2] We shall return to party-state relations in Chapter 7, after describing the organisation of the government, the background and the work of the deputies, or members of the Soviets. Here it is as well to point out that 'the government' is composed of two structures: a system of elected parliaments (or Soviets) which are something like western legislative bodies and are organised

---

[1] Boris Meissner, 'Totalitarian Rule and Social Change', *Problems of Communism*, vol. 15 (no. 6), Nov-Dec 1966, p. 59; Borys Lewytzkyj, 'Generations in Conflict', *Problems of Commuojsm* Jan-Feb 1967, vol. 16 (no. 1), pp. 36-38. Jerry Hough, 'The Soviet Elite: II', *Problems of Communism*, vol. 16 (no. 2), March-April 1967, p. 20. Michael P. Gehlin, *The Communist Party of the Soviet Union* (Bloomington, 1969) p. 45.

[2] *The Soviet Parliament* (Moscow, 1967), p. 8.

territorially and an executive, or ministerial structure, which in theory is responsible to the elected bodies. In Soviet constitutional theory all legislative power is vested in the working people of town and country as represented by the Soviets of Working Peoples' Deputies.[1] Legitimate power in the USSR lies in a series of Soviets which perform a role similar to parliaments in western states. 'Soviets' exist at all levels of government: from town or rural (village) Soviets carrying out local government, to the Supreme Soviet of the USSR which is the national government.

Soviet Federalism

First, let us consider the statutory, or formal organisation of the Soviet state by describing the federal structure. The reader must bear in mind that here (as in the whole of this chapter) we are considering the 'legal charter' rather than actual practice. By 'federal' is meant that powers are divided between a central (or federal) government and regional (or republican) governments. The individual republican governments, in theory, should have authority over certain aspects of social life while the central government has an overall authority over other aspects. Soviet federalism seeks to integrate the separate nations and areas into a single 'all union' state and economic order while giving an element of autonomy to the individual nations. The advantages of a federal system generally are that it has the virtues of a large market, a single monetary system and a common army and allows for local diversity: separate language, religion, culture and 'way of life'. The integrating institution is the federal or All-Union government of the USSR: the Soviet Republics promote local government.[2]

The formal federal structure is illustrated in a very simplified form in Chart 2. The USSR in 1969 is divided into fifteen Union Republics, in some cases these contain Autonomous Republics (of which there are 20). Autonomous Regions (eight) and National Areas (ten). Later we shall see how these lower units are divided among the Union Republics (see Chart 4 p. 146 and Table 46 pp. 435–9). All these units are based on the existence of a homogeneous national group, having its own written language. The units vary in status: Union Republics have their own Constitution and more powers than National Areas. The significance of the federal units is to give some authority and territorial integrity to a fairly well-defined *national* grouping. (National policy will be discussed later in the chapter on nationalities, Chapter 13.) The federal or All-Union parliament is bicameral (two chambers) having representatives both by density of population and by national areas (see p. 146 below) but all lower parliaments are unicameral (one chamber).

[1] *Constitution of the USSR*, Article 3.
[2] For the Soviet view see D. Zlatopolsky, *State System of the USSR* (Moscow, n.d.), pp. 23-25.

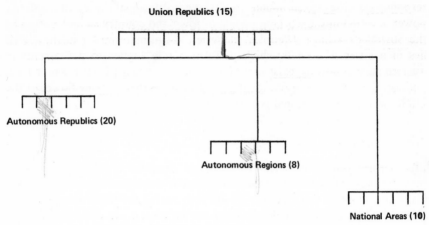

CHART 2   FEDERAL UNITS OF USSR (simplified)

The detailed powers of the All-Union and republican governments are defined in the Constitution (see Appendix C). We may summarise them here. The chief powers of the All-Union government are to issue currency, to declare war, to regulate external trade, and to develop a plan for the economic development of the Soviet Union. With the exception of the last condition, the formal constitutional powers of the All-Union government are similar to those of the federal government in the USA.

The Republics have the constitutional right to adopt and to amend their own constitution (as long as it remains consistent with the All-Union constitution), to approve a national plan and budget and to secede from the USSR. Each republic legally has the sanctity of its borders and the guarantee of republican citizenship.

Autonomous Republics are subordinate to the parent Union Republic in the establishment and interpretation of their constitutions. But a Union Republic has the right to suspend the laws of an Autonomous Republic and it may also intervene to ensure that economic planning is in conformity with the national plan.

The Autonomous Regions and National Areas are more limited in their powers. They are administrative bodies and do not have Supreme Soviets or constitutions like Republics. These units conduct business in the national language and like Republics they have the right to send delegates direct to the Supreme Soviet.

Within the federal structure are a number of administrative divisions on which local government is based. The exact configuration varies between Republics, and the details need not detain us here. The skeleton of the structure may be understood by references to Chart 3.[1] Directly subordinate to the Union Republican government are certain large cities (equivalent, say, to British county boroughs), which in turn are subdivided into small administrative districts (*rayons*). Some republics are divided into large territories or regions and then subdivided into districts, towns and villages, others are directly divided into regions, towns and villages.[2] At each lower level there is a Soviet or parliament which is directly elected, at two yearly intervals.

CHART 3

LEVELS OF SOVIET ADMINISTRATIVE UNITS

— Soviet of USSR

— Union Republican Soviets

— Soviets of Autonomous Republics, Territories (*kray*) Regions (*oblast*) and certain major cities

— Soviets of Autonomous Regions and National Areas (*okrug*)

— District (*rayon*) Soviets, certain towns outside District jurisdiction

— Soviet of towns, settlements and villages (or rural soviets)

While election to the Soviets is direct, the administration is centralised and indirect: 'all organs of state power and organs of state administration form a single system, based on the strictest subordination of lower organs to the direction and control of higher organs; the acts of higher organs are binding on lower organs.'[3] This results in a vertical chain of command with a strong element of centralisation in the All-Union or Union Republican ministry (see Chapter 9). Finance is centralised and apportioned to the Union Republics. The local units tend to be organs of administration, rather than independent organs of local decision-making.

---

[1] For a full discussion of Soviet local government see L. G. Churchward, *Contemporary Soviet Government* (1968), Chapter 12.

[2] For details of organisation, D. Zlatopolsky, *State System of the USSR* (Moscow, n.d.), Chapter 7, and *SSSR Administrativno-territorial'noe delenie Soyuznykh Respublik* (Moscow, 1964).

[3] 'Demokraticheski Tsentralizm', *Bol'shaya Sovetskaya Entsiklopediya*, vol. 13, p. 656.

The Supreme Soviet

The Supreme Soviet is composed of two houses: the Soviet of the Union and the Soviet of Nationalities. The Soviet of the Union is elected according to density of population, with one deputy per some 300,000 inhabitants. In the 1970 election there were 767 deputies so elected. The Soviet of Nationalities is formed by representatives of the different federal units described above. Union Republics each send thirty-two delegates, each Autonomous Republic eleven, an Autonomous Region five and a national area one: this gives a total of 750. The composition of the Supreme Soviet by place of origin of delegate is shown in Chart 4. From this chart one can see the administrative subordination of the national administrative units to the various Republics.

CHART 4

ELECTION TO THE USSR SUPREME SOVIET, JUNE 1970

		32 Deputies from each Union Republic
	Supreme Soviet	11 Deputies from each Autonomous Republic
1 Deputy per 300,000 inhabitants	Soviet of the Union / Soviet of Nationalities	5 Deputies from each Autonomous Region
		1 Deputy from each National Area

By Republics:
    Deputies Elected (Union)   *Deputies Elected (Nationalities)*

	Union	Nat.	Nationalities breakdown
Russian Republic	423	243	32 + 176 from 16 Autonomous Republics, 25 from 5 Autonomous Regions, and 10 from 10 National Areas
Ukraine	150	32	
Byelorussia (White Russia)	28	32	
Uzbekistan	35	43	32 + 11 from one Autonomous Republic
Kazakhstan	39	32	
Georgia	15	59	32 + 22 from two Autonomous Republics, 5 from one Autonomous Region
Azerbaidzhan	15	48	32 + 11 from one Autonomous Republic, 5 from one Autonomous Region
Lithuania	10	32	
Moldavia	11	32	
Latvia	7	32	
Kirghiza	9	32	
Tadzhikistan	8	37	32 + 5 from one Autonomous Region
Armenia	7	32	
Turkmenistan	6	32	
Estonia	4	32	
	767	750	

The left-hand column shows the number of deputies in the Soviet of the Union: the Russian Federative Republics accounts for more than half the delegates (423), followed by the Ukraine (150). To the Soviet of Nationalities each Union Republic has the right to send 32 delegates, in addition, the lower federal units also send delegates, as defined above. This procedure gives the Russian Federative Republic a total of 243, Uzbekistan 43, Georgia 59, Azerbaidzhan 48 and Tadzhikistan 37.

The Supreme Soviet is directly elected every four years on the basis of universal suffrage and by secret ballot. Both chambers are equal in rights. Usually they meet separately. Joint sittings are presided over alternately by the chairman of each house. Laws are adopted if passed by both chambers by a simple majority vote in each. In the event of disagreement between them, questions are referred to a conciliation commission, formed by an equal number of members of each house. Failing agreement, the Presidium of the Supreme Soviet constitutionally has the power to order dissolution and new elections. The problem of resolving formal disagreement by vote either within or between the houses in fact never arises. Differences are ironed out before meetings of the Supreme Soviet and, in keeping with the myth of the political homogeneity of the USSR, divisive votes are not made. This practice might be likened to members of British parliamentary political parties disagreeing with party policy but nevertheless voting for the party line in Parliament. To be sure, in Britain, party splits and threatened splits do occur – not so in the USSR. Debates on proposed legislation take place in one chamber, when amendments are frequently put. The sessions are public, and representatives from non-parliamentary groups (such as trade unions) and other specialists may take part in proceedings.[1]

The Supreme Soviet at a joint sitting formally elects the Presidium, the Council of Ministers, the Supreme Court and the General Procurator; each house also elects ten commissions. This is shown on Chart 5.

The Presidium, headed by the President (at present Podgorny), has the right to take decisions when the Soviet is not sitting. As the Soviet meets only twice per annum for a session usually lasting three to five days, the Presidium's decrees, later approved by the Soviet, are quite numerous. During the Sixth Convocation (March 1962 to June 1966) 111 legislative acts were passed, including the approval of 60 decrees – which is roughly half the total.[2] The Presidium technically may annul the decisions of the Council of Ministers, it can interpret laws, ratify treaties, declare war, proclaim martial law, dismiss and appoint ministers – all subject to subsequent confirmation by the Supreme Soviet. (For full details see Article 49 of the Constitution.) The Presidium, including the President, is usually thirty-seven strong: it includes

[1] *The Soviet Parliament* (Moscow, 1967), pp. 14-15.
[2] *The Soviet Parliament* (1967), p. 16.

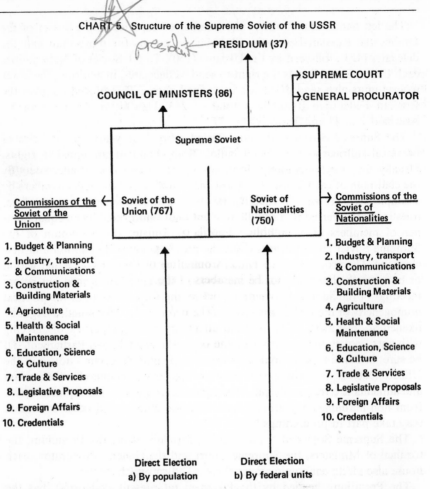

CHART 5 Structure of the Supreme Soviet of the USSR

president ——— PRESIDIUM (37)

→ SUPREME COURT

→ GENERAL PROCURATOR

COUNCIL OF MINISTERS (86)

Supreme Soviet

Commissions of the ← Soviet of the   Soviet of   → Commissions of the
Soviet of the   Union (767)   Nationalities   Soviet of
Union   (750)   Nationalities

Commissions of the Soviet of the Union
1. Budget & Planning
2. Industry, transport & Communications
3. Construction & Building Materials
4. Agriculture
5. Health & Social Maintenance
6. Education, Science & Culture
7. Trade & Services
8. Legislative Proposals
9. Foreign Affairs
10. Credentials

Commissions of the Soviet of Nationalities
1. Budget & Planning
2. Industry, transport & Communications
3. Construction & Building Materials
4. Agriculture
5. Health & Social Maintenance
6. Education, Science & Culture
7. Trade & Services
8. Legislative Proposals
9. Foreign Affairs
10. Credentials

Direct Election
a) By population

Direct Election
b) By federal units

fifteen vice-presidents (one from each of the Union Republics), a secretary and twenty members. The President is not in a comparable position to the President of the USA and he is, of course, not directly elected by the public. In practice, he performs many of the functions of head of state: he accepts foreign delegations, foreign ambassadors and signs official decrees.

The Council of Ministers

The Council of Ministers is the effective executive or government of the USSR. The Chairman of the Council, or Prime Minister, at the time of writing is A. Kosygin.   *Gromyko*

There are two types of Ministry – All-Union and Union-Republican.[1]

---

[1] In addition there are Republican Ministries which are directly subordinate to the Republican governments.

The former operate throughout the country as a whole, whereas the latter operate through corresponding ministries in the union republics and are therefore more decentralised. Most important bodies for co-ordinating government policy are the state committees: in 1966 there were nine – Procurement of Agricultural Products, Construction, Economic Relations with Foreign Countries, Labour and Wages, Materials and Technical Supplies, Planning, Timber Industry, Science and Technology, Vocational and Technical Education. Other important committees with chairmen in the Council of Ministers are: the People's Control Committee, the Board of the USSR State Bank, the Central Statistical Board, the State Security Committee and the Association for Supply of Agricultural Machinery. The Council of Ministers usually numbers over eighty (eighty-six in June 1966) including the heads of all Soviet ministries and a number of other high ranking officials – the fifteen chairmen of the Union Republic Councils of Ministers, the chairmen of the committees mentioned above. (For list see Appendix D.) These men are usually also members of the Central Committee of the party. The members of the Council, who need not be members of the Supreme Soviet, cannot be in the Presidium of the Supreme Soviet as the Council is responsible to it when the Supreme Soviet is not sitting. The tasks of the Council, as defined in Article 68 of the Constitution, are to direct and co-ordinate the work of the All-Union Ministries, to carry out the economic plan, to maintain law and order, to conduct foreign affairs, to organise the armed forces, and to set up state committees. With respect to those branches of the administration within its competence, it has the right 'to suspend the decisions and orders of the Councils of Ministers of the Union Republics and to annul orders and instructions of the Ministers of the USSR . . .'[1] In practice, the Council and its Ministries are the main sources of legislation and issue decrees and regulations governing the whole of economic and social life. As much of its activity is concerned with economic activities, we shall return to it later.

For clarity, we may summarise on a diagram the leading bodies of the three main political institutions: parliaments, ministries and the Communist Party (see Diagram 2). The parliamentary organs are elected, the members work part-time. In constitutional theory, they are supreme, they have authority over the ministries (shown in the second column). The ministries, and other committees, however, carry out the day-to-day policy; they are the effective government of the country. A body over 80 strong is unwieldy for policy making and there is a sort of unofficial 'cabinet' composed of the chairman of the Council, his deputies and other leading members. Its exact composition and its activity are not known. Finally, on the extreme right of the chart, is the party organisation. It seeks to influence and control the other two structures at all levels.

[1] Article 69, USSR Constitution.

F*

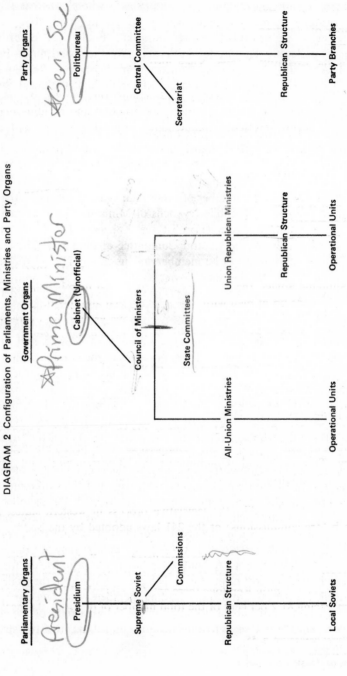

DIAGRAM 2 Configuration of Parliaments, Ministries and Party Organs

Commissions of the Soviet

A number of standing commissions are formed by members of the Soviet. They examine proposals put to the Supreme Soviet and they supervise the work of the executive bodies. They also put forward bills on their own initiative. In June 1966, the Soviet of the Union and the Soviet of Nationalities each had permanent standing commissions on: budget and planning, industry transport and communication, construction and building materials, agriculture, health and social maintenance, education science and culture, trade and services, legislative proposals, foreign affairs and a credentials commission. Other *ad hoc* commissions on specific subjects may also be formed. The commissions are set up during the first session of parliament and last for four years. They function even when the Supreme Soviet is not in session and it is here that much of the aggregation of interests takes place. Again a comparison may be made to the functions performed by parliamentary committees in Great Britain and the USA, though greater publicity is given to the work of the latter. The commissions provide specialist forums for the detailed study of various aspects of government work. In the 1966–70 session of the Supreme Soviet, the commissions had a total membership of 700. As each one is made up of men with different regional and institutional interests it is probable that in them the claims of various groups are expressed and compromises reached before being put to the relevant ministry or Supreme Soviet.

To ensure that interested parties involved in a bill have a chance to comment on it, a bill may be discussed in more than one commission. The bill on the Budgetary Powers of the USSR and the Union Republics was referred to the Budgetary Commissions of both chambers, and to the Economic Commission of the Soviet of Nationalities. On the draft of the Fundamentals of Land Use Bill the following commissions were involved: Agriculture, Industry Transport and Communications, Construction and Building Materials, Legislative Proposals.[1] It can be seen, therefore, that procedures are available by which proposals may be discussed and compromise made. On the other hand, unlike the legislative process in western states, not all bills go before commissions: of the 241 laws adopted by the Sixth Supreme Soviet (1962–6), only 53 had been before one.[2]

The standing commissions are paralleled at all levels of the Soviet parliamentary system – through the Union to the local Soviets. In the Soviet of the Ukrainian Union Republic there are, for example, 17 standing commissions embracing 81.2 per cent of the total number of deputies. At local levels,

---

[1] *The Soviet Parliament*, p. 55.
[2] O. E. Kutafin, 'Postoyannye komissii Verkhovnogo Soveta SSSR', *Sovetskoe gosudarstvo i pravo*, No. 4 (1966), p. 37.

Table 14. Membership of Sub-Commissions of Supreme Soviet.

Social Background of Members

Sub-Commission	Total Number of Members	Special- ists and Practical Workers	Scien- tific Workers	Represen- tatives of mass organisa- tions	Heads of Ministries and depart- ments	Managers of enter- prises, organisa- tions and establish- ments
Basic Principles of Land Use	31	10	8	3	5	5
Fundamentals of Matrimonial Law	32	11	9	4	5	3
Fundamentals of Legislation on Exploitation of Water Resources	50	19	10	6	9	6
Fundamentals of Legislation on Health Protection	44	17	12	6	5	4
Fundamentals of Corrective Labour Legislation	40	9	14	5	8	4
Basic Principles of the Exploitation of Mineral Wealth	28	11	8	3	3	3
Basic Principles of Forest Exploitation	40	12	15	3	5	5
Law on Accounting and Statistics	44	17	12	3	7	5

Cited in *The Soviet Parliament*, p. 134.

approximately four-fifths of all deputies are on commissions.

The commissions are not only composed of deputies: specialists on particular topics are drawn into their work, depending on the nature of the bill.
Representatives of the party, trade unions and Young Communist League are
also represented in subcommissions which are set up in addition and are
concerned with the analysis of particular problems. The wide social composition of a number of sub-commissions of the Supreme Soviet in 1965 is shown
in Table 14 where we may note that specialists and 'practical workers' make
up about a third of the participants.

Elections

The franchise is universal: all sane citizens over 18 years of age have the right
to vote, including soldiers and criminals. Formally elections to government
organs are direct, secret, and votes are cast on printed ballot papers. Any
person over 23 years of age is eligible for nomination to the USSR Supreme

Soviet, over 21 to the Soviets of a Union or Autonomous Republic and over 18 to a local Soviet.

Soviet elections, it should be added quickly, are not the same processes as in liberal-democratic states. For the voter there is no choice of candidate. He has, however, the opportunity of crossing off the name on the official ballot paper. In this way he can prevent the election of a candidate, who must receive more than fifty per cent of the votes on the voting register. In local elections such abstentions do happen: in March 1965, 208 candidates failed to get elected.[1] Of these 170 were in the RSFSR, where 1,059,255 deputies *did* get elected unopposed; generally, however, an overwhelming majority of the population votes for the nominated candidate. Voters absent from their own constituency may vote at another, provided that they have a Voting Right Certificate. The sick and invalid may vote at home by dropping their ballot papers into a ballot-box brought specially to them. Booths are also erected on long distance trains and ships. In the June 1970 elections to the Soviet of the Union, 99.74 per cent of the voters supported the official candidate; 396,343 voted against and 420 votes were invalid.[2] Similar figures apply to the Soviet of Nationalities. Though voting can be done secretly – a booth is provided for crossing off the name and the ballot paper is valid if dropped folded into the ballot box – a person entering the booth is most likely to be voting against the candidate, and this procedure has led to the accusation that the election cannot be 'secret'.[3]

The selection of candidates is when the crucial decisions over candidates are made. Nominations may be put forward to the state electoral commission by any public organisation – for example, party, trade union, or by the meeting of a collective farm. A person named at a meeting is discussed by the organisation concerned and, if approved, his name is put forward. All such nominated candidates are then discussed at a constituency 'pre-election meeting' attended by representatives from various organisations (party, unions) and a decision is reached on the candidate to be supported. As a Soviet source puts it: 'In order that collectives possessing the right to nominate candidates may come to an agreement on a general candidate, practice has developed such a form of consulting opinion at a meeting of representatives persons of collectives. At this meeting, not only do they decide on which candidate to put up for balloting in a given electorate, but how to develop the campaign for that candidate.[4] Those who do not receive support at this

[1] *Soviet News*, No. 5270, 3 May 1966.
[2] *Pravda*, 17 June 1970.
[3] Robert Conquest, *The Soviet Political System* (1968), p. 44.
[4] I. A. Azovkin, *Oblastnoy (kraevoy) Sovet deputatov trudyashchikhsya'* (Moscow, 1962), p. 40. Cited by Lloyd Churchward, 'Soviet Local Government Today', *Soviet Studies*, vol. 17 (no. 4), April 1966, p. 449.

meeting either gracefully withdraw their nomination or have it withdrawn for them by their nominating organisations.[1] It is here that the merits and faults of particular candidates are discussed, and possibly conflicting group and individual interests are manifested. The successful contender is registered with the District Electoral Commission in the name of the organisation nominating him. This commission is probably strongly controlled by the party and ensures its control of *cadres* or, in political science jargon, it ensures political recruitment. After selection by the pre-election meeting, the candidate must appear in public before his constituents. It is possible for objections to be made about his unsuitability: facts about unsavoury morals or unsatisfactory past work record, for example, may be brought to light, and he may be forced to withdraw. In the event of a candidate failing to get the necessary majority in the election, another election is called.

The Deputies

The election of government representatives also has the effect of directly involving in public affairs large numbers of people. In March 1965, for example, there were 2,010,540 deputies elected in local government.[2] Thereby many are drawn into activity who would not consider joining the Communist Party. At the June 1970 election to the Supreme Soviet, 27.7 per cent of those elected were non-party. Though non-party deputies are in a majority in *local* Soviets, it is not at all likely that they are dominant in decision-making or serious opponents to the party. Leading positions are usually held by party members. Taking the country as a whole, in the 1965 elections, whereas 45 per cent of deputies were party men, 72.1 per cent of members of executives of local Soviets were Communists.[3] In 1970, 72.3 per cent of delegates to the Supreme Soviet, and all of the members of the Council of Ministers and Presidium were party members. The party, by virtue of its organisation, plays a leading, but as we shall discuss later, not necessarily an omnipotent role.

The number of new deputies normally elected at the various levels is very large. For example, to the Supreme Soviet in 1966, 66.9 per cent of all deputies had not before been so elected; to the Supreme Soviets of the Union Republics, Autonomous Republics and to local Soviets, the figures were 68.1, 69.4 and 49.4 per cent respectively.[4] There are two conclusions to be drawn from these figures. First, they indicate much participation in civic affairs. Second, they probably mean that the high turnover of members gives some of them little

---

[1] *The Soviet Parliament*, pp. 30-31.
[2] *Sostav deputatov mestnykh sovetov deputatov trudyashchikhsya izbrannykh v marte 1965g* (Moscow, 1965), p. 12.
[3] *Sostav*, p. 201.
[4] *The Soviet Parliament*, p. 156.

lasting experience of administration, thereby weakening the element of lay control.

Soviet writers claim that the 'Soviet deputy is a true representative of the working people in the Soviets'.[1] A detailed occupational breakdown of Soviets at various levels is given in Table 15. Of the members of the Supreme Soviet, 26.6 per cent are factory workers, 19.4 per cent are collective farmers, 34 per cent, on the other hand, are engaged in government, party, or trade-union work. The non-manual strata account for only 16.2 per cent, though many others are concealed among the delegates working for government and other organisations. At lower levels, in town Soviets, workers compose 47.4 per cent of the total, and managers and other specialists 22.3 per cent. In rural Soviets, collective farmers make up only 42.9 per cent of the delegates. Women constitute 28 per cent of the total (425) of the delegates to the Supreme Soviet – more it is claimed than the total number of women elected to all parliaments in western countries. At the lower levels of local government, women figure prominently among the deputies, in 1967 they formed 42.8 per cent of the total.

Compared to advanced western states, the occupation of Soviet deputies shows some striking differences. The largest group is made up of engineers and technicians (20.5 per cent) followed by farming specialists (11.7 per cent). Lawyers, who form a large contingent among American Congressmen, constitute only 0.9 per cent of deputies to the Supreme Soviet.[2] Taking these figures as a whole, the occupational spread and the participation of women is much wider than in the west. The deputy, however, is not a full time parliamentarian. He continues his job though he must be given paid leave to attend the Soviet and to its affairs. He receives one hundred rubles[3] per month to cover expenses and is entitled to free transport (rail, ship and plane). However laudable the idea of a deputy being in constant contact with life at the bench and on the farm, it is probable that his effectiveness as a deputy is decreased by the necessity to continue another job.

A deputy may have his mandate revoked by his electors. More specifically, an organisation with the right to nominate may petition the Presidium of the Supreme Soviet. If it believes there is a case, then a writ is issued for a vote to be taken. Should a majority vote against the deputy, a new election is held. In the Fifth (1958–62) and Sixth (1962–6) Supreme Soviets ten deputies were recalled either for 'failing to justify the elector's trust' or 'for committing actions unworthy of their high calling'.[4]

[1] *Ibid.* p. 153.

[2] *Ibid.* p. 41.

[3] £1 equals 2.16 rubles (1 ruble equals $1.11 (USA)). This sum (100 r.) is approximately equal to the average wage.

[4] *The Soviet Parliament*, p. 99.

Table 15. Occupational Background of Deputies to the Soviets (1966, 1967)

	Total Deputies	Workers	Collective farmers	Managers, specialists and employees of enterprises and establishments	Workers in science, culture, art, education and health services	Workers of government bodies	Workers of party, trade union, Y.C.L. bodies and other mass organisations	Other workers
Supreme Soviet of the USSR (1966)	1,517	404	294	91	154	229	289	56
per cent		26.6	19.4	6.0	10.2	15.1	19.0	3.7
Supreme Soviets of the Union Republics (1967)	5,830	1,500	1,346	374	443	947	1,032	188
per cent		25.7	23.1	6.4	7.6	16.2	17.7	3.2
Supreme Soviets of the Autonomous Republics (1967)	2,925	700	561	286	233	525	563	57
per cent		23.9	19.2	9.8	8.0	17.9	20.8	2.0
Local Soviets (1967)	2,045,418	604,997	639,280	249,844	281,588	156,215	58,407	55,087
per cent		29.6	31.3	12.2	13.8	7.6	2.8	2.7
including								
Territory, Regional, Area Soviets	25,747	8,654	4,674	2,953	1,876	4,642	2,271	677
per cent		33.6	18.2	11.5	7.3	18.0	8.8	2.6
District Soviets	223,220	54,219	67,833	29,603	18,965	32,285	14,256	6,059
per cent		24.3	30.4	13.3	8.5	14.4	6.4	2.7
Town Soviets	238,250	112,902	3,437	53,233	31,037	15,789	11,273	10,579
per cent		47.4	1.4	22.3	13.0	6.6	4.7	4.5
Ward Soviets	86,642	41,965	46	19,457	11,777	5,241	5,064	3,092
per cent		48.4	0.1	22.5	13.6	6.0	5.8	3.6
Village or Rural Soviets	1,287,825	305,837	552,186	105,004	189,849	88,285	21,988	24,676
per cent		23.7	42.9	18.2	14.7	6.9	1.6	1.9
Township Soviets	183,734	81,420	11,104	39,594	28,084	9,973	3,555	10,004
per cent		44.33	6.0	21.5	15.3	5.4	2.0	5.4
All types of Soviets	2,055,690	607,601	641,481	250,595	282,418	157,916	60,291	55,388
per cent		29.6	31.2	12.2	13.7	7.7	2.9	2.7

Source: The Soviet Parliament (Moscow, 1967), p. 158.

The function of the deputy is to carry out political communication between government and Soviet citizen. He is expected to deal with individual complaints from constituents, to keep the law-making organs informed of his constituents' wishes. He reports to groups of constituents on the work of the Soviet, justifies its acts and explains the reasons for proposed legislation.

I try to use any opportunity I have to inform my electors of the Supreme Soviet's decisions and to mobilise them for their implementation. My official reports to the constituency apart, I pursue this line at the sittings of the District and Village Soviets, at the different meetings and conferences and at my meetings with electors in collective and state farms and in factory shops.[1]

Deputies of the Supreme Soviet give regular reports of their work to party and union meetings, speak on the radio and appear on television. Elected representatives often put certain days aside to meet constituents who have suggestions or grievances. Here, the intervention by a deputy can often lead to results after the exposure of inefficiency in administration. A deputy, for example, must by law have an answer within three days to a letter addressed to a minister or to the Council of Ministers. The existence of this regulation, of course, does not mean that he always gets a prompt or satisfactory reply.[2] Examples of the things the deputy gets done are: putting right faults in buildings, speeding up cultural development and improving railway services. Of 118 requests received by a deputy to the Supreme Soviet, 15 called for greater efficiency in the work of collective farms, nine mentioned the need for help in factories, 27 wanted help for municipal institutions (schools, hospitals, canteens etc.), 18 were on labour and citizen's rights, 27 were on housing problems, 22 asked for help in procuring building materials.[3]

Meeting such requests makes claims on Union and All-Union resources. Therefore, deputies most probably act to secure the interests of local groups – at an all-Union level to have favourable financial resources channelled to their area,[4] or to secure desirable industrial, educational or cultural development. Deputies, therefore, may act as articulators of regional interests. (See p. 286 and Reading No. 7, pp. 167–71.)

Rule Enforcement and Adjudication: The Police and Courts

In all modern societies a division of labour takes place between rule-makers (parliamentarians), rule-enforcers (executive) and rule-adjudicators (lawyers).

---

[1] Deputy V. P. Grishin, director of Proshursky state farm, quoted in *The Soviet Parliament*, p. 94.
[2] See Article 71 of the Constitution.
[3] *The Soviet Parliament*, p. 96.
[4] We should note that internally generated taxes are variably kept in Union Republics: e.g. 100 per cent in Uzbekistan, 82.8 per cent in Lithuania and only 13 per cent in Latvia (*Izvestiya*, 13 Oct. 1968). These figures probably conceal an interesting political process.

In liberal societies, a theoretical autonomy exists between the legislative, executive and judiciary: this gives the citizen a degree of independence from arbitrary treatment. A judiciary adjudicates in cases of conflict between the individual and the executive arm of government. The law-making *process* in the USA is bounded by the judiciary which can even declare Acts passed by Congress to be unconstitutional.

In Marxist theory the 'separation of powers' is an illusion. Law is not an 'independent' body of rules and the judiciary is not a group of men in any way independent of the ruling class. Laws, or the rules of society, are made by the ruling class and are the expression of it. Enforcement is in the interests of the ruling class. Justice is class justice. This Marxist viewpoint has influenced the structure of law in the USSR where it is considered to be an instrument of the political arm of the ruling class (the party), and it has a political role: 'The formal law is subordinate to the law of the revolution. There might be collisions and discrepancies between the formal commands of laws and those of the pro-letarian revolution . . . This collision must be solved only by the subordination of the formal commands of law to those of party policy'.[1] While this statement was made during the 'dictatorship of the proletariat', it strongly colours the present Soviet approach to law. A modern statement of Soviet theory is: 'Soviet law is a system of rules established by the state to promote the consolida-tion of the social order which helps society advance towards communism'.[2] Consequently, the *adjudicating* role of the Soviet courts and law is very weak, whereas its rule *enforcement* role is strong. If one identifies the achievement of communism with the development of the individual's freedom, rights and dignity, then of course there can be no contradiction between law enforcement which promotes it and individual interest. 'Soviet legislation is a juridical expression of the people's will and is designed to promote the fulfillment of the grand programme of communist construction.'[3]

As the extent of Soviet government is wide, so is the area of the courts and police jurisdiction over the citizen. The existence of law, or a set of rules binding on the members of a community, is held by liberals to be one of the greatest safeguards of individual freedom. Regularised processes of law depend to a large extent on a legal profession whose views of justice and whose norms are congruent with those of the law-makers. In the USSR, even during the Stalin period, law 'was for those areas of Soviet life where the political factor was stabilised.'[4] Where it was not, the secret police arrested, tried, imprisoned, and executed suspects.

---

[1] A. Vyshinski, *Sudoustroistvo v SSSR* (Moscow, 1935), p. 32. Cited by H. J. Berman, *Justice in the USSR* (New York, 1963), pp. 42-3.

[2] *Fundamentals of Soviet Law* (Moscow, n.d.), p. 20.

[3] *Fundamentals, op cit.*, p. 22.

[4] H. J. Berman, *op cit.*, p. 66.

The control of the internal security organs by Stalin was a crucial factor in the maintenance of his power and the enforcement of his policies. The security forces were subordinate to Stalin himself and their actions were not subject to judicial review: they had the power to exile, confine and execute the accused without trial. The importance of the secret police and the role of terror has already been described in the historical part of this book.[1] Obviously, after Stalin's death, Beria, as head of the secret police (then called the MVD, Ministry of Internal Affairs) was in a powerful position *vis-à-vis* both party and state bureaucrats. He was, however, destroyed by them and consequently, the powers of the security forces have been weakened.[2] The Chairman of the Committee for State Security is in the All-Union Council of Ministers. Under Khrushchev an attempt was made to give the Secret Police a new positive image.

The state's security agencies are no longer the bugbear that enemies – Beria and his aides – sought to make them not very long ago, but are truly peoples' . . . political agencies of our party . . . What is fundamentally new in the work of the state-security agencies is that, along with itensifying their efforts to deal with hostile intelligence agents, they have begun extensively applying preventive and educational measures in the case of Soviet citizens who commit politically improper acts, sometimes bordering on crimes, without any hostile intent but simply out of political immaturity or thoughtlessness.[3]

Recent trials, such as that of Sinyavsky, Ginzburg (see Readings No. 10 and 11), and Gerald Brooke, show the hand of the KGB in bringing men to trial. Such trials can in no way be compared to police activities in the Stalin period, though some commentators have pointed out that since Khrushchev's fall, secret police activity seems to have been on the increase. (See *Sunday Times*, 'Neo-Stalinism', 12 Jan. 1969. This and similar reports cannot be taken as representative of a *general* trend).[4]

The KGB is responsible for preventing all major crimes against the state (espionage, ideological subversion, and serious economic crimes) and for external intelligence. Border Guards also come under its jurisdiction. The KGB can arrest and hold a detainee for 24 hours after which a procurator, who is a member of the state legal service, must sanction the arrest or discharge the accused. A person may be detained for two months pending the investigation of a charge. (This may be extended to six months by order of a senior procurator).

[1] See Chapter 3.

[2] Beria and five other police officials were executed in December 1953.

[3] Shelepin, cited in Merle Fainsod, *How Russia is Ruled* (Cambridge, Mass., 1963), p. 450.

[4] Andrei Amalrik is probably right when he says: 'The regime has no wish either "to restore Stalinism" or "to persecute members of the intelligentsia" or "to render brotherly assistance" to those who do not ask for it. It only wants to go on as before . . .' 'Will the USSR Survive Until 1984?' *Survey*, no. 73 (Autumn 1969), p. 56.

Between 1962 and 1968 the ordinary police (the militia) came under the Ministry for the Preservation of Public Order. Since 1968 the title Ministry of Internal Affairs has been restored to this Union Republican Ministry. It is charged with detecting crime, apprehending criminals, operating the internal passport system, keeping order, controlling traffic and so on.[1]

The Supreme Court and the Procurator General are formally elected by, and responsible to, the Supreme Soviet. The Procurator General is charged with the administration of the legal apparatus and he should ensure that acts committed by ministries and their subordinate units (enterprises etc.) are legal. Excluded from the brief of the Supreme Court, as in English law, are acts or orders of the Council of Ministers and the Supreme Soviet.

The procurators have power to call for documents from institutions and to initiate proceedings against individuals or bodies against whom there is a *prima facie* case. After an investigation the procurator prosecutes in the courts.

A system of courts parallels the parliamentary system. At the apex is the Supreme Court of the USSR, then come the Supreme Courts of the Union Republics. Supreme Court judges are formally elected by the Supreme Soviet for a period of five years. At the base of the system are the People's Courts having a professional judge and two lay assessors who are directly elected for a two year period by 'general meetings of industrial, office and professional workers.'[2] The Supreme Court of the USSR is a final court of appeal, it resolves conflicts between lower judicial organs and can deal with cases of first instance only in exceptional cases.

Prosecution is based on the infringement of legal codes which are classified by subject: the criminal code, labour law, family law and so on. The details of the codes cannot be considered here.[3]

In sentencing policy an attempt is not only made to attribute blame but also to use penalties to 'reform' the accused. Law is an instrument to be used to adapt conduct and to mould behaviour to that of the 'new Soviet man'. In sociological jargon the process of law is a positive (and negative) part of socialisation.

The criminal code lays down the following three aims of punishment:

(1) Retaliation for the committed crime;
(2) Correction and re-education of the convicted persons in the spirit of an honourable attitude towards labour, of strict compliance with the laws, and of respect towards communal life;

---

[1] For details see E. L. Johnson, *An Introduction to the Soviet Legal System* (1969), pp. 138-142 and Robert Conquest, *The Soviet Police System* (1968), Chapter 1.

[2] For full details of elections of judges see Constitution articles 105-109, Appendix C below.

[3] For a detailed discussion see H. J. Berman, *Justice in the USSR* (New York, 1963), and E. L. Johnson, *An Introduction to the Soviet Legal System* (1969).

(3) The exercise of educational influence on the offender and other people in order to deter them from committing criminal offences.[1]

Under the first category comes the death penalty which can be given to criminals convicted of treason, espionage, banditry, intentional murder, speculation and theft of state property on a large scale. There are four kinds of 'correction colonies': general regime, used for first offenders convicted of minor crimes; strengthened regime, reserved for criminals sentenced for more serious crimes; strict regime for second or third offenders; special regime, for hardened criminals having been convicted of violent and serious crime.[2] Other penalties are deductions from wages (of from five to twenty per cent of earnings), fines, public censure, deprivation of medals, orders or other public titles.[3]

The 'withering away of the state' has involved the transfer of some legal tasks previously carried out by the state to social organisations. Voluntary people's militia formed through the trade unions and *Komsomol* have been charged with the maintenance of public order. Minor crimes are tried by comrades' courts which are elected at the place of work or place of residence. Their jurisdiction covers pilfering, hooliganism and labour relations and fines of up to 50 rubles, and reparation of loss up to the same amount may be imposed. Public reprimands may also be given. Since Khrushchev's departure from the political scene, however, the development of greater 'lay justice' has been curbed.[4]

Two points may be made to bring out the difference between the role of law in Britain and the Soviet Union. First, the pre-trial investigation of the alleged crime tends to diminish the importance of the court trial itself.[5] Second, the Marxist and Bolshevik conception of law as the political arm of the state militates against the development of the courts as independent adjudicators (at least in criminal cases). The lack of tradition of the presumption of innocence and the absence of a relatively autonomous legal profession contribute to strengthening the 'enforcement' elements in the Soviet political system, and weakening the function of adjudication.[6]

Having described the 'official' structure and the view of the political process we must now turn to some criticisms; objections on matters of fact, as it were,

[1] Cited by Ivo Lapenna, *Soviet Penal Policy* (1968), p. 87.
[2] B. S. Nikiforov, 'Soviet Criminal Law', *Anglo-Soviet Journal*, March 1967, p. 38.
[3] Special provisions exist for minors, see Ivo Lapenna, pp. 96-98.
[4] See below, pp. 215-6.
[5] This has led to the assertion that the court becomes 'little more than a rubber stamp'. Leonard Schapiro, 'Law and Legality in the USSR', *Problems of Communism*, vol. 14, no. 2 (March-April, 1965), p. 5.
[6] For an example of a case which was utilised as a 'mass political measure', see Peter Juviler, Mass Education and Justice in the Soviet Courts', *Soviet Studies*, vol. 18 (No. 4) April 1967.

of the official view. In later chapters, we shall consider from a more behavioural point of view, the actual political process.

Criticisms of the Official Analysis

In the first place many would deny that the notion of socialist harmony is true and that the working class is in power. Raymond Aron has objected that: 'It is possible that the party leaders govern in the interests of the proletarian and peasant masses, but the regime is not one in which the proletariat itself is in power . . .'[1] It is argued further that a distinction exists between the interests of the political leaders and those of the people. This criticism has been developed into various theories of bureaucratic and class rule which will be described in detail in the next chapter.

It must be admitted that Soviet theory is inadequate in some respects. It gives no explanation of the distribution of power between different institutions – economy, military and party. It also leaves unexplained such political processes as Stalin's 'excesses' which are put down by Soviet theorists to individual factors: 'the personality cult'. Another criticism is that in theory, there have been no 'antagonistic' classes or strata since 1936, yet in Marxist terms neither the state nor the party are 'withering away' in any politically significant way. If Soviet society is socially harmonious, then how can there be any justification for the continuation of the Communist Party, which originally represented the political arm of the working class? (This point is developed in Chapter 12). The criticism may be made that the Soviet description of Soviet society ignores political conflict which is endemic.

Another objection is that the Soviets are a facade and that political power lies mainly with the CPSU. A description of the Soviets takes up a considerable part of the Constitution of the USSR and a recent Soviet book on their parliaments says: 'The establishment of the Soviets, organs of popular rule, gave the people the real possibility of administering political, economic and social affairs. Soviet society gave birth to socialist democracy, which is the broadest most representative and just democracy known to men.'[2] The Communist Party of the Soviet Union, on the other hand, is only mentioned once in the Constitution: its structure and dominating role are not described. As Leonard Schapiro, a western writer on the CPSU has said, 'behind the formal organs of government . . . stands the real source of both legislative and executive power, the party'.[3] The point must be taken that the power of the party is far more pervasive and important than the official constitutional view suggests.

[1] R. Aron, *Democracy and Totalitarianism* (1968), p. 206.
[2] *The Soviet Parliament* (Moscow, 1967), p. 7.
[3] Leonard Schapiro, *The Government and Politics of the Soviet Union* (1965), p. 118.

Even the formal description of the party's political process given in its rules has been criticised in the west. First, critics claim that the party in practice is not organised on the democratic principle of election from the bottom up, but on the authoritarian method of control from the top down. Furthermore, the influence of party members over decision-making in the party is held to be very small indeed when compared to the party elite and to the secretariat. Obviously, the higher organs of the party and the secretariat are able to determine to a large extent the content of policy, its timing and implementation, and are able to bring pressure to promote or expel personnel —they perform the aggregation function and thereby play a dominant role in forming party policy. The secretariat organs are enforcement agencies. The organisational structure, with a strong full-time secretariat and centralised finance, a diffuse membership banned from forming factions and with emphasis on strict discipline from the top downwards, strengthens the power of the full-time secretariat. The indirect system of election in the party makes control of higher bodies by lower ones more difficult. During the Stalin period the manipulation of the party was mainly carried out by Stalin's control over the secretariat apparatus. These criticisms were also made by both Trotsky and Luxembourg even before the revolution. To view the party as a structure merely articulating the collective views of its total membership, a kind of 'general will' of the proletariat, therefore, is naïve. The full-time party secretariat plays a decisive role both in aggregating and in articulating general policy goals. Of utmost importance here are the specialised departments of the Central Committee, which are not mentioned in the party rules.

Rather less important is the formal criticism that even the minimum legal requirements concerning the timing of the party's meetings are not fulfilled. Though the party is now far removed from the time when no Party Congress could take place for over eleven years (i.e. from the Eighteenth Congress in Feburary 1941 to the Nineteenth in October 1952), the period between the Twenty-Second and Twenty-Third was four and a half years, not four as stipulated by the Rules. But nowadays this objection is legalistic.

The Communist Party of the Soviet Union then must be regarded as of at least equal importance to the government and in its process it should be considered as oligarchic rather than democratic.

The formal Soviet description of the state organisation is also naïve in many respects. The federal system gives to the Republics relatively few powers. No important aspects of policy are left to the Republics *independently* of the All-Union government. The Republics, Regions and Areas are units of administration. Policy is centrally decided but the implementation of policy is left to the Republics. Education, medical and social services, and welfare (for example, care of the old, child and maternity care) are their responsibility. Variation in standards exists between Republics, but the republican units are

not self-governing communities as local activities must be closely geared to
All-Union policy. The All-Union government's right of control of foreign
trade, economic planning and finance, makes it a dominant partner and in
practice, the government of the USSR is centralised. The clause that the
secession of a Union Republic from the USSR may take place is of little
practical consequence.

Of course, centralisation should not be thought of as characteristic only
of the USSR. It is a general tendency of all modern large industrial states, and
applies equally well to the USA. The main difference between liberal societies
and the USSR is the extent of state power, which gives to the Soviet central
government much more power than to its western counterpart. Direct local
subordination to the central government does not generally take place in
western states (except France), where more subtle methods of ensuring
conformity, such as financial control and inspection, are used.

The main factors which have led to centralisation are the All-Union
government's control of the budget (which it appropriates to the lower units);
the necessity for common technical standards in social services throughout
the whole society; the growth of a large complex economy which makes all its
parts interdependent; and the highly centralised Communist Party.

While politics is about conflict and about alternative policies, the 'official'
description denies any major political conflict. The sessions of the Soviets
show no fundamental criticism of policies. The amendments which are put
and accepted have been agreed to beforehand by the government, and represent
the end of a political process, rather than the initiation of one. This is said
by many western critics to show the absence of democracy.[1]

It can hardly be denied that in practice the formal operation of the Soviet
political system does not allow for the public airing of fundamental discontent
and for the articulation of alternative policy. Political opposition is not
institutionalised in the USSR.

The official description and the disclaimers made above are rather formal
and do not show how the political system actually 'works'. This is one of the
drawbacks of a formal 'institutional' approach. Constitutions have important
ideological implications. They are concerned with how the political system
should work and the political bodies defined in them are related to a theoretical
rather than to the actual state of the world. From the Soviet viewpoint, as
socialist society is socially and politically homogeneous, no institutional
system is necessary to reconcile political conflict. As there is no fundamental

---

[1] But speeches at meetings of the Soviet may reflect local and group interests, though its
meetings show unanimity and consensus. For instance in Reading no. 7 (an excerpt from the
Supreme Soviets' discussion of budget and plan) we see glimpses of local interests being articulated.
Deputy Yegorychev points out that Moscow has had its investment budget decreased. Deputy
Popov says that Leningrad's experience justifies the setting up of the regional economic councils
and he opposed a return to a centralised ministerial system.

conflict between social groups then, the logic runs, there is no need for competitive political elections and political parties resting on separate group interests. When government represents a common homogeneous social interest, then there can by definition be no political repression of the citizens by the government: therefore, there is no need for a balance of power (between executive, judiciary and legislative). In Soviet writings, the unity of Soviet state and society are emphasised. All this, of course, in some respects is unrealistic.

Reading No. 7
'Discussion of the Soviet State Plan and Budget in the Supreme Soviet'
Source:
Pravda, 11 Dec. 1964 *Izvestiya*, 11 Dec. 1964. Translated in the *Current Digest of the Soviet Press*, 13 Jan 1965, pp. 10-13.

Speech by Deputy I. P. Kazanets, Ukraine Republic.

It is necessary that the USSR State Planning Committee and the Supreme Council of the National Economy not only plan the dates for the opening of units but also concern themselves with questions of the placing of orders for equipment for these construction projects.

In his report Comrade Kosygin quite correctly pointed out the need for a rise in the responsibility of the design organisations for well-timed schedules and the high-quality preparation of design documents. This year we had to revise upward the estimated construction costs for almost half the projects. Yet many of these designs had been rated as of high quality, and their authors even received bonuses.

This situation can no longer be tolerated.

One result of the mistakes and miscalculations in planning in past years has been a lag in the building up of the capacities of the coal mines and pits. We request that the State Planning Committee, the State Committees and the republic agencies be charged jointly with working out fundamental measures for the further development of the Ukraine Republic's fuel industry.

The tasks set for 1965 require that we exert substantial efforts, put all reserves into operation and make more skilful use of such powerful economic levers as economic accountability, prices, credit and profits. A large role in this belongs to material incentives, which should be given to the republics, economic councils and enterprises. We therefore support the proposals of the Budget Committee of the USSR Supreme Soviet and consider it necessary that not less than 50 per cent of the turnover tax obtained through the sale of consumer goods produced above plan be left at the disposal of the republic's enterprises and channeled into expanding production and encouraging their collectives . . .

Speech by Deputy N. G. Yegorychev, Moscow.

. . . All Soviet people are labouring selflessly and achieving remarkable victories in the struggle for communism. At the same time, the socialist method of production makes it possible to achieve a substantially bigger economic effect if each enterprise makes more complete use of its internal reserves, if unconsidered and inexpedient experiments are not carried out on the scale of the entire national economy in the future, if shortcomings in the economic guidance of industrial and agricultural production are eliminated, if a decisive end is put to the constant reorganisations of the administrative apparatus, if officials are taught to be fully responsible for the sector under their charge and are not afraid to adopt decisions, do not shift responsibility to the shoulders of others. And finally, if the planning agencies, and primarily the USSR State Planning Committee, take their place in the guidance of the country's economy and approach planning only from the positions of Marxist-Leninist economic science, and the leaders of these agencies are more principled in their work.

Comrade Kosygin's report again emphasised the enormous importance of the problem of raising the quality and reliability of products. In recent years the collectives of Moscow enterprises have been waging an insistent struggle in this direction. In just three years the quality and reliability of 3,500 articles, of which more than 2,000 were machines, instruments and items of equipment, have been raised.

The work done by the Moscow enterprises has made it possible to save approximately 3,500,000 rubles a year in the national economy. The collective of the Electric Light Bulb Plant, for example, increased the service life of television picture tubes from 750 to 3,000 hours; this is equivalent to the additional output of several million tubes a year, for the manufacture of which two specialised plants would have had to be built. In this case one article replaces four articles, and not two, as the report said. Therefore one cannot agree with the groundless assertions of the authors of the article carried by *Pravda* under the heading 'The "Ladder" of Administration' to the effect that new articles of domestic industry are distinguished from the old ones 'only in a couple of nuts and a half-dozen size specifications'. These assertions wrongly disparage the work not only of Leningrad but of the whole of our industry . . .

Unfortunately, the State Committees for the branches of industry still do a poor job of co-ordinating and guiding this work on the scale of the country's entire national economy. The revision of existing standards and the elaboration of new standards that define present-day demands on the quality of raw materials, semi-manufactures, parts and finished articles are being carried out slowly. Thus far no solutions have been found to questions of the material incentive of enterprises to raise the quality of their articles.

We propose that the USSR Supreme Council of the National Economy be charged with working out a system that ensures the implementation of practical measures for raising the quality of products and with submitting it for the consideration of the government.

Moscow is the oldest economic region in the country. A majority of our enterprises were created during the years of the first five-year plans, and even earlier. Work conditions at these enterprises are difficult, and their equipment and especially the production premises are becoming obsolescent and worn out and insistently demand replacement and reconstruction.

However, an incorrect idea has taken hold in the USSR State Planning Committee that industrial reconstruction should not be carried out along a broad front in Moscow. The State Planning Committee officials are proceeding here not from economic considerations but merely from formal ones. . .

The State Planning Committee ... has reduced state investments in housing construction every year. In particular, this year the plan for the opening of housing space in Moscow built with state capital investments was 20 per cent below the level achieved in 1962.

A substantial reduction in capital investments on housing construction has been permitted throughout the country as a whole. And this cannot be considered correct. Of all the problems of improving the living conditions of the working people, the housing problem has been and remains the most acute and the most difficult. Therefore we Deputies warmly hail the decision of the CPSU Central Committe and the government to correct in 1965 the situation that has evolved.

The Moscow City Party Committee and the Moscow City Executive Committee have submitted the technical and economic foundations of the general plan for the development of the city of Moscow during the period up to 1980 to the State Planning Committee and the State Committee for Construction Affairs for a decision and a report to the USSR government. However, almost two years have passed and the discussion of the materials presented to the staffs of the State Planning Committee and the State Committe for Construction Affairs has not yet been completed . . .

Speech by Deputy G. I. Popov, Leningrad.

. . . It is now evident to everyone that many of the decisions that have been adopted in recent years on reorganising the management of the national economy have not facilitated the fuller utilisation of the material and labour resources of the country but, on the contrary, have begun to hamper the development of productive forces. The structure of economic agencies has proved to be very cumbersome. The excessive centralisation of guidance, the multiplicity of agencies, parallelism in the activities of state organs – all this complicates the work of industry and does not facilitate the development of local initiative. The Izhorsky Plant, for example, is under the jurisdiction of nine State Committees, four economic councils and two State Planning Committees. Some 70 different officials of the above-mentioned organisations (administrations, departments, and so on) have the right to give the plant instructions. Under the conditions that have been created, a large number of the most highly skilled industrial officials are forced to waste an enormous amount of time resolving various questions in the central agencies. This year executives of Leningrad enterprises spent more than 500,000 days on business trips to Moscow. The number of State Committees has been increased unjustifiably. A majority of them do not fulfil the tasks entrusted to them and do not bear proper responsibility for ensuring the high technical level of the products turned out or for improving the technology and organisation of production.

Industry barely feels the practical assistance of the State Committees in deciding questions of technical progress, although a majority of the research and design organisations and experimental shops have been turned over to them. Furthermore, the handing over to the State Committees of a number of plant design bureau has, in our view, substantially weakened the technical possibilities of the enterprises.

Life demands the careful and painstaking elaboration of an optimum system for the management of production on the basis of the rational combination of the territorial and branch principles, with due regard for the accumulated experience of economic construction in our country as well as in other states of the socialist commonwealth.

In this connection I should like to touch upon what seems to me a very important problem. In recent times more and more voices are being heard expressing the advisability of abolishing the economic councils and returning to the old system of managing production through ministries. In our opinion, such proposals are unjustified. We feel that the system of economic councils is completely progressive and has fully justified itself.

The experience of the Leningrad Economic Council has made apparent the obvious advantages of this form of administration. Economic guidance has been brought closer to production, has become more effective and operational, and the manoeuverability of labour, material and financial resources has improved.

In the conditions of the economic council, extensive possibilities have appeared for the further improvement of the organisational structure of the enterprises. More than 400 factories and plants were combined recently in the Leningrad Economic Region.

In other words, we are in favour of the economic councils, but with substantially greater rights and authority.

In our opinion, it would be expedient to set up a single economic body to guide the country's industry, subordinating to it the present State Committees with the rights of chief branch administrations. These chief administrations must be charged with the responsibility for the integrated, comprehensive development of each branch of industry. They should carry out the function of operational guidance of the development of this or that branch on the basis of the national economic plan, check on the fulfilment of plan assignments and ensure technical progress in the enterprises under their jurisdiction.

It seems expedient to us to free the chief administrations from operational guidance of the numerous design and drafting organisations that are directly linked with production, returning these agencies to the plants.

In addition to improving the system of administration of the national economy, it is necessary to improve the style and methods of work of the state apparatus, to eliminate the elements of bureaucratism and red tape in certain of its links.

At recent sessions of the USSR Supreme Soviet, Deputies from Leningrad and other provinces of the country have repeatedly introduced a proposal on the transition to the integrated planning of capital investments for housing, cultural, everday-service and communal construction. The advisability of resolving this question is so obvious that it evokes no objections from anyone. And yet this problem has not yet been solved.

Cases of the ineffectiveness, and sometimes simply the lack of discipline, of some central-agency officials in fulfilling certain government assignments are conspicuous. In recent years the construction workers of Leningrad and other provinces of the country have repeatedly proposed the introduction of a method of financial accounts for fully completed projects, without intermediate payments. Such a practice stimulates better work on the part of the construction organisations and contributes to the quicker opening of new structures. The government has approved this initiative, but through the fault of the USSR State Planning Committee this completely progressive method of financing construction work has not yet been introduced.

A no less important condition for successful work is a further rise in the incentive of all categories of workers in the national economy in the growth of labour productivity, technical progress, and improvement of the quality of the articles produced. Discussions on this question have been conducted for a fairly long time, and more than a few interesting opinions have been advanced. But in practice, these exceptionally important questions are being resolved extremely slowly.

When the plan for 1965 was being drawn up, Leningraders proposed an 85,000,000-ruble increase in the output of additional cultural and everyday goods by our industry. For the successful solution of this task, we ask that the USSR State Planning Committee be charged with intensifying the rates of reconstruction of enterprises of the former local industry by stipulating the necessary financing for 1965.

Speech by Deputy N. N. Kachalov, Minister of Construction, Russian Republic.

In our opinion, the chief shortcoming is the unscientific, arbitrary planning that has taken root in many cases. Departmentalism and local allegiances lead to the fact that the construction of more and more new projects is launched while at the same time already built production premises and units are being poorly utilised and technological processes are not completely operational. This occurs because there is inadequate responsibility for the working out of the technological part of the designs for enterprises.

Moreover, the compilation of the plans for capital construction is delayed until the end of the year. Furthermore, at the outset the plans are inflated, and then they begin to reduce and tighten them. Therefore decisions on inclusions in or exclusions from the draft plan are frequently made hastily. Where now is your meticulous economic verification of the designs and your genuinely scientific planning! . . .

The functions of the USSR State Committee for Construction Affairs should be somewhat revised. It is hardly expedient to invest this all-Union central agency in the future with the functions of the production-operational guidance of construction. Even now it is absolutely incorrect when its structural subdivisions are given direct supervision over the construction organisations – the trusts and construction project – including the right to allocate and reallocate resources, passing over the republic Councils of Ministers, the Construction Ministries and the chief territorial construction administrations . . .

INTRODUCTORY

Brzezinski, Z. K. and S. Huntington. *Political Power USA/USSR*. London: Chatto and Windus, 1964.

Churchward, Lloyd G. *Contemporary Soviet Government*. London: Routledge and Kegan Paul, 1968.

Conquest, Robert. *The Soviet Political System*. London: Bodley Head, 1968.

Hazard, John N. *The Soviet System of Government*. Chicago, Ill.: University of Chicago Press (Fourth Edition), 1968.

Meyer, Alfred G. *The Soviet Political System*. New York: Random House, 1965.

Schapiro, Leonard B. *The Government and Politics of the Soviet Union, 1965*. London: Hutchinson (Second Edition), 1967.

Scott, Derek J. R. *Russian Political Institutions*. London: Allen and Unwin (Fourth Edition), 1969.

BASIC

Conquest, Robert. *The Soviet Police System*. London: Bodley Head, 1968.

Fainsod, Merle. *How Russia is Ruled*. Cambridge, Mass.: Harvard University Press, 1961. Revised edition, 1963.

Gehlen, Michael P. *The Communist Party of the Soviet Union*. Bloomington: Indiana University Press, 1969.

Johnson, E. L. *An Introduction to the Soviet Legal System*. London: Methuen, 1969.

'KPSS v tsifrakh', *Partiynaya zhizn*', No. 10, May 1965, p. 8.

'KPSS v tsifrakh', *Kommunist*, No. 15, October 1967, pp. 89-103.

Obshchestvovedenie (Second Edition). Moscow, 1964.

Obshchestvovedenie (Third Edition). Moscow, 1965.

Obshchestvovedenie (Seventh Edition). Moscow, 1969.

Saifulin, M. (ed. & tr.) *The Soviet Parliament*. Moscow, Progress Publishers, 1967.

Zlatopolsky, D. L. *State System of the USSR*. Moscow, 1960.

SPECIALISED

Almond, Gabriel A. 'A Functional Approach to Comparative Politics', in Gabriel A. Almond and James S. Coleman, *The Politics of Developing Areas*. Princeton: New Jersey Princeton University Press, 1960, pp. 3-64.

Avtorkhanov, Abdurakhman. *The Communist Party Apparatus*. Chicago: Henry Regnery and Co., 1966.

Azovkin, I. A. *Oblastnoy (kraevoy) Sovet deputatov trudyashchikhsya*. Moscow, 1962.

Barsukov, N. A. and I. N. Yudin. *Sotsial'naya baza KPSS*. Moscow, 1967.

Berman, H. J. *Justice in the USSR*. Cambridge, Mass.: Harvard University Press, 1963.

Churchward, L. G. 'Soviet Local Government Today', *Soviet Studies*, Vol. 17, No. 4, April 1966, pp. 431-52.

'Constitution of the USSR', in *Sovetskie konstitutsii: spravochnik*. Moscow, 1963.

'Demokraticheski Tsentralizm', in *Bol'shaya Sovetskaya Entsiklopediya*, Vol. 13, p. 656.

Duverger, Maurice. *Political Parties: Their Organisation and Activity in the Modern State*. London: Methuen, 1964.

Easton, David. *A Systems Analysis of Political Life*. New York: J. Wiley and Son, Inc., 1965.

Fisher, George. *The Soviet System and Modern Society*. New York: Atherton Press, 1968.

Fundamentals of Soviet Law. Moscow, n.d.

Itgi vyborov i sostav deputatov mestnykh sovetov trudyashchikhsya 1969g. Moscow, 1969.

Kutafin, O. E. 'Postoyannye komissii Verkhovnogo Soveta SSSR', *Sovetskoe gosudarstvo i pravo*, No. 4, 1966, pp. 32-40.

Lapenna, Ivo. *Soviet Penal Policy*. London: Bodley Head, 1968.

Lewytzkyj, Borys. 'Generations in Conflict', *Problems of Communism*, Vol. 16, (No. 1), Jan.-Feb. 1967, pp. 36-40.

Longo, L. *Problemi e Realtà dell' URSS*. Rome, 1958.

Meissner, Boris. 'Totalitarian Rule and Social Change', in *Problems of Communism*, Vol. 15, No. 6, Nov-Dec. 1966.

Mickiewicz, E. P. *Soviet Political Schools: The Communist Party Adult Instruction System*. New Haven, Conn.: Yale University Press, 1967.

Izvestiya, 13 October 1968. (Article on tax proportions to union republics).

'Soblyudat' ustavnye trebovaniya o chlenstve v KPSS', *Partiynaya zhizn'*, No. 18, September 1966, pp. 3-8.

Nikiforov, B. S. 'Soviet Criminal Law', in *Anglo-Soviet Journal*, March 1967.

Petrenko, F. 'Printsipy partiynoy demokratii', in *Kommunist*, No. 18, 1965, pp. 36-42.

Rigby, T. H. 'Social Orientation of Recruitment and Distribution of Membership in the Communist Party of the Soviet Union', in *The American Slavic and East European Review*, Vol. 16 (Oct. 1957), pp. 275-90.

Rigby, T. H. *Communist Party Membership in the USSR, 1917-1967*. Princeton, New Jersey: Princeton University Press, 1968.

Rules of the CPSU (English Edition). London, 1961.

Schapiro, Leonard. 'Prospects for the Rule of Law', in *Problems of Communism*, Vol. 14, No. 2, March-April 1965, pp. 2-7.

Sostav deputatov mestnykh sovetov deputatov trudyashchikhsya izbrannykh v marte 1965g. Moscow, 1965.

SSSR Administrativno-territorial'noe delenie Soyuznykh Respublik. Moscow, 1963.

Vyshinski, A. *Sudoustroistvo v SSSR*. Moscow, 1936.

6

CRITICAL THEORIES OF
SOVIET SOCIETY

If Soviet society is not 'socialist' in the way it is officially defined, then what kind of socio-political system is it? Theorists outside the USSR have attempted to describe it in the following ways. The first is in terms of bureaucratic power, resting on a Weberian approach. Second, there is the model put forward by Marxist critics of the USSR, who try to combine elements of bureaucratic and class theory. The third may be described as the 'industrial society' or convergence model. Fourth, is the paradigm of totalitarianism.[1]

Bureaucratic

The search for a theory to describe the modern USSR has led many writers in the 1960s to favour a 'bureaucratic' approach.[2] Bureaucracy, however, is an ambiguous word and this is particularly the case with 'bureaucratic' studies of the USSR which have utilised this approach.

Alfred G. Meyer, for instance, has described contemporary Soviet society as follows:

The USSR is best understood as a large, complex bureaucracy comparable in its structure and functioning to giant corporations, armies, government agencies, and similar institutions – some might wish to add various churches – in the West. It shares with such bureaucracies many principles of organisation and patterns of management . . . All human beings must live in a world they themselves did not make; but in modern bureaucracies, they live in worlds someone is constantly seeking to remake.[3]

Kassof's description is somewhat narrower. He defines the USSR as an

---

[1] See Daniel Bell, 'Ten Theories in Search of Reality', in *The End of Ideology* (New York, 1961).

[2] Alfred G. Meyer, *The Soviet Political System* (New York, 1965), Chapter 22. Allen Kassof, 'The Administered Society', *World Politics*, vol. 16 (July 1964). T. H. Rigby, 'Traditional, Market and Organisational Societies and the USSR', *World Politics*, vol. 16 (July 1964). L. G. Churchward 'Bureaucracy – USA:USSR', *Coexistence*, vol. 5 (1968). Carl Beck, 'Bureaucratic Conservatism and Innovation in Eastern Europe', *Comparative Political Studies*, vol. 1 (no. 2), July 1968. John A. Armstrong, 'Sources of Administrative Behaviour: Some Soviet and Western European Comparisons', *American Political Science Review*, vol. 59 (1965).

[3] *Op. cit.*, pp. 477-8.

'administered society' that is 'one in which an entrenched and extraordinarily powerful ruling group lays claim to ultimate and exclusive scientific knowledge of social and historical laws and is impelled by a belief not only in the practical desirability, but the moral necessity, of planning, direction and co-ordination from above in the name of human welfare and progress.'[1]

Rigby comes the nearest to adopting Weber's theory of bureaucracy. He argues that while simpler societies have the characteristics of contract (a commitment by each party to perform certain actions to further goals) and custom ('objectives, roles, and methods are all "given" '), in modern industrial society it has 'become technically possible to run a large nation as a single corporation.'[2] For Rigby, Soviet society is a *command* society. 'Command is a relationship in which one party is active and the other is passive in the determination of what is done. The complement of command is obedience. One actor formulates or transmits goals, assigns tasks, and prescribes methods; the other carries out his assigned tasks in the manner prescribed.[3]

Objections which might be made to these theories are that organisations in practice do not conform to a simple command type stereotype and that in practice, 'giant corporations, armies, government agencies' do not have similar organisational features. To describe the USSR as (in Meyer's words) 'a modern corporation writ large', ignores the styles of activity which may characterise bureaucratic organisations. His description focuses on the extent to which third parties regulate behaviour, rather than on the style in which behaviour is regulated. Alvin W. Gouldner, for example, has shown that in one industrial organisation three patterns of bureaucracy occur: 'mock', representative and punishment-centred.[4] 'Mock' rules (for example, 'No smoking' notices) are not enforced and entail no conflict between management and men. 'Representative' rules (about safety) are enforced by both sides and generate little overt conflict. 'Punishment-centred' rules (appropriation of materials) are enforced by one side and evaded by the other; they involve tension and conflict. Gouldner stresses the importance of the values and sentiments for compliance to authority and rules: where the formal rules violate the values of both sides, they are broken; where they are supported by the sentiments of both sides, they are voluntarily obeyed; where they are violated by the sentiments of one side but supported by the values of the other side, they are enforced by punishments. An examination of Soviet society in these terms has not yet been attempted.

Gouldner's 'representative' type of bureaucracy suggests that bureaucracy as such need not have 'a special nightmare quality of its own'.[5] Indeed,

[1] *Loc. cit.*, p. 558.
[2] *Loc. cit.*, p. 545.
[3] *Loc. cit.*, p. 539.
[4] *Patterns of Industrial Bureaucracy* (New York, 1964).
[5] Kassof, *loc. cit.*, p. 574.

democracy and bureaucracy are incompatible if the former is concerned with preserving individual rights and bureaucracy can be progressive in so far as it promotes certain social goals[1] (such as equality of the consideration of individuals).

There are some obvious points which may be made about Soviet administrative behaviour which follow Max Weber's model.[2] Organisations are formally hierarchical – i.e. they are based on levels of authority. 'Officials' are experts, they receive special training and they consider their jobs to be a career. Promotion is based on ability and seniority. Management is based on conduct regulated by rules or norms.

A more detailed study of Soviet administrative behaviour[3] has suggested that it is *similar* to that of Western Europe in respect of the extent of *departures* from hierarchical command principles in industrial production and foreign trade. In other words, Soviet industrial enterprises are as much under 'one-man management' as western firms. Armstrong points out that a 'considerable measure of adherence to hierarchical administrative principles is necessary to the highly modernised economies . . . in both Western Europe and the Soviet Union.'[4] But this command structure is not rigid. Second, informal relationships also play an important part in Soviet administration. Informal groupings spring up within organisations which defend them against the pressures generated by the formal structures. While these links are ignored in Weber's approach, they play an important part also in the behaviour of western organisations. Third, the motivational factors influencing Soviet administrators are, like their Western European counterparts, highly utilitarian. Material rewards and high social status go with administrative success. Purely normative incentives, 'building communism' play a very unimportant role. Fourth, as in western organisations, authority is acquired by staff (or functional agencies) by virtue of their power to report to the top of the command structure: research and design staffs, for instance, have access to the top line authority.[5] Finally, there is considerable friction in Soviet industrial administration between staff and line: between production and research. This friction is not unusual in western firms but says Armstrong, it is greater in the USSR.

On the other hand, there are some important ways in which Soviet administrative practice seems to differ from Western European. Formal communication is very inefficient. Clerical facilities are poor, there is less reliance on written than on oral communication. (In 1960, it has been estimated that there

[1] See Franz Neumann, *Behemoth* (1944), pp. 368-9.

[2] Max Weber, 'The Essentials of Bureaucratic Organisation', in R. K. Merton (ed.) *Reader in Bureaucracy* (New York, 1952), pp. 19-21.

[3] John A. Armstrong, *loc. cit.*

[4] *Ibid.*, p. 645. The whole of this paragraph is based on Armstrong's data.

[5] Armstrong, *loc. cit.* pp. 645–6.

were only 130,000 shorthand-writers and typists compared to 559,000 in Britain in 1951.)[1] An engineering or 'technocratic approach' is more characteristic of Russian than Western European administrators. Armstrong reports that they tend to be less willing to consider sociological or psychological factors than technical. Norman Kaplan has also shown that in Soviet research organisations, administrators have much less authority and scientists much more than in comparable American organisations.[2]

Elements of Weber's theory which do not lend themselves so easily to the character of Soviet society, at least at the macro level, are as follows. Areas of official authority are not ordered in a 'stable manner': there tend to be violent shifts in official duties (for instance the changes in structure of industrial ministries, see Chapter 9). As we have seen above, legal norms and the role of the legal profession are not independent binding forces. While individual organisations are hierarchical, there is an intermixing of organisational structures (in the factory: party, trade union, ministerial) which belies the description of Soviet *society* as being *one* hierarchical organisation. Also, Soviet bureaucracy has had an important role in *changing* the structure of Soviet society. Here it departs from the Weberian model which stresses the more conservative administrative process. As we shall see in a later chapter, Soviet administration relies to a considerable extent on active participation rather than passive management: it encourages the participation of laymen and their intervention in the formal hierarchical procedure. (See Chapter 10). Bureaucracy is not only the administration of things, but involves the manipulation of people. It is sometimes objected to, because it is said that a small group of people may manipulate the majority and thereby curtail individual freedom.[3] The theorists which we shall discuss next develop this line of thought and attempt to add to a bureaucratic critique, elements of a Marxist class analysis.[4]

State Capitalism

Non-Soviet, or rather anti-Soviet, Marxists have tried to adapt Marxism to the features of the Soviet state. They argue that the October Revolution did not carry out the classical socialist revolution. They point out that Tsarist Russia was backward, the proletariat was small, the Bolsheviks did not have wide popular support and that a necessary condition to fulfil a *socialist* revolution was a class conscious proletariat forming the majority of a highly developed capitalist society. As Russia had not a fully developed capitalist

[1] Alec Nove, *Was Stalin Really Necessary?* (1964), p. 277.

[2] Norman Kaplan, 'Research Administration and the Administrator: USSR and US', *Administrative Science Quarterly*, No. 6 (June 1961) pp. 51-72.

[2] See Reinhard Bendix, 'Bureaucracy and the Problem of Power', in R. K. Merton *et. al. op. cit.*

[4] For an introduction see Nicol P. Mouzelis, *Organisation and Bureaucracy* (1967), Chapter 1.

type economy, Marxist laws of social development had to take their inexorable course and paradoxically, therefore, the Communist Party, when in power, had to carry out 'capitalist' economic development and with it the exploitation of the subject classes. Class rule was a necessary concomitant of this process, but with the difference that the Soviet ruling class was not based on private property, but on state property: the ruling class was (and still is) a *state capitalist* class.

Djilas is perhaps the best known exponent of such views. He argues that the Communist Party in its *initial* revolutionary seizure of power did not establish the rule of a new exploiting class:

> . . . the new class was definitely formed after it attained power . . . This is not to say that the new party (i.e. the Communist Party) and the new class are identical. The party, however, is the core of that class, and its base. It is very difficult, perhaps impossible, to define the limits of the new class and to identify its members. The new class may be said to be made up of those who have special privileges and economic preference because of the administrative monopoly they hold . . .
>
> In loose terms, as the new class becomes stronger and attains a more perceptible physiognomy, the role of the party diminishes. The core and the basis of the new class is created in the party and at its top, as well as in the state political organs. The once live, compact party, full of initiative, is disappearing to become transformed into the traditional oligarchy of the new class, irresistibly drawing into its ranks those who aspire to join the new class and repressing those who have any ideals.
>
> The party makes the class, but the class grows as a result and uses the party as a basis. The class grows stronger, while the party grows weaker; this is the inescapable fate of every Communist Party in power.[1]

In other words, the incumbents of higher positions in the ministerial system come to dominate the power structure. A network running from the Council of Ministers down to factory directors and their immediate subordinates is able to exert the interest of an elite, even if opposed by the lower-level party secretaries and (or) the elected organs of the Soviets. It is, therefore, in the bureaucratic stratum, by virtue of its *control* over the means of production that the new ruling class is located. It may overlap with the Communist Party apparatus, but only in so far as the apparatus has any control. According to Djilas, with time the party weakens and power passes to the bureaucracy.

The bureaucratic power of the new ruling class has been emphasised by Tony Cliff and Bruno Rizzi. Cliff points out that:

> The state bureaucracy . . . possesses the state as private property. In a state which is the repository of the means of production the state bureaucracy – the ruling class – has forms of passing on its privileges . . . Every bureaucrat will try more to pass on to his son his 'connections' than he would, let us say, a million rubles (even though

[1] Milovan Djilas, *The New Class* (1966), pp. 48-9.

this has importance). Obviously, he will at the same time try to limit the number of competitors for positions in the bureaucracy by restricting the possibilities the masses have of getting a higher education etc.[1]

The state takes the place of the political and economic market as a co-ordinator of activity; it dominates the economic and social spheres. The Soviet state has basically the same social relations as the capitalist. From this viewpoint a ruling class, based on property, exploits the proletariat.

The social origin of the new class is proletarian. In the first instance it is anti-capitalist and after the seizure of power, it relies on proletarian support to 'asure a normal flow of production' and to achieve industrialisation.[2] With the consolidation of its power, however, the new class establishes a monopoly. The 'monopolists of the administration' constitute 'a narrow and closed stratum', while 'the mass of producers (farmer, workers and intelligentsia) . . . have no rights'.[3]

Elsewhere, Djilas argues that mobility is high between the new class and the masses. 'In the new class, just as in other classes, some individuals constantly fall by the wayside while others go up the ladder. In private ownership classes an individual left his property to his descendants. In the new class no one inherits anything except the aspiration to raise himself to a higher rung of the ladder. The new class is actually being created from the lowest and broadest strata of the people, and is in constant motion. Although it is sociologically possible to prescribe who belongs to the new class, it is difficult to do so; for the new class melts into and spills over into the people, into other lower classes and is constantly changing'.[4]

But such a ruling-class theory as adapted from Marxism, would seem to be inappropriate to the Soviet Union, for the following reasons. State capitalist and bureaucratic state theory is open to the objection that the Marxist notion of class depends on the *ownership* of the means of production and that the ruling class extracts surplus from the exploited. The state capitalist shifts the ownership relations of private property to the *control* of the state over property. Here it needs to be proven that state power does confer the property relations crucial to Marxist analysis, and it is yet to be demonstrated that the incumbents of Soviet state power possess and inherit property as the landed aristocracy in feudal society or as shareholders

---

[1] T. Cliff, *Russia: A Marxist Analysis*, (London n.d. but 1964), p. 122. I shall not deal with the differences between Cliff on the one hand and Bruno Rizzi and Schachtman on the other. See the somewhat sectarian article: T. Cliff, 'The Theory of Bureaucratic Collectivism – a Critique', *International Socialism*, no. 32 (Spring, 1968). For a more recent statement with reference to Poland, see J. Kuron and K. Modzelewski, *An Open Letter to the Party* (London, n.d.).

[2] Djilas, pp. 50-51.

[3] M. Djilas, p. 53.

[4] M. Djilas, p. 66.

under capitalism. The ruling class's privileges are derived, according to Marx, from surplus which is a variable left after the workers have been paid wages. But the Soviet ruling class, if it is such, receives a salary drawn from employment. If unemployed it draws no salary – unlike its capitalist counterpart which can live quite happily from dividends – and is therefore in the same *market* position as other wage-earners. It is difficult to understand how such a group of stratum may be equated with a ruling 'class' in a Marxist sense.[1]

The dynamics of the society would indicate that factors outside the dictates of the ruling class account for mobility: for example, achievement based on educational qualification rather than family ties, though family background affects educational chances. (See Chapters 11 and 12). The boundaries of the 'new class' are characterised by such flexibility in Djilas's theory, that it is impossible to conceive of it developing any consciousness of its class position which, by definition, in Marxist theory, is an essential trait of a ruling class.

Cliff, and to a lesser degree Djilas, assume that the ruling bureaucracy is composed of both party and state personnel. But this leaves the boundaries of the ruling class too generally defined. Does it include the members of government organs (Soviets), industrial administrators, factory directors and party officials and does it exclude rank-and-file party members? Not all enjoy the same powers, or even the same relations to the means of production. Differences between the government and party are particularly important; for the party, unlike government authorities, has no *legal* authority over the activity of the enterprise, or over the administration of law.

Degenerate Workers' State

The 'degenerate workers' state' theory, associated with Trotsky, accepts some of the above criticisms. The USSR is regarded as a society dominated by a social stratum, but not by a class in the Marxist sense; the society is a workers' state, though having undesirable 'degenerate' characteristics. This view is rather similar to the orthodox Menshevik criticism raised after the Bolshevik Revolution by Kautsky. He coined the well-known expression that the Soviet system was 'not the dictatorship of the proletariat but the dictatorship of the party over the proletariat'.

Trotsky, in *The Revolution Betrayed*,[2] argued that the Soviet Union by having nationalised property and having a planned economy is fundamentally different from capitalist society. It is 'a contradictory society, halfway between capitalism and socialism'. While nationalised property is a step towards

---

[1] It is true that in a capitalist society some members of the ruling class (such as judges) also draw salaries, but one should not confuse such groups with the proper industrial and commercial bourgeoisie, who do not.

[2] See adaptation, 'Is the Bureaucracy a Ruling Class?' Reading No. 10.

socialism, the low level of technology is inadequate to give the USSR a socialist character. Trotsky writes:

> ... Experience has taught us that the workers' state is still a state, that is ... doubly barbaric in a backward and isolated country; that under unfavourable conditions it can degenerate to the point of being unrecognisable; that it may require a supplementary revolution in order to be regenerated. But the workers' state nonetheless remains an inevitable stage on our road. This stage cannot be overcome except by the permanent revolution of the international proletariat.[1]

The crux of the matter, for Trotsky, was that the Soviet system, having abolished in the October Revolution the class relations of capitalism, had degenerated into a new form of elite rule. The party had betrayed the revolution and, with the bureaucracy ensconced in a privileged position, acted as a privileged stratum or caste which might have to be overthrown by revolution.

The 'degenerate workers' state' theorists argue, I think quite correctly, that the USSR cannot be regarded as 'capitalist' in a Marxist sense because the property relations have been destroyed. A social group or stratum controls the society; but not entirely in the same way as a capitalist maintains his own rule and supremacy, for the Soviet ruling stratum defends *nationalised* property. But it is from a political and moral point of view that Trotsky criticises the USSR: workers' democracy does not exist, a clique misrules the country, the creative role of the party is undermined, the international aspects of socialist revolution are neglected.

Trotsky, unlike totalitarian theorists whom we shall describe later, does not underestimate the economic growth and 'development' aspects of Soviet power. Indeed, the 'backward' character of the Tsarist heritage and the positive results of planning are brought out. But he does ignore the degree of public participation in the Soviet regime. His emphasis on 'degenerate leaders' fails to consider how those leaders may have been abetted, and their policies enthusiastically implemented, by their supporters, especially the rank-and-file members of the Communist Party. Presumably, the revolutionary consciousness which the toiling masses had at the time of the revolution, at some time changes to a false 'consciousness' when given to the ruling party. This has resulted in somewhat unsatisfactory attempts by such theorists to say when this change took place. Though Trotsky admits that the economic position of the masses is bettered by the new bureaucracy, revolutionary action is still required for them to achieve socialism. As a *Marxist* theory, one would have expected much more emphasis on social and economic factors to explain the rise and basis of power of the undesirable political elite. We are left, however, with a criticism of Stalin's Russia rather like the

---

[1] *The Class Nature of the Soviet Union* (W.I.R. Publications, London, n.d.), p. 4. See also *The Revolution Betrayed* (1957), p. 255.

orthodox Soviet Marxist, mainly based on the condemnation of the personality of certain individuals and their manipulation of political institutions.

Let us turn now from considering those who accept a Marxian class approach to society to those who do not. There are two main models in this respect: 'urban-industrial society' and 'totalitarianism'.

Industrial Society

Clark Kerr

An important school of sociologists has attempted to adapt a form of industrial or technological determinism to the analysis of modern society, by stressing the way *technology* influences social structures. This might be called simply the 'industrial society' model. In this theory, the class conflict engendered by ownership relations posited by Marxists is rejected, but industrialism is regarded as the prime determinant of social relations.

Such theorists argue that social class in a Marxist sense is irrelevant in modern industrial societies. In the West, they argue, class polarisation has not led to a revolutionary overthrow of the bourgeois social order. The affluent working class does not see itself as a class for itself. It regards work as instrumental to maintaining a higher standard of living. Life becomes privatised, focused on the family group. In the West the broader relevance of political parties to the trade union struggle is not perceived. For the Marxist view of political polarisation between capitalists and proletariat, political conflicts are seen to be of a more differentiated kind representing 'interests' on 'issues'.

The Marxist analysis of power and society, it is argued, has also been shown to be inappropriate to the states of the socialist world. Here the abolition of private ownership has not led, it is alleged, to social and political harmony but to inequality of power and to privilege and a hierarchical social scale similar to that of the West. The dichotomy between capitalism and communism posed in the 1930s and 1940s has given way to a set of dichotomies between freedom and organisation, between participant democracy and elite rule, between equality and equality of opportunity. Bureaucracy and organisations are seen to be greater foes to the emancipation of man than the old bogies of the ruling class and private ownership. The social and political characteristics of modern society are dependent on industrialism. Clark Kerr sums up this perspective as follows: 'In our times it is no longer the spectre of communism which is haunting Europe, but rather emerging industrialisation in many forms that is confronting the whole world. The giant of industrialisation is stalking the earth, transforming all the features of older and traditional societies'.[1]

Marxist analysis, however, is not discarded by 'industrial society' theorists. Three elements of Marxist theory are retained. These are: first, the 'inner

[1] Clark Kerr *et al.*, *Industrialism and Industrial Man* (1962), p. 28.

logic and necessities of the industrialisation process'; second, the effects of technology on social institutions and on the character of the family, the role of education, the nature of values and beliefs; third, the process of capital accumulation, the sources and rates of which vary from one country to another.[1] This theory is a kind of technological determinism: given a certain industrial structure, then one can expect a 'relevant' social structure. But, unlike the Marxist model, this structure contains no irreconcilable class contradictions. What then are its characteristics? Here I shall summarise its main features under eight headings.[2]

First, there is rapid growth of the population and control of this growth. Labour becomes more valuable relative to capital. For the first time in history there is no expendable class (such as beggars or untouchables). While the population grows because of longevity, the size of the family falls. The extended or consanguine family structure shrivels and the nuclear family supersedes it. Women are emancipated, relations between the spouses are 'democratic'.

Second, there is a diffusion of political power and greater equality of wealth. As rulers can no longer alone provide protection for their subjects, one man rule in its many forms is no longer an acceptable form of government. Knowledge is spread among the population and as a consequence there is mass literacy. Government requires participation by the people and their consent. Non-elites are able to bargain for concessions, for higher standards of living and human rights (for instance, inviolability of the person).

Third, there is a highly developed division of labour, entailing differentiated roles (for example, the roles of a man as father and as worker are separate in an industrial society, whereas they are fused in a peasant one). The family provides fewer social functions. There are market mechanisms for the exchange of commodities and for labour. Mobility between occupations is rapid and access to higher positions in the social hierarchy is open to all – equality of opportunity becomes a watchword. A highly differentiated social hierarchy based on education and occupation is a feature of the industrial order.

Fourth, a system of values exists in all industrial societies which puts a premium on work, on economic production for the market involving a high level of industrial and economic productivity. The ideology of hard work, technical change, 'progress', science, and status differentiation provides a cement to bind together the disparate groups of industrial society and to provide consensus in the new industrial state. The search for a utopian social

[1] Kerr, *op. cit.*, p. 27.

[2] See C. Kerr *et al.*, *Industrialism and Industrial Man* (1962); G. E. Lenski, *Power and Privilege* (New York, 1966), esp. Chapter 10; Talcott Parsons, 'Characteristics of Industrial Societies', in C. E. Black, *The Transformation of Russian Society* (Cambridge, Mass., 1960).

order, for a 'true democracy', for a 'communist' society is abandoned. Ideologies are dominant which sustain the social structure, rather than utopias which seek to change it.[1]

Fifth, the legal system applies a more or less common law to individuals of all status groups, and is relatively independent of the government. Compared to earlier societies laws are extensive, complex and detailed. Rule-making and enforcement finally rest with the government, but are shared to a greater or lesser extent with private associations (firms, unions) and quasi-state bodies – the judiciary. The legal provisions are 'universalistic' rather than 'particularistic': they apply to all incumbents of given roles, rather than to individuals or members of status groups.

Sixth, while the forms of government control vary, the national government organises the whole society in the interest of collective goals, it has authority to coerce and exercise sanctions. Its direct and indirect role in the control of the economy, science and education distinguishes it from non-industrial societies.

Seventh, human relations tend to be specific, achievement-oriented, rather than diffuse and ascribed. For example, the role of one's boss or teacher is restricted to work or educational tasks. One's promotion is determined by one's capabilities at work rather than by social origin. Relations between individuals tend to be affectively neutral: that is, not concerned with the immediate gratification of interests, but controlled and in pursuit of specific goals; for instance though a pupil might like to imprison or assassinate his teacher for his political views, neither side is expected to let political considerations detract from the process of learning.

Eighth, large-scale urbanism generates a form of social life and social relationships independently of the political setting. Relationships are impersonal, superficial and differentiated. The individual is anonymous, freed from the constraint of intimate groups. The city is supreme both economically and culturally over the surrounding rural hinterland. The size of communities necessitates that communication becomes indirect: representatives dominate the political sphere, and newspapers, T.V. and radio, the cultural. The city performs specialised functions; it has business, entertainment and other areas in which separate modes of life are pursued. Routine and formal controls take the place of the emotional ties of simple societies. As Louis Wirth has graphically put it: 'The clock and the traffic signal are symbolic of the basis of our social order in the urban world.'[2] The hubbub and the lay-out of the city's central business area are common to all major cities of the world. Mass

---

[1] See for instance, Daniel Bell, *The End of Ideology* (New York, 1961), p. 398. We shall discuss this in more detail below, pp. 216–19.

[2] L. Wirth, 'Urbanism as a Way of Life', in *On Cities and Social Life*, ed. A. J. Reiss Jr. (Chicago, 1964), p. 75.

art and culture ranging from the Beatles to Beethoven are common cultural symbols of modern urban life, quite independent of the geographic or political setting.

The characteristics of urban-industrial society are world-wide. While no two societies are identical, when compared to pre-industrial societies the similarities abound. 'The empire of industrialism will embrace the whole world; and such similarities as it decrees will penetrate the outermost points of its sphere of influence and its sphere comes to be universal.'[1]

Below we shall be concerned with a detailed examination of the structure of Soviet society, but here it is apposite to cite the views of some specialists who, on the basis of empirical work, take an 'industrial society' view of the USSR. The most important works are by Inkeles and Bauer and by Brzezinski and Huntington.

The findings of Inkeles and Bauer are based, not on the study of structures, but on examination of the attitudes of Soviet refugees interviewed after the Second World War. They write:

We have observed that the *patterning* of values about the occupational structure of opportunities for mobility, of the evaluation of education, of ideas about child rearing, of communications behaviour, and many other realms of experience is broadly similar in the Soviet Union and other large scale industrial societies. This seems a finding of substantial general significance for social science, since it so strongly suggests that the industrial social order carries with it certain inherent propensities which influence individual values and experience relatively if not completely, *independently* of the political setting.[2]

In *Political Power: USA/USSR* Brzezinski and Huntington relate and contrast the Soviet and American political systems. They say:

To name only a few key similarities: the governments are on a continental scale; they involve the commingling of a variety of peoples, often with consequent racial (or ethnic) tensions; the societies have experienced rapid technological and economic change and share in some regard a similar respect for material and technical values; historically each society was closely related to but not an integral part of the Western European political system; each society sees itself as the particular embodiment of universally true principles; international responsibilities have become increasingly important in shaping their major domestic political dilemmas. When compared to the complex political systems of Western Europe, with their intricate class structures and multiplicity of political cultures, the political systems of the United States and the Soviet Union seem to share a homogeneity, a unity, and a simplicity which are missing on the Continent. Confronted today with many of the same challenges – economic, military, and political – the two systems have not reacted along entirely different lines. (p. 8).

[1] C. Kerr *et al*, p. 46.
[2] *The Soviet Citizen* (Cambridge, Mass., 1959), p. 391.

In both these extracts we see the 'convergence' of the USA and USSR, but underlying it is the notion of the common characteristics of urban industrial societies.

The reader, at this stage, may, in view of these similarities, begin to wonder why international relations have in recent years been dominated by conflict between capitalist and communist states. The answer is to be found in the political sphere. It is not being suggested by these writers that the USSR is merely another copy of the USA. In both books important differences between these countries are noted. Inkeles and Bauer point out that the state or the polity plays a dominant part in Soviet society, unlike in America. The state uses its resources 'to secure the total mobilisation of all resources and above all personal human resources, in the assault on the goals set for the society by its ruling elite.'[1]

Ossowski has also stressed the way the 'political authorities can overtly and effectively change the class structure; where the privileges that are most essential for social status . . . are conferred by a decision of the political authorities . . .'[2] While the culture of industrial society may have characteristics common to both state socialist and capitalist countries, the polity and its relationship to the social system are significantly different.

Raymond Aron has defined four major characteristics of a capitalist economic system which differentiate it from the Soviet. These are: a great diversity in types of property, the integration of national economies with the world market, the dominant influence of consumers over the allocation of national resources, free trade unions.[3] Aron points out that though western and state socialist systems have large enterprises in common, in the West, family business continues in industry, agriculture and commerce. The USSR, he argues, has maintained a large measure of self-sufficiency and independence of the world market, unlike countries of the capitalist West. Though state intervention influences the balance between consumption and investment, the cycle of investment (ironing out booms and slumps), and the distribution of the national income, consumers still play 'a dominant role in the allocation of collective resources'. In a state socialist society, the state is a corporate entity, with trade unions being an organic part of the state apparatus, but in the West there is a greater plurality, a 'permanent rivalry between individuals and groups, and between these groups and the state.'[4]

---

[1] *The Soviet Citizen*, p. 385.

[2] S. Ossowski, *Class Structure in the Social Consciousness* (1963), p. 184. This point has also been made by J. Goldthorpe, 'Social Stratification in Industrial Society', *The Sociological Review Monograph* (ed. P. Halmos), no. 8, Oct. 1964, p. 111. See also Jan Szczepanski, 'Possibility of a Theory of Socialist Society', *Empirical Sociology in Poland* (Warsaw, 1966), p. 146.

[3] R. Aron, *18 Lectures on Industrial Society* (1967), p. 103.

[4] *Ibid.*

These differences serve to introduce us to our fifth and final theory, that of totalitarianism.

Totalitarianism

Most western political theorists concerned with Soviet society have defined its characteristics in terms of 'totalitarian' theory. Here we shall consider the views of William Kornhauser, and C. J. Friedrich and Z. K. Brzezinski. Kornhauser (see above pp. 47–8), has shown how the conditions of mass society lead to the totalitarian state. The population is 'massified' (i.e. highly fragmented and powerless) and highly available to politically organised groups. Whereas in a 'mass' society the elite is highly accessible to the non-elite, in a totalitarian society, accessibility is low. State and society are fused, the individual is isolated and oppressed.

Totalitarian dictatorship involves total domination, limited neither by received laws or codes (as in traditional authoritarianism) nor even the boundaries of governmental functions (as in classical tyranny), since *they obliterate the distinction between state and society*. Totalitarianism is limited only by the need to keep large numbers of people in a state of constant activity controlled by the elite.[1]

In Kornhauser's theory the crucial factors are the wide control over the society exercised by the polity and the absence of any participation by the masses or constraint of the totalitarian dictatorship by law, custom or mores.

A second distinguishing factor of totalitarianism is the group structure. Intermediate groups such as trade unions, parent-teacher associations, professional bodies and welfare groups are both weak and 'inclusive' – they tend to be state run and encompass much of an individual's life. The trade unions or youth organisations are agents of the government – they are 'weak' because they have little autonomy from it, they are 'inclusive' because they organise many aspects of the individual's life. (Soviet unions run clubs, lease houses, organise holidays and rest-homes, administer social security and have responsibility for work discipline).

Such a society, argue totalitarian theorists, is typified by the USSR, Nazi Germany and Mao's China.

A more detailed model of totalitarianism specifically related to Soviet society has been devised by C. J. Friedrich and Z. K. Brzezinski,[2] who not only accept Kornhauser's distinctions but fill out the details of the role of ideology, party, leader, police and propaganda. In the first edition of their book, totalitarianism has six main characteristics:

[1] William Kornhauser, *The Politics of Mass Society* (1960), p. 123.
[2] *Totalitarian Dictatorship and Autocracy* (New York, 1956).

1. an official ideology, consisting of an official body of doctrine covering all vital aspects of man's existence to which everyone living in that society is supposed to adhere, at least passively; this ideology is characteristically focused and projected toward a perfect final state of mankind, that is to say, it contains a chiliastic claim, based upon a radical reflection of the existing society and conquest of the world for the new one;

2. a single mass party led typically by one man, the 'dictator' and consisting of a relatively small percentage of the total population (up to ten per cent) of men and women, a hard core of them passionately and unquestioningly dedicated to the ideology and prepared to assist in every way in promoting its general acceptance, such a party being hierarchically, oligarchically organised, and typically either superior to, or completely intertwined with the beaucratic government organisation;

3. a system of terroristic police control, supporting but also supervising the party for its leaders, and characteristically directed not only against demonstrable 'enemies' of the regime, but against arbitrarily selected classes of the population; the terror of the secret police systematically exploiting modern science and more especially scientific psychology;

4. a technologically conditioned near-monopoly of control, in the hands of the party and its subservient cadres, of all means of effective mass communications, such as the press, radio, motion pictures;

5. a similarly technologically conditioned near-complete monopoly of control (in the same hands) of all means of effective armed combat;

6. a central control and direction of the entire economy through the bureaucratic co-ordination of its formerly independent corporate entities, typically including most other associations and group activities.[1]

In terms of Soviet society, the 'official ideology' obviously refers to Marxism-Leninism and its goal of a classless, free and harmonious society. The single mass party led by the 'dictator', controlling mass communications and the economy through terror is meant to sum up the Soviet regime under Stalin: hence the stress in most western books on terror and dictatorship. 'Totalitarian' theory, particularly during the Stalin period, has the merit of making the political system central. Ideology, mass communication, polity and economy are seen as integrated and operating to constrain the individual. But a criticism which may be made is why only the six factors mentioned above have been selected. Indeed, in the latest edition of Brzezinski and Friedrich's book another two traits – expansion and the administrative control of justice and the courts – are added to the list.[2] Equally relevant and important to the Stalinist regime were rapid economic growth, the rise in educational standards, high population movement and mobilisation, the growth of urbanism and the social relationships accompanying it.

The typology had important political usages in the West during the Cold

[1] *Totalitarian Dictatorship and Autocracy* (New York, 1956), pp. 9-10.
[2] *Totalitarian Dictatorship and Autocracy* (New York, 1966), p. 22.

War: it focused on the more horrendous and anti-liberal aspects of Soviet rule. As Herbert J. Spiro has suggested, the word has become 'an anti-Communist slogan in the cold war'.[1] Applied comparatively to Nazi society, it is revealed that the analogy is not a good one. Fascist and communist ideology are antithetical: communism postulates an ideal of man and a classless society quite foreign to fascism. The Soviet regime is founded on nationalised property and central planning whereas the fascist had private ownership and much weaker control of the economy. The rates of economic growth and social change were much lower in Germany than in the USSR.

One of the main criticisms of the totalitarianism theory is that it is 'static'.[2] It does not pay sufficient attention to the ends pursued by the Soviet political leaders. Emphasising that the population is kept in a 'state of constant activity' and that the elite pursues a 'chiliastic claim', tends to ignore the momentous social change accomplished by the Stalin regime. A more dynamic model is necessary to evaluate properly this era.

Elites

While neo-Marxist theorists depict a ruling class in the USSR, those of totalitarianism postulate a ruling elite. Before describing attempts by political scientists to apply this concept to the Soviet Union, we may distinguish between two kinds of elite theory.

One refers to groups of individuals who are eminent in a particular field; a second delineates *the elite* composed of the eminent in many different spheres. In the first kind of model there are many elites: the holders of high positions in economic institutions, religious orders, trade unions, government and voluntary societies. Such groups have high status, wield power and control values in a limited functional field. In the second type of model, a distinction is made between the various social or intellectual elites and *the elite* composed of the top persons from those institutions, which perform the act of governing the society in key sectors, such as in government, in the economy, in communications and in values. It is a minority which rules over society, it is a ruling elite. Such a minority may not be impermeable like a ruling class; it may interact with society, new elements or social forces may arise and either displace the existing elite or be accommodated in it. A widely accepted definition of elite rule is that of H. D. Lasswell: 'The political elite comprises the power holders of a body politic. The power holders include the

[1] Herbert J. Spiro, 'Totalitarianism', *International Encyclopedia of the Social Sciences*, vol. 16 (Macmillan, 1968), p. 112.

[2] Karl Wittfogel's theory of oriental despotism is a combination of bureaucracy and totalitarianism. Its main drawback when applied to the Soviet Union is that Soviet society has been dynamic not static. This is recognised by Wittfogel, see *Oriental Despotism* (New Haven, Conn., 1963), p. 440.

leadership and the social formations from which leaders typically come and to which accountability is maintained, during a given generation'.[1] To avoid ambiguity, 'elites' shall refer to any high status group and 'ruling elite' shall be used to describe that minority drawn from key sectors (as defined above). Raymond Aron has said that the essential characteristic of pluralist (western) society is a number of accessible elites whereas a totalitarian society has an inaccessible unified elite.

There is a small number of men who in practice run the industrial undertakings, command the army, decide what proportion of the national resources should be allocated to saving and investment and fix scales of remuneration. This minority has infinitely more power than the political rulers in a democratic society, because both political and economic power are concentrated in their hands. They control the public departments and industrial undertakings. The planning office distributes raw materials and workers between industries according to plan. The whole society comes to resemble a single business in which the managers, or possibly *the* one manager, apportion men and things as they see fit, in the name of technical efficiency.

Politicians, trade union leaders, public officials, generals and managers all belong to one party and are part of an authoritarian organisation. The unified elite has absolute and unbounded power. All intermediate bodies, all individual groupings and particularly professional groups, are in fact controlled by delegates of the elite, or if you prefer it, representatives of the state. The trade unions are no more expressing the claims of the workers, they are an instrument of the state, intended to bring the workers into line. A classless society leaves the mass of the population without any possible means of defence against the elite.[2]

This is the totalitarian model of Soviet society. It is not distinguished from other elites which tend to be lumped together with it.

In addition to a ruling elite of this kind totalitarianism also logically entails that the Soviet Union is a classless society. Socially, the society is divided into a Communist Party ruling elite – and a fragmented and groupless *mass*. Group formations, whether they be of trade unionists or of a privileged 'upper class' are inimical to the hegemony of the party. A ruling elite, with high power, high social prestige and control of the means of production, exploits a groupless, diffuse though changing *mass*. Such an absence of group formations does not inhibit social change. On the contrary, the high turnover, caused by the purges, and arrests on the one hand, and by individual promotion and achievement on the other, help keep the society in a state of flux and prevent the formation of enduring social groups.

Most totalitarian writers, including Aron, modify this model to include intermediary organisations, through which the party elite exercises power.

[1] H. D. Lasswell, D. Lerner, and C. E. Rothwell, *The Comparative Study of Elites* (Stanford, California, 1952), p. 13.

[2] Raymond Aron, 'Social Structure and the Ruling Class', in L. S. Coser, *Political Sociology* (New York, 1966), pp. 81-2.

The ruling elite operates both directly on the population and indirectly through other structures which are completely penetrated. This is shown diagrammatically in Chart 6.

CHART 6
'TOTALITARIAN' ELITE MODEL

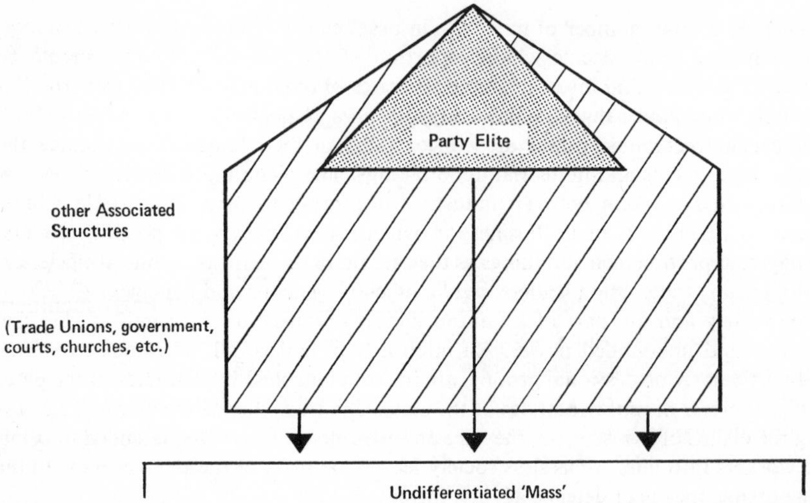

Party Elite

other Associated
Structures

(Trade Unions, government,
courts, churches, etc.)

Undifferentiated 'Mass'

Recruitment into, and movement from, the ruling elite to the mass is not dealt with in any detail in totalitarian theory. It is likely to be both self-recruiting and to accept socially mobile aspirants from the mass. Upward mobility provides both an 'escape' and a positive channel of activity for the masses. Mobility helps maintain a state of flux and discourages the formation of associations. 'Access' in terms of *influencing* the elite, on the other hand, is precluded.

The more extreme totalitarian models are inadequate to explain the facts of contemporary Soviet social and political life. It is doubtful whether a regime could last for long if it is completely impervious to demands made by the non-elite. The professional groups which have grown significantly under Soviet power (e.g. scientists, professors, writers, journalists) cannot be ignored or regarded simply as forming 'front' organisations. The fact that the elite is drawn from one social group (in this case the intelligentsia) does not imply that it acts mainly in the interests of that group. This model, like that of Djilas, discussed earlier, suffers from crudely lumping together the political elite with others of a different kind (social, economic, professional). Further-more, the operation of the party through intermediary associations (writers, trade-unions, the police) does not ensure their subordination; in fact such associations have acted to modify the party elite's demands and have performed interest articulation functions.

A more complex political model is that of A. G. Meyer,[1] who compares the Soviet ruling elite to Wright Mills's power elite model of the United States. Mills's theory, it will be recalled, depicted three interrelated groups at the apex of power in the USA: the top military ('the warlords'), leading business executives ('the corporation chieftains') and the heads of government ('the political directorate').[2] Mills gives these groups parity of status in his description of the structure of American politics. The triumvirate possess 'the most of what there is to have: money, power, prestige'.

Meyer's Soviet ruling elite is composed of 'industrial and administrative executives, military and security officers, leading scientists, opinion makers (including both social scientists and journalists), and finally, professional politicians, who constitute the party *aktiv*.[3] The party *aktiv* for Meyer is the dominant group. He compares it with the Board of Directors in a modern western corporation. The rank and file Communist Party members are as powerless to influence it as western shareholders with a single share are to control the Board. The party *aktiv* is 'the group which behaves as if it owned the Soviet Union, and which, therefore in fact does own it.'[4]

Mobility exists between the top elites and access is open to all according to 'ability, application, success . . . and conformism'.[5] The open recruitment pattern, therefore, does not make the USSR a class society in which the rulers would be selected predominantly from property-owning or controlling families.

The contrast between Mills's and Meyer's model may be shown diagrammatically. (See Chart 7.)

The models can be seen to differ in one chief respect. Meyer gives prime place to the party, unlike Mills who regards the parts of the ruling trinity as equal in power. Mills does allow for interaction between masses and government in what he calls the middle ranges of power. By this he means the activity of 'pressure groups' (unions, local interest) and the political process of local politics. Meyer's model of the USSR is more realistic than the others I have so far described. It takes into account group formations at the highest level and it stresses the importance of social mobility. It allows for change and for movement between the elites, or at least for the 'pressuring' of the dominant institution (the *Aktiv*) by other groups. For both Mills and Meyer,

[1] A. G. Meyer, 'USSR Incorporated', in *The Development of the USSR*, ed. D. W. Treadgold (Seattle, 1964).

[2] C. Wright Mills, *The Power Elite* (New York, 1956), Chapter 1.

[3] A. G. Meyer, *loc. cit.*, p. 21.

[4] *Ibid.*

[5] Meyer, p. 23.

CHART 7

C. W. MILLS' and A. G. MEYER'S ELITE MODELS

C. WRIGHT MILLS' POWER ELITE

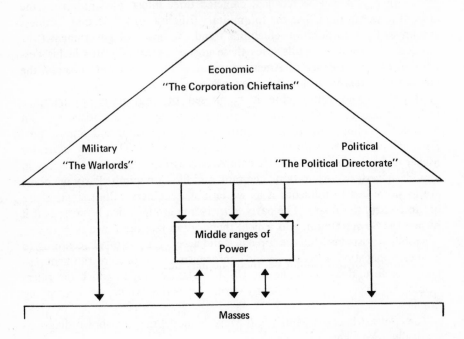

A.G. MEYER'S POLITICAL ELITE

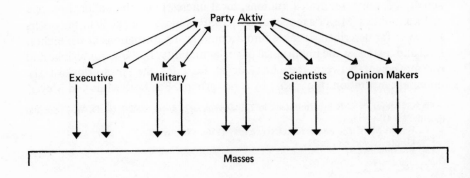

at the bottom of the pyramid rests the undifferentiated mass, which is acted on by the ruling elite.

Meyer also takes into account the political process, or the relationship between the party and other groups composing the ruling elite. He points out:

> Although relations between the various elements have fluctuated in the past and can be expected to do so in the future, one might generalise that in governing the society the professional politicians must carefully steer a middle course by balancing various groups of experts against each other as well as against the hard shell ideological dogmatists. Their problem is somewhat similar to that of professional politicians in constitutional governments who steer between various interest groups and the watchdogs of democratic and constitutional purity.[1]

Here Meyer seems to be suggesting that the party elite to some extent takes into consideration the preference of others. If this is so, then the notion of a ruling elite is undermined. Let us, in criticising elite theories, therefore, look more closely at what the notion of a ruling elite implies.

R. A. Dahl has pointed out that to define satisfactorily a ruling elite, its composition first, 'must be more or less definitely specified', second, the preferences of this elite must 'regularly prevail in cases of difference on key issues'.[2] If the wishes or desires of the elite do not regularly prevail, it follows that it is not a 'ruling' elite, for other groups or interests take preference in such cases over the wishes of the elite. To be meaningful, the ruling elite must be identified, for if it cannot be, then one may not assert that it, rather than other groups, wields decisive power.

The ruling elite must be unified in ideology and aim: there cannot be different parts of the elite pulling in opposite directions or advocating different policies. Were Mills's elite not unified, for example, then the triumvirate would constitute countervailing forces: say, the government elite wanting peace, low military expenditure and high control of the economy; the military demanding and supporting firm government control of the economy, a hawkish foreign policy and high military expenditure; big business seeking low government taxes, little control over the economy, but much military spending.

It must also be shown, therefore, that the groups forming the ruling elite (if there are more than one) do in fact have a common interest and not just a possible or theoretical one.

The models I have described earlier in this chapter (of bureaucracy, ruling class, degenerate workers' state, industrial society, and totalitarianism) are contradictory. Even those which define a ruling elite are not agreed on what constitutes it. Is the ruling elite composed of the party, or the bureaucracy, or both? At what level does the elite finish and shade off into the mass?

[1] A. G. Meyer, p. 21.

[2] R. A. Dahl, 'A Critique of the Ruling Elite Model', *American Political Science Review*, vol. 52 (June 1958), p. 464.

The bureaucratic, class and elitist models we have considered provide little empirical evidence to justify their assertions. Neither Aron, nor Djilas relate their *a priori* interpretation to the stratification system; rather they assume that the socio-political relationships they describe are self-evident.

Methodologically, the studies (excepting Armstrong's) are weak in that they ignore the decision-making process. Little attention is given to a number of decisions to test the extent to which the ruling elite gets its way against the wills of others. No attempt is made to determine the scope of the ruling elite, save that the totalitarian model by definition means that it is unlimited.

But it is possible to some extent to reconcile these models. The degenerate workers' state theory, the bureaucratic and the totalitarian model see a dichotomy between an elite and a mass; together with the state capitalist criticism, they all emphasise the bureaucratic elements of political power. The industrial society approach concentrates on aspects of the social system which are neither dichotomous on the one hand nor necessarily harmonious on the other. It emphasises differentiation, the interdependence of role structures and institutions; it regards 'interests' rather than classes or elites as being at the core of the political system. If one could distinguish between a higher and a lower level of decision-making in a modern society, the 'conflict' theories may best explain the former and the 'industrial society' the latter. Elements of both must be utilised if we are properly to understand Soviet society. Let us now turn from the discussion of purely theoretical or *a priori* models to describe empirically the Soviet power structure.

Reading No. 8
'Is the Bureaucracy a Ruling Class?'
Source:
L. Trotsky, *The Revolution Betrayed* (London: Plough Press, 1957), pp. 248-52.

Is the Bureaucracy a Ruling Class? Classes are characterised by their position in the social system of economy, and primarily by their relation to the means of production. In civilised societies, property relations are validated by laws. The nationalisation of the land, the means of industrial production, transport and exchange, together with the monopoly of foreign trade, constitute the basis of the Soviet social structure. Through these relations, established by the proletarian revolution, the nature of the Soviet Union as a proletarian state is for us basically defined.

In its intermediary and regulating function, its concern to maintain social ranks, and its exploitation of the state apparatus for personal goals, the Soviet bureaucracy is similar to every other bureaucracy, especially the fascist. But it is also in a vast way different. In no other regime has a bureaucracy ever achieved such a degree of independence from the dominating class. In bourgeois society, the bureaucracy represents the interests of a possessing and educated class, which has at its disposal innumerable means of everyday control over its administration of affairs. The Soviet bureaucracy has risen above a class which is hardly emerging from destitution and darkness, and has no tradition of dominion or command. Whereas the fascists, when they find themselves in power, are united with the big bourgeoisie by bonds of common interest, friendship, marriage, etc., the Soviet bureaucracy takes on bourgeois customs without having beside it a national bourgeoisie. In this sense we cannot deny that it is something more than a bureaucracy. It is in the full sense of the word the sole privileged and commanding stratum in the Soviet society.

Another difference is no less important. The Soviet bureaucracy has expropriated the proletariat politically in order by methods of *its own* to defend the social conquests. But the very fact of its appropriation of political power in a country where the principal means of production are in the hands of the state, creates a new and hitherto unknown relation between the bureaucracy and the riches of the nation. The means of production belong to the state. But the state, so to speak, 'belongs' to the bureaucracy. If these as yet wholly new relations should solidify, become the norm and be legalised, whether with or without resistance from the workers, they would, in the long run, lead to a complete liquidation of the social conquests of the proletarian revolution. But to speak of that now is at least premature. The proletariat has not yet said its last word. The bureaucracy has not yet created social supports for its dominion in the form of special types of property. It is compelled to defend state property as the source of its power and its income. In this aspect of its activity it still remains a weapon of proletarian dictatorship.

The attempt to represent the Soviet bureaucracy as a class of 'state capitalists' will obviously not withstand criticism. The bureaucracy has neither stocks nor bonds. It is recruited, supplemented and renewed in the manner of an administrative hierarchy, independently of any special property relations of its own. The individual bureaucrat cannot transmit to his heirs his rights in the exploitation of the state apparatus. The bureaucracy enjoys its privileges under the form of an abuse of power. It conceals its income; it pretends that as a special social group it does not even exist. Its appropriation of a vast share of the national income has the character of social parasitism. All this makes the position of the commanding Soviet stratum in the highest degree contradictory, equivocal and undignified, notwithstanding the completeness of its power and the smoke screen of flattery that conceals it.

Bourgeois society has in the course of its history displaced many political regimes and bureaucratic castes, without changing its social foundations. It has preserved itself against the restoration of feudal and guild relations by the superiority of its productive methods. The state power has been able either to co-operate with capitalist development, or put brakes on it. But in general the productive forces, upon a basis of private property and competition, have been working out their own destiny. In contrast to this, the property relations which issued from the socialist revolution are indivisibly bound up with the new state as their repository. The predominance of socialist over petty bourgeois tendencies is guaranteed, not by the automatism of the economy – we are still far from that – but by political measures taken by the dictatorship. The character of the economy as a whole thus depends upon the character of the state power.

A collapse of the Soviet regime would lead inevitably to the collapse of the planned economy, and thus to the abolition of state property. The bond of compulsion between the trusts and the factories within them would fall away. The more successful enterprises would succeed in coming out on the road of independence. They might convert themselves into stock companies, or they might find some other transitional form of property – one, for example, in which the workers should participate in the profits. The collective farms would disintegrate at the same time, and far more easily. The fall of the present bureaucratic dictatorship, if it were not replaced by a new socialist power, would thus mean a return to capitalist relations with a catastrophic decline of industry and culture.

But if a socialist government is still absolutely necessary for the preservation and development of the planned economy, the question is all the more important, upon whom the present Soviet government relies, and in what measure the socialist character of its policy is guaranteed. At the 11th Party Congress in March 1922, Lenin, in practically bidding farewell to the party, addressed these words to the commanding group: 'History knows transformations of all sorts. To rely upon conviction, devotion and other excellent spiritual qualities – that is not to be taken seriously in politics.' Being determines consciousness. During the last fifteen years, the government has changed its social composition even more deeply than its ideas. Since of all the strata of Soviet society the bureaucracy has best solved its own social problem, and is fully content with the existing situation, it has ceased to offer any subjective guarantee whatever of the socialist direction of its policy. It continues to preserve state property only to the extent that it fears the proletariat. This saving fear is nourished and supported by the illegal party of Bolshevik-Leninists, which is the most conscious expression of the socialist tendencies opposing that bourgeois reaction with which the Thermidorian bureaucracy is completely saturated. As a conscious political force the bureaucracy has betrayed the revolution. But a victorious revolution is fortunately not only a programme and a banner, not only political institutions, but also a system of social relations. To betray it is not enough. You have to overthrow it. The October Revolution has been betrayed by the ruling stratum, but not yet overthrown. It has a great power of resistance, coinciding with the established property relations, with the living force of the proletariat, the consciousness of its best elements, the impasse of world capitalism, and the inevitability of world revolution.

FOR FURTHER STUDY

INTRODUCTORY

Bell, Daniel. 'Ten Theories in Search of Reality: The Prediction of Soviet Behaviour in the Social Sciences', in *World Politics*, Vol. 10, No. 3, April 1958, pp. 327-65.

Churchward, L. G. 'Bureaucracy – USA:USSR', in *Coexistence*, Vol. 5, No. 2, 1968, pp. 201-10.

Mouzelis, Nicol P. *Organisation and Bureaucracy*. London. Routledge, 1967.

Rigby, T. H. 'Traditional, Market and Organizational Societies and the USSR', in *World Politics*, Vol. 16, July 1964, pp. 539-57.

Spiro, Herbert J. 'Totalitarianism', *International Encyclopedia of the Social Sciences*, Vol. 16, Macmillan 1968.

BASIC

Djilas, Milovan. *The New Class: An Analysis of the Communist System*. London: Unwin Books, 1966.

Friedrich, Carl J. and Z. K. Brzezinski. *Totalitarian Dictatorship and Autocracy*. New York: Praeger, 1956.

Friedrich, Carl J. and Z. K. Brzezinski. *Totalitarian Dictatorship and Autocracy*. (Revised Edition). New York: Praeger, 1966.

Inkeles, Alex and Raymond A. Bauer. *The Soviet Citizen*. Cambridge, Mass.: Harvard University Press, 1959.

Kuron, J. and K. Modzelewski. *An Open Letter to the Party*. London: International Socialism, n.d.

Marcuse, Herbert. *Soviet Marxism*. London: Routledge and Kegan Paul, 1958.

Meyer, Alfred G. 'USSR Incorporated', in D. W. Treadgold (ed.). *The Development of the USSR: An Exchange of Views*. Seattle: University of Washington Press, 1964, pp. 21-8.

Schachtman, Max. *The Bureaucratic Revolution*. New York: The Donald Press, 1962.

Szczepanski, Jan. 'Possibility of a Theory of Socialist Society', Institute of Philosophy and Sociology, Polish Academy of Sciences, *Empirical Sociology in Poland*. Warsaw: Polish Scientific Publishers, 1966, pp. 143-50.

Trotsky, L. *The Revolution Betrayed: The Soviet Union, What It Is and Where It Is Going*. New York: Pioneer Publishers, 1958.

Trotsky, L. *The Class Nature of the Soviet Union*. London: W. I. R. Publications, n.d.

SPECIALISED

Aron, Raymond. 'Social Structure and the Ruling Class', in L. S. Coser (ed.). *Political Sociology*. New York: Harper, 1966, pp. 48-100.

Armstrong, John A. 'Sources of Administrative Behaviour: Some Soviet and Western European Comparisons', in *American Political Science Review*, Vol. 59, Sept. 1965, pp. 643-55.

Beck, Carl. 'Bureaucratic Conservatism and Innovation in Eastern Europe', in *Comparative Political Studies*, Vol. 1, No. 2, July 1968.

Bell, Daniel. *The End of Ideology: On the Exhaustion of Political Ideas in the '50s.* New York: Collier Books, 1961.

Bendix, Reinhard. 'Bureaucracy and the Problem of Power', in R. K. Merton, *et. al.*, *Reader in Bureaucracy.* New York: Free Press, 1952, pp. 114-34.

Cliff, Tony. *Russia: A Marxist Analysis.* London: Socialist Review Pub., n.d., but 1964.

Cliff, Tony. 'The Theory of Bureaucratic Collectivism – A Critique', in *International Socialism*, No. 32, Spring 1968, pp. 13-18.

Dahl, Robert A. 'A Critique of the Ruling Elite Model', in *American Political Science Review*, Vol. 52, June 1958.

Fischer, George. *The Soviet System and Modern Society.* New York: Atherton Press, 1968.

Goldthorpe, J. 'Social Stratification in Industrial Society', in P. Halmos (ed.). *The Sociological Review Monograph*, No. 8, October 1964, pp. 97-122.

Gouldner, Alvin W. *Patterns of Industrial Bureaucracy.* New York: Free Press, 1964.

Kassof, Allen. 'The Administered Society: Totalitarianism without Terror', in *World Politics*, Vol 16, July 1964, pp. 558-75.

Kerr, Clark, J. T. Dunlop, F. H. Harbison, and C. A. Mayers. *Industrialism and Industrial Man – The Problems of Labour and Management in Economic Growth.* London: Heinemann, 1962.

Lasswell, H. D., *et. al. The Comparative Study of Elites.* Stanford, California: Stanford University Press, 1952.

Lenski, Gerhard E. *Power and Privilege: A Theory of Social Stratification.* New York: McGraw Hill, Inc., 1966.

Mills, C. Wright. *The Power Elite.* New York: Oxford University Press, 1956.
'The Structure of Power in American Society', *British Journal of Sociology*, Vol. 9, 1958, pp. 29-41.

Neumann, Franz. *Behemoth.* London: Oxford University Press, 1944.

Nove, Alec. *Was Stalin Really Necessary?: Some Problems of Soviet Political Economy.* London: Allen and Unwin, 1964.

Ossowski, S. *Class Structure in the Social Consciousness.* London: Routledge and Kegan Paul, 1963.

Parsons, Talcott. 'Characteristics of Industrial Societies', in C. E. Black (ed.). *The Transformation of Russian Society.* Cambridge, Mass.: Harvard University Press, 1960, pp. 13-41.

Weber, Max. 'The Essentials of Bureaucratic Organisation', in R. K. Merton, *et al. Reader in Bureaucracy.* New York: Free Press, 1952, pp. 60-84.

Wirth, Louis. 'Urbanism as a Way of Life', in Alvin J. Reiss, Jr. (ed.). *On Cities and Social Life.* Chicago: University of Chicago Press, 1964, pp. 18-26.

Wittfogel, Karl. *Oriental Despotism: A Comparative Study of Total Power.* New Haven, Conn.: Yale University Press, 1963.

7

THE FUNCTIONS OF
THE PARTY

A Systems Approach

Let us briefly describe the terms used in modern political science to analyse political systems. The political system of modern societies may be considered in terms of demands and supports, the articulation of inputs, the aggregation of interests, output and enforcement.

Political inputs make claims for the use of legitimate compulsion – for the allocation of resources (say claims for nationalisation), for the use of sanctions (for instance, a demand for 'enforcing the law' against the infringement of civil rights). Through the use of (or the threat of) physical compulsion the political system can effectively integrate the demands on it and impose its will on society to fulfil given goals. All structures (e.g. churches, family groups) have political aspects in so far as they make claims on bodies which claim the legitimate use of force. A church in Russia may want the right to proselytise – such a claim is a demand on the political system – while most aspects of its dogma and church organisation do not spill over into the political arena. One of the characteristics of the Soviet system is a diffuse boundary between the political and other social institutions over which party and state claim the right to use sanctions.

The political system has a structure: it is composed of units which receive and process inputs and which turn some of them into output – that is, policies or activity affecting the society. The structure and process of a political system may be illustrated more clearly by considering Diagram 3. The 'supports' represent sentiments approving of the 'regime' and more or less supporting its laws and the structures through which inputs are converted into outputs. The 'demands' are expectations of action by individuals and groups; demands create stress in a society. 'Inputs' are demands which are communicated to a part of the political structure, they are claims of which the political system may take cognisance. Not all demands are articulated into 'inputs', the system may be insensitive to certain claims made on it, or others may be ignored. Aggregation is the process by which inputs are collated, they may be either 'dropped' or turned into policies or decisions. The aggregation process consists of the interaction between interested persons and groups in

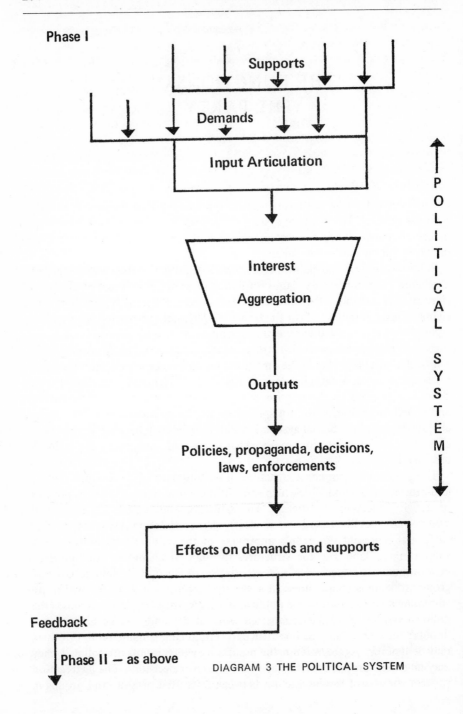

DIAGRAM 3 THE POLITICAL SYSTEM

which policies are thrashed out. Decisions or laws or actions, decided on in the polity, are the 'outputs' which affect the population. Finally, the effects of policies and enforcements on demands or supports are fed back by a similar process into the political system.

The stability or equilibrium of the social system as a whole, will depend on the way in which the political system can handle the demands generated in the society. Demands dysfunctional to the continued maintenance of the system (such as, say, the denationalisation of public property or the abolition of the Communist Party) must, in the USSR, be suppressed by the elites. Other demands, shared by a wide range of social strata (such as for better welfare facilities or more housing), may be channelled into 'outputs' which effectively reduce these areas of stress. The ability of a social system to flourish depends on the way the political system can adjust itself to the changing demands made on it. As Easton has put it: 'To persist, the system must be capable of responding with measures that are successful in alleviating the stress so created. To respond, the authorities at least must be in a position to obtain information about what is happening so that they may react insofar as they desire or are compelled to do so.[1] One of the striking facts about the Soviet regime, is its capacity to persist and to change.

CHART 8
LEADING POLITICAL BODIES

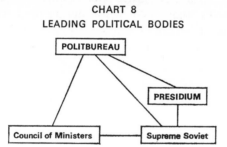

Notes:
At the time of writing (1969)
Brezhnev is Party General Secretary, and a member of the Supreme Soviet—not a member of the Council of Ministers or the Presidium, Kosygin is Prime Minister—a member of the Supreme Soviet (not Presidium) and the Politbureau, Podgorny is President—a member of the Supreme Soviet and Politbureau, but not of the Council of Ministers.
Membership of the Politbureau overlaps with that of the other organs as shown. Note the exclusion of members of the Presidium from the Council of Ministers.

How can we adapt this 'systems' model to the Soviet political system? Here we shall turn to discuss the political process as it affects the bodies described in a previous chapter: the party, the ministerial structure and the Soviets (parliaments). In the description of these bodies, it was asserted that the party's role was as important as that of the parliaments. We may begin to substantiate this statement by examining the way personnel overlaps between the elites. As shown in Chart 8 members of the Politbureau (party elite)

[1] David Easton, *A Systems Analysis of Political Life* (New York, 1965), p. 33.

H

are also in the Council of Ministers, the Presidium of the Supreme Soviet and, of lesser importance, the Supreme Soviet. At the highest reaches of state policy, the Politbureau may resolve conflicts or even deadlock reached in the Council of Ministers. Only in the Politbureau is there interlocking of party, ministerial and parliamentary elites.[1]

It seems logical to begin our analysis with the role of the party. We may examine its activity under three headings: the articulation and the aggregation of interests; the formation of values (ideology); an agency of enforcement.

The Articulation and Aggregation of Interests

It is notoriously difficult to describe the internal workings of a contemporary political party, even in western societies where many memoirs have been published and where party life is more accessible to observers. In state socialist societies the difficulty is compounded both by the general secrecy surrounding the political process and by the emphasis placed on party unity. Many western studies have described the process of Soviet politics, but they have done so in terms of individuals and their factionalism in the party.

We are fortunate, however, in having a good historical study of the party, based on original materials. The articulation of interests in the party has been described in Fainsod's study of Smolensk during the inter war period. He shows that while local secretaries played an important role in transmitting political instructions (or outputs) received from the centre, the process also worked the other way:

> There were also times when the *obkom*[2] secretary had to be a middleman or broker, mediating between the rock-bottom needs of his constituents and the niggardly resources which the centre made available to meet them. As a representative of the interests of the *oblast*, and indeed as a condition of his own survival, the *oblast* secretary had to press for allocations of supplies to the *oblast*, for budgetary appropriations which would enable him to fulfill the commitments which the centre imposed on him. In periods of distress, such as harvest failures, he had to plead for a lifting of the burden, for special assistance which was infrequently and only grudgingly forthcoming. What was required was negotiating skill of a high order, but it had to be supported by an overall record of successful performance of function. The long reign of Rumyantsev in Smolensk (1929-37) testifies to his adroitness in navigating between central and local pressures, though when disgrace finally came, it was complete and crushing.[3]

Written reports were sent to the Central Committee secretariat on all aspects of the local party's work. Officials frequently travelled to Moscow to make

[1] They overlap too in the party's Central Committee which is not shown on the chart.
[2] Regional or Province Party Committee.
[3] Merle Fainsod, *Smolensk Under Soviet Rule* (1958), p. 76.

oral statements. Sometimes special reports of failures were called for; here Fainsod cites an example of the local secretary asking for grain quotas to be reduced.[1] Of course, the local party organs tended to 'hush up' deficiencies and it is interesting to note that the secret police provided its own reports direct to Stalin and 'not infrequently they stimulated drastic intervention by the centre in the affairs of the oblast.'[2]

John Armstrong's study of the Ukrainian Party apparatus in the post World War II period, throws some light on the political process in the regions and the role of the party. Armstrong points out that 'types of training, career lines, and association in common activities tend to form cross-institutional alignments which, as power groups, may often be more important than formal structural divisions.'[3] The Ukrainian Party convened Congresses and Central Committee meetings regularly, even after the Great Purge. The Ukrainian Party elite tended to consult with other interested and affected groups when decisions were being made. Though rather circumspect on this score, Armstrong concludes: 'Whatever the reasons for the peculiarities of Ukrainian apparatus operation before 1953 as compared to other segments of the Soviet apparatus, they did tend towards the oligarchic, as contrasted to the auto-cratic system of rule.'[4]

Philip D. Stewart in a more recent analysis of a party committee in the Stalingrad *obkom* concludes: 'The evident tendency of the party secretaries to consult with interest groups in the policy-making process indicates that now many of these institutional interest groups may be able to translate their potential influence into actual influence'.[5] Channels of access to decision making are controlled by the First Secretaries. Conferences are transmission belts to convey top policy to the masses and access to the decision-making process: 'It does appear', continues Stewart, 'that a certain amount of criticism is directed by the speakers at particular officials, or at the way particular policies are implemented, or at the failure of the party officials to deal effec-tively with particular problems. At the same time, and this is the crucial point, the participants in the conferences . . . speak from a position of extreme weakness.'[6] But other non-party groups are consulted 'in open and frank dis-cussions in bureau sessions'.[7] The party articulates other group interests: of particular potential influence, says Stewart, are the Soviets, industrial managers, *Komsomol* and trade-union leaders, cultural-educational groups

---

[1] *Op. cit.*, p. 82.

[2] *Op. cit.*, p. 84.

[3] John A. Armstrong, *The Soviet Bureaucratic Elite, A Case Study of the Ukrainian Apparatus* (New York, 1959), p. 146.

[4] *Op. cit.*, p. 149.

[5] Philip D. Stewart, *Political Power in the Soviet Union* (Indianapolis, 1968), p. viii.

[6] *Ibid.*, p. 195.

[7] *Ibid.*, p. 197.

and the police. The party secretaries are key men in the interest articulation process: '. . . the observed tendency of the party secretaries to consult with interested groups, to listen to them, to encourage their participation in at least the public aspects of *obkom* activity must not be overlooked. Compared to the period of the thirties, more institutional interest groups now appear to have the opportunity to exert some influence in *obkom* decision making.[1]

Robert Conquest has also uncovered other examples of regional interests being articulated in the party. When discussing the Soviet policy of the merging of nations into a unitary state he points out that in a number of republics, there was resistance among the local party leaderships. 'In 1959, Azerbaidzhan was purged. The condemned First Secretary, Mustafeev, was accused at the Plenum of the local Central Committee on 16-17 June 1959 of "causing bewilderment in the completely clear language question" . . . The sending of the head of the Party Organs Department (Union Republics), Semichastny, to take over the key Second Secretaryship in Baku was a crisis move'.[2] 'Another example may be taken from Latvia where in September 1959, the new local secretary, Pelse, 'attacked "certain comrades" who had tried artificially to hold up the process of population movement specifically called for . . . Their motive was said to be "a false and groundless fear that the Latvian Republic would lose its national features." '[3]

These statements, which are probably only the tips of icebergs, indicate that the party sometimes articulates interests on a regional basis.

T. H. Rigby's discussion of the role of the party in modern Russia makes clear that the lower levels of the party organisation, party branches and regional committees, for instance, discuss issues and make recommendations. 'In these various ways, new ideas and facts are brought to the attention of the policy makers and they learn something about group preferences.'[4] The party apparatus acts as an information gathering and processing machine: it receives messages from the rank and file members and party groups, which are acted on at higher levels of the party secretariat. At this stage, the aggregation of interests is performed. The Central Committee, during Khrushchev's leadership, was an arena for interest articulation and aggregation. Zbigniew Brzezinski writes: 'Khrushchev's practice of holding enlarged Central Committee plenums, with representatives of other groups present, seems to have been a step toward formalising a more regular consultative procedure . . . Such enlarged plenums provided a consultative forum, where policies could be debated, views articulated and even some contradictory interests resolved.'[5]

[1] *Ibid.* pp. 200, 213.
[2] Robert Conquest, *Russia After Khrushchev* (1965), p. 208.
[3] *Kommunist Sovetskoy Latvii*, no. 9 (1959), cited by Conquest, *op. cit.*, p. 209.
[4] T. H. Rigby, *Communist Party Membership in the USSR 1917-1967* (New Jersey, 1968), p. 40.
[5] Zbigniew K. Brzezinski, *Ideology and Power in Soviet Politics* (New York, 1967), p. 119.
See M. P. Gehlen, *The Communist Party of the Soviet Union* (Bloomington 1969) pp. 66–70.

At lower levels of the party, Ralf Dahrendorf has aptly characterised the role of party groups as a medium of interest articulation as follows:

On the one hand, the party organisation and its varied affiliations serve as a gigantic institute of opinion research which, through meetings and 'discussions', tries to explore the 'wishes and feelings of the people'. On the other hand, the same meetings and 'discussions' that are necessary for this as well as for many another purpose bring in to contact the otherwise scattered members of the subjected quasi-group and form the nuclei of actual and future conflicts.[1]

The body which plays an important role in aggregation is the secretariat of the Central Committee.

It is generally believed in the West that the secretariat is dominant in the party. As Leonard Schapiro has put it: a feature of the party (in 1952) was 'the predominance within the party of the apparatus of officials and secretaries who formed a small minority of around three per cent. By virtue of the authority which they had acquired in the course of years, not without bloody conflict, these officials could dominate elections, discussions and decisions inside all party organisations throughout the country'.[2] But the role of the secretariat in decision-making is obscure. It is a field of Kremlinological speculation. Here is how a recent commentator describes the power position of Suslov, a party Secretary.

The question remains whether Suslov figured as the real second-in-command at and after the Twenty-third Congress. In terms of protocol this was undeniable. Throughout the Congress, he sat immediately on Brezhnev's right; in the Secretariat he was in second place, in the Politbureau fourth, after Brezhnev, Kosygin and Podgorny. Since the latter two were entitled to these positions by virtue of being Head of Government and Head of State, Suslov may be regarded as having been virtually in second or third place within the collective leadership, his influence being undoubtedly greater than Podgorny's and possibly even than Kosygin's.[3]

But this kind of methodology tells us nothing about the articulation or aggregation functions of the secretariat. We cannot say much more than that the various departments of the Central Committee, described above, define and clarify policy proposals for the Politbureau. We do not know how this advice is received, of whether it conflicts or augments that of other institutions and groups, such as the police, army or industrial ministries. Abdurakhman Avtorkhanov has constructed a very interesting and informative table in which the functions of the departments are defined. This is reproduced (shortened) in Table 16.[4] But its use is limited by the fact that it does not illustrate just how the functions described are performed.

[1] Ralf Dahrendorf, *Class and Class Conflict in an Industrial Society* (London, 1959), pp. 312-3.
[2] Leonard Schapiro, *The Communist Party of the Soviet Union* (London, 1960), p. 548.
[3] M. Tatu, *Power in the Kremlin* (1969), p. 509.
[4] Abdurakhman Avtorkhanov, *The Communist Party Apparatus* (Chicago, 1966), pp. 201-5.

Table 16. Distribution of Organs of State Administration and Public Organisations among the Departments of the Central Committee of the CPSU

Department of the Central Committee of the CPSU	*FUNCTIONS*
Party Organs Department	(a) selection of workers for apparatus of the Central Committee of the CPSU (b) registration, selection and allocation of workers in regional committees, provincial committees and central committees of constituent republics (c) leadership and allocation of trade union and *Komsomol* cadres (d) sanctioning appointment to military, secret police and diplomatic cadres (e) sanctioning appointments of leading workers in the USSR, constituent and autonomous republics.
Department of Propaganda Agitation	(a) registration, training and allocation of professional propaganda cadres (b) ensuring propagation of Marxism-Leninism in all spheres of party, state and public life (c) leadership of propaganda and agitation apparatus in party, state and public organisations.
Agricultural Department	(a) registration and allocation of agricultural cadres (b) issue of instructions to agricultural departments of regional committees, provincial committees and central committees of constituent republics (c) control and inspection of state agricultural organs.
Department of Science, Higher Education Institutes and Schools	(a) registration and allocation of scientific and school cadres (b) control and supervision of scientific and scholastic institutes (c) issuing of instructions to similar departments in regional committees, provincial committees and central committees of constituent republics.
Department of Culture	(a) registration and allocation of culture cadres (b) supervision and control of cultural educational institutes of state and public organisations.
Department of Heavy Industry	(a) registration and allocation of cadres (b) inspection and control of administrative organs of heavy industry.
Department of Light Industry	(a) registration and allocation of cadres (b) inspection and control of administrative organs of light industry.
Department for Machine Construction	(a) registration and allocation of cadres (b) inspection and control of machine tool industry.
Department of Defence Industry	(a) registration and allocation of cadres (b) inspection and control of administrative organs of defence industry.

Department of Chemical Industry	(a) registration and allocation of cadres (b) inspection and control of administrative organs of fuel industry.
Department for Construction	(a) registration and allocation of cadres (b) inspection and control of administrative organs of construction industry.
Transportation Department	(a) registration and allocation of transportation cadres (b) inspection and control of administrative organs of transportation and communications industry.
Department of Trade, Finance and Planning Organs	(a) registration and allocation of cadres (b) inspection and control of administrative organs for trade, finance and planning.
Administration Department	(a) registration and allocation of cadres (b) inspection of administration organs (the administration department of the Central Committee only inspects these organs; the corresponding secretaries of the Central Committee of the CPSU have direct control over them).
Foreign Department	(a) registration and allocation of international cadres of the CPSU (b) communications and controlling contacts with foreign Communist parties.
Department for Socialist (bloc) Countries	communications and contacts with Communist parties.
Department of Security	guard and security for members of the Central Committee and the government.
Chief Political Administration of Soviet Army and Navy	(a) registration and allocation of political cadres in army and navy (b) party and political leadership of the armed forces.
Special Sector	(a) secret registration and secret affairs of leading cadres (b) direction of personal secretariat of first secretary of the Central Committee.
Party Commission of the Central Committee	(a) party court for violation of party statutes and programme (b) supreme appeal court for party punishment and expulsion.
General Department	general office of the Central Committee of the CPSU.
Administration of the Central Committee of the CPSU	conduct of administrative and economic affairs of the Central Committee of the CPSU.

Source: Abdurakhman Avtorkhanov, *The Communist Party Apparatus* (1966), pp. 201-5.

Some examples of interest articulation in the party are available from studies of party congresses. Wolfgang Leonhard, for instance, has shown that at the Twentieth Party Congress many interested parties spoke about the reform of educational policy. The Chairman of the *Komsomol* (Young Communist League) said that insufficient training was given in practical skills. Khrushchev advocated the setting up of boarding schools, presumably to reduce the influence of family background in children's socialisation. The President of the Academy of Sciences spoke against an 'excessively "practical approach" '. Another scientist advocated a closer link between theory and practice.[1] These are only glimpses of political reality which may be caught by the observer. In the party behind the scenes, many interests – teachers, regional authorities, industry, universities and the Academy of Sciences – articulated their views before the leadership finally put forward the educational reforms. As much of this activity was performed outside the party it is the subject of the next chapter.

The Central Committee of the party is an arena in which various interests may be voiced. It is composed of members of the CPSU Politbureau and secretariat, the first secretaries of the republican communist parties, the chairman of the Council of Ministers and some of the chairmen of the republican Councils of Ministers; in addition some other government ministers, the first secretary of the *Komsomol*, the chairman of the Trade Union Council and the president of the Academy of Sciences are also members. The meetings of the Central Committee serve for the various interests of these groups to be articulated. Gehlin has shown that under Khrushchev speakers at Central Committee plenums were specialists and many were not even members of the Central Committee; under Brezhnev, however, party secretaries have been more conspicuous.[2] The meetings are, to use Gehlin's term, 'information forums' and though different points of view are expressed, no opposing sides are publicly taken. The Central Committee then may be regarded as one of the important bodies in which information is articulated which is necessary for effective decision-making in the USSR. While the Central Committee enables the articulation of interests to take place, its size (in 1966 there were 195 full members and 165 candidates) and the shortness of its duration as a deliberating body (it usually has about two or three sessions a year each lasting not more than a week) make it a less important instrument in the aggregation process.

It is at the highest levels of the party apparatus that policy decisions are aggregated and factional differences finally resolved. The Politbureau is a crucial organ. To accommodate the greater activity in Soviet society, it has grown in size from five (1919-21) to eleven in 1966-67; in 1960 it had twenty

[1] W. Leonhard, *The Kremlin Since Stalin* (1962), pp. 149-50.
[2] Gehlin, *op. cit.* pp. 63–6.

members.[1] Group conflict may be illustrated by the struggle between Khrushchev and his rivals (the 'anti-party' group). Amongst other things, Molotov and his associates opposed Khrushchev's softer foreign policy: 'He [Molotov] opposed the fundamental proposition worked out by the party on the possibility of preventing wars in the present conditions, on the possibility of different ways of transition to socialism in different countries, on the necessity of strengthening contacts between the CPSU and progressive parties abroad'.[2] In June 1957, other disagreements at the summit of the party came to the fore. The 'anti-party' group opposed Khrushchev and his policies: 'It recruited supporters, held secret meetings behind the Presidium's back, placed cadres with the intention of seizing power'[3] and Khrushchev's opponents had a majority in the Presidium. The issues at dispute were the policies of industrial administration, the virgin lands campaign and foreign policy. Bulganin has recalled: 'In my office the anti-party group (Malenkov, Kaganovich and Molotov) gathered and intrigued about its anti-party factional work. Thus, if at a definite stage I behaved correctly and adhered to party principles, later I in fact shared with them the entire anti-party dirt.'[4] Khrushchev appealed to the Central Committee which reversed the decision and a new Presidium and Secretariat was elected. Khrushchev's opponents were relegated to obscurity. Here personal and policy differences were resolved by the exclusion of one group. In most instances, it is likely that conflicts are internally resolved by compromise. One of the tasks of party leadership is to contrive policies which do not alienate social and political interests. Khrushchev in turn fell from grace because he violated this principle of politics.[5] As a Soviet commentator put it:

... in recent years there had been more and more defects in his methods of leadership. The principles of collective leadership were violated. When an idea entered his head he hurried to put it into operation without due thought and without discussion with others. This applied especially to agriculture.

There had been many discussions and disagreements with Khrushchev in the Presidium, which finally felt that his methods had exceeded all possible limits and had become an obstacle.[6]

The aggregation of interests in the USSR is a more intractable problem than in liberal democracies. As pointed out earlier, the ideology finds no place for

---

[1] Dan N. Jacobs, 'The Politburo in the First and Fifth Decades of Soviet Power', in Kurt London, *The Soviet Union: A Half Century of Communism* (Baltimore, Maryland, 1968), p. 61.

[2] Radio Moscow's English Service, 3 July 1957. Cited by R. Conquest, *Power and Policy in the USSR* (1961), p. 265.

[3] *Pravda*, 7 July 1957, cited by Conquest, *op. cit.*, p. 311.

[4] *Pravda*, 19 December 1958, cited by Conquest, p. 314.

[5] See below, pp. 240–3.

[6] Report of British Communist Party visit to Moscow, cited by L. Churchward, *Contemporary Soviet Government* (1968), p. 287.

H*

group dissensus. No open institutional channels exist to resolve fundamental disagreements. The party plays an important role in articulating interests. The succession of the head of state is not institutionalised through regular popular election, as in the USA. There are, therefore, intense *internal* struggles within the party elite, which have the character of personal rivalry. These manoeuvrings are the food of the Kremlinologists. (Elite conflict is discussed further below pp. 236–43.)

The Aggregation and Articulation of Values: Ideology

In Chapter 1 was mentioned the importance of ideology as a means of power, as a manipulative device by which elites may ensure conformity of the masses to their will. This is the particular means at the disposal of the party to ensure compliance. The party itself has no armed forces directly under its command, neither does it have legal power over economic production enterprises. It does have a monopoly, however, in the aggregation and articulation of values. It defines the charter, the general goals of the society.

The Transition from Socialism to Communism

In earlier chapters of this book were described the main 'stages' or ideal types of society which are defined by Marxist thinkers. We have seen that Soviet Russia has passed through the dictatorship of the proletariat to the socialist stage. One of the chief roles of the party now is the articulation of policies and programmes for the achievement of the future, for the creation of a communist society. In doing so, the party must take into account a number of factors. Ideological values (say the primacy of Marxism) generated in the past cannot be ignored, but neither can specific popular demands (say for better housing). The last party programme, published in 1961,[1] is an example of the width and nature of the party's ideological output. It has, of course, been modified by subsequent development and 'brought up to date' by other pronouncements, but it still provides a good indication of Soviet official ideology.

The New Programme of the CPSU was an attempt by Khrushchev to spell out some of the general goals deriving from the communist belief system. It is instructive to study them, not because they are 'true' in a philosophical sense, but because they indicate the kinds of expectations generated by the party elite, and their view of social change. *The Programme* covered a wide range of activities: economic growth and management, the standard of living, the growth of democracy, the role of the state and party, the tasks of international relations, education and science. We shall discuss some of the alterations to

[1] *The Programme of the CPSU* (Adopted at the 22nd Congress 1961) Reprinted in *Soviet Booklet No. 83* (London, 1961).

this policy which have been made since Khrushchev's departure, but we may use the Programme to illustrate the kind of values the party articulates.[1]

No radical changes were envisaged in the 'coming of communism'. Money as a means of exchange was to continue. Income differentials for specialised and skilled work would persist but decline. Some services and commodities were planned to be taken out of the price system, transport and public catering being important in this regard. In the economic sphere, the principle of 'one-man management' was to be modified by the institution of various advisory committees within the factory (see Chapter 10). While power was to be delegated to the factory level, no far-reaching proposals, say for 'workers' control' were put. The position of women was to be improved by the provision of collective services, but the monogamous family as a unit was to continue. Khrushchev advocated the development of boarding schools to reduce the disparities between various social groups, but this policy has since been modified.

In Marxist theory, the abolition of capitalism and the advent of communism leads to the 'withering away' of the state. Lenin made this explicit in *State and Revolution*: 'So long as the state exists, there is no freedom; when freedom exists, there will be no state'. In the USSR, though certain aspects of administration have been taken over by 'voluntary institutions', the form of government apparatus advocated by Khrushchev was that of the 'state of the entire people, expressing the interests and will of the people as a whole'.[2] A state apparatus, he argued, would be necessary (at least until 1980) for the organisation of material construction, to 'exercise control' over work and consumption, to maintain 'law and order' and socialist property and to fortify the regime against external attack.[3] Indeed, only with the 'triumph and consolidation' of socialism in the world arena would the state become unnecessary. Until such a time, however, some of the functions of the existing government would be transferred for administration to voluntary bodies. Trade unions, and the Young Communist League (*Komsomol*) would take over responsibility for aspects of the management of enterprises, for supervising personal conduct and for the enforcement of law and order. The 'withering away' of the state was to begin with greater participation in administration at the lower levels. Soviet policy here, if implemented, would certainly have meant an increase in participation in the decision-making processes and a decline in the authority of the state. Also, the provisions were intended to give much more power to the party at the expense of the state. Since Khrushchev's

[1] *The Programme* is still cited in the school textbook of social studies, where reference is also made to other party pronouncements. See *Obshchestvovedenie* (Moscow, 1969), especially pp. 324–5 and the English edition of this work: G. Shakhnazarov (ed.), *Man, Science and Society* (Moscow, 1965).

[2] *The Programme*, p. 68.

[3] *Ibid.*

demise the role of voluntary organisations has been played down and the role of the state apparatus has been re-emphasised. The idea of 'public self-government' has been given rather less prominence.

One of the more extravagant claims of the Programme was that Soviet growth, economically speaking, would 'surpass the strongest and richest capitalist country, the USA', and by 1980 the Soviet Union would outdistance American *per capita* production.[2] Since Khrushchev's fall these predictions have been dropped.[3] This is an interesting example of the way in which, when ideological output (propaganda) and reality get too obviously incongruent, the ideology undergoes a modification. In this case it was simply not further mentioned. Here we may draw attention to the flexibility of Soviet doctrine on particulars. As Barrington Moore has pointed out: 'On the whole, one is likely to be more impressed with the flexibility of Communist doctrine than with its rigidity. Its elasticity has proved its value in the ideology of that strange alloy of authoritarian and populist practices, the Soviet Union itself, as well as in its adaptive forms in the Soviet satellite states . . .'[4]

The role of the Soviet Union in international relations[5] as defined in the Programme is two-fold: on the one-hand, to support national-liberation movements struggling against foreign colonial powers, and on the other, to maintain peaceful relations with the leading capitalist states. Revolutions by oppressed peoples were to be the prime responsibility of the oppressed and not of the USSR, aid being limited to material and moral support, though excluding military intervention. This modest policy might be contrasted with a more thoroughgoing Marxism (as adopted by Mao) emphasising the antagonistic contradictions in the world.

The ideological programme of the CPSU envisaged very few radical changes. The emphasis was, and still is, on catching up with the West. There is no intention of abolishing money, or the state, or the party, or the monogamous family. The 'official goals' are to increase the Gross National Product within the framework of a publicly-owned, but more decentralised, industry; to involve more citizens in the administration of public affairs within the framework of a strong state apparatus; to keep family and social life on the same lines as at present. These then are the goals of the Soviet regime, as described

[1] Roger E. Kanet, 'The Rise'and Fall of the All-People's State', *Soviet Studies*, vol. 20 (July 1968), p. 88. See also discussion of party-state relations in Chapter 10.

[2] *Ibid.*, p. 46.

[3] See M. Tatu, *Power in the Kremlin* (1969), pp. 491-3.

[4] Barrington Moore Jr, *Soviet Politics – The Dilemma of Power* (1965 ed.), p. 416. For further discussion of detailed changes since Khrushchev, see Carl A. Linden *Khrushchev and the Soviet Leadership 1957-1964* (The Johns Hopkins Press, Baltimore, 1966), Chapter 10. See also Wolfgang Leonhard, 'Politics and Ideology in the Post-Khrushchev Era', in A. Dallin and T. B. Larson, *Soviet Politics since Khrushchev* (New Jersey, 1968), pp. 71-72.

[5] See also Chapter 4, above.

by the Communist Party's latest official programme. They are significantly different from the notion of a communist society as conceived of by classical Marxists.

The ideology of Soviet communism as summarised in its *Programme* and subsequent developments, mark a shift in the role of Marxist theory. In Chapter 1, we saw that Marxism-Leninism emphasised the values of internal class war. Now the official Soviet doctrine is one of social harmony; the chiliastic vision of a Utopia has to a great extent been replaced by the goals of higher standards of living. Daniel Bell has remarked that the notion of the transformation of the world, an important aspect of Marxist theory, has become exhausted (at least in the 1950s).[1] In the USSR, present ideological trends seem to confirm Bell's view.[2] Recent developments under the collective leadership, have minimised the emotional appeal of communist ideology even more; the communist Utopia has been replaced by the more pragmatic utilitarian and practical policy of Kosygin and Brezhnev. At the Twentieth Congress, Stalin and the personality cult were denounced; at the Twenty-Second (1961), the *The Programme of the CPSU* attempted to redefine goals for the 1980s; the Twenty-Third Congress (1966) saw the adoption of a more cautious policy.[3] These changes over time also indicate a different emphasis given to the kinds of sanctions mentioned earlier. In destroying Stalin's reliance on terror and coercive sanctions, Khrushchev sought to replace them with normative controls. Since his fall these in turn have been replaced by utilitarian sanctions (i.e. financial rewards – see p. 1 above).

Here, however, we must be sure not to confuse the *official* ideology, propagated by the Communist Party, with ideological undercurrents, the views of alienated groupings, who reject communist ideology or, at least, do not take it seriously. Such ideological alternatives are broadly three in number. First, are groups who want a return to 'Genuine Marxism-Leninism', second, are those who advocate the 'Christian ideology', and third, is a group believing in a 'liberal ideology', wanting 'a transition to a Western-type democratic society . . . [maintaining] the principle of social and state property'.[4]

The question arises as to what kind of effect party ideology now has: does it effectively bind elites and masses, does it realistically explain to Soviet man his 'historical and social setting'? Is it simply a verbal gloss to justify political action, or is it even irrelevant meaningless verbiage? The brief answer is that it

[1] See *The End of Ideology* (New York, 1961), pp. 396-7.

[2] See his 'Marxism-Leninism: A Doctrine on the Defensive', in M. M. Drachkovitch, *Marxist Ideology in the Contemporary World* (New York, 1966); also my paper 'Ideology and Sociology in the USSR', *British Journal of Sociology*, vol. 21 (March 1970).

[3] See L. Schapiro, 'The Twenty-Third Congress of the CPSU', *Survey*, no. 60 (July 1966), and Gehlin's description of goals specified in *Pravda* editorials, *op. cit.* p. 105.

[4] Andrei Amalrik, 'Will the USSR survive until 1984?' *Survey*, no. 73 (Autumn 1969), p. 51. See below p. 252 *et seq.*

has all these effects. As Alfred G. Meyer has pointed out, Soviet citizens do talk the language of *Pravda* editorials.[1] In a very nebulous sense individuals accept the goals of communism, just as not very religious citizens in Christian countries still believe in the existence of God. As far as policy-making is concerned, purely ideological considerations restrict the range of policy decisions: for example, the abolition of collective farms, a return to a 'free enterprise' economy in either agricultural or industrial products, freedom of religious and anti-communist propaganda are all precluded on *ideological* grounds. This can perhaps be put another way: the elites who shape policy would lose some of their power if any of these policies were effected. The ideology defends their political interests, it is a method of ensuring compliance. On the other hand, the passage of time itself has enabled some aspects of the 'world view' of communism to be internalised by Soviet citizens. In the absence of a scientific social survey,[2] it is extremely difficult to estimate how far the party's ideology is rejected by Soviet citizens, how far reality so conflicts with the ideological explanation that belief in it is lost. An attempt has been made by Peter Reddaway to show how Soviet literature portrays such a loss of faith. From Tarsis's *Ward Seven*, he cites the character Almazov who: 'lost any notion of what the people round him meant by good, evil, morality, convictions, belief; it seemed to him that for a long time none of all these things had existed in his country . . . Words had ceased to have any resonance, they had no force, they rustled like dry, fallen leaves – a sort of lifeless garbage'.[3] The rejection of party ideology by other Soviet writers, such as Sinyavski and Daniel is some evidence of ideological dissent. Important here is the point that unlike Tarsis, they do not oppose the values of the Soviet state, rather they oppose the violation of these values by the present elites. Not only at their trial but also in one of the letters recently smuggled out of the USSR, Daniel calls for the proper enforcement of the law and not its violation.[4] Similarly, the demands voiced by Tatars to return to the Crimea are based on the rights guaranteed in the Constitution.[5] Here we have an example of a more independent role played by official ideology: it is a measure of conduct, to which the elites should conform. But the apparently sincere denunciation of such writers as Kuznetsov by many Soviet citizens and the ready acceptance by them of 'official' explanations – 'anti-Soviet propaganda',

[1] 'The Functions of Ideology in the Soviet Political System', *Soviet Studies*, vol. 18, (no. 3), 1966, p. 276.

[2] Amalrik has estimated that more than a thousand people have protested against illegality between 1966 and 1969. Most are intellectuals and are isolated pockets of resistance, *loc. cit.*, p. 53. Again, because one opposes some aspects of Soviet life, it does not mean that one rejects all aspects.

[3] P. B. Reddaway, 'Aspects of Ideology in the Soviet Union', *Soviet Studies*, vol. 18 (no. 4), 1966, p. 475.

[4] *The Observer*, 29 June 1969.

[5] See *The Observer*, 27 July 1969.

'pro-capitalist sentiments' – leads to caution in generalising from such sources. As an antidote to them is a letter sent to the West by a teacher of Marxist philosophy: '. . . I joined the party firstly because I believe in the victory of what it stands for, secondly because it filled my own life with great things and gave me good, genuine comrades. Understand me . . . the party is for me the most precious thing in life, it has fused for me with the idea of mother and people, conscience and honour'.[1]

It seems likely that some values of the regime, of the October Revolution and its aspirations, embodied in ideology are generally accepted, 'compliance' here has been successfully achieved. It provides an orientation to the past, present and future for the majority of the Soviet people. The development of science and social science is a limiting factor to the application of ideology. In specialised professionalised studies, such as physics, engineering and even sociology new vocabularies and explanations of segments of the universe make historical materialism irrelevant. In these specific areas of life, lip-service is paid to and sometimes an ideological gloss is put on the macro-theory discussed above. The language, tools and outlook of science become world-wide and replace aspects of ideology embodied in the political creeds of the West and state socialist societies. But they do not replace it completely.

Political ideology is not politically neutral: it tends to support those in positions of power, and behind ideological statements are social groups which ideology serves. The fact that since Khrushchev's replacement by Kosygin and Brezhnev there have been slight shifts in the emphasis of doctrine, suggests that there may be group interests in Soviet society to which the ideological elite is responding. Such changes in ideology may represent the climax of their efforts to reduce political 'stress'. There can be no doubt that since the October Revolution the dominant official ideology of Soviet Marxism has changed. It has adapted itself to a new world: from challenging a *status quo* to defending it. The content of the ideology has also altered in response to the modern technical-industrial structure of Soviet society and to the groups thrown up by it: now there is not only a party-political elite but also other institutional groups of whom the party ideologists must take cognisance. Let us now turn to analyse the interaction of the party with other such social groups.

The Party as an Agency of Political Output and Social Control

The party not only articulates and aggregates interests, but has the function of enforcing its policy. The two most important ways it does this are by an ideological monopoly, discussed above and by the control of personnel, or cadres (the *nomenklatura*). The enforcement activity of the Soviet political

---

[1] Cited by Jack Miller, *Life in Russia To-day* (1969), p. 7.

system, however, is less a function of the party than of the government apparatus.

The recruitment and placement of personnel in the highest decision-making posts remains the party's prerogative. Even officially, when Kosygin put his list of ministers to the Supreme Soviet for its considerations he reported that its composition had been approved by the Party's Central Committee.[1] In this respect the CPSU is not unlike ruling parties in western societies, though membership of the party is necessary for a much wider range of jobs in the USSR than here. How far party membership is merely a formal requirement, demanding no firm ideological position or political conviction, cannot at present be accurately assessed. Much may depend on the post: for engineering and scientific work, party membership is probably a formality, but for leading jobs in literary journals or foreign affairs, or the secret police, not only party membership, but also reliable political beliefs are necessary.

At all levels, the party organisation is responsible for the supervision of the selection of personnel to leading positions – in factories, unions, collective farms, administration. Under Stalin, between 1934 and 1939, party organs selected and promoted to 'leading state and party posts' over a half-million Bolsheviks and others 'standing close to the party'.[2] Lloyd Churchward has estimated that in the mid-60s more than 600,000 or upwards of 35 per cent of all administrative positions are subject to party control.[3] The party, however, is confronted with the personnel (or 'cadres') departments of Ministries and enterprises, which are responsible for appointments in their respective fields. The party may veto a nomination on political criteria, but it seems doubtful whether this is necessary now in the large majority of cases. Though it does sometimes happen that 'party men' may be rewarded with sinecures, appointments in industrial ministries are made on functional grounds and it is in the interest of both party and ministry to select the most efficient person. This may be demonstrated by examining the background of party secretaries and government administrators.

Jerry F. Hough's study of the party and industry[4] shows that the leading administrators in ministries tend to be men of a different type from the party secretaries in ideological and even industrial posts. The available data on new USSR ministers and deputy ministers (a total of 63) appointed in the 1950s showed that they joined the party on average at the age of 28 or 29 years, and that all had had an engineering education. 'By the 1950s the men

<hr>

[1] See report of proceedings of first session of Seventh Supreme Soviet, *Soviet News*, 5 August 1966, p. 64.

[2] J. Stalin, *Problems of Leninism* (Moscow, 1941), p. 652. Cited by Louis Nemzer, 'The Kremlin's Professional Staff', *American Political Science Review*, vol. 44 (1950), p. 64.

[3] L. G. Churchward, 'Bureaucracy – USA:USSR', *Co-existence*, vol. 5 (1968), p. 206.

[4] Jerry F. Hough, *The Soviet Prefects: The Local Party Organs in Industrial Decision-making* (Cambridge, Mass., 1969).

rising to ministerial rank increasingly came to have characteristics indicating that political factors were becoming even less of an influence on promotion within the industrial hierarchy'.[1] On the other hand, Party first secretaries (25 in all) of the studied *industrialised* regions (*oblasti*) had entered the party on average at 23 years of age, and only 12 out of 22 had had an engineering education.[2] But Hough points out that the position is not as bad as it would appear from Bulganin's statement in 1955 that, 'The industrial departments of the party organs are frequently staffed by inexperienced officials, who do not have the necessary technical and economic knowledge and who cannot deeply analyse the work of the enterprise'.[3] Since the mid-1950s the party has been improving the educational standards of its full-time men and many secretaries have moved into the party after a period of service (at a junior level) in industry. Another qualification which must be made is that an 'engineering education' can differ significantly in quality. Some engineering graduates who consequently enter party work may have spent a considerable part of their student time in political activities (i.e. as *Komsomol* secretary),[4] to the detriment of their scientific training.

The creation of Regional Economic Councils (*sovnarkhozy*) in 1957, was hailed (probably rightly) as an attempt by Khrushchev to increase party control over the ministries. But it is interesting to note that the leading officials of the *sovnarkhozy* were recruited from the industrial ministries. Of 97 *sovnarkhoz* chairmen, only six had previously been party officials; the remainder were men who had been senior state administrators (8 had been USSR ministers, 30 USSR deputy ministers, 9 lower ministerial officials, 8 deputy chairmen of a republican council of ministers, 16 republican ministers, 6 republican deputy ministers and 14 directors of plants or combines).[5] Industrial ministers are men with outstanding industrial experience. In 1965, 88 per cent of the ministers had been enterprise directors or above for at least 15 years, and 55 per cent of them for at least 20 years. Senior ministerial 'staff have stability of tenure and are promoted from within the state, rather than from the party structure. Of 33 USSR industrial and construction ministers appointed in 1965, 12 had been USSR ministers in 1957, 10 had been deputy ministers, 4 had been in charge of industrial boards and one had been a minister in the Russian Federation.[6] As Hough concludes, 'Even if the top Soviet industrial officials may not be ideally equipped to carry through any revolution in industrial planning and administration, they remain men with great technical authority and they remain formidable

[1] *Op. cit.*, pp. 47-8.
[2] *Op. cit.*, p. 51.
[3] *Pravda*, 17 July 1955, p. 6, cited by Hough, *op. cit.*, p. 52.
[4] See Hough, *op. cit.*, p. 67.
[5] Hough, *op. cit.*, pp. 58-9.
[6] *Op. cit.*, p. 75.

opponents in bureaucratic struggles on planning and technical questions'.[1]

The men who become party First Secretaries in industrial areas nearly all came from previous party posts. Their engineering background, therefore, may not be of much use as knowledge quickly gets out of date. Such men are also inferior in quality to their ministerial counterparts. Hough describes the position as follows:

> Despite the number of managerial personnel transferred into the party apparatus, during the *sovnarkhoz* period, the local party organs still remained at somewhat of a disadvantage *vis-à-vis* the industrial hierarchy. The directors of the very largest plants still (with a few exceptions) were promoted into the *sovnarkhoz* rather than into the party apparatus, and, as a consequence, the top industrial administrators had personal authority that the managers among the secretaries of the local party organs usually could not match. The managers who entered party work usually had directed plants that were important, but not quite important enough to give them reasonable hope of rising directly to the ministerial level. They often were men for whom responsible party work might offer an attractive alternate route to higher levels.[2]

In local government, on the other hand, there can be no doubt that the party plays a most important role. The attempts by the government to increase voluntary participation in local government activity have led to the local party branches taking the initiative.

> Only the party can unite and give correct political direction to all forms of organisation of the public, hasten the development of socialist democracy in the work of Soviets, raise their role as mass organisations. Thus the development of socialist statehood into communist self-administration is impossible without the development of the leading role of the party in the work of all mass organisations of workers both state and social.[3]

The party controls Soviets through factions of its members, which influence the appointment of the leading officials of the Soviets (Chairman, Vice-Chairman and Secretary).[4] Local government elections too are regulated by the Communist Party. While many nominations do not originate in party groups, no candidate can receive the approval of the electoral committees without party approval. 'The central party organisations decide the social and political . . . composition of the Soviets'. The party also controls the agencies which nominate candidates.[5]

---

[1] *Op. cit.*, pp. 78-9.

[2] *Op. cit.*, p. 69.

[3] E. V. Barabashev and K. F. Sheremet, *Sovetskoe gosudarstvo i obshchestvennost' v usloviyakh razvernutogo stroitel'stva kommunizma* (Moscow, 1962), p. 57. Cited by Lloyd Churchward, 'Soviet Local Government Today', *Soviet Studies*, vol. 17 (4) (April, 1966), p. 443n.

[4] Lloyd Churchward, *loc. cit.*, pp. 443-4.

[5] Lloyd Churchward, *loc. cit.*, p. 451.

In the Soviet Union there are a large number of 'voluntary' or 'social' organisations (*obshchestvennye organizatsii*). A list is shown on Table 17.

Table 17. Data on Social Organisations in the RSFSR (1964)

Type of Organisation	Number of Organisations	Number of Members
Street and house committees	170,346	919,722
Parents' Committees in schools, kindergartens, creches and flats	172,388	1,138,507
Councils in Medical Institutions	10,600	127,451
Councils of Clubs and Libraries	64,549	454,524
Councils for assisting the improvement of living conditions	7,174	99,537
Women's Councils	32,607	297,904
Pensioners' Councils	9,531	194,479
Volunteer Fire Brigades	38,072	707,269
Volunteer Militia	85,182	3,351,078
Comradely Courts	112,371	693,434
Commissions on Control of socialist property	3,391	25,688
Technical-Production Councils in enterprises, state and collective farms	12,201	164,030
Councils of kolkhoz brigades	16,554	95.947
Shop and Restaurant Commissions	107,402	386,282
Councils of Elders	1,151	13,487
Sanitary posts and brigades	90,811	485,423
Pensioners' Commissions in establishments and enterprises	2,498	16,535
Other organisations	29,583	571,075
Total	966,412	9,774,372*

* [The figures add up to 9,742,372. The discrepancy is in the original. ED.]
Source: Data cited by Lloyd Churchward, 'Soviet Local Government Today', *Soviet Studies*, 17 (4), p. 440.

In theory these groups are to take over the management of certain aspects of state affairs, at least they provide services and assist local government authorities. Here the party plays an active role. It mobilises the population into such groups to perform social and political activity. In the town of Rostov (660,000 population) for example, it was reported that in 1962 there were 2,000 social organisations: 380 street and apartment committees, 700 comrade courts and 152 volunteer bureaux of the local Soviet executive committees.[1] In 1963, it has been estimated, 23 million were involved in local

[1] Robert G. Wesson, 'Volunteers and Soviets', *Soviet Studies*, vol. 15 (no. 3), 1964, p. 232. In 1966, half a million citizens participated as assessors in the Peoples Courts, *Izvestiya*, 7 December 1967.

government and another 17 million in other voluntary work.[1] Such groups are initiated and directed by the party. Their control is recognised in the statutes of the *druzhiny* (vigilantes).[2] In such organisations, the party is supreme and performs social mobilisation and some enforcement roles.

In Soviet (parliamentary) and trade union elective posts, party nomination and oversight is most important. Here specific techniques are less relevant than in ministerial posts and personal and 'political' considerations may be taken more into account. Party activists may sometimes be rewarded for their energy. In these spheres the party performs the political recruitment role. In 'elective' posts, therefore, one may generalise that party control is dominant, whereas in work roles, the bureaucracy is so.

In the sphere of political output and enforcement, the party is now probably less important than the government ministries. General political pronouncements, 'propaganda' and political education are the most important elements of party activity. Government output in quantitative terms is predominant: it is made up of ministerial decrees, orders and everyday ministerial activity. Enforcement is largely a state affair under the surveillance of the police and courts. The party also has a role to play here. Voluntary control commissions, formed of party activists, supervise the execution of state laws. Such groups attempt to 'control' production in the factories and keep order in the streets. But in industrial management, party 'control' is less effective than state management. We saw above that the party is circumscribed in its control of personnel. What makes it even more difficult for the party to exercise power over the industrial ministries is its small staff. The Leningrad *sovnarkhoz*, for instance, had a staff numbering over a thousand, whereas the industrial department of the Leningrad Party Committee had only 25 officials.[3] The party relies to some extent on part-time auxiliaries, but in practice, the sheer volume of work, its technical character, and the lower competence of party officials, must leave the state bureaucracies with a relatively free hand.[4]

We have seen earlier that the Communist Party articulates an ideology to which social and economic life should conform, it shapes the structure of the political system, and the form in which inputs should be made. But the party's incapacity both to aggregate inputs and to perform specialist output functions has in my view led to its decline as a political power, and has increased the

---

[1] Lloyd Churchward, *Contemporary Soviet Government* (1968), p. 182. In 1969, it was reported in *Ekonomicheskaya Gazeta* that seven million voluntary inspectors and controllers were working in close contact with Party, *Komsomol* and trade union organisations. See No. 4, Jan 20 1969, p. 7.

[2] Lloyd Churchward, 'Soviet Local Government Today', *Soviet Studies*, vol. 17 (no. 4), 1966, p. 444.

[3] Hough, *The Soviet Prefects*, p. 69.

[4] This is discussed in more detail in Chapter 10.

power of other institutions, the strongest of which is the state ministerial system.

This has not always been the case. Historically, in the years immediately following the October Revolution, the party had a more dominant position. It provided the general staff of the revolution and it largely controlled the processes of interest articulation, aggregation and enforcement. The party penetrated social institutions and groups and was a means of social integration. The social structure was characterised by weak intermediary groups; the professional classes were small, the dislocation through the war and the upheaveals of 1917 had pulverised the middle and upper classes. The party was not only centrally organised and disciplined but was the only group having links with all social institutions in the USSR. This is shown on Chart 9. The horizontal bars show the main social groupings. The group formations were fragmented and the professional strata relatively small. Government ministries were weakly organised. The party was able, by virtue of its centralised and disciplined organisation, to exert control over the social groupings by horizontal penetration, as shown by the arrows on Chart 9.

Under Stalin not only was the party decimated and the police used as an enforcement agency, but also the ministerial apparatus was enlarged in size. It developed a vertically integrated structure. While the party played an important role in enforcement, interest articulation and political recruitment, the state ministries, especially the police, were more important agencies of socio-political change. Under Stalin, the party was weakened. As Conquest has pointed out, 'Stalin's later Politbureaus consisted of figures from the government apparatus. And Stalin himself, in decrees proceeding from both government and party, signed first as representative of the government, allowing his senior subordinate in the Party Secretariat to sign, second, for the party'.[1]

While this confirms my point, it is, nevertheless superficial evidence. A better example is cited by Casinelli, who points out that in Smolensk while the party was said to be playing a 'leading role' in fact Stalin used the secret police to decimate its leading members.[2]

Khrushchev attempted to strengthen party control. By 1957, two-thirds of the Party Presidium (now the Politbureau) were party men. The power of the police was curbed. By 1961, only the Chairman of the KGB (Committee

[1] Robert Conquest, *Power and Policy in the USSR* (1961), p. 31. Armstrong has made the point that at the middle levels there is considerable interchange between state and party, *The Soviet Bureaucratic Elite* (New York, 1959), p. 144. This may have been a characteristic of the mid and late fifties. Even if generally true, it does not entail the absence of institutional loyalty at any given time to one *or* other of the state or party machines. Men who start out as engineers and move over to the party with time become cut off from their professional or previous institutional allegiance. Other groups, such as that headed by Khrushchev, are noted by Armstrong to be focussed on the party, *ibid.*, p. 147.

[2] C. W. Casinelli, 'The Totalitarian Party', *The Journal of Politics*, vol. 24 (1962), p. 140.

for State Security – Secret Police) remained a voting member of the Central Committee. Police representation has continued to decline in the higher organs. A study of the Central Committees of six republican parties shows that in 1954 there were eleven heads of police having full membership, in 1961 there were five and in 1966 only one.[1]

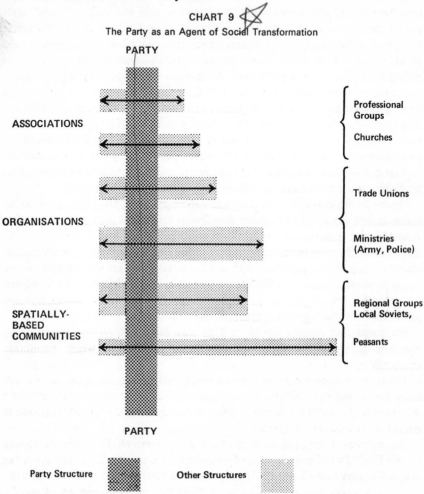

CHART 9

The Party as an Agent of Social Transformation

PARTY

ASSOCIATIONS

Professional Groups

Churches

ORGANISATIONS

Trade Unions

Ministries (Army, Police)

SPATIALLY-BASED COMMUNITIES

Regional Groups Local Soviets,

Peasants

PARTY

Party Structure   Other Structures

The industrial maturation of Soviet society has also created a different kind of socio-economic structure in which new groups have arisen. The ministries are particularly important. In the succession struggle with Khrushchev, Malenkov based his bid for power on the state bureaucracy. As the party

[1] Jerry Hough, 'The Soviet Elite', *Problems of Communism*, vol. 16 (no. 1), Jan./Feb. 1967, pp. 29-30.

journal put it: 'Members of the anti-party group departed from the Leninist understanding of the leading role of the party in the system of the dictatorship of the proletariat . . . Some of them . . . seeking to substantiate the [alleged] necessity of the primacy of state organs over party, distorted the Leninist doctrine on the role of the party after the victory of the proletarian revolution'.[1] This highlights institutional conflict in Soviet society, and the endemic tension between the party and other forces. While Khrushchev strengthened the power of party *apparatchiks*, the Brezhnev/Kosygin collective leadership has diminished it. Writing of the changes at the Twenty-Third Party Congress (1966) Boris Meissner has suggested that they reflect 'the sociological effects of the Kosygin economic reform, by which the power position of the state and economic bureaucracy has been greatly strengthened in relation to the party bureaucracy. This has restored the situation that existed prior to 1957'.[2] In his study of the composition of Republican Party Bureaux, Hough also shows that the membership of state bureaucrats in the Central Committee of six Republican parties increased from 33 in 1962-64 to 48 in 1966.[3] Let us now generalise about the interaction of the party with other groupings.

Chart 10 illustrates the group formations in modern Russia, it shows three major divisions: ministries, professional social groups and regional groups. Resistance to party control (shown by the arrows from the top of chart) varies, being greatest in the economic and military ministerial hierarchies and least among the spatially organised social groups. This is a consequence of the strength of the organisational structure. Another factor here is the knowledge and expertise of organised professional groups (scientists, managers and technologists) which gives them greater bargaining power.

The industrial ministries possess their own chain of command. The party straddles group interests but its integrating function is weak. Economic ministries have specific tasks on which their criteria for success are determined, and have no time for party political dabbling. To maintain morale, to increase output, the ministries must be allowed considerable independence. Their specialist technical expertise gives them a strong bargaining position against purely 'political' interests (say party secretaries) located in other structures. At the top levels of policy-making the ministries are faced by the specialised bureaux of the Central Committee, which probably have a large say in the final aggregation of policy (we do not really know how they interact). In the articulation of their own interests and in the carrying out of plans the ministries are in all probability highly independent of party control.

---

[1] *Kommunist*, no. 10 (July 1957), p. 5. Cited by Myron Rush, *Political Succession in the USSR* (New York, 1965), p. 60.

[2] Boris Meissner, 'Totalitarian Rule and Social Change', *Problems of Communism*, vol. 15 (no. 6) 1966, p. 59.

[3] Jerry Hough, 'The Soviet Elite', *loc. cit.*, p. 30.

CHART 10

A Model of the Party and other Structures in Modern Russia

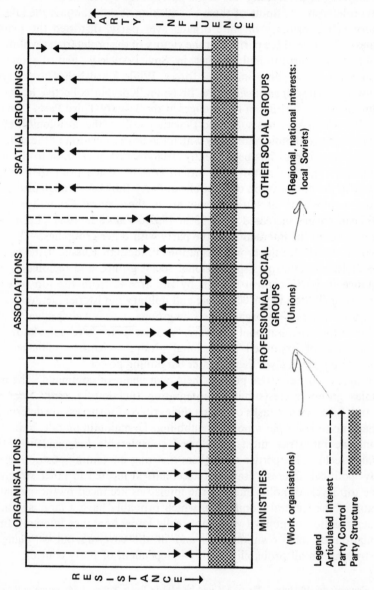

Professional strata, such as writers, cherish their professional code and interests but are less autonomous than ministries and, therefore, are less able to assert their own interests. They are more likely to participate in 'anomic'

interest activity and to demonstrate in public places.[1] The weakest group ties are among the third category, which includes nationalities and regional interests. Such territorial or spatial solidarity tends to be weakly aggregated in modern societies because territorial groups suffer disintegration through the organisations and associations which criss-cross them. (More examples of group activity will be considered in the next chapter.)

Why, then, it may be asked, does the party continue to attempt to control, direct and organise social life? The answer to this partly lies in the absence of conflict in the ideology sustaining Soviet society and in the absence of formally constituted channels to resolve any conflict. And it is partly explained by the self-interest of the party elite in perpetuating its own power. In Marxist-Leninist theory it is only the party which can be politically legitimate. It has a political authority not possessed by other institutions in Soviet society. The ideology of Soviet society gives the party an important leading role. People are led to believe that the party is supreme. This suits the elites for the party promises a Utopia, it presents a vision of the classless society, of the working out of the laws of human destiny. This may be a myth. But it is an important myth: it helps integrate the individual and gives an aura of legitimacy to the various elites.

Party-state relations are bedevilled by a fundamental role conflict. The party seeks a diffuse, particularistic role whereas the ministries have specifistic and universalistic tasks. The party tends to be concerned with who a person is, rather than with what he does – it is more concerned with (political) qualities than with performance capabilities. Under conditions of urban-industrial society, specifistic, universalistic and performance relationships seem to result from the highly specialised division of labour and differentiation of relationships. The party's attempt at wide-ranging political and social control is probably now anachronistic. Khrushchev recognised that the party had to be strengthened and he encouraged the recruitment of technical specialists. But this process has not yet succeeded in strengthening the party *vis-à-vis* the state in industrial administration.

The ideological rigidity of Soviet society has precluded the development of a social theory which both recognises conflict and which suggests mechanisms for its resolution. On the other hand, it has afforded an opportunity to the party elite for strengthening its position. Its present form creates resentment among managerial, professional and intellectual groups. Such resentment was epitomised in Czechoslovakia with the reforms of early 1968, when the political role of the Czech Communist Party was weakened. It is probably significant that Brezhnev, the Party General Secretary, was said to be more

---

[1] Amalrik shows that 72 per cent (N =738) of those signing their names to protests were academics, artists or students. 'Will the USSR Survive until 1984?' *Survey*, no. 73 (Autumn 1969), eadings 10 and 11 below.

strongly opposed to the Czech reforms than was Premier Kosygin. While there is conflict between the elites we must not overlook the fact that *there is also consensus*. This is of an ideological kind, which accepts the structure of Soviet society – the goal of communism, the nationalisation of property, the system of stratification, of inequality, of a one-party as opposed to a multi-party state. In these respects the party and state bureaucrats have an identity of interest.

Let us now summarise the function of the Communist Party of the Soviet Union in Soviet society. Unlike the view taken by many contemporary writers[1] the CPSU here is not regarded as a 'ruling party'. Such writers exaggerate the party's power: they tend to ignore or minimise the real powers of social forces and institutions outside it; they too readily accept Soviet and 'totalitarian' ideological beliefs. On the other hand, we should not, like Casinelli, relegate the party to a position of obscurity, excluding it even from the most important instruments of rule.[2] The party retains its power by virtue of normative controls – it articulates an ideology (constrained, it is true, by other groups); it has considerable powers in political mobilisation, recruitment and placement. It plays an important role in input articulation. While much aggregation of interests takes place within and between the ministerial apparatus, *the final aggregation process occurs in the Politbureau*. This is a party body; in recent times it has been held responsible to the Central Committee of the party who elect it. At the apex, to be sure, non-party interests attempt to secure their claims and the state apparatus provides the greatest resistance to party control. Let us now turn to consider wider issues to illustrate the group process of politics.

[1] T. H. Rigby, 'Traditional, Market and Organisational Societies and the USSR', *World Politics*, vol. 16 (1964); Allen Kassof, 'The Administered Society', *World Politics*, vol. 16 (1964). See above, Chapter 6.

[2] C. W. Casinelli, 'The Totalitarian Party', *The Journal of Politics*, vol. 24 (1962).

FOR FURTHER STUDY

INTRODUCTORY

Brzezinski, Zbigniew K. *Ideology and Power in Soviet Politics*. New York: Praeger, 1967.

Churchward, Lloyd G. *Contemporary Soviet Government*. London: Routledge and Kegan Paul, 1968.

Moore, Barrington, Jr. *Soviet Politics: The Dilemma of Power* (Revised Edition). New York: Harper and Row, 1965.

Rigby, T. H. 'Traditional, Market and Organisational Societies and the USSR', in *World Politics*, Vol. 16, July 1964, pp. 539-57.

Schapiro, Leonard. *The Communist Party of the Soviet Union*. London: Eyre and Spottiswoode, 1960.

BASIC

Casinelli, C. W. 'The Totalitarian Party', in *The Journal of Politics*, Vol. 24, Feb. 1962, pp. 111-41.

Churchward, Lloyd. 'Soviet Local Government To-day', in *Soviet Studies*, Vol. 17, No. 4.

Conquest, Robert. *Power and Policy in the USSR: The Study of Soviet Dynastics*. London: Macmillan, 1961.

Dallin, A. and T. B. Larson. *Soviet Politics since Khrushchev*. New Jersey: Prentice Hall, 1968.

Fainsod, Merle. *Smolensk Under Soviet Rule*. London: Macmillan, 1958.

Gehlin, Michael P. *The Communist Party of the Soviet Union*. Bloomington: Indiana University Press, 1969.

Hough, Jerry F. *The Soviet Prefects: The Local Party Organs in Industrial Decision-Making*. Cambridge, Mass.: Harvard University Press, 1969.

Hough, Jerry F. 'The Soviet Elite', in *Problems of Communism*, Vol. 16, No. 1, Jan.-Feb. 1967, pp. 28-35.

Linden, Carl A. *Khrushchev and the Soviet Leadership, 1957-1964*. Baltimore, Maryland: Johns Hopkins University Press, 1966.

Nemzer, Louis. 'The Kremlin's Professional Staff; The "Apparatus" of the Central Committee, Communist Party of the Soviet Union', in *American Political Science Review*, Vol. 44, March 1950, pp. 64-85.

Meyer, Alfred G. 'The Functions of Ideology in the Soviet Political System', in *Soviet Studies*, Vol. 17, No. 3, 1966, pp. 273-85.

Stewart, Philip D. *Political Power in the Soviet Union*. Indianapolis: Bobbs-Merrill, 1968.

SPECIALISED

Amalrik, Andrei, 'Will the USSR Survive Until 1984?', *Survey*, No. 73, Autumn 1969, pp. 47-79.

Avtorkhanov, Abdurakhman. *The Communist Party Apparatus*. Chicago: Henry Regnery and Co., 1966.

Barabashev, E. V. and K. F. Sheremet. *Sovetskoe gosudarstvo i obshchestvennost' v usloviyakh razvernutogo stroitel'stva kommunizma*. Moscow: 1962.

Bell, Daniel. 'Ten Theories in Search of Reality: The Prediction of Soviet Behaviour in the Social Sciences', *World Politics*, Vol. 10, No. 10, April 1958, pp. 327-65. 'Marxism-Leninism: A Doctrine on the Defensive', in M. M. Drackhovitch (ed.). *Marxist Ideology in the Contemporary World*. New York, 1966.

Easton, David. *A Systems Analysis of Political Life*. New York: J. Wiley and Sons Inc., 1965.

Kanet, Roger E. 'The Rise and Fall of the All-People's State', in *Soviet Studies*. Vol. 20, No. 1, July 1968.

Kassof, Allen. 'The Administered Society: Totalitarianism Without Terror', *World Politics*, Vol. 16, July 1964, pp. 558-75.

Kommunist. No. 10, July 1957. (on Khrushchev's succession over the Anti-Party group).

Lane, David. 'Ideology and Sociology in the USSR', in *British Journal of Sociology*, Vol. 21, No. 1, March 1970.

Leonhard, Wolfgang. *The Kremlin Since Stalin*, translated by Elizabeth Wiskemann and M. Jackson. London: Oxford University Press, 1962.

The Observer, 27 July 1969 (*on dispossessed Crimean Tartars*).

The Observer, 29 June 1969 (*review of dissident writers' trials*).

Obshchestvovedenie, Seventh Edition. Moscow, 1969.

Pravda, 19 December 1958 (*on Khrushchev's dealings with the Anti-Party group*).

Pravda, 7 July 1957 (*on dealings with the Anti-Party group*).

Reddaway, P. B. 'Aspects of Ideological Belief in the Soviet Union: comments on Professor Meyer's essay', *Soviet Studies*, Vol. 17, No. 4, April 1966, pp. 473-83.

Rigby, T. H. *Communist Party Membership in the USSR, 1917-1967*. Princeton, New Jersey: Princeton University Press, 1968.

Rush, Myron. *Political Succession in the USSR* (Second Edition). New York: Columbia University Press, 1968.

'Report of the Proceedings of the first session of Seventh Supreme Soviet', *Soviet News*, 5 August 1966.

Schapiro, Leonard. 'The Twenty-Third Congress of the CPSU', in *Survey*, No. 60, July 1966, pp. 72-84.

Stalin, J. V. *Problems of Leninism*. Moscow, 1941.

Tatu, Michel. *Power in the Kremlin: From Khrushchev's Decline to Collective Leadership*, translated by Helen Katel. London: Collins, 1969.

Wesson, Robert G. 'Volunteers and Soviets', in *Soviet Studies*, Vol. 15, No. 3, January 1964, pp. 231-49.

8

THE GROUP PROCESS
OF POLITICS

The foregoing chapter suggests that the Soviet political system is characterised not by the rule of a class or a unitary power elite, but by the interaction of a number of elites both between themselves and with other groups. Rather than viewing the party or the state bureaucracy as a monistic structure 'ruling' the USSR, both are seen as providing an apparatus through which interests are articulated, aggregated and outputs are enforced. It is sometimes said that the distinctive character of 'totalitarian systems' is to 'suppress demands coming from their societies' and to be 'unresponsive to demands coming from the international environment'.[1] The view adopted here is that the Soviet political system *functions* in a similar way to western ones. While *there is a difference* in the degree of suppression of demands on the system, in any system demands which threaten its integrity are suppressed or suppression is attempted. Another important difference between it and liberal-democratic societies is (in Almond's and Powell's terms), the stronger *distributive* capability of the Soviet political system: the boundaries between it and other social subsystems are weak and the polity (in practice, the party and the bureaucracy) is able to exert its power in areas of social life from which it is excluded in the west – except in times of emergency here such as war. Let us now turn to consider the groups which characterise the political system.

H. Gordon Skilling has pointed out that in analysing Soviet society, group interest and group conflict cannot be excluded.[2] In the USSR, as in advanced western political systems, interest groups 'on the basis of one or more shared attitudes' make claims on other groups 'through or upon any of the institutions of government'.[3] An interest group then, makes claims on the legitimate power wielders though it does not seek legitimate power itself.

In the USSR, while there are restraints on the formal organisation of political groups, this does not entail the absence of what Skilling calls an 'informal

[1] G. A. Almond and G. B. Powell, *Comparative Politics* (Boston, 1966), p. 28. Later in the book however, they describe the political conversion process in group terms (pp. 277-9).

[2] 'Interest Groups and Communist Politics', *World Politics*, no. 18 (1966), pp. 441-2, 446-7.

[3] D. B. Truman, *The Governmental Process* (New York, 1951), pp. 33, 37, cited by Skilling, *loc. cit.*, p. 450.

group' or an 'interest grouping'.[1] Such a grouping may be defined as 'any mass of human activity tending in a common political direction'.[2] This does not imply that all groups necessarily participate in the political process. Social groups in the West, such as women or 'old boys' reunions', may not be interest groupings because they make no claims on the political system as such. When groups make a claim or articulate an interest they become 'pressure groups' or 'interest groupings'.

The existence of a number of elites, either in the USA or the USSR, does not exclude conflict and group activity at the middle or lower levels of the system. Party secretaries, factory managers, government executives, directors of scientific institutions, army generals, trade union leaders, who all hold official positions of one kind or another, are, if the conclusions of political science are to be given any credibility, likely to form their own professional sectional view of the public good. Such men are likely to intermingle with others of a similar occupational role and on that basis to advocate and to support policies which they believe to be in their interest. Those excluded from elite positions, but who perform functions important for the continuation of the regime, such as teachers, journalists, doctors, skilled workers, are also likely to conceive of the national interest in terms of their own interests and, unless oppressed by violence or terrorism, are likely to express their views. The recent history of the world would suggest that it is extremely difficult to suppress ideas which are alien to those of the elites: it is, therefore, likely that in modern Russia those estranged and alienated from the values of the regime will voice their disapproval and try to secure their own safety and values. All these groups will make claims on the basis of their own interests.

The making of claims involves the definition of issues on which groups may have separate interests. It is probable that any given 'group' may be indifferent to certain issues: army generals may have no opinion or interest *as generals* as to whether jazz is inimical to communism. It is, therefore, somewhat unreal to describe 'interest groups' without specifying the issues on which the groups may politically intervene. First, we must consider the group structure in a more systematic way than suggested above in Chapter 7. Second, we must define the issues which unite groups and on which they make claims on the political system.

Groups in terms of their *political* articulation may be defined at five levels: the political elites, groups with an institutional position in the apparatus, 'loyal dissenters', amorphous social groupings and unincorporated (or estranged) groupings.[3]

---

[1] H. Gordon Skilling, *Interest Groups in Soviet Politics* (Duplicated paper), p. 21.

[2] *Ibid.*

[3] Brzezinski and Huntington define three groupings: policy, specific interest and amorphous social forces – see *Political Power USA/USSR*, pp. 195-6. H. Gordon Skilling has defined four types of 'oppositional tendency': 'integral opposition', 'fundamental opposition', 'factional

The *political elites* are the incumbents of positions at the apex of the Soviet political structure: members of the Politbureau, of the Cabinet, of the Presidium, below them are a second string – members of the Central Committee, of the Council of Ministers, of the Supreme Soviet. These groups have direct access to the law-making and law-enforcement mechanisms. It would be incorrect to regard them as a unitary or monistic elite.

Institutional groups are those which are quasi-incorporated into the political apparatus; some are formally part of it – such as local Soviets, others are formally outside it, for example, the trade unions, the *Komsomol*, or the Academy of Sciences. All these institutions, however, are closely entwined with the law-making and enforcement agencies.

'*Loyal dissenters*' are groupings which accept the parameters of Soviet society, but whose group associations are not closely integrated with the law-making machinery. Examples here are writers, town planners, teachers, doctors, managers, social scientists. These are the professional and technical groups who are equivalent to the 'professions' in the West. They must be differentiated from the *political elites*; they are vertical social strata rather than horizontal, but cognisance must be given to them at many levels of decision-making. Such groups, though loyal to a socialist system, may be critical of certain arrangements under it.

Amorphous social groupings are those which may share a given occupation, or a similar social or national position but which are only partially conscious of their own identity and which have little opportunity for interest articulation. Examples of such groupings are the peasantry, white collar workers, manual workers, various national or religious minorities and consumers.

Finally, *unincorporated or estranged groups* are those which have a strong antipathy to the Soviet regime. Such antipathy is likely to be nourished by values stemming from the pre-revolutionary social structure, or from the capitalist West or from moral conviction. Soviet law-makers and enforcers attempt to isolate and eliminate such groups. For example, the elimination of the *kulaks* was fairly successfully carried out in the late twenties. But such groupings persist among the peasants, religious bodies (such as Baptists), dissident intellectuals and writers (Tsarsis, Amalrik, Sinyavski and Daniel), and some of the youth.

These groupings are only 'interest groups' in so far as they are able to communicate their interest (i.e. a common attitude on a particular matter) to the law makers. This possibility is extremely high for the first three groups mentioned above – the elites, institutional groups, the loyal oppositions, but lower for the last two – the amorphous and the estranged groupings.

---

opposition', 'specific opposition'. See 'The Party, Opposition, and Interest Groups in Communist Politics', in Kurt London (ed.) *The Soviet Union: A Half Century of Communism* (Baltimore, Maryland, 1968), pp. 123-4.

In the Soviet Union communication between, and organisation of, such interests are subject to greater constraints than in liberal-democratic systems. In the latter, the ideology sustains free bargaining by autonomous groups in politics as between buyers and sellers in the economic market. Therefore, the group political process in Soviet society is more muted, more informal, less organised and conducted usually behind closed doors, within the bureaucratic structure. Sanctions against 'disloyal' oppositions which may espouse political leadership or seek to replace elite incumbents may be severe – involving loss of office, deportation, imprisonment, or even (during the Stalin era) death. Any general appeal for support or for organisation between interests is particularly likely to result in sanctions – for the aggregation of interests or of issues into an alternative policy is a challenge to the authority of the Communist Party.

Garthoff, in discussing Soviet military policy has ably summed up the relation of the party to other elite group interests:

The party is dominant – but not too omnipotent – in Soviet society. The party leadership, comprising the Presidium[1] and Central Committee, is responsible for political decision making; it also provides the arena in which policy conflicts are decided. The top leaders function as party representatives in their other assignments, but in the top party councils they represent those other interests and institutions with which they are associated. If the interests of the party are all-encompassing, so too is the range of interests which are brought to bear in its deliberations. Only a powerful minority of the top party leaders are fully and exclusively identified with the party machine, those in the party's chief executive body, the Secretariat. All believe that the party's requirements – for defence, security, heavy industry, light industry and consumer goods, agriculture, ties with other communist parties, and foreign policy – must be met; but, not surprisingly, they differ on the relative weight that should be assigned to each. Moreover, these interests not only complement one another, they also compete and conflict. . . .[2]

To illustrate the role in the political process of the five types of groups mentioned above we shall consider first the political elites.

The Political Elites

The study of political leadership and political succession in the USSR has highlighted the role of group interests at the apex of power. While Kremlinologists in their demonic art have emphasised the existence of rivalry and competition for leadership among the members of the elite, they have characterised such conflict as being personal in substance; individual poli-

---

[1] Now the *Politbureau.*
[2] Raymond L. Garthoff, *Soviet Military Policy* (London, 1966), p. 58.

ticians being primarily motivated by their thirst for political power, rather than by the desire to implement any policies.[1] As the group structure of Soviet society has been regarded by such writers as exceedingly weak, any possible linking of policy with social groupings was not considered possible.[2] From a theoretical political science point of view, it is impossible to conceive of men wanting 'power' without specifying for what power is wanted.

A first attempt was made in Britain by Roger Pethybridge to examine Soviet elite politics in interest group terms,[3] and has been further developed by Carl A. Linden's study of the Soviet leadership between 1957 and 1964.[4] Linden sees

> .... those around Khrushchev ... not as nonentities or toadies, but men of power who represent real political and organisational interests. At no point do they appear as wholly malleable to the leader's purposes and, while opportunistic and skilled tacticians, they also are seen as men who more often than not possessed political identities which placed them to one side or other in the political spectrum of the party. It was through such territory and with such company that Khrushchev made his way and finally stumbled ... The major, but not the exclusive, focus here is the narrow circle of a few dozen figures at the level of the Party Presidium and Secretariat.[5]

Who, then, are the political elites? Michel Tatu, though emphasising power at the top, defines 'the lobbies' in Soviet politics. (The use of the term 'lobby' is rather misleading, for in the USA it includes persons employed in promoting or defeating bills: no process of the American kind takes place in the USSR.) Tatu's list includes the army, the police, the 'steel eaters' (supporters of heavy industry), the party *apparatchiki* and economic administrators – the last two being the most important.[6] Tatu's discussion, however, centres around the struggle for supreme political control. He says, 'The party's grip over the population is as firm as ever, but the machinery of power now tends to split into separate entities (major state administrations, "steel-eaters", army, police,

---

[1] Probably the best recent account is to be found in Michel Tatu, *Power in the Kremlin* (1969). He sees the power structure of the following men: Kosygin, Podgorny, Shelepin, Suslov and Brezhnev, pp. 494–523. See Alec Nove. 'The Uses and Abuses of Kremlinology', in *Was Stalin Really Necessary?* (1964).

[2] Robert Conquest, *Power and Policy in the USSR* (New York, 1961). Kremlinologists have been concerned with predicting Soviet political behaviour and have tried to use personnel changes as indicators. Unfortunately, they have had no consistent success. None predicted the downfall of Khrushchev in the short run before his ousting. Robert Conquest rightly said that the Soviet invasion of Czechoslovakia would take place; but his prediction that a 'decisive split at the highest level' in the USSR would develop 'in the fairly near future' has not materialised by 1970. R. Conquest, *Russia After Khrushchev* (1965), p. 264. See also M. Page and David Burg, *Unpersonned* (1966).

[3] See his *A Key to Soviet Politics* (1962).

[4] *Khrushchev and the Soviet Leadership 1957-1964* (Baltimore, Maryland, 1966).

[5] Linden, *op. cit.*, pp. 7-8.

[6] *Power in the Kremlin*, pp. 429-60.

CHART 11 Political Spectrum USSR

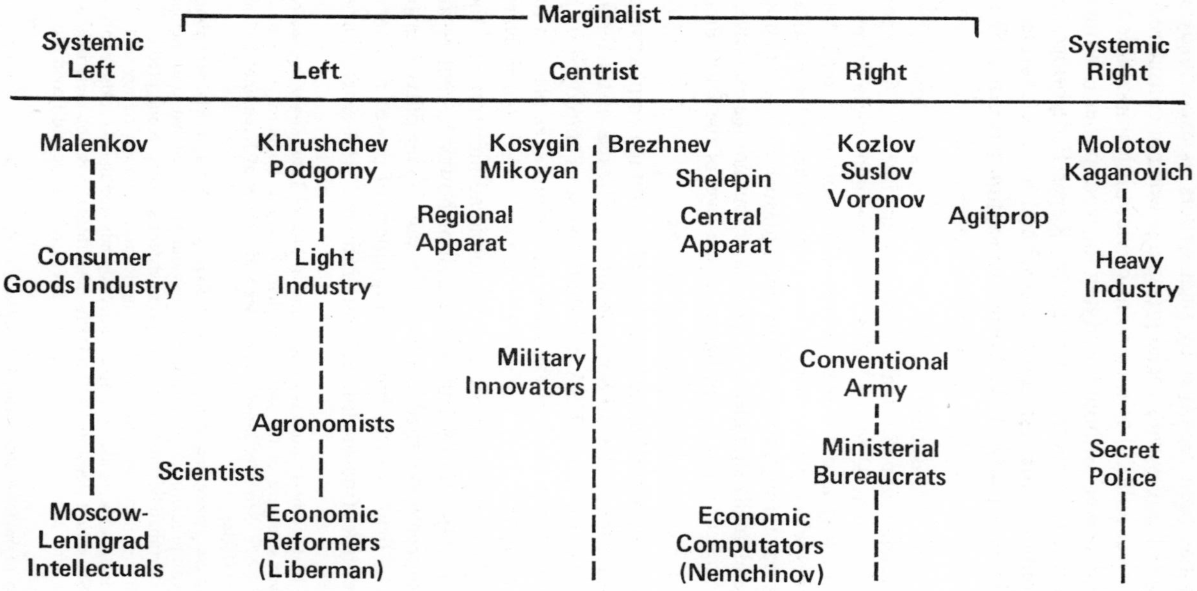

Marginalist

Systemic Left	Left	Centrist	Right	Systemic Right
Malenkov	Khrushchev Podgorny	Kosygin Mikoyan	Brezhnev	Kozlov Suslov Voronov	Molotov Kaganovich

| Consumer Goods Industry | Light Industry | Regional Apparat | Shelepin Central Apparat | Agitprop | Heavy Industry |

Military Innovators — Conventional Army

Scientists — Agronomists

Economic Reformers (Liberman) — Economic Computators (Nemchinov) — Ministerial Bureaucrats

Moscow-Leningrad Intellectuals — Secret Police

Source : Z.K. Brzezinski, Ideology and Power in Soviet Politics (Praeger, New York 1967) p. 117.

regional groupings). None of them can as yet either gain the upper hand or be subdued'.[1]

Vernon V. Aspaturian in discussing Soviet foreign policy has identified the armed forces, the heavy-industrial managers, professional party *apparatchiki* and ideologues as groups which appear to benefit from an aggressive foreign policy, while those who would benefit from a relaxation of international tension are the state bureaucracy, the light-industrial, consumer goods and services, and agricultural managers, the cultural-professional scientific groups and the Soviet 'consumer'.[2] A more elaborate and general description of groups has been devised by Brzezinski who shows both individuals and group interest at the top levels of power (see Chart 11). By 'systemic left' he means 'a radical reformist outlook, challenging the predominant values of the existing system'; and 'systemic right' he defines as 'an almost reactionary return to past values'.[3] The chart shows at the extreme right the secret police, the heavy industry interests and at the extreme left consumer goods industry and the Moscow-Leningrad intellectuals. Brzezinski's approach performs a very useful service in establishing the groups and their interests, but it is quite another matter to demonstrate how they interact and how their interests are articulated and aggregated. We have given one example in Chapter 7 of elite group conflict within the party, here we shall consider three issues: the role of the military in Khrushchev's rise to, and fall from, power, the problem of party control of the economy, and the groups involved in Khrushchev's ousting.

The political role of the military is always important, for the armed forces have the ability to assert their will against other groups by the use of arms. In a modern industrial society, the technology of war is not only expensive, but involves military strategy depending on specialised professional advice, which the armed forces possess or think they possess. The effective waging of war also depends on the morale of the armed forces and their capability to innovate and to show initiative. The military can be expected to play quite an important role in shaping policies in modern industrial societies. Thomas W. Wolfe has suggested that there are three areas in which the military exerts influence on Soviet policy-making: '(1) the high-level sphere of party-state policy formulation; (2) the lesser level of military-technical considerations relating to the development and management of the military establishment itself; (3) the area of internal Soviet politics'.[4] The first is concerned with the

[1] *Ibid.*, p. 527.

[2] Vernon V. Aspaturian, 'The Soviet Case: Unique and Generalisable Factors' in R. Barry Farrell, *Approaches to Comparative and International Politics* (Evanston Ill., 1966), pp. 261, 278–82.

[3] Z. K. Brzezinski, *Ideology and Power in Soviet Politics* (New York, 1967), pp. 116-7.

[4] T. W. Wolfe, 'Political Primacy vs. Professional Elan,' *Problems of Communism*, vol. 13 (no. 3) 1964, p. 50. For a more detailed account of the changing role of the military see Roman Kolkowicz, *The Soviet Military and the Communist Party* (Princeton, New Jersey, 1967) espec. pp. 345-6.

domain of military strategy in an era of nuclear power. The second with the use of military knowledge in the deployment and use of military resources. The third with the policy implications, with financial priorities, entailed by military objectives. It is difficult to find data on the role of the military in strategic policies, for the Soviet Union, as any other power, attempts to ensure strict secrecy in this area.

We know, however, that Khrushchev, when pitted against Malenkov, had come to power with much military support.[1] After assuming power, Khrushchev became involved in the policy issue of missiles versus ground forces, and he came down forcibly on the side of the missiles: of 'fire power' rather than the number of 'army great coats'. At the Supreme Soviet in January 1960, Khrushchev argued that large armies, navies and bomber forces were obsolete. The conventional military leaders opposed Khrushchev. Marshall Malinovski in reply said:

> The rocket troops are indisputably the main arm of our armed forces. However, we understand that it is not possible to solve all the tasks of war with any one arm of troops. Therefore, proceeding from the thesis that the successful conduct of military operations in modern war is possibly only on the basis of the unified use of all means of armed struggle, and combining the efforts of all arms of the armed forces, we are retaining all arms of our armed forces at a definite strength and in relevant sound proportions.[2]

The implications here and elsewhere in the military press were that undue reliance on a rocket defensive arm was inimical to successful defence. Western commentators are agreed that the military had differences with Khrushchev and believed his defence policy to be incorrect. Garthoff comments:

> On this issue [the reduction of the armed forces], the political leadership prevailed only in part. As a whole, the military leaders accepted and implemented the decision, but they also fought an effective rear-guard action. They were apparently given the deciding vote in allocating military reductions and in shaping the force structure under the politically imposed manpower ceiling.[3]

In the spring and summer of 1961, with the worsening of international relations (the U-2 incident, the failure of the Paris summit and a new crisis over Berlin) some concessions were made to the military. The manpower cuts were suspended, defence expenditure was increased by one third and the release of servicemen was stopped. In June 1961, Khrushchev made a formal concession: 'The strengthening of the defence of the Soviet Union depends on the perfection of all services of our armed forces – infantry and artillery,

---

[1] For an account see R. L. Garthoff, *Soviet Military Policy* (1966) Chapter 3.
[2] *Pravda* 15 January 1960. Cited by Linden, p. 93n.
[3] *Soviet Military Policy*, p. 58.

engineering corps and signal corps, armoured tank divisions and the navy, the air force, and the missile force.'[1]

While military support, especially that of Zhukov, was an important factor in Khrushchev's rise to power, it seems that it did not play a very active part in his downfall. But this does not diminish the importance of the military as a political interest: the *neutrality* of the military to the anti-Khrushchev coalition helped secure the Brezhnev-Kosygin leadership. As Garthoff has pointed out when commenting on his removal, 'the military were only a part of a coalition involving individual leaders and interest groups'.[2]

It cannot be doubted that the military has a voice which it makes heard in the inner councils concerned with policy in the USSR. Military leaders defend their interest against party and other groups. They provide resistance when changes which threaten them are muted. ' . . . While the military's influence on policy is no doubt limited, the extent to which Khrushchev – and with him the entire political leadership – can ignore military opinion also seems to have its limits.'[3]

A second issue on which opinions differed and around which elitist group interest diverged was party control of the economy. While all members of the Council of Ministers and Central Committee are party members, one must distinguish between that group from which sprang Khrushchev, which is wholly dependent on a party career, full-time *party* officials, and a group which mans the government ministerial system. The conflict in 1957 over top political leadership between the 'party group' (Khrushchev, Mikoyan, Kirichenko) and the 'anti-party' group (Malenkov, Molotov, Bulganin) was between the interests of these two factions. Khrushchev when in power strengthened party control of industry and split up economic administration into regional, rather than ministerial units, which coincided with party administrative boundaries. (We shall examine party control at the factory level below. Chapter 10.) This was not simply a move designed to improve administrative efficiency. Khrushchev's motives included, in Armstrong's words: 'the weakening of the influence of his "anti-party" rivals in the central administrative apparatus; and the strengthening of his supporters in the territorial party organisation'.[4] Later Khrushchev divided the party organisation into industrial and agricultural hierarchies. By increasing the number of units he in effect reduced the power of many former party first secretaries who, of course, resented the policy.

Khrushchev then found himself very unpopular with the chief ministerial

[1] *Pravda*, 22 June 1961. Cited by M. P. Gallaher, 'Military Manpower: A Case Study', *Problems of Communism*, vol. 13 (no. 3) 1964, p. 64.

[2] *Op. cit.*, p. 60.

[3] Matthew P. Gallaher, *loc. cit.*, p. 62.

[4] John A. Armstrong, 'Party Bifurcation and Elite Interests', *Soviet Studies*, vol. 17 (no. 4) 1966, p. 418.

bureaucrats and with some of the 'old' party secretaries. The latter may have played an important role in his downfall, for many of them held positions in the Central Committee, which the secretaries who benefitted by the reorganisation did not. '*All* of the Ukrainian and RSFSR *obkom* secretaries who appeared to be threatened by reorganisation measures were Central Committee members or candidates, while *none* of the 'new' secretaries who were beneficiaries of the bifurcation belonged as yet to that body.'[1]

In October 1964, subsequent to Khrushchev's fall, the party was reunified. The industrial ministerial system was re-centralised, and the 'collective leadership' has included Kosygin, the Chairman of the Council of Ministers. The 'reinstated' party secretaries were those who held their posts prior to bifurcation.[2]

Above, and in Chapter 7, I have identified three interest groups at the top of the Soviet power structure. First, the leaders of the armed forces who tend to identify Soviet national interests with a strong defence capacity and who actively supported Khrushchev against Molotov in 1957, and whose neutrality to the Brezhnev-Kosygin *coup* ensured his removal in 1964; second, the *party* secretariat wishing the predominance of the party over the ministries; third, the state bureaucracy which was at loggerheads with Khrushchev over industrial administration during the whole period of Khrushchev's supremacy. It would be superficial to explain elite politics solely in terms of these interest groups. To account adequately for the demise of Khrushchev one must look at other aspects of his policy – on Berlin, Cuba, China, agriculture, education – to gauge how other groups reacted to his leadership.[3]

To discuss the downfall of Khrushchev would require a whole book. Here we may mention some of the main groups and issues which caused the upheaval in October 1964. It seems improbable to suggest that Khrushchev was ousted over one policy by a single interest group. Rather, a combination of factors was responsible. We have noted some of them already. Khrushchev tried to establish the supremacy of the party over state organs. He succeeded in smashing police power. He weakened, but did not decimate the state bureaucratic machine. He discredited the secret police by his anti-Stalin campaign which, at least initially, secured him public, and a good deal of party, support. But his policy here backfired. His anti-Stalinism unleashed tremendous political demands. Eastern Europe was in upheaval. Soviet writers questioned the very basis of party control. He met such stress and demand on the political system by repression – thereby weakening his popularity. While Khrushchev had strengthened the party *vis-à-vis* the 'anti-party' group, he now became

[1] Armstrong, *loc. cit.*, p. 426.

[2] Armstrong, *ibid.*

[3] For the best account using Kremlinological methods, see Michel Tatu, *Power in the Kremlin* (1967) Part Four. For a case study of agriculture: Sidney I. Ploss, *Conflict and Decision Making in Soviet Russia* (New Jersey, 1965).

more dependant on the party to maintain his own power. But here he was faced by men of his own ilk, party secretaries and officials reared in the Stalin era. While he could not resort to Stalinist methods of terror and coercion – both the social framework and his destruction of the police apparatus prevented this – his attempt at normative controls (the *Party Programme*) and policy changes created resistance. For instance 'peaceful coexistence' led to criticism from the Chinese which destroyed the hitherto unity of the Socialist camp.

His other main policy was the wager on utilitarian means. His policy was instrumental in providing the goods of a mature industrial system. Here he promised a rapid rise in living standards: the American standard of living by 1980. To achieve this goal, he had to shift resources: away from the military to chemicals; from heavy to light industry. He offended the army by his emphasis on nuclear power and his reduction of military manpower. His Cuba gamble, which would have increased Soviet nuclear strike capability, had it come off, failed. This had repercussions outside the military interest groups. Against the opposing groups, Khrushchev resorted to a flamboyant political style. He convened enlarged meetings of the Central Committee, presumably attended by outsiders who were more sympathetic to his policy, and he tended to appeal to the public in the style of an American president. These tactics probably led to revulsion on the part of the more traditional formal politicians.

Khrushchev's last desperate gamble was with the party machine itself. By dividing it, he increased its size: the number of first secretaries doubled. The new men were younger, probably more progressive, more instrumental than ideological in orientation. But Khrushchev had not politically eliminated his opponents in the party. This was his final undoing. They had a majority in the Central Committee. With the Presidium by now hostile he could not stay in power.

Quasi-Institutional Groups

The second interest grouping mentioned above were groups with a quasi-institutional position in the political apparatus. Here we shall take two examples: a study of the groups within the Academy of Sciences which articulated an interest during Khrushchev's proposed reorganisation of this body, and the role of regional interests in the reform of education.

The Academy of Sciences embraces most post-graduate research and some post-graduate teaching in all disciplines: law, social studies, the humanities and the natural sciences. The Academy is divided geographically, with each Republic having its own institution, and vertically, each subject forming a department. The USSR Academy of Sciences is responsible for the co-ordination of research throughout Soviet higher education. It is a body separated from the Universities and from other higher educational institutions. In conducting and co-ordinating research, the Academy plays a crucial part in the development of a modern society, as innovation in science and its application in industry is a source of economic and military strength.

Under Stalin, firm political control was at least ostensibly maintained over the fields of biology and social studies – though physical sciences were less subject to direction. Khrushchev, in line with his thinking on bringing together education and practical problems of life, suggested that research work be co-ordinated to prevent duplication and that the more applied aspects of research be the responsibility of industrial enterprises.

> . . . Let us set up laboratories at plants and factories, establish scientific institutes and other scientific centres under the economic councils, and assign more young people to them, along with experienced and well-known scientists. Think over this problem, comrades, and make suggestions on it. I think the policy will prove correct . . . We shall ask the USSR Academy of Sciences, its Presidium, to draft proposals for further improving the activity of the Academy.[1]

This suggestion led to the emergence of two opposed groups in the Academy. On the one hand, pure scientists tended to support applied work being carried out in industry but saw science as an autonomous institution generating its own laws and processes. On the other hand, applied scientists tended to emphasise the unity of theory and applied practice – and opposed any movement of engineering away from the Academy.

The pure scientists led by a chemist, Nikolay Semenov, proposed that the Academy be re-shaped, in practice to resemble its non-Soviet predecessor in Tsarist Russia. Semenov's proposals included removal of the narrow engineering institutes, concentration on fundamental research by the Academy, reduction in the size of the Presidium of the Academy, the abolition of planning of theoretical research and the right of the Academy to retain the top ten to fifteen per cent of its post-graduates.[2]

Semenov's views were opposed by the engineers who, led by Ivan Bardin, argued that science and technology could not be divorced. Engels, it was pointed out, had noted that: 'Technology depends to a considerable extent on the state of science, science depends to a far greater degree on the state and requirements of technology'.[3]

The issue of reform of the Academy was not restricted to conflict between engineers and scientists. The members of the Academy of the Republican institutes also feared that their independence would be undermined by greater

---

[1] *Pravda*, 2 July 1959. Cited by L. R. Graham, 'Reorganisation of the USSR Academy of Sciences', in P. H. Juliver *et al*, *Soviet Policy-Making* (1967), p. 139.
[2] L. R. Graham, *loc. cit.*, p. 141.
[3] Cited by Graham, *loc. cit.*, p. 144.

'co-ordination'. A spokesman of the regions said: 'We must reject the idea that a central organ can plan and co-ordinate all the scientific work being conducted in the various institutes, laboratories, and higher educational institutions in the Soviet Union'.[1] Scientific councils or co-ordinating councils, organised on a subject, rather than a geographical, principle were advocated to co-ordinate research.

Yet another group interest voiced its disapproval of Semenov's and, indirectly, Khrushchev's proposals. This was composed of the university teachers. Here the status of the Academy was resented and its control over research opposed. Professor Kurosh wrote:

Academician N. Semenov's suggestion that the universities . . . should regard their main scientific activity as being the development of already extant branches of science gives rise to serious objections . . . It is precisely the universities that are best adapted to the establishment and development of fundamentally new trends in theoretical mathematics . . . since it is there that the opportunity exists to draw into research young students who are just taking their first steps in science and are therefore better able to grasp new ideas.[2]

The universities were regarded, by the university teachers, as being more virile institutions, more associated with 'life' and its pressures, whereas the Academy was 'academic', an ivory tower, aloof, and not able to play such a positive role as the universities.

The configuration of interests in the reorganisation of the Academy then appears as Khrushchev and the pure scientists, against the applied scientists, the universities and regional Academicians.

The reforms carried out since 1960 have tended to be along the lines advocated by Semenov. The narrow engineering institutes have been removed from the Academy, though engineers concerned with advanced engineering research remained in it. The State Committee of the Council of Ministers of the USSR for the co-ordination of Scientific Research[3] has been set up to co-ordinate all scientific work. In 1963 the co-ordinating role of the USSR Academy in the activities of Republican Academies and the higher education sector was re-emphasised.

This example illustrates the articulation of interests of those in institutions closely intertwined with the bureaucratic apparatus. As Graham concludes:

The reforms of the Academy illustrate that the leaders of the Communist Party of the Soviet Union rely on the expert opinion of specialists making decisions related to specific sectors of cultural and economic activity . . . Within the framework of

---

[1] A. Kirillin, 'Nauka i zhizn' ', *Pravda*, 13 March 1959. Cited by Graham, *loc. cit.*, p. 145.
[2] A. Kurosh, 'Dorogu smelym ideyam', *Izvestiya*, 18 Aug. 1959. Cited by Graham, *loc. cit.*, p. 146.
[3] Re-named State Committee for Science and Technology in 1965.

I*

strict political control by the party, the Soviet Union has devised a workable, but constantly evolving system for the inclusion of scientific advice in the process of making governmental decisions.[1]

The educational reforms of 1959 illustrate the role of regional groupings in the political process. This has been well illustrated by Vernon Aspaturian's study.[2] The reforms proposed by the Central Committee and the Council of Ministers, recommended that non-indigenous pupils of various Republics would have the right to opt out of the Republican language (i.e. Estonian in Estonia); also the indigenous population, attending Russian language-schools, were no longer to be obliged to learn the language of the Republic. This proposal threatened the non-Russian speaking nationalities. Dissent was expressed in the Supreme Soviet. Some republics, the Ukraine, Georgia, Armenia, Azerbaidzhan and the Baltic states vigorously championed their rights and the obligation they had to teach the indigenous language. 'We must not set up the Russian and the local indigenous language one against another by allowing people to choose between them. For us both languages are native languages, both of them are indispensable, and both are obligatory.'[3] The spokesmen of the Central Asian Republics and Moldavia were less hostile. The upshot of this pressurising was that the recommendations were left out of the all-union law. Each republic could decide the issue for itself. In the Russian Republic (RSFSR), the original proposals were incorporated in the laws and similar proposals were introduced in Uzbekistan, Tadzhikistan, Turkmenistan and Kirgizia. In the Ukraine, Russian was to be compulsory. In Armenia, Estonia and Georgia the laws would be 'implemented so as to strengthen the native languages rather than Russian'.[4] In Azerbaidzhan and Latvia the importance of the indigenous languages was emphasised. The central authorities however, had the last word and the legal requirements were later made more uniform – how they were enforced in the Republics is a different matter. The point to be made here, is that regional interests were articulated within the framework of the federal system. The central authorities had the last word, as Aspaturian puts it: 'the elites of the various nationalities are forced to play two social roles, each responding to different pressures and constituencies, often pulling in opposite directions. Since the political constituency of the non-Russian Soviet official is in Moscow, though his natural constituency is his national republic, he is more likely to be responsive to the interests of Moscow than to those of his republic.'[5]

---

[1] *Loc. cit.*, pp. 155-9.

[2] 'The Non-Russian Nationalities', in Allen Kassof, *Prospects for Soviet Society* (1968). For an excellent study of groups in education, see P. D. Stewart, 'Soviet Interest Groups and the Policy Process', *World Politics*, vol. 22, No. 1 (Oct. 1969).

[3] Speech at Supreme Soviet, cited by Aspaturian, p. 170.

[4] Aspaturian, *op. cit.*, p. 171.

[5] *Op. cit.*, p. 173.

'Loyal Dissenters'

The third group interest, which I have defined as 'loyal dissenters', is less well integrated than those already mentioned. Here, first, the technical and managerial groups and second, lawyers will be considered. The role of the former in politics has been long debated: as we have seen, some critics regard this group as a new Soviet ruling class (see pp. 178–83). Pethybridge has described the 'technocracy' as one of the 'minor' interest groups involved in Khrushchev's struggle for power.[1] The importance of professional groups and particularly of 'economic technicians' has been noted by Myron Rush in his study of political succession.[2] Probably the best study of managerial politics in contemporary Russia is that of Jeremy Azrael.[3]

Azrael says that

> the available data confirm that the managers have played [a significant role in Soviet political development] in a manner that justifies their treatment as a political group rather than as an aggregate of discrete political actors. In the first place, it is evident that managerial status has had an important influence on the political behaviour of the men concerned . . . In addition, most industrial executives have consciously recognised that they have important interests in common . . . Finally, there is good reason to believe that the managers have sometimes collectively engaged in more or less disciplined and co-ordinated political action. So far as one can judge on the basis of the available evidence, they have never emerged as a formally organised 'faction', but they do seem occasionally to have developed a common political strategy for the purpose of influencing public policy in a pre-determined direction. (p. 8).

Azrael describes the influence of the Red Directors during the Stalin era, and of managers under Khrushchev. For the later period he shows that the demands made by the managerial group did not transcend the boundaries defined by the elites. While they gained by the curbs on police action and the greater freedom of expression they sought to preserve their privilege and did not want a full-blooded destalinisation.[4]

It is difficult to find evidence of the articulation and aggregation of a *managerial* interest; rather the findings seem to point to fragmentation and particularisation of managerial interest. The ministerial industrial system[5] gives managers a loyalty to their industry in a way similar to that which managers give to their firm in the West. Soviet managers tend to be specialists tied to a production process rather than generalists, which reinforces institu-

---

[1] *Op. cit.* While he defines a technical elite (p. 33), he is also concerned with a much wider group of factory managers, construction chiefs and chief engineers – see p. 34.

[2] *Political Succession in the USSR* (New York, 1968), pp. 85–6.

[3] *Managerial Power and Soviet Politics* (Cambridge, Mass., 1966).

[4] See Azrael, *op. cit.*, Chapter 5.

[5] See Chapter 9.

tional loyalty. As industries compete for resources, then managerial interests too tend to be divided.

In the post-Stalin succession struggle, 'the managers' did not play a direct part in either Khrushchev's rise or fall. It is more likely that they played a supporting part, and that elitist groups advocated policies which would appease managers. Malenkov, for example, indicated 'that he was acutely aware of the need for more realistic planning. Nor was the appeal of his position on planning diminished by his simultaneous advocacy of greater investment in light industry'.[1] As I have argued above, party control was opposed by the ministerial elites and managers, and therefore Malenkov might also be regarded as a spokesman or articulator of managers' interests. The point must be made, however, that the managers were unable formally to aggregate and articulate such an interest themselves – this was left to members of the political elites.

The reorganisation of industrial ministries into a hundred or so economic regions (sovnarkhozy) again provides an indication of the ways a managerial interest was manifested. In 1955 George Glebovsky, the director of Uralmash, had publicly opposed the dismantling of the industrial ministries, and he too came out against Khrushchev's decentralisation plan.[2] Other 'extremely influential directors' also opposed Khrushchev on this issue.[3] While the managers as a group supported the 'anti-party' political faction, the political leadership of the managers was taken over by members of the government elite. At the time of Khrushchev's fall, the managers as a group do not seem to have played a very direct part in the succession struggle though their hostility to Khrushchev's economic policies and support for ministerial (as against party) power no doubt provided considerable backing for the anti-Khrushchev counter-elites. Kosygin, by background and attitude closely akin to the managers, has probably voiced their views. Certainly policy since Khrushchev's fall has been geared more closely to their interests – for instance, the strengthening of the ministerial system, the greater powers of managers over factory-level decisions and the emphasis now put at enterprise level on profit maximisation (see below, Chapter 9).

The foregoing discussion illustrates that managers have interests which are voiced and of which cognisance is taken by the political elite. In the crucial areas of group interest articulation and aggregation we lack adequate information to show how effective managers are as an interest group. The work of Azrael must be taken as tentative until we are able to study in detail the decision-making process. At present, the state of research on Soviet politics enables one to do no more than piece together scraps of information about

---

[1] Azrael, p. 125.
[2] *Pravda*, 4 April 1957, cited by Azrael, *op. cit.*, p. 135.
[3] *Ibid.*

what has happened and the lack of open channels of communication makes research in this field extremely difficult.[1]

As a second case study of 'loyal dissenters' we may consider the role of lawyers in effecting a change in article 89 of the Principles of the USSR and the Union Republics.[2] This article is concerned with government tort liability. Donald Barry shows that the campaign for 'socialist legality' led to a number of papers being written in professional journals. In *Sovetskoe gosudarstvo i pravo*,[3] a jurist asserted that 'the time has come to decide in legislative order the question of compensation for damages caused to a citizen by the illegal instituting of criminal proceedings, arrest or conviction in the event of his rehabilitation.'

In 1957, at the Supreme Soviet, the question of government tort liability was raised by a lawyer, Stefanik, and the existing statute was criticised. Barry goes on to show that Stefanik's views were echoed by members of the Lvov University Law Faculty (Stefanik was chairman of the executive committee of the Lvov *oblast*). It is interesting to note that the issue was discussed at an inter-university law conference in Moscow in 1958.[4] The topic was also discussed by other lawyers from Kharkov and Leningrad. It seems likely that professional interests are articulated and aggregated at such meetings.

Government lawyers were also involved in drafting new principles of civil legislation. In December 1959, the RSFSR Ministry of Justice held a meeting attended by other lawyers and legal scholars. At this meeting it was proposed 'that a rule be included in the draft of the Civil Code according to which governmental institutions would bear material liability according to general principles for injury caused by improper acts of officials.'[5]

Barry points out that when a draft of the new code was drawn up in 1959 it contained a clause essentially similar to the existing law. Therefore, he asserts, the proposals mentioned above must to some extent have been in opposition to the draft. He cites a Soviet writer commenting on the draft who says: 'it would be difficult to find another question which would manifest such *unanimous opinion among scientific and practical workers* as the question of the establishment of liability of government institutions for injury caused by administrative acts.'[6] The quotation would seem to suggest quite strongly that a professional opinion was here in evidence.

---

[1] We should note that in Albert Parry's study, the technical intelligentsia are shown to have a strong socio-political consciousness: see *The New Class Divided* (New York, 1966). Parry, moreover, doubts the loyalty of this group to the regime.

[2] Donald D. Barry, 'The Specialist in Soviet Policy-making: the Adoption of a Law', *Soviet Studies*, vol. 16 (no. 2) 1964.

[3] 1956, no 4.

[4] Barry, *loc. cit.*, p. 155, n.15.

[5] *Pravovedenie* 1957 (no. 1), p. 53. Cited by Barry, *loc. cit.*, p. 156.

[6] *Pravovedenie*, 1960 (no. 4), p. 45. Cited by Barry, *loc. cit.*, p. 157. Italics added.

After the publication of the draft Principles in 1960 (with no concessions to the above views), many lawyers explicitly opposed them. Discussion at conferences in a number of union republics ' "had shown that among both judicial workers and legal scholars there were almost no advocates of the preservation" of article 407' (the old Code).[1] Barry makes the excellent point that this particular statement was made by leading civil law authorities of the All-Union Institute of Juristic Sciences, which had worked out the draft with the RSFSR Ministry of Justice. Therefore, it would seem that the Ministry lawyers were opposing the introduction of wider ministerial liability, against. the professional workers outside.

In another publication a correspondent said 'the compilers of the draft of the Principles should listen to the voice of the wide scientific public and of authoritative practising jurists and radically change their approach to the liability of governmental institutions for injury caused by administrative acts.'[2] The protests culminated in an article signed by the complete faculty of the Leningrad Department of Civil Law, which advocated liability for improper official acts committed by governmental institutions.[3]

In December 1961, a revised version of the Principles of Civil Legislation was passed by the Supreme Soviet of the USSR. It contained in Article 89 a liability for tort by government institutions:

> Governmental institutions shall be liable for injury caused to citizens by improper official acts of their officials in the sphere of administrative governing according to general principles (Article 88 of the present Principles) if not otherwise provided by special law. For injury caused by such acts of officials to organisations, governmental institutions shall be liable under a system established by law.
>
> For injuries caused by improper official acts of officials of the organs of inquiry and preliminary investigations, of the procuracy and of the courts, the corresponding governmental organs shall bear property liability in cases and within limits specially prescribed by law.[4]

The significance of this case study is that there are certain areas of Soviet life, in which relatively free discussion may take place and in which opposing views may be publicly aired. Of course in not all cases of legal change do such exchanges publicly take place. Over the extension of the death penalty and anti-parasite laws in 1961 and 1962 no public discussion occurred.[5] But the case above does show, however, that lawyers *as a group* seem to have articulated a policy. We are unable to describe for lack of information the way in which specialists within the governmental ministries in practice help create

[1] *Sovetskaya yustitsiya*, 1960 (no. 8), pp. 6-7, cited by Barry.
[2] *Pravovedenie*, 1960 (no. 4), p. 45. Cited by Barry, p. 158.
[3] *Sovetskoe gosudarstvo i pravo*, 1961 (no. 2), p. 101.
[4] Article 89. Cited by Barry, *loc. cit.*, p. 153.
[5] Barry, *loc. cit.*, p. 159.

policy. It seems likely, however, that their advice and expertise is brought to bear on a large number of decisions.

'Amorphous' Social Groupings

'Amorphous' social groupings are even more difficult to pin down than the ones described above. We are concerned here with a group consciousness which may not be clearly articulated or measurable, such as the collective wishes of consumers. Consumers regularly interact as purchasers of commodities or services, but by virtue of the atomistic nature of individual purchasing, they lack group solidarity. If consumer interests are ignored, the government may find that 'tension' increases and morale falls – thereby thwarting other desirable policies and increasing political instability. 'Amorphous' interest groups, therefore, may indirectly influence decision-making. To maintain morale and to fulfil popular expectations concessions may be given to such interests and decisions may thereby be shaped by them. Alternatively, play may be given to consumer taste, by allowing consumers some choice through the market.

Maurice Friedberg has shown the influence of consumer preference in literature.[1] He shows that since 1953 Soviet publishing policy has paid much greater attention to public taste – the proportion of belletristic books to political ones rose from 79.5 per cent in 1946-53 to 191 per cent in 1959-62. This change was related to consumer demand. In city libraries political books were borrowed half as frequently as the average for all books.[2]

From the mid-1950s, Soviet publishers began to publish what the public wanted – light reading mainly originating from the West. For instance, between 1956 and 1957, Sherlock Holmes stories were printed in 1.5 million copies; 2 million and 3 million copies of Jules Verne and Dumas respectively were sold. The sale of *The Three Musketeers*, *The Count of Monte Cristo* and *Queen Margot* 'consumed almost twice as much paper as is used annually by the publishing house Sovetski Pisatel' for the printing of all new Soviet fiction, poetry, and drama'.[3]

Similarly, the theatre was affected by the same considerations. Theatre managers were required to make their performances pay. To the surprise of many western tourists, many plays and films on show in the USSR are of a low cultural standard and play to packed houses. In 1957, for instance, *Sovetskaya Rossiya* wrote:

The theatre season in Leningrad began in a rather disquieting manner. And not only because it was in Leningrad that the notorious *Telephone Call* (*Dial M for*

---

[1] 'Coexistence in Culture', in Juviler and Morton, *op. cit.*
[2] Friedberg, *loc. cit.*, p. 125.
[3] Friedberg, *loc. cit.*, p. 127.

Murder) was first rung. [It had been staged in 1956.] The fact is that nearly every Leningrad theatre got such a 'telephone call'. At one theatre it was called *Commotion at Night*, at another, *What Every Woman Knows*, at a third, still something else. The theatre managers, anxious to fill up the house, plainly lowered their repertory standards. They looked around to see what their neighbours were doing and eagerly took up the production of detective plays and farce comedies.[1]

These examples show the influence of public demand in an important political and ideological field. Friedburg concludes that various 'centrifugal forces' have resulted in a partial decentralisation of power in the Soviet Union.[2] The interpretation given here to the examples cited above is that the incumbents of power replacing Stalin were astute enough and had sufficient political *savoir faire* to accept consumer demands for light literature and light entertainment. Thereby they helped maintain a political equilibrium.

Estranged Groups

Social groupings which consider themselves estranged from the regime are the final category which makes a claim on the political authorities. Such groups advocate policies which the political elites consider to be harmful to the integrity of the Soviet order. The activity of such groups is usually ignored in the Soviet press and they campaign outside recognised channels by demonstrating, and by appeals in the foreign press. Considerable group activity takes place which is 'alien' to the dominant ideology.[3] Modern art and literature circles meet to discuss books such as *Cancer Ward* and other unpublished writings which are officially proscribed. Minority religious groups proselytise and conduct religious meetings outside the bounds of the legitimate religious orders.[4] Here we are not concerned with the structure and ideas of these groups but with the articulation of their demands into political inputs. Protests have been made in recent years over the trial and subsequent imprisonment of Sinyavski and Daniel, and public demonstrations have taken place in which religious and national minorities have demanded 'rights' or concessions from the regime. The political elites respond to these demands by making concessions and by suppression. Here we shall consider two examples: dissident literary intellectuals and the Baptists.

One of the traditional roles of literature in Tsarist Russia was to act as a medium of criticism of the political authorities. Since the late 1920's the

[1] *Sovetskaya Rossiya*, 16 May 1957. Cited by Friedburg, p. 128.

[2] *Ibid.*, p. 130.

[3] The Soviet writer Andrei Amalrik has said that by 1969 the 'cultural opposition' had given birth to a 'real political opposition to the regime'. Several groups have been tried and the social movement, claims Amalrik, is known by the title of the Democratic Opposition. See 'Will the USSR Survive Until 1984?' *Survey*, no. 73 (Autumn 1969), p. 50. See also above, p. 217.

[4] See M. Bourdeaux, *Religious Ferment in Russia* (1968), p. 127.

Communist Party has attempted to harness creative literary work to the goals of the party: literature was to be pervaded with the 'party spirit'. This has involved the description of a desirable state rather than the actual condition of Soviet society. Writers who have not written in this way according to the party line have suffered repression; most have had to circulate their works in the underground or have had them published abroad.[1]

Some of these writers consider themselves as 'loyal oppositions' rather than as groups opposed to the Soviet order as such. Some writers, such as Evtushenko, have at times received official approval. His poem 'The Heirs of Stalin' was published in *Pravda*. Here is an extract which shows the extent of 'officially approved' criticism in the early 1960s.

> *We bore him out of the mausoleum.*
> *But now, out of Stalin, shall we bear Stalin's heirs?*
> *Some of his heirs trim roses in retirement*
> *secretly thinking their discharge is temporary.*
> *Others, from rostrums, even heap abuse on Stalin*
> *but, at night, hanker after the good old days.*
> *No wonder Stalin's heirs seem stricken*
> *with heart attacks these days. They, once the stalwarts,*
> *detest this time of empty prison camps*
> *and halls packed with people listening to poets.*
> *The Party forbids me to be smug.*
> *'Why bother?' some urge me – but I can't be quiet.*
> *While the heirs of Stalin walk this earth,*
> *Stalin, I fancy, still lurks in the mausoleum.*[2]

The official party attitude to writers with critical thoughts about certain aspects of Soviet society (political corruption, anti-Semitism, individual morality) has fluctuated. At one time, Khrushchev gave his blessing to anti-Stalinist literature. But after the initial cultural thaw initiated by the publication of Dudintsev's, 'Not by Bread Alone', there has been an attempt by the Soviet cultural authorities to clamp down on the more outspoken criticism of the regime associated with the works of Evtushenko, Voznesensky, Nekrasov, Akhmadulina, Vinokurov and others. Khrushchev came out strongly against them. 'Anyone who advocates the idea of political coexistence in the sphere of ideology is, objectively speaking, sliding down to positions of anti-communism. The enemies of communism would like to see us ideologically

[1] There are numerous groups of such writers. McClure has divided them into five groups: the Dogmatists, the Slavophiles, the Russian Traditionalists, the Liberal Conservatives, the Modern Liberals. *Problems of Communism*, vol. 16 (no. 2) 1967, pp. 30-31. These are artistic and literary rather than political categories.

[2] 'The Heirs of Stalin', published in Patricia Blake and Max Hayward, *Half-Way to the Moon* (1964), pp. 220-1.

disarmed.'[1] In March and April 1963, party officials and 'Stalinist' writers combined to try to restrain the more outspoken intellectuals. Meetings were held and it was reported that Evtushenko has said that he had 'committed an irreparable mistake'. '(He) attempted to dispute the sharp criticism directed at him . . . but under the influence of the exacting, principled atmosphere of the plenary session [of the USSR Writers' Union] Evtushenko was nevertheless forced to talk of his mistakes.'[2] Others, however, have held firm. Some such 'progressive' writers, it is said, have been removed from positions in the cultural apparatus and from the boards of journals.

Others still have chosen to send their books abroad for publication. This provides a method not only for their views to be known, but also for them to be rebroadcast to the USSR and Eastern Europe by anti-Communist radio stations. The stories published in the West by such writers vividly show the kind of criticism which is voiced against the Soviet system by a minority in modern Russia. There is a constant battle behind the scenes between 'liberal' groups and the established cultural elites. Sometimes aggrieved intellectuals petition the elites to right some grievance suffered by one of their number.[3]

The trial of Daniel and Sinyavski is instructive in showing the way estranged groups are prevented from articulating their interests: they are suppressed because their activity threatens (at least in the eyes of the elites) the integrity of the system. The charge against the two authors was that they broke article 70, section 1 of the Criminal Code of the RSFSR:

Agitation or propaganda carried out with the purpose of subverting or weakening the Soviet regime or in order to commit particularly dangerous crimes against the state, the dissemination for the said purposes of slanderous inventions defamatory to the Soviet political and social system, as well as the dissemination or production or harbouring for the said purposes of literature of similar content, are punishable by imprisonment for a period of from six months to seven years and with exile from two to five years, or without exile, or by exile from two to five years.[4]

The public prosecutor argued that the work of the 'so-called "Soviet literary underground" was a form of "ideological subversion" in the interests of the "imperialist reactionaries" '. Sinyavski, it was alleged, had ridiculed the Soviet system and the principles of Marxism-Leninism; he had 'maliciously slandered Marxist theory and the future of human society'. Similar charges

---

[1] Cited by Patricia Blake, 'Freedom and Control in Literature 1962-63', in A. Dallin and A. F. Westin, *Politics in the Soviet Union* (New York, 1966), p. 188.

[2] *Literaturnaya Gazeta*, cited by Patricia Blake, *loc. cit.*, p. 192.

[3] See Readings nos. 10 and 11, and the protests at the trial of Sinyavski and Daniel published in *On Trial*, edited by L. Labedz and M. Hayward (London, 1967). On Soviet writers see *Soviet Literature in the Sixties* (1965), P. Blake and M. Hayward, *Half-Way to the Moon* (1964). A rather more positive view is taken by H. T. Willetts, 'New Directions', *Survey*, no. 36 (1963).

[4] Cited in *On Trial*, edited by Leopold Labedz and Max Hayward (1967), p. 149.

were made against Daniel who had depicted 'Soviet society as being in a state of moral and political decay. The story suggests that the entire Soviet people is to blame for the cult of personality, that 'our prisons are within us', that 'the Government is unable to give us our freedom', that 'we sent ourselves to prison'.[1] Sinyavski was sentenced to seven years and Daniel to five years in a labour camp.

The point here is not to pursue whether the charges, trial and sentences were just in any ethical sense, but to note that certain groups whose values are perceived to be hostile to those of the elites are forcibly restrained.[2] The Secret Police also plays a role in repressing anti-Soviet literature[3]; they play a similar role in relation to it as do the British police to pornography and pornographers. All police forces, of course, try to repress activities which threaten a given social order.

A second example of an estranged group is that of the Soviet Baptists. The persecution of Baptists has led to protests by them to change the *status quo*. Two Baptists wrote to Khrushchev in 13 August 1963 complaining that: 'Today all doubts have been removed that the church, formally separated from the state, is completely under the illegal control of various state organs, for whom both secret and open access to the church has been opened up by the apostate ministers who have entered into illegal deals and collaboration with organs of the government and the KGB'.[4] These views were articulated by two members of a 'reform movement' of the Baptist Church (an unofficial breakaway group from the state-sponsored All-Union Council of the Evangelical Christians and Baptists – AUCECB).

The Soviet government attempted to reduce this stress: the official Baptist organisation tried to unite the church and, according to Bourdeaux and Reddaway, other reformists were persecuted. But the persecution led to renewed protests: an account of the alleged torture of a church member in Kulunda was circulated and signed by 120 Baptists.[5] Even a conference of the relatives of prisoners of the reform church took place to collect information and to make the nature of persecution more widely-known.

As a result, a statement was published saying that the arrested were imprisoned for their religious beliefs – not for any violation of Soviet law. The conference decided to petition Khrushchev – whether this was done or not is unknown; but a delegation of twenty-six released Baptists did petition the Procuracy.[6] Other letters and interviews for the improvement of the Baptists' situation were sent to, and sought with, the Soviet political elite. In

---

[1] Cited in *On Trial*, pp. 152-4.
[2] See also Timothy McClure, 'The Cultural Scene', *Problems of Communism*, vol. 16 (no. 2) 1967.
[3] A. Anatol, 'Russian Writers and the Secret Police', *The Sunday Telegraph*, 10 Aug. 1969.
[4] Cited by M. Bourdeaux and P. Reddaway, 'Soviet Baptists Today', *Survey*, Jan. 1968, p. 55.
[5] See Bourdeaux, *Religious Ferment in Russia*, pp. 78-83.
[6] Bourdeaux and Reddaway, pp. 58-9.

September 1965, Mikoyan agreed to receive a delegation. And in May 1966, 500 delegates from 130 towns descended on Moscow to interview Brezhnev.

Brezhnev at first refused to see them and the petitioners sat down in the yard. But after a wait of a day and a half it was agreed to receive a delegation of ten. As the Baptists did not agree to this, they were arrested and imprisoned for ten to fifteen days. Bourdeaux and Reddaway point out that later in 1966 further legislation was passed which penalised those organising or participating in 'group actions which grossly violate public order, involve clear disobedience to the lawful demands of representatives of authority, or entail the disruption of the operation of transport, state and public enterprises or institutions'.[1] This does not seem to have had the effect of stopping illegal Baptist activity. The production and 'mass distribution' of religious literature still continued.[2] Many examples are available of the similar ways in which other estranged groupings articulate their interest to redress grievances. Protests have been made by way of petitions against the trial and subsequent imprisonment of writers demanding civil rights – freedom of speech, of assembly, of the press. The trials of Sinyavski and Daniel and others led to petitions concerning aspects of their legality. Two are included in the readings.

As Reddaway and Bordeaux point out, these activities are 'a remarkable form of challenge to the state's *de facto* authority in a particular sphere' (p. 66). The activities mentioned above expose only a small proportion of the ways alienated groupings aggregate and articulate their interest. Here the regime's response has been to attempt to dissipate the demands. From the point of view of the political process, action is taken which seeks to reduce stress.

One of the features of the Soviet Baptists' and intellectuals' campaign is the use of channels outside the USSR: the publication of letters and news of their persecution in such Bulletins as *Religion in Communist Dominated Areas*,[3] and the publicity subsequently received have the effect of *articulating* a demand into the Soviet political system, which may reinforce direct action at home. Not only foreign sources, such as the BBC and the Voice of America, but foreign communist newspapers, report news and comment which lead to internal interest articulation.[4] The political system, therefore, must be conceived of as a behavioural unit which transcends the geographical boundaries of the USSR. Even the articulation of amorphous groups'

[1] Cited by Bourdeaux and Reddaway, pp. 62-3.
[2] Many documents showing the forms of protest are reprinted in *Problems of Communism*, vol. 17 (no. 4) 1968.
[3] See vol. 7 (no. 3-4) 1968 for items on the Baptists.
[4] See for instance, the 'Petition of 46 Residents of Novosibirsk', who learned of the writers trials from foreign Communist newspapers, *Problems of Communism*, vol 17 (no. 4) 1968, p. 68.

interest can be shown to be influenced by geographically exogenous factors.

Before turning to discuss the structure of the Soviet economy, the salient features of the Soviet power structure and political process may be summarised. We have seen that the USSR is far from being a stereotyped form of totalitarianism with a dictatorial monistic ruling elite. As a state socialist political system, it has structural characteristics which differentiate it from liberal-democratic states: the state has a larger share of public ownership and a wider range of social control, there are no formal checks and balances between political institutions, social group interests are restricted in the ways they may be articulated. While the structures differ, the political *process* is essentially similar in all modern industrialised states. The political elites attempt to secure their own privileges by defending the existing social order, but the group structure of modern society and the demands engendered by it require the reconciliation of diverse interests. The presence of a single party is a distinction the USSR does not share with liberal societies, and communist ideology and the goals of a classless society too are unique characteristics. The party has changed from a narrow vertically integrated unit – the 'vanguard' of Lenin's theory of revolution – and it retains an aura not shared by other ruling parties. But the modern party operates in a society criss-crossed with specialised group and institutional interests. One of its main current functions is to integrate Soviet society; it seeks to promote a consensus conducive to the 'building of communism'. To do this it articulates a social programme, it aggregates interests and it adjudicates between conflicting interests. In these respects it acts like ruling parties in other large scale industrialised states but on a much wider scale. Also it includes within its structure representations of the major interest groups.

In a recent series of articles in *Problems of Communism*, the question has been posed as to whether the political system of the USSR can adapt to the demands made on it in the next twenty years.[1] If there is one thing a study of writing on the Soviet Union can teach, it is this: one should not attempt to predict the course of Soviet behaviour. Brzezinski's last article (May-June 1968), for instance, asserted that there was 'no one in effective power in the Soviet Union', and that the effect of the collective leadership is 'a kind of partial policy paralysis'.[2] Yet in August 1968, the Red Army and other Warsaw Pact countries forcibly occupied Czechoslovakia. This may have been mistaken, bloody or evil, but it is not indicative of a lack of effective

[1] See Zbigniew Brzezinski, 'The Soviet Political System: Transformation or Degeneration?', *Problems of Communism*, vol. 15, 1966; and articles on the same theme in the subsequent numbers of this journal. The final article appeared in the May-June issue 1968, 'Reflections on the Soviet System', vol. 17, no. 3.

[2] *Loc. cit.*, p. 47.

power, or of the paralysis of decision-making. Let us here therefore confine ourselves to an appraisal of past changes in the Soviet polity.

The Soviet political system has passed through a number of stages which may be described in terms of the compliance model and the use of sanctions which have been mentioned in Chapter 1. In the Stalin era, coercion and normative sanctions were predominant and the political institutions which were supreme were the police and the ministries. Under Khrushchev, the forms of sanctions changed to bring them into line with the more complex social structure. The police lost their arbitrary power and the role of the party was enhanced. The sanctions utilised by Khrushchev depended more on utilitarian factors: on providing greater individual material means, a higher level of services, more and greater financial incentives in industry. The *Programme of the CPSU* (1961) might well be said to be a blueprint for catching up with the West. The use of coercion was minimised: Stalin and the police regime were renounced; men were freed from the concentration camps; there has been no major political trial since 1956. To be sure, violence and coercion continued, as it does in all modern states, but it was not the predominant pattern. Khrushchev too, attempted to revive normative sanctions: people were to be guided in their activity by reference to the norm of the 'new Soviet man'. This was very much a secondary and not very effective mechanism of compliance. Under the new leadership of Brezhnev and Kosygin, the use of sanctions has changed slightly. The predominant pattern is still utilitarian (this will be discussed in more detail in the chapter on the economy). Somewhat greater use has been made of coercive powers. 'Dissident' intellectuals (such as Sinyavski) have been imprisoned. Abroad the military intervention in Czechoslovakia is another example. But coercion is still very much a subsidiary mechanism: there has been no recourse to terror, no return to the political trials of the Stalin era or to the use of forced labour. On the other hand, the use of utilitarian sanctions in the economy has increased considerably. One might well argue that the political system is now more utilitarian, slightly more coercive and less normative than it was under Khrushchev. These changes in political style illustrate the adaptive capacity of the Soviet political system, of its attempts to grapple not only with the problems of revolutionary change, as during and after 1917, but also to come to grips with the control and direction of a complex modern economy.

But all this does not entail the absence of considerable problems in the Soviet political system. In terms of interest articulation, the many amorphous groupings cannot make their claims known. The existence of a single candidate at elections does not encourage vigorous political activity on the part of deputies. The part-time nature of elected deputies makes their interest articulation role less effective than it might be. Interest aggregation is also less effective in the process of reconciling divergent views than in advanced western states. The notion that there is one policy, divined by the leaders of the CPSU, may deter the full discussion of the many-sided aspects of policy. The appraisal and reappraisal of policy is not always frank because the participant may be said to question the authority of the party. This may have the advantage that the public tends to follow government policy (say over Czechoslovakia) and it avoids the impression of division and weakness, but in fact, policies may change violently over time (for instance the policy on economic organisation discussed in the next chapter). Such changes and the sudden departure of personnel (such as Khrushchev) do not promote the confidence of the masses. The fact that institutional and group rivalries are not recognised and institutionalised, means that almost everything becomes politicised. In an institutionalised system of political conflict, one's interest is recognised and one is consulted through the relevant mechanisms. Without such institutionalisation, political conflict becomes more bitter, one must continually be on guard to defend one's interest. Finally, the enforcement policy of the Soviet state appears crude. The trials of writers and the invasion of Czechoslovakia are examples of the resort to coercion which cannot in the long run achieve the intended reduction of political stress. Indeed, they weaken the ideological sanctions entailed in the notion of 'the building of communism'. Here the political elites appear bound by the legacy of coercion, by previous responses. In a complex modern society, diversity and disagreement are inevitable; innovation is necessary for growth and change. Enforcements which sanctify only a rigid *status quo*, have the undesirable effects of creating a social environment unconducive to creativity: this applies as much to science and technology as it does to art and literature.

Reading No. 9
Open Letter from 176 Evangelical Christians and Baptists on the persecution of one of their number.
Source:
Published in *Problems of Communism*, July-August 1968, pp. 101-102.

In 1963 our Kiev community of Evangelical Christians and Baptists, together with the other communities [of believers in Kiev], authorised one of our members, preacher Georgi P. Vins, to represent us in the Organising Committee of the All-Union ECB Congress (now termed the Council of Churches of the ECB [CCECB]). As a member of this committee and later as its secretary, G. P. Vins was commissioned by the believers to submit petitions to the central authorities, as well as to ensure the reform of the spiritual ministry to all ECB communities throughout the country . . .

Nevertheless, no sooner was G. P. Vins elected to this office than he suffered persecution of various kinds – slander, attacks in the press, insults, threats of arrest, summonses to the procurator's office, etc. Nor was he the only one to suffer persecution. His wife was dismissed from her job with a compromising statement in her work record, so that up to now she has been unable to enjoy the constitutional right to work. His daughter was terrorised at school.

In May 1966, G. P. Vins was arrested in the reception room of the Central Committee of the CPSU, where he had been sent as a delegate by the CCECB to submit a petition addressed to L. N. Brezhnev requesting that the All-Union delegation of ECB believers, arrested on 17 May 1966, be released and received. On 29-30 November 1966, G. P. Vins and CCECB representative G. K. Kriuchkov were sentenced by the Moscow City Court to three years' imprisonment in a normal corrective labour camp under Article 142, para. 2, of the Criminal Code of the RSFSR, notwithstanding the fact that the court failed in fact to prove them guilty of any of the crimes of which they had been accused . . .

In February 1967, G. P. Vins was sent to serve his sentence in one of the camps of the Perm region, but in the summer of the same year he was transferred to another camp. (His address is P.O. Box 2040 A, Taly Postal District, Kizil, Urals). The conditions under which he is being kept in the new camp indicate the real reason for his transfer and the intentions of the responsible authorities.

The Kiev ECB community possesses reliable information as to the intent of certain agencies to liquidate Georgi Petrovich Vins by means of camp conditions. Vins has now been reduced to a state of complete physical exhaustion. Violating the existing regulations of the Ministry of Public Order governing the treatment of prisoners in camps, the authorities made Vins, a member of the building brigade, walk five to six miles every day under guard to his place of work and back over rugged, mountainous terrain (ten to twelve miles daily in all). Though an engineer by profession, he was employed as a manual hauler, dragging logs from the forest for the construction of railway buildings.

According to the regulations, Vins should be released before serving his full sentence, as he has never infringed camp rules. The camp administration recommended him for early release but the Taly administrative commission refused to grant it. This fact also reveals that Vins is being discriminated against for his religious convictions, and in the light of all the above our fears for Vins' life have increased . . .

1. We consider the transfer of G. P. Vins to a job suited to his present state of health absolutely essential. If this is not done, our fears will be confirmed that he is being liquidated wittingly and with the sanction of the authorities.

2. We request that a government commission be set up to investigate the treatment of G. P. Vins in camp, as well as the conditions under which all other ECB believers are detained, since several of those sentenced for their faith in God are facing death in labour camps.

3. Once more we bring before the Procuracy of the USSR the question of reviewing the cases of Vins and of all other imprisoned ECB believers in order that they may be rehabilitated.

We pray to our Heavenly Father that He may give you wisdom. We ask all ECB believers to increase their prayers for brother Vins and all those fulfilling their mission in bondage.

25 February 1968

On behalf of the 400 ECB believers of Kiev,
[signed by 176 members]

Reading No. 10
Petition on the Trial of A. Ginzburg.
Source:
Novoe russkoe slovo, 7 April 1968. Reprinted in *Problems of Communism*, July-August 1968, pp. 42-3.
To the Moscow Municipal Court
Copy to Defence Counsel B. A. Zolotukhin

According to rumours circulating around Moscow, the Moscow Municipal Court will hear the case of A. Ginzburg within the next few days.

Many circumstances connected with the trial of A. Ginzburg, who was arrested about a year ago, cannot fail to arouse the alarm of the public: the unprecedented duration of the twelve-month preliminary imprisonment before trial, the absence in our press of any word whatsoever about the reasons for A. Ginzburg's arrest and the prolonged investigation. Those of us who know A. Ginzburg personally do not doubt his integrity and decency. His basic interests lie in the field of culture; he has not been engaged in political activity as such. The collection of documents he compiled (which included articles from our press as well as official documents) concerning the Siniavsky-Daniel case, which so deeply disturbed our society, cannot constitute sufficient reason for his arrest and trial. This trial cannot sanitise the atmosphere of a society which not long ago witnessed mass rehabilitations of persons who had been sentenced on false charges.

The abnormal circumstances noted above compel us to ask the Moscow Municipal Court to take the case of A. Ginzburg under special consideration and to ensure the airing of public testimony, the unprejudiced selection of witnesses, and wide coverage of the trial in the press.

Copies to the following:
Chairman of the Council of Ministers of the USSR, A. N. Kosygin.
Secretary General of the CPSU Central Committee, L. I. Brezhnev.
Chairman of the Presidium of the Supreme Soviet of the USSR, N. V. Podgorny.

Signatures:
V. Aksionov, Member of the Writers' Union
B. Akhmadulina, Member of the Writers' Union
A. Babaev, Member of the Writers' Union, Candidate in Philological Sciences
B. Birger, Artist, Member of the Artists' Union
K. Bogatyrev, Member of the Writers' Union
V. Veisberg, Artist, Member of the Artists' Union
I. M. Gelfand, Corresponding Member, Academy of Sciences, USSR
Yu. Glazov, Candidate in Philological Sciences
Ye. Golysheva, Member of the Writers' Union
Ye. Grin, Editor
A. Dobrovich, Doctor
M. Zand, Fellow of the Institute of the Peoples of Asia, Academy of Sciences, USSR
V. Ivanov, Deputy Secretary of the Institute of Slavic Studies, Academy of Sciences, USSR
M. Ivanov, Member of the Artists' Union
F. A. Iskander, Member of the Writers' Union
L. Keldysh, Professor, Doctor of Physical-Mathematical Sciences
E. Liakhovich, Interpreter
P. Novikov, Full member of the Academy of Sciences, USSR
N. Otten, Member of the Writers' Union
A. M. Piatigorsky, Candidate in Philological Sciences
I. Revzin, Doctor of Philological Sciences
Rozenfeld, Professor, Doctor of Biological Sciences
K. Rudnitsky, Member of the Writers' Union
M. Segal, Fellow of the Institute of Slavic Studies, Academy of Sciences, USSR
Ye. Semeka, Candidate in Historical Sciences
N. Stoliarova, Member of the Literary Fund

T. *Tsivian*, Candidate in Philological Sciences
I. R. *Shafarevich*, Corresponding Member, Academy of Sciences, USSR
Yu. *Edlis*, Member of the Writers' Union
A. *Yaglom*, Professor, Doctor of Phys.-Math. Sciences

Reading No. 11
Petition on the Legality of the Trial of Ginzburg, Galanskov, Dobrovolsky and Lashkova.
Source:
Novoe Russkoe slovo, 27 Feb., 7 March 1968. Reprinted in *Problems of Communism*, July-August 1968, pp. 52-4

To: Procurator General of the USSR Rudenko
  The USSR Supreme Court
In December 1967, letters were sent to various procuratorial and judicial offices requesting that those who wished to do so be allowed to attend the [then] impending trial of Ginzburg, Galanskov, Dobrovolsky, and Lashkova. The signers of these letters considered it their civic duty to press the authorities to make the trial public, since in the past our society had repeatedly been faced with flagrant violations of legality committed in court cases where the proceedings were either hidden from or falsified to the public. Such was the case, for example, in the trials of Siniavsky and Daniel, of Khaustov, and of Bukovsky. All these trials were declared to be public, but in reality were not. Only persons with special passes were allowed into the court-room, and the criteria for the issuance of these passes and the person(s) who issued them are not known. In sum, a specially selected 'public' was present in the court-room, while friends and even several close relatives of the defendants were not permitted to attend.

Only through the device of keeping the public ignorant of the proceedings was the KGB able to settle accounts with the dissidents. Indeed the accused, who acted within the framework of our Constitution and our laws, and who in several instances used the Constitution as their defence, demanded that legality be observed, but were nevertheless committed to harsh sentences without genuine evidence of their guilt. In any event, the public has no knowledge of such evidence. Only in the absence of open hearings could our press have printed reports which distorted the trial proceedings and grossly deceived readers regarding the trials' true nature. (For example, the only published notice concerning the Bukovsky's trial, in the newspaper *Vecherniaia Moskva*, informed the public that Bukovsky had admitted his guilt, although this was completely false.)

There have been no answers to the letters [mentioned above], and not one of the signers of the letters has received permission to attend the trial, which has just been completed. Furthermore, the trial of Ginzburg, Galanskov, Dobrovolsky, and Lashkova was characterised by even more scandalous violations of legality and turned out to be a repetition, in still more sombre form, of the other previously-mentioned trials.

All entrances to the Moscow Municipal Court building were guarded by numerous KGB functionaries, as well as by *druzhinniki* and policemen, who refused entry to anyone who did not possess special authorisation (the nature of which they stubbornly refused to disclose). During the days of the trial, the 'Commandant of the Court' was Tsirkunenko, a colonel of the KGB. Characteristically, even the relatives of the defendants were not all, and not immediately, admitted to the court-room, even though many of them carried legal summonses. Relatives of the defendants, witnesses, and other citizens were subjected to rude treatment, threats, and insults; they were photographed in order to intimidate them, their conversations were subjected to eavesdropping. Throughout the trial, constant surveillance was maintained over the relatives and close friends of the defendants with the express purpose of blackmailing them.

All this was done so that no objective information could leak out of the court-room. For example, the wife of Galanskov and the fiancée of Ginzburg received threats that added reprisals would be taken against the defendants if accounts of the trial were written down. Unknown persons coming out of the courtroom attempted to give completely false information to foreign correspondents, who themselves had not been admitted to the court session.

Many of us were witnesses to these facts and are prepared to corroborate them

The fact that the organisation which carried out the investigation [of the accused) was constantly involved in efforts to keep the trial from being public is a mockery of justice which should not be permitted in a civilised society. No one who respects himself and his calling as a judge had the right to conduct a court hearing under such conditions. And the fact that the trial proceedings were in every way kept hidden from the public appears to be sufficient grounds for a vote of non-confidence in the court and its verdict.

Therefore we cannot believe either in the justice of the [court's] prosecution of the case of Ginzburg, Galanskov, and Lashkova, or in the truth or sincerity of Dobrovolsky's testimony, on the basis of which the former were alleged to have had ties with the NTS. This testimony compels us to recall the even more menacing aspects of the trials of the 1930s, when accused persons were subjected to coercion during the period of investigation and forced to admit their own guilt and that of others, with the result that millions of people were executed, tortured, or incarcerated in labour camps for decades. In this connection, it must be noted that in this case the accused were held in isolated confinement for investigation during an entire year, which far and away exceeds the investigatory periods stipulated under the Complete Procedural Code of the RSFSR.

It is generally known that Ginzburg compiled a collection of materials relating to the trial of Siniavsky and Daniel, which evoked a reaction on the part of both the Soviet and the world public; that Galanskov was editor of the mimeographed journal *Phoenix*, the contents of which had included, specifically, protocols of the discussion of the draft of the third volume of the *History of the Party* by Old Bolsheviks and documents of the Writers' Union recording the expulsion of Boris Pasternak from the Union; and finally, that Lashkova typed these materials. These things had been done openly. They [Ginzburg and Galanskov] placed their signatures on all the manuscripts. They attempted to make these materials public so that they could circulate openly. Soviet laws do not prohibit such activity.

Do these actions of the defendants consitute a just basis for their arrest? Isn't the indictment accusing them of having ties with subversive organisations (NTS) a typical means of reprisal utilised in the days of Stalin?

Such questions naturally arise as a result of the violations of the public's right to be informed that were perpetrated during this trial. Is it not incredible that people who acted openly and supported openness were in fact judged and sentenced secretly? A court organised and acting lawfully would not only have no fear of publicity but would welcome it in every way.

We demand a retrial of the case of Ginzburg, Galanskov, Dobrovolsky, and Lashkova by a reconstituted court acting in conformity with all the norms of legal procedure and with full publicity.

We also demand that those officials guilty of gross violations of legality in this trial be brought to account.

Yu. Apresian, Candidate in Philological Sciences

Afanaseva, Member, USSR Union of Journalists

L. Alekseeva, Editor

K. Babitsky, Linguist

S. Belokrinitskaia, Linguist

K. Bogatyrev, Member, Union of Soviet Writers

L. Belova, Candidate in Philological Sciences; Member, Union of Cinematographers

N. Vvedenskaia, Candidate in Phys.-Math. Sciences

N. Viliams, Instructor, MITKhT [Moscow Institute of Precise Chemical Technology]

Ye. Vinogradova, Candidate in Fine Arts

A. Velikanov, Physicist

T. Velikanova, Mathematician

Ye. Volkovmokaia, Linguist

S. Gindikin, Candidate in Physical-Mathematical Sciences

Yu. Gastev, Teacher, Moscow State University

M. Grabar, Lecturer, Moscow Institute of Aviation Technology

Yu. Glazov, Candidate in Philological Sciences

S. Goffe, Artist

P. Gaidenko, Candidate in Philosophical Sciences

Yu. Gerchuk, Critic; Member, USSR Union of Artists

I. Golomshtok, Art historian; Member, USSR Union of Artists

R. Dobrushin, Doctor of Physical-Mathematical Sciences

V. Dybo, Candidate in Philological Sciences

Yu. Davydov, Candidate in Philosophical Sciences

M. Domshlak, Art historian

V. Ivanov, Candidate in Philological Sciences

Ye. Kopeleva, Proofreader, Publications Section, State Radio Committee

G. Korpelevic, Graduate Student, MGU [Moscow State University]

Kasatkin, Candidate in Philological Sciences

L. Kapanadze, Candidate in Philological Sciences

L. Krysin, Candidate in Philological Sciences

O. Kiselev, Actor
R. Minlos, Candidate in Physical-Mathematical Sciences; Senior Scientific Worker, MGU
I. Milchuk, Candidate in Philological Sciences
V. Meniker, Economist
A. Ogurtsov, Candidate in Philosophical Sciences
B. Poliak, Candidate in Physical-Mathematical Sciences
S. Pozharitskaia, Candidate in Philological Sciences
A. Piatigorsky, Candidate in Philological Sciences
L. Pazhitnov, Candidate in Philosophical Sciences
Sedov, Candidate in Historical Sciences
N. Sadomskaia, Candidate in Historical Sciences
V. Skvirsky, Geographer
Ye. Semeka, Candidate in Historical Sciences
M. Taniuk, Director
Yu. Telesin, Mathematician
M. Ulanovskaia, Bibliographer
M. Feigina, Historian
I. Faleeva, Sociologist
B. Shragin, Candidate in Philosophical Sciences
A. Yakobson, Translator

Send answers to this appeal to the following address:
Moscow G-117 Pogodin Street, House 2/3, Apt. 91, B.I. Shragin.
27 January 1968

26 Additional Signatures:
N. Belogorodskaia, Engineer
G. Bulatov, Actor
Yu. Blumental, Musician
N. Blumental, Student at the Institute of Culture
P. Grigorenko, Construction Engineer, SU-20 Moscow Building Trust; former Major-General; Candidate in Military Sciences; Lecturer
A. Grigorenko, Senior Technician
Yu. Gubanov, Electrician
D. Daniel, Schoolboy, son of Yuli Daniel
N. Yemelkina, Civil Servant
D. Zhitomirsky, Doctor of Art History
A. Kosterin, Writer; spent 17 years in Stalinist labour camp, 3 years in a Tsarist prison; member of the CPSU; father of Nina Kosterina
A. Kaplan, Candidate in Physical-Mathematical Sciences
M. Kazartev, Worker
G. Kravtsova, Plumber
O. Leonteva, Candidate in Art History
V. Nikolsky, Senior Engineer, Physicist
A. Pavlova, Construction Engineer

S. Pisarev, Scientific Worker
M. Puzikov, Engineer
I. Rudakov
V. Teterin, Civil Servant
M. Shaposhnikov
Yu. Yukhnovets, Worker
A. Khrabrovitsky, Literary Scholar
A. Tsvetopolskaia, Senior Engineer
Utinka, Senior Engineer
6 February 1968

INTRODUCTORY

Almond, G. A. and G. B. Powell. *Comparative Politics: A Developmental Approach.* Boston: Little, Brown and Co., 1966.

Brzezinski, Zbigniew, K. *Ideology and Power in Soviet Politics.* New York: Praeger, 1967.

'The Soviet Political System: Transformation or Degeneration?', *Problems of Communism*, Vol. 15, Jan.-Feb. 1966, pp. 1-15.

Brzezinski, Z. K. and S. Huntington. *Political Power USA/USSR.* London, Chatto and Windus, 1964.

Pethybridge, Roger. *A Key to Soviet Politics: The Crisis of the 'Anti-Party' Group.* London: Allen and Unwin, 1962.

Skilling, H. Gordon. 'Interest Groups and Communist Politics', in *World Politics*, Vol. 18, No. 3, 1966, pp. 435-51.

'Soviet and Communist Politics: A Comparative Approach', in *Journal of Politics*, Vol. 22, 1960, pp. 300-13.

'Interest Groups in Soviet Politics', (*Duplicated Paper*).

'The Party, Opposition and Interest Groups in Communist Politics: Fifty Years of Continuity and Change', in Kurt London, *The Soviet Union: A Half Century of Communism.* Baltimore: The Johns Hopkins Press, 1968.

BASIC

Amalrik, Andrei. 'Will the USSR Survive Until 1984?' in *Survey*, No. 73, Autumn 1969, pp. 47-79.

Aspaturian, Vernon. 'The Non-Russian Nationalities', in Allen Kassof (ed.). *Prospects for Soviet Society.* London: Pall Mall Press, 1968, pp. 143-98.

Azrael, Jeremy. *Managerial Power and Soviet Politics.* Cambridge, Mass.: Harvard University Press, 1966.

Brzezinski, Z. K. 'Reflections on the Soviet System', in *Problems of Communism*, Vol. 17, No. 3, May-June 1968, pp. 44-48.

Gallagher, M. P. 'Military Manpower: A Case Study', in *Problems of Communism*, Vol. 13, No. 3, May-June 1964, pp. 53-62.

Granick, David. *The Red Executive: A Study of the Organisation Man in Russian Industry.* Garden City, New York: Doubleday, 1960.

Ploss, Sidney I. *Conflict and Decision Making in Soviet Russia: A Case Study of Agricultural Policy, 1953-63.* Princeton, New Jersey: Princeton University Press, 1965.

Rush, Myron. *Political Succession in the USSR* (Second Edition). New York: Columbia University Press, 1968.

K

Stewart, Philip D. 'Soviet Interest Groups and the Policy Process: the Repeal of Production Education', in *World Politics*, vol. 22, No. 1, October 1969.

Tatu, Michel. *Power in the Kremlin: From Khrushchev's Decline to Collective Leadership*. London: Collins, 1969.

Wolfe, T. W. 'Political Primacy vs. Professional Elan', in *Problems of Communism*, Vol. 13, No. 3, May-June 1964, pp. 45-52.

SPECIALISED

Armstrong, John A. 'Party Bifurcation and Elite Interests', in *Soviet Studies*, Vol. 17, No. 4, April 1966, pp. 417-30.

Barry, Donald B. 'The Specialist in Soviet Policy-Making: the Adoption of a Law', in *Soviet Studies*, Vol. 16, No. 2, October 1964, pp. 152-65.

Blake, Patricia. 'Freedom and Control in Literature, 1962-63', in A. Dallin and A. F. Westin (Eds.), *Politics in the Soviet Union: Seven Case Studies*. New York: Harcourt 1966, pp. 165-206.

Bourdeaux, M. *Religious Ferment in Russia: Protestant Opposition to Soviet Religious Policy*. London: Macmillan, 1968.

Bourdeaux, M. and P. Reddaway. 'Soviet Baptists Today', *Survey*, No. 66, January 1968, pp. 48-66.

Conquest, Robert. *Russia after Khrushchev*. London: Pall Mall Press, 1965.

Evtushenko, E. 'The Heirs of Stalin', in Patricia Blake and Max Hayward (eds.), *Halfway to the Moon, New Writing from Russia*. London: Weidenfeld and Nicolson, 1964, pp. 220-21.

Friedberg, Maurice. 'Coexistence in Culture', in P. H. Juviler and H. W. Morton (eds.), *Soviet Policy-Making: Studies of Communism in Transition*. London: Pall Mall Press, 1967, pp. 121-32.

Graham, L. R. 'Reorganisation of the USSR Academy of Sciences', in P. H. Juviler and H. W. Morton (eds.), *Soviet Policy-Making: Studies of Communism in Transition*. London: Pall Mall Press, 1967, pp. 135-62.

Kirillin, A. 'Nauka i zhizn',' *Pravda*, 13 March 1959.

Kolkowicz, Roman. *The Soviet Military and the Communist Party*. Princeton, New Jersey: Princeton University Press, 1967.

Kurosh, A. 'Dorogu smelym ideyam', in *Izvestiya*, 18 August 1959.

Labedz, L. and M. Hayward (eds.), *On Trial* (documents). London: Collins and Harvill Press, 1967.

Lasswell, H. D., D. Lerner, C. E. Rothwell. *The Comparative Study of Elites*. Stanford, California Hoover Institute Studies: Stanford University Press, 1952.

Literaturnaya Gazeta. March or April, 1963.

McClure, Timothy. 'The Politics of Soviet Culture, 1964-7' in *Problems of Communism*, Vol. 16, No. 2, March-April 1967, pp. 26-43.

Nove, Alec. 'The Uses and Abuses of Kremlinology', in Alec Nove, *Was Stalin Really Necessary?* London: Allen and Unwin, 1964.

Page, M. and David Burg. *Unpersoned: The Fall of Nikita Sergeyevitch Khrushchev*. London: Chapman and Hall, 1966.

Parry, Albert. *The New Class Divided – Science and Technology versus Communism.*
    New York: Macmillan, 1966.
Pravda, 4 April 1957 (opposition to industrial reorganisation).
Pravda, 2 July 1959 (on reorganisation of the Academy of Sciences).
Pravda, 15 January 1960 (on Khrushchev's military reorganisation).
Pravda, 22 June 1961 (on Khrushchev's concession to the military).
Problems of Communism, Vol. 17, No. 4, July-August 1968. (Baptist protest docu-
    ments).
Religion in Communist Dominated Areas, Vol. 7, No. 3-4 Feb. 1968 (items on
    Baptists).
Soviet Literature in the Sixties. London: Methuen, 1965.
Truman, David B. *The Governmental Process.* New York: A. A. Knopf, 1951.
Willetts, H. T. 'New Directions', in *Survey*, No. 46, 1963, pp. 3-8.

9

THE ECONOMY,
GENERAL FEATURES

We have seen that the Russian Marxists were opposed to the economic relationships which existed under a capitalist system. But though they were guided by Marxist ideas, they had no blueprint on which a socialist economic order could be constructed. In this chapter we shall discuss the economic system the Russian communists have devised. First we shall briefly describe the structure of the Soviet economy, the mechanism of planning, and second we shall study comparatively the standard of living it generates. In the next chapter we shall focus on the industrial enterprise to consider management, trade unions and the worker's attitude to work.

Socialist Forms of Economy

The Soviet system is one which is called state socialist. It is not the only form a 'socialist' economy could take. We may briefly outline four forms of ownership and economic organisation in a socialist system in contrast to modern western capitalism. These are syndicalism, managerial socialism, state socialism and communism.[1]

Syndicalism is a system in which the owners of enterprises are the workers employed in them. Individual work units determine output. In the Yugoslav state, where elements of a syndicalist system have been adopted, a director, who may be removed by the workers, is responsible for the administration of the factory, workers are paid a wage but in addition a part of profits or surpluses accruing to the enterprise are distributed to the workers or used for the enterprise's benefit (e.g. for reinvestment or for workers' housing). Such a system of ownership may exist in a market type economic exchange system, or in one where a central planning agency may take macro decisions (it may control investment, have a monopoly of foreign trade, and control the flow of money). Syndicalist factories existed in the USSR after the revolution when workers spontaneously expropriated private property and instituted workers' control believing that socialist democracy involved the abolition of factory

[1] For further discussion see P. Wiles, *The Political Economy of Communism* (1964).

administration. As we saw earlier, syndicalism was opposed by the Bolsheviks.

Managerial socialism is a mixed system in which privately owned production units coexist with a state sector under government ownership and control. In addition, the state exercises overall control by fiscal and other measures. Such a mixed system exists today, on a small scale, in East Germany (GDR) and existed in the Soviet Union, on a larger scale, during the New Economic Policy.[1]

Under *state socialism*, ministries and local authorities own and manage production enterprises. Prices and output of individual firms are largely determined by central or regional boards. Industries and their sub-units (enterprises) operate like ministries in western countries. Profits and losses accrue to the state exchequer. No distinction is made between such industrial or trade ministries and social ministries such as that between nationalised boards and ministries in Britain.

Analytically, it is preferable to call such a system state socialism and reserve the term state capitalism[2] for societies in which industry is privately owned but state controlled (such as in Britain or Germany during the Second World War). This conforms to the generally accepted distinction between capitalism being based on private ownership and socialism on public or state ownership.

Under *communism*, an abundance of consumer goods exists: there are no shortages, there is no scarcity. Therefore, goods and factors of production have no price. Individuals work 'according to their ability' and receive 'according to their need'. The achievement of communism is the goal of the Soviet state. It is a utopian goal, rather than an actual socio-economic system.

Today, the USSR comes most closely to the state socialist model described above: it is an administered or command economy in which the influence of individual consumers and producers is replaced by administrative bodies which make decisions for the whole economy. It determines what and how much is to be produced and the price at which things must be sold. This entails decisions by the central planners about which collection of goods is to be produced. In industry, all prices (of goods and labour) are fixed by the planners. The individual has little control over the economy; the state monopoly of production, distribution and exchange replaces the market: the consumer is less powerful in the USSR than his counterpart in the USA. Such a stark model is modified in practice. We shall see that though the Soviet economy is predominantly of the command type, market elements exist.

The fundamental distinction between a capitalist 'market' economy and a Soviet 'command' one is that in the former, in theory, *individual interests* are dominant, the state providing mechanisms to promote them; in the latter case, *collective* or state interest is dominant, the government acting to destroy the

[1] See Chapter 3.
[2] 'State capitalist' theories of the USSR have been discussed above, Chapter 6.

individual articulation of interest. In a 'free economy' property is privately owned, and the state intervenes to protect the consumer and worker against exploitation. In a 'command' or state socialist economy property is communally owned, the state directly controls the economy. This is not to say, as Galbraith[1] has pointed out, that contemporary western societies are composed of small competing private businesses: many large American corporations are closely geared to the demands of the government. But western societies contain a large number of private businesses, small manufacturers, retail shops, garages, farms, which depend on the market and give consumer demand a power unknown in Soviet society.

As we have seen in the historical chapters, government control was ensured by the nationalisation of industry and the land. It is now illegal for one man to employ another for trade or production. Ownership is vested in the state and control in government ministries. There are some areas of economic activity outside direct government control. A small co-operative industrial sector continues which is based on the group activity of a number of workers who own and market their produce. Individual craftsmen (cobblers, watch repairers) and some professional specialists (dentists, doctors) may still give private services – provided that they are registered. Secretaries and domestic helps may be hired privately.

A generally held view is that in state socialist societies control is highly centralised: 'In the totalitarian societies the process of concentration of power in a small elite reached its zenith.'[2] This, however, is far too oversimplified. In agriculture, the produce of farmers' private plots is completely outside government control: it is sold at a price fixed by supply and demand in the free market. Some of the produce of collective farms is also sold in this way.

Industrial enterprises and 'state' farms (not 'collective' farms) are organised by the government which decides what shall be produced: what proportion of output is devoted to consumption and investment; it is responsible for fixing the price of inputs: raw materials and basic wage rates, and outputs: the prices of finished and semi-finished products.

In a nutshell, the Soviet planning process enables key policy decisions to be taken centrally: the 'aggregation' of economic decision-making is centralised. The carrying-out of decisions is delegated: 'output and enforcement' are performed in practice by ministries.

The Structure of the Soviet Economy

We must now consider just how the government organises the economy: how it comes to make decisions, how it chooses between alternative policies, and how it enforces decisions.

[1] J. K. Galbraith, *The New Industrial State* (1967), Chapter 35.
[2] T. B. Bottomore, *Sociology* (1962), p. 140.

In theory, it might be claimed that the ministerial industrial system has the advantages of a 'rational bureaucracy'.[1] We discussed the bureaucratic model of Soviet society above in Chapter 6; here Weber's theory may be summarised. Policy is made at the top where all knowledge is available. Decisions are not based on a lower individual's personal judgement and, therefore, 'arbitrary' decisions are not made: each case is decided according to the application of the rules, and rational decisions may be made fairly rapidly. Personal feelings between individuals are minimised and replaced by the authority and duty of the office. Appointment and promotion are determined by ability and effort, and not by personal influence or family connection. But the Soviet Union as a bureaucratic organisation has differed from those studied by Weber in that it has been an agency of social transformation, rather than one simply of the administration of rules,[2] though at present it has a more conservative function.

The above points are advantages given by an efficient bureaucratic apparatus but large-scale bureaucracy also has disadvantages. Problems are not studied from all point of view but merely as features of prescribed factors. While central decision-making may reduce arbitrariness, the ideas and initiative of lower officials may be stifled. The application of rules may be slow and decisions may be passed from one official to another. The rules themselves become inflexible and difficult to apply to new tasks. Appointment is subject to obsolete criteria and advancement determined by seniority.

The Soviet economic system has attempted to have the advantages of a centralised bureaucracy whilst mitigating the 'dysfunctional' elements outlined above. Particularly important, in the second respect, is the existence of a dual chain of 'control' at all levels of the industrial (and government) hierarchy by which the Communist Party of the Soviet Union is especially charged with the task of circumventing such evils. Before turning to the party's role we must consider how the Soviet economy is organised in practice.

In our discussion of the government apparatus we saw that centralisation was achieved through the All-Union government and the Communist Party, and decentralisation of administration through the federal units. This is paralleled in the economy and is shown diagrammatically on Chart 12. The key decisions are taken in the Council of Ministers/Politbureau: such decisions are concerned with the rate of growth, the priority of different industries and regions.[3] Much of the detailed policy formulation is performed both in the

---

[1] See Max Weber, 'The Essentials of Bureaucratic Organisation: An Ideal-Type Construction', in R. K. Merton (ed.) *Reader in Bureaucracy* (New York, 1952), pp. 18-26.

[2] This point is made by L. Churchward, *Contemporary Soviet Government* (1968), p. 3. See also the discussion, above, pp. 175-8.

[3] Apart from Chapter 5 above, I have ignored the historical development of industrial management. For details see G. Bienstock *et al.*, *Management in Russian Industry and Agriculture* (1944) Chapter 1. A much more detailed account is to be found in B. M. Richman *Soviet Management* (1965). For 1970 economic plan see: *Soviet News* 23 Dec. 1969.

CHART 12 Soviet Economy

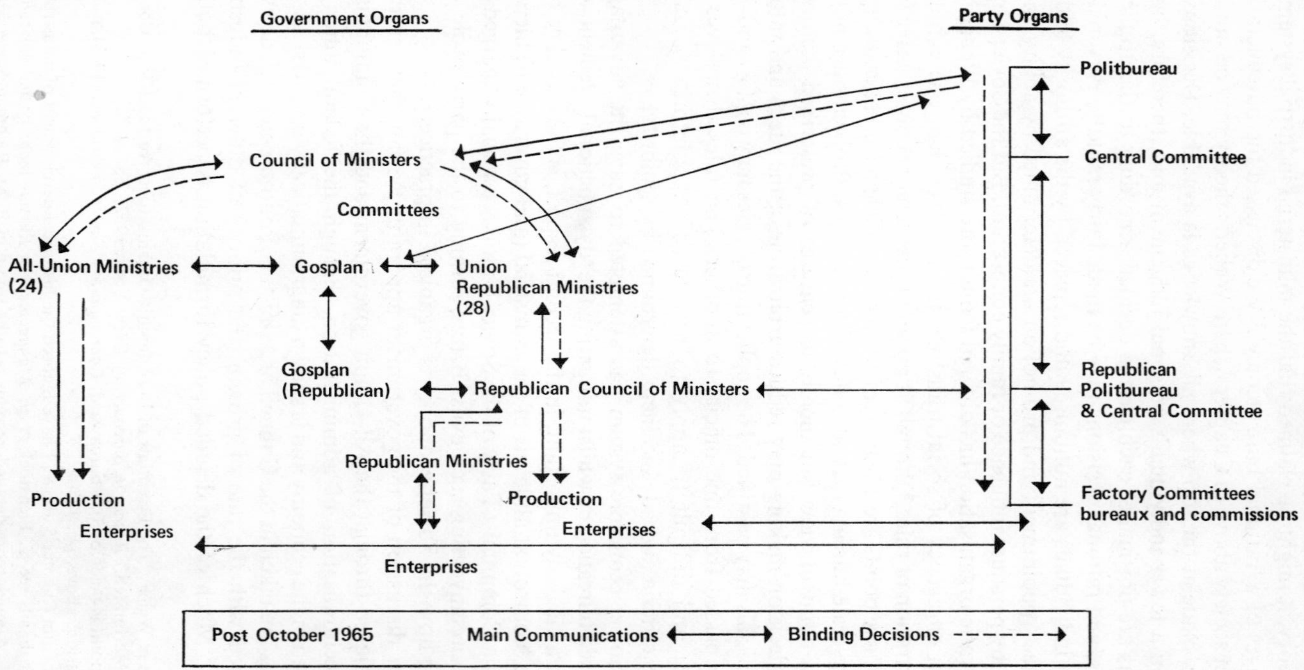

Party Organs

Politbureau

Central Committee

Republican Politbureau & Central Committee

Factory Committees bureaux and commissions

Government Organs

Council of Ministers

Committees

Gosplan

Gosplan (Republican)

Union Republican Ministries (28)

Republican Council of Ministers

Republican Ministries

Republican Ministries

Production Enterprises

Enterprises

Enterprises

All-Union Ministries (24)

Production Enterprises

Post October 1965

Main Communications ⟷

Binding Decisions ⟵----⟶

industrial ministries and on the committees of state concerned with various problems.

Specific plans are devised in the government apparatus to supplement these general policies and are passed for enforcement (a) to All-Union ministries or (b) to Union-Republican ministries. Outside this network and subordinate to the republican and local government authorities are republican industrial ministries. These are relatively unimportant (e.g. local building and transport, some food and local handicraft factories) and need not detain us here.[1] The All-Union Ministries accounted for 47 per cent of the industrial product in 1968.[2]

Co-ordination is attempted both centrally and regionally. The bodies which attempt this co-ordination are the central and republican State Planning Committees (or *Gosplans*). The central, or All-Union, body is by far the most important.

Production enterprises are organised and co-ordinated in ministries which are responsible for fulfilling certain definite plans. These plans are drawn up by Gosplan after consultations between the individual ministries. Ministries in turn discuss projected plans with the directors of production enterprises. The general priorities are laid down by the chief party and state bodies: Politbureau and Council of Ministers.[3]

Binding decisions are seen on the chart to operate from the top downwards. Communication goes both ways. At the centre of the system is Gosplan. This may be likened to a nerve centre: it is responsible for drawing up detailed plans for the consideration of the government. It is, therefore, not only in a position to advise, but also to influence policy at the highest levels. In the past, reluctance by Gosplan to implement economic policy with which it disagreed has led to friction between its leaders and the government. In the thirties, and even as late as 1948–9, some of its leading personnel were executed; the reasons for this are not precisely known.

General five-year plans define the rates of growth of the economy for sectors and products: they indicate the major capital investment projects. The All-Union Gosplan, Council of Ministers and Politbureau are the most important organs involved in drawing them up. (The Ninth Five Year Plan runs between the years 1971–75).

Annual plans are the specific concern of the ministries and Gosplan. They define for each ministry its output targets for the given period. These plans are arrived at after detailed discussion between the heads of enterprises, ministry representatives and officials of Gosplan. The ministry allocates to individual enterprises specific quantitative inputs and outputs, and such minis-

[1] See A. Nove, *The Soviet Economy* (1968), Chapter 2.
[2] *Narodnoe khozyaystvo SSSR v 1968g* (Moscow, 1969), p. 184.
[3] For a full list of All-Union and Union-Republican Ministries, see Appendix D.
K*

terial directives are binding on the enterprise – it 'must' fulfil its quantitative output targets (that is, with so much resources of materials and labour, so many units of cars or tables must be produced). The prices of inputs and outputs are defined by the plan. The enormous task involved in central planning may be illustrated by the fact that from eight to nine million prices have to be fixed by the various price control organs located in the various Gosplans.[1] It has been estimated by Soviet researchers that in the mid 1960s, the Soviet apparatus performed some ten thousand fewer operations than were needed for efficient management.[2]

While material inputs and outputs of individual factories are government controlled, it is important to note that not all aspects of economic activity are 'planned' by the government agencies. While minimum wages are fixed, labour is not controlled: enterprises must recruit and retain their labour force; workers may change their job and their place of work, and frequently do so. Consumption of consumer goods is not 'planned': prices are fixed, but individuals are paid with money and can choose between the assortment of goods available. Obviously, to control labour and individual consumption by some form of direction or rationing would involve a tremendous administrative apparatus.

'Market' forces,[3] therefore, directly operate on the factory director: unless his organisation can provide continual work and payments above the minimum, he may lose skilled workers. Similarly, shoddily-made, wrongly-sized, and unfashionable goods may not be 'sold' and will remain on the hands of the retailers. Both high labour turnover[4] and unsold consumer goods have been problems in recent years. These 'market' forces are important and they are often overlooked by those who simply define a priori the Soviet economy as a 'planned' one.

The economic ministries are important political entities. Almost the sole criterion for their success is fulfilment (or preferably, overfulfilment) of their plans. At all levels success and promotion follow 'plan fulfilment'. The ministries are, therefore, as argued earlier, in a strong position vis-à-vis party organisations and groups.[5] Not only have they the organisational experience and 'know-how' of certain areas of economic production, but they are legally responsible for carrying out the plan.

The dangers to 'political' groups, located in the party are obvious. Faced by

[1] R. Belousov (ed.), *Sovremennaya praktika tsenoobrazovaniya* (Moscow, 1965).

[2] I. G. Petrov, *Predmet i metody sotsiologicheskikh issledovanii* (Moscow, 1964); English extract in *The Anglo-Soviet Journal* (London), vol. 26 (no. 1/2) 1965, p. 23.

[3] I have put market in inverted commas to indicate that supply may be responsive to demand with the price remaining constant.

[4] For example, *Trud* reports that on average 9,000 workless men per day seek new jobs in Leningrad. They remain unemployed from 8 to 12 days. *Trud* 6.x.1967.

[5] See Chapter 7.

the well-organised opposition of bureaucrats with the material means of economic ministries at their disposal, extensive control of the economy may only be achieved by party functionaries at the expense of severe economic disruption. While this may not worry a strongly entrenched dictator too much, it affects a party elite which is trying to justify itself by results, and particularly by economic results. It is unrealistic to argue that control of a few 'key' decisions only is necessary. Decision-making involves competence, knowledge and the ability to pose alternatives, which only specialists possess.

As Max Weber has pointed out, bureaucracy is a 'power instrument of the first order – for the one who controls the bureaucratic apparatus . . . And where the bureaucratisation of administration has been completely carried through, a form of power relation is established that is practically unshatterable.'[1] But Weber goes on to say that other factors in the modern state, 'seem to run directly against the bureaucratic tendency'. He gives as examples the inclusion of lay representatives, the establishment of local, regional, central, parliamentary or other representative bodies, and of occupational associations[2]. He concludes that 'the "political master" finds himself in the position of the "dilettante" who stands opposite the "expert", facing the trained official who stands within the management of administration.'[3]

If Weber is correct, it would suggest that ministries in the Soviet state are all-powerful, for they have the control of financial means and are staffed by experts. Though it must be conceded that within an economic ministry the leading bureaucrats have much power, it would be wrong to categorise the USSR as one giant bureaucracy. The individual ministries have functional responsibilities. Their scope of interest is narrowly focused. Some general direction is necessary to balance the demands of one ministry against another, and it is by no means true that they share similar interests. The extent of their internal unity is a matter for empirical investigation and should not be assumed *a priori*.[4]

Under Stalin, the final aggregation of ministerial interests was performed to a large extent by the master himself. When the industrial apparatus was set up in the 1930s the economy was relatively simple, but since 1928 the *industrial* labour force has risen from some four millions to over twenty-eight millions in 1966, when the *total* employed work force was 79.7 millions.[5] Under Stalin, the system could be relatively easily directed from Moscow, but with a complex economy, centralisation has led to unnecessary delay in decision-making.

Economically, the system led to excessive vertical industrial integration.

[1] H. H. Gerth and C. W. Mills, *From Max Weber* (1948), p. 228.

[2] *Ibid.*, p. 232.

[3] *Ibid.*

[4] See the discussion of ministerial and managerial pressure groups, Chapter 8.

[5] *Strana Sovetov za 50 let* (Moscow, 1967), p. 218.

For instance, in order to ensure supplies of materials a motor-car factory might have its own tannery to secure its supply of leather for seats and its own glass works to provide for car windows. Such proliferation of small-scale production may lead to cases where, say tyres produced in town A were sent to factory X in town B, and identical products made in town B were sent to firm Y in town A. This created obvious waste.

Politically, it meant that individual ministries were subject to little external control, and were over-centralised. Initiative was stifled, decisions were passed from one official to another. Khrushchev's proposed economic reforms had two objectives: first, to increase economic efficiency, second, to assert greater party control over the ministries. In this section we shall mention the first objective and consider party control in the next chapter.[1]

Between 1957 and 1964 Khrushchev attempted to shake up the central administrative apparatus, to give the party greater power of control, to give more power to the 'man on the spot' and to break up the self-interested industrial ministries. The country was divided into 104 geographical economic units in which nearly all factories came under a Regional Economic Council. The council (or *sovnarkhoz*) attempted to co-ordinate industrial economic activity in the area. This was to prevent wasteful transfers as shown in the example above, and to give an impetus to regional interests. To obviate 'localism', much of the central industrial organisation was maintained. The centralisation of the ministerial bureaucracies was weakened, but economic administration was complicated by conflicting lines of authority between factory, ministry and *sovnarkhoz*.

In 1965, after the demise of Khrushchev, the Regional Economic Councils were abolished and the ministerial system with All-Union and Republican ministries, as earlier described, was set up. The detailed control of production by ministries was replaced by giving greater power to the individual enterprise. To prevent waste and to encourage efficient use of materials, a larger part of surplus was to remain in the enterprise. After meeting its costs (including a planned surplus which is paid to the government), up to forty per cent of any 'excess' profits may be kept by the enterprise. Such profit may be used either as direct financial reward to employees, or for social services – the provision of factory crèches or housing. In 1968, 54 per cent of enterprises producing 72 per cent of industrial produce were on the new system.[2] Minimum wage rates are still determined centrally, but no constraints are now placed on the way the wage fund may be divided. Higher wages may be paid by reducing the number of men employed or steeper differentials may be introduced. Before

[1] A third way in which 'bureaucracy' was to be combatted was by voluntary participation. This has been referred to above, Chapter 7. See also L. G. Churchward, 'Bureaucracy – USA:USSR', *Coexistence*, vol. 5.
[2] *Narodnoe khozyaystvo SSSR v 1968g* (1969), p. 184.

1965, plan completion was measured in quantities of output produced (e.g. five million tons of cement, one thousand iron bedsteads). This did not alwys ensure the correct allocation of sizes. For example, too many large nails may have been produced because output was measured in weight, too few large hats because materials could be economised on smaller sizes, and consumer goods were often distasteful or old-fashioned. Since 1965, output has only been credited to an enterprise after it has been accepted by a purchasing unit. In this way, the influence of factor or consumer demand in theory was strengthened. In fact, purchasing units may still have to accept unsatisfactory commodities because of the lack of alternatives.

The Kosygin reforms, described above, retain the framework of the traditional physical planning system, but graft onto it elements of a market type: particularly, the 'stimulus' of demand. The national economic plan is still drawn up on the basis of physical inputs and outputs, though the final product-mix is less detailed than hitherto. (Parts of Kosygin's speech on economic reform are given in Appendix G.)

Agriculture aside, Soviet central planning has been relatively more successful in pioneering methods of economic planning in a relatively simple economy than in a complex large-scale industrial order. The present problem is to develop methods and a structure which can cope with the very large number of economic variables generated by a modern economy. This involves optimising inputs to produce a given desired combination of outputs, and evolving a mechanism to determine more accurately consumer demand.

Two main general approaches have been put forward to solve this problem: greater reliance on the market mechanism advocated by such economists as Professor Liberman, and improved central planning with the aid of the computer as suggested by the late Academician Nemchinov. These writers did not advocate either method exclusively but emphasised the importance of one in conjunction with the other.[1]

The use of market stimuli to determine the detailed final product-mix is likely to be extended, especially in the consumer sector. There seems to be no reason why, within the framework of central planning, the length, colour and shape of men's jackets should not be determined by their wearers – a principle which might be applied to most consumer goods. But the development of a wider 'market system' is unlikely. At present the prices of commodities do not reflect the balance of supply and demand; therefore, either a limited amount of price competition would create a large number of distortions, or a full-blooded free market might result in catastrophe. In the short run, the inadequate economic infrastructure (for instance, the absence of advertising) would mean that the market was imperfect. In the long run, free market conditions

[1] For detailed discussion see E. Zaleski, *Planning Reforms in the Soviet Union* (Chapel Hill, N.C. 1967) and Michael Ellman, *Economic Reform in the Soviet Union* (1969).

may have the undesirable consequences they have had in the West, particularly those of unemployment and uneven growth. Perhaps most important of all are the political objections. Not only would a free market economy lead to the development of individual 'capitalist' interests; it would enhance a pattern of social stratification inimical to the norms of Soviet society. Finally such a development, if carried to its logical conclusion, would completely undermine the notion of a planned economy.

A computer network is more likely to be adopted. This involves the general economic plan being divided into a number of segments, by area and by industry. For the end output of each segment a computer programme is made to match, most efficiently, inputs to outputs. Each segment is linked to the overall plan for the economy. Thus decentralisation of detail is achieved within the framework of a national plan. In 1969, however, such procedures were limited to a number of experimental regions.

While industrial production is organised by state ministries and by factories run by appointed managers, which are similar in structure to their western counterparts, Soviet agriculture has units of production unknown to farming in the West – the collective farm, or *kolkhoz*. The collective farm is one of three distinct economic units of the agricultural sector: the state farms (*sovkhozy*), the collective farms and private plots. At one end of the scale are the state farms where, as in industry, the 'command' principle operates; at the other end, we find the private plots which are completely outside government control and are in many ways similar to western agricultural small-holdings. The collective farms occupy a central position on the 'control' continuum. As they provide the bulk of Soviet agricultural production we shall discuss them first.

The Collective Farm

The collective farm is a producers' co-operative. It uses nationalised land leased to the farm in perpetuity. *In theory*, individual leaseholders have joined together to work the land and market their produce collectively and, unlike in the factory, the management is elected by the farmers. In fact, considerable pressure and force was initially put on individual peasants to farm collectively and the farm chairman is often appointed or removed by the authorities. The farm is only indirectly subordinate to the economic planning authorities.

The collective farm is a form of co-operative rather than a unit of state socialism. It will be recalled that in 1917 the land was nationalised, but given to the peasantry to use with their own tools, seeds and livestock. Collectivisation changed the basis of production from an individual to a co-operative one. The land was state-owned, but the tools (excepting large-scale agricultural machinery), seeds and produce were the property of the collective. In an industrial enterprise, of course, the state owns the tools and the produce.

The supreme body is the collective farm meeting composed of its working members over sixteen years of age. It elects its managing committee, chairman, and auditing commission. To the chairman and the committee, responsibility for the work of the collective is given. Certain decisions are reserved for the general meeting of the farm: the admittance or expulsion of members, the adoption of the farm's charter, the election of chairman, the adoption of the farm's annual plan, changes in boundaries of the farm and the determination of the size of various funds.[1] The general meeting takes place at least four times per year. It can express a motion of no confidence in the chairman (and management) and has the right to remove him and elect another. Members wishing to leave the farm have to apply to the executive committee and to the general meeting.

The executive committee and chairman appoint charge-hands responsible for various aspects of farm work, who in turn control the work of different sections or work gangs and maintain discipline.

The collective farm is not an independent self-governing unit; even in Soviet theory, it is guided by government economic administration. Its decisions must be in conformity with the Soviet Constitution, with the laws and with the economic plans. In fact, a collective farm general meeting cannot decide the content of the annual production plan. This is determined by the state planning authorities to whom it is subject. It must hand over to the state procurement bodies quotas defined by them. The farms are paid by the government for such deliveries. Thus main decisions about farm output and the control of planting are the prerogative of a body outside the farm. While the Ministry of Agriculture is for the collective farm sector the equivalent of the industrial ministries, it does not directly organise production. The district Soviet passes output quotas to the farms, and gives technical advice through its agricultural specialists on rotation, produce and methods.

The machine-tractor stations (MTS) were important instruments of control by the government over the collective farm. They were units under state management which carried out all machine work on the farms. In addition, of course, they facilitated intensive use of scarce machines. They were abolished in 1958, and now the farms own their machinery.

The farm chairman is subject to the strong influence of state and party bodies which are also able to reject unco-operative or inefficient chairmen. In recent years, with the growth of collective farm party membership, the control of leading personnel can be managed by the party group, rather than externally. But the following extract from a Soviet novel shows how the farm chairman is subject to external authority.

[1] See 'Text of the Model Collective Farm Charter.' *Current Digest of the Soviet Press*, vol. 21, no. 50, p. 14. See also A. Vucinich, *Soviet Economic Institutions* (Stanford, 1952).

THE FIRST TELEPHONE CALL:

'Ananiy Yegorovich? Hello, hello. Well, what good news have you got? A lot of work going on, you say? They've all gone out to the hayfields? Good, good. But what about the silage? You're hard at it? All right, carry on.'

THE SECOND TELEPHONE CALL:

'I don't see any mention of silage in your report. Your kolkhoz is holding the whole district back. What? Using the dry weather to push on with the haymaking? Push on, then. But just bear in mind that the district committee won't pat you on the back for not making a big effort over rich fodder. You of all people ought to know *that* bit of basic politics.'

Yes, he knew all about politics at the district level (thank God, he'd trudged around as a district official for pretty nearly thirty years): silage should never lag behind hay in the report. But, damn it all, whether it's laid down or not, surely the *kolkhozniki* can use their own heads occasionally? And at the general meeting the *kolkhozniki* had decided to wait with the silage. Silage can be picked up even in wet weather, but hay can't.

THE THIRD TELEPHONE CALL:

'Comrade Mysovsky? (A form of address that promised nothing good). And how, may I ask do you want me to take your stubbornness? Sabotage? Or just a stupid, muddle-headed failure to understand our basic economic task?'

'But look, after all,' – Ananiy Yegorovich burst in – 'who's boss in the *kolkhoz*? The Party has given the farms freedom, and now you're putting a spoke in their wheel again . . .'

AND HERE'S THE DECISION

'1. Member of the Party Comrade A. E. Mysovsky, Chairman of the "New Life" collective farm, to be given a severe reprimand for his failure politically to appreciate the importance of silage as the main source of fodder for stockbreeding on collective farms.

2. Comrade Mysovsky to be held responsible for liquidating in the next fifteen days the "New Life" collective farm's intolerable delay in the preparation of rich fodder.'[1]

While the district Soviet can and often does interfere with planning and planting, the collective farm has considerably more control over finance, general operations and investment than has the management of an industrial enterprise.

The output of the collective farm is sold to the state at fixed prices. The earnings of the collective are then allocated to various funds by the general meeting: insurance, capital and cultural and wages fund are the most important recipients. Until 1958, most collective farmers were paid according to the *trudo-den'* or 'work-day' system. The wage-fund was divided among the collective farmers according to the number of 'work-days' performed by the individual farmer. The number of 'work-days' is determined by the time a

---

[1] Fyodor Abramov, *The Dodgers* (Flegon Press, London, 1963), pp. 21-2.

kolkhoznik works, multiplied by a coefficient which varies with each job. A 'skilled' job will have a high coefficient, whereas an unskilled will have a low one. Since 1958, payment has been introduced at similar rates for the job as in state farms and payment has been more regularly made to the collective farmer. This is part of the attempt of the Soviet authorities to 'merge' the collective and state farms (see below, Chapter 12). Most farms in fact have a combination of work-day and monthly cash payments.[1]

The State Farm

The Soviet *sovkhoz* has the same legal status and organisational subordination as a Soviet industrial enterprise. The management is appointed by the Ministry of Agriculture, it is not elected as in the collective farm. Its organisation, internal order and budget are the concern of the Ministry.

As the produce of the farm is state property, the state farm agricultural worker receives a wage from state funds related to his skill in the same way as a factory worker is paid. The state farmer participates in a trade union and has similar rights as factory workers to welfare services. The management, technical and clerical staff are classified as non-manual workers as they are in industry; agricultural labourers and other workers engaged full time on the *sovkhoz* are classified as 'workers'.

The Private Plot

While individual private agricultural production on a large scale was abolished with the development of the collectives, individuals were allowed to keep a small number of animals and a private plot. (At present, plots average $1\frac{1}{2}$ acres of ground per household.)

The produce from the plots, together with any surpluses from the collective farm, may be freely sold at the collective farm markets which are provided in urban areas for the sale of produce. The collective farmer, therefore, is not only employed on the collective's lands, but is also a smallholder in his own right and this, as we shall see, provides much of his income.

Agricultural Production

The bulk of Soviet agricultural production is provided by the collective and state farms. The number of units is shown on the following table:

---

[1] For details, see R. Conquest, *Agricultural Workers in the USSR* (1968), pp. 99-100. The average field workers recommended wage is 2.15 roubles per day: for scales see A. S. Pankratov, *Zakonodatel'stvo o proizvodstve, zagotovkakh i zakupkakh sel'khozproduktov* (*sbornik*) Moscow 1967, p.270.

Table 18. Numbers of State and Collective Farms, 1940, 1950, 1960 and 1968

	1940*	1950*	1960*	1968*
No. of state farms	4,159	4,988	7,375	13,398
No. of collective farms	235,500	121,400	44,000	35,600

* 31 December

Source: Narodnoe khozyaystvo SSSR (Narkhoz) v 1968g (Moscow, 1969), p. 313 and Narkhoz v 1967g (1968), p. 325

Though the numbers of collective farms have significantly fallen, and those of state farms risen over the past twenty-five years, collective farms are still nearly three times as numerous as state. State farms are larger units as is evident from the distribution of land. Collective farms utilise 440.6 million hectares of land, state farms 614.4 million, collective farm plots 5.0 million and private plots utilised by workers and employees 3.64 million.[1] The *area* of land used by various types of agricultural unit, however, may be misleading, for the intensity of cultivation affects yields. In 1966, private plots contributed about 17 per cent of agricultural output: 6 per cent of the crops, 30 per cent of livestock, 60 per cent of the potatoes, 40 per cent of the vegetables, over 40 per cent of the meat, 39 per cent of milk and 68 per cent of all eggs.[2] The area privately farmed, however, was about one five hundredth of the total cultivated area. Industrial agricultural commodities (flax, cotton) were mainly produced on state and collective farms. It is sometimes argued that the collective farmer neglects 'collective' work in favour of activity on his own plot. Soviet research suggests that female labour is primarily expended on the plots – over a third of all female labour time in the RSFSR (Russian Federation) was spent this way, compared with only 9 per cent of the male.[3]

Since the early 1950s, Soviet agricultural production has shown a steady increase: the index of total agricultural production being 155 in 1958 and 171 in 1965 (1950=100): crops increased to 143 and 141 and livestock to 172 and 212 in the two years respectively.[4] The total agricultural output has increased fairly constantly since 1950, though grain output has fluctuated.[5] But Soviet agricultural production is backward compared with the American. Apart from potato and sugar production which is larger than gross American output, food production is well below American. In 1955–8 the USSR produced only 57.3 per cent of the output of the USA in vegetables, and only 42.4 per cent of

[1] *Narodnoe khozyaystvo SSSR v 1967g.* (Moscow, 1968), p. 342.
[2] M. Makeenko, 'Ekonomicheskaya rol' lichnogo podsobnogo khozyaystva', *Voprosy ekonomiki*, no. 10, 1966, p. 61.
[3] *Ibid.*, p. 63.
[4] D. B. Diamond, 'Trends in Output, Inputs and Factor Productivity in Soviet Agriculture', Joint Economic Committee, US Congress, *New Directions in the Soviet Economy* (Washington, 1966), p. 346.
[5] For details see *Narodnoe khozyaystvo v 1967g.* (Moscow, 1968), pp. 326-7.

her meat.[1] While the Soviet population is larger than the American, grain, vegetable, milk and meat production is lower.

The data shown on Table 19, dramatically sum up the differences and highlight the main problems of Soviet agriculture. While the Soviet population is

Table 19. Agricultural Resources, USA/USSR

Item	Year	Unit	USA	USSR	USSR as % of USA (per cent)
Population	1964	Millions	192.1	227.7	119
Civilian labour force (work experience)	1964	,,	85.1	116.0	136
Annual average employment	1964	,,	70.4	103.4	147
Agricultural labour force (work experience)	1964	,,	7.1	46.5	655
Annual average employment in agriculture	1964	,,	4.8	39.1	815
Farm share of total labour force (work experience)	1964	Per cent	8.3	40.1	—
Farm share of total employment (annual average)	1964	,,	6.8	37.8	—
Sown cropland	1964	Millions of acres	306	526	172
Sown cropland per capita	1964	Acres	1.6	2.3	144
Tractors on farms	1965	Thousands	4,625	1,539	33
Motor trucks on farms	1965	,,	2,925	954	33
Grain combines on farms	1965	,,	990	513	52
Agricultural consumption of electricity	1964	(American) Billions of kilo-watt-hours	29.9	18.4	62
Use of commercial fertiliser in terms of principal plant nutrients:					
Total	1964	1,000 short tons	8,131	5,500	68
Per acre of sown area	1964	Pounds	59	21	36

Source: Harry E. Walters, 'Agriculture in the United States and USSR', Joint Economic Committee, *New Directions in the Soviet Economy.* (Washington, 1966), p. 476.

[1] D. Gale Johnson and Arcadius Kahan, 'Soviet Agriculture: Structure and Growth', Joint Economic Committee, US Congress, *Comparisons of the United States and Soviet Economies* (Washington, 1959), pp. 209, 223.

only 19 per cent larger than the American, agricultural employment is eight times as large. While the Soviet sown area is 172 per cent of the American, the number of tractors used is only 33 per cent and the number of grain combines 52 per cent. Particularly important is the small amount of fertiliser employed; it is only 36 per cent of the American, per pound per acre. Soviet yields both per man and per acre are much below the American, corn yield per acre is only 44 per cent, and potatoes 59 per cent.[1]

Table 20. Comparative dollar values of Gross National Product in 1964 (market prices)

Country	Ranked by GNP (billions)	Country	Ranked by per capita (dollars)
United States	629	United States	3,273
USSR	293	West Germany	2,154
West Germany	126	France	1,953
United Kingdom	104	United Kingdom	1.910
Japan	101	USSR	1,289
France	96	Italy	1,187
Italy	61	Japan	1,040

Source: S. H. Cohn, 'Soviet Growth Retardation: Trends in Resource Availability and Efficiency', Joint Economic Committee, US Congress, New Directions in the Soviet Economy (Washington, 1966), p. 108.

The Standard of Living: post 1956

Having considered how the forces of production are organised, we may turn to consider the size of output and the level of the standard of living. First, we must define the size of the Soviet Gross National Product,[2] its division between different kinds of end use (consumption, investment, defence); second, we may compare the standard of living of the Soviet consumer with his western counterpart. In 1955, the size of Soviet GNP has been estimated at between a quarter and a half of the American, depending on whether Russian or American price comparisons are used.[3] In the same year, Soviet consumption has been estimated at from a fifth to two-fifths of the American, and defence expenditure from 75 to 94 per cent.[4] Measured by market prices in 1964, Soviet GNP was 47 per cent of that of the USA and about three times that of the United

[1] Harry E. Walters, loc. cit., p. 478.

[2] The growth of Soviet GNP after 1917 was described in Chapter 3 above.

[3] For example, suppose 1 ruble exchanges for 1 dollar, and a car costs $3,000 in the USA and 30,000 rubles in the USSR, a common production of 100 cars would be worth $300,000 in the USA and 3,000,000 rubles in the USSR, i.e. in a common currency, $300,000 or $3,000,000.

[4] M. Bornstein, 'A Comparison of Soviet and United States National Product', in Joint Economic Committee, US Congress, Comparisons of the United States and Soviet Economies (Washington, 1959), p. 385.

Kingdom. In *per capita* terms the USSR ranks fifth, behind the UK but above
Italy and Japan (see Table 20). The same source estimates that in 1964 private
consumption accounted for 46.5 per cent of Soviet GNP and defence 11.3 per
cent, whereas the American figures were 58.9 per cent and 10.8 per cent.[1]
But these overall figures do not tell us about individual or family consumption.

Lynn Turgeon has drawn up tables for the USA and USSR showing the
income and expenditure of both a 'subsistence' and an 'average' family in 1958.
This is shown in Table 21. As a proportion of total money income, we see that
necessaries (shelter, medical, transport, insurance) account for some 15
per cent of Soviet money income, whereas it comes to about 50 per cent of the
American family's. In the USSR rent, heating and light are provided very
cheaply, other services, (medical, dental, child care) are highly subsidised.
Philip Hanson has constructed a comparative table of estimated Soviet
average expenditure and British low income expenditure, he shows that the
Soviets spend five per cent of their income on housing, fuel, light and power
whereas the British spend twenty-seven per cent.[2] Hanson and Turgeon come
to essentially the same conclusion that the Soviet family has more for dis-
cretionary purchasing after shelter has been paid for. Next we must examine
what collection of goods the individual may purchase with this residual.

Turgeon goes on to convert Soviet prices to their dollar equivalents at the
average and *subsistence* family income levels.[3] She concludes that the average
Soviet family in 1959 'probably eat reasonably well by American standards'.[4]
Clothing is relatively more expensive than food, however, and after satisfying
both food and clothing needs, she concludes that 'not a great deal of family
disposable income remains after the purchases of the more essential food and
clothing'.[5] Soviet *per capita* consumption of food, she estimates in absolute
terms at just over half the American, and of clothing just under half. For
durable goods the American level is considerably above that of the Russian.

However, consumption has been regularly increasing since the early 1950s.
The consumption of consumer durables increased five-fold between 1950 and
1964–5.[6] As stated above, the calorific food value was roughly equal to the
American in the early 1950s, since then consumption of meat and processed
foods has increased at the expense of basic foods. Nevertheless, between 1960
and 1964 starchy foods accounted for about sixty-two per cent of the calorie

---

[1] *Ibid.*, p. 106. See also above p. 116.

[2] Philip Hanson, *The Consumer in the Soviet Economy* (1968), p. 73.

[3] Tables of Soviet prices and their equivalents are cited in detail by Lynn Turgeon in Joint
Economic Committee, US Congress, *Comparisons of the United States and Soviet Economies*
(Washington, 1959), pp. 335-6.

[4] *Ibid.*, p. 336.

[5] *Ibid.*

[6] D. W. Bronson and B. S. Severin, 'Recent Trends in Consumption and Disposable Income
in the USSR', US Congress, *New Directions . . .* (1966), p. 501.

Table 21. Average and Subsistence Family Income, USA, USSR

	UNITED STATES		USSR	
	Subsistence family (dollars per month)	Average family (dollars per month)	Subsistence family (rubles per month)	Average family (rubles per month)
Gross family income before taxes	250	435	600	1,400
Family income after taxes	235	380	600	1,315
Less following expenditure for items other than food, clothing, durable consumer goods, personal care, and recreation:				
Shelter and household operations	70	100	40	100
Medical, dental and child care	15	20	5	15
Transportation expenses	25	50	30	40
Insurance contributions, savings, etc.	10	30	5	40
Total deductions	120	200	80	195
Family disposable income remaining for food, clothing, durable consumer goods, personal care and recreation expenditures	115	180	520	1,120

Source: Based on Joint Economic Committee, US Congress, Comparisons of the United States and Soviet Economies (Washington, 1959), p. 329

intake compared to 24 per cent in the USA.[1] The changes in Soviet food consumption have been estimated by a Soviet study as follows:

	1913	1950	1965
		Kg. per capita	
Bread products	200	172	156
Potatoes	—	241	141
Vegetables and pulses	40	51	73
Sugar	8.1	11.6	34.2
Vegetable oils	—	2.7	7.1
Meat and meat products	27	26	41
Milk and dairy products	154	172	252
Fish and fish products	6.7	7.0	12.2
Eggs	48*	60*	124*

Source: Sovetskaya Torgovlya, No. 8, 1967, p. 8
* Eggs, per capita

Though house building has increased since the early 1950s, the amount of room per person in 1965 was 6.42 square metres (5.40 sq. m. in 1958).[2] In Western Germany, the comparable figure is more than 13 square metres. In 1965, the average density per room in the USSR was 2.33 persons – much more than in modern Western European countries.[3] In 1961, Sosnovy has estimated that 57.3 per cent of floor space was provided with running water, and 30.6 per cent with a bath.[4] In the USA the comparable figures were 93.1 per cent, and 81.2 per cent (bath or shower).[5] In Leningrad in 1963, only 70 per cent of the flats had central heating and in 1965 less than a quarter had gas.[6] There can be little doubt that the USSR's housing provision is still very much inferior to that of western states.

An index more favourable to the Soviets is that of house construction which has, in recent years, outstripped that of the West. This can be seen by studying the figures cited below (see p. 292).[7]

Also the Soviet Union compares well with the USA in the provision of health services and education. The number of doctors (per 10,000 persons) in 1964 was 20.5, whereas in the USA it was only 14.7, and the ratio of hospital beds (per 10,000) was 94 and 88 respectively. The number of students per teacher

[1] *Ibid.*, p. 502.
[2] T. Sosnovy, 'Housing Conditions in the USSR', *New Directions in the Soviet Economy*, pp. 544-5.
[3] *Ibid.*
[4] *Loc. cit.*, p. 551.
[5] *Ibid.*
[6] Donald D. Barry, 'Housing in the USSR', *Problems of Communism*, vol. 18 (no. 3) 1969, p. 5.
[7] Nothing can be inferred here about the absolute size of housing stock in the various countries, as the *size* of dwellings cited may differ. The average Soviet unit is probably smaller than that of Britain or the USA.

Dwelling Construction per 1,000 inhabitants

	1954	1959	1961	1963
USSR	7.0	14.5	12.4	11.1
Italy	3.7	6.0	6.3	8.1
Great Britain	7.0	5.5	5.9	5.9
West Germany	11.1	10.7	10.1	9.9
USA	8.8	8.7	7.5	8.6

Source: Economic Commission for Europe, *Annual Bulletin of Housing and Building Statistics for Europe, 1963.* (New York: United Nations, 1963), pp. 8-11.

was 19.2 in the USSR and 25.1 in the USA.[1] Though it is sometimes claimed that the quality of teachers and doctors is better in the USA, this is an assertion which cannot be easily proved.

Between 1951 and 1958, the production of consumer durables increased by 16.5 per cent per year and between 1959 and 1965 by 8 per cent per year.[2] The stocks of consumer durables in the USA and USSR, shown in Table 22 illustrate the tremendous gap between the consumption patterns of both

Table 22. USSR and United States: Estimated Stocks of Selected Consumer Durables, Selected Years, 1955-64. (Units per thousand persons)

	USSR				United States
	1955	1958	1960	1964	1963
Sewing machines	31	64	92	n.a.	135*
Radios†	66	105	130	161	974
Television sets†	4	12	22	56	318
Motorcycles and scooters	4	8	13	23	4
Refrigerators	5	8	13	27	288
Washing machines	1	6	13	47	216
Electric vacuum cleaners	2	5	8	18	211

* Electric only
† Based on official figures
Source: D. W. Bronson, B. S. Severin, 'Recent Trends in Consumption and Disposable Income in the USSR', in *New Directions in the Soviet Economy,* p. 504

societies. In addition, the ratio of cars to people in 1964 was 1 to 250 in Russia, whereas it was more than 1 to 3 in the USA. The standards of service are also low in the USSR. This is illustrated by the fact that the number of workers employed in trading establishments was (in 1964) 76 per 1,000 of the population in the USA, whereas the Soviet figure was only 16.[3]

[1] T. Sosnovy, *loc. cit.,* p. 503.
[2] D. W. Bronson, B. S. Severin, 'Recent Trends in Consumption and Disposable Income in the USSR', in *New Directions in the Soviet Economy,* p. 504.
[3] E. L. Manevich, *Problemy obshchestvennogo truda v SSSR* (Moscow, 1966), p. 51.

The Soviet Union is at a relatively early stage of industrialisation. It has completed its basic capital investment. In *per capita* output it already exceeds Italy and Japan. In the provision of some social services it ranks even above the USA. These statistics bring out the fact that whereas in the West the economy is consumer and sales orientated, in the USSR it is producer and supply-based. The social services which, it is often alleged, are neglected in the West are relatively privileged in the USSR. The tendency from 1958 to 1969, however, has been for the Soviet Union to increase expenditure relatively, on consumer goods.

INTRODUCTORY

Bergson, Abram. *The Economics of Soviet Planning*. New Haven, Conn.: Yale University Press, 1964.

Campbell, Robert W. *Soviet Economic Power: Its Organisation, Growth and Challenge*. London: Macmillan, 1967.

Churchward, L. G. *Contemporary Soviet Government*. London: Routledge and Kegan Paul, 1968.

Conquest, R. *Agricultural Workers in the USSR*. London: Bodley Head, 1968.

Ellman, Michael. *Economic Reform in the Soviet Union*. London: PEP Broadsheet 509, 1969.

Nove, Alec. *The Soviet Economy*. London: Allen and Unwin, revised edition, 1968.

BASIC

Bornstein, M. 'A Comparison of Soviet and United States National Product', in Joint Economic Committee, US Congress, *Comparisons of the United States and Soviet Economies*, Part II. Washington: Government Printing Office, 1959, pp. 377-95.

Bornstein, M. and Daniel Fusfeld. *The Soviet Economy: A Book of Readings*. New York: Irwin, 1962.

Bronson, D. W. and B. S. Severin. 'Recent Trends in Consumption and Disposable Income in the USSR', in Joint Economic Committee, US Congress, *New Directions in the Soviet Economy*. Washington: Government Printing Office, 1966, pp. 495-529.

Churchward, L. G. 'Bureaucracy – USA:USSR', in *Coexistence*, 1968, Vol. 5, No. 2, pp. 201-9.

Cohn, S. H. 'Soviet Growth Retardation: Trends in Resource Availability and Efficiency', Joint Economic Committee, US Congress, *New Directions in the Soviet Economy*. Washington: Government Printing Office, 1966, pp. 99-132.

Conquest, Robert. *Industrial Workers in the USSR* (Soviet Studies Series). London: Bodley Head, 1967.

Diamond, D. B. 'Trends in Output, Inputs and Factor Productivity in Soviet Agriculture', in Joint Economic Committee, US Congress, *New Directions in the Soviet Economy*. Washington: Government Printing Office, 1966, pp. 339-81.

Johnson, D. Gale, and A. Kahan. 'Soviet Agriculture: Structure and Growth', in Joint Economic Committee, US Congress, *Comparisons of the United States and Soviet Economies*. Washington: Government Printing Office, 1959, pp. 201-36.

Shaffer, Harry. *The Soviet Economy. A Collection of Western and Soviet Views*. New York: Appleton-Century-Crofts, 1963.

Walters, Harry E. 'Agriculture in the United States and USSR', in Joint Economic Committee, US Congress, *New Directions in the Soviet Economy*. Washington: Government Printing Office, 1966, pp. 473-81.

Wiles, P. J. D. *The Political Economy of Communism*. Oxford: B. Blackwell, 1964.

Zaleski, E. *Planning Reforms in the Soviet Union, 1962-66. An Analysis of Recent Trends in Economic Organisation and Management*. Chapel Hill, North Carolina: University of North Carolina Press, 1967.

SPECIALISED

Abramov, F. *The Dodgers*. London: Anthony Blond and Flegon Press, 1963.

Barry, Donald D. 'Housing in the USSR', in *Problems of Communism*, Vol. 18, No. 3, May-June, 1969, pp. 1-11.

Belousov, R. (ed.). *Sovremennaya praktika tsenoobrazovaniya*. Moscow, 1965.

Bienstock, G. *et al. Management in Russian Industry and Agriculture*. Ithaca, New York: Cornell University Press, 1944.

Economic Commission for Europe. *Annual Bulletin of Housing and Building Statistics for Europe, 1963*. New York: United Nations, 1963.

Gerth, H. H., and C. W. Mills. *From Max Weber*. London: Routledge and Kegan Paul, 1948.

Hanson, Philip. *The Consumer in the Soviet Economy*. London,: Macmillan, 1968.

Kazantsev, N. D. 'Stalinski ustav sel'skokhozyaystvennoy arteli – osnovnoy zakon kolkhoznoy zhizni', *Sovetskoe gosudartsvo i pravo*, No. 12, 1949, pp. 79-94.

'Kem byt' o nekotorykh nazrevshikh problemakh professional'noy orientatsii', *Trud*, 6 October 1967. (on labour turnover in Leningrad).

Makeenko, M. 'Ekonomicheskaya rol' lichnogo podsobnogo khozyaystva', *Voprosy ekonomiki*, No. 10, October 1966, pp. 57-67.

Manevich, E. L. *Problemy obshchestvennogo truda v SSSR*. Moscow, 1966.

Nazarov, R. 'Rost i uluchshenie struktury potrebleniya produktov pitaniya', in *Sovetskaya torgovlya*, No. 8, 1967, p. 6-9.

Petrov, I. G. *Predmet i metody sotsiologicheskikh issledovanii*. Moscow, 1964. English extract in *The Anglo-Soviet Journal* (London), Vol. 26, Nos. 1/2, Summer, 1965, p. 23.

Sosnovy, T. 'Housing Conditions and Urban Development in the USSR', in Joint Economic Committee, US Congress, *New Directions in the Soviet Economy*. Washington: Government Printing Office, 1966, pp. 531-54.

'Text of the Model Collective Farm Charter', *Current Digest of the Soviet Press*, Vol. 21, No. 50.

Tsentral'noe statisticheskoe upravlenie. *Narodnoe khozyaystvo SSSR v 1960g*. Moscow, 1961.

Tsentral'noe satisticheskoe upravlenie. *Narodnoe khozyaystvo v 1968g*. Moscow, 1969.

Vucinich, A. *Soviet Economic Institutions*. Stanford, California: Stanford University Press, 1952.

10

MANAGEMENT, TRADE UNIONS AND
THE PARTY IN INDUSTRY

In the preceding chapter the general features of Soviet economic organisation were described. Other important aspects of the economy are work relations. What is the attitude of the worker to authority, how is the worker paid, what motivates him to work? What is the relation of the political order to the control of the economy?

Let us begin to answer these questions firstly by considering the role and powers of the production head of the Soviet enterprise, the factory director, or manager. Secondly, we shall turn attention to the workers' organisation, the trade union, and thirdly, to the Communist Party. Finally, we shall describe the Soviet worker's attitude to his work.

Industrial Management

While the industrial ministry is legally vested with the ownership and control of the Soviet enterprise, the factory director and the management are in *de facto* control. The question which poses itself is whether a shift of control from ministry to management has taken place in the USSR resulting in something like a 'managerial revolution'.

In the early days of industrial capitalism the entrepreneur combined the role of owner and manager of an enterprise. In the twentieth century, the joint stock company vests ownership with shareholders who generally play no direct part in the operation of the enterprise, and control in directors who often own only a small proportion of the shares. James Burnham[1] has argued that effective control lies with managers and is based on their technical skill and competence. A divorce has taken place then, it is said, between ownership and control. The interest of the 'controllers', it is argued by the managerial revolutionaries, is contrary to that of the owners: they seek, for example, expansion of the firm and re-investment, rather than profit distribution. This analysis, if true, would seriously undermine a Marxist critique of society, for it postulates a managerial, bureaucratic stratum controlling the means of production, rather than an owning class.

[1] *The Managerial Revolution* (1945).

T. B. Bottomore, for example, has pointed out that

Many sociologists would argue that the concept of 'ownership of the means of production' needs re-examination. In the USSR, as in Britain and the USA, a small number of individuals manage the giant enterprises upon which material well-being depends and decide the major economic issues as to the use of resources. In all cases they have great power, and it is increasingly difficult for the mass of the population to exercise control over their use of power. Contrary to the orthodox Marxist view, popular control may well be greater in the capitalist countries, where independent trade unions can bring pressure to bear upon managements and where the competition among political groups prevents the emergence of a single, omnipotent elite.[1]

This extract has been cited because it illustrates the widely held view that the ownership and control of western firms or corporations have been separated. But this is a contentious issue. Control of large-scale industry is vested in the boards composed of directors who are substantial shareholders in their companies[2] and who, therefore, have similar interests to shareholders: they distribute the proceeds of production. There is no evidence to suggest that with the rise of the joint stock company, the share of production accruing to shareholders has declined.

Before considering this problem in relation to the USSR, it will be as well to consider the structure of the typical production unit in each society: the capitalist firm and the socialist enterprise. Their structure is summarised on Diagram 4.

Under conditions of modern capitalism, the ownership of the means of production, of the typical corporation or firm, is vested in a joint stock company. Shareholders contribute capital to the company, they elect its officers and receive a share of its produce (profits, interest) but they do not individually contribute to its activity. At the company's general meeting they elect a board, who run the company primarily to secure a profit for the shareholders.

The legal unit of production is the firm (or company). The economic production unit is the factory or plant producing and marketing a product. A firm such as ICI may embrace a whole variety of products in separate independent production units.

In the Soviet Union there are no 'firms' in the western sense of the word. Ownership and control are vested in government ministries, as defined above. The minister, aided by secretaries (*nachal'niki*), is responsible to the Council of Ministers for the organisation of an industry. He appoints directors who are in

[1] T. B. Bottomore, *Sociology* (1962), pp. 139-40. This is not necessarily Bottomore's own view. In *Elites and Society* (1964), he says it is at best a half truth. (p. 74).

[2] Ralph Miliband, *The State in Capitalist Society* (1969), pp. 34-7; P. Sargant Florence, *The Logic of British and American Industry* (1953); *Ownership, Control and Success of Large Companies* (1961).

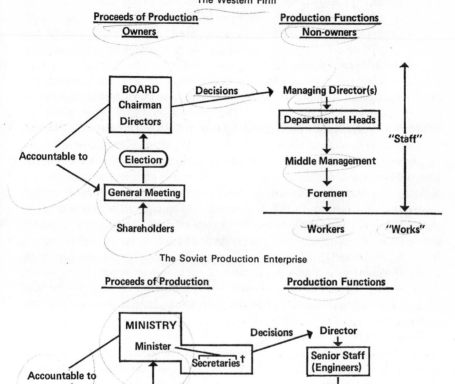

DIAGRAM 4
The Western Firm

Proceeds of Production
Owners

Production Functions
Non-owners

BOARD
Chairman
Directors

Decisions → Managing Director(s)
↓
Departmental Heads
↓
Middle Management
↓
Foremen
↓

"Staff"

Accountable to

Election ↑

General Meeting ↑

Shareholders

Workers   "Works"

The Soviet Production Enterprise

Proceeds of Production

Production Functions

MINISTRY
Minister
Secretaries †

Decisions → Director
↓
Senior Staff
(Engineers)
↓
Middle Management
↓
Foremen
↓
Workers

Accountable to

Council of Ministers

Supreme soviet ↑

Deputies ↑

Election ↑

Electors

*Here I have considered an All-Union Ministry.
For "Republican" industries and local ones, subordination
is to the Republican and local Soviet, respectively.

† "Secretaries" are senior permanent high-ranking officials,
similar to "administrative" class civil servants in Britain.
They are in Russian terminology heads (nachal'niki)
of branches (glavki).

charge of 'enterprises', or production units. These are analogous to factories and plants in capitalist states. The Soviet 'enterprise', therefore, has the standing of a subsidiary or branch. As a production unit, however, it is similar, save that less distinction is made between 'staff' and workers. (There are, however, official and technical groups – 'leading personnel', 'engineering-technical staff', and 'workers'.)

In the West, the firm or company is a private venture, the board is not responsible, or answerable to society at large – though, of course, business is subject to government intervention. The greatest similarity between the two production units is in the production functions. Both the Soviet enterprise and the western firm have in common a managing director solely responsible for the operation of the factory, beneath the managing director is a hierarchy with the industrial worker at the bottom.[1] Here it is pertinent to note that the ministry and the managers are not synonymous. It is, therefore, extremely misleading to argue, as Burnham does, that 'The captain of industry is, by virtue of his function, at the same time a state official. The 'supreme planning commission' is indistinguishably a political and an economic institution . . . In managerial society, the managers become the state. To say that the ruling class is the manager is almost the same as to say that it is the state bureaucracy. The two have, by and large, coalesced.'[2] It is the state bureaucrats who have the power and organisation to run the state, the industrial manager is a subordinate.[3]

The western joint stock company's *raison d'être* is to make a profit for its shareholders. The activities of the firm are geared to this: if it continuously makes a loss on business and it cannot meet creditors then it is declared bankrupt and the employees lose their jobs and the shareholders lose their money.

In the Soviet Union there is no profit maximisation as a *general principle* of industrial administration. The Soviet enterprise is geared to fulfil its plan, given by the ministry. The tasks of an enterprise director have been put as follows: 'What I strive for and what I believe all good managers must follow is this: All tasks set by the government must be fulfilled; and to fulfil them it is necessary to have 'authority', respect, from those he works with.'[4] Management has a strong incentive to fulfil the plan for which it is paid a bonus or premium. One of the problems to which the 'plan fulfilment' system gives rise is that managers are loath to risk short term production losses by introducing new techniques and 'innovating'. Furthermore, such innovation as does take place in the plant is concerned with improving the production of the existing

[1] For details see J. S. Berliner, *Factory and Manager in the USSR* (1957).

[2] James Burnham, *The Managerial Revolution* (1945), p. 147.

[3] See discussion on managers as a pressure group, Chapter 8, pp. 247-8.

[4] 'Textile director', cited by E. C. Brown, *Soviet Trade Unions and Labor Relations* (Cambridge, Mass., 1966), p. 175.

product, rather than designing a new product, which is more characteristic of American industry.

The Soviet factory is run by men with an engineering background; 'sales' is unimportant (though 'procurement' of materials is). In the United States, it is the financial expert, the administrator and sales director who have the upper hand over production decision-making. On the other hand, as Granick has pointed out, the similarities between the American and Soviet scene are the tendency to have middle and top management with higher education, the growing importance of the functional departments (research, finance) and the declining role of the foreman.[1]

While the calculation of premia (or bonus) varies between industries, in general, in the mid 1960s, management receives about fifteen per cent of their basic wage for fulfilling the plan and an additional three to five per cent for overfulfilling it. While premia in the nineteen forties and fifties sometimes came to as much as 75 per cent of income for the director of a chemical enterprise,[2] by the 1960s the proportion had fallen. Perhaps as important as the premia payments is the status which goes with 'plan fulfilment', on which the efficiency of the enterprise is judged and promotions are made. Therefore, it acts as a measure of the Soviet enterprise's success in the same way as prices on the stock exchange do for the western firm. But the premia system has led to some abuses, for example, production has been achieved at all costs and at the expense of quality and 'finish'.

Since 1964, a number of firms have changed to a new system of 'material incentives' and by 1968, 72 per cent of industrial output was under this method.[3] This gives the manager (and the enterprise as a whole) a financial incentive to cut costs and increase output. After fulfilling the 'planned profit', up to 40 per cent of excess profits may be utilised by the director for the enterprise's benefit; all proceeds from the use of 'waste materials' are at the disposal of the director.

The introduction of the 'profit motive' in this way has led to accusations that capitalism is being introduced in the Soviet Union. While it cannot be denied that directors have been given more power, in the context of Soviet industrial organisation it is clear that they are not yet equivalent to a western company chairman with an effective voting majority on the board. First, a Soviet director cannot produce or market new products: he cannot shift production from radios to typewriters to meet an unfulfilled demand. Such entrepreneurship, which is a characteristic of the western firm, does not exist at the enterprise level in the USSR. Second, the director has detailed orders given to him by the ministry, which also hires and fires him. Third, the

[1] D. Granick, *The Red Executive* (1960), p. 7.
[2] J. Berliner, *Factory and Manager* . . ., p. 30.
[3] *Narodnoe khozyaystvo SSSR v 1968g.* (Moscow, 1969), p. 184.

L

enterprise director works in an economic-political milieu with party and union organisations. What the 'profit motive' does signify, is the importance of monetary or utilitarian incentives in the operation of the plant and in the motivation to work.

The Soviet manager then, may be said to have control over the *process* of production, but he has little power over its proceeds. Probably the best description of him is, in Kerr's terms, that of a 'constitutional manager', whose authority is circumscribed by state, party and unions, but who, nevertheless, has directly subordinate to him the work force.[1]

The similarity between the western and Soviet system lies in the production process and in particular the work roles in the factory. The main differences result from the setting of the production unit and are more political and social than economic. Therefore, let us now turn to examine the activity of trade unions and the Communist Party.

Trade Unions

One of the most widely accepted definitions of a trade union is that of the Webbs: 'A trade union . . . is a continuous association of wage earners for the purpose of maintaining or improving the conditions of their working lives.'[2] Trade unions are composed of workers, organised either by trade or industry. They aim to improve the condition of life for members. Their main object, especially in western societies, is to increase wages, usually at the expense of management (or owners) and this may be classified as an 'industrial' objective. Wider political goals are pursued and include parliamentary representation to ensure favourable labour legislation. In the West, however, such activity is secondary to industrial activity, and unions work within the structure of society rather than in opposition to it. The final sanction a union can employ against the employer is the withdrawal of labour, or strike. Unions are enduring institutions with a membership usually, but not always, voluntary in character and with full-time salaried officials elected by the membership.

In western societies the improvement of workers' conditions, particularly wages, is paramount and the right to enforce sanctions against the employers by withdrawing labour is considered a fundamental right of unions and even a necessary condition for their existence. In liberal-democratic states, the separate and conflicting interests of employers and employed is institutionalised through collective bargaining between both sides. The roles of union and management are highly specific: the management is primarily concerned with production

---

[1] C. Kerr *et al.*, *Industrialisation and Industrial Man* (1960), pp. 156-7.
[2] Sidney and Beatrice Webb, *The History of Trade Unionism* (1920), p. 1.

and associated problems (product design and quality, trade training, hiring and firing) and the union with the improvement of workers' conditions. One of the conditions for a 'pluralist' society is that various groups of persons may form associations to pursue their common interests. As we have seen above (Chapter 6), Raymond Aron has specified the existence of separate workers' and employers' associations as one of the most important distinctions between a totalitarian and democratic society.

Under state socialism, as it prevails in the USSR, rather than a number of separate and conflicting interests, one common interest is assumed. The representation of a separate workers', or employers' interest, therefore, is alien to the dominant Soviet ideology. Unions are formed in western states, it is argued, to protect the worker from the oppression of capital. But in a society where the means of production are nationalised, controlled by the state, where the state in the last analysis is answerable to the people, it follows from the Soviet standpoint that antagonistic interests cannot occur between workers and state management.

In the early days of the Soviet regime, there was much controversy concerning the role to be played by the unions. There was one group who saw the existing unions as 'cells of the coming socialist social order' and another who referred to them as 'living corpses'.[1] The former view, later shared by the workers' opposition led by Shlyapnikov, was that the unions should strengthen their structure and should dominate over the state apparatus and its economic administration. Control of the enterprise should rest with the union committee, and of the economy with the trade unions. This was essentially a syndicalist position. The other group, led by Trotsky, wanted the 'stratification' of the unions. A workers' state was organised under the party for the well-being of the working class as a whole. Therefore, the unions should be brought under the economic administration and perform a management function. Lenin's position was between these two extremes: the unions were to stand between party and state, albeit performing a rather limited number of functions.[2] The power of the unions as an independent bargaining group defending specific groups of workers' interests was broken following the Eighth Trade Union Congress in 1929. During the First Five-Year Plan (1928–32), the central planning agencies asserted full control over labour. A trade union structure remained, however, and to it were left many aspects of worker welfare.

In theory, at the present time the Soviet unions act in harmony with the Soviet state which plays the major part in planning the economy; they

---

[1] E. H. Carr, *The Bolshevik Revolution 1917-1923* (1952), vol. 2, pp. 106-7.

[2] The history of trade-unionism in the USSR is discussed in detail by I. Deutscher, *Soviet Trade Unions* (1950). For early history see also Frederick I. Kaplan, *Bolshevik Ideology and the Ethics of Soviet Labor* (New York, 1968).

enhance the material and spiritual position of labour in the building of communism.

The trade unions . . . play a major part in implementing measures to improve working conditions and, as mass organisations with extensive rights, collaborate with the state authorities on the most important questions relating to labour and remuneration. They encourage workers' initiative in developing new forms of work – socialist emulation, the shock-worker movement, the Communist labour brigades and enterprises – and help workers to acquire experience in dealing with production, state and community matters. As society has developed and its material level has risen, the unions have taken over functions previously performed by the state. They at present participate directly in public administration in fields closely related to workers' needs such as social insurance, the running of sanatoria and rest homes, physical culture and sports.[1]

The Central Council of Trade Unions has to be consulted by the Soviet government on matters concerning labour. The Council, in conjunction with appropriate government departments issues 'rules and standards on occupational safety and health'. Centrally, then, the unions act as advisory bodies on labour problems and also as government agencies.

One of the most important tasks of the unions is to administer some of the schemes of social insurance. These include sickness, maternity, industrial injury, family allowances, old-age, disability and dependants' pensions. Unions supervise the collection of premia and determine the amount of benefits. Workers not belonging to a union receive only half the benefit accorded to a union member, which is an important stimulus to join.[2] Health and safety regulations are supervised by the unions. The work of health and safety inspectors is administered by them, and local union officials are responsible for ensuring that labour legislation is enforced. Social services are administered by the unions and numerous rest homes and sanatoria come under their jurisdiction.

Union Structure

The membership of trade unions in the USSR is open to all workers. As we have seen, a collective farmer is not classified as a 'worker' and therefore is not eligible for trade union membership. (But some workers on collective farms – specialists, book-keepers, machine-operators – do join unions.) Membership is voluntary and workers are required to pay a subscription.

Unions are industrial and cover the whole of the USSR (i.e. are 'All-Union',

[1] A. Piatakov, 'Labour Administration by the State and Trade Unions in the USSR', *International Labour Review*, vol. 85 (June 1962), pp. 558-9.
[2] For details of scales of payment, which vary according to the kind of labour and the duration of work and average earnings see *Gosudarstvennoe sotsial'noe strakhovanie* (Moscow, 1965).

referring to the federal structure). In 1964 there were twenty-two unions:[1] Aircraft and Defence Industry; Aviation; Communications and Road Transport; Education and Scientific Institutions; Geological Prospecting; Cooperative and State Trade; Government Employees; Railways; Cultural Workers; Timber, Paper and Woodworking; Engineering; Metallurgical; Sea and River Transport; Health Workers; Local Industry and Municipal Enterprises; Oil and Chemical; Food and Food Industry; Agricultural and State Purchasing; Construction and Building Materials; Textile and Light Industries; Coal Mining; Power and Electrical.[2]

Workers are organised by their industry: *all* workers from clerks to engineers employed on the railways belong to the railway union. The occupational structure is not a criterion for union organisation: an electrician will be attached to the coal mining union if he works in a coal mine, or to the railway union if he works on the railways. No divisions of the work force by skill or position are reflected in union structure. The factory director, administrative and technical personnel and unskilled workers in a given factory all belong to the same union. An exception is made for medical workers who, despite their location, are members of the Health Workers' Union. Employees of factory clinics are employed by the Ministry of Health – not by the enterprise. Obviously, the union structure helps promote unity and solidarity and weakens the professional and occupational stratification on which western (and especially British) unions are organised. The industrial unions make it relatively easier for the planning authorities to alter trade differentials, as there are no organised interest groups to defend particular trade interests.

Soviet trade unions are voluntary organisations and membership is not compulsory. In 1964 (1 July), total membership was 71,229,000.[3] In 1963, 94 per cent of the employed were union members;[4] in certain industries the membership figure (in 1964) was between 95 and 98.1 per cent.[5] Union dues are generally one per cent of earnings (they are reduced somewhat for the lowest-paid categories of workers).

The unions have an organisational structure similar in pattern to the Communist Party. Unions are 'constructed on the basis of democratic centralism according to the production principle'.[6] The structure of Soviet

[1] See I. Vladychenko, *Uchastie rabochikh i sluzhashchikh v upravlenii proizvodstva* (Moscow, 1967), p. 4.

[2] I.L.O., *The Trade Union Situation in the USSR*, (Geneva 1960) p. 70. Some sources mention a twenty-third union, 'medium machine building' (atomic energy); see discussion in E. C. Brown, *Soviet Trade Unions* . . . p. 68.

[3] *Spravochnaya kniga o professional'nykh soyuzov SSSR* (Moscow, 1965), p. 51.

[4] Cited by E. C. Brown, *Soviet Trade Unions* . . ., p. 66.

[5] *Spravochnaya kniga* . . ., *ibid.*

[6] 'Ustav professionaln'ykh soyuzov SSSR', in *Spravochnik profsoyuznogo rabotnika* (1962), Art. 13.

unions is shown on Diagram 5. At the bottom is the primary union group
formed at the place of work. This is at least 15 strong. The factory committee
is directly elected (sometimes on a workshop basis depending on the size of

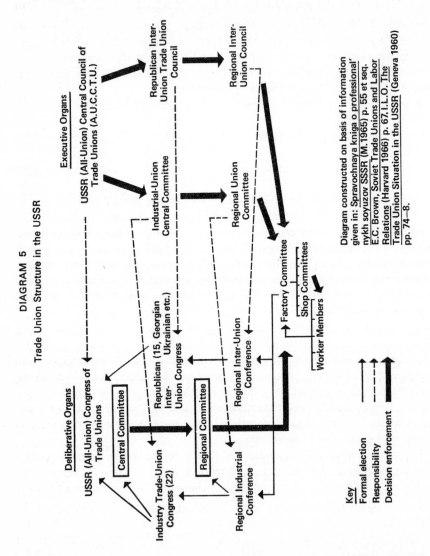

DIAGRAM 5
Trade Union Structure in the USSR

Diagram constructed on basis of information
given in: Spravochnaya kniga o professional'
nykh soyuzov SSSR (M.1965) p. 55 et seq.
E.C. Brown, Soviet Trade Unions and Labor
Relations (Harvard 1966) p. 67.I.L.O. The
Trade Union Situation in the USSR (Geneva 1960)
pp. 74–8.

the factory) or sometimes indirectly by deputies elected by union members.[1]
Factory committees elect delegates both to industrial regional conferences
(i.e. conference of men from *one* union) and to regional inter-union con-

[1] See chart.

ferences. These in turn elect to the trade unions' own congress and to the Republican inter-union conference. Finally, delegates are elected to the All-Union (Federal) Congress of Trade-Unions.

The union structure, therefore, ensures considerable overlap between unions and, particularly as some two-thirds of the delegates to the Federal Trade Union Congress[1] are elected by the regional inter-union conferences, gives the central authority considerable control over the lower organs. Furthermore, the 'centralism' of union structure demands the subordination of lower units to higher ones. The implementation of central decisions is mainly the responsibility of the executive organs which are linked as shown on the diagram. In Britain, on the other hand, the unions are strongly organised on a trade basis and inter-union co-operation is minimal; the Trade Union Congress has no authority over the individual unions which make up its membership. The two union structures reflect the pluralist and unitary theories on which each society is politically based.

The Central Council, elected by the Congress, plays a leading role in the union movement. Among its activities are

to determine the immediate tasks of unions generally, to participate in the elaboration of the national economic plan, to submit to legislative organs draft laws and decrees, to exercise the direction of the state social insurance system, to approve the budget of the trade unions and the state social insurance budget, to define the general structure of trade unions and their staffs, and to represent Soviet trade unions in the international trade union movement.[2]

It has staff throughout the lower echelons of the union administration. Thus while the Republican Inter-Union Trade Union Council is elected by the Republican Union Congress, the full-time officials have a responsibility to the secretariat in Moscow. The power of this central body is in contrast to the weak control which western union secretariats have over individual unions. During the decentralisation of industrial management, for example, the number of unions was halved by order of the All-Union Central Committee of Trade Unions (AUCCTU). Each union, however, elects its own central committee, both at a federal and at a regional level. Work peculiar to that union is carried out by the secretariat of the union.[3]

In the west, Soviet unions are regarded by many commentators as mere 'puppets' of the central authorities. Indeed, there can be no doubt that the unions are not workers' organisations divorced from, and opposed to man-

[1] i.e. At the Twelfth Federal Union Congress in 1959, 400 delegates were elected by the trade union congress and 900 by the inter-union regional conference (I.L.O. *The Trade Union Situation in the USSR*, p. 74).

[2] *Ustav professional'nykh soyuzov SSSR*, paragraph 29 (Moscow, 1968).

[3] The duties of the respective organs are defined in the Statutes of the Trade Unions, *Ustav professional'nykh soyuzov SSSR* (Moscow, 1968). See also R. Conquest, *Industrial Workers in the USSR* (1967), Chapter 5.

agement as they appear in Great Britain. (On the continent and in the USA unions and management often work in closer harmony). But this does not entail that the 'management' and the 'unions' are equally intermeshed at all levels. Mary McAuley has argued that at the regional level and above the unions' organisations are 'more closely tied in with the administrative apparatus – both in terms of personnel and functions – than at the enterprise'.[1] At the higher levels, the promotion of the more general interest can be pursued without any loss to either side; also an industrial union and ministry (or a branch of it) may combine to promote their common interest against other competitors. At the enterprise level, however, the process of production gives worker and management different roles which may give rise to strife. Let us consider first the formal structure of unions in the enterprise, and then turn to look at labour disputes.

Trade Union Activity in the Factory

The main differences between western unions and the Soviet kind may be illustrated by considering the kind of activities performed by the union at the place of production.

The Soviet factory union committee has the following responsibilities:
(a) mobilisation of all workers and employees in the enterprise, building site, state farm or establishment for fulfilment and over-fulfilment of the state plan, strengthening of labour discipline and development of socialist emulation and the movement for communist labour;
(b) elaboration and putting into effect of practical measures aimed at steadily raising labour productivity, the maximum utilisation of internal production reserves, improving quality and lowering production costs;
(c) enlisting workers and employees into active participation in questions of the activity of the enterprise and establishment and in the administration of production and social matters;
(d) organising the popularisation of advanced experience, the latest achievements of science and technology, the development of the mass movement of rationalisers and inventors; raising the level of general education and technical knowledge of the working people;
(e) daily concern for the improvement of labour protection, the improvement of the material position and everyday conditions of workers and employees; carrying out among working people and their families mass cultural, physical culture and sports activity, the development of tourism;
(f) fostering in workers and employees, high political consciousness, dedication to the public interest, honesty and truthfulness, high moral qualities,

[1] Mary McAuley, *Labour Disputes in Soviet Russia 1957-1965* (1969), p. 72.

the struggle against anti-social tendencies and survivals of the past in people's minds;

(g) fulfilling obligations taken under the collective agreement;

(h) implementing decisions of higher trade union organs and resolutions of general meetings;

(i) enlisting all workers and employees into membership of the trade union;

(k) development of criticism and self-criticism, educating trade union members in a spirit of intolerance to shortcomings, to manifestations of bureaucracy and to the issuing of false returns, to mismanagement and waste and a negligent attitude to public property.[1]

As we saw earlier, Soviet unions play an important role in the production process unlike in the West where they have no such duties. A second difference is in membership, where in the Soviet case management can and does participate in union affairs. The factory director or other supervisory staff might well be members of the factory union committee. McAuley, for instance, says that of 25 members of the Skorokhod factory committee, five were full-time union officials; seven were specialists, the chairman had been the former chief engineer, and the vice-chairman was an official from the production department; but at another plant, the Mikoyan sweet factory, none of the 15 members was from top management.[2]

The range of Soviet union activities also includes many aspects of production problems (wages, output). The union has a specific duty to increase output, to encourage more effective use of labour, to root out practices which restrict production, to encourage workers to improve their qualifications and to devise more efficient production methods. 'Socialist emulation' or comradely co-operation and mutual assistance in the labour process is to be encouraged at the point of production – not only to improve output but to develop a co-operative spirit towards work.[3] In the factory a number of commissions are organised under the union committee. They are shown on Diagram 6. Under the factory union committee come shop committees, mainly concerned with production. They act, at the point of production, as liaison units between the factory director and the worker.

The 'commissions' of the union are charged with specific duties, often defined by the USSR Central Council of Trade Unions.[4] For example, a commission will have particular responsibilities concerning insurance and will administer the housing constructed for factory personnel. A group will be responsible for encouraging invention and rationalising production. In practice there is considerable overlap of personnel between these commissions and much

---

[1] Source: *Ustav professional'nykh soyuzov SSSR*, paragraph 47 (Moscow, 1968).

[2] *Labour Disputes in Soviet Russia 1957-65* (1969), pp. 76-7.

[3] See I. Dvornikov *et al*, *Professional'nye soyuzy SSSR* (Moscow, 1961), pp. 22-3.
See *Spravochnaya kniga . . .*, p. 53.

L*

inefficiency. As McAuley has described their operation: '...under the *fabkom* [factory committee] we have commissions devoted to production, to socialist competition, to rationalisation proposals, and to the production conferences; at the same time, the party organisation would have a section devoted to the improvement of production.[1] All these different commissions would be considering some of the same questions and, in many cases, the membership

DIAGRAM 6

Factory Union Committee and Sub-units

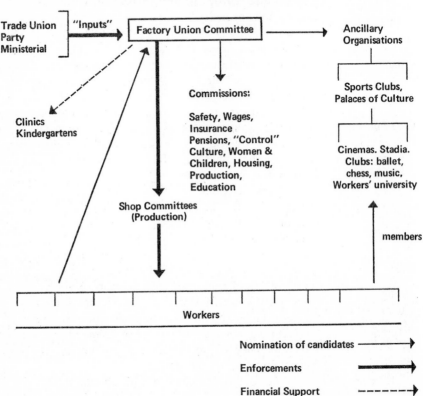

would be overlapping.'[2] Much of the union's activity comes under what western firms would call 'personnel' work. It is required to deal with workers' personal problems, to issue holiday and sanitoria vouchers, besides dealing with grievances and disputes.

To the right of the diagram are 'ancillary organisations' run by the local union committee. 'Palaces of culture' are the equivalent of the English

[1] See Chapter 13.
[2] *Labour Disputes in Soviet Russia*, p. 71. See also below, p. 323.

workingman's club. The larger factories have premises (often literally former palaces) where artistic (painting, sculpture) and general leisure activities can take place. Sports clubs and stadia, cinemas and theatres often form part of the Palace of Culture complex. Such well-known teams as Moscow Dynamo and Riga Zef are 'union' teams. The sports clubs embrace a wide variety of sports: in 1964 there were 13,700,000 participants in union sports societies.[1] They are administered by a director and a committee responsible to the factory committee. The finance of the Palaces is the concern of the union. Income from dances, cinema shows and football matches accrues to the union.

The equivalent of the British Workers' Educational Association is organised by unions. In 1964, 4,844 'peoples' universities' were organised, with a membership of over a million workers.[2] Such sections arrange for series of talks on social, political and economic themes and organise day-schools.

On the left of Diagram 6, joined by a dotted line, are institutions which come under the administration of separate government departments but which may be sponsored by the local factory committee. A district polyclinic located in the factory's catchment area might receive financial help to buy special equipment and a local kindergarten might be helped to provide toys and equipment for the children.

Locally, at the level of the enterprise, the unions participate in the drawing up of the collective agreement (*koldogovor*) which defines the level of output and the division of bonus between workers and its utilisation for collective provision (e.g. new housing). The workers themselves, of course, participate in meetings to discuss aspects of the agreement. This discussion may be an important means of reducing stress in industrial relations. The fact that the workers may keep a certain proportion of profits for their own use helps to strengthen collective responsibility. As a trade union pamphlet puts it: 'The agreement has a great influence on the most diverse aspects of the factory's life. The better the collective works, the more profit it receives, which it may use at its own discretion'.[3] The extent to which the unions and the rank and file workers participate in drawing up the collective agreement has not been thoroughly studied. In McAuley's study of six Leningrad factories, the contentious points were not very important. Extra holidays, the opening of a new cafeteria and the shortage of children's crèches were the most important areas of dispute between management and union.[4]

In the elaboration of the economic plan and its execution, local union committees participate with management. They must help the management to promote efficiency and maintain discipline, they encourage workers to

[1] *Spravochnaya kniga* . . ., p. 93.
[2] *Spravochnaya kniga* . . ., p. 83.
[3] I. Vladychenko, *Uchastie rabochikh i sluzhashchikh v upravlenii proizvodstva* (Moscow, 1967), p. 36.
[4] Mary McAuley, *Labour Disputes in Soviet Russia 1957-1965* 1969), p. 80.

improve their qualifications and to suggest improvements in productive capacity. Workers, management and the state in theory have a common interest – to increase production. This view of industrial relations is not unlike that of progressive western firms (such as ICI) which have introduced profit-sharing and other 'workers' participation' schemes in order to bring management and worker closer. The attempt of the British government and unions in recent years to relate wage increases to increases in productivity and to secure the workers' agreement to this is a policy similar to that adopted in the USSR.

There is, however, evidence of conflict between the various interests. On the one hand, factory management and the factory union committee share a common interest against the higher industrial administration to secure as large a wage fund as possible. On the other, conflict takes place between the union and the factory administration on the grading of jobs. Here is how a British study comments on wage scales.

At the Leningrad enterprises, it seemed usual for all decisions or suggestions to come from management. The *fabkom* [factory TU committee] saw its task to be that of checking a proposed list of changes and making the occasional query or objection to a particular point. But if subsequently a change brought protests from the workers involved, the *fabkom* then felt entitled to take the matter up and take a decision on it . . . The *fabkom* acted . . . as a body for resolving disputes.[1]

It is also interesting to find that as the management's bonus partly came from economies on the factory wages fund, this caused opposition from the workers who wanted, of course, to overspend this fund.[2] It seems most probable that considerable bargaining goes on about the wage structure of the enterprise and that the union committee plays an important part in resolving the conflict of interests. Here it acts more like the personnel department of a western firm than a workers' organisation.

The existence of disputes is recognised by Soviet commentators, who explain them as due to 'inadequate knowledge of labour legislation on the part of individual management representatives or workers, or through its faulty application.' There are three channels for the resolution of conflict: the labour disputes board (made up of equal numbers of members of the trade union and management), the local trade union committee, the people's courts. The disputes board is the most important medium and deals with cases which have been passed to it after preliminary investigation by the trade union committee.

The procedure of the labour disputes board is quite informal. After an aggrieved worker hands in his complaint, if it cannot be resolved by the management, the board must meet within five days. The number of disputes per

[1] McAuley, *op. cit.*, p. 97.
[2] McAuley, *op. cit.*, p. 101.

annum brought before these boards, according to McAuley's study is equal to three to ten per cent of the labour force.[1] It is interesting to note that, as far as cases in 138 enterprises were concerned, nearly twice as many decisions went in favour of the worker as against him.[2] The disputes referred to these boards were on the following topics (in order of frequency): holidays, wages, dismissals, subtraction from pay, bonus, transfer to other work, disciplinary procedure. (Based on 32 Urals factories cited by McAuley, p. 160.) The employees may appeal, if dissatisfied, to the trade union committee and from there to the people's court; the management, if it considers the trade union committee's decision illegal, may also appeal.

Unlike the practice in western countries, the local union in the USSR has to agree with the management before a worker may be dismissed. Here the case may be referred to the people's court and yet again an appeal may be made to a higher court. Soviet labour relations are characterised more by judicial procedures than they are in Great Britain. How far union committees ensure that workers' rights are respected is extremely difficult to estimate. The union newspaper *Trud* often complains that unions do not protect workers' rights. McAuley's study shows that of requests for dismissal of workers about half were agreed to by the unions. In such cases workers had either been previously threatened with dismissal or frequently reprimanded. Requests for dismissals were dealt with as follows:

it was usual to call the worker before the *fabkom*. This meant that discussion of management's request could be turned into a discussion of the worker's behaviour in his presence. At Karl Marx [factory], workers who did not bother to attend were more likely to find themselves dismissed. At Mikoyan, where the requests were not frequent and where the *fabkom* laid great stress upon educational measures, one worker who refused to listen to the *fabkom*'s discussion of his behaviour and became extremely rude was, as a consequence, dismissed.[3]

The unions therefore, are not official 'rubber stamps'.

Workers receive, without payment, legal help through their union in order to defend their legal rights. Workers may appeal to the court against the decision. In McAuley's study only one case went to court. 'The worker had been dismissed for repeated infractions of labour discipline; he claimed before the court that he should have been dismissed for 'unsuitability at the job' because his health was poor and he could not manage his work. The court granted the claim and ordered the enterprise to make the corresponding change in his work-book.'[4] Claims for reinstatement dominate court proceedings,

---

[1] *Op. cit.*, p. 154, i.e. in a factory employing 300 men, there would be from 9 to 30 disputes per annum brought before the boards.

[2] *Op. cit.*, p. 156.

[3] *Labour Disputes in Soviet Russia*, p. 124.

[4] *Labour Disputes in Soviet Russia*, pp. 124-5.

followed by claims over wages[1]; in the early 1960s about half the claims for reinstatement were granted by the courts[2]; this entailed reimbursement of back pay.

While the factory TU committee seems to have had some effect in preventing dismissals, it takes a rather different attitude to workers who want to leave; in this case it seems to interpret its role as a defender of the plan and management. As skilled labour is scarce, leaving workers may seriously disrupt the plan – and the wages of other workers. The trade union committee, therefore, assumes that it has a responsibility to reduce labour turnover. At one factory a TU commission was established to investigate turnover and those who had given in their notice were referred to it. This body could bring pressure to bear on workers who wanted to leave by saying that they first had to investigate the case.[3]

The function of the union to engender a 'collective consciousness' would seem to operate to strengthen the worker's allegiance to his present place of work. The more general social consciousness would, on the other hand, appear to suffer at its expense. Management and TU branch sometimes unite against the central authorities and likewise both have a common interest against a worker who saw better opportunities elsewhere. The local interest therefore may come before the national interest.

Strikes are not specifically prohibited by law, though there are laws covering acts which undermine or weaken the Soviet state which possibly could be used against strikers. In fact, strikes are rare in the USSR. Workers sometimes go slow or walk out because of poor conditions. According to Soviet trade union officials, sufficient negotiating channels exist and, therefore, there is 'no need' for strikes.[4] We have seen above how minor disputes are resolved. It is also important to note that the belief system, in which homogeneity of interests and social harmony is emphasised, may condition workers to use existing channels and discourage violent confrontations with management. Furthermore there is now no tradition of unions organising strikes to improve wages or conditions. The participation by the unions in 'management functions' and their identification with the production goals of the enterprise keep their objectives within the bargaining process of the 'collective agreement', through which tension may be released at regular intervals. Soviet industrial relations, therefore, should not be regarded as the 'bottling down' of legitimate workers' grievances by the trade unions as they are sometimes characterised in the West. Rather, Soviet unions have successfully helped to reduce stress in the factory and have played a most important part in stimulating the workers to increase production.

[1] McAuley, p. 206.
[2] McAuley, p. 213.
[3] McAuley, pp. 126-7.
[4] I.L.O., *The Trade Union Situation in the USSR* (Geneva, 1960), pp. 53-66.

Soviet trade unions, therefore, cannot be seen as 'equivalents' of their western namesakes. But it is absurd not to call them trade unions because the strike weapon is never used. They fully contribute to 'maintaining' and 'improving' the conditions of life of the working man as defined by the Webbs. Indeed, the range and extent of the Soviet unions' activity far surpasses anything known in western states. This difference in function is related to the ideological beliefs of the society's elites. Unions in the USSR are organised on the basis that society is politically homogeneous, and that a union member as such can have no individual interest above or separate from that of society as a whole which is represented by the government. But in practice there are conflicts of interest: between union branch and management; between the enterprise and the central administration; between individual enterprises – who want to keep their own skilled workers and entice others from competitors. Rather than articulating a 'workers' interest' against other parties and aggregating a workers' interest as a whole, the unions seek to resolve disputes, to see that law is enforced in favour of the worker. In western societies, in contrast, it is held that group relations are essentially conflicting: an equilibrium is maintained through competition between sectional interests, an important one of which is the trade union which articulates and aggregates a specific workers' interest.

Yet another, and perhaps more important, institution is organised at the Soviet place of work, the Communist Party of the Soviet Union. We have discussed generally its role in Soviet society, next we shall concentrate on its activity in the economy and the enterprise.

Party Control of the Economy

All political parties attempt to influence, in some respects, the operation of the economy. Their role in the economy of a liberal society is mainly to unify and co-ordinate.[1] To this end parties formulate general economic programmes for public approval. Under normal circumstances, they aggregate demands to maintain a political equilibrium. In the aggregation process some groups will be favoured relative to others, though, to be sure, party statements will attempt to show, perhaps disingenuously, how all groups will benefit. In the West party policies usually procliam targets of economic growth for a given period and define the distribution of resources between different headings – such as, for example, investment and consumption, foreign aid and defence. One of the distinguishing characteristics of state socialism is the leading role of the party. Indeed, in the West it is widely believed that 'In Socialist societies, the public ownership and control of the means of production has been carried much further, so that in the USSR, the party machinery effectively controls

[1] A. Leiserson, *Parties and Politics* (New York, 1958).

the entire production process'.[1] We have already discussed the economic goals of the CPSU in the chapter on the functions of the party and we have seen that the party's economic programme is comprehensive. We have noted that the Constitution defines the party as the leading organisation of Soviet society and the trade-union rules say that 'the trade-unions carry out their work under the leadership of the CPSU – the leading and directing force of Soviet society'.[2]

How do economic policies become translated into practical plans and activity? The short answer is through the government organisations already considered: the ministerial apparatus. The party *itself* does not directly organise the economy, it has no economic establishments under its command, which are legally and organisationally under government ministries. (See above pp. 274–82.) Party organisations must *not* 'act in place of Soviet, trade union, co-operative or other public organisations . . . they must not allow either the merging of the functions of the party and other bodies or undue parallelism in work.' (*Party Rules*, article 42.) In theory then, the party does not aspire to administer but 'to guide' or to bring influence to bear on industrial organisations controlled by the government. Between 1940 and 1953 under Stalin, and from 1958 to 1964 under Khrushchev, the leadership of party and government was unified; one man held both the top jobs in party and state. But the existence of separate party and government organisations may lead to dualism and conflict. (See Chapter 7.) This is less frequent and less important in the USA where national parties are weakly organised and have little, if any, ideological identity. But it is not unknown in Great Britain, where many examples of friction and differences between the leadership of the Parliamentary Labour Party when responsible for government and the executive of the Labour Party representing the views of the Labour Party annual conference and Labour Party members as a whole, may be cited. In the Soviet Union, personnel overlap between party and state to a much greater extent and party influence is stronger than in liberal-democratic states. The existence of only one party in the USSR means that if interests are to be effectively articulated, they must be represented within its framework. As with parties in Great Britain and the United States, the CPSU is responsible for the formulation of general policy goals, the government for carrying them out.

The degree of responsibility and the extent of public control over industry are of crucial importance in a socialist system where industry is a government responsibility. For it is possible that ministries, if dominated by factory directors and executives, could embrace a new ruling stratum. Party control in such a case would either be too weak to assert its own values over the ministerial elites or the party elites would be corrupted and act in their own

---

[1] S. Cotgrove, *The Science of Society* (1967), p. 120.
[2] *Spravochnik profsoyuznogo rabotnika 1967* (Moscow, 1967), p. 157.

interest and not for the popular good. While having no ownership rights over industry, such groups could secure a commanding or controlling position. Indeed, some critics of Soviet society have suggested that this is the predominant characteristic of the USSR – bureaucrats forming tight social groups based on self-interest.[1] It is also true that popular control of the executive by the legislature is ineffective in the USSR. Deputies are part-time and Soviets meet infrequently; ministerial industrial enterprises are outside local government control and All-Union factories are answerable to headquarters in Moscow. Therefore, the role of the party, especially where a strong government apparatus is necessary, is to act as a guardian of the revolution and the class its triumph represents. In some ways, it may be considered as providing a form of public control which is carried out by elected bodies (councils) in Britain and the USA. In industry, in the same way as shareholders are seen in Marxist theory to be the dominant class in capitalist society, the party safeguards the interests of the dominant class under socialism. David Granick has argued that 'in one basic sense, both groups (i.e. capitalist shareholders and the Russian Communist Party) play the same role in the respective societies. Each represents legitimacy of power'.[2] He sees the Party Presidium (now Politbureau) at the 'apex of an all-embracing administrative system'.[3]

The factory manager's authority, however, is legally based on the Supreme Soviet, and his appointment is made by an organ of the Council of Ministers. The party committees in the factories protect the interests of the party, in the same way as directors should protect the interests of shareholders in capitalist firms. The party committees, argues Granick, are more active in this respect than are 'their counterparts in American business', and have 'injected themselves into the management function'.[4] Let us briefly look at the history of the party's role in industry.

During the immediate post-revolutionary period, when the Communist Party was relatively small, it was necessary for it to exercise control over the economic and government apparatuses which were filled with men hostile to the Bolsheviks. Party commissars were directed and party groups were formed to see that the political goals of the new Soviet state were being carried out.

By 1934 the need for such political control had lessened. The Seventeenth Party Congress, on the one hand, liquidated these party control groups but, on the other, reaffirmed the need for party control. The dominant form of authority over the economic enterprise at this time was one-man leadership[5] and such regulations as existed for party supervision were not

---

[1] See above, pp. 178-8 and Max Schachtman, *The Bureaucratic Revolution*, New York, 1962), p. 50.

[2] *The Red Executive* (New York, 1960), p. 188.

[3] P. 194.

[4] Pp. 203-4.

[5] See I. V. Stalin, 'Report to 17th Party Congress', *Collected Works*, vol. 13.

fully implemented. Not only did direct party influence decline in industrial enterprises but also at the higher levels the government apparatus became most important; though not to the exclusion of the party.

At the Eighteenth Party Congress (1939) the party rules gave basic party organs the prerogative to 'control'[1] the work of the administration of production enterprises. This gave them the right to see papers concerned with production, to have meetings with, and information from the management and to make recommendations to promote efficiency.[2] In practice, this took the form of party groups being able to question the enterprise's management at party meetings. According to a recent Soviet writer, party basic organisations had greater influence than hitherto in economic decision-making[3] but in fact they were still not very decisive. Most western experts consider that practice varied considerably in the USSR. '. . . There is no single 'typical' relationship between party secretary and director. At one extreme are cases in which secretary Golovkin of the party committee of the administration stamps as O.K. any anti-party action of his boss. On the other hand, there are sharp conflicts, over personal matters of authority or privilege.'[4]

Under Stalin there was considerable confusion between factory manager and party secretary. It has been suggested, even, that this was intentional and 'a carefully nurtured system of parallel competing bureaucracies' had been set up in which Stalin had a 'vested interest in confusion'.[5] The literature on the subject abounds with examples showing the supremacy of one or the other. R. C. Gripp cites a case where the power of a factory director was sufficient to scorn a party secretary's advice, and, if need be, even to threaten dismissal if orders were not carried out.[6] Berliner quotes an émigré who says that 'since the late thirties the party secretary has participated in the solution even of technical problems. But no rule can be established about his influence. This depends on his personal qualities. His influence increases with his technical competence.'[7] Jerry Hough interviewed a number of Soviet officials between 1958 and 1962. They all agreed that the powers of the party secretary are limited to persuasion and appeal to higher officials. 'Those interviewed stated that the decision of a meeting of the primary party organisation or its bureau does not bind the manager unless he has concurred in the decision. Even a non-party director of a textile factory insisted that the primary party organisation would take no decision concerning the economic side of the enterprise's

[1] I have followed the usual practice of translating the Russian *kontrol* by 'control'. The Russian is not as strong as the English and refers more to supervision or checking-up.

[2] 'Edinonachalie i pravo kontroliya', *Partiynoe stroitel'stvo*, no. 18 (1940), p. 34.

[3] A. A. Agapova, *Obshchestvennye kontrolery partii* (Moscow, 1965), p. 7.

[4] Joseph S. Berliner, *Factory and Manager in the USSR* (Cambridge, Mass., 1957), p. 265.

[5] Jeremy R. Azrael, *Managerial Power and Soviet Politics* (Cambridge, 1966), p. 117.

[6] M. Grozhev, 'K chemu vedet bezkontrol'nost', *Partiynaya zhizn'*, no. 4 (Feb. 1955), pp. 65-6. As cited by R. C. Gripp, *Patterns of Soviet Politics* (Chicago, 1963), p. 201.

[7] J. Berliner, p. 267.

life without clearing it with him first.'[1] The director is 'first among equals'.

One should not assume *a priori* that conflict is either necessary or endemic between party secretary and director, any more than it is between managing director and shareholder in western firms. Both manager and party secretary have a common interest and stake in the success of the enterprise. As Richman has pointed out, the party secretary is 'evaluated in terms of enterprise success indicator performance' and he receives a bonus on the same conditions as the management gets premiums.[2] The secretary through his party organisation and connections may well be able to aid the management – for example, to ensure the supply of scarce materials.[3] The party's membership at all levels of the factory gives it 'eyes and ears' among the employees. When working in concert with the party such links can be well utilised by the management. On the other hand, it provides a 'non-management' organisation with access to information about the activity of the plant which might embarrass the management, especially if it has acted inefficiently or unwisely. The party also may be effectively used to mobilise or discipline the work force and may serve the factory management in a similar way to the personnel and welfare departments of capitalist firms. The party organisation at the plant level, therefore, should be considered as a partner to management. Normally it functions in support with the manager being responsible for fulfilling technical goals of the plant.[4] If the factory is well-managed, a working partnership may be achieved between manager and secretary; if it is not, and especially should the party secretary be forceful or technically qualified (or both), then the party may more directly enter the sphere of management relations, usurping the manager's authority. It also, however, supervises the legality and honesty of the management and in these respects (securing 'socialist legality') may be able to limit or even to remove it.

Though one should be wary of making generalisations about managerial-party relations under Stalin at the factory level, it seems likely that the management was relatively strong and the party a more subsidiary influence. This conclusion is in agreement with party-state relations at top levels.[5] Changes introduced by Khrushchev after the Twentieth Congress sought to strengthen the influence of the party generally and particularly its control over the administration of the economy. Party membership was increased among production workers and the party's powers as a 'controller' were enlarged. In this respect it is interesting to note that by 1962 two-thirds of Moscow

[1] Jerry F. Hough, *The Soviet Prefects* (Cambridge, Mass., 1969), p. 94.

[2] B. M. Richman, *Soviet Management* (New York, 1965), pp. 220-1.

[3] David Granick, *Management of the Industrial Firm in the USSR* (New York, 1954), p. 206.

[4] See Granick, *Management . . .*, pp. 208-9.

[5] This has been discussed above, Chapter 7. See also R. Pethybridge, *A Key to Soviet Politics* (1962), p. 32 and L. Schapiro, *The Communist Party of the Soviet Union* (1960), p. 549.

raykom (district) party secretaries had had higher technical education.[1] Party secretaries at the factory level, of course, would have lower technical qualifications than factory managers, the majority of whom have higher technical education. Under Khrushchev the party was to be a 'balance' at the higher levels of administration and a 'check' at the lower ones. The element of party control in Soviet industry was to be strengthened and bureaucratic tendencies on the part of ministries weakened and control 'commissions' of various types outside the formal government apparatuses were set up to supervise ministerial activity.

Party Control Commissions

In June 1959, the Central Committee passed a decree on the formation of party control commissions in industrial enterprises and regulations were published concerning their activities.[2] These regulations are based on, and further develop, the party rules which give the CPSU far greater powers in industry than any liberal-democratic party. Party basic organisations 'enjoy the right to control the work of the administration'.[3] Excluded from this obligation are party groups in the following organisations: 'at ministries, state committees, economic councils and other central and local government or economic agencies and departments'.[4] In such institutions, party members are obliged to: 'actively promote improvement of the apparatus, cultivate among personnel a high sense of responsibility in their work, promote state discipline and better service to the population, firmly combat bureaucracy and red tape, inform the appropriate party bodies in good time of shortcomings in the work of the respective offices and individuals, regardless of what posts the latter occupy'.[5] At the upper levels, then, the dualism of party control is absent, though its members may collectively act to expose individuals and to remedy administrative faults in the party's name.

Our empirical knowledge of such internal occurrences does not allow us to say how frequent or important such activity is. But it is doubtful whether the party group in the ministerial apparatus has much influence on the day-to-day activity of ministries at the highest levels.[6] The integrated ministerial command, charged with definite economic plans, understanding the technical

---

[1] J. Azrael, 'Politics and Management', *Survey*, no. 49 (October 1963), p. 98. There is little movement between party and industrial hierarchies. Staffs are specialised. See Jerry Hough, *op. cit.*, pp. 274, 276.

[2] See Reading no. 12.

[3] Paragraph 59, *The Rules of the Communist Party of the Soviet Union* (1961).

[4] Paragraph 59.

[5] Paragraph 59.

[6] The role of the party central committee's secretariat is another question. This has more power in the aggregation of interests (see Chapter 7). This body is able to intervene at the top of the ministerial hierarchy.

complexity and problems of a given industry, is strongly positioned against daily party meddling. Khrushchev's attempt to decentralise industry by breaking up many of the all-union ministries, replacing them with regional economic councils (*sovnarkhozy*) controlling most of the industrial units within their areas might have enhanced party control, had they been long lasting. The final abolition of the *sovnarkhozy* and the strengthening of the ministerial system in 1965 moved the balance very much in the latter's favour.

At the lower levels, at the grass roots, in 'industrial enterprises, trading establishments, state and collective farms, design and drafting offices and research institutes directly related to production'[1] party control becomes more significant. The *Handbook for the Secretary of a Basic Party Organisation* defines the activity of party groups in establishments to include the promotion of improvements in the organisation of production, the introduction of new methods and advanced technology, the support of invention and rationalisation and the development of 'socialist emulation'.[2] To secure these ends special party commissions, or groups, already mentioned are organised at enterprises.[3]

At this stage, it may be useful to draw up an organisational scheme of a 'typical' Soviet factory. We may distinguish between three separate organisations in the factory: production (the ministry), political (the party), social and educational (the trade union). These are shown on Chart 13 (p. 322).

The factory manager is responsible to the ministry by whom he is appointed. Under him are production departments headed by assistant managers, and production shops, by foremen. The production aspects of Soviet factories are similar to factories in western countries. There are some differences: quality control and inspection are usually organised under production, rather than in separate independent departments. It is notable that, unlike in western firms, sales departments generally are very small and have little, if any, influence over production. The director is solely responsible to the ministry for the operation of the plant. This is responsible to the Council of Ministers, (in which the minister in charge of the industry will have a place) which in turn is answerable to the Supreme Soviet – at least in theory.

Running parallel with the ministerial chain of command are the party and union hierarchies. These are shown on Chart 13, to the left and right of the ministerial hierarchy. The party committee is charged with a general political supervision of the plant, and the union is particularly responsible for workers' welfare. In Soviet theory, the three groups work in harmony. In Soviet parlance, they have to 'speak the same language'.

We saw earlier that the unions assist the management in drawing up the

[1] Paragraph 59.

[2] *Spravochnik sekretarya pervichnoy partiynoy organizatsii* (Moscow, 1960), p. 470.

[3] See Reading 13, 'Regulations concerning the commissions under basic party organisations of production and trade establishments on the realisation by party organisations of the right to control the activity of the administration'.

CHART 13
Party, Ministerial and Trade Union Hierarchies

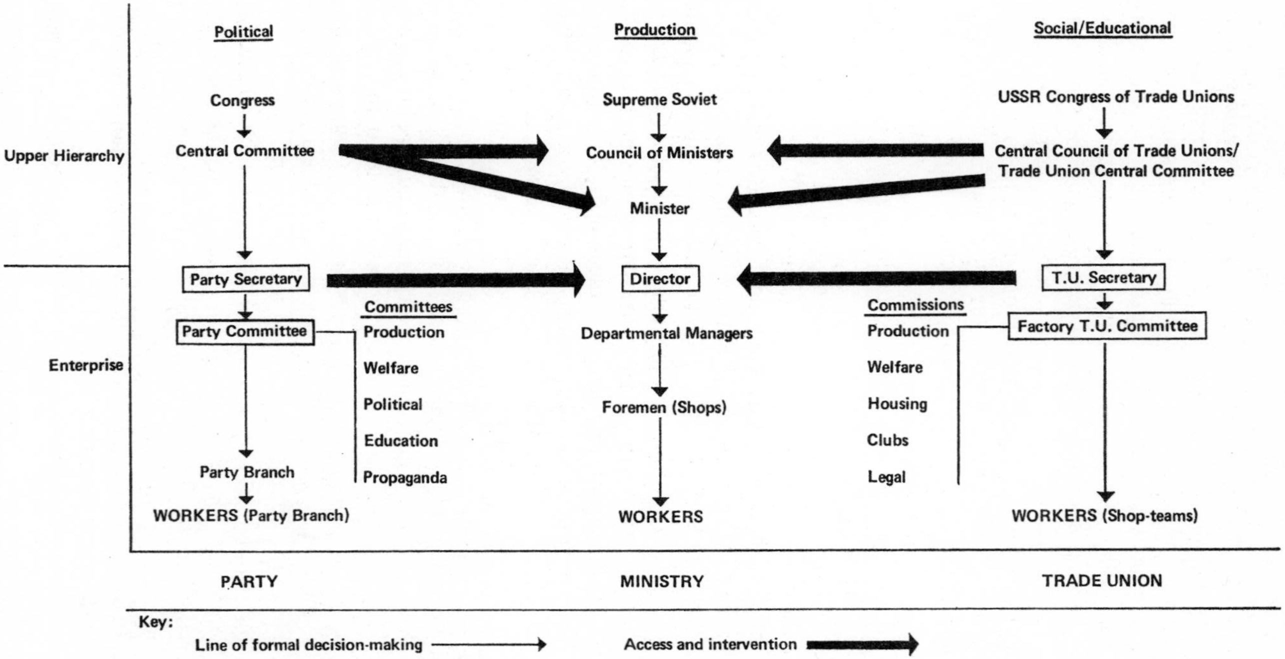

<u>Political</u>

Congress

Central Committee

Party Secretary

Party Committee

Committees
Production
Welfare
Political
Education
Propaganda

Party Branch

WORKERS (Party Branch)

<u>Production</u>

Supreme Soviet

Council of Ministers

Minister

Director

Departmental Managers

Foremen (Shops)

WORKERS

<u>Social/Educational</u>

USSR Congress of Trade Unions

Central Council of Trade Unions/
Trade Union Central Committee

T.U. Secretary

Factory T.U. Committee

Commissions
Production
Welfare
Housing
Clubs
Legal

WORKERS (Shop-teams)

Upper Hierarchy

Enterprise

PARTY   MINISTRY   TRADE UNION

Key:

Line of formal decision-making →

Access and intervention ◄

plan.[1] Since 1957, the unions have had greater opportunity to participate in the drawing up of collective agreements between the factory directorate and the workers. In this process, the factory trade union committee and shop committees consider ways the factory plan may be fulfilled and workers' suggestions and complaints are often taken into consideration.[2] These, however, are within the context of the financial resources of the enterprise and involve changing priorities rather than a fundamental appraisal of the plan. Disagreements over rates of pay for particular jobs may be referred to the commissions concerned with these matters. The management's authority over the workers is also restricted by the union's responsibility for labour discipline. Comrades' courts in the factory act under the unions composed of its members and decide sanctions. The unions do not control the hiring of workers but as we saw above they *must* legally be consulted before a dismissal of a worker takes place and they must sanction such action.

In the production process, the Soviet factory manager must learn to get on with union factory standing production commissions. In Byelorussia in 1966, for example, there were 4,000 standing production committees with 148,000 members. They were concerned with production, problems of labour, wages, technical standards, improvement of quality and cost reduction, vocational training and the efficient use of labour.[3] It should be remembered, of course, that engineers and 'administrative' staff may join such commissions. It is claimed that in 1964, the all-union society of inventors and rationalisers had 3,344,600 members in 45,800 societies, and their work saved 2,912 million rubles.[4]

Under the Communist Party, similar commissions have been set up. In some factories both party and union committees work side by side, sometimes specialising in separate aspects of production. On the eve of the Twenty-Second Congress, more than one hundred thousand party commissions existed with a membership of six hundred thousand communists, whose task it was to 'control production'.[5] Other party-government groups also existed concerned with control and supervision of the firm: in October, 1961, there were 'several hundred thousand groups and smaller units (*posty*) comprising about four million communists and non-party people'.[6] At the November 1962 plenum of the Central Committee of the CPSU a single party-state committee was formed subordinate to the Central Committee and the Council of Ministers. In September, 1964, 3,390 committees of party-government control,

[1] See p. 311.

[2] For examples, see E. C. Brown, *Soviet Trade Unions* . . ., pp. 184-6.

[3] A. P. Obukhovich, 'Participation by Workers' Organisations in Planned Social and Economic Development in Byelorussia', *International Labour Review*, no. 94, 1966, p. 454.

[4] *Spravochnaya kniga o professional'nykh soyuzakh SSSR* (Moscow, 1965), p. 65.

[5] 'Partiyny kontrol' na proizvodstve', *Partiynaya zhizn'*, no. 6, May 1964, p. 40.

[6] 'Partiyny kontrol' . . .', p. 41.

19,000 extra voluntary (*vneshtatnykh*) sections and commissions, and 765,000 groups and posts of joint activity had been set up at enterprises, buildings, collective and state farms, establishments and schools.[1] Until December 1965, these groups were called 'party-government' control agencies, and thereafter 'people's control agencies.'[2] We do not have detailed figures of the distribution of control groups between different industries though we know that in 1961 not all primary organisations having the right to form them had done so and rural party groups were especially laggardly in this respect.[3]

To avoid duplication of activity and clashes of authority, the different control commissions should be responsible for separate areas of activity. At one factory, for example, the party groups exercised control over the use of the factory's equipment, over capital building and over the carrying out of organisational-technical measures. The party-government groups' responsibility lay with supervision of the use of machinery, with quality of production control and with overseeing the utilisation of materials.[4] Though the stipulation is not always carried out in practice, the control commissions should be composed of specialists or men knowledgeable about the relevant process of production.

These 'control' units may interfere and hinder the execution of the factory director's proper work, which is probably why they have been played down since Khrushchev's departure from the political scene. For example, one director complained to a journal that a sign he had erected calling for full workers' discipline had been criticised by a party district committee member who objected that it undermined democracy. The journal's commentator pointed out that the director had the right to call for obedience – which the party had to help the workers understand.[5] On the other hand, party secretaries may be instrumental in bringing about the downfall of the director. Richman gives an example of a director 'who was brought to trial for "shoes of poor quality, for maintaining substandard output . . . for regularly causing material damage to customers and still greater moral damage to the state." '[6] In such cases the party apparatus administratively performs a similar function in the Soviet Union as bankruptcy entails in the West.

The Soviet press carries a large number of articles on the achievements of the 'control' groups in raising production and cheapening output.[7] Sometimes savings of as much as ten per cent are claimed resulting from innovations

[1] Agapova, p. 10.

[2] L. Brezhnev, Report to December Plenum of Central Committee, 6 Dec. 1965, reported in *Pravda*, 7 Dec. 1965.

[3] 'Partiyny kontrol' . . ', p. 41.

[4] 'Partiyny kontrol' . . .', p. 42.

[5] *Agitator*, no. 11 (1966), pp. 13-16.

[6] B. M. Richman, *Soviet Management* (New York, 1965), p. 222.

[7] E.g. A. Cherepenin, 'Partiyny kontrol' – sredstvo uluchsheniya rukovodstva khozyaystvom', *Partiynaya zhizn*', no. 5 (March 1962), pp. 30-3.

introduced by the party.[1] The significance of these groups, however, is more likely to lie in their social and political role.

The growing dependence of enterprises on 'market forces' (in practice their ability to determine the precise details of output and the amount of labour employed, their ability to keep and distribute a proportion of the earnings of the enterprise) makes the enterprise less amenable to central control, increases the possibility of fraud and embezzlement and the utilisation of the plant for private ends. As a party secretary has pointed out: the duty of party factory committees 'is to restrain too ardent businessmen and to see that in the search for high profitability preference is not given to the most lucrative type of production to the detriment of state interests'.[2] One of the results of the recent economic reforms is that enterprises may retain all profits accruing from the sale of consumer and industrial goods made from 'waste materials'. Obviously, such a provision could lead to abuse. In the absence of sophisticated accountancy methods or professional 'watch-dog' committees, party and other voluntary bodies may serve as useful constraints. Also, such groups carry out unpaid much of the welfare and personnel work which is necessary in modern industry and which is professionalised in the West.

Internal changes in production processes, the responsibility of management departments in the West, are often organised by party commissions. An account of the Ordzhonikidze factory in *Kommunist*[3] says that the party organisations, at the request of the director, planned and implemented in detail the automation of the factory. The existence of the party group, more than a thousand strong spread through the factory, probably made the change-over easier than in a western (or at least British) factory where resistance to, and suspicion of, change is rife on the factory floor. The Soviet author who cites these examples argues that the administration is increasingly relying on voluntary commissions for advice and co-operation.[4]

The emphasis on the 'assistance' given by these groups to the enterprise administration which is still legally responsible for its performance, is in contrast to the situation in Yugoslavia where the workers' committees have more power and can even remove factory directors. The regulations defining party commissions make clear that the management is responsible for managing, the commissions are auxiliaries having no legal powers over the enterprise. Under Brezhnev and Kosygin, commissions have been retained

---

[1] V. Shivrinski, 'Gorkom i pervichnye partorganizatsii', *Partiynayazhizn*' No. 18, Sept. 1966 pp. 40 - 41. An element of special pleading may be put into these accounts.
[2] M. Sergeev, 'Khozyaystvennaya reforma-vazhny rychag pod"ema ekonomika', *Partiynaya zhizn*', no. 12 (1966), p. 28.
[3] I. Naydis, 'Zavodskoy kollektiv, partorganizatsiya, direktor', *Kommunist* 18 (Dec. 1965), pp. 43-9. Another example of the help given by party groups to the management of the Yaroslavl motor works may be found in G. Belyaev, 'Stopyatidesyaty kvadratny koren', *Agitator*, no. 2, Jan. 1966, pp. 29-31.
[4] *Loc. cit.*

though the emphasis has been more on the partnership of party and government with a subsequent weakening of the former's influence.

The Soviet enterprise will probably develop features different from its counterpart in the West, with more of the quality control, personnel, education, welfare and even accounting, coming within the realm of party and union supervision. This represents a form of structural differentiation in the enterprise. It is too early to say how efficient such a system will be. Khrushchev's solution to bureaucratic delays and inefficiencies lay in strengthening party control. This most probably resulted in the duplication of government and party channels and on occasions led to resented 'meddling' of party groups in the administration. Under Brezhnev and Kosygin economic efficiency has been 'stimulated' by market incentive and party administrative control made less important. Nevertheless, control commissions are to continue. In future they will probably remain secondary to the management and, with the trade unions, their major role will be to give it help and assistance. If an analogy may be made with the function of shareholders in private companies who act in their own financial interest as a check on management efficiency, in the USSR commissions under party guidance try to check up on the administration in terms of a much more general and less easily definable public interest.

The party organisation may prove useful in getting the compliance of workers for changes required by technological advance and by the changing needs of the economy. The party with the union may carry out much of the welfare required in enterprises working under large scale industrial production. But its role as a 'controller' may decline with government departments strengthening their own checks over factories. 'Economic stimulation' may be a better way of encouraging innovation and introducing new techniques than the exhortations of party activists. Perhaps most important is that under Brezhnev and Kosygin greater reliance is put on utilitarian sanctions to achieve compliance, rather than on the normative.[1] The position of the factory manager cannot be described as hegemonic in the USSR. Though one of the most important social forces outside the elites in Soviet society, the factory director is constrained by the party and, to a lesser extent, by the union. These groups give him help, they provide him with information, they mobilise the work force, they suggest how improvements may be made, they give him links in other geographical areas and with different industries.

The Attitude of the Worker to Work

According to Marx, the most important determinants of social relations are

[1] On the distinction between normative and utilitarian sanctions see Chapter 1, p. 1.

those of production. (See Chapter 1.) What does this imply for the worker under capitalism and socialism respectively? Under capitalism, for Marx, the worker finds himself in a state of *alienation*. This word is used with a variety of meanings in numerous contexts in modern sociology. The traditional Marxist concept is relatively simple to understand.[1] Under capitalism, the bourgeoisie owns the tools of production and controls the industrial process. The worker is a factor of production, labour. The worker expends his labour in production, but he neither owns his tools, nor his product and he has no control over the process of production. The capitalist employer appropriates the worker's product. He therefore becomes estranged, or alienated, from his work. This estrangement is not only expressed in political relations (the formation of class parties), but is also reflected in his state of mind:

> What, then, constitutes the alienation of labour?
> First, the fact that labour is external to the worker, i.e. it does not belong to his essential being; that in his work, therefore, he does not affirm himself but denies himself, does not feel content but unhappy, does not develop freely his physical and mental energy but mortifies his body and ruins his mind. The worker therefore only feels himself outside his work, and in his work feels outside himself, he is at home when he is not working, and when he is working he is not at home. His labour is therefore not voluntary, but coerced; it is *forced labour*. It is therefore not the satisfaction of a need; it is merely a *means* to satisfy needs external to it. Its alien character emerges clearly in the fact that as soon as no physical or other compulsion exists, labour is shunned like the plague. External labour, labour in which man alienates himself, is labour of self-sacrifice, of mortification. Lastly, the external character of labour for the worker appears in the fact that it is not his own, but someone else's, that it does not belong to him, that in it he belongs, not to himself, but to another. Just as in religion the spontaneous activity of the human imagination, of the human brain and the human heart, operates independently of the individual – that is, operates on him as an alien, divine or diabolical activity – in the same way the worker's activity is not his spontaneous activity. It belongs to another; it is the loss of his self.[2]

We may sum up Marx's alienation thesis as follows. First, as ownership relations require a division between managerial and worker functions, the worker is excluded from decision-making in the firm, and, due to the increasing division of labour, the production process becomes meaningless to him. Second, because the proceeds of his work are expropriated in the form of profits, the worker loses any sense of identity with his work and becomes isolated from it. Third, his separation from the ownership and control of the industrial firm results in the worker's feeling of powerlessness. Therefore, fourth,

---

[1] For an interesting commentary on Marx's views on alienation see D. Bell, 'The Debate on Alienation', in Leopold Labedz, *Revisionism* (1962).

[2] K. Marx, *Economic and Philosophic Manuscripts of 1844* (Moscow, 1961), pp. 72-3.

feelings of meaninglessness and isolation are common to the worker under capitalist conditions.

If ownership relations are the determining factors of alienation, then the abolition of private capitalist ownership must also eliminate the estrangement that goes with it. Under socialism one should *a priori* expect no alienation of labour but a set of relationships the opposite to those under capitalism. The worker, far from being powerless before the production process, should be able to see its wholeness. He controls it, the fruits of his labour are not expropriated from him but accrue to him. The creativity and meaning of work are restored to him. He participates and takes initiative in the work process. A Soviet theorist contrasts capitalism and socialism as follows:

The productive forces of socialism differ basically from the productive forces of capitalism in their social form, although they have much in common with the latter from the material and technical standpoint. The new social system has opened up for them great additional possibilities and advantages; a planned and rational use of productive capacities, greater efficiency in the organisation of production, balanced development, higher rates of economic growth, unlimited overall technical progress, new incentives for labour, and the creation of a new man.[1]

The attitude of the worker in the Soviet Union to his work, therefore, is of crucial importance. For, if alienation does not exist, it might help demonstrate the determining character of capitalist property relations. Should 'alienation' continue, either the USSR is some *de facto* form of capitalist society, or other factors in industrial society create alienating attitudes.

In the discussion of the organisation of the Soviet economy, we saw that enterprises had fairly specific production tasks allocated to them by their respective ministries and that under state socialism the factory director was solely responsible for the organisation of the plant. The director, however, is required to consult fully with workers' organisations, and both the trade unions and the Communist Party are able to exert pressure on the manager and are also responsible for some management functions – such as labour discipline.

While the unions, the party and other commissions undoubtedly give the worker a greater opportunity for participation than under private enterprise capitalism, we do not know how effective such participation is, or how it influences the psychological attitudes of the worker.

Some Soviet 'concrete sociological research' has attempted to measure the Soviet worker's attitude to his work. One of the best studies is that of A. G. Zdravomyslov and V. A. Yadov.[2] This study surveyed a sample of 2,665

[1] A. A. Zvorykin, 'The Development of the Productive Forces in the Soviet Union', in G. V. Osipov (ed.), *Industry and Labour in the USSR* (1966), pp. 16-17.

[2] 'Effect of Vocational Distinctions on the Attitude to work', in G. V. Osipov, *Industry and Labour in the USSR* (1966).

workers aged under 30 employed in 25 Leningrad factories. The investigation recorded the workers' fulfillment of quota, and constructed an index of their initiative and discipline and sense of responsibility. The workers were ranked into six groups according to the degree of technical skill. Fifty per cent of the total interviewed fell into these six groups. The authors found that 'satisfaction with occupation' varied from a negative attitude among heavy, unskilled manual labour to a highly positive one among the most highly skilled – panel operator setters. The 'appreciation of the social significance of work' also varied similarly. A part of the table is shown below (see Table 23).

The table shows that greater interest in the job tends to be associated with the more complex situations demanding high skill. It is notable that the fifth group (fitters, electricians, loom-setters) had a high score. This probably reflects their greater independence and the opportunity such men have to control the tempo of their work. On the other hand, manual workers had a negative attitude.

The authors of the study go on to analyse the factors in the work situation which give rise to satisfaction or dissatisfaction in work. These are ranked as follows (index):

1. Control of work (does it require ingenuity or not)   0.72
2. Pay   0.61
3. The possibility of improving skill   0.58
4. Variety in work   0.48
5. Organisation of labour   0.38
6. Management's concern for workers   0.35
7. Physical effort   0.32[1]

It is interesting to note here the high rank given to pay as a factor involving job satisfaction. Possibly, pay may have an instrumental effect – a good job being one in which one has sufficient pay to buy consumer goods. The factors above do not seem very different from western studies of job satisfaction.[2] Therefore, we cannot easily accept Zdravomyslov and Yadov's conclusion that:

> The Soviet worker is aware that advance lies not through consumption but through labour. He is most concerned not with pay and distribution but with the business of production. This is a novel attitude to work, which is unthinkable under capitalism. Our survey shows that work in a Soviet society is the workers' main interest . . .

> In the assessment of work, it never enters the head of the Soviet worker to wonder whether work is guaranteed. He is never afraid of being left without employment for his abilities or of being left stranded without a means of livelihood. Consequently he is not concerned merely to get a job, but to get one which conforms to his own interests and inclinations. Material motivations are still important, of course, but they are quite different in kind. The American worker's interpretation of the material

[1] Zdravomyslov and Yadov, p. 114.

[2] See, for example, Blauner's discussion, *Alienation and Freedom* (Chicago, 1964), p. 29.

Table 23. Attitude to Work Indexes

	Total	Grade of Occupation					
		6	5	4	3	2	i
		Heavy, unskilled manual labour	Skilled manual labour	Machine tool operators	Machine operators, skilled conveyor labour	Panel operators	Panel operators, setters
	$N=2665$	146	285	411	307	54	46
Satisfaction with occupation	+0.21	−0.14	+0.43	+0.24	+0.15	+0.27	+0.35
Appreciation of social significance of work	+0.08	−0.31	+0.19	+0.05	+0.15	+0.18	+0.26

Source: A. G. Zdravomyslov and V. A. Yadov, 'Effect of Vocational Distinctions on the Attitude to Work' in G. V. Osipov (ed.), *Industry and Labour in the USSR* (1966) p. 108.

incentive in work, is explained by the American researchers S. Strauss and L. Sayles in their observation that, in American society, money was all-important not only to pay for food, clothing, and housing, but also as an indication of 'having made it', of success and social standing. To 'have made it' means to have a high income. A 'good job' means it is well paid. To have opportunities for promotion means chances for making more money. In a socialist society, on the contrary, money has lost its importance as a symbol of wealth and, the main thing, wealth itself is not the basic yardstick of a person's worth.[1]

Another criticism which may be levelled at these conclusions is that the Soviet study is not directly comparable. We are not told whether the workers were questioned about stability (or availability) of employment. As the survey is concerned only with one area (Leningrad) it may not apply over the whole USSR. Measures of social standing or status were not reported as being in the survey. While pay would seem to play an important part in the worker's motivation, in a society where many material rewards are outside the market (social benefits, housing), one would expect earned income to be given less weight than in the West. Money may not be the same symbol of wealth as it is in the West, but this does not mean that money itself is no longer an important social yard-stick. As noted above money figured quite prominently as a factor leading to job satisfaction.

High subjective 'satisfaction' with a job does not exclude alienation from work: for work may have an instrumental role in fulfilling the desire for a certain pattern of consumption. The implication of the Zdravomyslov and Yadov survey for alienation is to be found in the indexes showing the appreciation of the social significance of work. Here a gradation can be detected. The workers performing heavy, unskilled manual tasks have a negative ranking (−0.31) probably implying considerable alienation; machine operators only just have a positive index (0.05). It is interesting to note that the most skilled workers have the highest index (0.26). We may use Shkaratan's 'participation in social work' as a second index of alienation (see Table 41, p. 408). Here again we see considerable differences between the groups of workers. The unqualified workers and the semi-skilled press and machine operators both have low scores (respectively 35.1 and 54.3 per cent participating in social work) while the well qualified have high ones (82.4 and 70.4 per cent). Party membership follows the same pattern: only 13.8 per cent of manual workers were in the party or komsomol compared to 42.8 per cent of qualified non-manual workers. This suggests 'alienation' on the part of the unqualified manual workers. It would appear that under the conditions of Soviet state socialism greater alienation exists among the unskilled performing repetitive jobs than among the more skilled workers. Manual workers, like those in western society, have no control over the flow and rhythm of factory

[1] *Loc. cit.*, pp. 119-20.

work. Their participation in political and other voluntary groups is less than that of higher strata and they are relatively more powerless.

Our study of attitudes towards work in the USSR allows us to make some general points about the Marxist theory of alienation. The abolition of the private ownership of the means of production does not *per se* appear to abolish alienation. Soviet conditions give the worker many opportunities for control of the work situation, the numerous workers commissions and the participation of workers in rationalisation and invention are unique factors of Soviet industrial production. The more paternalistic attitude of the state to the worker, the absence of structural unemployment and the unions' legal right to veto sackings give the worker greater job security. But feelings of powerlessness and the meaninglessness of labour have probably not been abolished in the USSR. In addition to *ownership* relations, the technological requirements of modern industry and the effects of the division of labour would seem to be factors of universal application. Workers of superior skill and those in the higher echelons of factory administration are involved in decision-making and have greater control over the work process than machinists and manual workers. Modern technological production, therefore, both under capitalism and socialism, would appear to generate similar attitudes towards work. At least, the empirical Soviet research we have considered does not show that work attitudes are significantly different from those under capitalism.

In the fifty or so years of Soviet rule, the Soviet authorities have been faced with different kinds of economic problems. In the Stalin era, to ensure economic growth, the movement of the peasantry from village to town, to maintain labour discipline, the use of normative or ideological means (see below, Chapter 12) were replaced by administrative control of labour and by a greater emphasis on monetary or utilitarian stimuli. The economy was a 'command' one and the ministerial apparatus was dominant. After Stalin, Khrushchev sought to strengthen normative sanctions and the power of the Communist Party. To this end his decentralisation schemes were related. To combat the negative aspects of the state bureaucracy (localism, suspicion of innovators) Khrushchev tried to revive the party as an administrative unit of control and, at the same time, he strengthened the lay control of administration ('control' and innovation commissions). Here the problem was not primarily one of inducing rapid economic change, but of efficiently managing a diverse economy. The Brezhnev-Kosygin leadership has relied more on utilitarian means – 'economic stimulation'. They have strengthened the ministerial system, and have increased somewhat enterprise competition along market lines.

The Soviet ideology of management has consistently emphasised the unity of interest between party, state and worker. Unions promote this 'general interest'. Compared to factories organised on a western capitalist model, there probably is greater homogeneity of interest and co-operation between worker and manager, between union official and worker and between union official and manager. Party and union help mobilise the worker. Party and union provide management with information about morale and about factory problems; they help to integrate the worker into the enterprise.

The controversy over economic planning has probably weakened belief in this theoretical unity. 'Profit' has been differentially distributed between management and worker. There is also in some respects a conflict of wills between ministries, between ministry and party, between management and ministry, between management and party, between union, management and party, between enterprises and between the worker and authority. Both the Soviet theory of a harmonious, and the western criticism of an oppressive totalitarian social system are inaccurate.

There is no evidence to substantiate the claim that the managers as such constitute a ruling class or stratum. Neither do the party secretaries. The ministerial bureaucracies vie with each other. But the unions are probably the weakest institution. While there is not a single unitary will in Soviet society there is not an *equal* plurality of interests either. All these groups, to some extent, articulate an interest. The ministries and the party are probably the most effective. In the factory the ministerial interest is probably supreme but in the control of the economy, in the final aggregation process, the party performs an adjudicating role. At the bottom, not unlike his western counterpart, is the worker. He largely regards work as instrumental, as a means to a better life. While he works to promote communism in a ritualistic way, the methods used to motivate him are partly normative but largely utilitarian.

There are also important structural differences between Soviet and western societies. While the *process* of production is becoming more alike (more technocratic) the *proceeds* of production are quite differently apportioned. In the USA, as Galbraith has pointed out: 'no grant of feudal privilege has ever equalled, for effortless return, that of the grandparent who bought and endowed his descendents with a thousand shares of General Motors or General Electric. The beneficiaries of this foresight have become and remain rich by no exercise of effort or intelligence beyond the decision to do nothing . . .'[1] There is no such apportionment in the USSR and this socially and politically gives each society unique features.

In the foregoing chapters we have outlined the development of the USSR at the societal level and have described the institutions which have generated

[1] J. K. Galbraith, *The New Industrial State* (1967), p. 394.

M

social change. In the chapters which follow we shall examine the social structure. We shall describe the family and then turn to the social network in which the family is enmeshed: the system of social stratification and differentiation. Finally, we shall consider the educational system.

Reading No. 12

REGULATIONS CONCERNING THE COMMISSIONS UNDER BASIC PARTY ORGANISATIONS OF PRODUCTION AND TRADE ESTABLISHMENTS ON THE REALISATION OF THE RIGHT BY PARTY ORGANISATIONS TO CONTROL THE ADMINISTRATION'S ACTIVITY[1]

Commissions of party members and candidates are formed in basic party organisations of productive and distributive enterprises to implement the right to control the activity of enterprises' administration. The aims of the commissions are to advance the responsibility of basic party organisations for the fulfilment of state plans, to exercise more completely the right to control economic activity granted by the Rules of the CPSU, to widen internal party democracy and to develop party members' initiative and activity.

THE TASKS OF PARTY ORGANISATIONS' COMMISSIONS, THEIR RIGHTS AND DUTIES

1. Constant organisational work among the masses which has successfully guided the realisation of the plans for the development of the Soviet economy is the most important task of basic party organisations. Party commissions must carry out systematic control to ensure the timely fulfilment by the enterprise of production tasks, state orders and deliveries, with the highest regard for quality. They must see that state discipline is strictly observed by all the enterprise's workers and must struggle against the development of a formal and narrow bureaucratic approach which puts local interests first and harms general state interests.

Commissions in themselves are not a special organ of control existing parallel to party organisations. They are one of the organisational forms, through which basic party organisations carry out their right of control of the administration given by the Rules of the CPSU. Commissions work under the leadership of party committees, party bureaux and the secretaries of primary organisations.

2. In order to exercise party control over all the varied activity of industrial undertakings, transport and building as well as 'project'[2] organisations, design bureau and scientific research institutes carrying out orders for enterprises and construction sites, at the discretion of party organisations and dependent on the character of production, the following may be set up:

control commissions for effecting the fulfilment of state orders and cooperative deliveries to other enterprises and economic administrative districts;

control commissions for the fulfilment of special, specialist, and export deliveries;

---

[1] *Partiyny kontrol'* (Gosudarstvennoe izdatel'stvo politicheskoy literatury SSSR, Kiev 1960), pp. 6-11.

[2] *proeknye.*

control commissions for quality of manufactured products;

control commissions for price reductions and quality improvement in building work;

control commissions for the rational use of transport;

control commissions for the fulfilment of plans introducing new techniques, mechanisation and the automation of production processes.

party organisations in shops and the catering and retail trades may form control commissions:

for the uninterrupted provision of goods;

for observation of Soviet trade regulations;

for the reduction of distribution and production costs.

Basic party organisations in industry, transport, construction and trade as well as planning and design offices and scientific institutes fulfilling orders for enterprises, form commissions for other problems as well, depending on local conditions and on the importance of the tasks which the enterprise, department, organisation or institute is working on.

3. Commissions must attentively study the state of affairs in those sections for which they directly exercise control. On the appearance of shortcomings in the work of the various establishments (shop, organisation or institute) they must quickly communicate the facts both to the party committee (or party bureau, or party meeting) and to the responsible persons of the enterprise (shop, organisation, etc.) and jointly take steps to eliminate the exposed irregularities. In such cases when the management does not promptly remedy the irregularities revealed by the commissions, the party committee or the party meeting implementing the right of party organisations to control the activity discusses the question at its meeting and the full pressure of the party is brought to bear on the institution's management. If these measures are inadequate, the party organisation may appeal for assistance to district, town, area and republican party and government organs and to the regional economic council (*sovnarkhoz*).

Should these leading organs not take the necessary measures called for by the basic organisations, the latter may report this fact to the Central Committee of the CPSU and the Council of Ministers of the USSR.

4. Through party committees or party bureaux, commissions have the right to put forward questions for discussion at meetings of workers and employees concerning the improvement of the work of the shop, factory, enterprise or institute. With the aim of mobilising the collective for the elimination of shortcomings, separate questions may be put at party meetings for preliminary consideration and for working out proposals. Relying on public support and an active membership, the commissions must persistently strive to ensure that the questions they raise are fully resolved and the shortcomings completely eliminated.

5. Party committees, bureaux and secretaries of party organisations must prevent the activity of commissions being turned into unnecessary paperwork. It is necessary to ensure in the work of the commissions the avoidance of stoppages in the enterprise or on any other job to prevent the accumulation of defects and to take prompt action for their elimination. The commission gives periodic reports about its work

to the party committee, the party bureau or the general meeting of the party organisation.

6. The commissions of basic party organisations checking up on the state of production, cannot abrogate or give administrative directions of any kind, as this would be a violation of the principle of one man management. At the same time, the management must help the commissions in all ways with the carrying out of their. work, must acquaint them with necessary materials and data on questions of interest to them and must give objective information on the state of affairs, must immediately examine the proposals of commissions and promptly take measures for the elimination of revealed shortcomings.

THE PROCEDURE FOR THE FORMATION AND ACCOUNTABILITY OF COMMISSIONS

7. The size and membership of commissions depend on the volume and character of their work. Members are elected by open voting at the general party meeting of the basic party organisation or party conference. The commissions are elected for one year and re-elected when they give their reports at the usual party election meetings.

If, in the course of the stipulated period, it is necessary to form a new commission or change the composition of existing ones, then the question is brought for review to the usual party meeting, and in large party organisations where the party conference takes place once a year, it is decided at the meeting of the party committee.

It is essential to include in the commissions the most suitable, stable and active communists – workers, employees, engineers – able to exercise real control over the implementation of party and government directives.

8. Strict observance of the existing instructions for the keeping of government secrets must be followed by the commissions organised at defence and classified establishments and workshops. All members of such commissions must be selected from communists working in the sections concerned and having admittance to the work there. The activity of commissions in classified establishments and workshops must fully observe the regulations for maintaining the secrecy of production and must eliminate all possibilities of divulging state secrets.

9. In small basic party organisations, commissions are formed at the discretion of the general party meeting. Where it is considered unsuitable to form a commission, control of economic activity is carried out by all communists under the leadership of the basic party organisation's secretary.

10. At enterprises where there are no basic organisations, the functions of control and informing party organs concerning the violation of state discipline is carried out by the trade unions and the *Komsomol* as provided for in the trade union regulations and in the Rules of the CPSU concerning the *Komsomol*.

11. Into the work of the commissions, party committees and bureaux should draw trade union and *Komsomol* activists, the best of the non-party workers, specialists and people having a good knowledge of production. They should secure a firm interrelationship between the commissions' work and other well-tried forms of public control existing in party, trade union and *Komsomol* organisations (for example, hearing accounts of the management at party meetings, permanent production conferences, mass public production commissions of the trade union

committees, through *Komsomol* activities, lightning checks and so on). The unity and co-ordination of activity between the different forms of party and public control must promote the elimination of excessive checking-up by different bodies and unnecessary dislocation of the enterprise's administration. Normal conditions for the administration to carry out its functions must be ensured.

12. If joint deliveries are disrupted because of other establishments or institutions, party committees and bureaux of party organisations may bring such matters to the attention of the party organisations of the enterprises or institutions concerned. Party organisations receiving such notification are under an obligation to discuss it without delay, to take proper measures and to answer immediately the points raised.

FOR FURTHER STUDY

INTRODUCTORY

Brown, E. C. *Soviet Trade Unions and Labour Relations*. Cambridge, Mass.: Harvard University Press, 1966.

Deutscher, I. *Soviet Trade Unions, Their Place in Soviet Labour Policy*. London: Royal Institute for International Affairs, 1950.

Granick, D. *Management of the Industrial Firm in the USSR*. New York: Columbia University Press, 1954.

Granick, D. *The Red Executive*. London: Macmillan, 1960.

Gripp, R. C. *Patterns of Soviet Politics*. Chicago: Dorsey Press, 1963.

See also introductory books on the economy.

BASIC

Azrael, J. R. *Managerial Power and Soviet Politics*. Cambridge, Mass.: Harvard University Press, 1966.

Azrael, J. R. 'Politics and Management', in *Survey*, No. 49, October 1963, pp. 90-101.

Berliner, J. S. *Factory and Manager in the USSR*. Cambridge, Mass.: Harvard University Press, 1957.

Hough, Jerry F. *The Soviet Prefects: The Local Party Organs in Industrial Decision-Making*. Cambridge, Mass.: Harvard University Press, 1969.

International Labour Organisation. *The Trade Union Situation in the USSR*. Geneva: United Nations, 1960.

Kerr, C., *et al. Industrialisation and Industrial Man*. London: Heinemann, 1962.

McAuley, Mary. *Labour Disputes in Soviet Russia, 1957-1965*. Oxford: Clarendon Press, 1969.

Piatakov, A. 'Labour Administration by the State and Trade Unions in the USSR', in *International Labour Review*, Vol. 85, June 1962, pp. 558-72.

Richman, B. M. *Soviet Management*. Englewood Cliffs, N.J.: Prentice Hall, 1965.

The Rules of the Communist Party of the Soviet Union. London, 1961.

SPECIALISED

Agapova, A. A. *Obshchestvennye kontrolery partii*. Moscow, 1965.

Bell, D. 'The Debate on Alienation', in Leopold Labedz (ed.). *Revisionism*. London: Allen and Unwin, 1962, pp. 195-214.

Belyaev, G. 'Stopyatidesyaty kvadratny koren', in *Agitator*, No. 2, January 1966, pp. 29-31.

Blauner, Robert. *Alienation and Freedom*. Chicago: University of Chicago Press, 1964.

Bottomore, T. B. *Elites and Society*. London: Watts, 1964.

Brezhnev, L. 'Report to December Plenum of Central Committee', 6 December 1965, reported in *Pravda*, 7 December 1965.

Burnham, James. *The Managerial Revolution*. London: Pelican, 1945.

Carr, E. H. *The Bolshevik Revolution, 1917-1923*. London: Macmillan, 1952.

Cherepenin, A. 'Partiyny kontrol' – sredstvo uluchsheniya rukovodstva khozyay-stvom', *Partiynaya zhizn'*, No. 5, 1962.

Dvornikov, I., *et al. Professional'nye soyuzy SSSR*. Moscow, 1961.

'Edinonachalie i pravo kontroliya', *Partiynoe stroitel'stvo*, No. 18, 1940.

Ekonomicheskaya Gazeta, No. 15, April 1968 (on Material Incentives method of production).

Florence, P. Sargant. *The Logic of British and American Industry*. London: Routledge and Kegan Paul, 1953.

Florence, P. Sargant. *Ownership, Control and Success of Large Companies*. London: Sweet and Maxwell, 1961.

Grozhev, M. 'K chemu vedet bezkontrol'nost', *Partiynaya zhizn'*, No. 4, February 1955, pp. 65-8.

Kaplan, Frederick I. *Bolshevik Ideology and the Ethics of Soviet Labour, 1917-1920: The Formative Years*. New York: Philosophical Library, 1968.

Kaziev, M. Ya (ed.). *Gosudarstvennoe sotsial'noe strakhovanie*, Fourth Edition. Moscow: Profizdat, 1965.

Leiserson, A. *Parties and Politics*. New York: A. A. Knopf, 1958.

Marx, K. *Economic and Philosophic Manuscripts of 1844*. Moscow: Foreign Languages Publishing House, 1961.

Naydis, I. 'Zavodskoy kollektiv, partorganizatsiya, direktor', in *Kommunist*, No. 18, December 1965, pp. 43-9.

Nove, Alec. 'Industrial Planning System: Reform and Prospect', in *Soviet Studies*, Vol. 14, July 1962, pp. 1-15.

Obukhovich, A. P. 'Participation by Workers' Organisations in Planned Social and Economic Development in Byelorussia', *International Labour Review*, Vol. 94, No. 5, November 1966, pp. 449-64.

'Partiyny kontrol' na proizvodstve', *Partiynaya zhizn'*, No. 6, May 1964, pp. 40-3.

'Prav li direktor?', *Agitator*, No. 11, 1966, pp. 13-16.

Schachtman, Max. *The Bureaucratic Revolution*. New York: The Donald Press, 1962.

Sergeev, M. 'Khozyaystvennaya reforma-vazhny rychag pod"ema ekonomika', in *Partiynaya zhizn'*, No. 12, 1966, pp. 23-30.

Shivrinski, V. 'Gorkom i pervichnye partorganizatsii', in *Partiynaya Zhizn'*, No. 18, September 1966, pp. 40-45.

Spravochnaya kniga o professional'nykh soyuzax SSSR. Moscow, 1965.

Spravochnik sekretarya pervichnoy partinoy organizatsii. Moscow, 1960.

Stalin, I. V. 'Report to the 16th Party Congress', *Works*. Moscow, 1955, Vol. 13.

'Ustav professionalnykh soyuzov SSSR', in *Spravochnik profsoyuznogo rabotnika*. Moscow, 1962.

Vladychenko, I. *Uchastie rabochikh i sluzhashchikh v upravlenii proizvodstva*. Moscow, 1967.

Zdravomyslov, A. G. and V. A. Yadov. 'Effect of Vocational Distinctions on the Attitude to Work', in G. V. Osipov (ed.). *Industry and Labour in the USSR*. London: Tavistock Publishers, 1966, pp. 99-125.

Zvorykin, A. A. 'The Development of the Productive Forces in the Soviet Union', in G. V. Osipov (ed.). *Industry and Labour in the USSR*. London: Tavistock Publishers, 1966, pp. 15-25.

11

THE FAMILY

The family is recognised to be a universal social phenomenon. In this chapter we shall discover the ways in which the Soviet family differs from its counterpart in the West and why conditions of Soviet communism have not displaced it altogether.

First, let us define what a family unit is and describe its major functions. The human family may be defined as a more or less permanent bio-social group composed of at least two cohabiting adults of the opposite sex and children towards whom they act as parents. The family has four major functions: the physical reproduction of individuals, the nourishment and maintenance of children, their placement in the occupational system or status hierarchy and the socialisation of children (that is, the teaching of social behaviour and mores).[1] Each of these functions, of course, is not exclusive to the family: reproduction may be illegitimate as with the offspring of prostitutes, maintenance of children may be the responsibility of children's homes or orphanages, placement is often carried out by market relations; and socialisation is performed by educational institutions. Nevertheless, in all societies, including the USSR, the family provides to a greater or lesser extent, all these functions.

To avoid confusion, we must distinguish between two kinds of family structure: *conjugal*, consisting of husband, wife and children to whom they act as parents; *consanguine*, being all the blood relatives forming several conjugal units. Hence, though every typical adult is a member of one consanguine family, he is a member of two conjugal families: a family of orientation, into which he is born and by which he is reared, and a family of procreation established by his own marriage and birth of offspring (or adopted children). Though there are many types of family in the USSR, the pattern of the Soviet family structure over the last fifty years has changed from the larger family grouping of several conjugal families in the consanguine unit, to a more independent or 'nuclear' family of the conjugal type. This shift parallels the movement from a predominantly peasant agrarian to an urban-industrial society.

We may begin our discussion of the family in the USSR with a brief summary of family structures before the revolution, for they have influenced to some extent the family orientation of Soviet citizens.

[1] Kingsley Davis, *Human Society* (New York, 1959), pp. 394-5.

During the nineteenth century, the Russian Empire was predominantly rural. The peasant family was monogamous—at least in the European areas of the country—based on the consanguine unit. It was patriarchal and authoritarian: the head of the family being the grandfather, or his eldest brother or son. 'The wife is obliged to love, respect and obey her husband implicitly and must please and follow him in every way.'[1] The family transmitted property, which was legally vested in the family head. The family was a work unit: typically, the fields were tended collectively. The peasant remained largely untouched by educational and government institutions and the chief non-familial influence on his life was the church and, perhaps, army service. The family unit was the dominant social institution in his life.

During the nineteenth century, the population grew rapidly following the pattern of other developing industrial nations, with a high infant mortality rate and a higher birth-rate: in 1913 the birth rate was 47 per thousand of the population and the death rate 30.2.[2] Population grew, mainly due to an increase in the number of live births. Large families predominated, especially in the countryside.

With the development of industry and commerce, the *gemeinschaft* (or communal) relations of the peasant family broke down. Men moved to the town for work, thereby breaking the geographical unity of the family. Though wife and children remained in the village, where the new town worker may have been legally domiciled, urban life began to assert its own values on the village community. The traditional head lost much of his power because of his urban working sons' comparative wealth (money was sent from town to the country).[3] The growth of towns encouraged an agricultural market which tended to undermine the peasant subsistence economy. For the townsmen and other permanent urban dwellers family life approximated to that of Western Europe: for the bourgeoisie it was an important economic unit.

In the non-European areas of Russia, many different forms of family life existed. Polygamy was general and many brides were under sixteen years of age. Marriage contracts were arranged through parents and patriarchal authority predominated. In Central Asia, family structure and relations were similar to those of the family in the Middle East today. Usually the family was organised on a consanguine basis and Kislyakov has shown that still in the early 1930s, family units of up to 50 strong persisted among the Tadzhiks, and in Turkestan in the early 1940s, there were similar large family units.[4] But

[1] *Svod zakonov Rossiyskoy imperii*, Spb. 1857, vol. 10, part 1, p. 18. Cited by A. G. Kharchev, *Brak i sem'ya v SSSR* (Moscow, 1964), p. 129.

[2] See Chapter 2. In 1913, it was estimated that the infant mortality rate was 273 per thousand. *Narkhoè v 1968g* (Moscow, 1969), p. 36.

[3] For an example of this see E. W. Burgess and H. J. Locke, *The Family* (New York, 1945), pp. 180-2, and D. Lane, *The Roots of Russian Communism* (Assen 1969), pp. 145-6.

[4] N. A. Kislyakov, *Sem'ya i brak u Tadzhikov*, Trudy instituta etnografii, vol. 44 (Moscow, 1959) p. 31.

there were exceptions to this: for example, the Kirgiz in the nineteenth century had developed a more nuclear family structure.[1]

Soviet Marxist Ideology of the Family

After the October Revolution, the attitude of the Soviet government to the family, as to everything else, was determined partly by Marxist theory and partly by expediency. Marx and particularly Engels had attempted to explain forms of family life in terms of the requirements of the economic structure of society.[2] Under capitalism, monogamy allows the regular transfer of property from father to son, thereby strengthening the motive for capitalist accumulation. Spouse relationships are not based on equality but on the subjugation of the female by the male. Love, at least for the property-owning or bourgeois family, rarely exists: the sexual relationship between husband and wife is a form of legalised prostitution which takes place in addition to frequent sexual liaisons outside marriage.[3] As Engels put it in his description of the bourgeoisie: 'the wife differs from the ordinary courtesan only in that she does not hire out her body like a wage worker, but sells it into slavery once for all',[4] and, in the Communist Manifesto—'bourgeois marriage is in reality a system of wives in common. . . .'[5]

For the subject class, the proletariat under capitalism, family relationships are sustained more by love and less by property relations, because the workers are propertyless. The wife is less subjugated by the husband, for industrial conditions enable her to take up paid employment. To this extent, therefore, no economic basis exists for the exploitation of one sex by the other,[6] and mutual love is more frequent. On the other hand, the brutalising effects of industrial capitalism, the ruthless and merciless employment of women and children degrade family relationships. Nevertheless, common industrial employment creates a basis for equality between spouses unknown to the bourgeoisie.

Engels also applied his analysis to the exploration of family life under

[1] Kharchev, op. cit., p. 131. See also O. A. Sukhareva, M. A. Bukzhanova, Proshloe i nastoyashchee seleniya Aykyran (Tashkent, 1955), S. Lyubimova, V pervye gody (Moscow, 1958).

[2] I cannot consider here how this theory is related to the various stages of society. Suffice it must to say that in the first form of primitive communism there was complete sexual licence with no marriage and family bonds. This developed into group marriage distinguished by the absence of incest. A third type was that of monogamy, which was the dominant family form under capitalism.

[3] F. Engels, 'The Origin of the Family, Private Property and the State', Marx and Engels, Selected Works (Moscow, 1951), vol. 2, pp. 208-9. See Reading no. 13. Galsworthy's Forsyte Saga is well known in the USSR: Soames's marriage to Irene, his rape and her subsequent adultery might be considered an example of Engels's 'typical' bourgeois family.

[4] 'The Origin of the Family' Marx-Engels Selected Works, vol. 2, p. 209.

[5] 'The Communist Manifesto' ,Marx-Engels, Selected Works, vol. 1, p. 224.

[6] Engels, p. 210.

socialism. Given the abolition of private wealth – which lay at the root of the prostitution (i.e. sexual relations without love) of monogamous marriage – prostitution itself, he argued, would disappear. But monogamy, as a form of social relationship, would prevail: in fact, only under socialism would mono-gamy 'finally become a reality'.[1] Women would have equality with men: the care of children and housekeeping would be the concern of society. Contrac-ting out of marriage, extremely difficult to do in Engels's day, would be easy and available to either spouse. Marriage would be a union reflecting free choice between partners.[2] 'The monogamous family has improved greatly since the commencement of civilisation, and very sensibly in modern times, it is at least supposable that it is capable of still further improvement until the equality of the sexes is attained.'[3]

The chief points embodied in Engels's work may be summarised as follows: under capitalism, monogamy has an economic foundation necessary for the transmission of property and is corrupted by private wealth; mono-gamy provides for the fulfilment of human love which, under capitalism, exists more in working class families than in capitalist; under socialism, the monogamous family would continue but entry into and release from marriage would be based on individual free choice unrestricted by legal barriers.

The Soviet Family After the Revolution

Soviet communists in the days after the Revolution interpreted Marxist theory in different ways. Alexandra Kollontay[4] argued for a looser family union based more on sexual desires.

> The old type of family has seen its day. . . . needlessly holds back the female workers from the more productive and far more serious work. Nor is the family any more necessary to the members themselves, since the task of bringing up children . . . is passing more and more into the hands of the collectivity.[5]

In the days of the Civil War such views were cited to justify promiscuity, 'free love' and the 'nationalisation of women': for example, in Vladimir a decree was passed making every virgin over eighteen years state property. This, of course, was not official Leninist policy and was a popular vulgarisation of Marxism in which human equality (not the ownership of women) was emphasised.

The period following the October Revolution was one of relatively un-

[1] *Ibid.*, p. 213.
[2] *Ibid.*, p. 218.
[3] *Ibid.*, p. 219.
[4] A. Kollontay *The New Morality and the Working Classes* (1918). See also Reading no. 14.
[5] *Ibid.*

restricted sexual activity: many families broke up and children were conceived outside marriage.[1] The breakdown of traditional morals was not solely due to the actions of the communist government, it was caused by the breakdown of the old society, and the impact of war and revolution. One should not exaggerate the extent of this dislocation: it was greatest in the towns; in the countryside and the non-European areas family life was less affected. Nevertheless, the consequences of uninhibited sexual activity caused concern and some communists called for sublimation of the sex drives. Opposing the 'old wives tale' that sexual indulgence was necessary to health, Semashko wrote in *Izvestiya*: 'Drown your sexual energy in public work. . . . If you want to solve the sexual problem, be a public worker, a comrade, not a stallion or a brood-mare.'[2]

In addition to changes in ownership and control of the economy, legislation was enacted specifically concerning the civil status of husband, wife and children. This was more conservative than the views held by Kollontay. The legislation of 1917 and 1918,[3] though it intentionally weakened family bonds (the 'obliteration' of the capitalist family), by no means abolished it as a social institution, as demanded by Kollontay and other more utopian communists. While inheritance was abolished in 1918 and property was transferred to the state, the law was soon amended; by 1922 one could inherit up to 10,000 rubles, and after 1926 the upper limit was abolished. (Private ownership of the means of production, of course, was illegal.)

The principal aspects of Soviet family legislation (the foundation of a 'socialist' family) were to sustain the principle of monogamy; to recognise *de facto* or common-law marriage—if registered at the registrar's office or if proven in court of law; to abolish all class, national or religious restraints on marriage; to allow easy divorce—through the court if one spouse desired it, through the registry office if both agreed; to make equal the legal status of husband and wife (especially in respect of property and children); and to recognise birth (whether parents were of legal standing or not) as the basis of the family.

The Code of 1926[4] contained provisions similar to the above and gave legal status both to registered marriage and marriage in 'common law' the latter being a union where 'the fact of cohabitation, combined with a common household . . . the manifestation of marital relations . . . could be shown' (Article 11). Soviet legislation differed from that of western states at that time

---

[1] The Petrograd Commission for Juvenile Affairs from 1918 to 1924 handled some 35,000 cases, most of which concerned homeless children, Kharchev, p. 138.

[2] *Izvestiya*, 15 May 1925, cited in E. H. Carr, *Socialism in One Country* (Part One) (London, 1958), pp. 33-4.

[3] See G. Sverdlov, *Marriage and the Family in the USSR* (Moscow, 1956).

[4] Code on Marriage. The Family and Guardianship of RSFSR. On Soviet family law see E. L. Johnson, *An Introduction to the Soviet Legal System* (1969).

in that children of 'common law' marriage were given the same rights before the law as those of 'civil law' marriage. In fact the Soviet state sanctioned many unions which had occurred outside the framework of state legality. The decree of 1917 had made marriage a civil and not a religious procedure. Yet in 1925 about a third of urban marriages were still performed in church[1] (therefore the comparative figure in the countryside must have been about three-quarters). The effects of the 1926 Code were to allow marriages to be both easily formed and ended.

If by marriage we mean the regular cohabiting of a man and woman with the intention of founding a family, then the Soviet practice during these times would properly be defined as 'marriage'. If, however, we wish to restrict the usage to unions given public recognition and conferring a special legal status on children, then Soviet 'marriage' of the 1930s might be excluded. Kingsley Davis, for example, has argued that control by society over parenthood (distinguished from control over sexual relations) and the legal obligations and rights associated with it are the most important attribute of the family.[2] Soviet family law, it might be argued, did not distinguish closely between such unions and other less permanent liasions, for both parents and offspring could claim that a 'common law' marriage had taken place. Therefore, it might be said, 'marriage' as an institution did not exist.

It is perhaps best to adopt a wide definition of the family (to include practices on the Israeli kibbutz as well as in the Soviet Union at the time under discussion) and to bear in mind the differences which may exist between nations. It seems arbitrary to define marriage as a sociological phenomenon in terms of western (and particularly Catholic) conventions. The Soviet family, during this period (1926–1944) was certainly of a looser, more informal 'common law' type than in western states.

Up to 1944, when the laws were changed, Soviet law was permissive and tended to encourage family disintegration. A weakened family unit was in the interests of the new regime in that it made easier the accomplishment of social change. By weakening the family, the relationships over which the state could have no direct control, it made the individual open to pressure by other social institutions. The socialising influence of the parents and their traditional (or anti-socialist) values were minimised.

In fact the 1930s were a period of tension between parents and children. Inkeles and Bauer[3] have given examples of conflict in family life reported by post-1945 Russian émigrés.

---

[1] Speech delivered to the Second Session of the Central Executive Committee of the RSFSR. Reprinted in R. Schlesinger, *The Family in the USSR* (1949), p. 84.

[2] Kingsley Davis, *op. cit.*, pp. 400-1. See also R. Savatier, 'Le Communisme et le mariage', *Revue catholique des institutions et du droit*, novembre-decembre (1936), p · 523.

[3] *The Soviet Citizen* (Cambridge, Massachusetts, 1959).

. . . We can understand why conflicts over religion and political belief permeated the reports on family life given by those from peasant and worker backgrounds. From the parents' point of view it seemed that their children were being torn away from them and won over to or at least significantly influenced to be irreligious and to support the Communist regime. The children, in turn, often felt their parents to be backward or ignorant, and thus were alienated from them. This was especially evident when the children were advancing themselves and thus coming ever more under the influence of values which ran counter to those of the parents. A Komsomol member, who was a student at the time the war began, reported that when he came home from school he demanded that the ikon which his peasant mother kept in plain sight be removed from the home. 'When younger,' he said, 'I had been afraid to discuss the matter with them, but growing older and *being away from home* I found the courage to do this.' He hid the ikon, but his mother found it, and after a scene he agreed not to remove it again. Thus a resolution was achieved, but it is clear that the residue must have been a sense of alienation between parent and child.[1]

The economic and legal position of the wife was ameliorated, not only for moral reasons but also because it enabled an increasing number of women to be employed in the economy.[2] During the inter-war period the tasks of child-minding and upbringing were still the main responsibility of the wife: in 1927, there were only 2,100 kindergartens.[3] The wife, sometimes helped by her mother or mother-in-law, looked after the children and was responsible for the household: her duties included the latter whether she worked or not.

From 1935 a number of decrees strengthened the family: in that year parents were made responsible for the disorderly conduct of their children, divorce was made a little more difficult and expensive, and in 1936 abortion became a criminal offence. But the chief provisions of the 1926 Code were kept intact until 1944, when the position of the family was made much more stable. The deprivation and chaos of the war had resulted in unrestrained sexual relations: some four million Soviet women had children with no legal father.[4] The main provisions of the 1944 decree were four-fold: only registered marriages were recognised; divorce was made much more expensive[5] and

---

[1] *The Soviet Citizen*, p. 216.

[2] In 1928 women constituted 24 per cent of the employed population, 39 per cent in 1940 and 50 per cent in 1968. *Narkhoz v 1968g* (Moscow, 1969), p. 552.

[3] 28,400 in 1945, 43,600 in 1960 and 78,300 in 1968. *Narkhoz v 1968g* (Moscow, 1969), p. 676.

[4] Gerhard Neubeck, 'Notes on Russian Family Life Today', *Acta Sociologica*, vol. 8 (1965), p. 324.

[5] From 1936 to 1944, the cost of a divorce was 50 rubles on the first occasion; 150 rubles on the second and 300 rubles on the third; there was no formality – divorce was registered, expressing the wish of the couple concerned. From 1944, marriage breakdown had to be shown before the People's Court and (if accepted) before a Higher Court. A fee of 100 rubles was payable, plus the cost of publicity (i.e. newspaper notices, etc.) of the case. In the event of a divorce being given, either or both parties were to pay a sum ranging from 500 to 2,000 rubles decided by the court. The payments are here shown in old rubles (10 old rubles equals 1 new ruble). In 1965 the estimated average weekly wage was 225 (old) rubles.

obtainable only through court action; the family was strengthened—children born outside wedlock had no right to the father's name, or his possessions, and the father had no legal obligations to maintain them. (On the other hand, the mothers of such children received a state grant.) In 1968, the law on marriage and the family[1] decreed that children born outside marriage have the right to the father's name if paternity can be established—either by a joint statement or through a court. This was designed to strengthen an unmarried mother's rights for her children. On 10 December 1965, a decree eliminated the publication of notice of divorce in the local press. The second (or final) hearing is now conducted in the people's court. The cost of divorce was reduced marginally: the 40 ruble publication fee was abolished, but other costs remained.[2] Further restrictions on divorce were introduced in 1968. A husband cannot start divorce proceedings without his wife's consent if she is pregnant or during the year following the birth of a child.

The legal position of the Soviet family between 1917 and 1944 had turned full circle; from being weakened to being strengthened by state laws. Robert S. Lynd has argued that, in contrast to western societies, the Soviet state actively promotes and supports the family.

. . . The family *as an institution* is different in the Soviet Union, and importantly different, in that society *intends* it to function strongly and is building a kind of security and social role for the family that is different from the casual fate of our own struggling, largely unsupported family units. The building of a healthy family life is on the agenda of the Soviet Union – a claim which may scarcely be made for western liberal society, with the exception of Sweden.[3]

The strengthening of the Soviet family is an indication of the Soviet belief that new families are no longer likely to inculcate values at variance with the dominant ideology; rather than being a potential opposition to the regime, their conservatism helps to sustain it. Though Kollontay's proposals are occasionally voiced in the USSR, they are regarded as eccentric.[4] The history of the Soviet family in the period 1916–1969 helps illustrate that the character of the family is determined by other institutions. In the USSR the driving agents of social change were located in the political system: the character of the family changed in response to it.

The Family in the Modern Soviet Union

Let us begin our description of marriage in the modern USSR by considering

[1] Articles 16 and 17. See below, Appendix I.

[2] *Vedomosti verkhovnogo soveta SSSR*, no. 49 (1965), point 275.

[3] Robert S. Lynd, 'Ideology and the Soviet Family', *American Slavic and East European Review*, vol. 9, no. 4 (1950), p. 177.

[4] See S. Strumilin, 'Rabochi byt i kommunizm', *Novy mir*, no. 7 (1960).

the age of union. Until 1968, the legal minimum age of marriage varied from one republic to another: in some, girls under 16 could legally marry. The all-union law[1] on marriage and the family (1968) made the minimum age 18 for men and women, but republics were given the right to lower the minimum by two years. Though no comprehensive statistics exist for our purpose, the median age of marriage has been reported to be 24–25 for men and 21–23 for women.[2] In the United States in 1962, the median age was 22.7 for men and 20.3 for women.[3] Studies of localities show that considerable differences exist between areas of the Soviet Union.

Table 24.Changes in Marriage Ages in Uzbekistan 1937–1957 (Percentages)*

Age of Marriage	1937		1946		1957	
	Men	Women	Men	Women	Men	Women
18 and under	2.2	35.0	4.0	16.8	2.4	12.8
19–22	19.0	27.7	16.4	37.7	19.4	36.3
23–26	31.1	17.1	19.0	19.0	28.2	15.3
27–	47.7	20.2	60.6	26.5	50.0	35.6
	100	100	100	100	100	100

* Cited in A. G. Kharchev, *Brak i sem'ya v SSSR* (Moscow, 1964), p. 184

In Uzbekistan, the age of marriage for women and men has risen since 1937, as shown in Table 24. No doubt the large number of women (35 per cent in 1937) married at eighteen or younger, is due to the Uzbek tradition of early marriage set before 1917. The fall to 12.8 per cent in this age group in 1957 is due, on the one hand, to the pressure brought by the Soviet authorities to prevent marriage under eighteen and, on the other, to the large number of Russian and Ukrainian immigrants after the war. The figures for men show a rise in the age of marriage in 1946, when the average was over 27; this is probably accounted for by the returned ex-service men who had necessarily postponed marriage until the end of the war. Comparing the figures for 1937 and 1957, we see that men tended to marry only slightly later, whereas for women there has been a considerable shift to later marriage: 20.2 per cent of the women marrying were over 27 years old in 1937, whereas 35.6 per cent were of this group in 1957.

Data collected on differences in age between brides and grooms in Kiev, Tyurmen and the Mga district of Leningrad give a general indication of the average age of marriage. (See Table 25.) From these figures we can see that the modal age of marriage is from 20 to 24 for women and 21 to 26 for men.

[1] Basic Principles of Legislation on Marriage and the Family, see below, Appendix I.
[2] G. Neubeck, 'Notes on Russian Family Life Today', *loc. cit.*, p. 324.
[3] US Department of Commerce, Bureau of the Census, *Historical Statistics* (1965), p. 3.

Figures for Latvia confirm these conclusions, the average for men being 24 to 25 and women 21 to 23.[1] These data lead us to conclude that marriage takes place at ages not unlike those in advanced western societies.

Marriage is popular in the USSR, and proportionately more males are

Table 25. Age of Marriage, Kiev, Tyurmen, Mga*

	Brides		Grooms	
Place	Per cent of Total	Age	Average difference in age between husband and wife	Approx. modal average of male age of marriage
Kiev	56	20—24	+2 years	22—26
Tyurmen	45	20—23	+2 years	21—25
Mga	45	20—24	+1 year	21—25

* Adapted from data for 1959 cited by Kharchev, pp. 186–7

married[2] than in England and Wales. Comparative figures for 1959 and 1961 are shown on Table 26. Obviously the imbalance between the sexes in Soviet Russia (there were 20 million more females than males in 1959) may have exerted pressure on all available males to marry and the pattern in future

Table 26. Comparative Marital Status of Males in USSR (1959) and England and Wales (1961). Number Married as Proportion of Age Group (per 1,000)*

Age of Males	England and Wales 1961	USSR 1959
21—34	610	697
35—44	866	957
45—54	881	960
55—64	860	934
65—	599	800

* Itogi vsesoyuznoy perepisi naseleniya 1959 g. SSSR (svodny tom) (Moscow, 1962), Table 18 (notes), p. 73 Census 1961 (England and Wales): Age, Marital Condition and General Tables (London, 1964), Table 13

may be for the Soviet figures to fall somewhat. As Table 26 shows, at all ages a higher proportion of Russian men are married compared to their English peers. In 1965, the USSR came second in an international table of marriage rates, with 8.7 marriages per thousand of the population: in the USA the

[1] Cited by Kharchev, p. 184.

[2] Marriage takes place after an acquaintance by the spouses in most cases lasting from one to three years, of one sample, 23 per cent knew each other from one to two years, 35.6 per cent from two to three years. Kharchev, op. cit., p. 205.

comparative figure was 9.2, in West Germany 8.3, Sweden 7.8, and in England and Wales (1964) 7.6.[1] Of course, the marriage rate depends on the age structure of the population, but we may safely say that marriage as an institution is as popular in the USSR as in the West.

Family Relations

What does marriage mean in terms of interpersonal relations? Soviet historical materialism defines relations generally under socialism to be 'based on principles of comradely cooperation and mutual assistance'.[2] Sverdlov applies this view to the Soviet family:

> The Soviet family, the latest type of family in the history of humanity, is based on entirely new principles compared with other types . . .
>
> In a society based on exploitation, all the natural and necessary human relationships, including family relationships are wholly subordinated to the laws of private ownership. In a society with antagonistic classes, love and the interests of preserving private property contradict each other to a large extent.
>
> The family in socialist society is of an entirely different nature.
>
> Socialist society has brought about conditions for a really free marriage. Consolidation of the socialist system, the growing well-being of the people and the emancipation of women mean that the overwhelming majority of marriages in the USSR have nothing to do with considerations of gain. Mutual love of men and women and the affection for children is the guiding force of marriage in the Soviet Union. Here, as Marx put it, family life for the first time becomes the life of the family, the *living love*.[3]

Unfortunately, Sverdlov provides no empirical data to substantiate his *a priori* generalisation. In fact, Soviet families differ in character.

In the countryside attitudes continue much in the same way as before the revolution. The traditional marriage ceremony and ritual is still performed and the agreement of parents for the marriage is still usually socially required.[4] A peasant woman cited by Geiger describes her family relations as follows: 'In the majority of good families the wife subordinates herself to the husband. Now with us, when my son comes home my daughter-in-law takes off his boots, cleans them for him, you see how it is. She is obedient and devoted to her husband. There is no other way.' Another says: 'If my husband shouted at me because of the children I just remained silent, so there could be no quarrels.'[5] Even here patriarchal authority has crumbled: in the collective

---

[1] *Narodnoe khozyaystvo SSSR v 1965g* (Moscow, 1966), p. 118. In 1968 the marriage rate was 8.9. *Narodnoe khozyaystvo SSSR v 1968g* (Moscow, 1969), p. 40.

[2] *Fundamentals of Marxism-Leninism* (Moscow, 1961), p. 695.

[3] G. Sverdlov, *Marriage and the Family in the USSR* (English Edition, Moscow, 1956), pp. 5-6.

[4] P. I. Kushner, *Selo Viryatino v proshlom i nastoyashchem* (Moscow, 1958), p. 226.

[5] K. Geiger, *The Soviet Family* (New York, 1968), p. 217.

farm the individual rather than the head of household is the unit of payment for work. Choice of occupation, spouse and leisure pursuits are now generally regarded as the right of individual members – and not of the family as a whole.

In the towns romantic love is usually the basis for marriage, though examples of the abduction of brides and the payment of *kalym* still sometimes occur.[1] But in the countryside, a less romantic attitude to mate selection is predominant. A recent Soviet study cites a young *kolkhoznik* as saying: 'We don't seek a great friendship. If one likes a girl, then one gets married,'[2] though of course, this agreement must be mutual. Such popular Soviet films as *Ballad of a Soldier* and plays such as *Warsaw Melody* emphasise the romantic and emotional ties between the sexes which are probably more typical in the town.

The urban family as a unit provides love (or emotional satisfaction) and companionship for its members. It is not as 'isolated' from other social organisations as in the West. The mass-produced private car which binds the nuclear family in the West has yet to appear in large numbers in the USSR. The 'companionship' role between spouses and children in the Soviet Union is less important than in the western nuclear family. Collective activity (for example, leisure pursuits and holidays) is mainly the prerogative of social clubs, unions and schools. The members of families often take their holidays separately: husband and wife may attend a union rest home, and the children a Pioneer or *Komsomol* camp. A Soviet refugee reported: 'The wife may want to go into the *Komsomol* or do something, and she does what she wants, not what her husband wants.'[3] The gradual appearance of the family car is changing this; a visit to any Eastern European camping site will show that the 'family holiday' is becoming as popular as in Western Europe.

Urban spouses often specialise in their marital roles: cooking and cleaning being the wife's tasks and decorating that of the husband. Equality and consideration often characterise marriage. A marriage between a university professor's daughter and an army officer has been described as follows: 'Relations between them were very affectionate and they did a lot of things together, though she did not share his occupational life. Surprisingly, he was more for equal rights in the marriage than she, who preferred to be somewhat subordinate and made no use of the liberties he was ready to extend to her.'[4]

But the 'equality-companionship' motif is absent in many cases: marriage provides a mechanism for sexual gratification, feeding and resting. A returned German prisoner-of-war (POW) described one family – army officer married to a peasant girl – as follows:

[1] *Molodoy Kommunist*, no. 2, 1966, pp. 112-14.
[2] P. I. Kushner, *op. cit.*, p. 226.
[3] Cited by Geiger, p. 226.
[4] Report of returned German POW, cited in Geiger, p. 222.

Basically . . . they lived together without any relationship; each followed his own interests . . . The partners were together solely at mealtimes and at night. In addition there are regular visits to her relatives, which, however, serve mainly as an opportunity for them to eat their fill. They do not think about the future nor eventual children, because each of the two partners is happy and satisfied in his situation.[1]

Here is an example of spouse relations which provide the very minimum. Unfortunately we have insufficient quantitative data to say how 'typical' these examples are.

A survey of 500 couples carried out in Leningrad in 1962 found that 76.2 per cent considered the chief condition for a 'healthy and happy marriage' to be 'love or mutual love with a community of outlook, confidence, sincerity and friendship; 13.2 per cent, equality and mutual respect; 4 per cent, love and housing conditions; 1.6 per cent, love and material wellbeing; 0.6 per cent, children; 0.2 per cent, practical views on life; the remainder (4.2 per cent) did not answer'.[2] While this survey refers to what brides and grooms think constitutes a happy marriage (and is not direct evidence of 'happy marriage') it does bring out the emphasis put on mutual love and respect.[3] A report by another returned German POW illustrates the deep emotional ties felt by husband and wife in some Soviet families: 'They cared for each other not only in the usual sense of marriage, but took an interest in each other's work. Thus she visited him on her free days at his construction site. They also shared the same values and opinions . . . when they had nothing to do, they sat together in front of the door of the house, the wife played the balalaika and the family sang, or the husband and wife played chess.'[4] Mutual love and a community of interest is paramount in mate selection. 'Equality' is only stated by 13.2 per cent of the couples to be a prime condition for a happy marriage. This is just as well for in practice, as both contemporary Soviet fiction and other studies have shown, Soviet women do not enjoy full equality with men. In addition to their full-time work, they bear the brunt of house-cleaning and cooking.[5] This is illustrated by Table 27 which is based on a survey of 2,682 persons working in factories in Gorki *oblast'* (1962) and shows the following use of time.

The burden of housekeeping and looking after children is still largely that of the woman as shown by column 3: women spent 40.34 hours on this compared with the men's 25.45 hours. Men work slightly longer, but they have more leisure-time, spend more time on improving their professional and cultural standards (this category includes social and party activity), column 2 probably

[1] Cited by Geiger, p. 232.
[2] A. G. Kharchev, *Brak i sem'ya*, p. 179.
[3] The play 'The Promise', by the modern writer Arbuzov, shows how marriage fails when one spouse loses the respect of the other.
[4] Cited by Geiger, *The Family in Soviet Russia*, p. 223.
[5] David and Vera Mace, *The Soviet Family* (New York, 1963), pp. 190-191.

means that they often spend more time even in bed. Other research cited by Kharchev shows that while women in Leningrad spend on average 30.5 hours in household labour, the comparable figure for men is only 10.5.[1]

Talcott Parsons has argued that the division of sex role in the occupational sphere is a mechanism which minimises rivalry and promotes family stability. Women are more often occupied in menial jobs and therefore do not rival

Table 27. Use of Leisure Time: Men and Women*

Sex:	Activity:				
	1	2	3	4	5
		Self-	Housework and		Improvement of
	Work	renewal	Self-service	Leisure	professional
	(including	(sleep,	(inc. buying	time	qualifications
	travel etc.)	eating	food, looking	use	and improving
		washing)	after children)		cultural level
Men	48.48	64.07	25.45	11.92	18.16
Women	47.56	61.19	40.34	7.08	11.65

* As written in the original, the figures do not total 168 hours.
G. V. Osipov and S. F. Frolov, 'Vnerabochee vremya i ego ispol'zovanie', *Sotsiologiya v SSSR* (Moscow, 1966), vol. 2, p. 238
The table is based on a survey of 2,682 persons employed in factories in Gorki *oblast'* (1962)

husbands.[2] A statement which may be modified in view of the fact that in the USSR, women enjoy a greater parity with men in the professional occupational sphere. They account for 52 per cent of the 'specialists' (i.e. professional employees with higher education): 72 per cent of doctors, 68 per cent of teachers, 63 per cent of economists and only 30 per cent of engineers.[3] But male dominance is still evident though it is probably moderate,[4] and the amount of marital disharmony is not significantly different in the USA and USSR, as we shall see later.

To improve the status of the wife, in future, it is planned that collective bodies will take more responsibility for child care and domestic duties. More nurseries, and restaurants are advocated.[5] A few housing complexes are being built in which considerable collective provision for social needs is provided. For example, in two 16-storey buildings of 812 flats, there will be 30 communal eating rooms (accommodating 15 to 20 people), two Finnish

[1] A. G. Kharchev, *Brak i sem'ya v SSSR* (Moscow, 1964), p. 258.
[2] T. Parsons, 'The Kinship System of the United States', *Essays in Sociological Theory* (New York, 1964), pp. 192-3.
[3] *Trud v SSSR* (Moscow, 1968), p. 275.
[4] Husband and wife have the right to choose as a joint surname the name of either, or they may keep their own names. When asked, Soviet urban families cite the husband as head of the household. (Evidence cited in Geiger, 227-8).
[5] 'Sem'ya yacheyka obshchestva', *Pravda*, 25 July 1966.

baths, a hair-dressing salon, workshops, a sports hall, a polyclinic, numerous rooms for children to play, various rooms for leisure (cinema, billiard room, dance terrace).[1] These complexes are as yet few in number and experimental. They do not envisage, it should be noted, a different *family* structure, with collective child care and group marriage or even relatively unrestricted sexual relations.

With urbanisation, the size of the family in the USSR has fallen. In 1939, its average size was 4.1: 3.6 in urban and 4.3 in rural areas. In 1959, the census shows that the average size had declined to 3.7: 3.5 in the town and 3.9 in the countryside. There were still important differences between the Republics. In Tadzhikistan the average size was 4.7 (5.1 in rural areas) and 4.8 in Armenia (5.1 in rural areas); the Baltic republics had much smaller families: 3.1 in Estonia and 3.2 in Latvia.[2] In 1966 the average size of family was estimated at around 4.0.[3]

Republican statistics, however, do not refer to separate national groups – and most republics are nationally mixed. The size of family by nationality ranges from 5.2 among Tadzhiks, 5.0 among Turkmens and Uzbeks to 3.1 for Latvians and 3.0 for Estonians.[4] The differences show that traditional attitudes still linger and affect family size. The prevalence of the very large family in Central Asia is brought out by research comparing the family structure in the Russian villages of Viryatino and Darkhan (Kirgiziya). In Darkhan 51 per cent and in Viryatino, 34 per cent of the families live in units with over five members.[5]

Table 28, which illustrates five separate communities, shows the persistence of the extended family in both town and countryside. With the exception of Latvia, in all areas in town and country more than a fifth of the family units are composed of three generations. Usually the family unit is made up of a parent of one of the spouses who helps around the house and looks after children.

The extended family, therefore, is a more frequent phenomenon in the USSR than in Great Britain or the USA. In Britain, for example, Peter Townsend has shown that 59 per cent of old people (not of families) live in a single generation group, 31 per cent live in a two-generation group and 10 per cent live as part of a three generation unit.[6] The larger Russian family unit is probably due to the acute housing shortage, the large number of war widows

---

[1] *Literaturnaya gazeta*, 6 Nov. 1968.

[2] Table 59, *Itogi vsesoyuznoy perepisi naseleniya 1959 g. SSSR* (*Svodny tom*) (Moscow, 1962), pp. 242-3.

[3] 'Sem'ya – yacheyka obshchestva', *Pravda*, 25 July 1966.

[4] See table in Appendix F.

[5] S. M. Abramzon, K. I. Antipina, *et al, Byt kolkhoznikov Kirgizskikh seleniy Darkhan Chichkan* (Moscow, 1958), p. 218.

[6] P. Townsend, *The Family Life of Old People* (1963), p. 36.

Table 28. Distribution of Families by Number of Generations in the Family Group (as a proportion of the total)*

Composition of Family	Village of Viryatino (Tambov RSFSR)	Villages in Zakarpat (Ukraine)	Villages in Latvia	Village o, Darkhan (Kirgiz)	Urban Leningrad Workers
With one Generation	19.3	6.6	13.2	not known	17.0
With two Generations†	60.3	64.2	65.3	55.1	53.0
With three Generations	20.0	24.2	13.0	21.7	24.0
Remaining Families	0.4	5.0	8.1	not known	6.0

* Information based on numerous surveys carried out in late 1950s in USSR, cited by Kharchev, p. 231
† Includes widows and unmarried mothers

and the low geographical mobility. (The new Siberian towns may show a different pattern.) Invalid parents must be maintained by their children.

The number of large families in the USSR is falling. Comparing the figures of family size for 1939 and 1959, we see that families composed of two persons had increased 129 per cent, whereas families five strong had decreased 83

Table 29. Number of children under sixteen in families of different social groups*

	Manual Workers	Collective Farmers	Non-manual Workers
	%	%	%
All families having children	100	100	100
With one child	46	40	50
With two children	39	32	41
With three children	12	19	8
With four or more	3	9	1

* Zhenshchiny i deti v SSSR. Statisticheski sbornik (Moscow, 1963), p. 68

per cent and families of nine had declined by 67 per cent.[1]   By 1962 the single child family was most typical, as shown by Table 29. This table may under-estimate family size, as it includes only children under 16 years of age. The figures confirm that the family is still relatively large in the countryside where 28 per cent of all families have three or more children, Non-manual workers have the smallest families—half having only one child. This tendency

[1] Figures refer to town and country population. SSSR v tsifrakh v 1961g. (Moscow, 1962), p. 59.

to small families has established itself despite substantial financial aid given to and orders[1] bestowed on, mothers who beget large families.

The fall in birth rate follows a pattern similar to that of western societies, as can be seen from Table 30: the Soviet birth rate having fallen from 47 in 1913 to 19.7 in 1964 a figure below the American on the latter year. (By 1968, the Soviet birth rate had dropped to 17.3)[2].

Table 30. Crude Birth-Rate* in USSR, USA and England and Wales: 1913, 1940, 1958, 1964†

	1913	1940	1958	1964
USSR	47.0	31.3	25.3	19.7
USA	35.0	17.9	24.3	21.7
England and Wales	24.3	14.6	16.8	18.4

* Per thousand of total population
† *SSSR v tsifrakh v 1961 g.* (Moscow, 1962), pp. 368-9 and *SSSR v tsifrhah v 1964 g.* (Moscow, 1965), pp. 42-3.

These figures, it should be remembered, are insufficient for a detailed analysis of fertility[3] which is affected by changes in the proportion of sexes of different ages and the age of marriage. The large number of men killed in the war reduced the birth rate not only during the period 1941–45, but also had effects for twenty years afterwards. It has meant that the male death rate will be 'artificially' reduced from 1960 to 1985, as fewer men than usual will be between the age of 60 and 80 years. While the Soviet total population is greater than the American, the latter's male stock aged over 35 (in 1960) is greater.[4] The losses incurred in the war largely account for the lower Soviet death-rate, as shown in Table 31.

Table 31. Crude Death-Rate* in USSR, USA and England and Wales: 1913, 1940, 1958, 1964†

	1913	1940	1958	1964
USSR	30.2	18.1	7.2	7.0
USA	13.2	10.8	9.5	9.6
England and Wales	14.2	14.4	11.7	12.2

* Per thousand of total population
† *SSSR v tsifrakh v 1961 g.* (Moscow, 1962), pp. 368-9 and *SSSR v tsifrakh v 1964 g.* (Moscow, 1965), pp. 42-3.

[1] Mothers who give birth to and rear ten children have the title 'Heroine Mother'.
[2] *Narkhoz SSSR v 1968g.* (Moscow, 1969), p. 36.
[3] The frequency of births, which should not be confused with fecundity which refers to productive capacity.
[4] See James W. Brackett, 'Demographic Trends and Population Policy in the USSR', *Dimensions of Soviet Economic Power*, Joint Economic Committee US Congress (Washington, 1962), p. 538.

The lowered birth-rate has not simply been due to publicity about, and the availability of, contraceptives. Sex education is virtually unknown, and family planning advice is not very widespread in Soviet Russia. Unlike married women in the United States, of whom one survey shows that 70 per cent used contraceptive devices,[1] 52 per cent of a sample of Soviet married women practised no form of contraception; condoms were used by 20 per cent of couples; 10 per cent resorted to coitus interruptus, 8 per cent relied on lactation, 5 per cent employed douches, and 5 per cent used a diaphragm or jelly.[2] Abortion, which was legalised from 1920 to 1936 and again from 1955,[3] is the chief method of birth control. Unless carried out on medical or social grounds, a fee of 50 rubles is payable for an abortion.[4] It has been estimated that in 1958-9 the abortion rate was as high as if not higher than the birth rate.[5] The number of fatherless children (aged under eighteen) was roughly four million in 1954 and it has been estimated that 300,000 births with no legal father take place annually.[6] These are much lower figures than in 1947, when there were eleven million fatherless children in the USSR and 3,312,000 unmarried mothers received grants.[7] In one *oblast'* (district) in 1965 the number of births 'outside marriage' was 17 per cent of all births – 13 per cent in 1967; these figures were 13.1 and 9.4 per cent in the towns and 19.6 and 17.2 per cent in the countryside for 1965 and 1967 respectively.[8] The 1968 law on marriage and the family gave the wife a right to maintenance by her husband both during and for one year after pregnancy.

Family size is one area in which a government finds it extremely difficult to exercise control. While childbirth has been regarded as a right of the citizen, the falling birthrate induced the government to prohibit abortion (in the '30s and '40s) and to give family allowances. The size of the Soviet family seems to have followed the pattern of other industrialised countries. As in modern western societies, there is an inverse relation between income and

[1] Ronald Freeman *et al*, *Family Planning, Sterility and Population Growth* (New York, McGraw Hill, 1959), p. 68, cited by David M. Heer, 'Abortion, Contraception and Population Policy in the Soviet Union', *Soviet Studies*, vol. 17 (no. 1) July 1965, p. 82.

[2] Cited by David M. Heer, *loc. cit.*, p. 82.

[3] Abortion was made legal in 1955 due mainly to the prevalence of criminal abortion taking place outside hospital. It was considered a temporary measure until contraception which is now encouraged could be effective.

[4] See *Maternal and Child Health in the USSR* (Geneva, 1962), pp. 21-2.

[5] Heer, *loc. cit.*, p. 81. See also B. Berelson, *Family Planning and Population Programs* (Chicago, 1966).

[6] Peter H. Juviler, 'Family Reforms on the Road to Communism', in P. H. Juviler and H. W. Morton, *Soviet Policy-Making* (1967), p. 34.

[7] P. H. Juviler, 'Marriage and Divorce', *Survey*, 48 (1963), p. 115.

[8] *Literaturnaya gazeta*, 4 Dec. 1968.

fertility and between income and infant mortality.[1] Infant mortality in the Soviet Union has been much higher than in the USA. In the late 1950s, it was 40.6 deaths per thousand births of children aged under one year, compared to 29.5 in the USA. By 1968, however, the Soviet infant mortality rate had fallen to 26.[2]

As in western societies, the role of the family in maintenance during sickness, incapacity and old age has declined. Social security covering illness, maternity, industrial injury, family allowances, old-age, self and dependents' disability is provided by the state through the trade union organisation.[3] Even so, the family seems to play a more important role in the maintenance of the old than it does in Britain or the USA.

The discussion so far shows that the functions of procreation and maintenance have continued to be important for the Soviet family. Let us now look at its roles of 'placement' and 'socialisation'.

Placement

In all societies where individual achievement is highly values, the placement function of the family has declined. In the USSR the placement role has been seriously undermined by the state. Access to professions, education, ownership and wealth lie outside the family circle. While it is true that one can inherit one's parents' personal possessions, the illegality of private ownership of productive property means that the family as such transmits no wealth. But attitudes and motivations may be transferred to children making them more 'educable'. Though education cannot be privately bought, opportunities provided by schools and universities may be more highly valued and exploited by professional or white collar groups than by manual or peasant strata. Education becomes a form of property and one of the most important determinants of status. 'In the USSR there is no capital except education. If a person does not want to become a collective farmer or just a charwoman, the only means you have to get something is through education'.[4] We shall see later that the children of higher occupational groups have a greater likelihood of receiving higher education than the children of parents in lower groups.

The relationship between parents' social status and children's occupational aspirations may be seen by studying Table 32.

[1] James W. Brackett, 'Demographic Trends and Population Policy in the Soviet Union', Joint Economic Committee US Congress, *Dimensions of Soviet Economic Power* (Washington, 1962), p. 544.

[2] Figures for USA in 1959 and USSR 1958-9. Cited by Brackett, *loc. cit.*, p. 499. For 1968, *Narkhoz SSSR v 1968g* (Moscow, 1969), p. 36.

[3] For details of amounts paid see *Gosudarstvennoe sotsial'noe strakhovanie* (Moscow, 1965), *Social Security Programs in the Soviet Union* (Washington, 1960).

[4] A Soviet refugee, cited by K. Geiger, *The Family in Soviet Russia*, p. 156.

Table 32. Parents' Social Status and Children's Aspirations*†

Children want to become (as percentage of total)

Groups to which Parents belong	Industrial and Building Workers	Agricultural Workers and Collective Farmers	Public Service Workers	Intelligentsia	Total
Industrial and Building Workers	35	—	5	60	100
Agricultural Workers and Collective Farmers	87	12	—	—	100
Public Service Workers	56	4	4	36	100
Intelligentsia	25	1	3	71	100

* V. N. Shubkin, 'Social Mobility and Choice of Occupation' in G. V. Osipov (ed.), *Industry and Labour in the USSR* (1966), p. 93
† The data refer to questionnaires answered by 289 children in secondary schools in Novosibirsk and Kyzyl. The table has many shortcomings – particularly the proportion of parents in each category and the number of children in each group are not given.

Any results from the table must be regarded as tentative, as it refers to a very small sample of the Soviet population. It is obvious from it that in most social groups children do not aspire to their parents' social position: only in the intelligentsia category, where three-quarters of the children are inclined to their parents' profession is this so. Of the children of agricultural workers and collective farmers, only 12 per cent desire to take up agricultural work and, surprisingly, none aspires to intelligentsia status. Probably agricultural workers and collective farmers strongly advise their children to take up factory or building work and may be ignorant of the advantages of and avenues to intellectual labour; similarly, the gravitation to intelligentsia status by the children of workers and intellectuals may be explained in similar fashion.

The relationship between family background, children's aspirations for education and their fulfilment may be illustrated by Table 33 on page 362. This table clearly indicates the importance attached by all social groups to higher education. Of the total number of school leavers, 83 per cent wished to continue to study and another 10 per cent wanted to study part-time. Even three-quarters of the children of agricultural workers wanted to continue to study, as did 93 per cent of the children from intelligentsia backgrounds. The degree of inequality is shown by the proportion of school leavers who subsequently did full-time study: of the urban intelligentsia, there were 82 per cent, of the village intelligentsia 58 per cent, and of agricultural workers, only 10 per cent.

The results of this survey are also borne out nationally. A Soviet source has pointed out the unequal 'class chances' of the children of collective

Table 33. School Leavers' Aspirations and their Fulfilment

Groups to which parents belong	Proportion of school leavers wishing to:			Proportion of school leavers subsequently actually engaged in:		
		Work with			Work with	
	Work %	Study %	Study %	Work %	Study %	Study %
Urban intelligentsia	2	5	93	15	3	82
Village intelligentsia	11	13	76	42	—	58
Workers in industry and building	11	6	83	36	3	61
Workers in transport and communications	—	18	82	55	—	45
Agricultural workers	10	14	76	90	—	10
Service workers	9	15	76	38	3	59
Others	12	38	50	63	12	25
Per cent of total	7	10	83	37	2	61

V. N. Shubkin, *Voprosy filosofii* (May 1965), p. 65

farmers and workers. Of students in specialised secondary and higher education, manual workers and children of manual workers constituted 39.4 per cent; white collar workers and their children 41 per cent, collective farmers and their children 19.6 per cent. Evening class students were divided socially as follows: workers and their children 50.6 per cent, collective farmers and their children 2.3 per cent, white collar workers 47.1 per cent. Among correspondence students the weight of white collar workers was even stronger: they accounted for 67.3 per cent of the total, workers and the children made up 25.7 per cent and collective farmers and their children 7 per cent. (The figures are for the 1963/4 school year).[1] We shall return to the analysis of inequality when we consider social stratification.

Socialisation

Compared to the USA and Great Britain, the family, at least on the surface, has less power in the USSR to influence the informal ways children learn to deal with problems and adopt attitudes. This is because to a much greater extent than in western societies, the state is responsible for child welfare and for the provision of social and cultural amenities for young people. We have seen that a large number of children in the USSR are 'fatherless'. Many are orphans and some live only with their mothers. Since 1944, children may be adopted[2] or, if the mother has no living mate, reared in a children's home.

[1] E. L. Manevich, *Problemy obshchestvennogo truda v SSSR* (Moscow, 1966), p. 63.
[2] See Article 24 of *Basic Principles of Marriage and the Family*, below Appendix I.

The local authority also has the right – as in England – to deprive a family of its children if it considers them to be in need of care and protection. Many of them go to boarding schools which have none of the pomp and ceremony of the English variety and they are weaker socialising institutions. Children may go home at weekends. Few staff live on the premises and the staff-pupil ratio appears to be less favourable than in good English public schools. In 1960, there were some half million children in Soviet boarding schools,[1] about 1.4 per cent of the school population. Most of these had only one parent: of 422 children in one Leningrad boarding school, 325 had only a mother, 15 only a father and 16 were orphans.[2] The family, however, has an important part to play in the process of socialisation. This too, is also a Soviet view of the family. 'In the sphere of spiritual life the most important function of the family is child education. This function is linked up closest of all with the natural and social essence of the family as the propagator of the human race. Besides, it represents a direct concentration of economic functions in as much as the education of a child starts properly, with his upkeep and care.'[3]

As a larger proportion of married women work in the USSR than in Great Britain or the USA, the state has greater necessity for providing collective child care. More than 83 per cent of all women in the 15 to 59 years age group are at work;[4] and 70 per cent of all children under 16 have mothers who work.[5] Though the Soviet authorities have made great efforts at providing the collective care of young children, the burden of their upbringing still falls on the family (usually the grandmother) or neighbours. In 1960, only about one tenth of all children under three years old were in nurseries and 15.6 per cent of those aged between three and seven in kindergartens,[6] although the figures rose to 22.9 per cent in 1965.[7] After reaching school age provision is wider; even so, in 1960 facilities provided only for a small proportion of the child population: only 1.4 per cent attended boarding schools and 9.1 per cent pioneer camps.[8] Kaser has estimated that in 1966, less than a million out of a

---

[1] Geiger, p. 268.

[2] A. Kharchev, *Brak i sem'ya v SSSR* (Moscow, 1964), p. 273.

[3] A. Kharchev, *Brak i sem'ya v SSSR*, p. 261. See also English shortened edition, *Marriage and Family Relations in the USSR* (Moscow, 1965), p. 41.

[4] K. H. Mehlan, 'The Socialist Countries of Europe', in B. Berelson, *Family Planning and Population Programs* (Chicago, 1966), p. 214.

[5] M. Yanowitch, 'Soviet Patterns of Time Use and Concepts of Leisure', *Soviet Studies*, vol. 15, no. 1 (1953), p. 27. (In Britain in the early 1960s, 30 per cent of married women were at work).

[6] The number of children in all pre-school establishments rose from 4,428,000 in 1960 to 8,534,000 in 1967. *Zhenshchiny i deti v SSSR* (Moscow, 1969), p. 126. More than three-quarters of the provision was in urban areas.

[7] *Zhenshchini i deti v SSSR* (Moscow, 1961), p. 591, *50 let Sovetskogo zdravookhraneniya* (Moscow, 1967), p. 116.

[8] K. Geiger, *The Soviet Family*, p. 194.

total enrolment of 48 million were in boarding schools (about 2 per cent).[1]
The socialisation process in the early years is still the prerogative of the
family. How, then, are children brought up in the USSR? The short answer,
is that it depends on the kind of parents the child has. Here we may consider
a number of different family relationships.[2] Again we must bear in mind that
we cannot say how 'typical' these examples are.

A description of a metal worker's family by a released German prisoner of
war reported to Malte Bischoff was as follows:

> The children were growing up amidst it all just like the pigs, who themselves lived
> together with the family. They experienced everything possible and became accus-
> tomed to everything at an early age. No-one worried especially about them nor took
> any special interest in them. The parents were not unloving toward them, but super-
> vised them little, so that all the children had a somewhat neglected look. In the
> summer, for example, they ran around clad only in little shirts. Some of the children
> were already going to school, but this had little influence upon them . . . The births
> were not planned; the children simply came. A birth meant only a short interruption
> in sexual intercourse . . . The children were not punished, they were only shouted at.[3]

This example illustrates a general lack of parental supervision and control.
The children are given much independence as shown by this reminiscence:

> I had many friends, and sometimes I didn't come home for the whole summer,
> especially I and my older brother. For three months I didn't come home, we used to
> play on freight trains. There were many like this . . . in poor families they don't pay
> any attention to the children. Very little boys often play cards, and do whatever
> they want . . . As soon as the weather got warm we were rarely found at home.
> Only mama and papa lived peacefully.[4]

Obviously, the existence of such weak parental control may make the task of
socialisation at school relatively easier. The extent of such absence of control
is not readily quantifiable, nor is the influence of particularly 'Soviet' factors
or child rearing patterns. Indeed, the kind of relationships cited above may
also be found among 'rough' English working class families.

Among urban families, and perhaps particularly among the middle class,
children became the centre of attention, and the family becomes 'child-
centred'. Children in such homes are planned, fed at regular intervals and
very much loved. A nurse married to a University lecturer recalls: 'Because we
had a dearly loved only child, we lived and worked for him. He was the main
aim of our life. My husband and I wanted to make him a decent, honest and
diligent man.'[5] Concern about education, an intense desire for upward

---

[1] M. Kaser, 'Soviet Boarding Schools', *Soviet Studies*, vol. 20, no. 1 (July, 1968), p. 94.

[2] These families are based on reports cited in K. Geiger, *The Soviet Family* (1968).

[3] Cited by K. Geiger, p. 270.

[4] Harvard Project on the Soviet Social System, cited by K. Geiger, p. 271.

[5] Cited by Geiger, p. 276.

mobility are characteristics of such families. Here again, the child-centred family like that in the West supplies an aim in life for the parents and provides them with emotional satisfaction. It is difficult to know whether values stemming from the family influence the child more than those of the environment outside. The incidence of religious views is probably an indication of still strong family influence. (See Chapter 13 on religion.) Even so, there is resistance to religious indoctrination. A Soviet refugee recalls: 'I used to see my mother standing and praying to herself, but I was not interested. She sometimes got angry, and said: "Why don't you pray to God?" I laughed at her. I knew nothing about religion. The history of the Communist Party said that religion is an enemy of communism.'[1] This example of intergenerational conflict (between communism and religion) is now probably less important than it was in the Stalin period. Other conflicts, perhaps of a more political nature, may take place: for example, the condemnation by the young of a parent's involvement in the party during Stalin's time.

A third kind of family type is that of the professional career-centred family. Here both parents work and are to varying degrees engrossed in their profession. The mother suckles the child for six months or so, and may even take a year off work. The child is well cared for and loved. But a surrogate quickly enters his life. This is either the staff at the local *yasli* (or nursery) or, perhaps more frequently, a grandmother. Sometimes a private children's nurse is employed. Here, while the surrogates have an important influence in the formative years, the role of factors outside the home is extremely strong. An army officer recalls: 'The education of children who grew up before the Revolution is very different. Then the basic influence was that of their parents, while in the USSR it is that of school, Pioneer and Komsomol organisations.'[2]

This type of family structure is probably now the most typical in the USSR. It involves care and love for the child who is often looked after by surrogates and who in later years comes very much under the influence of groups outside the home, enjoys a considerable amount of independence, and freedom of choice in his activities. Perhaps the most important factor is the career interests of both parents. Talcott Parsons has argued that only *one* of the members of a family has an occupational role which is of determinate significance for the status of the family as a whole. 'The wife and mother is either exclusively a "housewife" or at most has a "job" rather than a "career".'[3] This view must be modified in the light of Soviet experience. The larger number of married women in professional and higher engineering jobs, reflecting more equal

---

[1] Harvard Project, cited by Geiger, p. 301.
[2] Cited by K. Geiger, p. 287.
[3] 'The Kinship System of the Contemporary United States', *Essays in Sociological Theory* (Free Press, New York, 1964), p. 192.

N

Table 34. Marriage and Divorce in Uzbekistan and Kiev 1939-1958 (Selected years)

Year	Uzbek SSR		Samarkand Areas of Uzbek SSR				Kiev: 3 Districts	
			Urban		Rural			
	Marriages	Divorces	Marriages	Divorces	Marriages	Divorces	Marriages	Divorces
1939	52,700	9,617	2,977	52	2,326	20	7,458	2,063
1946	48,400	653					6,592	824
1949			3,701	41	4,026	7		
1950	64,100	673						
1953	65,100	780	3,323	69	5,888	8		
1956	81,600	1,272						
1957			3,471	109	8,603	15	7,577	1,733
1958								

Data cited by A. G. Kharchev, *Brak i sem'ya v SSSR* (Moscow, 1964), pp. 168-70.

educational opportunities distinguishes the Soviet family from its western counterpart. Many middle class Soviet women are 'career' women.

Divorce

Earlier in this chapter we noted the changes in the regulations for divorce; we saw that the 1944 decree made divorce more difficult and that the 1968 law gave certain safeguards to pregnant wives. In addition the 1968 law gave a divorced partner, of either sex, the right to maintenance by the other if he (or she) becomes incapacitated within a year of divorce. Though no comprehensive statistics are available, it would appear that the divorce rate fell in 1944, but since that time it has again been rising, until in 1958 it reached, and in 1960 it surpassed, the 1940 figure.[1] Divorce rates vary both between different parts of the country and between rural and urban areas. This can be seen on Table 34 where in addition to the divorce rate, the marriage rate is also cited for comparative purposes.

An important difference shown is the lower divorce rate in rural areas compared with urban: since 1946 the rate in Kiev has been at least eight times that of Uzbekistan. Note the very low divorce rate in rural Uzbek Samarkand: in 1957, only 15 divorces, and 8,603 marriages. A striking difference also exists in Uzbekistan (Samarkand) where in 1949 divorce occurred five times as often in urban as in rural areas. Most probably here the low rural divorce rate is accounted for by the religious and national positions of the indigenous population.

More figures have been published for Kirovograd province. Here in urban areas the divorce rate rose from 20.3 (per 10,000 of the total population) in 1965 to 44.7 in 1967; whereas in the countryside the respective numbers were 7.1 and 16.8.[2]

Where there are no obvious ethno-cultural factors, the explanation of these urban-rural differences probably lies in the greater social pressure which may be brought against possible divorcees in rural areas. The publication of proceedings and the reconciliation function of the Comrades' Court probably has had little effect – witness the very large increases in the divorce rate from 1965 to 1967. The more heterogeneous and anonymous life of the town gives greater opportunity for marital infidelity and consequent strife. Again the statistics may be unreliable, many families break up and others are formed with no official record.

[1] Registered divorce, per thousand of the total population fell from 1.1 in 1940 to 0.4 in 1950. Thereafter it rose to 0.7 in 1956, 1.3 in 1961, 2.8 in 1966 and was 2.7 in 1968. See G. M. Sverdlov, 'Zakon o razvode i statistika', *Sovetskoe gosudarstvo i pravo*, no. 10 (1964), p. 33, and *Narodnoe khozyaystvo SSSR v 1964g* (Moscow, 1965), p. 41, *Narodnoe khozyaystvo SSSR v 1965g* (Moscow, 1966), p. 118, *Narodnoe khozyaystvo SSSR v 1968g* (Moscow, 1969), p. 40.

[2] *Literaturnaya Gazeta*, 4 Dec. 1968.

Extra-marital relations are not uncommon and adultery figures prominently in divorce proceedings. In Kirovograd *oblast*, in 1965 the percentage of births outside marriage was 17 and in 1967, 13[1] and a survey of a thousand divorces in Latvia gave the reason for divorce as infidelity in 128 cases; other factors were: drunkenness in 160, 'egoistic tendencies' of the husband/wife, heartless, callous relations to other members of the family 640, not serious or fickle attitude to marriage 51, others 21.[2] An interesting illustration of morals and their bearing on marriage is given by Solzhenitsyn in *Cancer Ward*:

> . . . The young men she met all danced and went for walks with the same aim in mind: to warm themselves up a bit, have their fun and then clear out. They used to say among themselves, 'I could get married, but it never takes me more than an evening or two to find a new "friend", so why should I bother?'
>
> Indeed, why marry when women were so easy to get? If a great load of tomatoes suddenly arrived in the market, you couldn't just triple the price of yours, they'd go rotten. How could you be inaccessible when everyone around you was ready to surrender?
>
> A registry office wedding didn't help either. Zoya had learnt this from the experience of Maria . . . Maria had relied on the registry office, but a week after the marriage her husband left her, went away and completely disappeared.[3]

In Bischoff's study, of wives observed, about one third were known to have been unfaithful to their husbands.[4] A returned German POW describes a lorry driver's marital life as follows:

> He was interested only in his stomach and his pleasures—women and vodka . . . In the two years of observation (1945-7) he married (that is registered with) four different wives, but after a time divorced them again and took his first wife back. He threw each of the women out if she did not accomplish her duties precisely, if she began to bore him, or if he became interested in another woman. During the entire period that he would live with a new wife, his very first wife, together with their two-year-old child, would sleep on the very threshold of his room and wait patiently until he threw the new wife out. Then she would return, without ever showing any jealousy.[5]

In the 1960s Soviet writers have claimed that the divorce rate in the USA is twice as high as that of the USSR: one quarter of marriages ending in the divorce court in America, compared with only one in nine in Soviet Russia.[6] Expressed as a proportion of the population,[7] the comparative figures cited in 1965 were: England and Wales 0.6, USSR 1.6, USA 2.2, France 0.6, West

[1] *Literaturnaya Gazeta*, 4 Dec. 1968.
[2] *Literaturnaya Gazeta*, 4 Dec. 1968.
[3] *Cancer Ward* (1968), p. 184.
[4] Cited by Geiger, p. 249.
[5] Cited by Geiger, pp. 245-246.
[6] G. M. Sverdlov, 'Zakon o razvode . . .', *Sovetskoe gosudarstvo i pravo*, no. 10 (1964), p. 33.
[7] Per 1,000 of the total population.

Germany 0.8.[1] Such comparisons can only be superficial and may be misleading – measuring the ease of divorce, rather than family disintegration –
and are partly determined by the population's age and sex structure; for
example, a very young population might have a lower proportion of marriage-
able age and therefore, other things being equal, would have a lower divorce
rate. Again, as we have seen above, the Soviet divorce rates have shot up
to 2.7 in 1968 (a figure above the American shown above). The expense
involved in getting divorce may encourage separations, and new families may
be formed outside formal marriage. Of a survey on divorce carried out in
Leningrad, it is reported that 'already one or both of the divorcees have, in
one fifth of the cases, formed another marriage (in practice) of which they have
children'.[2] This poses a problem for measuring family break-up, not only in
the USSR, but in all countries where there are impediments to divorce. Most
probably, the amount of 'real' family disintegration in Russia is closer to the
American figure than suggested by the statistics quoted. Indeed as
Literaturnaya Gazeta has pointed out, in 1966 the official divorce rate showed
that for every three marriages, there was one divorce.[3] It has been estimated
that in Moscow ten per cent of marriages last for less than a year.[4]

Some interesting data are available on divorce in Leningrad: on the basis
of a sample of 1,000 divorces, 3.1 per cent of marriages had lasted half a year,
7.3 per cent of marriages a full year, 10.7 per cent two years, 20.5 per cent
up to four years.[5] In the period from 1960 to 1965, the divorce rate was 'highest
among couples who have lived together for five to nine years'.[6] Another report
on divorce in Lithuania shows that 33.7 per cent were of marriages which had
lasted from five to nine years, 28.8 per cent from ten to nineteen years, only
1.5 per cent lasted less than a year. It is also interesting to note that in
Lithuania there are two age ranges for men to marry, when they are between
22 and 27 years and from 40 to 42 or more; for women, on the other hand,
there is only one age range, between 20 and 24. We also know that there is a
large number of remarriages – in 1966 there were 5,370 divorces and 3,777
second weddings.[7] It seems probable, therefore, that many men marry
twice and on the second occasion take once more a young bride in her
twenties or even younger. This may be an adaptive mechanism to help correct
the demographic sex imbalance[8] – giving more women the chance of marriage
and bringing up children.

---

[1] Figures for 1965, *Narodnoe khozyaystvo SSSR v 1965g* (Moscow, 1966), p. 117.
[2] A. K. Kharchev, *Brak i sem'ya v SSSR* (1964), p. 212.
[3] *Literaturnaya Gazeta*, 6 Nov. 1968.
[4] *Literaturnaya Gazeta*, 3 September 1969.
[5] *Pravda*, 23 November 1966.
[6] *Soviet News* (London), 30 May 1967.
[7] *Literaturnaya Gazeta*, 16 Oct. 1968.
[8] We saw earlier that there is an excess of 20 million women.

Let me now sum up the principal characteristics of the family in the USSR. Over the past fifty years or so, the main change has been away from the consanguine family structure to a smaller and more homogeneous unit. Though conjugal families tend to be small in size, the extended family exists to a greater extent than in Britain or the USA. Spouse relations have changed. Woman is now equal in rights – before the law – with man: she is usually a breadwinner, like her husband, but she is still mainly responsible for household chores. Family relationships are more 'democratic': children are more independent, more performance-oriented. The functions of the Soviet family have followed the trend of its counterpart in the West: the family has lost its control over 'placement', and socialisation is more the prerogative of the state. Its main function is the provision of regular sexual gratification between the spouses, procreation and maintenance of children and, to a lesser degree, companionship between its members. The state assists rather than replaces the family. This 'assistance' is of a similar kind to that provided in advanced Western European states. While the monogamous family exists under Soviet Communism, we cannot conclude that society must necessarily be dependent on it. The USSR has never seriously attempted to experiment with different forms of group living. Housing is still designed with the monogamous family unit in mind.

How have the polity and family interacted over the years since 1917? In the days after the October Revolution, the communist power took measures to weaken the solidarity of the family. Its economic power vested in the control of property was broken. The law gave it no support; divorce was easily available; children born in wedlock had no greater status than children born out of it. Probably more important, however, has been the influence of industrialisation and urbanisation, which has resulted in the smaller family, the working wife and 'achievement-oriented' children. From 1936, and even more so from 1944, the Soviet political system attempted to strengthen the family. Marriage was given civic recognition, divorce made more difficult to achieve, and stable parenthood encouraged. As a socialising agency, the family after the Revolution was potentially more hostile to the Soviet state: in it were embodied the values of the 'ancien regime'. Today, shorn of its wider functions, indoctrinated with Soviet norms, the family can be relied upon by the regime for support.

Reading No. 13
Frederick Engels, 'The Origin of the Family, Private Property and the State' (1884).
Source:
K. Marx and F. Engels, *Selected Works*, Moscow, 1951, Vol. 2.

Bourgeois marriage of our own times is of two kinds. In Catholic countries the parents, as heretofore, still provide a suitable wife for their young bourgeois son, and the consequence is naturally the fullest unfolding of the contradiction inherent in monogamy – flourishing hetaerism on the part of the husband, and flourishing adultery on the part of the wife. The Catholic Church doubtless abolished divorce only because it was convinced that for adultery, as for death, there is no cure whatsoever. In Protestant countries, on the other hand, it is the rule that the bourgeois son is allowed to seek a wife for himself from his own class, more or less freely. Consequently, marriage can be based on a certain degree of love which, for decency's sake, is always assumed, in accordance with Protestant hypocrisy. In this case, hetaerism on the part of the man is less actively pursued, and adultery on the woman's part is not so much the rule. Since, in every kind of marriage, however, people remain what they were before they married, and since the citizens of Protestant countries are mostly philistines, this Protestant monogamy leads merely, if we take the average of the best cases, to a wedded life of leaden boredom, which is described as domestic bliss. The best mirror of these two ways of marriage is the novel; the French novel for the Catholic style, and the German novel for the Protestant. In both cases, 'he gets it': in the German novel the young man gets the girl; in the French, the husband gets the cuckold's horns. Which of the two is in the worse plight is not always easy to make out. For the dullness of the German novel excites the same horror in the French bourgeois as the 'immorality' of the French novel excites in the German philistine, although lately, since 'Berlin is becoming a metropolis', the German novel has begun to deal a little less timidly with hetaerism and adultery, long known to exist there.

In both cases, however, marriage is determined by the class position of the participants, and to that extent always remains marriage of convenience. In both cases, this marriage of convenience often enough turns into the crassest prostitution – sometimes on both sides, but much more generally on the part of the wife, who differs from the ordinary courtesan only in that she does not hire out her body, like a wageworker, on piecework, but sells it into slavery once for all. And Fourier's words hold good for all marriages of convenience: 'Just as in grammar two negatives make a positive, so in the morals of marriage, two prostitutions make one virtue.' Sex love in the relation of husband and wife is and can become the rule only among the oppressed classes, that is, at the present day, among the proletariat, no matter whether this relationship is officially sanctioned or not. But here all the foundations of classical monogamy are removed. Here, there is a complete absence of all property, for the safeguarding and inheritance of which monogamy and male domination were established. Therefore, there is no stimulus whatever here to assert male domination. What is more, the means, too, are absent; bourgeois law, which protects this domination, exists only for the propertied classes and their dealings with the proletarians. It costs money, and therefore, owing to the worker's poverty, has no validity in his attitude towards his wife. Personal and social relations of quite a different sort are the decisive factors here. Moreover, since large-scale industry has transferred the woman from the house to the labour market and the factory, and makes her, often enough, the breadwinner of the family, the last remnants of male domination in the proletarian home have lost all foundation – except, perhaps, for some of that brutality towards women which became firmly rooted with the establishment of monogamy. Thus, the proletarian family is no longer monogamian in the strict sense, even in cases of the most passionate love and strictest faithfulness of the two parties, and despite all spiritual and wordly benedictions which may have been received. The two eternal adjuncts of monogamy – hetaerism and adultery – therefore, play an almost negligible role here; the woman has regained, in fact, the right of separation, and when the man and woman cannot get along they prefer to part. In short, proletarian marriage is monogamian in the etymological sense of the word, but by no means in the historical sense.

. . . The modern individual family is based on the open or disguised domestic enslavement of the woman; and modern society is a mass composed solely of individual families as its molecules. Today, in the great majority of cases, the man has to be the earner, the breadwinner of the family, at least among the propertied classes, and this gives him a dominating position which requires no special legal privileges. In the family, he is the bourgeois; the wife represents the proletariat. In the industrial world, however, the specific character of the economic oppression that weighs down the proletariat stands out in all its sharpness only after all the special legal privileges of the capitalist class have been set aside and the complete juridical equality of both classes is established. The democratic republic does not abolish the antagonism between the two classes; on the contrary, it provides the field on which it is fought out. And, similarly, the peculiar character of man's domination over woman in the modern family, and the necessity, as well as the manner, of establishing real social equality between the two, will be brought out into full relief only when both are completely equal before the law. It will then become evident that the first premise for the emancipation of women is the re-introduction of the entire female sex into public industry; and that this again demands that the quality possessed by the individual family of being the economic unit of society be abolished.

We are now approaching a social revolution in which the hitherto existing economic foundations of monogamy will disappear just as certainly as will those of its supplement – prostitution. Monogamy arose out of the concentration of considerable wealth in the hands of one person – and that a man – and out of the desire to bequeath this wealth to this man's children and to no one else's. For this purpose monogamy was essential on the woman's part, but not on the man's; so that this monogamy of the woman in no way hindered the overt or covert polygamy of the man. The impending social revolution, however, by transforming at least the far greater part of permanent inheritable wealth – the means of production – into social property, will reduce all this anxiety about inheritance to a minimum. Since monogamy arose from economic causes, will it disappear when these causes disappear?

One might not unjustly answer: far from disappearing, it will only begin to be completely realised. For with the conversion of the means of production into social property, wage labour, the proletariat, also disappears, and therewith, also, the necessity for a certain – statistically calculable – number of women to surrender themselves for money. Prostitution disappears; monogamy, instead of declining, finally becomes a reality – for the men as well.

At all events, the position of the men thus undergoes considerable change. But that of the woman, of *all* women, also undergoes important alteration. With the passage of the means of production into common property, the individual family ceases to be the economic unit of society. Private housekeeping is transformed into a social industry. The care and education of the children becomes a public matter. Society takes care of all children equally, irrespective of whether they are born in wedlock or not. Thus, the anxiety about the 'consequences', which is today the most important social factor – both moral and economic – that hinders a girl from giving herself freely to the man she loves, disappears. Will this not be cause enough for a gradual rise of more unrestrained sexual intercourse, and along with it, a more lenient public opinion regarding virginal honour and feminine shame? And finally, have we not seen that monogamy and prostitution in the modern world, although opposites, are nevertheless inseparable opposites, poles of the same social conditions? Can prostitution disappear without dragging monogamy with it into the abyss?

Thus, full freedom in marriage can become generally operative only when the abolition of capitalist production, and of the property relations created by it, has removed all those secondary economic considerations which still exert so powerful an influence on the choice of a partner. Then, no other motive remains than mutual affection.

Since sex love is by its very nature exclusive – although this exclusiveness is fully realised today only in the woman – then marriage based on sex love is by its very nature monogamy. We have seen how right Bachofen was when he regarded the advance from group marriage to individual marriage chiefly as the work of the women; only the advance from pairing marriage to monogamy can be placed to the men's account, and, historically, this consisted essentially in a worsening of the position of women and in facilitating infidelity on the part of the men. With the disappearance of the economic considerations which compelled women to tolerate the customary infidelity of the men – the anxiety about their own livelihood and even more about the future of their children – the equality of woman thus achieved will, judging from all previous experience, result far more effectively in the men becoming really monogamous than in the women becoming polyandrous.

What will most definitely disappear from monogamy, however, is all the characteristics stamped on it in consequence of its having arisen out of property relationships. These are, first, the predominance of the man, and secondly, the indissolubility

N*

of marriage. The predominance of the man in marriage is simply a consequence of his economic predominance and will vanish with it automatically. The indissolubility of marriage is partly the result of the economic conditions under which monogamy arose, and partly a tradition from the time when the connection between these economic conditions and monogamy was not yet correctly understood and was exaggerated by religion. Today it has been breached a thousandfold. If only marriages that are based on love are moral, then, also, only those are moral in which love continues. The duration of the urge of individual sex love differs very much according to the individual, particularly among men; and a definite cessation of affection, or its displacement by a new passionate love, makes separation a blessing for both parties as well as for society. People will only be spared the experience of wading through the useless mire of divorce proceedings.

Thus, what we can conjecture at present about the regulation of sex relationships after the impending effacement of capitalist production is, in the main, of a negative character, limited mostly to what will vanish. But what will be added? That will be settled after a new generation has grown up: a generation of men who never in all their lives have had occasion to purchase a woman's surrender either with money or with any other means of social power, and of women who have never been obliged to surrender to any man out of any consideration other than that of real love, or to refrain from giving themselves to their beloved for fear of the economic consequences. Once such people appear, they will not care a rap about what we today think they should do. They will establish their own practice and their own public opinion, conformable therewith on the practice of each individual – and that's the end of it.

In the meantime, let us return to Morgan . . . He, too, regards the development of the monogamian family as an advance, as an approximation to the complete equality of the sexes, without, however, considering that this goal has been reached. But, he says, 'when the fact is accepted that the family has passed through four successive forms, and is now in a fifth, the question at once arises whether this form can be permanent in the future. The only answer that can be given is that it must advance as society advances, and change as society changes, even as it has done in the past. It is the creation of the social system, and will reflect its culture. As the monogamian family has improved greatly since the commencement of civilisation, and very sensibly in modern times, it is at least supposable that it is capable of still further improvement until the equality of the sexes is attained. Should the mono-gamian family in the distant future fail to answer the requirements of society it is impossible to predict the nature of its successor.'

Reading No. 14
A. M. Kollontay, 'The New Morality and the Working Classes' (1918)
Source:
Reprinted in R. Schlesinger, *The Family in the USSR*, London: Routledge, 1949, pp. 66-9.

Marriage No Longer a Chain

Let the working mothers be reassured. The communist society is not intending to take the children away from the parents, nor to tear the baby from its mother's breast; nor has it any intention of resorting to violence in order to destroy the family as such. No such thing! Such are not the aims of the communist society. What do we observe today? The wornout family is breaking up. It is gradually freeing itself from all the domestic labours which formerly were as so many pillars supporting the family as a social unit. Housekeeping? It also appears to have outlived its usefulness. The children? The parent-proletarians are already unable to take care of them; they can assure them neither subsistence nor education. This is the situation from which both parents and children suffer in equal measure. The communist society therefore approaches the working woman and the working man and says to them: 'You are young, you love each other. Everyone has the right to happiness. Therefore live your life. Do not flee happiness. Do not fear marriage, even though marriage was truly a chain for the working man and woman of capitalist society. Above all, do not fear, young and healthy as you are, to give to your country new workers, new citizen-children. The society of the workers is in need of new working forces; it hails the arrival of every new-born child in the world. Nor should you be concerned because of the future of your child: your child will know neither hunger nor cold. It will not be unhappy nor abandoned to its fate as would have been the case in capitalist society. A subsistence ration and solicitous care are secured to the child and to the mother by the communist society, by the Workers' State, as soon as the child arrives in the world. The child will be fed, it will be brought up, it will be educated by the care of the communist Fatherland; but this Fatherland will by no means undertake to tear the child away from such parents as may desire to participate in the education of their little ones. The communist society will take upon itself all the duties involved in the education of the child, but the paternal joys, the maternal satisfaction – these will not be taken away from those who show themselves capable of appreciating and understanding these joys.' Can this be called a destruction of the family by means of violence? – or a forcible separation of child and mother?

The Family a Union of Affection and Comradeship

There is no escaping the fact: the old type of family has seen its day. It is not the fault of the communist State, it is the result of the changed conditions of life. *The family is ceasing to be a necessity of the State, as it was in the past*; on the contrary, it is worse than useless, since it needlessly holds back the female workers from more productive and far more serious work. Nor is it any longer necessary to the members of the family themselves, since the task of bringing up the children, which was formerly that of the family, is passing more and more into the hands of the collectivity. But on the ruins of the former family we shall soon see a new form rising which will involve altogether different relations between men and women, and which will be *a union of affection and comradeship, a union of two equal members of the communist society, both of them free, both of them independent, both of them workers*. No more domestic 'servitude' for women. No more inequality within the family. No more fear on the part of the woman lest she remain without support or aid with little ones in her arms if her husband should desert her. The woman in the communist city no longer depends on her husband but on her work. It is not her husband but her robust arms which will support her. There will be no more anxiety as to the fate of her children. The State of the Workers will assume responsibility for these. Marriage will be purified of all its material elements, of all money calculations, which constitute a hideous blemish on family life in our days. Marriage is henceforth to be transformed into a sublime union of two souls in love with each other, each having faith in the other; this union promises to each working man and to each working woman, simultaneously, the most complete happiness, the maximum of satisfaction which can be the lot of creatures who are conscious of themselves and of the life which surrounds them. *This free union*, which is strong in the comradeship with which it is inspired, *instead of the conjugal slavery of the past – that is what the communist society of tomorrow offers to both men and women*. Once the conditions of labour have been transformed, and the material security of working women has been increased, and after marriage such as was performed by the Church – that so-called indissoluble marriage which was at bottom merely a fraud – after this marriage has given place to the free and honest union of men and women who are lovers and comrades, another shameful scourge will also be seen to disappear, another frightful evil which is a stain on humanity and which falls with all its weight on the hungry working woman: prostitution.

This evil we owe to the economic system now in force, to the institution of private property. Once the latter has been abolished, the trade in women will automatically disappear.

Therefore let the women of the working class cease to worry over the fact that the family as at present constituted is doomed to disappear. They will do much better to hail with joy the dawn of a new society which will liberate woman from domestic servitude, which will lighten the burden of motherhood for woman, and in which, finally, we shall see the disappearance of the most terrible of the curses weighing upon women: prostitution.

The woman who is called upon to struggle in the great cause of the liberation of the workers – such a woman should know that in the new State there will be no more room for such petty divisions as were formerly understood: 'These are my own children; to them I owe all my maternal solicitude, all my affection; those are your children, my neighbour's children; I am not concerned with them. I have enough to do with my own'. Henceforth the worker-mother, who is conscious of her social function, will rise to a point where she no longer differentiates between *yours* and *mine*; she must remember that there are henceforth only *our* children, those of the communist State, the common possession of all the workers.

Social Equality of Men and Women

The Workers' State has need of a new form of relation between the sexes. The narrow and exclusive affection of the mother for her own children must expand until it embraces all the children of the great proletarian family. In place of the indissoluble marriage based on the servitude of woman, we shall see rise the free union, fortified by the love and the mutual respect of the two members of the Workers' State, equal in their rights and in their obligations. In place of the individual and egotistic family, there will arise a great universal family of workers, in which all the workers, men and women, will be, above all, workers, comrades. Such will be the relation between men and women in the communist society of tomorrow. This new relation will assure to humanity all the joys of so-called free love ennobled by a true social equality of the mates, joys which were unknown to the commercial society of the capitalist régime.

Make way for healthy blossoming children: make way for a vigorous youth that clings to life and to its joys, which is free in its sentiments and in its affections. Such is the watchword of the communist society. In the name of equality, of liberty, and of love, we call upon the working women and the working men, peasant women and peasants, courageously and with faith to take up the work of the reconstruction of human society with the object of rendering it more perfect, more just, and more capable of assuring to the individual the happiness which he deserves. The red flag of the social revolution which will shelter, after Russia, other countries of the world also, already proclaims to us the approach of the heaven on earth to which humanity has been aspiring for centuries.

INTRODUCTORY

Burgess, E. W. and H. J. Locke. *The Family, From Institution to Companionship.* New York: American Book Company, 1945.

Davis, K. *Human Society.* New York: Macmillan, 1948, reprinted 1964.

Kharchev, A. *Marriage and Family Relations in the USSR.* Moscow, 1965.

Mace, V. and D. *The Soviet Family.* London: Hutchinson, 1964.

BASIC

Brackett, J. W. 'Demographic Trends and Population Policy in the Soviet Union', in Joint Economic Committee, US Congress, *Dimensions of Soviet Economic Power.* Washington: Government Printing Office, 1962.

Carr, E. H. *Socialism in One Country, 1924-1926.* Part I, London: Macmillan and Co., 1958.

Engels, F. 'The Origin of the Family, Private Property and the State', in Marx and Engels, *Selected Works,* Vol. 2. Moscow, 1951.

Geiger, K. *The Family in Soviet Russia.* Cambridge, Mass.: Harvard University Press, 1968.

Heer, David M. 'Abortion, Contraception and Population Policy in the Soviet Union', *Soviet Studies,* Vol. 17, No. 1, July 1965, pp. 76-83.

Inkeles, A. and R. A. Bauer. *The Soviet Citizen.* Cambridge, Mass.: Harvard University Press, 1959.

Juviler, P. H. 'Marriage and Divorce', in *Survey,* No. 48, 1963, pp. 104-17.

Juviler, P. H. 'Family Reforms on the Road to Communism', in P. H. Juviler and H. W. Morton (eds.), *Soviet Policy-Making.* London: Pall Mall, 1967, pp. 29-60.

Kharchev, A. G. *Brak i sem'ya v SSSR.* Moscow, 1964.

Kushner, P. I. *Selo Viryatino v proshlom i nastoyashchem.* Moscow, 1958.

Lynd, Robert S. 'Ideology and the Soviet Family', in *American Slavic and East European Review,* Vol. 9, No. 4, 1950, pp. 268-78.

Neubeck, Gerhard. 'Notes on Russian Family Life Today', in *Acta Sociologica,* Vol. 8, No. 4, 1965, pp. 324-6.

Osipov, G. V. and Frolov, S. F. 'Vnerabochee vremya i ego ispol'zovanie', in *Sotsiologiya v SSSR,* Vol. 2, pp. 225-42. Moscow, 1965.

'The 1926 Family Code and the Practical Application of Soviet Family Law. Discussion of the drafts of the code', Doc. 6, in R. Schlesinger, *The Family in the USSR.* London: Routledge and Kegan Paul, 1949, pp. 81-153.

Social Security Programs in the Soviet Union. Washington: Government Printing Office, 1960.

Solzhenitsyn, A. *Cancer Ward,* Part 1, translated by Nicholas Bethell and David Burg. London: The Bodley Head, 1968.

SPECIALISED

Abramzon, S. M., K. I. Antipina, *et al. Byt kolkhoznikov Kirgizskikh seleniy Darkhan i Chichkan.* Moscow, 1958.

Aleksandrov, G. 'Sostav prestupleniya', in *Molodoy Kommunist*, No. 2, 1966, pp. 112-14.

Berelson, B. (ed.). *Family Planning and Population Programs.* Chicago: University of Chicago Press, 1966.

'Facts and Figures about Families', in *Soviet News.* London, 30 May 1967, No. 5338, p. 112.

Freeman, R., *et al. Family Planning, Sterility and Population Growth.* New York: McGraw-Hill, 1959.

Gosudarstvennoe sotsial'noe strakhovanie. Moscow, 1965.

Kaser, M. 'Soviet Boarding Schools', in *Soviet Studies*, Vol. 20, No. 1, July 1968.

Kharchev, A. 'Eshche o sem'ye, problemy sotsial'noy zhizni', in *Pravda*, 23 November 1966, pp. 2-3.

Kharchev, A. 'Sem'ya yacheyka obshchestva, problemy sotsial'noy zhizni', in *Pravda*, 25 July 1966, pp. 2-3.

Kislyakov, N. A. 'Sem'ya i brak u Tadzhikov', in *Trudy instituta etnografii*, Vol. 44. Moscow, 1959.

Kollontay, A. *Communism and the Family.* London: Workers' Socialist Federation, 1920.

Lane, D. *The Roots of Russian Communism.* Assen: Van Gorcum, 1969.

Literaturnaya gazeta, 4 December 1968 (on divorce in Kirovograd).

Literaturnaya gazeta, 6 November 1968 (divorce and marriage).

Literaturnaya gazeta, 16 October 1968 (divorce in Lithuania).

Lyubimova, A. *V pervye gody.* Moscow, 1958.

Marx, K., and F. Engels. 'The Communist Manifesto, in Marx and Engels, *Selected Works*, Vol. 1. Moscow, 1951.

Maternal and Child Health in the USSR. Geneva: World Health Organisation, 1962.

Mehlan, K. H. 'The Socialist Countries of Europe', in B. Berelson (ed.). *Family Planning and Population Programs.* Chicago: University of Chicago Press, 1966, pp. 207-26.

Parsons, T. 'The Kinship System of the United States', in *Essays in Sociological Theory.* New York: The Free Press 1964, pp. 177-96.

Savatier, R. 'Le communisme et le mariage', in *Revue catholique des institutions et du droit*, novembre-decembre 1936.

Shubkin, V. N. 'Molodezh' vstupaet v zhizn' ', in *Voprosy filosofii*, No. 5, May 1965, pp. 57-70.

Shubkin, V. N. 'Social Mobility and Choice of Occupation', in G. V. Osipov (ed.). *Industry and Labour in the USSR.* London: Tavistock, 1966, pp. 86-98.

Stavovski, V. 'Pervye i togi perepisi naseleniya', in *Kommunist*, No. 7, 1959, pp. 74-81.

Strumilin, S. 'Rabochi byt i kommunizm', in *Novy mir*, No. 7, June 1960, pp. 203-20.

Sukhareva, O. A., and M. A. Bukzhanova. *Proshloe i nastoyashchee seleniya Aykyran.* Tashkent, 1955.

Sverdlov, G. *Marriage and the Family in the USSR.* Moscow, 1956.

Sverdlov, G. M. 'Zakon o razvode i statistika', *Sovetskoe gosudarstvo i pravo*, No. 10, 1964, pp. 31-41.

Svod zakonov Rossiyskoy imperii, Vol. 10, Part 1, p. 18. Spb. 1857.

Townsend, P. *The Family Life of Old People: An Inquiry in East London.* London: Routledge and Kegan Paul, 1963.

Trud v SSSR Statisticheski sbornik. Moscow, 1968.

Tsentral'noe statisticheskoe upravlenie.

    Itogi vsesoyuznoy perepisi nasleniya 1959g. SSSR (svodny tom). Moscow, 1962.

Tsentral'noe statisticheskoe upravlenie

    Narodnoe khozyaystvo SSSR v 1960g. Moscow, 1961.

    Narodnoe khozyaystvo SSSR v 1964g. Moscow, 1965.

    Narodnoe khozyaystvo SSSR v 1965g. Moscow, 1966.

    Narodnoe khozyaystvo SSSR v 1968g. Moscow, 1969.

Tsentral,-noe statisticheskoe upravlenie

    SSSR v tsifrakh v 1961g. Moscow, 1962.

    SSSR v tsifrakh v 1964g. Moscow, 1965.

Tsentral'noe statisticheskoe upravlenie

    Zhenshchiny i deti v SSSR: Statisticheski sbornik. Moscow, 1963.

Tsentral'noe statisticheskoe upravlenie

    Zhenshchiny i deti v SSSR. Moscow, 1969.

Vedomosti verkhovnogo soveta SSSR, No. 49, 1965.

Yanowitch, M. 'Soviet Patterns of Time Use and Concepts of Leisure', *Soviet Studies*, Vol. 15, No. 1, 1963, pp. 17-37.

50 let Sovetskogo zdravookhraneniya. Moscow, 1967.

12

SOCIAL
STRATIFICATION

Many radicals seek, in one way or another, to make society more egalitarian, to reduce the distance between social strata: to give the powerless more power, the poor more riches, the social outcasts more status. The study of social stratification is concerned with these and related problems. In the first place, a student of society is interested to know the forms social inequality may take. Second, he seeks to describe the extent of this inequality in specific societies. Third, he is anxious to know why it is that inequality exists in society: is it a necessary condition to maintain the equilibrium of a social order? Is it a functional requirement necessary 'to ensure that the most important positions are conscientiously filled by the most qualified persons'?[1] Or is it a process by which the privileged have seized an unfair share of the desirable things in life and, thereafter, by force and fraud (of which the ideology of inequality is a part), maintain a *status quo* which is mainly in their own interests? The case of the USSR may be used to illustrate these problems and to answer some of them.

Let us first attempt a definition of social stratification. It means the division of society into a hierarchy of strata, each having an unequal share of society's power, wealth, property or income and each enjoying an unequal evaluation in terms of prestige, or honour or social esteem. There are two aspects of stratification which must be distinguished: the *objective* inequality between groups and the *subjective* ranking of individual group members by others. Marxist writers tend to emphasise objective inequality between classes based on the ownership or non-ownership of property, even if this does not give rise to a subjective feeling of class identification on this 'objective' basis. Non-Marxist sociologists tend to define strata in subjective terms of status or honour.

Subjective inequality involves interpersonal evaluations of honour or status. Talcott Parsons defines stratification as '. . . the differential ranking of the human individuals who compose a given social system and their treatment as superior and inferior relative to one another in certain socially important

[1] Kingsley Davis, *Human Society* (New York, 1948), p. 367.

aspects'.[1] Not all persons, of course, bestow honour on the same criteria. Some may rank highly professional footballers, other cabinet ministers. Thus the kind of evaluations, the degree of consensus or disagreement among the members of a society as to what determines 'honour', the ranking of individuals' status, and the groups of persons who enjoy common evaluation as equals, all vary between societies and the ways sociologists classify them. There is no unique configuration of grades of social evaluation, though we shall see later that there are similarities between major societies.

Studies of stratification attempt to delineate the 'socially important' groups, to determine the relationship between political privilege, economic inequality and social rank. In this chapter we shall consider first Marx's attitude to inequality, second, the policies adopted by the communists after the revolution, third, the profile of the main social groups today (intelligentsia, workers and peasants) and finally, we shall discuss the implications of Soviet experience for social restructuring.

The Dictatorship of the Proletariat

Marx and Engels made ownership the fundamental determinant of class position. The owners of the means of production constitute the ruling class over the non-owners. Originally, the division of labour in society gave rise to economic classes. (See Chapter 1.) Associated with class position and dependent on it are social status and political power. In capitalist society, the industrial *bourgeoisie* owns the means of production and employs labour; its superior financial and organisational resources give control over the state; its wealth gives access to culture and education and gives rise to a style of life. The *proletariat* is distinguished by the fact that it sells its labour power on the market (where it has a bargaining disadvantage); it has little participation (power) in the affairs of the state; it is deprived educationally and culturally. For Marx, class, power and honour in society are inextricably related and are highly correlated.

As we saw in Chapter 1 above, capitalist society is characterised by the contradiction between the bourgeoisie and proletariat, only with its resolution and the subsequent creation of socialist society can classes be eliminated. In the *Communist Manifesto* Marx wrote: 'When in the course of development class distinctions have disappeared and all production has been concentrated in the hands of a vast association of the whole nation, then public power will lose its political character.' As social and political inequality was sustained by economic class inequality, the abolition of private property and of the capitalist class based on it would entail the elimination of political and social inequality. Only in communist society would '. . . all the springs of co-operative wealth

[1] 'An Analytical Approach to the Theory of Social Stratification', *Essays in Sociological Theory, Pure and Applied* (Glencoe, Ill., 1949), p. 166.

flow more abundantly – only then can ... society inscribe on its banners:
From each according to his ability, to each according to his needs!' Under
communism, there would be no division of labour and therefore no antithesis
between mental and manual labour.[1] From the point of view of social stratification, the October Revolution was to create conditions for a truly equal and
classless society. In place of a system of stratification determined by class relations and by the forces of the market, it was thought that social relations would
be determined by the ideology and goals of the Communist Party.

After the revolution, the Bolsheviks' main concern was to abolish the
ownership relations on which capitalism rested. Nationalisation of property,
the seizure of land and factories, helped destroy the old possessing classes and
the middle strata associated with them. But, as we have noted in the historical
survey (see Chapter 3), before and during the New Economic Policy private
ownership and private trade continued. In market terms, separate classes still
existed: the proletariat and a property owning class (particularly among the
peasantry).

The proletariat was, in theory, the political base of the new order. To safeguard the revolution the Bolsheviks thought it necessary that the proletariat
act initially as the *ruling class*. During the period up to 1936, the official
definition of Soviet society was that of 'the dictatorship of the proletariat'.
From the communist viewpoint the proletariat consisted of three strata –
workers, landless peasants and employees. The strata hostile to the proletariat
were made up (during the New Economic Policy) of private traders (*nepmen*),
rich peasants (*kulaks*) and the technical intelligentsia having sympathy for a
bourgeois order. These 'hostile' groups had restricted political rights: they
were barred from official positions, they had no vote and could not join the
Communist Party.[2]

In terms of social esteem a most complex situation existed: the values of the
old regime still lingered on in people's consciousness, while the communists
attempted to assert the mores of a new order. Official policy was egalitarian, an
attempt was made to give higher status to skilled and unskilled factory workers.
In April 1917, Lenin had said that the pay of officials must not exceed that of
'competent workmen'. The status of the old managerial and executive groups
was undermined: for example in 1917, the Council of People's Commissars
fixed salaries at 500 rubles basic for Commissars. Soviet policy was to reduce
high salaries to the earnings of the average worker.[3] Wage differentials were
reduced, giving government employees of the lowest category of office worker
350 r. a month.[4] This, however, should not be taken as the 'introduction of

[1] 'Critique of Gotha Program', in Marx and Engels, *Selected Works* (1950), vol. 2, p. 23.

[2] In addition, the clergy and members of the royal family had restricted political rights.

[3] V. I. Lenin, 'The Immediate Tasks of the Soviet Government', *Collected Works* (1965), vol.
27, pp. 249, 581n.

[4] See A. Bergson, *The Structure of Soviet Wages* (Cambridge, Mass. 1954), p. 190.

communism'; wage equalisation and the rationing that went with it (see Chapter 3) were temporary measures intended to distribute the scarce resources available under 'War Communism'. In January 1919, a wage scale approved by the Second Trade Union Congress laid down wages of the highest grades of workers and employees at only 1.75 times those of the lowest paid grade in each category – a drastic reduction of the differentials pertaining before the revolution.[1] In practice, however, it was difficult to enforce these trade union statutes and the wages of 'scarce' workers went above the ceiling. In 1921, when Lenin introduced the New Economic Policy, a wage structure with 17 divisions covered all grades of workers and employees. The differential was widened; highly skilled workers received 3.5 times the wage of the lowest category and the ratio of the highest salary to the lowest was eight to one.[2] It is interesting to note that in the 1920s the differentials between workers followed a ranking similar to the pre-revolutionary pattern: printers, tanners and workers in the food industry receiving more than miners, metallurgists and engineers.[3] Here is an example of the way the forces of tradition were stronger than Bolshevik policy at this time. In 1926 the law was again changed and differentials were reduced to much below the pre-war levels. This was part of a policy by the communists to ameliorate the position of the most deprived strata. Even so, as Bergson has pointed out, income inequality among Soviet industrial workers in 1928 'was closely proximate to that among American industrial workers in 1904'.[4]

But this egalitarian policy was cut short and replaced under Stalin by a system of greater wage differentiation. Only under full communism, Stalin argued, would individuals receive according to need, under socialism wages must be paid according to work performed. The 'Marxist formula of socialism' stated: 'From each according to his ability, to each according to his work'.[5]

In 1932, in an interview with Emil Ludwig, Stalin made clear his views on equalitarianism.

The kind of socialism under which everybody would get the same pay, an equal quantity of meat and an equal quantity of bread, would wear the same clothes and receive the same goods in the same quantities – such a socialism is unknown to Marxism . . . Equalitarianism owes its origin to the individual peasant type of mentality, the psychology of share and share alike, the psychology of primitive 'communism'. Equalitarianism has nothing in common with Marxist socialism. Only people who are unacquainted with Marxism can have the primitive notion that the

---

[1] A. Bergson, *The Structure of Soviet Wages* (Cambridge, Mass., 1954), p. 182.

[2] Bergson, p. 185. See also *Trud i zarabotnaya plata v SSSR* (Moscow, 1968), p. 323.

[3] L. Kostin, *Wages in the USSR* (Moscow, 1960), p. 16.

[4] *The Structure of Soviet Wages* (1954), p. 92. In the sphere of education, workers and peasants were given preference for admission to higher educational institutions (see Chapter 14). At the same time laws weakening the family were passed (see Chapter 11).

[5] J. V. Stalin, 'Talk With Emil Ludwig', *Collected Works*, vol. 13, p. 120.

Russian Bolsheviks want to pool all wealth and then share it out equally. That is the notion of people who have nothing in common with Marxism.[1]

Accordingly, a steeper gradation between skills and occupations was introduced and wage ratios increased between the lowest and highest paid.[2] Stalin's immediate justification for the change was the need to reduce labour mobility and to introduce incentives for the unskilled to become skilled – a policy substantiated, at least in part, by the most authoritative western writer on this subject.[3]

Post-revolutionary experience, therefore, saw, after an initial egalitarian phase, the assertion of wage inequality. The Russian communists, in this sphere of social life as in others, found themselves faced with introducing socialism in a backward underdeveloped country. Without the economic basis provided by an advanced industrial economy, a system of differentiation based on egalitarianism could not come to fruition, especially when introduced after a revolution, a civil war, a general famine and economic collapse. In practice, the inequality between occupational strata of other industrial societies became also a characteristic of Soviet Russia. As Robert Hodge and others have suggested, economic development depends upon the recruitment and training of men in skilled, clerical and administrative positions and a system of differential social evaluation is therefore a necessary condition of rapid industrialisation.[4]

To attract workers to the industries essential for the industrialisation effort, wages in them were increased. In 1934, the highest wages were paid in engineering, followed by the power industry, ferrous metallurgy, oil, coking, iron ore and coal industries.[5] While it is sometimes thought that Stalin personally created a system of severe social inequality, it is more accurate to view the changes in social stratification of the early 1930s as determined by the demands of industrialisation and the forces to which they gave rise. The centrally *administered* economy recognised these demands. In doing so a system of wage payment was introduced in which 'the principles of relative wages in the Soviet Union are also capitalist principles'.[6]

The USSR as a Socialist State

In 1936 the USSR was proclaimed a 'socialist society'. In Soviet Marxist terms this implied that no contradictory class relationships existed. The owners of the means of production had finally been expropriated, but

---

[1] J. V. Stalin, 'Talk with Emil Ludwig', pp. 120-1.

[2] See comparison computed by Bergson, *op. cit.*, pp. 101, 118.

[3] See Bergson, pp. 200-1, 203-4.

[4] Robert W. Hodge *et al*, 'A Comparative Study of Occupational Prestige', in R. Bendix and S. M. Lipset, *Class, Status and Power* (1967), p. 320.

[5] L. Kostin, *Wages in the USSR* (Moscow, 1960), p. 16.

[6] Bergson, p. 208.

inequality persisted. Under socialism men were paid according to their work. The 1936 USSR Constitution defined three friendly co-operative groups each with full civil rights: the workers, the intelligentsia (sometimes defined as employees or non-manual workers) and the collective farm peasantry. The first two groups are the main subdivisions of the working class which is seen in a firm friendly union with the collective farm peasantry. Two social (but not antagonistic) 'classes' therefore exist, differentiated by their relationship to the means of production. Though the means of production (the land) on collective farms is owned by the state, the products of collective farms belong to collective farmers, they are sold to the state and the proceeds of sales are shared. Manual and non-manual workers, including farmers on state farms, directly employed by the state which owns their produce, are paid wages.

The social structure of Soviet state *socialism* (not communism) involving social inequality is not as contradictory as is sometimes supposed. In Soviet terms, property relations have been changed: private ownership has been abolished. But this does not imply that inequality has been eliminated. Unequal incomes giving rise to privileges in consumption and status differences have been officially admitted, with differential access to power position, or political stratification. To understand adequately the process of social stratification, much more than a crude mechanical relationship between ownership relations, on the one hand, and honour and political power, on the other, is required. We must bear in mind that in the USSR 'socialism' is defined in terms of Marxist property relations. In western social-democratic theory, socialism is *defined* in terms of egalitarianism. As Roy Jenkins pointed out in 1952: 'The desire for greater equality has been part of the inspiration of all socialist thinkers and of all socialist movements. The absence of this desire, indeed, provides the most useful of all exclusive definitions of socialism.'[1]

In Marxist theory, under capitalism, wealth is determined by the ownership of the means of production, under socialism income is determined according to one's work and only in a communist society does one receive according to need. The introduction of graded wage scales in place of the more egalitarian early post-revolutionary policy has important social implications, for it shows that wage incentive is necessary to reward workers for greater effort and for gaining higher qualifications. As Stalin wrote:

> The consequence of wage equalisation is that the unskilled worker lacks the incentive to become a skilled worker and is thus deprived of the prospect of advancement; as a result he feels himself a 'visitor' in the factory, working only temporarily so as to 'earn a little' and then go off to 'seek his fortune' elsewhere . . .
>
> Hence, the 'general' drift from factory to factory; hence the heavy turnover of labour power.

[1] 'Equality', in *New Fabian Essays* (1952), p. 69.

In order to put an end to this evil we must abolish equalisation and discard the old wage rates. In order to put an end to this evil we must draw up wage scales that will take into account the difference between skilled and unskilled labour, between heavy and light work. We cannot tolerate a situation where a rolling-mill hand in a steel mill earns no more than a sweeper.[1]

Though the lack of skilled manpower may be partly accounted for by the rapidity of industrialisation, Stalin's statement should not be derided by egalitarians. (Nor should it be inferred on the other hand that egalitarianism is impracticable). The significance of Soviet experience is that to achieve a rapid rate of industrial growth from a relatively low level of industrial development income differentials seem to be necessary, or at least useful, levers of labour recruitment.

Social Stratification in Modern Russia

We have seen that in a state socialist society there can be no class conflict, in the sense that Soviet sociologists use the term. This does not mean, even in theory, that there is complete harmony, or that no system of social stratification prevails. An authoritative article in *Kommunist*[2] emphasises the conflict inherent in present Soviet society. Glezerman quotes Lenin's description of social classes as 'large groups of people differing from each other by the place they occupy in the historically determined system of social production, by their relation (in some cases fixed and formulated in law) to the means of production, by their role in the social organisation of labour, and, consequently, by the dimensions and mode of acquiring the share of social wealth of which they dispose.'[3]

This definition of class is much wider than Stalin's interpretation of Marx defined above in strict terms of ownership. The place one occupies in 'the social organisation of labour' and by 'the dimensions and mode of acquiring the share of social wealth' of which one disposes may be independent of one's ownership relations. Here the division of labour could be a basis for differentiation.

Glezerman continues by defining four main kinds of social distinction under socialism: first, a class division proper between workers and peasants; second, distinctions between rural and urban populations; third, those between manual and mental labour; fourth, those between 'people of different trades, skills and incomes within the working class, peasantry, intelligentsia and office workers'. Before considering these distinctions we may begin by turning to the empirical composition of Soviet social strata. First, we may

[1] J. Stalin, 'New Conditions – New Tasks in Economic Construction', in *Problems of Leninism* (Moscow, 1952), pp. 463-4. See Reading No. 15.
[2] G. Glezerman, 'Sotsial'naya struktura sotsialisticheskogo obshchestva', no. 13, 1968. See also *Soviet News*, 12 Nov. 1968.
[3] *Selected Works*, vol. 3, p. 248.

describe the broad groupings as defined by Soviet sociologists in official classifications. Second, we shall consider the significance of social stratification in the USSR as seen by western sociologists. Finally, we shall turn to social mobility.

Manual and non-manual workers (*sluzhashchie*) include all engaged in state and co-operative institutions and members of collective farms regularly employed in industry, building, transport (etc.) and only part or not at all employed on the collective farm. Collective farmers include members of the *kolkhoz* and their families engaged in agricultural production.[1] A collective farmer is in a different *class* because he is not employed by an enterprise for a wage, he is a member of the collective which owns the seeds and their produce. The 1968 handbook of the Soviet economy[2] defines manual and non-manual workers as comprising 77.7 per cent of the population and collective farmers and co-operative handicraftsmen 22.27 per cent. Only 0.03 per cent were self-employed peasants or craftsmen. These crude divisions do not preclude further sub-classification which may first be most conveniently analysed in terms used by Soviet writers.

The Soviet 'Intelligentsia', Non-Manual Workers

Under socialism, the existence of separate 'mental and manual' strata is determined 'above all else by the different role of these groups in the social organisation of labour'.[3] A Soviet theorist notes that under socialism the division of labour gives rise to a 'qualitative difference' between non-manual and manual labour[4] which is abolished only under communism.

Such a definition of 'mental labour' includes a very wide range of employees —from storemen to cabinet ministers. Sometimes, the term *intelligentsia* is restricted to an exclusive group of specialists possessing higher educational qualifications, and the word *sluzhashchie* is used to describe unqualified or junior white collar workers.

Another Soviet writer divides non-manual workers into eight main social groups; the first four being *intelligentsia*, executives in government administration and public organisations, the technical and economic intelligentsia, the scientific cultural intelligentsia; the last four being *sluzhashchie*, including counting-house employees, transport employees, those in communications, and subordinate employees in local and municipal utilities (watchmen, porters).[5] The literature on the subject is, therefore, highly ambiguous. In the

[1] P. G. Pod'yachich, *Naselenie SSSR* (Moscow, 1961), p. 154.

[2] *Narodnoe khozyaystvo SSSR v 1968g* (Moscow, 1969), p. 35.

[3] M. N. Rutkevitch, 'Izmenenie sotsial'noy struktury sovetskogo obshchestva i intelligentsiya', *Sotsiologiya v SSSR*, vol 1 (Moscow, 1965), p. 401.

[4] F. Konstantinov, 'Sovetskaya intelligentsiya', *Kommunist*, no. 15 (1959), p. 50.

[5] V. S. Semenov, 'Ob izmenenii intelligentsii i sluzhashchikh v protsesse razvernutogo stroitel-'stva kommunizma', *Sotsiologiya v SSSR* (Moscow, 1963), vol. 1, p. 418.

widest sense the *intelligentsia* and *sluzhashchie* are synonymous—'non-manual workers'. But the more specific use of intelligentsia is to define a highly qualified creative executive and technical stratum.

If we consider the number of employed persons with higher and specialist secondary education, the total size of the intelligentsia was 12.1 million in December 1965, but using the wider above definition the number rises to 25.3 million. Manevich's attempt to define the main groups in terms of function as shown on Table 35 gives a total of over 17 millions.

The Soviet *intelligentsia* cannot be considered a homogeneous social group. Rutkevitch distinguishes between 'mental labour' as a general category and those of this stratum engaged in a leading or directing capacity. This group

Table 35. Division of Soviet Intelligentsia (End 1965)

	000s
Chiefs of organs of government administration and social organisations and their structural sub-divisions	392.1
Chiefs of enterprises (of which directors of state farms and chairmen of collective farms and their deputies 102.8)	955.2
Teachers and professors of higher educational institutes (including heads)	431.3
Those occupied in art, literature and publishing	294.8
Urban technical intelligentsia	4,205.9
Village technical intelligentsia	477.2
Medical personnel and teachers in junior schools and all secondary schools (and secondary courses)	3,725.3
Planning, accounting, control and inspection personnel	3,501.9
Employees in catering, trade, procurement, supply and marketing, municipal services, and welfare services	2,545.3
Employees in the cultural field and secretarial personnel	998.2
	17,527.2

E. L. Manevich, *Problemy obshchestvennogo truda v SSSR* (Moscow, 1966), pp. 20-1

he estimates to be some 1.8 million strong. To the chiefs of government administration and factory directors (see Table 35) he adds head doctors and other health chiefs (44,000), heads of educational institutions (114,000), directors of wholesale and leading retail organisations (334,800).[1]

Manevich also points out that the level of income, culture and education varies between the sub-groups. Teachers in primary schools, those in inspection and control are not very much different (in their way of life) from manual workers, whereas the heads of state administration, higher scientific workers and those in art, literature and publishing are significantly differentiated in their way of life from workers, collective farmers and other non-manual

[1] M. N. Rutkevitch, 'Izmenenie sotsial'noy struktury Sovetskogo obshchestva i intelligentsiya', *loc. cit.*, p. 412.

workers. This kind of analysis of *intra-class* differences has occupied Soviet attention only from the late 1950s, and reveals the existence of status gradations between strata within a given Soviet-defined *class*. Table 35 shows the non-manual groups and, if we bear in mind the social structure before 1917, it illustrates the success the regime has had in training a large number of people for specialised professions. Perhaps the most important in terms of income, status and power are the first two – chiefs of organs of government administration and of enterprises.

The Manual Working Class

The working class as shown in Soviet statistics may be divided into those occupied in agriculture (on state farms) and those employed in industry. In 1958, a sixth of those defined as 'workers' were employed on state farms.[2] In 1967, out of a total 'working class' of 82 million, nearly nine million were in agriculture (state farms and related enterprises) and another seven and a half million were in forestry.[3]

Workers are divided for purposes of pay into strata according to skill. Such divisions vary from one industry to another.[4] A Soviet sociologist has distinguished between three main strata or divisions of workers: first, those with physical skills (stevedores, dockers, draymen, labourers); second, those whose jobs require physical labour and knowledge (turners, lathe operators, milling machine operators, polishers, etc.); third, those whose work requires mainly knowledge (laboratory assistants, furnace-men, electricians). Soviet labour theorists contend that, with the development of the economy, the first division will die out and that eventually all workers will be in the third category. In support of this view, it is pointed out that in the Ukraine between 1959 and 1962, the first group declined by 10 per cent, the second increased by 30 per cent and the third increased by 50 per cent.[5]

There are, therefore, clear divisions of pay and education between unskilled, semi-skilled and skilled workers. In Soviet theory, the development to communism will see the merging of these three groups.

The Peasantry

The factors which generally distinguish the peasantry as a socio-economic group are: residence in a rural habitat, labour on the land with the family

[1] E. L. Manevich, *op. cit.*, p. 21.

[2] G. Smirnov, 'Rabochi klass SSSR', *Kommunist*, no. 4 (March, 1960), p. 43.

[3] *Trud v SSSR* (Moscow, 1968), pp. 24-5.

[4] In 1965, 72 per cent of workers were employed in industries with six basic wage divisions. See *Trud v SSSR*, pp. 150-1.

[5] The workers are now divided between the three groups in these proportions: 29.3 per cent, 43.7 per cent and 27 per cent. 'Sotsialisticheskoe proizvodstvo i razvitie rabochego klassa', *Klassy, sotsial'nye sloi i gruppy v SSSR* (Moscow, 1968), pp. 52-4.

being the fundamental unit, an ideology of attachment to the soil, to the family and to the local community. The peasantry, as a social group has a certain self-sufficiency and isolation from the social world but is nevertheless part of a wider society and is to a greater or lesser extent influenced by urban areas. Unlike an agricultural worker, the peasant is largely sustained by the produce from the land he works. Though he may not own it, he determines to a large degree the inputs (both in terms of hours worked and kinds of crops to be produced) and has control over the distribution of products.

Soviet classification of social classes is dependent on the individual's relationship to the means of production. To understand the Soviet concept of 'state' and 'collective' farmer one must examine the chief characteristics of the two forms of agricultural production: 'state' and 'collective' farms. On state farms workers are paid a wage, and all proceeds accrue to the state. The farm director is appointed by the state. Such men (*sovkhozniki*) are defined as part of the working class – not the peasantry. On the collective farm, the land is collectively tilled. The produce is, in theory, owned by the collective. 'The means of production belong to the state, the products of production belong to the individual collective farms, as their own property (as is labour and seeds).'[1] Their *class* position, therefore, is not that of hired labour; collective farmers (*kolkhozniki*) are in co-operative production and, in Soviet theory, form a separate class. But as ownership of the land is vested in the state, the collective farmers do not form a class with antagonistic interests to the workers, they are a 'non-antagonistic' class forming a 'friendly union' with, although under the leadership of, the working class.

The extent to which collective farmers constitute a 'proper' peasantry has been disputed by non-Soviet writers on the peasantry. Basile Kerblay, for instance, has argued that in the collectivised sector the control over labour-input by the peasant has been vitiated: 'his work has become subject to the same direction as in industry, except that its remuneration is still a residual income and not a fixed wage', and a collective farmer, in this respect, therefore 'cannot be considered a peasant'.[2] While it is true that crucial input-output decisions are taken out of the collective farmers' hands by the Soviet planning agencies, it should not be forgotten that all peasants are subject to urban pressures and especially to market forces and, therefore, the difference is not as sharp as Kerblay suggests. It must be conceded then that the Soviet collective farm peasantry, in so far as it works on the *collective's lands*, is neither a family work unit nor has it control over decisions concerning planting. But in

---

[1] J. Stalin, 'Ekonomicheskie problemy sotsializma' (1952), *Sochineniya*, vol. 16 (Stanford, 1967), p. 205. See also above Chapter 11, pp. 282-3.
[2] Basile Kerblay, 'The Russian Peasant', *St Antony's Papers*, no. 19 (1966), p. 15. Also many collective farmers are now paid regular wages at the same rates as *sovkhozniki*.

other respects it has some of the characteristics of a more traditional 'peasantry'. The collective farmer decides the amount of time he spends and the kind of crops he will produce on his own plot. His mode of work is manual and much of his labour is expended in the traditional peasant fashion. He has no internal passport and his geographical mobility is limited. More important, he conceives of himself as part of a distinct social group attached to working the land.

To analyse the social strata of the Soviet peasantry, Soviet sociologists use a number of criteria: the character of work, and the qualifications, culture and income level, and class consciousness of the farmers.[1] On these criteria not all members of collective farms are simply 'peasants'. One Soviet writer suggests a three-fold grouping of strata. The first is engineering/technical and administrative personnel – the farm chairman and his subordinates, econo-mists, agronomists, vets, engineering mechanics, bookkeepers, and others with middle and higher education. In the mid-sixties these men made up from six to nine per cent of *kolkhozniks*. The second group is constituted of those utilising farm machinery (*mekhanizatory*) – tractor and machine-harvester drivers and operators. These totalled from ten to thirteen per cent of the collective farm labour force. The remainder, the third group, are collective farmers having no trade or speciality being occupied only in physical labour,[2] and form the 'peasantry' proper. The first two groups by occupation and culture form separate as it were 'non-peasant' strata for they have no par-ticular attachment to traditional forms of land working and have been influenced through training and education by urban values and skills. While about three-quarters of collective farmers are of the unskilled manual worker or 'peasant' category, the relative proportion of state farmers is only 41 per cent – showing their higher technical and cultural level.[3]

While workers and peasants live 'in harmony', the working class is the leading social force; it is politically, economically and socially superior to the peasantry and acts as a model for it. Gradually, argue Soviet theorists, with the building of communism, the peasantry will wither away and the differences between town and country will be obliterated. The countryside will be 'pulled up' to the level of the town. It is said that there are three ways in which this levelling will take place.

First, the 'growing together' of the urban working class and the collective farm peasantry is related to the mechanisation of agriculture which will increase the number of machine workers and operators in the countryside. (Group 2 above). By virtue of their trade such men are 'brought near to the

---

[1] 'Strukturnye izmeneniya v krest'yanstve', *Klassy, sotsial'nye sloi i gruppy v SSSR*, p. 102.

[2] 'Kolkhoznoe krest'yanstvo i sovetskaya derevnya na puti k kommunizmu', *Klassy, sotsial'nye sloi i gruppy v SSSR* (Moscow, 1968), pp. 85-6.

[3] 'Kolkhoznoe krest'yanstvo . . .', p. 92.

working class'.[1] The point Soviet theorists are trying to make here is that a highly mechanised and capital-intensive agriculture undermines the traditional 'peasant' mentality and that on this basis an agricultural working class rather than a peasantry will grow.

On what Soviet writers call the 'development of intra-collective relations' rests the second main way to change the character of the collective farms. By this it is meant that conditions of production and consumption will move closer to the practice in the towns: that wages will be paid on guaranteed monthly rates and that social services (pensions, provision of schools and medical care) will be provided on the same basis as in the town.

Thirdly, the structure of the collective farm alters through migration of people from the country to the town, and the consequent reduction in the rural population. At the same time the level of skill in the countryside will rise and labour productivity will increase and thus the living standards of the peasant will be brought into line with workers in the towns.[2]

Having described some of the features of the Soviet system of social classes, we may now turn to discuss the inequality which exists between them.

Social Inequalities

The liberal ideology of western societies accepts inequality and many claim that it is not only inevitable but necessary in modern societies: for example, it is argued that unequal power is essential for the organisation of production, unequal rewards are desirable to encourage the development of scarce skills. Rather than the abolition of inequality, many progressive social-democratic thinkers emphasise *equality of opportunity*:[3] that is, the opportunity for the deprived to ameliorate their existing position, so as to give all persons an equal chance of becoming unequal. American and, to a lesser extent, British sociology has been preoccupied with measuring social inequality between strata and with the degree to which individuals may better or worsen their status (or class) position.

In Soviet society, status or power ranking is not part of the official ideology. The classes of peasantry and workers live in 'friendly collaboration', only distinguished by the leading role of the working class in building communism. As Ossowski has pointed out, the Soviet image of contemporary Russia 'is of a society without class stratification . . . nor are there upper classes and lower classes in the sense in which we encounter them in the American scheme of gradation. . . . In the Soviet Union economic privileges and discriminations

[1] I. I. Bodyul, *Preodolenie sushchestvennykh razlichiy mezhdu gorodom i derevney v usloviyakh Moldavskoy SSR* (Kishinev, 1967), p. 86.

[2] One Soviet estimate is that the productivity of labour will rise from five to six times between 1960 and 1980 resulting in a 20-30 per cent reduction of the labour force. ('Strukturnye izmeneniya . . .', p. 119).

[3] C. A. R. Crosland, *The Future of Socialism* (1956).

have, in accordance with Soviet doctrine, nothing in common with class divisions'.[1] The grading or ranking of individuals into groups of superior or inferior status is alien to the Soviet concept of socialism. Sociological work investigating such grading therefore is not carried out – or is done only indirectly. Unlike in the United States, where a plethora of empirical work has been carried out into status differences, in the USSR very little is known about such stratification.

Soviet official ideology impels sociological research to describe inequalities between town and country, between worker and peasant. Such research illustrates the gulf between these strata, which we may describe before considering other forms of stratification.

Table 36. Educational Level of Workers and Collective Farmers

| Social Group | Per 1,000 persons of a given social group aged 10 and over having the following education: | |
	Higher, incompleted higher and middle specialist	Middle Education
Workers		
Both sexes	18	50
Men	21	55
Women	15	46
Collective Farmers		
Both sexes	9	24
Men	13	33
Women	5	18

Source: *Itogi vsesoyuznoy perepisi naseleniya 1959g.* (*Svodny tom*), pp. 112-4. Cited by E. Manevich, *Problemy obshchestvennogo truda v SSSR* (Moscow, 1966), p. 39

The level of education of collective farmers is considerably lower than that of the working class as shown in Table 36, where we see that twice as many workers have a higher and middle education compared to collective farmers. Collective farm women are also shown to be underprivileged. While it is true that the age structure of the village influences the figures – the larger number of older relatively uneducated women to some extent explains the very low number of women with the highest qualifications – it is striking that only five collective farm women per thousand of the population have higher education compared to fifteen per thousand of the working class.

The differences in social structure between town and country may be illustrated by the educational standards of workers in a collective farm, a state

[1] S. Ossowski, *Class Structure in the Social Consciousness* (1963), pp. 112-3.

farm, a settlement and a suburb of Sverdlovsk. The figures are divided between manual and 'specialist' non-manual workers and are shown in Table 37.

A clear pattern emerges from the table. If we study those with middle and higher education, the numbers increase as we read across the page from *kolkhoz* to the town suburb. For example, in Table A we see that only 1 per

Table 37. Distribution of Manual Workers and Specialists by Educational Level between Collective Farm, State Farm, Settlement and Town.

A. Manual Workers

	Kolkhoz (Collective farm)	Sovkhoz (State farm)	Settlement	Town (Sverdlovsk suburb)
N =	507	994	1,026	318
Education	%	%	%	%
Middle specialist	0	0.2	0.4	2.5
Middle general	1.0	2.6	5.2	16.3
8–9 classes	5.3	4.8	7.9	17.3
7 classes	16.6	16.0	26.6	27.8
5–6 classes	21.9	19.5	20.7	16.8
4 classes	27.6	31.6	19.4	10.6
Under 4 classes	27.6	25.3	19.8	8.6

B. Specialists

	Kolkhoz (Collective farm)	Sovkhoz (State farm)	Settlement	Town (Sverdlovsk suburb)
N =	38	86	111	206
Education	%	%	%	%
Higher	15.8	23.3	31.7	37.3
Middle Specialist	29.0	32.5	53.0	38.5
Middle General	29.0	24.4	7.2	15.5
8–9 classes	2.6	4.7	—	3.4
7 classes	7.9	13.9	3.6	1.4
5–6 classes	5.2	—	0.9	3.4
4 classes	7.9	1.2	0.9	0.4
Under 4 classes	2.6	—	2.7	—

Source: Klassy, sotsial'nye sloi i gruppy v SSSR (Moscow, 1968), p. 130

cent of *kolkhoz* manual workers have a middle general education, the figure rises to 2.6 in the *sovkhoz*, 5.2 in the settlement and 16.3 in the town; in Table B specialists with higher education are 15.8 per cent of the *kolkhoz* non-manual staff, but 23.5 per cent, 31.7 per cent and 37.3 per cent for the *sovkhoz*, settlement and town. On the other hand, if we study the distribution of the lowly educated, we see that they are clustered in the bottom left hand corner of the chart – as we move from collective farm to town the numbers decline. For example, in Table A, 27.6 per cent of *kolkhoz* manual workers had under four years of schooling, whereas the proportion was 25.3 per cent in the *sovkhoz*, 19.8 per cent in the settlement and 8.6 per cent in the town.

The provision of services is also very much more rudimentary in the village than in the town, as shown below:

Number of persons occupied in service trades in town and village

	Per 10,000 of the population	
	Town	Village
All persons engaged in service trades	1507	716
Of which: education	260	186
health services	230	90

Source: E. Manevich, Problemy . . ., p. 40

Obviously, the collective farm community is underprivileged. It has less than its proportional share of scarce educational and medical facilities. The figures show that the urban areas have two times more workers (doctors, nurses, radiographers etc.) and 40 per cent more teachers per head than the villages. Some of this difference may be accounted for by the location of regional hospitals and educational institutions in the towns but, as the population is widely scattered in the countryside, one should not expect such a large difference. Similarly, the provision of retail services (shops, cinemas) is much worse in the village than the town.

The general cultural level is also lower in the village than the town. The distribution of television sets and radios is uneven: in the Moldavian Republic in 1967, per 100 inhabitants, in the towns 13.5 had televisions and 22.3 radios, while in the villages the numbers were 3.3 and 7.2 respectively.[1] In the survey of Siberia cited above it was found that in no household either in the *kolkhoz* or *sovkhoz* was there a television set, whereas 22 per cent of households had one in the settlement and 59 per cent in the Sverdlovsk suburb. The number of radios was lower in the countryside (34.8 per cent of households in the *kolkhoz* and 78.1 per cent in Sverdlovsk) but radio relay points were much more frequent – in 48 per cent of peasant households and only 20.7 per cent of those in Sverdlovsk suburb. The number of books in the house and the frequency of subscription to journals was significantly lower in the rural than in the urban communities.[2] In a collective farm only 0.9 per cent of peasant labourers' families had a library holding 51–100 books, for non-manual workers (*sluzhashchie*) on the farm, the figure was 33.3 per cent, whereas for 'specialists' the figure rose to 66.6 per cent. Similar rankings were found for newspaper subscriptions: 6.7 per cent of labourers, 33.3 per cent of clerical workers and 83.4 per cent of specialists subscribed to three or more newspapers or journals.[3]

[1] I. Bodyul, *Preodolenie sushchestvennykh razlichiy mezhdu gorodom i derevney v usloviyakh Moldavskoy SSR* (Kishinev, 1967), p. 80.

[2] 'Pod"em kultury kolkhoznogo sela', n *Klassy, sotsial'nye sloi i gruppy v SSSR* (Moscow, 1968), p. 127.

[3] 'Pod"em kultury . . .' In *Klassy . . .*, p. 128.

O

Income

An important kind of inequality is that of income. Soviet theorists regard income as generating differentiation rather than a status hierarchy. A high income may differentiate groups of workers, but it may not lead to the creation of strata with a definite ranking on a scale of social worth – some being 'superior' to others.[1] In the USSR it is denied by some sociologists that there is a definite 'style of life' associated with income differentials.

While we have no adequate survey data to test whether *social* status by income exists, we may describe the form income differentials take. Earlier in this chapter we saw that rewards were related to skill and output, and that differentials were sharpened under Stalin. Since the early 1950s, a reversal of this inegalitarian trend has occurred. Among workers, for example, the ratio of highest paid to the lowest paid has fallen from 3.6:1 to 2.6:1 in the ferrous metals industry, in light industry from 2.6:1 to 1.8:1 and in machine-building from 2.5:1 to 2:1.[2] Here again we see an example of the way the economic and social structure influences wage differentials. In 1956, Mikoyan, envisaging the elimination of the 'excessive gap' between the highest and lowest paid, said:

During the period when we were carrying out industrialisation in a peasant country, this gap was natural, since it stimulated the rapid formation of cadres of highly skilled workers of whom the country was in dire need. Now, when there exists a working class which is highly skilled and has a high cultural level, and which is annually replenished by people graduating from seven and ten-year schools, the difference, though necessarily preserved, must be reduced. This proceeds from the new level of our development and signifies a new step forward in the advance towards Communism.[3]

Wages are regarded as an important 'lever' to influence the workers' choice of occupation and place of work. Differential wage rates attempt to attract workers to the more needed occupations and to reward them for improving their skill. The harsher climate and lack of amenities in some parts of the USSR have induced the Soviet authorities to relate pay to various 'zones' of the country. Pay is from 10 to 20 per cent higher in the Urals, Kazakhstan and Central Asia, and up to 70 per cent greater in the extreme north. Extra earnings are also derived from higher qualifications: Doctors of Science receive an extra 100 rubles per month while Candidates (a lower post-graduate degree) receive 50 rubles.[4] (At the official rate of exchange, 1 ruble is equivalent to $1.1; £1 is exchanged for 2.16 rubles).

[1] See M. Tumin, 'On Inequality', *American Sociological Review*, vol. 28, 1963.
[2] Figures cited in *Klassy, sotsial'nye sloi i gruppy v SSSR* (Moscow, 1968), p. 53.
[3] *XX S"ezd KPSS*, vol. 1, p. 307, cited by Robert Conquest, *Industrial Workers in the USSR* (1967), p. 50.
[4] For details see G. Mustinov, *Raschety po zarabotnoy plate rabochikh i sluzhashchikh* (Moscow, 1965), pp. 11-12.

As to actual earnings, a minimum wage of 40–45 rubles per month (the lower figure is for rural, the upper for urban areas) was decreed in 1965, and raised to 60 rubles in 1967.[1] Average monthly money wages for manual and non-manual workers in 1968 were 113 rubles (just over double the minimum wage) – an estimated real income of 151 rubles including services in kind.[2] Figures are also published showing averages for many different sectors of the economy: in 'industry' in 1968 the average monthly money wage was 121.9 rubles, in building it was 131.2 rubles, on state farms and in agricultural enterprises 92.1 rubles, in transport 126 rubles (railways 116 rubles, on water 154.4 rubles, road haulage, including chauffeurs and town transport 128.8 rubles), communications 88 rubles, trade, catering, supplies 90.6 rubles, housework and service (*zhilishchnokommunalinoe khozyaystvo*) 87.9 rubles, health and social services, 90 rubles, education 102.8 rubles, science 129.4 rubles, credit and insurance 103.7 rubles, public administration 118 rubles.[3] Though these figures are only averages, the occupational composition of different industries indicates a hierarchy with sailors and scientists at the top and post-office workers and those in household service and agriculture at the bottom. Figures have also been published showing average earnings of manual workers, 'engineering and technical' personnel and white collar employees in different industries. In 1966, the highest paid workers were in coal mining (192.6 rubles per month) and the lowest in the sugar production industry (78.8 rubles). Of engineers and technical workers the highest paid were in the fish industry (281.4 rubles) and the lowest (107.5 rubles) in the sewn goods branch of light industry.[4]

These broad 'industrial' categories obviously mask differences between occupations. A Soviet booklet published in 1960 gives details of various incomes. The monthly salary of a technician in the metal-working industry ranged from 75 to 90 (new) rubles, that of a departmental chief from 190 to 220 rubles and a top grade director received from 350 to 400 rubles.[5] This is a range of only about one to five. Other wage rates give a miner 60 rubles per month and the lowest grade worker in the food industry about 30 rubles.[6] A ratio of thirteen to one between the basic pay of a top director and one of the lowest workers.

Other earnings are not systematically collected in official statistics. N. DeWitt has estimated earnings for certain occupations. A government minister he says earns a minimum of $700 per month (the maximum may be perhaps five times this amount); an academician (research scientist) ranges from

[1] *Pravda*, 27 Sept. 1967. Payable from 1 Jan. 1968.
[2] *Narodnoe khozyaystvo SSSR v 1968g* (Moscow, 1969), p. 554.
[3] *Ibid*, pp. 555-6.
[4] *Trud v SSSR* (Moscow, 1968), pp. 140-4.
[5] See table in L. Kostin, *Wages in the Soviet Union* (Moscow, 1960), pp. 60-1.
[6] Kostin, pp. 17, 19.

$880 to $1,650, a manager of an industrial enterprise $330–$1,100, an engineer $110 to $330, a secondary school teacher $94 to $165, and an unskilled worker earns between $30 and $55 per month.[1] Journalists such as John Gunther have also made estimates of earnings. Composers may earn 8,300 (new) rubles a month in a good year. Research professors in the Academy of Sciences earn 1,050 rubles per month basic with additions for royalties and other lectures. The President of an Institute of the Academy of Sciences receives 1,500 rubles, a rector of a large educational institution 800–1,200 rubles, a senior government official 600 rubles, an army colonel 400 rubles. At the other end of the scale, a rural doctor receives 140 rubles, a Moscow taxi-driver gets 110 rubles and a waiter 85 rubles.[2]

The money income of agricultural workers is generally below that of indus-trial workers. In 1968, the average monthly income of a state farmer was 92.1 rubles.[3] To this, of course, must be added income from private plots – both produce consumed and sold – which is something of an unknown quantity, but it might increase income by 20 rubles which brings up the wage near to the average of workers and employees: 112.6 rubles in 1968.[4] Though collective farm incomes have risen by 232 per cent between 1953 and 1963 (collective farmwork only, excluding other income)[5] the earnings of collective farmers are probably still below the average of all workers and employees. In 1966 it has been estimated by Soviet writers that *kolkhoz* family income was only 75 to 83 per cent of that of a *sovkhoz* family.[6] Since July 1966, collective farmers have been paid at similar rates to state farmers, though this has not resulted in equal 'take-home' pay because the collective farmer is only em-ployed for about 185 days per year, whereas the state farmer is in paid employ-ment all the year round. The collective farmer's income is made up by employment outside the farm and by the sale of his own produce, which has been estimated at 28 per cent of his income.[7] Whereas in 1964 the state farmer had a wage of 70.6 rubles, the collective farmer received from the collective 31 rubles.[8] If we make allowances for other income (outside employment and

[1] Figures for 1960, N, DeWitt, *Education and Professional Manpower in the USSR* (Washington, 1961), pp. 541-4. Cited by Barry M. Richman, *Management, Development and Education in the Soviet Union* (Michigan, 1967), p. 124.

[2] John Gunther, *Inside Russia Today* (1962), pp. 49-50.

[3] *Narodnoe khozyaystvo v 1968g* (Moscow, 1969), p. 555.

[4] *Ibid.*

[5] D. B. Diamond, 'Trends in Output, Inputs and Factor Productivity in Soviet Agriculture', Joint Economic Committee US Congress, *New Directions in the Soviet Economy* (Washington, 1966), p. 358.

[6] M. Palladina, L. Grebennikova, 'Garantirovannaya oplata truda v kolkhozakh', *Voprosy ekonomiki*, no. 11, 1966, p. 27.

[7] M. Makeenko, 'Ekonomicheskaya rol' lichnogo podsobnogo khozyaystva', *Voprosy eko-nomiki*, no. 10, 1966, p. 61.

[8] J. F. Karcz, 'Seven Years on the Farm: Retrospect and Prospects', *New Directions in the Soviet Economy* (Washington, 1966), pp. 359-6.

sales from plots) total money income would have been about 55 rubles. A figure not too far out from the Soviet estimated differential. A social survey carried out in a village in the Caucasus showed that three-quarters of the income of the collective farmers was made up from collective farm earnings. Average total *family* income here ranged from 150 rubles to 208 rubles per month; the richest families received as much as 333 rubles a month.[1]

Another form of discrimination is that between the sexes. Earlier we saw that women enjoy legal equality, they predominate in some professions, such as medicine and teaching but they still bear the burden of household chores (see Chapter 11). Even in the occupational sphere, at the highest levels, women are relatively underprivileged; while in 1967 there were 14,700 Academicians, corresponding Members of the Academy and Professors, women accounted for only 1,200 – less than ten per cent of the total; similarly, they constituted less than a fifth of the university teachers.[2] Women are mainly occupied in health (85 per cent of the labour force), education (72 per cent), banking and insurance (74 per cent) and trade, catering, procurement and supply (73 per cent). While the average money wage in 1968 was 112.6 rubles, it is interesting to note that *all* these branches of the economy were below it: the figures are health – 90 rubles, education – 102.8 rubles, banking and insurance 103.7 rubles, and trade etc. – 90.6 rubles.[3]

In a survey of sex differentiation in a number of Urals factories, it was found that women still made up a large proportion of the unskilled workers and clerical staff. For instance, at one factory women accounted for 44 per cent of the work force, but 92.7 per cent of the white collar workers and 91.9 per cent of the junior ancillary staff, and their share of the skilled technical engineering jobs was only 26.8 per cent. Of men employed in the factory, 68.7 per cent wanted to continue to study but only 45.5 per cent of the women did; those actually studying came to 30.1 per cent of the men and only 14.8 per cent of the women. Perhaps a more telling statistic is that of earnings: whereas the average wage of men and women was 122 rubles 80 kopecs that of the women was only 98 rubles – the differential between men and women, therefore, must have been considerably greater than this.[4]

The prevalence of discrimination by sex shows that, despite the genuine attempts of the authorities to emancipate women, the attitudes engendered by centuries of male domination cannot be eradicated by the passing of laws or by giving access to previously male occupations, though these measures help. Let us now turn to wage differentials between other groups.

---

[1] *Sovremennoe Abkhazskoe selo* (Tbilisi, 1967), pp. 22-3.

[2] *Trud v SSSR* (Moscow, 1968), p. 247.

[3] *Narodnoe khozyaystvo SSSR v 1968g* (Moscow, 1969), pp. 555-6.

[4] E. P. Obchinikova and S. V. Brova, 'O likvidatsii ostatkov sotsial'nogo neravenstva rabochikh i rabotnits na promyshlennykh predpriyatiyakh', in *Protsessy izmeneniya sotsial'noy struktury v sovetskom obshchestve* (Sverdlovsk, 1967), pp. 37-40.

The differentials between technically qualified personnel ('engineering technical personnel') and other manual workers and between 'non-manual' and 'physical' labour have declined considerably since the 1930s. This is shown on the table, which refers to earnings (not rates).

Table 38. Wage Ratios between Non-Manual and Manual Workers

Year	Average Earnings of Engineering-Technical Personnel in Per Cent of Average Earnings of Workers	Average Earnings of Non-Manuals in Per Cent of Average Earnings of Workers
1932	263	150
1935	236	126
1940	210	109
1950	175	93
1955	165	88
1960	150	n/a*

* Yanowitch says that where data are available on an industry basis the trend is in the same direction.

Source: Yanowitch, 'The Soviet Income Revolution', Slavonic Review, No. 22 (1963), p. 688.

Figures released since Yanowitch's article was published confirm the trend. The average monthly wages in rubles of manual workers, technical personnel and white collar staff are shown below.

Table 39. Wages between Groups of Workers.

	1940	1950	1960	1966
Workers	32.3	68.7	89.9	104.4
Engineering and technical workers	68.9	120.8	133.0	150.1
White collar workers	35.8	63.6	73.2	88.2

Source: Trud v SSSR (Moscow, 1968), pp. 138-9

As in the advanced West, the Soviet income structure shows how wage and salary rates are similarly related to the forces of demand and supply. With the growing maturity of the Soviet economy, differentials between manual and white-collar workers have shown a similar tendency as in the West – a growing equalisation, an improvement in the income of unskilled manual workers at the expense of clerical and similar strata. The new 'incentive fund' payments for fulfilling plans may swing the balance back in favour of engineering-technical workers. For example, in 43 enterprises the material incentive fund was divided as follows: to engineering and technical workers 46.6 per cent, 15.5 per cent to workers and 37.9 per cent went to non-manual employees.[1]

The averages, however, conceal the range of income. We saw earlier that the 'official' differential between the pay of a top director and the lowest paid worker was 13 to 1 (see p. 399) though Bottomore cites a 25–30 to 1 ratio (in 1953), between the income of a factory manager (director) and a manual worker.[2]

Inter-society comparisons are extremely difficult to make. The official ratio of 13 to 1 is much below the equivalent in Great Britain. If we take into consideration individual *unearned* income in capitalist states, the income differentiation in Soviet society is certainly less than in most western states. Comparative figures collected by Lenski indicate that in the USA the maximum income is 11,000 times the minimum and 7,000 times the average, whereas the comparative Soviet figures are only 300 times and 100 times respectively.[3] The ideology of 'building communism' together with collective ownership probably accounts for the much lower Soviet differential.

The changes described above in Soviet policy since the revolution indicate that the political elite in the USSR has been constrained by economic and social laws which operate in a similar way as in western society. The history of the changes in wage differentials illustrates that the system of wage differentiation could only be changed within limits. The inequality demanded by a quickly industrialising social structure overcame the leaders' early egalitarian aims and induced a change in the belief system to justify it. As Margaret Dewar has concluded:

The organisational structure of the Soviet labour force up to the time of Stalin's death displayed no essentially novel or advanced methods of disciplining labour and increasing productivity which had not been employed in the West. By and large, the industrialisation of the USSR showed features also inherent in the periods of

---

[1] K. Kedrova, 'Tekhnicheski progress i material'naya zainteresovannost', *Planovoe khozyaystvo*, no. 6, 1966, p. 12.

[2] T. B. Bottomore, *Classes in Modern Society*, p. 47.

[3] Gerhard E. Lenski, *Power and Privilege* (New York, 1966), pp. 312-3. See also J. A. Newth, 'Income Distribution in the USSR', *Soviet Studies*, No. 12 (1960/61), p. 196.

industrialisation of other countries, modified, of course, by contemporary methods of production and labour incentives . . .[1]

While such income differences give rise to privilege in consumption, we must bear in mind that many goods and services are excluded from the market and therefore *income* inequality may not be as significant as in western societies. Let us now turn from the study of income inequality to other forms of social hierarchy.

Hierarchy in Soviet Society

Inkeles has used a combination of measures to determine stratum membership: occupation, income, power and authority being the main elements.[2] Though he does not explain precisely how he measures group cohesion he defines ten 'major social-class groups' as follows. The intelligentsia he divides into four main units:

1. The ruling elite, a small group consisting of high party, government, economic, and military officials, prominent scientists, and selected artists and writers.
2. The superior intelligentsia, composed of the intermediary ranks of the categories mentioned above, plus certain important technical specialists.
3. The general intelligentsia, incorporating most of the professional groups, the middle ranks of the bureaucracy, managers of small enterprises, junior military officers, technicians, etc.
4. The white collar group, largely synonymous with the Soviet term for employees, which ranges from petty bureaucrats through accountants and book-keepers down to the level of ordinary clerks and office workers.

The working class Inkeles groups into three main strata:

1. The working class 'aristocracy', that is, the most highly skilled and productive workers, in particular large numbers of the so-called Stakhanovites [i.e. highly paid 'rate busters'].
2. The rank-and-file workers, those in one of the lesser skilled grades slightly above or below the average wage for all workers.
3. The disadvantaged workers, estimated to include as many as one-fourth of the labour force, whose low level of skill and lack of productivity or initiative kept them close to the minimum wage level.

[1] M. Dewar, 'Labour and Wage Reforms in the USSR, *Studies on the Soviet Union* (Munich) vol. 3, no. 3 (1962), p. 80. See also for a similar view E. C. Brown, *Soviet Trade Unions and Labour Relations* (Cambridge, Mass., 1966), p. 44.
[2] A. Inkeles, 'Social Stratification and Mobility in the Soviet Union 1940-1950', *American Sociological Review*, vol. 15 (1950), reprinted in A. Inkeles and K. Geiger, *Soviet Society* (1961).

The peasantry had two main sub-groups:

1. The well-to-do peasants, consisting of those particularly advantaged by virtue of the location, fertility, or crop raised by their collective farms – i.e. those living on the so-called 'millionaire' farms – and those whose trade, skill or productivity pushes them into the higher income brackets even on the less prosperous farms.
2. The average peasant, shading off into the least productive or poor peasant groups.

Finally, a separate group of those in forced labour camps who according to Inkeles, were 'outside the formal class structure' and had its own social structure derived from the structure of the society as a whole.

While the ranks within each main stratum are shown above, they do not coincide with the ranking of each sub-group within the society as a whole which Inkeles says was as follows:[1]

1	Ruling elite
2	Superior intelligentsia
3	General intelligentsia
4	Working class aristocracy
5.5	White collar
5.5	Well-to-do peasants
7	Average workers
8.5	Average peasants
8.5	Disadvantaged workers
10	Forced labour

The main drawback to Inkeles's classification is that the subjects were drawn from a group living in Russia before the Second World War. Another estimate is that of Wädekin who, on the basis of the 1959 census, has attempted to define and quantify the social strata. His hierarchy has four main divisions: upper, upper-middle, lower-middle and lower.[2] In fact it is very similar to Inkeles's, save that the latter's final two categories are ignored. While Inkeles's top three groups follow quite closely the economic stratification, there are some examples of an economic sub-group being ranked in a different order in the status hierarchy i.e., the working class aristocracy coming above the white collar worker, and the well-to-do peasants are ranked above the average workers. Inkeles asserts that these groups 'had begun to develop fairly definitive styles of life, to elaborate differential patterns of association and to manifest varying degrees of group-consciousness'.[3] Such a pattern of stratification including occupational prestige, level of income and political authority brings the social structure of Soviet society closer in kind to that of other

---

[1] A. Inkeles, *op. cit.*, p. 560.

[2] See Karl-Eugen Wädekin, *Ost Europa*, no. 5 (1965).

[3] Inkeles, p. 561.

O*

Table 40. Ranking of Soviet Occupations According to their General Desirability, Material Position, Personal Satisfaction, Safety and Popular Support*

Occupation	General desirability	Material position	Personal satisfaction	Safety (from arrest)	Popular regard
Doctor	1	7	3	2½	1
Scientific worker	2½	5	4	9	2
Engineer	2½	6	5	12	3
Factory Manager	4½	2	2	13	10
Foreman	4½	9	7½	7	6
Accountant	6	8	7½	5½	8
Officer in armed forces	7	3	6	10½	9
Teacher	8	11	10	4	4
Rank and file worker	9	12	12	1	5
Farm brigade leader	10	10	11	5½	11
Party secretary	11	1	1	8	13
Collective farm chairman	12	4	9	10½	12
Rank and file collective farmer	13	13	13	2½	7

* Based on written questionnaires completed by 2,146 former Soviet citizens, who were in displaced persons' camps in Germany (1,505) or who had emigrated to the USA (1950–51).

Inter-Correlations among Ratings

	Desirability (1)	Material position (2)	Personal satisfaction (3)	Safety (4)	Popular regard (5)
Desirability (1)	—	+.67	+.898	−.401	+.525
Material position (2)	+.67	—	+.92	−.818	−.180
Personal satisfaction (3)	+.898	+.92	—	−.644	+.167
Safety (4)	−.401	−.818	−.644	—	+.301
Popular regard (5)	+.525	−.180	+.167	+.301	—

Source: P. H. Rossi, A. Inkeles, 'Multidimensional Ratings of Occupations', Sociometry, Vol. 20, No. 3 (1957), p. 247.

modern industrial societies than Stalin's view of the USSR as a morally and politically unique society.

The relative honour or status of different occupations may be shown quantitatively by data from the Harvard project reported in *Sociometry*. Table 40 lists 13 different occupations ranked by 'general desirability', 'material position', 'personal satisfaction', 'safety' and 'popular regard'.[1] Even if the nature of the sample and the conditions in Europe at the time of the survey lead to caution in accepting the findings as typical for the USSR as a whole, by considering the differences in the four columns we may make at least three fairly safe inferences. Party secretaries are ranked highly in both material position (1) and personal satisfaction (1), while low in terms of 'desirability' (11) and popular regard (13); we may infer that political stratification and status stratification are not highly correlated. A second important implication of the table is that material position is not highly correlated with social esteem. The top four in the popular regard column are not in the top four of the material means. A third characteristic, to which I shall return later, is the similarity of the high social status groups (i.e. general desirability) with their counterparts in capitalist countries.

The intercorrelation matrix shown on Table 40, brings out more clearly the relationship between the variables. Row 2 shows the very high positive correlation between material position and personal satisfaction (0.92); and row 1 the high correlation again between desirability and personal satisfaction (0.898). The negative association (-0.818) between material position and personal safety indicates a feeling of 'high risk' for the higher occupational positions – particularly for the factory manager. It might be inferred from this that social mobility was hindered by the terror of the Stalin era; more competent men preferring a safe but modest occupation, rather than the risky highly paid. The authors of the study conclude that 'the *personal satisfaction* which inheres in the job is the prime determinant of its rated *desirability*'.[2] The 'popular regard' (row 5) associations do not show highly positive correlations on all scores, and with material position (column 2), there is even a negative association. The data here suggest rather a differentiated social system, with values being allocated separately on criteria – such as power, safety, popular regard, and material position – rather than a highly stratified society with such indexes showing a positive correlation throughout. This result is what one perhaps should expect when a society is in flux and characterised by rapid social and political change.

The Rossi and Inkeles survey is now rather dated and unfortunately we have no recent comparable survey from Soviet sources. Research in Leningrad

---

[1] Based on data given in P. H. Rossi and A. Inkeles, 'Multidimensional Ratings of Occupations', *Sociometry*, vol. 20, no. 3 (1957).

[2] *Ibid*, pp. 250-1.

Table 41. Some Aspects of the Social Structure of Leningrad Engineering Workers

Group of Workers	Education (Years)	Wages Rubles (monthly)	Party/Komsomol membership (%)	Participation in social work (%)
1. Management (Factory directors, shop superintendents)	13.6	172.9	60.8	84.2
2. Workers in highly qualified technical-scientific jobs (designers)	14.0	127.0	40.2	70.4
3. Qualified non-manual workers (technologists, book-keepers)	12.5	109.8	42.8	82.4
4. Highly qualified workers in jobs with mental and manual functions (tool setters)	8.8	129.0	37.6	79.2
5. Qualified workers of superior manual work (fitters, welders)	8.3	120.0	37.4	60.7
6. Qualified manual workers (machine-tool operators, press operators)	8.2	107.5	39.5	54.3
7. Non-manual workers of medium qualifications (inspection and office workers)	9.1	83.6	27.1	54.5
8. Unqualified manual workers	6.5	97.5	13.8	35.1

Source: Adapted from O. I. Shkaratan, 'Sotsial'naya struktura sovetskogo rabochego klassa', *Voprosy filosofii,* No. 1 (1967), p. 36.

illustrates how earnings are related to other factors – education, party membership and voluntary participation in social work. Some of the results of the survey are shown on Table 41. The wage differential shows that managerial personnel receive on average, just under double the income of unqualified workers. This does not exclude, of course, a greater range between the factory director and labourers as bonus payments and other non-monetary rewards may not have been counted in the survey.[1] Highly qualified production workers are the second most highly paid in the factory. Clerical workers, despite their relatively higher education, are the lowest paid, receiving even less than the unqualified manual workers.

The striking conclusion to be drawn from the table is the high positive correlation between the four factors: education, wages, party membership and social work. This is shown on the intercorrelation matrix below.

Spearman Rank Correlation Matrix

	Education	Wages	Party Membership	Social work
Education	—	.52	.71	.76
Wages	.52	—	.67	.79
Party Membership	.71	.67	—	.81
Social work	.76	.79	.81	—

From the data presented we may make some inference about stratification. At one end of the table (Group 1) we see a group which is highly educated, has high income, very high Party/Komsomol membership (60.8 per cent) and good participation in voluntary work. At the other end, the unqualified manual workers seem to constitute a relatively deprived group having low incomes, with a very short education (only 6.5 years), a small proportion of party members (only 13.8 per cent), and their participation in voluntary work (35.1 per cent) is also minimal. Unlike the Rossi and Inkeles survey, this work, with the positively correlated factors of education, wages, party membership and voluntary work, suggests a 'consistent' system of stratification.

While Soviet research is deficient on the status of particular social groups, studies conducted in the west on the prestige given to different occupations show a high correlation between their ranking in the USSR and other industrial countries. The correlation of matched occupations between the Soviet Union and other countries is highly positive: with Japan it was 0.74, Great Britain 0.83, New Zealand 0.83, United States 0.9 and Germany 0.9.[2] Some notable differences, however, show up in Inkeles's and Rossi's research. The 'worker' was given a relatively higher ranking in the USSR than in the USA,

[1] Also the factory director is included in these statistics with other managerial personnel.

[2] Soviet data were derived from interviews with emigres. A. Inkeles and P. H. Rossi, 'National Comparisons of Occupational Prestige', *American Journal of Sociology*, January 1956, no. 61 (4), p. 333.

Great Britain and New Zealand; and engineers were also given a higher rating in the Soviet Union than in the USA. At the other extreme, farmers were all rated lower in the USSR than in the USA, Great Britain and New Zealand, and scientists have less prestige than in the USA.[1] It is difficult to measure and compare how these status perceptions and 'ranks' manifest themselves in social relations. We have no detailed studies to go by but only personal observations and subjective opinions. While the feeling that 'Jack's as good as his master' is widespread in the USSR, status differences are also important and are illustrated in the following quotation from Solzhenitsyn's *Cancer Ward* in which a party official discusses his son's marriage.

> He was such a naïve boy, he might be led up the garden path by some ordinary weaver girl from the textile factory. Well, perhaps not a weaver, there'd be nowhere for them to meet, they wouldn't frequent the same places . . . Look at Shendyapin's daughter, how she'd very nearly married a student in her year at teachers' training college. He was only a boy from the country and his mother was an ordinary collective farmer. Just imagine the Shendyapin's flat, their furniture and the influential people they had as guests and suddenly there's this old woman in a white headscarf sitting at their table, their daughter's mother-in-law, and she didn't even have a passport. Whatever next? Thank goodness they'd managed to discredit the fiancé politically and save their daughter.[2]

This extract makes clear that in the USSR some social groups are inferior to others and are treated as such.

While the data available to us do not allow very firm conclusions to be drawn, it does seem likely that despite the ways in which Soviet society is structurally different from western industrial systems, 'there is a relatively invariable hierarchy of prestige associated with the industrial system, even when it is placed in the context of larger social systems which are otherwise differentiated in important respects'.[3] The relatively lower rank given to 'farmers' in the USSR, is partly a reflection of the different structure of agriculture and coincides not only with their lower political standing in the USSR but also with the relatively unskilled work of the collective farmer. The higher status given to 'workers' in the USSR is quite important and shows the influence of political ideology in the social sphere.[4] What is particularly interesting to note in the

[1] *Ibid.*, p. 334.

[2] Solzhenitsyn, *Cancer Ward*, pp. 212-3. Internal passports are not generally issued to peasants, thereby their occupational and geographical mobility is restricted.

[3] Inkeles, *loc. cit.*, p. 339. See also the extension of this work by Robert W. Hodge *et al*, 'A Comparative Study of Occupational Prestige', in R. Bendix and S. M. Lipset, *Class, Status and Power* (second ed., 1967).

[4] It is relevant here to point out that a recent study in Poland explicitly using the methods of Inkeles and Rossi shows a positive correlation of the rankings of occupational prestige hierarchies between Warsaw and USA to be 0.884, Warsaw/England 0.862, Warsaw/West Germany 0.879. Adam Sarapata, 'Stratification and Social Mobility', in *Empirical Sociology in Poland* (Warsaw, 1966), p. 41. Skilled workers are rated higher and white collar workers lower in Poland than in western advanced societies (*ibid.*, p. 42).

Soviet case are not only the high status given to the worker, a value engendered by Marxist ideology, but also the high evaluation of the professional employees – a factor shared with the West.

Social Mobility

The hierarchical arrangement of Soviet social strata raises the question of social mobility between them. How far are there distinct self-recruiting strata and how far are the top positions equally accessible to different social groups lower down the hierarchy?

During the Stalin era not only were wage differentials increased but other privileges also accrued to the rich. During the Second World War, access to higher education (and the top three classes of secondary schools) was made conditional, in most cases, on the payment of fees. The rationing system and shops restricted to higher strata strengthened status differentials as did inheritance being taxed at lower rates[1] and the highest decorations in the armed forces being restricted only to the top ranks. In addition, after the Second World War, the family as a unit was strengthened. These factors tended to reduce mobility.

Other factors worked in an opposite direction. Very rapid industrialisation, particularly between 1928 and 1939, provided a large number of skilled and executive jobs associated with the factory system. The changes in the social structure are illustrated by the official figures cited below. (Table 42). The proportion of manual and non-manual workers rose from 17.6 per cent to 50.2 per cent of the employed population, though these figures included, of course, workers on state farms.

Table 42. Official Figures of Soviet Social Change 1913–1968

	1913	1928	1939	1959	1968
Manual and non-manual workers	17.0	17.6	50.2	68.3	77.7
Collective famers and co-operative handicraftsmen	—	2.9	47.2	31.4	22.27
Independent peasants and handicraftsmen	66.7	74.9	2.6	0.3	0.03
Bourgeoisie	16.3	4.6	—	—	—
	100.0	100.0	100.0	100.0	100.0

Source: Narodnoe khozyaystvo SSSR v 1968g. (1969), p. 35

Between 1928 and 1937 the numbers employed in industrial production increased by 268 per cent and between 1931 and 1961, the number of manual workers increased three-fold, that of engineers five-fold and other non-manual

[1] For details see A. Inkeles, 'Social Stratification and Mobility', loc. cit.

employees by 33 per cent.[1] In addition to the effects of industrialisation the purges depleted the higher ranks of the bureaucracy and provided extra opportunity for upward mobility and the war, with the terrific loss of older experienced manpower, also created greater possibilities for rapid social mobility.

The table and figures cited illustrate the changes in the general composition of Soviet society since the revolution. They imply considerable upward social mobility, for the increase in the size of the intelligentsia and working class presumes recruitment from the peasantry (in at least one of the categories) though this does not preclude a high rate of internal recruitment from the intelligentsia itself. The results of the survey of Russian émigrés reported by Inkeles and Bauer show that access to higher education and therefore to high status occupations was differentially related to social background. (This will be discussed in the section on education, see Chapter 14). Inkeles has generalised this tendency by saying that 'as stratification has become institutionalised there has been a noticeable tendency for social mobility to decline and for the system to become less an open class structure.'[2]

However, it certainly would not be correct to think that the social horizons of lower social strata have been lowered. Aspiration for higher social position is widespread. Of 2,518 parents surveyed in Sverdlovsk, 64 per cent wanted a higher education for their children. The aspirations were greatest among the 'specialists' (workers with professional qualifications) of whom 89 per cent wanted higher education for their children, the figure fell to 64.9 per cent for workers and 36.2 per cent for collective farmers.[3] These figures show a terrific demand for higher education and, indirectly, high social position. The 'institutionalisation' of status position referred to by Inkeles, therefore, must take place in the process of educational selection.

It is likely, as Inkeles points out, that those who have legitimately acquired privilege in the system will seek to preserve it and pass it on to their children. In 1938, for instance, 47 per cent of the student body was made up of children with intelligentsia background.[4] Again we have no comprehensive statistics for recent Soviet developments. Soviet sociologists tend to emphasise the opportunities for upward mobility. For example, a study by Rutkevitch of full-time students in the Sverdlovsk Mining Institute illustrates the changing composition of its full-time students which is shown on Table 43.

[1] See V. S. Semenov, 'Ob izmenenii intelligentsii i sluzhashchikh v protsesse razvernutogo stroitel'stva kommunizma', *Sotsiologiya v SSSR*, vol. 1, p. 422. A. G. Rashin, 'Dinamika promyshlennykh kadrov SSSR za 1917-58gg,' *Izmeneniya v chislennosti i sostave sovetskogo rabochego klassa* (Moscow, 1961), p. 29.

[2] *Loc. cit.*, p. 571.

[3] Ya M. Tkach, 'Roditeli o sud'bakh svoikh detey', *Protesessy izmeneniya sotsial'noy struktury v Sovetskom obshchestve* (Sverdlovsk, 1967), p. 145.

[4] *Kul'turnoe stroitel'stvo SSSR* (Moscow, 1940), p. 114. Cited by A. Inkeles, *loc. cit.*, p. 572.

Table 43. Social Structure of Full-time Students in Sverdlovsk Mining Institute 1940, 1955, 1961, 1963

Year of	Social Origins (%)*			Social Position (%)†			
Observation	Workers	Employees	Peasants	Workers	Employees	Peasants	Students
1940	33.4	30.2	36.4	4.6	5.9	—	85.5
1955	27.7	57.3	15.0	5.1	9.6	—	84.3
1961	59.8	25.0	15.2	62.8	20.2	3.0	14.0
1963	61.7	25.0	13.3	61.9	25.0	—	13.1

Source: M. N. Rutkevitch, 'Izmenenie sotsial'noy struktury sovetskogo obshchestva i intelligentsiya', Sotsiologiya v SSSR, Vol. 1, p. 412

* Social origin denotes occupation of father.
† Social position is first or current occupation of person.

The table shows the increasing number of children of working class origin entering the institute: a rise of 28.3 per cent between 1940 and 1963. The increase in numbers of students with a working class 'social position' (from 4.6 per cent to 61.9 per cent), reflects the practice of selecting students from men who had already had production experience after school. Of course, one might expect such a large proletarian intake in a technological institute and Rutkevitch goes on to cite other statistics. In 1963 children from working class families accounted for 51 per cent of full-time students at the Urals university, and 42 per cent at the Sverdlovsk medical institute. At a teacher's training college in 1962–63, children from working class families constituted 66.8 per cent of the intake.[1]

Rather greater inequality has been found among evening and correspondence course students. Of students at various institutes of higher education in Sverdlovsk, 47.1 per cent of the evening students and 63.5 per cent of the correspondence students were either non-manual workers or the children of this stratum. It is clear that non-manual workers predominate among the students to a far greater extent than in the population as a whole. The lack of opportunity for peasants is also noteworthy: of evening students they accounted for 0.4 per cent and 0.9 per cent of the correspondence group. The working class students tend to be clustered in the polytechnic, the railway and mining institute, and the economics institute, whereas in teaching and law, at the conservatory and university, non-manual workers or their children are predominant.[2]

Advancement to positions of authority in industry would probably be more open to children of manual workers than to other strata. In Shkaratan's survey of Leningrad workers 54.2 per cent of factory chiefs were of manual worker and

[1] Loc. cit., pp. 412-3.
[2] See Protsessy izmeneniya sotsial'noy struktury v Sovetskom obshchestve (Sverdlovsk, 1967), pp. 133, 139.

Table 44. Composition and Social Origin of Directing Personnel in Factories GPZ-6 and UKZ (%)

Category of Worker	Social Origin			Began work as:			Specialist	Party Membership
	Worker	Peasant	Non-Manual Worker	Worker	Peasant	White-Collar		
Directors of work on a factory scale:								
GPZ-6	28	48	24	52	12	16	20	76
UKZ	27	27	46	23	12	11	54	73
Shop Managers:								
GPZ-6	46	38	16	77	—	—	23	61
UKZ	67	33	—	67	—	—	33	83

Source: Protsessy izmeneniya sotsial'noy struktury v Sovetskom obshchestve (Sverdlovsk, 1967), p. 194.

collective farm family background.[1] Most seem to have worked their way up through the factory. This evidence is corroborated by S. T. Guryanov, who found that of a thousand workers in a Moscow electrical engineering factory who started work as semi-skilled operators, 14 were promoted after ten years experience to engineer or technical status.[2] E. C. Brown, on a visit to 19 factories, found that at least fourteen of the factory directors had begun as manual workers. 'In their family origin and in part their work experience most of these directors and their chief engineers and other technical and adminis-trative people had a common bond with workers and union officers'.[3]

A survey of staff and workers at two factories in the Urals shows that a large proportion of the 'directing personnel' are of worker and peasant background. Some of the data in this survey are given above (Table 44).

Here we see that 48 per cent of the top management at GPZ-6 and over 27 per cent at UKZ were of peasant social origin. Note also the high proportion who began work as manual workers: at GPZ-6 52 per cent of the directors and 77 per cent of the shop managers. These men worked their way up and many were able to study in their spare time.

A second index of the degree to which the 'middle class' is passing on its privilege, is another study by Rutkevitch of scientists employed at the Eastern Coal-Chemical (Research) Institute. Here 56.6 per cent of the scientists were from non-manual families which make up 25 per cent of the total population. Of scientists under 30 years of age, 23.4 per cent were of parents from the higher intelligentsia, and 46.8 per cent from other middle class strata. While of the scientists aged over 50 years, 17.5 were of peasant origin, only 4.3 per cent the young scientists (under 30) were of such stock.[4]

Opportunities would seem to be more generally available for upward social mobility in industrial production than in research where the superior cultural background of the non-manual worker gives his children a great advantage. This tendency seems to have been strengthened in recent years in the USSR. Even so, compared to western societies, social promotion is probably relatively easier.

These figures confirm what was said earlier about the ways family back-ground influenced fulfilment of children's educational aspirations. There can be no doubt that in the USSR the social position of parents plays a most important role in determining the education and, therefore, the subsequent social standing of children.

It is not wished to imply that the Soviet regime intentionally restricts mobility. After 1956, tuition fees were abolished in education and in recent

[1] *Loc. cit.*, p. 39.

[2] 'Vertical mobility of employees in an enterprise', in G. V. Osipov, *Industry and Labour . . .*, p. 126.

[3] E. C. Brown, *Soviet Trade Unions and Labor Relations* (Cambridge, Mass., 1966), p. 175.

[4] *Klassy, sotsial'nye sloi i gruppy v SSSR* (Moscow, 1968), p. 160.

years children of lower educational strata (manual workers and collective farm peasantry) were given special consideration for admission to *vuzy*.[1] For instance, in Lvov Polytechnic admission standards are related to the social position of candidates – the children of workers, peasants and lower employees having to fulfill lower requirements than those of the intelligentsia.[2] In 1969, arrangements were announced for setting-up special preparatory departments in universities to prepare workers and peasants lacking formal requirements.[3] The regulations demanding practical work experience also tended to work in favour of lower strata children. Other acts have been passed intended to reduce social distance between strata: wage differentials have been reduced, minimum wages have been raised and old age and disability pensions have been increased.

Nevertheless, despite the attempts of the Soviet government to reduce inequality, the operation of general social laws has inhibited social mobility in the USSR as they have in western societies. Social position, based on the division of labour, is a common characteristic of all modern urban industrial societies. Perfect social mobility is prevented because those with scarce skills and specialist training are able within their family sphere to perpetuate the advantages which these skills and training give them. The strengthening of the Soviet family has encouraged this tendency, though the family's right to transmit a claim on the appropriation of the social product does not pertain as in the West. On the other hand, upward social mobility has probably been greater in Soviet Russia than in contemporary western societies. This upward mobility may only partially be accounted for by 'communist' values. Forces engendered by the rapid industrialisation process entailed the recruitment, training and upward mobility of previous lower strata.

Socialism and Egalitarianism

What then are the implications of Soviet experience for the more general questions raised at the beginning of the chapter?

First, the evidence shows that Soviet society is not and has never been at any time in its history, 'classless': social inequality is a universal social phenomenon.

Second, the forms of social stratification in the USSR differ from those of western liberal societies. There is no property-owning class; large-scale industrial societies, therefore, can function without the *private* accumulation of property and the inequalities to which it gives rise. This is now an obvious, though most important, conclusion to be drawn from Soviet experience.

Third, the functionalists' view that inequality is necessary – (a) to induce

---

[1] Higher Educational Institutions.
[2] K. Tidmarsh, *The Times*, 20 Nov. 1968.
[3] See *Soviet News*, 28 Oct. 1969, p. 46, and below, p. 508.

individuals into positions requiring special skills and abilities; (b) to reward them differentially so that their tasks may be efficiently carried out – has been substantiated in Soviet conditions. It is sometimes said, by radicals and egalitarians, that if one could change the values or socialisation pattern of a society, then inferiority could be abolished. In other words, if people do not believe in inequality they do not take cognisance of income, power, or occupational differentials in their social relationships. The trouble with this argument is that it does not explain the conditions under which such a value pattern or socialisation process can take place. Both the process of the division of labour and the maintenance and socialisation functions of the family preclude such a development in modern society. Occupations differentiate the roles of individuals, and as long as these are specific, intellectual or creative occupations will always be more highly valued by members of society because they are inherently more agreeable, they also promote a way of life culturally distinct from those occupied in routine, manual jobs. A necessary condition of a truly classless society, is, as Marx long ago pointed out, the absence of the division of labour. The family, even if its legal rights over property are abolished, differentially socialises children; by doing so, it makes the inculcation of universal social mores difficult; it also makes some children more capable of benefitting from education than others. Thereby inequality is perpetuated. Under the conditions of industrial production known to us, both in state socialist and capitalist societies, the division of labour is more specialised and the family is as persistent as it ever has been. As far as Marxist theory is concerned, the existence of social inequality *under the industrial conditions inherited by the Soviet communists* has never been in doubt. The main dispute in the USSR has been over the ratio between the richest and the poorest and in practice this ratio is now very much lower than in western societies.

Fourth, political elites play an important role in *defining* the inequalities, or the system of positions in which one is rewarded more than in another. In the USSR, engineers, Academicians and coal miners get higher pay than doctors. The recruitment of doctors does not depend on a high reward 'commensurate with the sacrifice' necessary to undertake medical studies.[1] This reflects the political priorities of a society, which become embodied in an ideology that justifies a certain income inequality.

Fifth, while the political authorities may influence certain kinds of privilege, particularly income and education, they are subject to external social constraints. Some elements of a subjective status hierarchy transcend societies: here control over life itself, exercised by doctors, gives honour; those with technical qualifications in industrial societies and those who transmit knowledge similarly have a high status ranking.

Sixth, political values may affect the status of occupations: 'the worker' in

[1] Kingsley Davis, *Human Society*, p. 369.

Soviet society is more highly rated than in liberal-democratic ones; and perhaps more important, the ideology of 'building communism' has minimised the range of inequality between the richest and poorest and between men and women.

The last general conclusion to be drawn is that social inequality of one kind or another seems to be inevitable as long as societies are characterised by a division of labour, and as long as the family plays an important role in the maintenance of children.

Reading No. 15
J. Stalin on Wage Differentials in Soviet Society
Source:
'New Conditions – New Tasks in Economic Construction', in *Problems of Leninism*, Moscow, 1952, pp. 462-6.

WAGES

I have just spoken about the organised recruiting of workers for our factories. But recruiting workers is only part of the job. In order to ensure the necessary labour power for our factories we must see to it that the workers remain in the factories and that the latter have a more or less permanent personnel. It need hardly be proved that without a permanent labour force who have more or less mastered the technique of production and have become accustomed to the new machinery it will be impossible to make any headway, impossible to fulfil the production plans. Unless this is achieved, we shall have to keep on training new workers and to spend half the time on training them instead of making use of this time for production. What is actually happening now? Can it be said that our factories have a more or less permanent labour force? Unfortunately, this cannot be said. On the contrary, we still have a *heavy turnover* of labour power in our factories. Moreover, in a number of factories the turnover of labour power is not shrinking, but, on the contrary, is increasing and becoming more marked. At any rate, you will find few new factories where the personnel does not change at least to the extent of 30 to 40 per cent of the total in the course of a half year, or even in one quarter.

Formerly, during the period of restoration of our industry, when its technical equipment was not very complex and the scale of production not very large, it was more or less possible to 'tolerate' this so-called turnover of labour power. Now it is another matter. Conditions have changed radically. Now, in the period of intensive reconstruction, when the scale of production has become gigantic and technical equipment has become extremely complex, the heavy turnover of labour power has become the plague of production, which is disorganising our factories. To 'tolerate' the heavy turnover of labour power now would mean disintegrating our industry, it would mean wrecking the opportunities of fulfilling production plans and ruining the opportunities of improving the quality of the articles produced.

What is the cause of the heavy turnover of labour power?

The cause is the wrong structure of wages, the wrong wage scales, the 'Leftist' practice of wage equalisation. In a number of our factories wage scales are drawn up in such a way as to practically wipe out the difference between skilled and unskilled labour, between heavy and light work. The consequence of wage equalisation is that the unskilled worker lacks the incentive to become a skilled worker and is thus deprived of the prospect of advancement; as a result he feels himself a 'visitor' in the factory, working only temporarily so as to 'earn a little' and then go off to 'seek his fortune' elsewhere. The consequence of wage equalisation is that the skilled worker is obliged to wander from factory to factory until he finds one where his skill is properly appreciated.

Hence, the 'general' drift from factory to factory; hence, the heavy turnover of labour power.

In order to put an end to this evil we must abolish wage equalisation and discard the old wage scales. In order to put an end to this evil we must draw up wage scales that will take into account the difference between skilled and unskilled labour, between heavy and light work. We cannot tolerate a situation where a rolling-mill hand in a steel mill earns no more than a sweeper. We cannot tolerate a situation where a locomotive driver earns only as much as a copying clerk. Marx and Lenin said that the difference between skilled and unskilled labour would exist even under socialism, even after classes had been abolished; that only under communism would this difference disappear and that, consequently, even under socialism 'wages' must be paid according to work performed and not according to needs. But the equalitarians among our business executives and trade union officials do not agree with this and believe that under our Soviet system this difference has already disappeared. Who is right, Marx and Lenin, or the equalitarians? We must take it that it is Marx and Lenin who are right. But if that is so, it follows that whoever draws up wage scales on the 'principle' of wage equalisation, without taking into account the difference between skilled and unskilled labour, breaks with Marxism, breaks with Leninism.

In every branch of industry, in every factory, in every shop, there is a leading group of more or less skilled workers whom it is our immediate and urgent duty to retain in industry if we really want to secure for the factories a permanent labour force. These leading groups of workers are the essential element in production. By retaining them in the factory, in the shop, we can retain the whole personnel and put an end to the heavy turnover of labour power. But how can we retain them in the factories? We can retain them only by promoting them to higher positions, by raising the level of their wages, by introducing a system of wages that will give the worker his due according to qualification.

And what does promoting them to higher positions and raising their wage level imply as far as unskilled workers are concerned? It implies, apart from everything else, opening up prospects for the unskilled worker and giving him an incentive to rise higher, to rise to the category of a skilled worker. You know yourselves that we now need hundreds of thousands and even millions of skilled workers. But in order to build up cadres of skilled workers, we must provide an incentive for the unskilled workers, provide for them a prospect of advancement, of rising to a higher position. And the more boldly we do this the better; for this is the principal means of putting an end to the heavy labour turnover. To economise in this matter would be criminal, it would be going against the interests of our socialist industry.

But that is not all.

In order to retain the workers in the factories we must still further improve the supply of food and consumer goods for the workers and improve their housing conditions. It cannot be denied that a good deal has been accomplished during the last few years in the sphere of housing construction and as regards improving the supply of food and consumer goods for the workers. But what has been accomplished is altogether inadequate compared with the rapidly growing requirements of the workers. It will not do to plead that there were fewer houses before than there are now and that therefore we can rest content with the results achieved. Nor will it do to plead that workers' supplies were far worse before than they are now and therefore we can be satisfied with the present situation. Only those who are rotten to the core can content themselves with references to what existed in the past. We must proceed, not from the past, but from the growing requirements of the workers today. We must realise that the conditions of life of the workers have radically changed in our country. The worker today is not what he was before. The worker today, our Soviet worker, wants to have all his material and cultural needs satisfied: in respect of food, housing conditions, cultural and all other requirements. He has a right to this, and it is our duty to secure these conditions for him. True, our worker does not suffer from unemployment; he is free from the yoke of capitalism; he is no longer a slave, but the master of his job. But this is not enough. He demands that all his material and cultural requirements be met, and it is our duty to fulfil his demand. Do not forget that we ourselves are now presenting certain demands to the workers – we demand labour discipline, intense effort, emulation, shock work. Do not forget that the vast majority of workers have accepted these demands of the Soviet government with great enthusiasm and are fulfilling them heroically. Do not be surprised, therefore, if, while fulfilling the demands of the Soviet government, the workers in their turn demand that the Soviet government should fulfil its pledge further to improve their material and cultural condition.

Hence, the task is *to put an end to the heavy turnover of labour power, to do away with wage equalisation, to organise wages properly and to improve the living conditions of the workers.*

This is the position with regard to the second new condition of development of our industry.

FOR FURTHER STUDY

INTRODUCTORY

Bottomore, T. B. *Classes in Modern Society*. London: Ampersand, 1955.
Conquest, R. (ed.). *Industrial Workers in the USSR*. London: Bodley Head, 1967.
Gunther, J. *Inside Russia Today*. London: Hamish Hamilton, 1962.
Kostin, L. *Wages in the USSR*. Moscow, 1960.

BASIC

Bergson, A. *The Structure of Soviet Wages: A Study in Socialist Economics*. Cambridge, Mass.: Harvard University Press, 1954.

Brown, E. C. *Soviet Trade Unions and Labor Relations*. Cambridge, Mass.: Harvard University Press, 1966.

Dewar, M. 'Labour and Wage Reforms in the USSR', *Studies on the Soviet Union* (Munich), Vol. 1, No. 3, 1962, pp. 80-91.

DeWitt, N. *Education and Professional Manpower in the USSR*. Washington: National Research Council, 1961.

Glezerman, G. 'Sotsial'naya struktura sotsialisticheskogo obshchestva', *Kommunist*, No. 13, 1968, pp. 28-39.

Hodge, R. W., *et al*. 'A Comparative Study of Occupational Prestige', in R. Bendix and S. M. Lipset (eds.), *Class, Status and Power*. London: Routledge and Kegan Paul, 1967, pp. 309-21.

Inkeles, A. and Rossi, P. H. 'National Comparisons of Occupational Prestige', in *American Journal of Sociology*, Vol. 61, No. 4, January 1956, pp. 329-39.

Inkeles, A. *Social Change in Soviet Russia*. Cambridge, Mass.: Harvard University Press, 1968.

Inkeles, A. 'Social Stratification and Mobility in the Soviet Union 1940-1950', *American Sociological Review*, Vol. 15, No. 4, 1950, pp.465-79. Reprinted in A. Inkeles and K. Geiger, *Soviet Society*. London: Constable, 1961, pp. 558-572.

Kerblay, Basile, 'The Russian Peasant', *St Antony's Papers*, No. 19. London, 1966.

Marx, K. 'Critique of the Gotha Program', in Marx and Engels, *Selected Works*, Vol. 2, London 1950, pp. 13-45.

The Poverty of Philosophy. London: Martin Lawrence, 1936.

Narodnoe khozyaystvo SSSR v 1968g. Moscow, 1969.

Newth, J. A. 'Income Distribution in the USSR', *Soviet Studies*, Vol. 12, 1960-61, pp. 193-96.

Obchinikova, E. P., and S. V. Brova. 'O likvidatsii ostatkov sotsial'nogo neravenstva rabochikh i rabotnits na promyshlennykh predpriyatiyakh', *Protsessy izmeneniya sotsial'noy struktury v sovetskom obshchestve*. Sverdlovsk, 1967.

Pod'yachich, P. G. *Naselenie SSSR*. Moscow, 1961.

Richman, B. M. *Management, Development and Education in the Soviet Union.* East Lansing, Michigan: Michigan University Press, 1967.

Rossi, P. H. and A. Inkeles. 'Multidimensional Ratings of Occupations', *Sociometry*, Vol. 20, No. 3, 1957, pp. 234-51.

Sarapata, A. 'Stratification and Social Mobility', in Jan Szczepanski (ed.), *Empirical Sociology in Poland.* Warsaw: Polish Scientific Publishers, 1966, pp. 37-52.

Stalin, J. 'New Conditions – New Tasks in Economic Construction', in *Problems of Leninism.* Moscow, 1952, pp. 459-82.

Sovremennoe Abkhazkoe selo. Tbilisi, 1967.

Trud v SSSR. Moscow, 1968.

Yanowitch, Murray. 'The Soviet Income Revolution', *Slavic Review*, Vol. 22, 1963, pp. 683-97.

SPECIALISED

Bodyul, I. I. *Preodolenie sushchestvennykh razlichiy mezhdu gorodom i derevney v usloviyakh Moldavskoy SSR.* Kishinev, 1967.

Crosland, C. A. R. *The Future of Socialism.* London: Cape, 1964 (abridged revised edition).

Diamond, D. B. 'Trends in Output, Inputs and Factor Productivity in Soviet Agriculture', Joint Economic Committee, US Congress, *New Directions in the Soviet Economy.* Washington: Government Printing Office, 1966, pp. 339-81.

Jenkins, Roy. 'Equality', in *New Fabian Essays.* London, 1952.

Karcz, J. F. 'Seven Years on the Farm: Retrospect and Prospects', Joint Economic Committee, US Congress, *New Directions in the Soviet Economy.* Washington: Government Printing Office, 1966, pp. 383-472.

Kedrova, K. 'Tekhnicheski progress i material'naya zainteresovannost', *Planovoe Khozyaystvo*, No. 6, 1966, pp. 10-18.

'Kolkhoznoe krest'yanstvo i sovetskaya derevnya na puti k kommunizmu', in *Klassy, sotsial'nye sloi i gruppy v SSSR.* Moscow, 1968, pp. 82-101.

Konstantinov, F. 'Sovetskaya intelligentsiya', *Kommunist*, No. 15, 1959, pp. 48-65.

Lenin, V. I. 'The Immediate Tasks of the Soviet Government', *Collected Works*, Vol 27. Moscow, 1965.

Lenski, G. E. *Power and Privilege. A Theory of Social Stratification.* New York: McGraw-Hill, 1966.

Makeenko, M. 'Ekonomicheskaya rol' lichnogo podsobnogo khozyaystva', *Voprosy ekonomiki*, No. 10, 1966, pp. 55-67.

Manevich, E. L. *Problemy obshchestvennogo truda v SSSR.* Moscow, 1966.

Mustinov, G. *Raschety po zarabotnoy plate rabochikh i sluzhashchikh.* Moscow, 1965.

Ossowski, S. *Class Structure in the Social Consciousness.* London: Routledge and Kegan Paul, 1963.

Parsons, T. 'An Analytical Approach to the Theory of Social Stratification', in *Essays in Sociological Theory, Pure and Applied.* Glencoe, Ill.: The Free Press, 1954, pp. 69-88.

Palladina, M. and L. Grebennikova. 'Garantirovannaya oplata truda v kolkhozakh', *Voprosy ekonomiki*, No. 11, 1966, pp. 25-33.

'Pod''em kultury kolkhoznogo sela', in *Klassy, sotsial'nye sloi i gruppy v SSSR*. Moscow, 1968, pp. 126-35.

Pravda, 27 Sept. 1967, pp. 1-2 (Decree on minimum wage).

Rashin, A. G. 'Dinamika promyshlennykh kadrov SSSR za 1917-58gg', in *Izmeneniya v chislennosti i sostave sovetskogo rabochego klassa*. Moscow, 1961.

Rutkevitch, M. N. 'Izmenenie sotsial'noy struktury sovetskogo obshchestva i intelligentsiya', in *Sotsiologiya v SSSR*, Vol. 1. Moscow, 1965.

Semenov, V. S. 'Ob izmenenii intelligentsii i sluzhashchikh v protsesse razvernutogo stroitel'stva kommunizma', *Sotsiologiya v SSSR*, Vol. 1. Moscow, 1963, pp. 416-30.

Shkaratan, O. I. 'Sotsial'naya struktura sovetskego rabochego klassa', *Voprosy filosofii*, No. 1, January 1967, pp. 28-39.

Smirnov, G. 'Rabochi klass SSSR', *Kommunist*, No. 4, March 1960, pp. 38-52.

'Sotsialisticheskoe proizvodstvo i razvitie rabochago klassa', in *Klassy, sotsial'nye sloi i gruppy v SSSR*. Moscow, 1968, pp. 47-81.

Stalin, J. 'Ekonomicheskie problemy sotsializma' (1952), *Sochineniya*, Vol. 16. Stanford. 1967.

Stalin, J. V. 'Talk with Emil Ludwig', in *Collected Works*, Vol. 13, Moscow.

Strukturnye izmeneniya v krest'yanstve', *Klassy, sotsial'nye sloi i gruppy v SSSR*. Moscow, 1968, pp. 102-25.

Tkach, Ya. M. 'Roditeli o sud'bakh svoikh detey', *Protsessy izmeneniya sotsial'noy struktury v sovetskom obshchestve*. Sverdlovsk, 1967.

Tumin, M. 'On Inequality', *American Sociological Review*, Vol. 28, No. 1, 1963, pp. 19-26.

Trud i zarabotnaya plata v SSSR. Moscow, 1968.

Tsentral'noe statisticheskoe upravlenie, *Kulturnoe stroitel'stvo*. Moscow, 1940.

Wädekin, Karl-Eugen. 'Sowjetisches Kleinstadtleben', *Osteuropa*, Vol. 15, No. 5, 1965, pp. 750-55.

13

SOCIAL DIFFERENTIATION

Social stratification is fundamentally concerned with hierarchy or inequality in society. But it is not the only or necessarily the most important basis for group differentiation. Nationality and religion are forms of group consciousness, which divide a society. They may transcend class and status boundaries, though they may also reinforce them. Nationality is a socio-cultural phenomenon, a sense of social unity being given by a common language, history, and literature. Religion is a system of values in which believers are united in their relationship to, and belief in, something sacred. Both nationality and religion are factors in the Soviet social structure. Today, the USSR is made up of over a hundred different national, tribal or linguistic groups. Great Russians constitute over half and twenty-two nationalities, 95 per cent of the population.[1] Though religious bodies have had a difficult time since the revolution, they still persist in an attenuated form. Both will be considered in this chapter.

NATIONALITIES

In general parlance a 'nation' is usually thought to be a large grouping of people united on the basis of a common culture. A nation is not always coterminous with a state or government, the Polish nation, for instance, has been divided between several states. A state or government is a political unit whereas a nation is a cultural community, having a common language, often a distinct religion, a sense of its own history and the consciousness of a common destiny. Stalin defined a nation as 'a historically constituted, stable community of people, formed on the basis of a common language, territory, economic life, and psychological make-up manifested in common culture'.[2]

Marxism and the National Question

How is the notion of nationality related to the Marxist view of class? This is a

---

[1] These are enumerated in Table 45, p. 43. As the birth rate of the Great Russians is falling relative to others, their share of the population is likely to fall in future.

[2] J. Stalin, 'Marxism and the National Question', *Collected Works* (Moscow, 1953), vol. 2. See Reading no. 16.

most complex matter and has resulted in much confusion in the literature of the subject. Theoretically, under conditions of socialism in which the proletariat is the ruling class and in which class contradictions have been abolished, class and nationality may be congruent: class providing the political basis of rule, and nationality, cultural values. Historically, however, the concept of nationality has developed with the emergence of the bourgeoisie for whom it provided an ideology. National conflict between states, Marxists argue, is epiphenomenal and a mere mask to their competing economic interests in the scramble for markets.

The concept of 'nation' engendered by the French Revolution involved the people or citizens of France as the repository of political power as opposed to the ousted monarchy. In Marxist analysis, the revolution only ensured the political supremacy of the bourgeoisie, for the workers had no share in the political control of the nation and therefore had no 'nation'. The struggle of the proletariat was not simply a class struggle against the bourgeoisie, but was also a struggle for the natural rights which the bourgeoisie proclaimed to belong to the workers. Therefore, a people's national liberation movement against the national bourgeoisie was an important stage in the class struggle.

Though not in substance, yet in form, the struggle of the proletariat with the bourgeoisie is at first a national struggle. The proletariat of each country must . . . first of all settle matters with its bourgeoisie. The working men have no country. We cannot take from them what they have not got. Since the proletariat must first of all acquire supremacy, must rise to be the leading class of the nation, must constitute itself *the* nation, it is, so far, itself national, though not in the bourgeois sense of the word.[1]

In other words, while national culture has developed under the bourgeoisie and under capitalism is controlled by it, the struggle for socialism by the workers involves them in securing their national heritage, making themselves the 'national' ruling class.

As nationalism was dependent on economic formations, it follows that as economic structures change, so does the nature of national consciousness. Marx observed that, with the growth of the world market, and uniform production relations, differences between national cultures would decline.

National differences and antagonisms between peoples are daily more and more vanishing, owing to the development of the bourgeoisie, to freedom of commerce, to the world market, to uniformity in the mode of production and in the conditions of life corresponding thereto . . .

In proportion, as the exploitation of one individual by another is put to an end, the exploitation of one nation by another will also be put to an end. In proportion,

[1] 'Communist Manifesto', *Marx & Engels, Selected Works*, vol. 1 (Moscow, 1958), pp. 217, 225.

POLITICS AND SOCIETY IN THE USSR

as the antagonism between classes within the nation vanishes, the hostility of one nation to another will come to an end.[1]

Economic development leads to larger economic and political units. Therefore the claims for independence of essentially rural national minorities (such as the Danes in Schleswig) were regarded by Marx as reactionary: the German right to the duchies was the 'right of civilisation against barbarism, of progress against stagnation'.[2]

Nationalism of the bourgeois era, therefore, according to the above extract from Marx, would develop into the internationalism of the socialist world. However, it is possible to interpret the development of society as entailing the abolition of national *antagonism* while encouraging *cultural* diversity. In fact, Marxists have differed in their attitude to national cultural values, some holding that under socialism they should flourish, others believing that with the development of internationalism, they would die a natural death. In the Soviet Union today a controversy rages between those supporting the assimilation of nations into one Soviet culture and others who stress the enduring nature of national sentiment and champion the cultural and political rights of minority nations.[3]

Nationalism has not been an important internal socio-political problem in Western European states in which, generally, the political order (the state) has been closely related to the national unit (Belgium, Switzerland and border areas of Germany are exceptions). In Eastern Europe, and especially in Russia before 1917, the national question was a major political issue. Nation and state generally did not coincide: Russia itself was made up of many national groups, though dominated by the Russian speaking, Orthodox Great Russians.

The Bolsheviks on the National Question

The national question raised itself in an acute form over the formation of a Russian social-democratic political party. Controversy raged over whether, after the bourgeois-democratic revolution, the Russian Empire should be balkanised or remain a single state. Advocates of the former asserted the rights of minority nationalities to form their own social-democratic parties. Lenin and the Bolsheviks supported the view that the class struggle was indivisible and that, therefore, the proletariat would weaken the class struggle by forming separate national parties. The Bund (The Jewish Social-Democratic Party in Russia and Poland), and socialist parties from the Baltic and Caucasus sought the exclusive right to represent the proletariat from their respective areas.

[1] *Loc. cit.*, p. 225.

[2] Engels, cited by E. H. Carr, *The Bolshevik Revolution 1917-1923*, vol. 1, p. 414.

[3] These views are discussed by Grey Hodnett, 'What's in a Nation?' *Problems of Communism*, vol. 16, no. 5 (Sept.-Oct. 1967).

Lenin and the Bolsheviks opposed this, arguing that the proletariat would be weakened by national autonomy.

But Lenin conceded that a nationality should have the right to secede. The party programme adopted in 1903 declared 'the right of self-determination for all nations comprising the state' (Para. 9).[1] Party policy also gave the right to national minorities of education in their own language and put native languages on equal terms with the main government language in all public affairs.

If one distinguishes between the bourgeois and socialist revolutions, some of the confusion over different statements by Lenin will be resolved. National independence had been associated with the bourgeois democratic revolution. Therefore, in support of it, the social-democrats had to recognise the right to secede. Otherwise, to deny it might sustain a feudal autocracy against a revolutionary democratic 'national' movement. For example, the fight for Finnish national independence was a struggle by the Finnish bourgeoisie against the Russian autocracy: such a *right* to independence, therefore, should not be opposed.[2]

But a right to secede did not imply favouring a balkanised form of independent states under socialism. For economic and political reasons, large units were preferable to small ones. Lenin likened the case of self-determination to divorce, which if granted would in some cases (but not necessarily all) strengthen family ties and the position of women. 'To accuse those who support freedom of self-determination, i.e. freedom to secede, of encouraging separatism, is as foolish and hypocritical as accusing those who advocate freedom of divorce of encouraging the destruction of family ties.'[3] Indeed, if secession should be against the interests of the proletariat, then it had to be opposed.

The demand for a 'yes' or 'no' reply to the question of secession in the case of every nation may seem a very 'practical' one. In reality, it is absurd; it is metaphysical in theory, while in practice it leads to subordinating the proletariat to the bourgeoisie's policy. The bourgeoisie always places its national demands in the forefront, and does so in categorical fashion. With the proletariat, however, these demands are subordinated to the interests of the class struggle. Theoretically, you cannot say in advance whether the bourgeois-democratic revolution will end in a given nation seceding from another nation, or in its equality with the latter; *in either case*, the important thing for the proletariat is to ensure the development of its class. For the bourgoisie it is important to hamper this development by pushing the aims of its 'own' nation before those of the proletariat. That is why the proletariat confines itself, so to speak, to the negative demand for recognition of the *right* to self-

---

[1] *Vtoroy s''ezd RSDRP: Protokoly* (Moscow, 1959), p. 421.

[2] See V. I. Lenin, 'The Right of Nations to Self-Determination' (1914), *Collected Works*, vol. 20 (Moscow, 1964), pp. 393-451.

[3] Lenin, 'The Right of Nations . . .', p. 422.

P

determination, without giving guarantees to any nation, and without undertaking to give *anything at the expense* of another nation.[1]

The national problem was essentially a short-term one. In the long-run, with the triumph of socialism, national boundaries would be destroyed and people would be united on a class basis. Under socialism, national autonomy would gradually be replaced by a measure of regional autonomy giving to local governments executive control in their area. This is how Stalin put it.

The advantage of regional autonomy consists . . . in the fact that it does not deal with a fiction bereft of territory but with a definite population inhabiting a definite territory. Next it does not divide people according to nations, it does not strengthen national barriers; on the contrary, it breaks down these barriers and unites the population in such a manner as to open the way for division of a different kind, division according to classes. Finally it makes it possible to utilise the natural wealth of the region and to develop its productive forces in the best possible way without awaiting the decisions of a common centre – functions which are not inherent features of cultural-national autonomy.[2]

National autonomy was necessary because the psychological consciousness of national identity would still prevail under socialism. Only in the communist epoch would nations merge. Until that stage was reached, under socialism nationality would persist in a different and even strengthened form:

The fact of the matter is that the elimination of the bourgeois nations signifies the elimination of not nations in general, but only of the bourgeois nations. On the ruins of the old, bourgeois nations, new socialist nations are arising and developing, and they are far more solidly united than any bourgeois nation, because they are exempt from the irreconcilable class contradictions that corrode the bourgeois nations, and are far more representative of the whole people than any bourgeois nation[3].

The main points in Bolshevik national policy may now be summarised. First, the equality of nations and languages was advocated. Second, a proletarian party divided on national lines was opposed. Third, the Bolsheviks supported the right of oppressed nations to secession and to form an independent state. Fourth, the granting of secession had to be reconcilable with the interests of the proletariat in the class struggle. Fifth, even in a socialist state concessions would have to be made to national consciousness, only under full communism would nations merge.

Soviet Nationalities Policy After the Revolution

The Tsarist Empire was multi-national.[4] The main slavonic groups are located in the Western and Central European parts of the country and eastwards,

[1] V. I. Lenin, 'The Rights of Nations to Self-Determination' *loc cit.*, p. 410.
[2] J. Stalin, 'Marxism and the National Question', *Collected Works* (1946), vol. 2, p. 375.
[3] J. V. Stalin, 'The National Question and Leninism', *Collected Works*, vol. 11, p. 355-56.
[4] For the national divisions of the population in 1897 and 1959, see Table 45.

Table 45. National Composition of the Population 1897, 1959*

	1897 Census Defined by language (Millions)	1959 Census Defined by nationality (Millions)
Total population	125.68	208.82
Russians	55.6	114.11
Ukrainians	22.3	37.25
Byelorussians	5.8	7.91
Uzbeks	.71	6.01
Tats	.94	—
Tatars	3.6	4.96
Kazakhs	4.0†	3.62
Azerbaidzhanies	1.47‡	2.93
Armenians	1.17	2.78
Georgians	.81	2.69
Lithuanians	1.20	2.32
Jews	4.9	2.26
Moldavians	1.11	2.21
Germans	1.78	1.61
Chuvases	.84	1.46
Latvians	1.42	1.39
Tadzhiks	.34	1.39
Poles	7.8	1.38
Mordvinians	1.01	1.28
Turkmenians	.27	1.00
Bashkirs	1.31	.989
Estonians	.99	.988
Kirgiz	4.0†	.968
Other nationalities§	—	7.000

Sources: Itogi vszsoyuznoy perepisi naseleniya 1959g. SSSR (svodny tom) (Moscow, 1962), pp. 184-9, *Pervaya vseobshchaya perepis' naseleniya rossiyskoy imperii 1897g.* (Obshchi svod), Vol. 2 (Spb. 1905), Table XIII.

* The statistics are not strictly comparable because the areas of the countries have changed, and for the 1897 census the basis of classification is language spoken, while for the 1959 census the basis is 'nationality'.

† Kazakhs and Kirgis undifferentiated in 1897 census.

‡ *Source:* R. Pipes, *The Formation of the Soviet Union* (Harvard University Press, New York, 1954), p. 12.

§ Most of the 103 other nationalities were less than a quarter of a million in 1959.

through emigration, to the Urals and Siberia (See Map 1, p. 31). Though slavonic, the Poles, Ukrainians and Great Russians formed distinct national groups with separate cultural identities; the Poles were Catholic by religion whereas the other slavonic groups were Orthodox. In the Baltic provinces (forming the present states of Estonia, Lithuania and Latvia), Indo-European languages quite different from Russian were spoken. Each of these countries has a distinct cultural tradition and history. Finland, though part of the Russian Empire, had a special status and was relatively more independent than other provinces having, even before the revolution, its own parliament, official language and currency, and separate army and educational system. In the Caucasus lived the Armenians, Georgians, Persians and Tatars, the most important and developed nationalities being the first two. In Central Asia and Siberia were a multitude of indigenous peoples, and some nomadic tribes. Colonisation and population movement meant that most areas had small Russian minorities. It is important to remember that the workers taking part in the industrialisation of the Ukraine were to quite a large extent Great Russian from the central areas. The skilled workers and overseers in the Azerbaidzhan oil industry were also Russians. In fact, excluding the Polish provinces, of the industrial working class, some three-quarters were Russian. What was to happen to national relations after the revolution?

The political fate of these national areas depended partly on geography, partly on the popular support enjoyed by the Bolsheviks and partly on the ability of the new Soviet government to enforce its decisions.[1] Poland, Finland, Lithuania, Latvia and Estonia all became established states. They were all (except Finland) under German occupation at the time of the revolution and had strong anti-Russian counter elites. Their geography allowed for successful intervention by the western powers in support of their independence. Despite the presence of Russian immigrants in some of the Baltic provinces, grass roots support for unification with Russia was miniscule. In these countries, national social-democratic parties were strongest and they favoured separation. In Finland, a capable bourgeoisie and in Poland a powerful land-owning elite led strong national liberation movements. Lenin's principle of secession was applied to these states. The Baltic states were established in the early 1920s until they were reoccupied by Soviet forces in the early 1940s and subsequently absorbed as national republics into the USSR.

The Ukraine had a more complex national and class structure. The land-owning elite was mainly Polish and Russian, and the petty-trading strata consisted largely of Jews: a Ukrainian *national* movement could not be led by such alien national strata. The industrial working class was largely Russian by nationality. National-social stratification, therefore, was much different than that in the Polish situation. The movement for independence was led by the professional middle strata: writers, teachers, lawyers and professors. And in the Ukraine the Bolsheviks had a considerable basis of support among the Russian-speaking working class.

In November 1917, a nationalist Rada proclaimed a Ukrainian People's

[1] The detailed history of each region may be consulted in E. H. Carr, *The Bolshevik Revolution 1917-1923*, vol. 1.

Republic. It disarmed the Bolshevik Red Guards and gave sustenance to the White Army. The Ukrainian Bolsheviks set up their headquarters in industrial Kharkov and, in December 1917, the All-Ukrainian Congress of Soviets 'assumed full powers in the Ukraine'. Later on, the Bolsheviks incorporated the Ukraine into the Soviet Union as a separate unit. Ukrainian culture (language, customs) was given official recognition, the socio-economic system, however, became 'socialist in form'; property was nationalised, anti-Bolshevik parties were banned, and a polity of the Soviet type was established. Bolshevik policy was to promote a 'culture national in form and socialist in content'.

Administratively, this involved the setting up of a federal state.[1] The powers of the Union government as defined by the Constitution of 1924 included the conduct of diplomatic affairs and the signing of treaties, the alteration of external frontiers and borders between republics, the transaction of foreign trade and loans, the determination of internal trade, the direction of the national economy and the organisation of the armed forces. To the individual republics (i.e. the equivalent of state governments such as California in the USA) was granted the formal right of secession from the USSR. They could amend their own constitutions as long as they conformed to the Union constitution, and the territory of a republic could not be altered without its own consent.

In the Caucasus, the socio-national structure was extremely variegated. There were eight indigenous national groups. The Georgians and Armenians, each about two million strong, had an ancient Christian non-industrial civilisation. The remainder were less developed and mainly illiterate peasant or tribal groups. In Georgia there was an established agrarian elite and in Armenia a commercial one. But in both countries no industrial proletariat had been formed. The main centre of industry was in the oil fields of Baku (Azerbaidzhan), where a substantial skilled Russian and unskilled Persian immigrant labour force had been recruited. National animosities were multilateral rather than bilateral and often based on class issues: peasant Georgians being hostile to Armenian traders, Russian industrial managers oppressing Persian worker immigrants.

Between 1917 and 1920 numerous national governments, often with English, German or Turkish support, were founded in the Caucasus. But following a Bolshevik rising in Baku, the Azerbaidzhan Socialist Soviet Republic was founded in January 1920. Then, after Turkish infiltration into Armenia, Soviet forces intervened and constituted the Armenian Socialist Republic in November of the same year. It was not until Feburary 1921 that the popular Georgian Menshevik government was overthrown by the Red Army and the Georgian Socialist Soviet Republic was proclaimed.

[1] Federalism has been discussed in detail above, Chapter 5, pp. 143-5.

The populations of the central and eastern areas of Russia were quite different in social composition from those influenced by European civilisation in the west and south. The peoples inhabiting the northern Caucasus, Central Asia, the indigenous population of Siberia and the Arctic reaches were non-Christian, often Muslim, Asiatic, agrarian and sometimes tribal in social organisation. These areas were before 1917 sparsely settled by Russian and Ukrainian immigrants who were clustered mainly in the towns. Politically, the situation was rather similar to that of the British colonies in the eighteenth century, save that Russia's eastern territories were joined to the homeland. There were important social differences, however, between the Russian and British colonies: in the 'White Dominions', the native population was small and British stock (in the early decades at least) largely settled in these areas. In other parts of the British Empire, such as India and West and East Africa, the British provided only an elite of administrators and traders.

At first, after the October Revolution, the indigenous national leaders in Asia supported the communists, who seemed more favourably disposed to national self-determination than the provisional government. Indeed, the communists received nationalist support at quite crucial periods of the Civil War.[1] In practice, however, the early policy of the Soviet government (such as national-isation) undermined the economic foundations of the national elites, and Bolshevik rule appeared as distant as that of the Tsars. Consequently, in-dependent national governments were formed among the Kazakhs, Bashkirs and Tatars which asserted autonomy for these peoples and independence from Petrograd.

In 1918, following the pattern of the Ukraine and Caucasus, the Soviet government militarily intervened against the 'bourgeois nationalist' governments to the east. Such nationalist states, it was argued, were inimical to the interests of the proletariat. Pro-Bolshevik governments were set up, ostensibly with the support of 'quasi-proletarian' strata.

But communist rule in these areas was not solely based on force. The central authorities abolished some of the more oppressive features of Tsarist admin-istration and they promised 'national self-determination'. In Central Asia, the Soviet government found support among the Russian settler population. This was not strictly proletarian by class but it represented a higher stage of civilisation than the indigenous population. The Russian communist govern-ment found itself denying, in practice, the right of the natives to independence because of their inferior cultural position.

In Asia, between 1920 and 1923, 17 autonomous republics and regions were created within the Russian Republic (RSFSR). These were administrative units based on the predominant national group in each area. The central

[1] R. Pipes, *The Formation of the Soviet Union* (Camb., Mass., 1964), p. 295. This book deals in detail with the national question 1917-1923.

government (i.e. the Russian Republic) had control over foreign affairs, economic planning, finance and defence, and the local bodies supervised education, health, social welfare (the old, childcare and so on). The units did not have the status of federal governments, but were rather like glorified regional counties in Great Britain. (At present, unlike Union Republics they do not have the right to secede from the USSR.)

By 1927, the communists had consolidated their rule: they suppressed hostile elements which were a mixture of national and class opponents. A federal state was founded in which, by 1936, were set up union republics, autonomous republics, autonomous regions, and national areas which gave the nationalities a degree of control over their own affairs.

The contemporary administrative structure of the USSR has been described above.[1] Here we may describe the main national groups in Russia. In Table 45, we have seen that the USSR, on the basis of the 1959 census, is made up of nearly 210 million people, of which the Great Russians make up more than half (114 million). The next largest nationality is the Ukrainians (37 million) followed by Byelorussians (White Russians) (nearly 8 million) and Uzbeks (6 million). Most of the other minor nationalities are under five million strong, the average being about two million. These peoples are still concentrated spatially in their traditional areas of Russia.

The Russian Federation (RSFSR) stretches the whole width of the country. It is mixed nationally, containing sixteen autonomous republics, five autonomous regions and ten national areas. The peoples inhabiting these national units are defined on Table 46. In the second column is shown the proportion of Great Russians and in the third and fourth the next two largest national groups. The table shows the high penetration of Russians in other areas:

Table 46. The Most Numerous Nationalities in the Union and Autonomous Republics, Autonomous Regions and National Areas. (1959 Census). Percentages.*

	Russians (%)	Other Nationalities (%)	
RSFSR	83.3	Ukrainians 2.9	
Autonomous Republics in RSFSR			
Bashkiriya	42.4	Bashkirs 22.1	Tatars 23.0
Buryat	74.6	Buryats 20.2	

* *Source: Itogi vsesoyuznoy perepisi naseleniya 1959g. SSSR* (Moscow, 1962). Adapted from Table 54.

[1] See Chapter 5.

Table 46—*continued*

Russians (%)		*Other Nationalities* (%)	
		Peoples of Dagestan	
Dagestan	20.1	69.3	
		Kabardintsy	
Kabardino-Balkaria	38.7	45.3	
		Kalmyks	
Kalmyt	55.9	35.1	
		Karelis	White Russians
Karelia	63.4	13.1	11.0
		Komis	
Komi	48.4	30.4	
		Maris	
Mari	47.8	43.1	
		Mordvinians	
Mordvinian	59.0	35.8	
		Osets	
North Osetinian	39.6	47.8	
		Tatars	
Tatar	43.9	47.2	
		Tuvins	
Tuvin	40.1	57.0	
		Udmurts	
Udmurt	56.8	35.6	
		Chechens	
Checheno-Ingush	49.0	34.3	
		Chuvashis	
Chuvash	24.0	70.2	
		Yakuts	
Yakutsk	44.2	46.4	
Autonomous Regions in RSFSR			
		Adygeyskis	
Adygeysk	70.4	23.2	
		Altais	
Gorno-Altay	69.8	24.2	
		Ukrainians	Jews
Jewish	78.2	8.9	8.8

Table 46—*continued*

	Russians (%)	Other Nationalities (%)	
Karachaevo-Cherkess	51.0	Karachaevs 24.4	Cherkesy 8.7
Khakass	76.5	Khakasi 11.8	

National Areas in RSFSR

	Russians (%)	Other Nationalities (%)	
Agin Buryat	48.6	Buryat 47.6	
Komi-Permyat	32.9	Komi-Permyats 58.0	
Koryak	60.6	'Peoples of the north' 27.7	
Nenetsk	68.8	Nentsis 10.9	Komis 11.0
Taymyr (Dolgano-Nenetsi)	65.3	'Peoples of the north' 9.0	Yakuts 11.8
Ust'-Ordyn Buryat	56.4	Buryaty 33.7	
Khanty-Mansiy	72.5	'Peoples of the north' 14.5	
Chukot	60.7	'Peoples of the north' 25.9	
Evenki	57.9	'Peoples of the north' 33.9	
Yamalo-Nenetsk	44.6	'Peoples of the north' 33.7	Komis 7.8
UKRAINIAN SSR	16.9	Ukrainians 76.8	
BYELORUSSIAN (WHITE RUSSIAN) SSR	8.2	White Russians 81.1	Poles 6.7

P*

Table 46—*continued*

	Russians (%)	Other Nationalities (%)		
UZBEKISTAN SSR	13.5	Uzbeks 62.2		Tatars 5.5
Kara-Kalpak ASSR	4.5	Karakalpaks 30.6	Uzbeks 28.8	Kazakhs 26.2
KAZAKHSTAN SSR	42.7	Kazakhs 30.0	Ukrainians 8.2	
GEORGIAN SSR	10.1	Georgians 64.3	Armenians 11.0	
Abkhaz ASSR	21.4	Abazis 15.1	Georgians 39.1	Armenians 15.9
Adzhar ASSR	13.4	Georgians 72.8	Armenians 6.5	
South-Osetian Autonomous Region	2.5	Georgians 27.5	Osets 65.8	
AZERBAIDZHAN SSR	13.6	Azerbaid- zhanies 67.5	Armenians 12.0	
Nakhichevan ASSR	2.2	Azerbaid- zhanies 90.2	Armenians 6.7	
Nagorno-Karabakh Autonomous Region	1.4	Azerbaid- zhanies 13.8	Armenians 84.4	
LITHUANIAN SSR	8.5	Lithuanians 79.3	Poles 8.5	
MOLDAVIAN SSR	10.2	Moldavians 65.4	Ukrainians 14.6	
LATVIAN SSR	26.6	Latvians 62.0		
KIRGIZ SSR	30.2	Kirgiz 40.5	Uzbeks 10.6	

Table 46—*continued*

	Russians (%)	Other Nationalities (%)	
		Tadzhik	Uzbeks
TADZHIK SSR	13.3	53.1	23.0
Gorno-Badakhshan		Tadzhiks	Kirgiz
Autonomous Region	1.9	89.7	7.4
		Armenians	Azerbaidzhanies
ARMENIAN SSR	3.2	88.0	6.1
		Turkmens	Uzbeks
TURKMENISTAN SSR	17.3	60.9	8.3
		Estonians	
ESTONIAN SSR	20.1	74.6	

in the Buryat Autonomous Republic, in 1959, 74.6 per cent of the population was Russian, and in the Mordvinian 59 per cent; in the Jewish Autonomous Region, 78.2 per cent of the population was Russian, and it was some 70 per cent in both the Adygeysk and Gorno-Altay regions. In other republics, with the exception of Kazakhstan where Russians constitute 42.7 per cent of the people and the Kirgiz Republic where they make up 30.2 per cent, the native inhabitants are preponderant. This is especially so in Lithuania, Latvia and Estonia where those nationalities make up respectively 79.3, 62.0 and 74.6 per cent of the population – see Table 46.

As there are more than one hundred nationalities in the USSR, one cannot study the impact the Soviet regime has had on all of them. I shall outline some of the features of Soviet rule focused on Central Asia and shall discuss the position of the Jews and political representation of nationalities.[1]

Soviet Rule in Central Asia

While most general studies consider the advanced European areas of the West, in fact, of the 140 million Soviet citizens of 1922, some 30 million, mainly Turkish peoples, still had a semi-feudal, pastoral or tribal form of life. Soviet experience of the 1930s, therefore, enables one to study the direct

[1] The empirical study of the 'national' problem in the advanced areas is not the subject of research in the Soviet Union. Much western writing is subjective, reflecting the interests of the national minorities. The reader may refer to *Problems of Communism*, vol. 16, no. 5 (Sept.-Oct. 1967), a special issue on nationalities and nationalism, and E. Goldhagen, *Ethnic Minorities in the Soviet Union* (New York, 1968).

impact of a socialist state on an underdeveloped area. Here I shall only cover
one area, Central Asia[1], in detail.

One of the major aims of the Russian government was to industrialise the
Asian areas. [Industrialisation would ensure economically, a rise in living
standards, and politically, a base on which Soviet power could rest. Soviet
development policy entailed, on the one hand, the despatch of Russian
specialists to the underdeveloped areas, and, on the other, the training of the
indigenous population in urban-industrial skills. This process has been said
to involve 'Russianisation': the Russian immigrants holding the chief positions
in the administration, and Russian language and culture dominating the
schools. The administrative control by the communists who had relatively
few members among the indigenous peoples can hardly be denied. But they
pursued a policy of promoting the indigenous population] The following
extract from a Soviet source shows the extent to which Russians dominated
among leading personnel in the Bashkir and Chuvash republics.

MAP 3 Central Asia

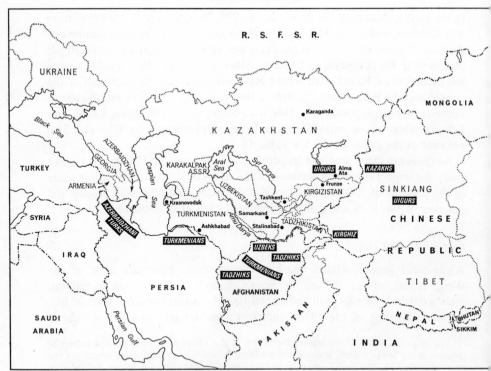

[1] The style Turkmenia, or Turkmen SSR, is used interchangeably for Turkmenistan and
similarly for some other republics.

Among the 398 leading and responsible officials of the district executive committee and village soviets in Kabardino-Balkaria, only 206 are indigenous . . . Of the 1,122 village soviet chairmen in the Bashkir Republic, only 340 are Bashkirs; of the 51 chairmen of the district executive committees, only 20; only 24 district executive committees have Bashkir secretaries, the rest have Russians. Yet 15 posts of district executive committee chairmen and deputy chairmen and 55 posts of district executive committee instructors have hitherto remained vacant. In the Chuvash Republic, of 2,232 officials of district executive committees and village soviets, 1,746 are indigenous. In the Adygei provincial executive committee, of the 40 Adygeis only 16 can write in their native language. In the provincial executive committee and party provincial committee, only Russian is spoken and even in some district organisations the Adygei language is avoided.[1]

While the Russian elite dominated the Central Asian Republics, it cannot be accepted that 'few events and no positive developments . . . could be said to have taken place on the initiative of the local inhabitants'.[2] The statistics above already show considerable participation by the indigenous population; over half of the 'leading and responsible officials' were indigenous. Participation was much greater than under the French in Algeria and the Belgians in the Congo.

The educational policy involved the setting-up of schools in which instruction took place in the native language. The second language was Russian. Instruction in higher education was often, though not always, carried out in Russian and in technical subjects, for Russians were the only ones able to teach them.

There can be no doubt that living and cultural standards have risen greatly in Soviet Central Asia. In 1900, only 0.5 per cent of the Kirghiz and 2 per cent of the Kazakhs were literate. In 1911, of the 20 million Muslim population, only 32,000 were enrolled in Muslim religious schools and 46,000 in Russian elementary schools. In Buryat-Mongolia the number of schools rose from 48 in 1917 to 700 in 1932-33, an increase from 1,000 to 67,000 pupils.[3] It was claimed that 99.3 per cent of children of school age were attending school in Bashkiria in 1932-33.[4] In Tataria, it was claimed that literacy, which had been 19 per cent before 1917, was over 90 per cent in 1932-33.[5] Among the national minorities, 80 per cent of teaching in the primary stage was in the native tongue.

Progress was not always smooth. In the Tatar republic, the Nenets schools

[1] A. Telikhanov, 'On National Soviet Cadres', *Revolyutsiya i natsionalnosti* (1935), no. 12, extract in R. Schlesinger, *The Nationalities Problem and Soviet Administration* (1956), p. 229.

[2] Geoffrey Wheeler, *The Modern History of Soviet Central Asia* (1964), p. 137.

[3] M. Nadezhdin and M. Solomonov, cited in R. Schlesinger, *The Nationalities Problem and Soviet Administration* (1956), p. 204.

[4] *Ibid.*, p. 205.

[5] *Ibid.*

had no language text books, and in other areas 'the needs of the national minorities' schools . . . are taken too little account of'.[1] This not only applied to non-Russian nationalities, but also to Russians who found themselves sometimes in a minority. Schlesinger recalls: 'I had myself in 1931 the opportunity to notice fantastic cases of disregard for the right of Russian workers to use their mother tongue: these cases cannot be described even as merely local excesses, as the underlying theory of Ukrainianisation was stubbornly defended by one of the leaders of the Ukrainian party organisation with whom I discussed it.'[2]

In higher education, of students admitted in the autumn of 1934, it was claimed that some 51 per cent of all students were from non-Russian nationalities: on 1 January 1935, 45.6 per cent of all students were of non-Russian national background.[3]

It should not be thought, however, that access to higher education was evenly distributed among the nationalities. This may be shown by the following table.

Table 47. Nationality and Higher Education 1934

Nationality	Percentage of the nationality:	
	of USSR population	of student intake 1934
Armenians	1.07	2.38
Georgians	1.24	3.16
Jews	1.82	12.5
Poles	0.53	1.05
Byelorussians	3.23	3.94
Tatars	1.99	1.44
Ukrainians	21.2	17.58
Chuvashis	0.76	0.59
Kazakhs	2.70	0.61
Kirghiz	0.52	0.81
Tadjiks	0.67	0.17
Uzbeks	2.66	0.57
Yakuts	0.16	0.02

Figures adapted from R. Schlesinger, *ibid.*, pp. 226-7.

Obviously, the bottom end of the table shows the serious inequality of the Central Asian nationalities. Here again, one should not unjustly condemn the Soviet authorities for the discrepancies which were mainly due to the policy of the Tsars. The *intentions* of the central government were to raise the standards of the national minorities. As Stalin put it:

What is needed is to nationalise – that is, to staff with members of the given

[1] *Ibid.*, p. 208.
[2] R. Schlesinger, p. 208n.
[3] B. R. 'On National Cadres of Specialists', in R. Schlesinger, p. 225.

nation – all the administrative apparatus, from party and trade-union to state and economic. What is needed is widely to develop the press, the theatre, the cinema and other cultural institutions functioning in the native languages. Why in the native languages? Because only in their native, national languages can the vast masses of the people be successful in cultural, political and economic development.[1]

Economic and industrial change was perhaps more fundamental than the cultural. Before 1914, about two-thirds of Russia's large-scale industry was located in the St Petersburg, Moscow and Donbas areas, despite the concentration of rich untapped mineral resources east of the Urals. Economic rationality therefore coincided with Stalin's desire to abolish national inequality. Industrial location favoured a shift of industry to the east.[2]

The low economic starting point of the Asian republics also meant that a relatively small absolute increase in industrial output would be reflected in a large percentage increase. The following table shows the increase of large-scale industry by republics.

Large-scale industry in selected Union Republics
(mil. rubles at 1926-27 prices)

	1913	1935	Growth
USSR	10,251	57,345	5.7 times
RSFSR	7,500	42,904	5.7 times
Georgian SSR	43	640.9	14.9 times
Turkmen SSR	20.9	171.1	8 times
Uzbek SSR	268.8	837.5	3 times
Kazakh SSR	50.9	432.4	8.5 times
Kirghiz SSR	1.2	99.8	83 times

Figures cited in Schlesinger, p. 260.

The main industries in Central Asia were started in connection with the development of the Karaganda coalfield in Kazakhstan. In Tashkent, textile, agricultural machinery and food-processing factories were built in the 1930s. Despite the low base, and other possible deficiencies in the statistics (a 1926-27 base results in the overweighting of scarce products in that year), the figures show a remarkable increase in the industrial capacity of the areas. True they were still less industrialised than the Soviet European areas,[3] but were much more so than, say, Britain's African colonies in the nineteenth and early twentieth century.

[1] J. V. Stalin, 'The National Question and Leninism', Collected Works, vol. 11, p. 370.
[2] Strategic considerations of having an industrial centre well away from a possible European front may also have played a part here.
[3] The percentage of the total employed population in 1939 occupied in industry, building and transport was as follows: USSR (average) 30.1, RSFSR 33.9, Uzbekistan 14.3, Kazakhstan 21.7, Kirgizia 13.9, Armenia 17.8, Tadzhikistan 10.9, Turkmenistan 20.3. Cited in A. Nove and J. A. Newth, The Soviet Middle East (1967), p. 41.

The Effects of Sovietisation on the Indigenous Peoples

The peoples of Central Asia were far less developed and, unlike the advanced nations in western Russia, had little consciousness of 'nationality' at the time of the revolution. There were two main groupings: the north (now Kazakhstan) made up of nomadic Turkish races, and the south peopled by Iranians and Turks who were pastoral.

In the western Christian areas of Russia, we shall see that Christianity in the form of the Orthodox Church provided some political opposition to the Bolsheviks. As a value system, or 'a way of life', it was not a serious obstacle. The Moslem faith was more at odds with the demands of an urban industrial civilisation. Daily prayers and fasting interfered with the rhythm of industrial life. Between 1928 and 1932 the leaders of the Muslim Church were imprisoned or deported, mosques were closed, and the ritual of the pilgrimage to Mecca and the payment of legal charity were forbidden.[1]

The communist authorities seem to have succeeded in suppressing Muslim religious beliefs. Pipes quotes the following statement by a Muslim emigrant as 'a typical opinion'. 'Religion is a superstition which keeps people backward. Look at the Arabs and Persians, where religion has gotten them: they are poor and ignorant. To achieve progress, we must not allow religion to interfere, though religion should not be persecuted because it does help some people in facing life.'[2]

A Soviet study of life in a Muslim collective farm shows how religious beliefs have declined:

> Until recently, in view of the numerous survivals of ancient beliefs, in particular the cult of trees . . . the practice of medicine men, the ancestral cult in clan cemeteries (a night spent in prayer among the tombs was supposed to help even against serious illness) . . . the influence of the Moslem clergy remained extremely strong during the first years of the *kolkhoz* . . .
>
> The authority and influence of the two *mullahs* among the inhabitants of the *kolkhoz* are declining from year to year. Only the old folk are remaining in their flock.[3]

While Muslim religious ritual seems to have suffered a decline, native customs have continued. Circumcision appears to be 'universally observed'.[4] Ceremonies at birth, weddings and burials continue, though in a less formal manner. Arranged marriages, polygamy and infant marriages and the bride price have

---

[1] See. A. Bennigsen and C. Lemercier-Quelquejay, *Islam in the Soviet Union* (1967), pp. 149-52.

[2] Pipes, 'Assimilation and the Muslims', in A. Inkeles and K. Geiger, *Soviet Society* (1961), p. 589.

[3] T. A. Zhdanko, 'Everyday Life in a Karakalpak Kolkhoz *aul*', *Sovestskaya Etnografiya* (1949), no. 2. Cited in R. Schlesinger, *The Nationalities Problem*, p. 292. Other examples in the Caucasus are given in *Sovremennoe Abkhazskoe selo* (Tbilisi 1967), pp. 27-52.

[4] Pipes, p 592.

been made illegal. Restraints on marriage between members of the same clan persisted at least to the late forties when other social taboos (such as women not pronouncing the names of their husband's relatives) were still observed.[1] Obviously, such customs do not conflict with the needs of an industrial order and may coexist with communist power, in the same way as the Cornish Floral Dance or Welsh Druid ceremonies coexist with managerial capitalism in modern Britain. While Muslim women have not yet been fully liberated, the impact of industrialisation, mixed schools, women's employment and education have gone a long way towards their emancipation.

The authorities had considerable impact on the native languages. First, the Persian-Arabic characters were latinised and then in 1939 a Cyrillic alphabet was introduced. The languages were 'enriched' by the introduction of Russian words to the native languages. Second, Russian was made a compulsory second language, taught in all schools, though the native languages remained predominant in Central Asia (at least among the natives). It is still the medium of instruction in secondary schools and the mode of communication in the family. Some of the Muslim emigrants, especially those from the countryside, interviewed by Pipes, knew hardly any Russian. An interesting example of this is given by Solzhenitsyn, when he describes an Uzbek hospital patient as follows: 'Before joining the army he had always lived in the *aul* and spoke only Uzbek. All his Russian words and ideas, his discipline and familiarity with friends, came from his days in the army.'[2]

In the towns, where the population is mixed, Russian is better known. It is the principle language for instruction in higher education (especially universities) in Central Asia. (This is not the case in the European national areas where Ukrainian, Latvian and Georgian are the mode in higher education.) Promotion in institutions with an all-Union complexion (such as the party or Supreme Soviet) would seem to depend on ability to speak Russian. This probably accounts for the higher enrolment by non-Russians in Russian-speaking schools. Table 48 shows, for example, that in the Georgian Republic where Russians constitute 10.8 per cent of the population, 20 per cent of the children are at Russian-language schools; in the Baltic, it should be noted, the differential is much lower – in Estonia where 21.7 per cent of the population is Russian, only 22 per cent of the schoolchildren are in Russian schools. In Central Asia and the European national republics, while the indigenous languages have persisted enrollment in Russian language schools is high.

While national schools have been set up at primary and secondary levels, in higher education, universities and other higher institutes have tended to be clustered in the Russian Republic, and particularly in Moscow and Leningrad. To overcome the traditional pre-revolutionary tendency for the 'European'

[1] Zhdanko, p. 290.
[2] *Cancer Ward* (1968), p. 121.

Table 48. Percentage of Students Attending Russian Language
Schools, 1955-56

Republic	% in Russian- Language Schools	% Russians in Republic
USSR	65	55.0
RSFSR	94	83.2
Ukrainian	26	17.1
Byelorussian	22	9.1
Uzbek	20	13.6
Kazakh	66	43.1
Georgian	20	10.8
Azerbaidzhan	23	13.9
Lithuanian	11	8.5
Moldavian	33	10.2
Latvian	33	26.6
Kirgiz	49	30.2
Tadzhik	16	13.3
Armenian	9	3.2
Turkmen	21	17.3
Estonian	22	21.7

Figures cited by V. V. Aspaturian, 'The Non-Russian Nationalities', in A. Kassof, *Prospects for Soviet Society* (1968), p. 174.

nations to be over-represented in higher education, and possible charges of
Russian domination, it has been asserted by some writers that a policy of
informal national quotas has been established giving preference to the
deprived nationals.[1] This, in addition to the construction of institutes in
Central Asia, has resulted in an increase in the share of students of the Central
Asian nationalities. For example, in 1927 the Kirgiz and Tadzhik each constituted 0.06 per cent and the Uzbek 0.3 per cent of the student population;
by 1965 they made up 0.4 per cent, 0.4 per cent and 2.4 per cent respectively.
The total number of Uzbek students rose from 500 in 1927 to 95,500 in 1965.[2]

Attempts were made to recruit the local indigenous population into the
industrial labour force. During the first five-year plan the number of Kazakh
workers trebled,[3] the initial base having been very small. Industrialisation of
the area has been promoted and has developed at a higher rate than in the
USSR as a whole.[4] Urbanisation of the population has continued: for
instance, the urban population of Kazakhstan rose from 10 per cent in 1913

[1] V. V. Aspaturian, 'The Non-Russian Nationalities', in A. Kassof, *Prospects for Soviet Society*
(1968), p. 176.
[2] Figures cited by V. V. Aspaturian, 'The Non-Russian Nationalities', in A. Kassof, *Prospects
for Soviet Society* (1968), p. 177.
[3] Figure cited by T. Zhdanko, 'The Nomads of Central Asia', in *International Labour Review*,
no. 93 (1966), p. 617n.
[4] T. Zhdanko, 'The Nomads . . .', pp. 616-8.

to 46 per cent in 1964, and in Kirgizia from 12 per cent to 38 per cent.[1] Associated with these rapid changes was immigration which has also had a profound effect on the area.

Russification

The chief factor which has brought about Russification in Central Asia is immigration. In 1897, there were about 700,000 Russians out of a total population of just over ten millions, roughly 6.8 per cent. By 1939, this proportion had risen to 27.1 per cent – a total Russian population of four and a half million.[2] With the exception of Kirghizia, where some immigrants were enagaged in agriculture, most of the migrants moved to the towns.

Settlement seems to follow the pattern of immigration to cities in the western world. The European immigrants have tended to live beside the indigenous population. The natives continued to live in the Oriental quarter of such cities as Bokhara, and the Russians in separate parts of the towns. With the redevelopment of towns in the 1960s, it is probable that more mixing has taken place. On the other hand, the provision of separate Russian-language and native-language schools tends to promote segregation.

In the countryside, the émigrés interviewed by Pipes reported that there were no racially mixed collective farms, which is also confirmed by Zhdanko's description.[3] State farms, however, are more mixed racially. Muslims have been hired both for white-collar work and as shepherds. This tendency has probably increased since the Second World War. On the other hand, a study of Darkhan and Chichkan villages reports that out of 648 collective farm families, 640 were Kirghiz, 5 were Russian, 2 Tatar and 1 Uygur.[4]

Intermarriage is the chief process by which a minor racial or national group may be absorbed by, or assimilated into, another culturally dominant nationality. Both before the revolution and during the Stalin era Muslims and Russians did not intermarry. Pipes puts this down to cultural differences, sexual customs, the control of Muslim parents over female children, and the problems of a mixed family in a Russian or Muslim community. Some émigrés asserted that a Muslim girl who married a Russian might be assassinated by her male relatives.[5] Those who do break the racial barriers are Russian women who marry Muslim men.

Pipes' work, though important, is only relevant to the early period of Russian rule. Since the Second World War, Russian emigration to Central Asia has considerably increased. The proportions of Russians and others by

---

[1] *Ibid.*, p. 618.

[2] Figures cited by Pipes, pp. 589-9.

[3] Printed in R. Schlesinger, *The Nationalities Problem*, p. 280.

[4] S. M. Abramzon, K. I. Antipina, *et al*, 'Byt kolkhoznikov Kirgizskikh seleniy Darkhan Chichkan', *Trudy Instituta Etnografii*, vol. 37, p. 212.

[5] Pipes, p. 601.

Republics and national areas at the 1959 Census are shown on Table 46 (pp. 435–9). Here the Russification of many areas is clearly brought out. In the Tatar Autonomous Republic, nearly 44 per cent of the population is Russian. The Chechens compose only 34.3 per cent of the Checheno-Ingush Autonomous Republic. In the Nenetsk National Area, 68.8 per cent of the population is Russian. Of the Kazakhstan population, only about 30 per cent are Kazakhs.

The war saw a movement of many people to Central Asia and Siberia. Not only were many voluntarily evacuated from western Russia, but the Volga Germans, the Crimean Tatars and the Kalmyks (each having their own Autonomous Republic) were also moved to the east.[1] The war also affected social mixing. Pipes points out that: 'The Red army represents the only Soviet institution – save for the forced labour camps – where Muslim and Russian societies are forcibly compressed together and where the cultural and ethnic walls usually separating them are to some extent broken down.'[2]

A more recent study in Tashkent and Samarkand reports that in these towns 20 per cent of marriages were nationally mixed, though only six to seven per cent between European and indigenous inhabitants. (In Leningrad in 1964, 17 per cent of marriages were also nationally mixed).[3]

According to post-1950 Soviet surveys the walls dividing nationalities are crumbling, if not breaking down. In Northern Turkmenistan, the Uzbek language is dying and Turkish is becoming more widely used. Mixed marriages between the different national groups are frequent and usually take place between Uzbeks on the one hand and Kazakhs and Karakalpaks, on the other.[4]

More detailed figures are available on intermarriage in Karachaevo-Cherkess in the Northern Caucasus.[5] Here mixed marriages range from 2.6 per cent of marriages among the Karachaev rural population to 56.2 per cent among the urbanised Abaziny. Among four national groups more than a quarter of all marriages were mixed, in the other four groups studied the range was from 3.3 per cent to 10.1 per cent. But marriage between Russians and 'non-Caucasian peoples' is infrequent, ranging over the eight groups from 0.6 per cent to 5.6 per cent, evidence of rather little racial intermixing with European national groups. A closer look at Smirnova's research suggests that in urban areas, 18.2 per cent of the Cherkesy, 25 per cent of the Abaziny and 33.3 per cent of the Nogaytsy married Russians and other non-Caucasians.

[1] For a detailed history see Walter Kolarz, *Russia and Her Colonies* (1952), Chapter 3.

[2] Pipes, p. 603.

[3] *Trud*, 'Lyubov, doverie, druzhba!', 22 Oct. 1965.

[4] G. P. Vasil'eva, 'Sovremennye etnicheskie protsessy v Severnom Turkmenistane', *Sovetskaya etnografiya*, no. 1, 1968, p. 13.

[5] Ya. S. Smirnova, 'Natsional'no-smeshannye braki u narodov Karachaevo-Cherkesii', *Sovetskaya etnografiya*, no. 4 (1967).

These high numbers probably reflect a low absolute number of mixed urban marriages: Russians constitute 78.5 per cent of the town population, Cherkesy 2.2 per cent, Abaziny 2 per cent, and Nogaytsy 0.6 per cent. Here we see a mixing of the national minorities, but relatively little intermarriage with Russians. That which did take place was again between native men and Russian girls.[1]

Another survey, conducted in the village of Abkhaz in the Adzhar Autonomous Republic, found that 'a significant per cent of the mixed marriages in the village were between Abazes and Russians', a male Abaz taking a Russian bride[2] or one from another nationality.

In cultural aspects of life, Russification does not seem to have penetrated very deeply. The native language is still spoken at home. In the eight-year schools instruction is in the Kazakh language, higher education in Turkish (in the towns of Urgench, Nukus or Tashkent). The changes in material aspects of life (clothing, food and housing) are all influenced by the Russians. But, as Vasil'eva points out, it is incorrect simply to call these changes Russification;[3] they are a synthesis of international features, and are as much related to urbanisation as Russification. The impact of the town and urban culture is also felt in the villages where the 'village intelligentsia' having had higher education in the town in turn influences the villagers. Smirnova observes, on the basis of her research, that in mixed marriages there is a tendency to generate a nationally mixed home culture. Of Cherkesi-Russian marriages, the family ate local and Russian food, the children wore local and Russian clothes, but the home language was Russian and the children went to the Russian language school.[4]

The Jews

The Jews first came into Russia with the partition of Poland in the late eighteenth century.[5] At the census of 1897, Jews constituted about 2.1 per cent of the Russian population – an absolute total of over 2,600,000. They were mainly urban and located in the western and south-western provinces of Tsarist Russia. Warsaw, with a Jewish population of 278,000 in 1908 was the largest Jewish community in Europe. Being urban, the Jews had a higher level of education than other national groups and they were prominent in industry, trade, education, the arts and professions.

---

[1] *Ibid.*, p. 141.

[2] *Sovremennoe Abkhazskoe selo* (Tbilisi, 1967), pp. 14-15.

[3] *Loc. cit.*, p. 15.

[4] Ya. S. Smirnova, 'Natsional'no-smeshannye braki u narodov Karachaevo-Cherkesii', *Sovestskaya etnografiya*, no. 4 (1967), p. 141.

[5] For the early history of Russian Jews see S. W. Baron, *The Russian Jew under Tsars and Soviets* (1964).

Under the Tsars, the Jews were restricted to particular areas of the country, the Pale – an area in the west and south-west, and their other traditional settlements in the Caucasus and Central Asia. Exceptions to this law were made for merchants of the highest guild and registered prostitutes.

In the countryside of the Polish and Ukrainian provinces, the Jews often were shopkeepers or money collectors, activities which encouraged anti-Jewish feeling and added to Christian-Jewish antagonism. They were not allowed to own and farm land. With the industrialisation of Russia in the late nineteenth century, the Jews, as entrepreneurs, began to play an important part in the metal industry, the sugar industry, railway building and transport, oil and finance.[1] In Poland, the Jewish share of commerce ranged from 80 to 95 per cent.[2]

On the other hand, a large proportion of the Jewish population was poor, often being unemployed; others were recruited into the growing industrial centres in Poland and the Ukraine, forming a Jewish proletariat. The social structure of the Jews, therefore elicited hostility both from those exploited by the Jewish bourgeoisie and from the authorities who held them responsible for public disorder.

Until 1884, when the Jews were brought under the jurisdiction of local courts, the Jewish community enforced its own laws – and in return collected taxes for the government. Social services were provided by Jewish voluntary societies; these provided for the poor and the sick. Jewish schools were also organised by their community and ensured a high standard of literacy and culture among their people.

But the communal solidarity of the Jews was being undermined from the late nineteenth century. Greater control of Jewish affairs was being exercised by the Russian government; not only was the legal autonomy of the community destroyed, but state education began to draw pupils from the Jewish to the state schools. The industrialisation process disrupted the guilds and also divided the Jewish community on class lines.

Of the political movements among the Jews, the Zionist movement and the Bund were the most important. The Zionists were imbued with Jewish culture; some sought the establishment of Palestine as a national home, others wanted national rights within the framework of the Russian Empire – particularly, the right to found and control institutions for national education, health, welfare, emigration and 'matters of faith'.[3] The Zionists insisted on the right to the use of the Hebrew language.

The chief socialist movement among the Jews was the Bund, or the Jewish

---

[1] In Berdichev, the ratio of money lenders per 1,000 Jewish residents was 33 to 35. For full details see Baron, pp. 101-15.

[2] Figures for 1914, cited by Baron, p. 117.

[3] Baron, p. 178.

Social-Democratic Party in Russia, Lithuania and Poland. While the Bund adopted a Marxist view of the class struggle and agitated for the improvement of wages and conditions, it insisted on the right of the Bund exclusively to represent Jewish workers; it also advocated national autonomy for the Jews in Russia.

The Bund found itself at odds with the Russian Social-Democratic Labour Party which sought a wider union of workers, rather than national workers' groups. To the Russian party belonged many Jewish intellectuals and workers who had to a greater or lesser degree rejected Jewish 'nationality'. Indeed, a higher proportion of Jews was in the RSDLP than in the population as a whole and many of them, such as Trotsky and Martov, held high office. Of the two factions of the party, fewer Jews joined the Bolsheviks, though they figured largely among the Menshevik leaders.[1]

Stalin, as we have seen, defined a nation as 'an historically constituted, stable community of people, formed on the basis of a common language, territory, economic life, and psychological make-up manifested in a common culture.'[2] And this viewpoint was incorporated into the communist's policy after the revolution. The Jews, on the basis of this definition did *not* constitute a single nation: they were economically disunited, inhabited various territories and spoke different languages. In practice, therefore, after the revolution, though the Jews in some areas were concentrated enough to form local Jewish Soviets, they were not at once constituted into an administrative national area.

Hostility to the Jewish community by the communists existed on many grounds. By class position, the relatively high proportion of self-employed craftsmen, entrepreneurs, and financiers among the Jews made some think that the Jews, as such, were of bourgeois class origin, and were therefore opposed to the communist regime. The demands of the Zionists for a national home outside Russia together with Zionism's international character, led some to doubt their loyalty to the new Soviet state.

In common with the other religious faiths, the religious aspects of Jewish culture were regarded as superstitions and inimical to the Marxist world view. Lenin regarded the demands for Jewish national culture as a 'slogan of rabbis and bourgeois',[3] showing the close links in Bolshevik eyes between Jewish national, religious and class aspirations. Many of the strongest proponents of the government's attack against the Jewish religion and Jewish nationalism were communists of Jewish ethnic stock and upbringing. *Yevsektsii*, or sections composed of Jews, were organised both in the Communist Party and in the League of Militant Godless. They conducted a propaganda

---

[1] See David Lane, *The Roots of Russian Communism* (Assen, 1969), Chapter 1.
[2] Stalin 'Marxism and the National Question', see Reading no. 16.
[3] Cited by W. Kolarz, *Religion in the Soviet Union* (1962), p. 372.

campaign against Judaism in the same way as others campaigned against Christianity.

While persecution of Jewish nationalist and religious sentiment took place, a more positive scheme for meeting the aspirations of the Jews was being worked out. A plan for settling the Russian Jews in a special area in the unpopulated Far Eastern territories of Russia had been devised. This had the political advantage that it countered the proposals of the Russian Zionists for a national home and it was practical, as it involved no dislocation of existing peoples, as might have been the case in the European parts of Russia. Another advantage was that it transferred to the east a hardworking people who could ably develop a new region. After a pioneering start in 1928, the Jewish Autonomous Region (Birobidyan) was proclaimed in 1934. Unfortunately, a large number of Jews moved away from the area (about half in the years 1928-1933) and non-Jews emigrated there giving it both in 1934 and today a non-Jewish majority (15,000 Jews out of a population of 170,000 – about 9 per cent.)

After the revolution, the traditional bourgeois occupations of the Jews (such as banking, trading and small-scale business) were gradually abolished. Jewish workers still pursued their traditional trades (such as shoe-repairing, tailoring, printing) and professions (medicine, teaching). Important changes in the occupational structure of the Jews paralleled the process of industrialisation. The number of Jews classified as wage-earners and salaried workers increased from 394,000 in 1926 to 1,100,000 in 1935.[1] The number of Jewish miners rose from 0.1 per cent of Jewish workers in 1926 to 3.3 per cent in 1936, metal workers increased from 14.1 per cent to 28.3 per cent.[2] The access of Jews to higher education and therefore to managerial and white-collar jobs was much greater than that of other nationalities. In 1926, Jews composed 1.8 per cent of the population whereas their share of students (in 1929) was 13.5 per cent, by 1956 their share had fallen to 4.1 per cent and by 1965 to 2.4 per cent. They still have a relatively privileged position, for their share of the population as a whole is only 1.1 per cent. Even the proportional fall between 1956 and 1965 noted above conceals an *absolute* increase in the number of Jewish students – from 51,600 to 94,600. The number of Jewish students expressed as a proportion per 10,000 of the Jewish population is 315, whereas the comparative figure for the USSR as a whole is 166 and for the Russian Federation 186.[3] Jews still have a higher proportion of white-collar workers than the average. While Jews number only 1.1 per cent of the population, they constitute 15.7 per cent of the doctors, 11 per cent of scientific

[1] Baron, p. 256.

[2] *Ibid.*, p. 257.

[3] Figures cited in S. Rabinovich, *Jews in the Soviet Union* (Moscow, 1967), p. 56, and V. V. Aspaturian, 'The Non-Russian Nationalities', in A. Kassof, *Prospects for Soviet Society* (1968), p. 177.

specialists, 10.4 per cent of jurists and 8.5 per cent of journalists and writers.[1]

Culturally, the Jews have fared less well than other minor nationalities in the USSR. Up to the middle 1920s, the Yiddish language used in the Soviet Jewish schools still flourished (Hebrew was also taught). In 1927, about 40 per cent of all Jewish pupils went to Yiddish schools.[2] Thereafter, Yiddish schools were progressively incorporated into other local schools. Yiddish was left at first as a subject of study, then later dropped from the curriculum. Today, there are no Yiddish schools in the USSR.[3]

The size of the Jewish congregation is declining rapidly. In the whole of the USSR in the mid 1960s there were 100 synagogues and 300 minians (a gathering under 10) compared to 1,034 in 1917. There is no Jewish seminary to train rabbis. Attendance at synagogues is poor and worshippers, like those in the Orthodox Church, are old. The proportion of avowed atheists among the Jewish population is, according to one survey, higher than that among other national groups – 98.5 per cent against an average of 65.1 per cent.[4] Possibly, this high figure was influenced by Jewish respondents being less secure than others and therefore feeling less willing to say they were Jewish. But the conclusion can hardly be escaped that Judaism has suffered the same fate as other religions in the USSR – it has become a relic of the pre-revolutionary past.

Publication of books in Yiddish has fallen dramatically since the revolution. In 1964 only two books, one periodical and one newspaper were published.[5] The Soviet explanation of such a small print is that there is little demand for media in the Yiddish language. But as the number of Jewish schools has dramatically declined, this is hardly surprising.

All forms of racial and national discrimination are illegal in the USSR, and this applies to the Jews as to other groups. But it is often alleged in the West that antisemitism is still practised. Alec Nove has said that Soviet Jews are 'all but barred from foreign trade organisations'.[6] Joel Cang in *The Times* (11 April 1968) asserts that Jews are not accepted in the Soviet diplomatic service. If true, this is probably due to the international nature of Jewry and the presence of Israel which has always been regarded as a puppet of the Americans. In fact, however, no statistical analysis of the national composition of the diplomatic service has been provided to substantiate these views, though on *a priori* grounds they seem likely to be true. Other commentators

[1] Figures cited by Z. Brzezinski and S. P. Huntington, *Political Power: USA/USSR* (1964), p. 131.

[2] Baron, p. 271.

[3] Zvi Gitelman, 'The Jews', *Problems of Communism*, vol. 16, no. 5 (Sept-Oct. 1967), p. 95.

[4] *Pritchiny sushchestvovaniya i puti preodoleniya religioznykh perezhitkov* (Minsk, 1965), p. 40, cited by Zvi Gitelman, *loc. cit.*, p. 93.

[5] Gitelman, p. 95.

[6] A. Nove, *Soviet Jewry and the Fiftieth Anniversary of the Russian Revolution* (World Jewish Congress, 1968), p. 17.

report on anti-Jewish prejudice in Russia.[1] A much larger proportion of Jews are sentenced for 'economic crimes' than is their share of the population as a whole. In the RSFSR Jews constitute 0.7 per cent of the population, whereas of those executed from July 1961 to August 1963, 64 per cent were Jews.[2] As Jews are disproportionately engaged in trade, one might expect a larger proportion to be involved in speculation. On the other hand, the law may be more strictly enforced against Jewish subjects than non-Jews, especially in areas with a history of anti-semitism.

The geographical dispersion of the Jews in the USSR together with Soviet social policy has tended to assimilate them into other national groups. Indeed, this is the official policy: *'The way to the future merging of nations lies through a long period of development of the nations, their cultures and languages.'*[3] The absence of family businesses and Jewish schools means that Jews are educated and employed with other nationalities. This encourages mixed marriages. In one Moscow district in one period of 1966, 66 per cent of the marriages involving one or both Jewish partners were mixed. It is also interesting to note a tendency for Jewish men rather than women to marry exogamously – as with other minor nationalities. The head of the Bukhara Jewish community has been quoted as saying: 'I don't know of any Bukhara Jewish girl marrying a non-Jew. But our men are not so zealous in observing the tradition. Many of them have married Russian, Uzbek or Armenian girls.'[4]

We might try to explain why the Jews seem to have fared less well than other national groups in the USSR. First, the Jews in Tsarist Russia had no definite territory, as did other national groups. Second, many Jews who had rejected the notion of an autonomous Jewish nationality had joined the Bolsheviks and, to counter Zionist sentiments, they vigorously supported and advocated an assimilationist policy. Whereas other national leaders were able to achieve considerable concessions, communists with a Jewish background were international in outlook. Third, the international role of Zionism, the large number of Jewish relations of Soviet Jews in capitalist states and, since the end of the Second World War, the presence of Israel, have led to a policy of assimilation for the Jews for political reasons. This policy has been politically expedient, but it has resulted in the suppression of the cultural identity of the Jews to a much greater extent than in modern western states. However, we should not attribute the assimilation of Jews in the USSR *solely* to Soviet political pressure, as a decline in Jewish religious faith has taken place in Great Britain and the United States, though the Jews here have

---

[1] John Gunther, *Inside Russia Today* (1962), pp. 370-2.
[2] Figures cited by Gitelman, *loc. cit.*, p. 97.
[3] *Pravda*, 7 Oct. 1966, cited in Rabinovich, *The Jews in the Soviet Union* (Moscow 1967), p. 62.
[4] Rabinovich, p. 62.

maintained their identity on a cultural and social basis. Soviet opposition to the Jews has been greater than in these two countries because the 'social' basis was regarded as maintaining bourgeois relations, and the cultural ties with abroad were suspect on political grounds.

Political Representation of Nationalities

We may now turn to discover how the social differences between national groups are manifested in the political sphere. We have already noted in the description of Communist Party membership the uneven representation of national groups,[1] but we have not considered possible national predominance at the elite level.

Brzezinski and Huntingdon in comparing American and Soviet political elites have identified the WASPS (white Anglo-Saxon protestants) and SRAPPS (Slavic-stock Russian-born apparatchikis) at the apex of each society.[2] While Soviet political leaders had a worker or peasant social background, they appeared to be drawn disproportionately from Slavic, and particularly Great Russian, stock. During the period 1919-1962, 75 per cent of the members of the Politbureau (Presidium) and Secretariat of the Party were of Russian nationality, whereas Russians composed only 54.6 per cent of the population.

One might expect the political elite to be weighted in favour of the Russians, who not only were among the most culturally advanced peoples of Russia, but also constituted a very large part of the Bolshevik Party before the revolution. Present policy is to recruit into the party and other political bodies antionalities in similar proportions as they are found in the population as a whole, though in practice this is not always carried out.[3]

Bilinsky provides the best analysis of national representation in the apparatuses of the Union Republics. He shows that the party first secretary in *all* the republican parties was a national of the indigenous population – e.g. a Moldavian in Moldavia. The party second secretary was sometimes of a different nationality: in 1966, six out of fourteen were Russians. The membership of the Republican Politbureaus in 1966 was overwhelmingly made up of nationalities of the titular republic: in the Ukraine, twelve out of fourteen were Ukrainians; in Uzbekistan, seven were Uzbeks, one was a Russian and the nationality of two could not be ascertained; in Moldavia, five were Moldavians, two were Russians and four were of unknown stock; in Latvia, seven

[1] See Chapter 5.
[2] *Political Power: USA/USSR* (1964), pp. 132-3.
[3] See J. Bilinsky, 'The Rulers and the Ruled', *Problems of Communism*, vol. 16 (Sept-Oct. 1967), p. 19.

were Latvians, one was Ossetian and the nationality of two was not known. In the Council of Ministers of the Republics, the Chairman was without exception a member of the titular nationality, as was the First Deputy Chairman in thirteen out of the fifteen Republics.[1] These findings are confirmed by George Fischer, who shows that executive posts at the USSR level (in 1958 and 1962) have more than an equal share of Russian incumbents but that the reverse is true for posts below the USSR level.[2] This evidence would not suggest that there is any deprivation of the nationalities by the union republics, at least as far as political representation is concerned. On the contrary, these figures would suggest that republics are able to aggregate a national republican interest.[3]

The representation of the various nationalities at the centre varies between different institutions. Russians are *under* represented in the Supreme Soviet, being 42.5 per cent of the deputies in 1966 and 54.6 per cent of the total population. In the CPSU, as I have pointed out earlier, they have more than their share – 62.4 per cent in 1965. Of the full members of the CPSU Central Committee in 1966, the Slavic nationalities (Russians, Ukrainians and White Russians) constituted 81.54 per cent of the total, their share of the Politbureau and Secretariat was 83.33 per cent, whereas their share of the population was 76.28 per cent. In the Council of Ministers of 1966, the Slavic nationalities constituted 94.2 per cent of the ministers and other functionaries. This figure, however, and this is important, ignores the fifteen chairmen of the Council of Ministers of the Union Republics, who are members of the Council of the USSR, and who are mostly non-Slavs.[4]

The smaller nationalities tend to be underrepresented, except in the Supreme Soviet where we have seen that the federal system assures their representation.[5] Jews come out particularly low: they make up 1.1 per cent of the population, but only 0.33 per cent of the Supreme Soviet (1966), 0.51 per cent of the Central Committee (1966), and their one member of the Council of Ministers gives them a 1.79 share. Professor Nove has said that this is unique both by comparison with the Russian past when Jews were most active politically and with other countries with a significant Jewish population.[6] But such low participation is accounted for in some respects by the institutional arrangements: as the Jews were not afforded the full status of a nationality and are geographically dispersed their share of members in the Soviet through the federal system is reduced. The 'quota system' of party membership tends to decrease their share – because of their geographical dispersion. It would be

[1] 'The Rulers and the Ruled', *loc. cit.*, p. 20.
[2] George Fischer, *The Soviet System and Modern Society* (New York, 1968), pp. 74-5.
[3] See Chapter 8 above, and Reading no. 7.
[4] Based on data cited by Bilinsky, *loc. cit.*, pp. 23-5.
[5] See Chapter 5.
[6] A. Nove, *Soviet Jewry . . .*, p. 17.

wrong, however, to infer that Jews are *excluded* from Soviet political institutions: in 1966, five were elected to the Supreme Soviet and 7,647 were chosen at all levels of government.[1]

Brzezinski and Huntingdon's characterisation of a national elite, therefore, needs some modification. The figures cited above would suggest that those of slavonic stock do predominate in all-union elite positions, and are rather more frequent than in the population as a whole. On the other hand, the republican political elites would seem not to be so constituted.

We have seen that considerable changes have taken place in the USSR and that these have altered the social and economic structure. Whether the non-Russian population is now 'worse off' than before or than they would have been under another non-Bolshevik government involves not only a comparison of objective indicators but also judgement of value. There seems to be little evidence to sustain the allegation of economic exploitation of non-Slavic areas. It is true that in the development of the more backward areas, a form of Russification has taken place: but again this may not be a bad thing, because with it social and cultural standards (such as welfare and education) were improved. There is some evidence to suggest the political exclusion of the minor nationalities from the top political and economic elites, but again not all nationalities (or professions) can be represented. In the republics the cultural importance of nationality persists, it seems to coexist with industrialisation, probably providing a sense of belonging in the growing diversification and anonymity created by an industrial society.

THE CHRISTIAN RELIGIONS

One of the widest definitions of religion is that of a system of *'belief, practice, and organisation* which shape an *ethic* manifest in the behaviour of their adherents'.[2] Belief involves an interpretation of the universe, usually in supernatural terms. The religious organisation defines the membership of the believers and lays down rules of conduct and ritual. The ethic involves interaction of the religious belief with the social environment – the effects of religious belief on social action. The essential characteristic of religion is a belief in the supernatural, or some sacred thing. Communism itself is said by some to be a religion. Communism, however, is a materialist, atheistic belief

[1] S. Rabinovich, *Jews in the Soviet Union* (Moscow, 1967), pp. 52-3.

[2] N. Birnbaum, 'Religion', in J. Gould and W. L. Kolb, *A Dictionary of the Social Sciences* (1964), p. 588.

system and while it certainly provides a Utopia in the form of a final state of society, it does not invoke any supernatural authority to do so and, therefore, in this book it will not be considered as a religion.[1] One can study a religious institution in terms of its dogma, its membership, the bonds between members, and the effects of an individual's membership of the religious body on other institutions of the society (the economy or the polity). This last aspect is what interests sociologists and political scientists and we shall consider it first before examining the structure of some religious organisations in Soviet Russia.

Marx on Religion

Marx's analysis of religion follows from his general theoretical outlook. Religious ideas reinforce the class relationships engendered by ownership relations. They reflect, on the one hand, the ideology of the ruling class and thereby act as cement in stabilising the social order; on the other, religion acts as a vent for the misery and degradation of the exploited class. Marx poignantly summed up his views on religion in a well-known passage: 'Religious belief is at one and the same time an expression of real poverty and a protest against real poverty. Religion is the sigh of an oppressed creature, the heart of a heartless world, just as it is the spirit of a spiritless situation. It is the *opium* of the people'.[2]

Marx here pointed out the more positive role played by religion in being a 'protest against real poverty': the role of religious sects is particularly important in this respect. But the dominant function of religious ideas, especially as expressed through established churches, is that of a soporific or opiate, which deadens the pain of oppression and which at the same time obscures class exploitation.

Membership of religious orders and belief in God as salvation are, in a Marxist sense, the 'false consciousness' of the oppressed. That is, the individual attributes his impoverishment to a false cause and his action can in no way improve his social being. Prayer, belief in God, in the supernatural and in religious salvation can only divert the individual's consciousness from class and revolutionary action.

Religion is the opium of the people . . . Religion is a kind of spiritual gin in which the slaves of capital drown their human shape and their claims to any decent life . . . All modern religions and Churches, all religious organisations, Marxism always regards as organs of *bourgeois* reaction serving to defend exploitation and to stupefy the working class.[3]

[1] Communism may provide for some people similar functions to a religious body. In this respect, of course, so do other creeds such as capitalism and libertarianism.

[2] Contribution to 'The Critique of Hegel's Philosophy of Law', K. Marx and F. Engels, *On Religion* (Moscow, 1955), p. 42.

[3] V. I. Lenin, cited in R. Conquest, *Religion in the USSR* (1968), p. 7.

The Bolsheviks regarded religion as being dependent on class relationships and exploitation. With the abolition of capitalism, they argued, religion would wither away. As an institution, the Bolsheviks opposed the Church, but the struggle against religion was secondary to the class struggle. Religious prejudices, it was thought, would disappear with the introduction of socialist planning and the kind of scientific education that goes with it. This would be the long-term tendency. In the short-run after the October revolution, measures had to be taken to combat the religious beliefs and institutions which flourished in Tsarist Russia.

The Russian Orthodox Church

Under the Tsars the Russian Orthodox Church was the national church of the Empire. As an official church, the Orthodoxy had special privileges and rights under the Tsars. It was closely linked to the government, it had official representatives in the Council of Ministers and in the provinces priests might be appointed to meetings of the *zemstva* (local councils).

The Orthodox Church was more than a simple expression of the misery of the poor.[1] It had its own lands and received financial support from the government. The Marxist view of an established religion closely bound to, and representing the interests of a dominant class fitted well the Russian Orthodox Church of the late nineteenth and early twentieth century. Not only did it have financial support and political privilege, it had also a monopoly of religious propaganda, it published its own literature and was able to forbid even other religious propaganda inimical to its interests. It alone gave religious instruction in schools, it had the right to perform missionary work and win converts, and the children of mixed religious marriages had to receive an Orthodox upbringing by law. The Orthodox Church was closely bound to the Tsar: he appointed its Over Procurator and the members of the supreme governing body (the Synod), and he had power of appointment and dismissal over bishops.

Politically, the Church in the early twentieth century adopted an extreme right wing position. It opposed atheistic socialist ideas, upheld the Tsarist order and the sanctity of private property. Many of the clergy supported the anti-Semitic *Union of the Russian People*. In the Third and Fourth Dumas (Parliaments) most of the forty or so clergy were extremely conservative. It is true that a minority of priests, such as Father Gapon, took a more liberal view. In general, however, there can be no doubt that the established Russian Orthodox Church was one of the mainstays of Tsarist power.

The belief system of Russian Orthodoxy did not involve strong evangelical

[1] For a detailed description of the Orthodox Church before the Revolution see J. S. Curtiss, *Church and the State in Russia* (New York, 1965).

fervour but stressed liturgy and ritual. It provided little in the form of popular charity. But its influence and ideological grip over the population were on the decline in the late nineteenth century. The intelligentsia generally was hostile to it. The prestige of the priest had fallen and in many villages the clergy were drunken or licentious or both.[1]

The Bolsheviks' Attitude to Religion

After the October Revolution, the Bolsheviks allowed 'freedom of religious and anti-religious propaganda'.[2] The Church was not closed, and services were allowed to continue. But other measures undermined the Church. The nationalisation of land deprived the Church of much of its wealth, and in January 1918, Church and state were legally separated and church property was nationalised.[3] Church schools were taken over by the government. Registration of births, deaths and marriages was made a secular and not a religious affair. Religious instruction of persons under the age of eighteen was prohibited by a decree published in June 1921. As the clergy was regarded as part of the property owning class – 'servants of the bourgeoisie' – they lost all civil rights under the Bolshevik government. They had no vote, either no ration cards or those of the lowest category, their children were barred from schools above the elementary grade and they had to pay higher rates of taxation.[4]

During the Civil War, the Church generally sided with the White Army and leaders such as Kolchak, Denikin and Wrangel. The Reds were condemned and appeals were made for help to Christian countries. After the Civil War, a period of conflict ensued between Church and state. Resistance to the communists was put up by the Church and disorders occurred as a result of which many priests and laymen were charged with counter-revolutionary activity and some were consequently executed.

A group of pro-Soviet priests, 'The Initiative Group of the Orthodox Church', was formed which felt that the government was justified in many of its actions during a national emergency. This group, which became known as the 'Living Church', accepted the political power of the Bolsheviks, advised church members to be loyal to the authorities who were 'fighting for the ideals of God's Kingdom.'[5] The Living Church introduced other reforms: services were performed in Russian and not Church Slavonic, married priests were able to become bishops, the eucharistic ceremony was performed openly,

---

[1] J. S. Curtiss, 'Church and State', in Black, *The Transformation of Russian Society*, pp. 407-8.
[2] See article 13, *Constitution of the RSFSR*, 10 July 1918.
[3] See the decree of the Council of People's Commissars, Reading no. 17.
[4] R. Conquest, *Religion in the USSR* (1967), p. 14.
[5] W. Kolarz, *Religion in the Soviet Union* (1962), p. 39.

not behind the altar screen. The Living Church was for a while given special privileges by the government: it was allowed a periodical, and it could train priests.

The more conservative members of the Orthodox Church opposed the new trends, but even here an accommodation with the Bolsheviks was to take place. The first development in this direction was the capitulation of Patriarch Tikhon who in 1922 gave his loyalty to the government and, in 1925 in his will, called churchmen to support Soviet rule. But opposition to the regime continued until 1927 when Tikhon's successor (Metropolitan Sergius) obtained official recognition for his part of the Church. This gave the Orthodoxy headquarters in Moscow and the right to publish the *Journal of the Moscow Patriarchate*. In return the Church was to refrain from politics and be loyal to the regime. This *modus vivendi* has continued to the present day. It did not mean, however, that the Church and church members were to go unpersecuted.

We have seen that the 1918 Constitution allowed anti-religious propaganda. The regime tried not only to weaken the Church but also to eradicate belief in God which it considered a superstition. In the early post-revolutionary years, violence and sacrilege had been perpetrated against the Church. From 1923, the Communist Party attempted to develop new ways of anti-religious propaganda. These included, the publication of 'popular scientific' literature devised to explain the origin and class nature of religion; the organisation of anti-religious propaganda put across by lectures; the setting up under the party of anti-religious study circles and the inculcation of materialist natural science among the masses.

Anti-religious newspapers flourished and the *League of Militant Godless* was formed in 1929. Anti-Christmas and anti-Easter campaigns were carried out accompanied by the ceremonial burning of ikons. The League campaigned for the closing of churches and often resorted to harsh measures to get them shut. By 1933, Moscow had only half the number of churches operating as before the revolution. Sometimes, the activity of the League was based on crude materialism: it campaigned for the removal of church bells because ferrous metals were needed by Soviet heavy industry.[1] In the early thirties, anti-religious evening courses were organised having an enrolment of some 150,000 students in 1933.[2] The activity of the League was not simply negative, it organised sections concerned with atheistic exhibitions, artistic forms of atheistic propaganda (the theatre and music), and with the creation of a new way of life. Through these groups it sought to alter the belief systems of the people. Its slogan was: 'the fight for godlessness is a fight for socialism'! The country was flooded with anti-religious posters and leaflets. The League

[1] For an account see Walter Kolarz, *Religion in the Soviet Union* (1962), p. 6.
[2] R. Conquest, *op. cit.*, p. 25.

Q

continued until the German invasion, had its main strength in the urban industrial areas, but in the countryside, where religious feeling was strong, it was weakest. The propaganda of the League might be considered as an ideological part of the industrialisation campaign. It provided in a very rudimentary way a belief system for the uprooted peasant drafted into the town for work. The League sought explicitly to contribute to the success of the economic plans and set up 'Godless Collective Farms' and 'Godless Shock Brigades'.

The persecution of the Church stopped during the Second World War. The Great Patriotic War demanded an end to internal dissension. Patriotism – always a strong element in Stalinist ideology – became dominant and the ideological schism between Church and state was ended. The Church actively supported the regime in the war against Hitler. As a result, the Church was given a higher status: it was recognised as a 'juridical person' able to own property and it was recognised as the principal religious body in the USSR. Church buildings were repaired. The Church for its part contributed financially to the war effort, it condemned collaborators with the Germans and offered prayers for 'our divinely protected land, and for its authorities headed by its God-given leader'.[1]

By the end of the Second World War, in theory the Russian Orthodox Church and the Soviet state each had separate areas of authority. The state was not to interfere with the internal life of the Church. It is still claimed by the Soviet authorities that no persecution of religious faith takes place in the USSR. Freedom of conscience is guaranteed by the Constitution. This view is echoed by many prominent Orthodox Churchmen who have officially said that in no country does the Church 'enjoy such favourable conditions of existence as in the USSR.'[2]

Paradoxically, therefore, one has a situation in which an avowedly communist state provides a framework for the development of a religious institution. In theory, it falls to the Communist Party (not the state officially) to counter religious teaching and the spread of superstition. In fact, the odds are weighed extremely heavily against the Church.

The Post-War Russian Orthodox Church

From the above we can see that sociologically the Orthodox Church had the role of an 'established' religion. Its external ethic, its recommendations for political and social action coincided with those of Soviet Russia's leaders. The Chinese Communists, criticising a Soviet children's book, *Tales from the Bible*, have even asserted that the Soviets use religion as a method of

---

[1] See Reading no. 18 on *rapprochement* between Church and state.
[2] *Journal of the Moscow Patriarchate*, no. 8 (1948), pp. 66-7, cited by Michael Bourdeaux, *Opium of the People* (1965), p. 77.

'enslavement and exploitation of the people'.[1] While this is not true, it illustrates the degree to which the regime had accommodated religion.

The Church since the death of Stalin has lost many of the privileges it had received. In 1958 under Khrushchev, a propaganda attack was launched, and many churches were closed. It has been estimated that nearly half of the Orthodox 20,000 churches operating in 1960 had been closed by 1965.[2] Closure of a church can be effected if it can be shown that there is no support for it. It is asserted in western church circles that often such decisions have been taken when a demand does exist.

Precise figures are not available on the number of worshippers attending church. In 1961, the Orthodox Church claimed 30 million regular worshippers, and Struve has estimated that in the period 1947-57, there were 90 million baptized Orthodox – roughly the same as in 1914.[3] The 'active' Church, however, has declined. The number of bishops has fallen from 163 in 1914 to 63 in 1962, the parochial clergy has declined in the same period from 51,105 to 14,000 and the number of seminaries from 57 to 4.[4] In the absence of detailed surveys, it is impossible to estimate the extent of religious belief. The Orthodox Church is not evangelical, it confines its work to within the walls of the Church. 'We do almost nothing outside the church building. We don't need to because . . . for the Orthodox Christian, liturgy is life'.[5]

According to Soviet figures, women constitute more than 70 per cent of all believers – and between 80 and 90 per cent of those in religious sects.[6] From personal observation of worshippers in Orthodox Churches, at least 80 per cent of those present are women, and of these, three-quarters are over 50 years old.[7] Kolarz has tried to explain the presence of women in church by arguing that women are not emancipated in the USSR and their family insecurity and the heavy work they perform create a need for religion which nullifies Soviet anti-religious arguments.[8] This would only be a partial explanation, for women in other respects – such as access to education and social security benefits – have done better under Soviet rule. Probably a more feasible explanation of female church attendance is the large number of older widows who lack family ties and who were themselves brought up to be religious. In such cases, the Church and its ritual and ceremonies may still provide a heart in a heartless Soviet world.[9] Laurens van der Post's view that, 'Three generations of Soviet indoctrination has destroyed all evidence of

[1] *Peking Review*, no. 20, 12 May 1967, p. 27.

[2] 'Russian Churchmen Face New Trials', *The Times*, 3 Jan. 1965.

[3] N. Struve, *Les Chrétiens en URSS* (Paris, 1963), p. 341.

[4] *Ibid.*

[5] Father Mikhail Zernov, cited in M. Bourdeaux, *Opium of the People* (1965), p. 74.

[6] *Nauka i religiya* (Moscow, 1957), pp. 61, 411.

[7] This view is also shared by Nikita Struve, *Christians in Contemporary Russia* (1967), p. 184.

[8] W. Kolarz, *Religion in the Soviet Union*, pp. 25-6.

[9] A good example of this may be seen in M. Bourdeaux, *Opium of the People*, pp. 82-4.

religion'[1] is too strong; it cannot be denied that religion has shown a certain resilience to communism.

Socially, the greatest number of believers is among the peasantry and the lowest is among the intelligentsia. This is what one would expect, for the peasantry is educationally relatively deprived and communist influence is lowest in the countryside. A recent Soviet social survey showed that 47 per cent of collective farm households had ikons: among pensioners the figure was 60 per cent.[2] Population movement from country to town has left the village and collective farm with a greater number of older female members who have in all probability been brought up to be religious.

Kolarz has estimated that some two to three per cent of Soviet youth is 'religious' – though exactly what is meant by 'religious' is not defined. He argues that there are probably two reasons for the persistence of religious beliefs among the young. First, the influence of older members of the family, particularly the grandmother who often has responsibility for the care of young children while the parents work and who inculcates religious beliefs at a formative age. Second, a communist regime creates frustrations: 'the unfilled hunger of the human soul awakes religious feelings in the young'.[3] After the initial religious indoctrination, religious beliefs lie dormant, as it were, for decades, and when the individual finds his life spiritually barren he turns again to the Church for religious salvation. While this is an interesting theory it has yet to be demonstrated empirically. The evidence taken as a whole seems to show that religion has little hold over the population,[4] but some evidence of a religious revival may be drawn from the activity of the non-conformist religious groups.

The Baptists[5]

At the beginning of this chapter, it was pointed out that religion in Marxist theory served both to reinforce the property relationships of society and to act as a vent for the misery engendered by a social order. 'Established' religions, such as Russian Orthodoxy, largely perform the first function, sectarian religious bodies, the second. Sectarian groups are often distinguished by being composed of lower, more deprived, social strata than those of the more established Church. As Stark has pointed out, religion acts

---

[1] Laurens van der Post, *Journey into Russia* (1964), p. 276.

[2] Yu V. Arutyunyan, 'Sotsial'naya struktura sel'skogo naseleniya', *Voprosy filosofii*, no. 6 (1966), p. 60.

[3] W. Kolarz, *Religion in the Soviet Union*, p. 24.

[4] See also A. Inkeles and R. A. Bauer, *The Soviet Citizen* (Cambridge, Mass., 1959), pp. 380-1.

[5] The Baptists only are taken as an example of the non-conformists. I have had to ignore the Catholics and other smaller sects. See also the section on nationalities where aspects of Moslem and Judaic faith are discussed.

as 'a kind of protest movement, distinguished from other similar movements by the basic fact that it experiences and expresses its dissatisfactions and strivings in religious (rather than in political or economic or generally secular) terms'.[1]

Many small eccentric groups such as the Molokans, Dukhobors, the Sect of the Castrated, the Fyodorist Crusaders, and the Innocents were founded in the Russian Empire.[2] Among the most important Protestant groups are the Evangelical Christians and the Baptists. To illustrate the position of the sects, only these will be commented on here.

Such sects were not regarded by Marxists in the same way as the Orthodox Church. Before the revolution they were as opposed to the autocracy as the Bolsheviks, except that their Utopia was a religious one based on spiritual precepts rather than on political revolution. After the revolution, the Baptists and Evangelical Christians were not regarded by the Bolsheviks as supporters of the *ancien régime*, for they had been persecuted by it. Much of the Bolsheviks' opposition to *established* religion was similar in character to what the sects had been saying for a long time, and in fact they were not persecuted or weakened by the new Soviet state for many years. Indeed, for their part many Baptists applauded the social and economic policies of the Bolsheviks.

The forms of communal living practised by many of the sects had none of the social consequences of capitalist production. Many of their village communities were based on thrift, the abolition of money and the rejection of private property. Their moral code also had similarities to the communist: it strongly disapproved of drinking, debauchery, hooliganism and sexual licence. In the first ten years of Bolshevik rule, the paradoxical position existed that sectarian groups, which had previously opposed and had been alienated from the state, were now given a secure position by Russia's atheistic leaders. The Baptists organised their own collective farms, formed their own youth movement, the *Khristomol*, and were allowed to publish the Bible (25,000 copies were published in 1926).

But with the collectivisation campaign and growing centralisation of political control from 1928, the attitude of the government to the sects began to change. Politically, they were charged with being connected with, and agents of, religious groups abroad. Economically, they were regarded as *kulak* elements, and were absorbed into collective farms and often deported east of the Urals. Ideologically, however similar some of the sects' moral teaching was to socialism, their religious ideals were at odds with historical materialism, and conflict with the state over education and the upbringing of the young ensued. Even on a Christian collective farm, one could not have

[1] Werner Stark, *The Sociology of Religion* (1967), vol. 2, p. 5.

[2] For details see W. Kolarz, *Religion in the USSR* (1962), Chapter 11; N. Struve, *Christians in Contemporary Russia* (1967), Chapter 10.

communism without the class struggle. The sects' position became more akin to what it had been before the revolution. Their periodicals stopped publication and their 'Preachers' School' was closed. To spread the faith they had to rely once more on face to face contact.

After the Second World War, the persecution of sects eased and a formal organisation, the 'All-Union Council of Evangelical Christians/Baptists' was set up. This had the right to represent all sectarians in the Soviet Union and brought under its wing the western, newly incorporated areas of the USSR which had relatively large sectarian populations.[1] Thus a number of Christian groups of all opinions were brought under the aegis of the All-Union Council.

The existence of a formal structure did not save the Baptists from the Communist Party's anti-religious propaganda. This, however, did not deplete the numbers or diminish the faith of the Baptist flock until the mid-fifties, when membership figures fell. At the end of 1947, there were 4,000 Baptist communities, 400,000 baptised and 4,000,000 attended services.[2] By 1954, there were 5,400 communities and 512,000 baptised.[3] Since the 1950s the size of the official Baptist community has declined, in 1966 there were about 2,000 communities with more than 200,000 members.[4] The strength of the Baptist Church has officially fallen by over three millions since 1954. The difficulty with these statistics is that they may reflect a genuine reduction in Church membership or a schism in the Baptist community, and the latter, according to Bourdeaux, is the most important.[5] The life of the breakaway sects is more dynamic and militant against the Soviet regime than the 'official' body, which has become more like an 'established church'. Illegal schools for the young, the circulation of leaflets, and public meetings have been reported.[6] The Baptists by some accounts, attract a large number of young people.[7] Soviet research, however, shows that the members of sects are old. Of the *Molokane* surveyed in Michurinsk district, only two were aged between 20 and 40 years, three between 40 and 50 years, the majority (14) were between 50 and 60 years

---

[1] The annexation of the western areas also brought the Jehovah's Witnesses, who now seem particularly strong in the east and north (areas of former deportation to the USSR). See Struve, pp. 240-3. The resettlement of Germans in the Perm region brought Baptism there: *Nauka i Religiya*, no. 11, 1966, pp. 32-3.

[2] *Bratski Vestnik*, no. 1 (1948), pp. 6-7. S. Bolshakoff, *Russian Non-Conformity* (Philadelphia, 1950), p. 128, cited by R. Conquest, *Religion in the USSR* (1968), p. 103.

[3] *Bratski Vestnik*, nos. 3-4 (1954), cited by Conquest, *ibid.*

[4] F. Fedorenko, *Sekty, ikh vera i dela* (Moscow, 1965), p. 166. An estimated 250,000 baptised members according to *Bratski Vestnik*, no. 6 (1966), p. 17, cited by Bourdeaux, *ibid.*

[5] The recent politics of the Baptists is dealt with by M. Bourdeaux and P. Reddaway, 'Soviet Baptists Today, *Survey* (Jan. 1968). See Reading No. 9, above pp. 261-2.

[6] Yu. Alexandrov, *The Times*, 22 September 1966, and examples were cited in Chapter 8 of the ways the Baptists pressurised the authorities.

[7] N. Struve, *Christians in Contemporary Russia* (1967), pp. 234-5.

and nine were over 60.[1] Similarly, of Baptists surveyed in this area, those over 60 years of age constituted 47 per cent of the total, between 50 and 60 years, 29 per cent and the younger generation aged between 20 and 40 made up only six per cent of the total.[2] It seems most likely that the Baptists and other sects are ageing like the members of the Orthodox Church.

The Baptists are particularly strong in the western areas of the USSR in the Baltic, Caucasus and Ukraine, though they also have houses of prayer in the Far East and the European part of Russia.[3]

The persistence of the sects shows that if beliefs are strong enough, non-communist ideals may persist even in a socialist state. The social ethic of the sects, it should be noted, is not hostile to the social ethic of the state. Work, modesty and frugality are virtues of the Baptists and presbyters who are implored to 'be exemplary in the fulfillment of civic duties and to educate the members of the church in this spirit. Your Church must ardently love your country and your people'.[4] The demonstrations by the Baptists are aimed at securing greater freedom within the framework of Soviet law and greater rights for propaganda and means to spread the message.[5] The form of protest, as with all religious sects, is not primarily political but concerned with securing concessions for the practice of spiritual and religious beliefs. The relationship between communism and Baptism has been summed up by a young Baptist as follows: 'There are many points in common between the *Komsomol* and the Baptist faith; both aim at the development of the moral virtues in men. But the communists have no fear of God, whereas the Baptists have, and that explains their greater success'.[6]

Christianity in Soviet Society

From our earlier discussion in this chapter we may conclude that organised Christianity has suffered a serious decline in the USSR, but this should not lead one to underestimate the persistence of religious belief. A decline has taken place in Great Britain, though it has not been so rapid as in the USSR. With industrialisation a secularisation of life has taken place. Mass media and entertainment have weakened the appeal of religious ceremony and ritual. The state has taken over the Church's role of provision for the needy and destitute. Science has provided an explanation of the physical world. But this does not entail that religion has 'withered away' in the West. In Britain, 72

[1] 'Sovremennoe sektantstvo i ego preodolenie', *Voprosy istorii religii i ateizma*, no. 9 (Moscow, 1961), p. 117.
[2] *Ibid.*, p. 127.
[3] See W. Kolarz, *Religion in the Soviet Union*, pp. 306-12.
[4] *Bratski Vestnik*, no. 3 (1946), p. 29. Cited by Kolarz, p. 313.
[5] See Bourdeaux and Reddaway, esp. p. 66.
[6] Cited by N. Struve, p. 236.

per cent of the population and in the United States 95.5 per cent say that they believe in God.[1] The large numbers of believers in the USA may not imply a high level of religious conviction but it may simply indicate a belief inculcated during childhood.

How can we account for the persistence of religious beliefs in Sovie society? Probably they provide an adaptive function. They help the individua to manage the tensions of his life, his fears and uncertainties. In so far as religion has an appeal, it provides something which the competing ideologies of communism and science cannot provide. The Church is most likely to provide a form of identity for individuals in a rapidly changing, fragmented and differentiated society. Those with no family and the aged are likely to find solace in religion. It provides a source of managing the tension which family bereavement and old age bring. It is impossible to say with any certainty why people join the religious sects. There is no evidence to suggest that their members are suffering from problems of adjustment any more than other Soviet citizens. Participants seem to be recruited from the less privileged social strata i.e. the peasantry and working class.[2] But one cannot infer from this very general statement that they are particularly *economically* deprived. The survival of Christian sects is probably due to the inadequate role of Communist Party organisations which do not fully satisfy individual citizens' needs. The welfare and companionship provided by the sects are important ways in which they win support. The commandments for presbyters require them to: 'Know [your sheep's] spiritual situation, their joys and sorrows, their family life. Visit the members of the Church in their homes. Show special love to the weak, the needy, those in sorrow and the sick'.[3]

Churches in any society cannot be regarded as institutions 'outside' the social structure. As we have seen, the economic ethic of the Baptists does not bring them into conflict with the Soviet state. But their religious beliefs are in contradiction to the belief system of the Communist Party. Consequently, Christians and other religious persons are penalised for their beliefs: they are barred from the highest political positions, for their values are at variance with those of communism. As the Church is not directly incorporated in the political system, this leads to stress between it and the state. This is not just a phenomenon of the USSR, but exists between Church and state in many countries (for example, France). In Great Britain, it is the humanists and atheists who are restricted in their access to television and radio. In Northern Ireland, it is the Catholics who are politically deprived. In Soviet society, the dominant ideology of Marxism is inimical to religion. The present *modus vivendi* makes it possible for believers to believe, but very difficult for religious

---

[1] Figures cited by S. Cotgrove, *The Science of Society* (1967), p. 191.

[2] Bourdeaux and Reddaway, p. 49.

[3] *Bratski Vestnik*, no. 3 (1946), p. 29. Cited by Kolarz, p. 313.

views to be spread or passed on to the young. The persistence of Christianity is the persistence of an alternative view and explanation of the world. While this may not appear particularly serious in western states, the authority of the Communist Party in the Soviet order is based to some extent on the theoretical validity of Marxism, which cannot be reconciled with the Christian religion.

Reading No. 16
J. Stalin, 'Marxism and the National Question'
Source:
Collected Works (Moscow, 1953), Vol. 2.

THE NATION

What is a nation?

A nation is primarily a community, a definite community of people.

This community is not racial, nor is it tribal. The modern Italian nation was formed from Romans, Teutons, Etruscans, Greeks, Arabs, and so forth. The French nation was formed from Gauls, Romans, Britons, Teutons, and so on. The same must be said of the British, the Germans and others, who were formed into nations from people of diverse races and tribes.

Thus, a nation is not a racial or tribal, but a historically constituted community of people.

On the other hand, it is unquestionable that the great empires of Cyrus and Alexander could not be called nations, although they came to be constituted historically and were formed out of different tribes and races. They were not nations, but casual and loosely-connected conglomerations of groups, which fell apart or joined together according to the victories or defeats of this or that conqueror.

Thus, a nation is not a casual or ephemeral conglomeration, but a stable community of people.

But not every stable community constitutes a nation. Austria and Russia are also stable communities, but nobody calls them nations. What distinguishes a national community from a state community? The fact, among others, that a national community is inconceivable without a common language. The Czech nation in Austria and the Polish in Russia would be impossible if each did not have a common language, whereas the integrity of Russia and Austria is not affected by the fact that there are a number of different languages within their borders. We are referring, of course, to the spoken languages of the people and not to the official governmental languages.

Thus, a *common language* is one of the characteristic features of a nation.

This, of course, does not mean that different nations always and everywhere speak different languages, or that all who speak one language necessarily constitute one nation. A *common* language for every nation, but not necessarily different languages for different nations! There is no nation which at one and the same time speaks several languages, but this does not mean that there cannot be two nations speaking the same language! Englishmen and Americans speak one language, but they do not constitute one nation. The same is true of the Norwegians and the Danes, the English and the Irish.

But why, for instance, do the English and the Americans not constitute one nation in spite of their common language?

Firstly, because they do not live together, but inhabit different territories. A nation is formed only as a result of lengthy and systematic intercourse, as a result of people living together generation after generation. But people cannot live together for lengthy periods unless they have a common territory. Englishmen and Americans originally inhabited the same territory, England, and constituted one nation. Later, one section of the English emigrated from England to a new territory, America, and there, in the new territory, in the course of time, came to form the new American nation. Difference of territory led to the formation of different nations.

Thus, a *common territory* is one of the characteristic features of a nation.

But this is not all. Common territory does not by itself create a nation. This requires, in addition, an internal economic bond to weld the various parts of the nation into a single whole. There is no such bond between England and America, and so they constitute two different nations. But the Americans themselves would not deserve to be called a nation were not the different parts of America bound together into an economic whole, as a result of division of labour between them, the development of means of communication, and so forth.

Take the Georgians, for instance. The Georgians before the Reform inhabited a common territory and spoke one language. Nevertheless, they did not, strictly speaking, constitute one nation, for, being split up into a number of disconnected principalities, they could not share a common economic life; for centuries they waged war against each other and pillaged each other, each inciting the Persians and Turks against the other. The ephemeral and casual union of the principalities which some successful king sometimes managed to bring about embraced at best a superficial administrative sphere, and rapidly disintegrated owing to the caprices of the princes and the indifference of the peasants. Nor could it be otherwise in economically disunited Georgia . . . Georgia came on the scene as a nation only in the latter half of the nineteenth century, when the fall of serfdom and the growth of the economic life of the country, the development of means of communication and the rise of capitalism, introduced division of labour between the various districts of Georgia, completely shattered the economic isolation of the principalities and bound them together into a single whole.

The same must be said of the other nations which have passed through the stage of feudalism and have developed capitalism.

Thus, *a common economic life, economic cohesion*, is one of the characteristic features of a nation.

But even this is not all. Apart from the foregoing, one must take into consideration the specific spiritual complexion of the people constituting a nation. Nations differ not only in their conditions of life, but also in spiritual complexion, which manifests itself in peculiarities of national culture. If England, America and Ireland, which speak one language, nevertheless constitute three distinct nations, it is in no small measure due to the peculiar psychological make-up which they developed from generation to generation as a result of dissimilar conditions of existence.

Of course, by itself, psychological make-up or, as it is otherwise called, 'national character', is something intangible for the observer, but in so far as it manifests itself in a distinctive culture common to the nation it is something tangible and cannot be ignored.

Needless to say, 'national character' is not a thing that is fixed once and for all, but is modified by changes in the conditions of life; but since it exists at every given moment, it leaves its impress on the physiognomy of the nation.

Thus, *a common psychological make-up*, which manifests itself in common culture, is one of the characteristic features of a nation.

We have now exhausted the characteristic features of a nation.

A nation is a historically constituted, stable community of people, formed on the basis of a common language, territory, economic life, and psychological make-up manifested in a common culture.

It goes without saying that a nation, like every historical phenomenon, is subject to the law of change, has its history, its beginning and end.

It must be emphasised that none of the above characteristics taken separately is sufficient to define a nation. More than that, it is sufficient for a single one of these characteristics to be lacking and the nation ceases to be a nation.

It is possible to conceive of people possessing a common 'national character' who, nevertheless, cannot be said to constitute a single nation if they are economically disunited, inhabit different territories, speak different languages, and so forth. Such, for instance, are the Russian, Galician, American, Georgian and Caucasian Highland *Jews*, who, in our opinion, do not constitute a single nation.

It is possible to conceive of people with a common territory and economic life who nevertheless would not constitute a single nation because they have no common language and no common 'national character'. Such, for instance, are the Germans and Letts in the Baltic region.

Finally, the Norwegians and the Danes speak one language, but they do not constitute a single nation owing to the absence of the other characteristics.

It is only when all these characteristics are present together that we have a nation.

Social-Democracy in all countries therefore proclaims the right of nations to self-determination.

The right of self-determination means that only the nation itself has the right to determine its destiny, that no one has the right *forcibly* to interfere in the life of the nation, to *destroy* its schools and other institutions, to *violate* its habits and customs, to *repress* its language, or *curtail* its rights.

This, of course, does not mean that Social-Democracy will support every custom and institution of a nation. While combating the coercion of any nation, it will uphold only the right of the *nation* itself to determine its own destiny, at the same time agitating against harmful customs and institutions of that nation in order to enable the toiling strata of the nation to emancipate themselves from them.

The right of self-determination means that a nation may arrange its life in the way it wishes. It has the right to arrange its life on the basis of autonomy. It has the right to enter into federal relations with other nations. It has the right to complete secession. Nations are sovereign, and all nations have equal rights.

This, of course, does not mean that Social-Democracy will support every demand of a nation. A nation has the right even to return to the old order of things; but this does not mean that Social-Democracy will subscribe to such a decision if taken by some institution of a particular nation. The obligations of Social-Democracy, which defends the interests of the proletariat, and the rights of a nation, which consists of various classes, are two different things.

In fighting for the right of nations to self-determination, the aim of Social-Democracy is to put an end to the policy of national oppression, to render it impossible, and thereby to remove the grounds of strife between nations, to take the edge off that strife and reduce it to a minimum.

This is what essentially distinguishes the policy of the class-conscious proletariat from the policy of the bourgeoisie, which attempts to aggravate and fan the national struggle and to prolong and sharpen the national movement.

And that is why the class-conscious proletariat cannot rally under the 'national' flag of the bourgeoisie.

That is why the so-called 'evolutionary national' policy advocated by Bauer cannot become the policy of the proletariat. Bauer's attempt to identify his 'evolutionary national' policy with the policy of the 'modern working class' is an attempt to adapt the class struggle of the workers to the struggle of the nations.

The fate of a national movement, which is essentially a bourgeois movement, is naturally bound up with the fate of the bourgeoisie. The final disappearance of a national movement is possible only with the downfall of the bourgeoisie. Only under the reign of socialism can peace be fully established. But even within the framework of capitalism it is possible to reduce the national struggle to a minimum, to undermine it at the root, to render it as harmless as possible to the proletariat. This is borne out, for example, by Switzerland and America. It requires that the country should be democratised and the nations be given the opportunity of free development.

THE NATIONAL QUESTION IN RUSSIA

It remains for us to suggest a positive solution of the national question.

We take as our starting point that the question can be solved only in intimate connection with the present situation in Russia.

Russia is in a transitional period, when 'normal', 'constitutional' life has not yet been established and when the political crisis has not yet been settled. Days of storm and 'complications' are ahead. And this gives rise to the movement, the present and the future movement, the aim of which is to achieve complete democratisation.

It is in connection with this movement that the national question must be examined.

Thus the complete democratisation of the country is the *basis* and condition for the solution of the national question.

When seeking a solution of the question we must take into account not only the situation at home but also the situation abroad. Russia is situated between Europe and Asia, between Austria and China. The growth of democracy in Asia is inevitable. The growth of imperialism in Europe is not fortuitous. In Europe, capital is beginning to feel cramped, and it is reaching out towards foreign countries in search of new markets, cheap labour and new fields of investment. But this leads to external complications and to war. No one can assert that the Balkan War is the end and not the beginning of the complications. It is quite possible, therefore, that a combination of internal and external conditions may arise in which one or another nationality in Russia may find it necessary to raise and settle the question of its independence. And, of course, it is not for Marxists to create obstacles in such cases.

But it follows that Russian Marxists cannot dispense with the right of nations to self-determination.

Thus, *the right of self-determination is an essential element* in the solution of the national question.

Further. What must be our attitude towards nations which for one reason or another will prefer to remain within the framework of the whole?

We have seen that cultural-national autonomy is unsuitable. Firstly, it is artificial and impracticable, for it proposes artificially to draw into a single nation people whom the march of events, real events, is disuniting and dispersing to every corner of the country. Secondly, it stimulates nationalism, because it leads to the viewpoint in favour of the 'demarcation' of people according to national curiae, the 'organisation' of nations, the 'preservation' and cultivation of 'national peculiarities' – all of which are entirely incompatible with Social-Democracy. It is not fortuitous that the Moravian separatists in the Reichsrat, having severed themselves from the German Social-Democratic deputies, have united with the Moravian bourgeois deputies to form a single, so to speak, Moravian 'kolo'. Nor is it fortuitous that the separatists of the Bund have got themselves involved in nationalism by acclaiming the 'Sabbath' and 'Yiddish'. There are no Bundist deputies yet in the Duma, but in the Bund area, there is a clerical-reactionary Jewish community, in the 'controlling institutions' of which the Bund is arranging, for a beginning, a 'get-together' of the Jewish workers and bourgeois'[1] Such is the logic of cultural-national autonomy.

Thus, *national* autonomy does not solve the problem.

What, then, is the way out?

The only correct solution is *regional* autonomy, autonomy for such crystallised units as Poland, Lithuania, the Ukraine, the Caucasus, etc.

The advantage of regional autonomy consists, first of all, in the fact that it does not deal with a fiction bereft of territory, but with a definite population inhabiting a definite territory. Next, it does not divide people according to nations, it does not strengthen national barriers; on the contrary, it breaks down these barriers and unites the population in such a manner as to open the way for division of a different kind, division according to classes. Finally, it makes it possible to utilise the natural wealth of the region and to develop its productive forces in the best possible way without awaiting the decisions of a common centre – functions which are not inherent features of cultural-national autonomy.

Thus, *regional autonomy is an essential element* in the solution of the national question.

Of course, not one of the regions constitutes a compact, homogeneous nation, for each is interspersed with national minorities, such are the Jews in Poland, the Letts in Lithuania, the Russians in the Caucasus, the Poles in the Ukraine, and so on. It may be feared therefore, that the minorities will be oppressed by the national

[1] See *Report of the Eighth Conference of the Bund*, the concluding part of the resolution on the community.

majorities. But there will be grounds for fear only if the old order continues to prevail in the country. Give the country complete democracy and all grounds for fear will vanish.

It is proposed to bind the dispersed minorities into a single national union. But what the minorities want is not an artificial union, but real rights in the localities they inhabit. What can such a union give them *without* complete democratisation? On the other hand, what need is there for a national union *when there is* complete democratisation?

What is it that particularly agitates a national minority?

A minority is discontented not because there is no national union but because it does not enjoy the right to use its native language. Permit it to use its native language and the discontent will pass of itself.

A minority is discontented not because there is no artificial union but because it does not possess its own schools. Give it its own schools and all grounds for discontent will disappear.

A minority is discontented not because there is no national union but because it does not enjoy liberty of conscience (religious liberty), liberty of movement, etc. Give it these liberties and it will cease to be discontented.

Thus, *equal rights of nations in all forms* (*language, schools, etc.*) *is an essential element* in the solution of the national question. Consequently, a state law based on complete democratisation of the country is required, prohibiting all national privileges without exception and every kind of disability or restriction on the rights of national minorities.

That, and that alone, is the real, not a paper guarantee of the rights of a minority.

One may or may not dispute the existence of a logical connection between organisational federalism and cultural-national autonomy. But one cannot dispute the fact that the latter creates an atmosphere favouring unlimited federalism, developing into complete rupture, into separatism. If the Czechs in Austria and the Bundists in Russia began with autonomy, passed to federation and ended in separatism, there can be no doubt that an important part in this was played by the nationalist atmosphere that is naturally generated by cultural-national autonomy. It is not fortuitous that national autonomy and organisational federalism go hand in hand. It is quite understandable. Both demand demarcation according to nationalities. The similarity is beyond question. The only difference is that in one case the population as a whole is divided, while in the other it is the Social-Democratic workers who are divided.

We know where the demarcation of workers according to nationalities leads to. The disintegration of a united workers' party, the splitting of trade unions according to nationalities, aggravation of national friction, national strikebreaking, complete demoralization within the ranks of Social-Democracy – such are the results of organisational federalism. This is eloquently borne out by the history of Social-Democracy in Austria and the activities of the Bund in Russia.

The only cure for this is organisation on the basis of internationalism.

To unite locally the workers of all nationalities of Russia into *single, integral* collective bodies, to unite these collective bodies into a *single* party – such is the task.

It goes without saying that a party structure of this kind does not preclude, but on the contrary presumes, wide autonomy for the *regions* within the single integral party.

The experience of the Caucasus proves the expediency of this type of organisation. If the Caucasians have succeeded in overcoming the national friction between the Armenian and Tatar workers; if they have succeeded in safeguarding the population against the possibility of massacres and shooting affrays; if in Baku, that kaleidoscope of national groups, national conflicts are now no longer possible, and if it has been possible to draw the workers there into the single current of a powerful movement, then the international structure of the Caucasian Social-Democracy was not the least factor in bringing this about.

The type of organisation influences not only practical work. It stamps an indelible impress on the whole mental life of the worker. The worker lives the life of his organisation, which stimulates his intellectual growth and educates him. And thus, acting within his organisation and continually meeting there comrades from other nationalities, and side by side with them waging a common struggle under the leadership of a common collective body, he becomes deeply imbued with the idea that workers are *primarily* members of one class family, members of the united army of socialism. And this cannot but have a tremendous educational value for large sections of the working class.

Therefore, the international type of organisation serves as a school of fraternal sentiments and is a tremendous agitational factor on behalf of internationalism.

But this is not the case with an organisation on the basis of nationalities. When the workers are organised according to nationality they isolate themselves within their national shells, fenced off from each other by organisational barriers. The stress is laid not on what is *common* to the workers but on what distinguishes them from each other. In this type of organisation the worker is *primarily* a member of his nation: a Jew, a Pole, and so on. It is not surprising that *national* federalism in organisation inculcates in the workers a spirit of national seclusion.

Therefore, the national type of organisation is a school of national narrow-mindedness and stagnation.

Thus we are confronted by two *fundamentally* different types of organisation: the type based on international solidarity and the type based on the organisational 'demarcation' of the workers according to nationalities.

Attempts to reconcile these two types have so far been vain. The compromise rules of the Austrian Social-Democratic Party drawn up in Wimberg in 1897 were left hanging in the air. The Austrian party fell to pieces and dragged the trade unions with it. 'Compromise' proved to be not only utopian, but harmful. Strasser is right when he says that 'separatism achieved its first triumph at the Wimberg Party Congress',[1] The same is true in Russia. The 'compromise' with the federalism of the Bund which took place at the Stockholm Congress ended in a complete fiasco. The Bund violated the Stockholm compromise. Ever since the Stockholm Congress the Bund has been an obstacle in the way of union of the workers locally in a *single* organisation, which would include workers of all nationalities. And the Bund has obstinately persisted in its separatist tactics in spite of the fact that in 1907 and in 1908 Russian Social-Democracy repeatedly demanded that unity should at last be

[1] See his *Der Arbeiter und die Nation*, 1912.

established from below among the workers of all nationalities. The Bund, which began with organisational national autonomy, in fact passed to federalism, only to end in complete rupture, separatism. And by breaking with the Russian Social-Democratic Party it caused disharmony and disorganisation in the ranks of the latter.

The path of 'compromise' must therefore be discarded as utopian and harmful.

One thing or the other: *either* the federalism of the Bund, in which case the Russian Social-Democratic Party must re-form itself on a basis of 'demarcation' of the workers according to nationalities; *or* an international type of organisation, in which case the Bund must reform itself on a basis of territorial autonomy after the pattern of the Caucasian, Lettish and Polish Social-Democracies, and thus make possible the direct union of the Jewish workers with the workers of the other nationalities of Russia.

There is no middle course: principles triumph, they do not 'compromise'.

Thus, *the principle of international solidarity of the workers is an essential element* in the solution of the national question.

Vienna, January 1913.

Reading No. 17
Separation of Church and State. Decree of the Council of People's Commissars, 23 Jan. 1918.
Source:
Reprinted in N. Struve, *Christians in Contemporary Russia* (London, 1967), pp. 378-9.

1. The Church is separated from the State.

2. Within the territory of the Republic, it is forbidden to promulgate any laws or local decrees which would hamper or limit freedom of conscience or establish advantages or privileges on the basis of the confessional membership of citizens.

3. Every citizen can practise any religion he wishes, or not practise one at all.

All loss of rights resulting from the practice of any faith or the non-practice of a faith, is repealed.

N.B. All indication of religious membership or non-membership of citizens is deleted from all official acts.

4. The activities of any State or other public, legal or social bodies will not be accompanied by any religious rites or ceremonies.

5. The free practice of religious rites is guaranteed in as far as it does not interfere with public order and is not accompanied by any attempt on the rights of the citizens of the Soviet Republic. Local authorities will be empowered to take all necessary measures in these cases, to protect public order and security.

6. No one may defect from the fulfilment of his public obligations by reason of his religious views.

Exceptions from this resolution, on condition one public duty is replaced by another, are permitted in individual cases, on the decision of a People's Court.

7. Religious oath taking or swearing in is annulled. Where necessary only a solemn promise will be given.

8. Marriage acts will only be drawn up by the civil authorities: by marriage and birth registration offices.

9. Schools are separated from the Church. The teaching of religious doctrines in all State and public as well as any private educational establishments where general subjects are taught, is prohibited.

Citizens may teach and be taught religion privately.

10. All ecclesiastical and religious societies are subject to the general regulations concerning private societies and associations and do not receive any privileges or subsidies either from the State or its local authorities and self-governing bodies.

11. The enforced gathering of collections and contributions, as well as any measures of enforcement or punishment on the part of these societies against their members is not permitted.

12. No ecclesiastical or religious society has the right to possess property. It does not enjoy any legal rights.

13. All the possessions of ecclesiastical and religious societies existing in Russia are declared to be national property. The buildings and objects specially intended for use in services, are made over, by special decree of the local or central state authority, for the free use of the aforesaid religious societies.

Chairman of the Council of People's Commissars,
V. Ulianov (Lenin)

People's Commisars:
N. Podvoisky, V. Aglasov, V. Trutovsky,
A. Shlikhter, P. Proshian, V. Menjinsky,
A. Shliapnikov, G. Petrovsky
Chargé d'affaires:
Vl. Bonch-Bruevich
Secretary:
N. Gorbunov

Reading No. 18
Rapprochement between The Orthodox Church and Soviet Government. Speech of M. G. Karpov at Council of the Orthodox Church, 1945.
Source:
Reprinted in N. Struve, *Christians in Contemporary Russia* (London, 1967), pp. 366-8.

Reverend bishops, priests and delegates of the faithful of the Russian Orthodox Church!

The Government of the USSR has instructed me to greet in its name this exalted assembly and to convey its wishes for the success of your labours in organising the higher administration of the Church.

The Soviet Government has also asked me to greet the guests of honour of the local Council, who have come from the Orthodox East – Patriarch Christophoros of Alexandria, Patriarch Alexander III of Antioch, Metropolitan Germanos representing the Ecumenical Patriarch, Archbishop Athenagoras representing the Patriarch of Jerusalem – as well as those who come from our Georgia – Catholicos Callistratos of all-Georgia – and from the Slav nations, our brothers – Metropolitan Joseph representing the Synod of the Serbian Church, and all the bishops and priests who accompany them.

The present local Council, called to elect the Patriarch of Moscow and all the Russias, and to adopt a rule for the administration of the Orthodox Church, will be a landmark in the history of the Russian Orthodox Church.

I am deeply convinced that the decisions of this Council will be of value in strengthening the Church, and will form an important starting point for the further development of its activity in helping the Soviet people to fulfil the major historical tasks which confront them.

The local Council of the Russian Orthodox Church has met at a time when all the nations of our great country, together with all the freedom-loving nations of the world, are fighting a holy war of liberation against the imperialist German bandits and are straining every nerve for victory at the cost of lives and possessions of millions of people sacrificed on the altar of patriotism.

Throughout the sore trials to which our country has so often been subjected in the past, the Russian Orthodox Church has never broken its links with the people: it has shared their needs, wishes and hopes and contributed its full measure to the common task. It was in its churches and monasteries that learning arose and the earliest chronicles of the life of our country were compiled; the walls of our churches and monasteries have more than once withstood the assault of foreign invaders, and many eminent churchmen have given their lives for their country.

And now, when the Hitlerite bandits have viciously attacked our sacred soil, when all the nations of the Soviet State have risen and surged forward to fight this great patriotic war in defence of their honour, their freedom and their independence, the Russian Orthodox Church has from the first taken the fullest part in defending the country with all the means at its disposal.

Having fully grasped the significance of the events, that eminent churchman, that wise and venerable man who was first Metropolitan, then Patriarch Sergius, bestowed his blessing upon the faithful in their task of participating in the defence of the frontiers of their country. In his many sermons and messages to the Church, he ceaselessly called upon her loyal sons to fight to the death against the barbarous enemy of the Soviet land – Hitler Germany.

Last year, the Patriarch Sergius died to the great loss of the Russian Orthodox Church. In accordance with his testament, the government of the Church passed into the hands of the senior Bishop, Metropolitan of Leningrad and Novgorod, Alexis, an outstanding churchman and an ardent patriot who never once left his post during the 900 days of the siege of Leningrad and who, in total unanimity with the other members of the Holy Synod, has guided the Church from the death of the Patriarch to this day.

The Church has not confined its patriotic action to letters and sermons but has collected funds for building tanks and aeroplanes and for helping the sick, the wounded and those crippled or orphaned by the war.

The Soviet Government has shown and continues to show deep interest in the Church's part in the struggle against the enemy.

In our country, the triumph of the new régime, a Socialist régime unprecedented in history and the most righteous in the world, has also brought about a new relationship between Church and State.

The great Socialist October Revolution which liberated our people from slavery and gave them freedom, has also freed the Church from the shackles which impeded its internal activity.

Freedom of conscience, promulgated by the Decree of 23 January 1918, has been consolidated by the basic laws of our country as embodied in the Soviet Constitution.

The Council of Church Affairs which, by Government decision, has been created and attached to the Council of People's Commissars of the USSR, forms a link between the Government and the Patriarch of Moscow and all the Russias, and provides liaison in all matters needing government approval.

Without in any way interfering with the spiritual life of the Church, the Council promotes normal relations between Church and State by seeing to the proper and timely application of government laws and decrees concerning the Russian Orthodox Church.

There is no doubt that the normal relations established between the Council and Patriarchate have helped to strengthen the Church administratively; the Council will continue in future to take all necessary steps to remove obstacles of whatever sort which may hinder the Soviet citizen in the exercise of the liberty of conscience granted by the Constitution.

Once again, I sincerely wish the members of the Council success in the task which awaits them.

FOR FURTHER STUDY

INTRODUCTORY

Aspaturian, V. V. 'The Non-Russian Nationalities', in A. Kassof (ed.). *Prospects for Soviet Society*. London: Pall Mall Press, 1968, pp. 143-200.

Curtiss, J. S. 'Church and State', in C. Black (ed.). *The Transformation of Russian Society. Aspects of Social Change since 1861*. Cambridge, Mass.: Harvard University Press, 1967. pp. 405-24.

Curtiss, J. S. *Church and State in Russia*. New York: Octagon Books, 1965.

Kolarz, W. *Religion in the Soviet Union*. London: Macmillan, 1962.

'Nationalities and Nationalism in the USSR'. Special issue of *Problems of Communism*, Vol. 16, No. 5, September-October 1967.

BASIC

Baron, S. W. *The Russian Jew under Tsars and Soviets*. London: Collier-Macmillan, 1964.

Bilinsky, J. 'The Rulers and the Ruled', *Problems of Communism*, Vol. 16, No. 5, September-October 1967, pp. 16-26.

Bourdeaux, M. *Opium of the People*. London: Faber, 1965.

Carr, E. H. *The Bolshevik Revolution, 1917-1923*. London: Macmillan, 1950.

Conquest, R. (ed.). *Religion in the USSR*. London: Bodley Head, 1968.

Gitelman, Zvi. 'The Jews', in *Problems of Communism*, Vol. 16, No. 5, Sept.-Oct. 1967, pp. 92-101.

Goldhagen, E. (ed.). *Ethnic Minorities in the Soviet Union*. New York: Praeger, 1968.

Hodnett, Grey, 'What's in a Nation?', in *Problems of Communism*, Vol. 16, No. 5, Sept.-Oct. 1967, pp. 2-15.

Lenin, V. I. 'The Right of Nations to Self-Determination' (1914), in *Collected Works*, Vol 20. Moscow, 1964, pp. 393-451.

Marx, K. and F. Engels. 'Communist Manifesto', in Marks and Engels, *Selected Works*, Vol. 1. Moscow, 1958, pp. 21-66.

Nove, A. and J. A. Newth. *The Soviet Middle East. A Model for Development*. London: Allen and Unwin, 1967.

Pipes, R. *The Formation of the Soviet Union*. Cambridge, Mass.: Harvard University Press, 1964.

Stalin, J. V. 'Marxism and the National Question', in *Collected Works*, Vol. 2. Moscow, 1953, pp. 300-81.

Stalin, J. V. 'The National Question and Leninism', in *Collected Works*, Vol. 11, Moscow, 1954, pp. 348-72.

Struve, Nikita. *Christians in Contemporary Russia*. London: Harvill Press, 1967.

Wheeler, Geoffrey. *The Modern History of Soviet Central Asia*. London: Weidenfeld and Nicolson, 1964.

SPECIALISED

Abramzon, S. M., K. I. Antipina, *et al.* 'Byt kolkhoznikov Kirgizskikh seleniy Darkhan i Chichkan', *Trudy Instituta Etnografii*, Vol. 37, Moscow, 1958.

Akaba, L. Kh. 'O nekotorykh religioznykh perezhitkakh u Abkhazov', *Sovremennoe Abkhazskoe selo, etnograficheskie ocherki*, Tbilisi, 1967, pp. 27-51.

Alexandrov, Yu. *The Times*, 22 September 1966.

Arutyunyan, Yu. V. 'Sotsial'naya struktura sel'skogo naseleniya', *Voprosy filosofii*, No. 5, 1966, pp. 51-61.

Bennigsen, A. and C. Lemercier-Quelquejay. *Islam in the Soviet Union*. London: Pall Mall, 1967.

Bolshakoff, S. *Russian Non-Conformity. The Story of 'Unofficial' Religion in Russia*. Philadelphia, Pa.: Westminster Press, 1950.

Bourdeaux, M. and P. Reddaway. 'Soviet Baptists Today', in *Survey*, No. 66, Jan. 1968.

B. R. 'On National Cadres of Specialists', in *R. Schlesinger* (ed.). *The Nationalities Problem and Soviet Administration*. London: Routledge and Kegan Paul, 1956, pp. 223-7.

Brzezinski, Z. K. and S. P. Huntington. *Political Power – USA/USSR*. London: Chatto and Windus, 1964.

'Chuvstvo druzhby i bratstva', *Pravda*, 7 October 1966.

Fedorenko, F. I. *Sekty: ikh vera i dela*. Moscow, 1965.

Geograficheski Atlas SSSR. Moscow, 1962.

Inkeles, A. and R. A. Bauer. *The Soviet Citizen*. Cambridge, Mass.: Harvard University Press, 1959.

Kolarz, Walter. *Russia and Her Colonies*. New York: Archon Books, 1967.

'Lyubov, doverie, druzhba! Sotsiologiya braka v SSSR', *Trud*, 22 October 1965, p. 4.

Marx, K. 'The Critique of Hegel's Philosophy of Law', in K. Marx and F. Engels, *On Religion*. Moscow, 1957.

Nadezhdin, M. and M. Solomonov. 'How the National School is made Indigenous; Results of an Investigation', *Revolutsia i Natsionalnosti*, 1935, No. 10 in R. Schlesinger (ed.). *The Nationalities Problem and Soviet Administration*. London: Routledge and Kegan Paul, 1956, pp. 204-11.

Nove, A. *Soviet Jewry and the Fiftieth Anniversary of the Russian Revolution*. London: World Jewish Congress, 1968.

Pipes, R. 'Assimilation and the Muslims', in A. Inkeles and K. Geiger (eds.). *Soviet Society*. London: Constable, 1961, pp. 588-606.

Pritchiny sushchestvovaniya i puti preodoleniya religioznykh perezhitkov. Minsk, 1965.

Rabinovich, S. *Jews in the Soviet Union*. Moscow, 1967.

'Russian Churchmen Face New Trials', *The Times*, 3 January 1965.

Smirnova, Ya. S. 'Natsional'no-smeshannye braki u narodov Karachaevo-Cherkesii', *Sovetskaya Etnografiya*, No. 4, 1967, pp. 137-42.

Solzhenitsyn, A. *Cancer Ward*. London: Bodley Head, 1968.

'Sovremennoe sektantstvo i ego preodolenie', *Voprosy istorii religii i ateizma*, No. 9. Moscow, 1961.

Stark, Werner. *The Sociology of Religion*. London: Routledge and Kegan Paul, 1967.

Telikhanov, A. 'On National Soviet Cadres', in *Revolutsia i Natsionalnosti*, 1935, No. 12, extract in R. Schlesinger, *The Nationalities Problem and Soviet Administration*, pp. 228-34. London: Routledge and Kegan Paul, 1956.

Tobolov, K. 'On National Cadres', *Sovetskoe Stroitelstvo*, 1933, Nos. 7-8, extract in R. Schlesinger, *The Nationalities Problem and Soviet Administration*. London: Routledge and Kegan Paul, 1956, pp. 212-22.

Tsentral'noe statisticheskoe upravlenie. *Itogi vsesoyuznoy perepisi naseleniya*, 1959g. SSSR (Svodny tom). Moscow, 1962.

Vasil'eva, G. P. 'Sovremennye etnicheskie protsessy v Severnom Turkmenistane', *Sovetskaya Etnografiya*, No. 1, 1968, pp. 3-17.

Zhdanko, T. A. 'Sedentarisation of the Nomads of Central Asia, including Kazakhstan, under the Soviet Regime', in *International Labour Review*, No. 93, 1966, pp. 601-20.

Zhdanko, T. A. 'Everyday Life in a Karakalpak Kolkhoz *aul*', *Sovetskaya Etnografiya*, No. 2, 1949, cited in R. Schlesinger, *The Nationalities Problem and Soviet Administration*. London: Routledge and Kegan Paul, 1956, pp. 280-94.

14

THE EDUCATIONAL SYSTEM

The layman regards 'education' as being largely concerned with schools and the learning of skills. For the sociologist, education has a much wider significance. Durkheim defined it as: 'a methodological socialisation of the young generation'.[1] This definition widens the layman's concept to include all actions performed by the older generation in introducing the young to the moral, social and intellectual tradition of a society. The word 'tradition' implies the inculcation of conservative notions; and educational institutions, therefore, normally stabilise a social order by passing on the values and codes of behaviour of the adult world or, more accurately, of the various social strata making up the adult world. This is an over-simplification, for the adult world is often not consensual itself and sometimes educational institutions may be hotbeds of social change. Learning involves discovering, and in educational institutions are also carried out research and innovation, presenting a dynamic element to the social system. In simple, relatively undifferentiated societies, the family is the chief agency for education. In complex ones, it becomes the task of specialised institutions: nurseries, schools, colleges and universities. These prepare individuals with the necessary skills and attitudes to perform specialised tasks given by the division of labour; the educational system, therefore, inculcates values demanded by the society as a whole and skills demanded by 'the special milieu for which (the individual) is specifically destined'.[2] Due to the tension sometimes created between the 'research' and 'teaching' elements, research or innovation is often organised separately, either in research units in universities or in special research institutes.

The importance of research activity and education in modern societies has led some sociologists to give educational institutions a central determining role:

Under conditions of advanced industrialism . . . the economy becomes increasingly dominated by the institutions of research and technical innovation, with the result that the differentiation of educational institutions and functions assumes new proportions. So much is this so that the educational system comes to occupy a strategic place as a central determinant of the economic, political and cultural character of society . . .[3]

[1] E. Durkheim, *Education and Society* (Free Press, Glencoe, 1956), p. 71.
[2] Durkheim, *ibid.*
[3] Jean Floud and A. H. Halsey, 'The Sociology of Education', *Current Sociology*, vol. 7, no. 3, 1958, pp. 169-70.

This statement, however, needs to take into account the demands made by other institutions on the educational system which help shape its character – particularly, the requirements of the state for defence and of the economy for skilled manpower. In the USSR, the educational system has also been an agent of the political, and it has played an important role in the inculcation of values. While the political aspect of education is often emphasised by writers on the USSR—especially by those with values opposed to the Soviet system – we should note that all educational systems inculcate political values. Schools in the United States, it has been said, are expected 'to preserve the capitalist system, to demonstrate that the enemy is always to blame for war, to prevent the intervention of government in business, to maintain permanent patterns of family relations, to teach respect for private property, and to protect the middle class by perpetuating the belief that the poor are inherently lazy 'no-count' people for whom nothing can be done'.[1] In Soviet society, the political role of the school is more obvious to western observers because some values run counter to liberal-democratic ones and because the schools were institutions used by the state to destroy the pre-revolutionary values and to inculcate Bolshevik ones.

Soviet education has been strongly influenced by the heritage of the Tsarist past, by the educational theories of the Bolsheviks and by the technological requirements of a modern economy. Let us consider each in turn.

Education Before the Revolution

Before 1917, the first steps had been taken in Russia to introduce an educational system on similar lines to that of Western Europe.[2] Schooling was organised both by the state through local government organs (the *Zemstva*) and by the churches. The churches were mainly concerned with primary education and the state with secondary and higher. By the end of the nineteenth century, the census showed that the literacy rate was 24 per cent for the total population (over the age of nine years). Important differences existed between town and country and between sexes: in the town, 52.3 per cent and in the countryside, 19.6 per cent were literate. Of the male population 35.8 per cent were literate, but only 12.4 per cent of the women were so.[3]

Among the young, literacy was much higher than the averages above and witnessed the achievement of the educational policies of the autocracy. A. G. Rashin has shown that of workers aged 15 to 16 in 1897, 73.3 per cent of the

---

[1] W. B. Brookover and D. Gottlieb, *A Sociology of Education* (New York, 1964), p. 74, cited by O. Banks, *The Sociology of Education* (1968), p. 201.

[2] Two interesting tables showing the growth in educational provision between 1801 and 1825, and the similarity of syllabuses in the Russian *gymnasia* and in the French *Écoles Centrales* are shown in N. Hans, *The Russian Tradition in Education* (1963), pp. 21-2.

[3] *Narodnoe obrazovanie v SSSR* (Moscow, 1957), p. 733.

men and 46.8 per cent of the women were literate.[1] By 1897, as shown in the
census, 63 per cent of males in the urban areas were literate.

As in other aspects of Russian life, important regional differences existed
in educational achievement. In Central Asia under 10 per cent of the male
population were literate, the figure rising to an average of 15 per cent in
Siberia. Top of the list were the Baltic provinces (Lithuania, Latvia and
Estonia) with male literacy ranging from 65.2 per cent to 79.2 per cent. In
the Great Russian areas, these figures were only equalled by St Petersburg.[2]

In 1914–15, there were nearly ten million pupils in primary and secondary
schools of all types. In higher education, at the same time, there had been
founded 105 institutions, including eight universities; total attendance was
127,400 students.[3] Institutes of higher education were mainly located in the
towns of European Russia. By 1914, a third of the students in higher educational institutions were enrolled in the universities.[4] A study of the social
background of students in Russian universities in 1914, shows that 37.6
per cent were of noble and state official background, 7.7 were of the clergy,
11.5 were 'honoured citizens' (i.e. members of the bottom five ranks of the
nobility) and merchants; townsmen's and shopkeepers' children accounted
for 24.2 per cent, and the children of cossaks and peasants came to 14.6 per
cent; this left a residual of 4.4 per cent.[5] The figures show a predominance of
the upper social status groups, though the 14.6 per cent from the peasantry
and cossaks is surprisingly high; approximately 6.3 per cent of students
received grants.[6]

The educational system inherited by the Soviet government was hierarchical
in structure and outlook. The universities were designed for the gentry and
other upper strata, the commercial and technical schools for the labouring
masses: in this respect Tsarist Russia was not unlike Great Britain in the nineteenth century. The educational system, though not as well developed as in
Western Europe, was already on the way to providing, at least in the towns,
literacy for the masses and the basis of higher education for the elite.

Marxist Views on Education

The Soviet leaders came to power with a Marxist philosophy as a guide to
educational policies in the new state. Under capitalism, according to Marxist

---

[1] A. G. Rashin, *Formirovanie rabochego klassa* (Moscow, 1958), p. 584.

[2] *Pervaya vseobshchaya perepis'* (1905), vol. 1, pp. 42-3.

[3] *SSSR v tsilrakh v 1963g* (Moscow, 1964), pp. 155-7.

[4] B. M. Remenikov and G. I. Ushakov, *Universitetskoe obrazovanie v SSSR* (Moscow, 1960),
p. 18.

[5] B. M. Remenikov and G. I. Ushakov, *Universitetskoe obrazovanie v SSSR* (Moscow, 1960),
p. 8.

[6] *Op. cit.*, p. 19.

theory, education, like the state, was part of the superstructure of society (see pp. 4–5); control of ideas and knowledge lay with the ruling class. Marx pointed out in the *Communist Manifesto* that 'the ruling ideas of each age have ever been the ideas of its ruling class'.[1] In the *German Ideology*, this view was put in more detail:

The ideas of the ruling class are in every epoch the ruling ideas: i.e. the class which is the ruling *material* force of society, is at the same time its ruling *intellectual* force. The class which has the means of material production at its disposal, has control at the same time over the means of mental production, so that thereby, generally speaking, the ideas of those who lack the means of mental production are subject to it. The ruling ideas are nothing more than the ideal expression of the dominant material relationships, the dominant material relationships grasped as ideas . . . [They rule] as producers of ideas, and regulate the production and distribution of the ideas of their age, thus their ideas are the ruling ideas.[2]

In capitalist society, education imparts class ideas: it indoctrinates men with the values of 'the system', it prepares them for class rule. From this viewpoint, educational ideas of egalitarianism or individual development are thwarted under capitalism because of the material basis on which social relations are based. But ideas and other sub-systems located in the superstructure also may have an important 'influence upon the course of the historical struggles and in many cases preponderate in determining their form'.[3] Therefore, according to Marx significant social change cannot be completed by altering the educational system, because it is organically related to the needs of the economy. But this relationship is not a mechanical one; within the educational system enclaves, as it were, may exist ideas at variance with the dominant ideology and the ruling class.

Marx and Engels were less precise about the nature of education under communism. Speaking of the educational policy of the Paris Commune, Marx pointed out that it provided free education for all without ecclesiastical interference and class domination and that there was open access to science and learning.[4] With the abolition of capitalism, society would be free to provide education unfettered by the needs of the ruling classes, based on man's needs to develop his potential to the full. But the Bolshevik government had to decide what precisely man's needs were and the ways his potential could be developed.

[1] Marx-Engels, *Selected Works*, vol. 1, p. 225.

[2] K. Marx and F. Engels, *The German Ideology* (1965), p. 61.

[3] F. Engels, 'Letter to J. Bloch', September 21, 1890 in *Karl Marx and Frederick Engels, Selected Works*, vol. 2 (Moscow, 1951), p. 433.

[4] 'The Civil War in France, Address of the General Council of the International Workingmen's Association', Charles Kerr and Co. Chicago, n.d., p. 44. Cited by M. Shore, *Soviet Education* (New York, 1947), p. 59. Shore considers Marx's views on education at some length.

Officially, in the new Soviet Republic, education was to reflect the dominance of the proletariat and its class aims. After a conference on proletarian culture in 1920, Lenin drafted the following:

1. All educational work in the Soviet Republic of workers and peasants, in the field of political education in general and in the field of art in particular, should be imbued with the spirit of the class struggle being waged by the proletariat for the successful achievement of the aims of its dictatorship, i.e. the overthrow of the bourgeoisie, the abolition of classes, and the elimination of all forms of exploitation of man by man.
2. Hence, the proletariat, both through its vanguard – the Communist Party – and through the many types of proletarian organisations in general, should display the utmost activity and play the leading part in all the work of public education.[1]

Early Soviet Educational Policy

From the above passage, we can see that the early Soviet educational system had a political role to play. In practical terms, the Bolsheviks defined three main aims for the educational system: first, to inculcate socialist and collectivist attitudes: second, to make literacy universal; third, to increase scientific and technological education.

In an attempt to abolish illiteracy, schools for adults were organised and existing buildings were utilised on a two or three shift basis. In 1930, compulsory attendance was introduced at the four-year school (eight to twelve years of age in the rural areas), and at the seven-year school (eight to fifteen) in the towns. It was not until 1949 that seven-year education was made compulsory in all areas, though it is doubtful whether the provisions in practice were fully enforced. As measured by official statistics, illiteracy, at least among the younger generation, was abolished in the USSR by the end of the 1930s. This is illustrated by the following table:

Table 49. Literacy in Russia and the USSR

		Per cent literate over nine years of age		
	Census	Men	Women	Total
Population of USSR	1897	35.8	12.4	24.0
(excluding Western Ukraine	1926	66.5	37.1	51.1
and Western White Russia)	1939	90.8	72.6	81.2

Source: Narodnoe obrazovanie v SSSR (Moscow, 1957), p. 733.

It should be pointed out that much of the increase between 1897 and 1926 was due directly to the educational provision before the revolution and the subsequent ageing of the population: nevertheless, some of the credit, especi-

V. I. Lenin, 'On Proletarian Culture', Collected Works, vol. 31 (1966), p. 316.

ally in the non-Russian areas, must go to the educational policies of the Soviet government.

In the 1920s, educational theory (as it applied to the organisation of the school), was similar to 'progressive' ideas current in America and Great Britain (i.e. Dalton and Dewey). In order to introduce a communist spirit, group and practical work was favoured; physical punishment was prohibited, 'discipline' was lax, and an element of self-government was introduced. Education was free of charge and based on comprehensive and co-educational principles. Whether, in fact, the 'progressive' system was adopted in all schools is a moot point; in practice it seems likely that many schools continued to operate in the traditional way, for teachers and lecturers very easily fall into routine ways and resist new ideas and changes. A leading communist in Solzhenitsyn's *Cancer Ward* points out: 'I could understand it in my day, when I was a school director. All the trained teachers were hostile to our authority, none of them were on our side. The main problem was to keep them in check'.[1]

From the beginning of the 1930s, the libertarian trend was reversed. Complaints were made from two sources: in industry and technology it was said that school leavers were incapable of fulfilling the tasks required of them; law enforcement and child-care institutions were concerned at the lack of discipline and hooliganism of school children and young people. Consequently formal studies based on book learning and assessed by grades (the usual continental five-point scale was used) were re-introduced. Emphasis in the general schools was placed on mathematics, language, geography, physics and chemistry. Authority was restored to heads and to teachers, and other social organisations (such as the Party and *Komsomol*) were called on to help assert authority. In 1943, co-education in urban areas was abandoned and single sex schools were re-established.

The Modern System of Soviet Education

For simplicity the present Soviet educational system may be divided into three main parts: pre-school, school and higher. This is shown on the diagram which is sub-divided horizontally by age and vertically by stream (see p. 492).

Pre-school education is neither compulsory nor free. Crèches (*yasli*) are available for children from three months to three years of age and kinder-gardens (*detskie sady*) for the three to six year olds. They are organised by factories, farms, Soviets and the Ministries of Education.

One of the aims of pre-school (or nursery) education is to release women for productive work. Though nurseries are cheap (costs ranging from £1 to £4 per month), accommodation is in short supply. DeWitt has estimated that in

[1] *Op. cit.*, p. 209.

1938–9 only seven per cent of all children in a given age group could attend a crèche.[1] In 1961, just over three and a half million children under seven were in nurseries: this is roughly ten per cent of the child population under seven. By 1965, approximately 22.9 per cent of children under seven years were in pre-school establishments.[2]

Children may stay in nurseries all day (from 8 a.m. to 6 p.m.). In certain circumstances, if the need of the parents warrants it, they may stay full-time as boarders (as, for example, may the offspring of University students).

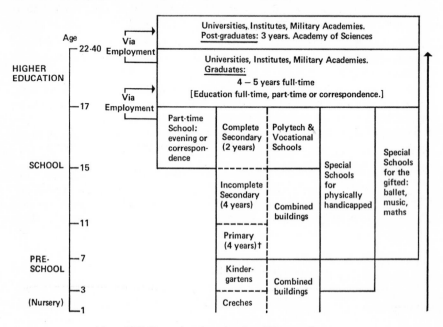

† From 1970 10 year secondary education will be compulsory.

DIAGRAM 7
Soviet System of Education: Post 1964

Education at this level consists of games, play and story-telling. Through stories about glorious deeds of leaders, children may learn a little about the history of the Soviet state and party. More important, the school routine teaches them ideas of order, neatness and personal relations.[3] But the significance of pre-school education generally as a socialising agency and its effectiveness in weakening the cohesion of the family is less than is sometimes

[1] N. DeWitt, *Education and Professional Employment in the USSR*, National Science Foundation (Washington, 1961), p. 73.

[2] *Zhenshchiny i deti v SSSR* (Moscow, 1963), p. 133, *50 let Sovetskogo zdravookhraneniya* (Moscow, 1967), p. 116.

[3] See Reading no. 19.

claimed because of inadequate provision. Most young children are brought up in the family (either by the mother or grandmother) or by friends. (See above Chapter 11.) The notion of the communist state seizing young children from their mothers after weaning is a fiction.

In school and higher education, the state has a monopoly over public provision: there are no private schools, though one can, of course, take private lessons. The aim of the first eight years of school education is to give a general education. This, in Soviet educational theory, has five main aspects:

1. *Physical education*, aimed at developing health and physical strength through curricular instruction and/or extracurricular participation in sports.
2. *Aesthetic education*, aimed at developing appreciation of 'artistic realism' among all students and/or mastery of a 'performing arts skill' by those who are particularly gifted.
3. *Mental education*, aimed at the mastery of all subjects of instruction; the development of a conscious scientific and materialistic outlook; mastery of the dialectical method; and orderly and systematic study and thought habits.
4. *Polytechnical education*, aimed at developing a specific manual skill; detailed familiarity with methods and general knowledge of production techniques and the organisation of socialist industry.
5. *Moral education*, aimed at creating a 'conscious communist morality', the elements of which are: conscious discipline; Soviet patriotism and proletarian internationalism; dedication to the goals of the community, the state and the Communist Party; dedication to socialist labour; and the acceptance of approved common rules of conduct and etiquette.

These components are said to represent a 'new, superior stage in the development of the theory and practice of education'.[1]

The Soviet regime has put the greatest emphasis on training in science and practical work. The following figures show how the emphasis has changed from 1871 to 1959.

Table 50. Curriculum for the eight upper years, 1871, 1915, 1959

| | *Hours per week throughout eight years* | | |
	*1871**	*1915†*	*1959‡*
Humanities	154	80	87
Maths. and Sciences	47	73	84
Physical culture, practical work and arts	—	34	93

* Classical *gymnasium*
† *Real* school
‡ Eight year school
Nicholas Hans, *The Russian Tradition in Education* (1963), p. 157.

[1] N. K. Goncharov, 'Sovetskaya pedagogicheskaya nauka', *Narodnoe obrazovanie*, no. 11, Nov. 1957, p. 70, cited by N. De Witt, *Education and Professional Employment in the USSR*, p. 78.

R

The table shows the near trebling of time taken for practical activity (1915–59). In other respects, the figures for 1915 and 1959 show much similarity – further activities have been added to the time-table, rather than a wholesale change of emphasis.

Before 1970, after the eighth year, students left school and finished education completely, or continued part-time or proceeded to more specialised study for another two years.[1] This is a form of educational selection. The children staying on to complete their general education (about 25 per cent of the total) constitute a high proportion of subsequent applicants to higher educational institutions.

It is interesting to note that the Russians seem to experience similar problems with 'early leavers' as in the West. A survey of evening school students in Ufa revealed that 50.7 per cent of students from working class families and 56.2 per cent from peasant backgrounds left school after the eighth form in order to contribute to family income.[2]

Again, Osipov has shown that children entering these last two forms tend to be recruited disproportionately from the upper strata groups. The relevant figures for Gorki *oblast'* are cited below.

Occupation of Father	Per cent of children	
	Fourth Class	Tenth-Eleventh Classes
Specialist	25.8	42.8
Skilled worker	43.6	23.1
Unskilled worker	6.6	1.5
Pensioner or invalid	4.6	7.9
No father	13.4	16.6

Source: G. Osipov, *Rabochi klass i tekhnicheski progress* (Moscow, 1965). Cited by M. Matthews, *New Society*, 19 Dec. 1968.

In the last two forms (the ninth and tenth), students prepare for higher education or begin more specialised courses related to their future work. In general polytechnics, one quarter of the time is spent on specialist subjects (machine-tool production, textile technology), and in vocational schools trade training (of draughtsmen, librarians, nursery school teachers) takes up to two-thirds of the time.

Under Khrushchev, practical training was increased partly to ensure that school students were well versed in the affairs and activity of the real world and not merely imbued with book-learning and theory. After eight years secondary education, another three (not two, as above) were spent in com-

[1] Ten year compulsory education is to be introduced in 1970. (Decree 19/20 November 1966).
[2] *Molodoy kommunist*, no. 7 (1966), p. 78.

Table 51. Curriculum for Secondary Polytechnical School: pre and post 1964.

| | | Plan before the 1964 reform revision | | | | | Plan after the 1964 reform revision | | | |
| | | Number of hours a week for grades | | | Total hours | | Number of hours per week for grades | | Total hours | |
No.	Subject	IX	X	XI	By the week	By the year	IX	X	By the week	By the year
1	Literature	3	3	3	9	339	5/4	4/3	8	280
2	Mathematics	4	4	4	12	452	6	6	12	420
3	History	2	3	4	9	335	3/4	3/4	7	245
4	Social science	—	—	2	2	70	—	2	2	70
5	Geography	—	2	2	4	148	—	2	2	70
6	Physics	4	4	2	10	382	5	5	10	350
7	Astronomy	—	1	—	1	39	—	1	1	35
8	Chemistry	2	3	2	7	265	4	3	7	245
9	Biology	3	—	—	3	117	2	—	2	70
10	Drawing (mechanical)	2	—	—	2	78	1	—	1	35
11	Foreign language	2	2	3	7	261	2	2	4	140
12	Physical training	2	2	2	6	226	2	2	4	140
	Total	24	24	24	72	2,712	30	30	60	2,100
13	Production (theoretical and practical) training	12	12	12	36	1,356	12	8	20	708
	Total	36	36	36	108	4,068	42	38	80	2,808
14	Electives	2	2	2	6	226	2	2	4	140

Source: S. M. Rosen, *Significant Aspects of Soviet Education*, US Department of Health, Education and Welfare (Washington, 1965), facing p. 22. For post-1964 syllabus see also *Uchitel'skaya gazeta*, 20 August 1964.

pleting school education. Much of this time was taken up with practical work. The curriculum of a general polytechnical school before and after the reforms of 1964 are shown in Table 51. The syllabuses show the wide range of subjects studied in the last two school years: much wider in fact than that of a British sixth-form and more akin to the syllabuses in a German *gymnasium* or American High School. The emphasis on acquiring vocational skills in the upper forms of secondary school is greater than in the West. One other difference is the longer period of direct instruction (42 and 38 hours per week) compared with Great Britain and the USA (but not with continental European countries). Homework is additional and compulsory. Technical or trade-training, acquired under apprenticeship in the West, is performed within the school system in the USSR. The factories in turn provide facilities for practical training and may send skilled workers to the schools to give instruction.

The polytechnical secondary schools should not be thought of simply as 'trade schools'. They aim to provide an education relevant to the needs of an industrial order; Soviet polytechnical education 'is based on the notion that labour is a basic form of activity, essential not only to man's survival (and therefore undertaken merely as a necessary evil) but also to his satisfaction as a human being'.[1] The pupils study mathematics, literature, history, a foreign language, physics, the practical use of tools, and physical training (see syllabus, Table 51). Khrushchev, particularly, stressed the importance of polytechnical education. He supported the view that academic study and work activity should be united, unlike in practice where, he asserted, Soviet educational institutions were training students with little knowledge of the practical problems of the world. On more social grounds polytechnical education is sometimes seen as a means by which manual and white collar workers can be drawn together in an educational process.

Soviet education is based on comprehensive co-educational principles.[2] We noted earlier that sex segregation was introduced in 1943. It was short-lived; since 1945 all schools, including boarding schools, have been made co-educational. The comprehensives are based on the theory that the environment is the most important determinant of ability. The aim of the school is to make good the deficiencies in the home background of the child. An article in *Komsomolets Turkmenistana* reported that the initial advantage of some school beginners is only ironed out after the third form (i.e. by the age of ten years).[3] Pupils therefore, are not segregated according to performance (there are exceptions to this discussed below); intelligence testing is not practised. Children are allocated to classes on the basis of their surnames. All classes pursue

[1] Kenneth Charlton, 'Polytechnical Education', *International Review of Education*, vol. 14, (1968) no. 1, p. 45.

[2] Some schools work on a shift system. In 1967 about 70 per cent of schools were single shift. *inansy SSSR*, no. 5, 1967.

[3] Cited in *Soviet News* (London), no. 5398, 8 August 1967.

a common syllabus. At the end of each year an examination is conducted on the results of which promotion is made to the next grade. Though Soviet teachers and educationalists deny that an undue number of students repeat the year, it is sometimes asserted in the West that this procedure results in ability streaming 'by age'. Khrushchev has said that before the 1958 reforms, 20 per cent of children in the seven-year schools repeated so often that they did not complete the course.[1] *Literaturnaya gazeta* has reported that in 1964 approximately four per cent or nearly two million children were repeating a year.[2] This, of course, is a form of 'streaming', technically called grading, and it is common not only in the USSR, but also on the continent and in the USA. Such a system is unlawful in Britain, where children must be taught in homogeneous age groups. Age grading has the effect of making the teaching groups more homogeneous, but in a cruder less systematic way than the English streaming principle.

Outside the general schools are others giving specialist training. At one end are schools for the mentally and physically handicapped, while at the other end are those for the artistically gifted (ballet and music schools) and for children with exceptional ability in physics, chemistry and mathematics. In between are schools specialising in teaching foreign languages: in 'English schools' after a certain level has been reached, general subjects are taught in English.[3] An informal streaming system *between schools* is denied by the Soviet authorities, but the possibility nevertheless exists. Within the schools, children with special aptitudes may join voluntary 'circles' in which more advanced work is pursued. In mathematics and physics, outside school competitions are held and summer courses take place. A common and relatively high general standard is achieved in the general secondary schools and outstanding performance is attained through special schools and extra-curricular activities. Perhaps the most important aspect of Soviet comprehensive education is the effect it has on social attitudes. The sense of inferiority associated with 11 + failures in England and with the allocation to the fifteenth graded stream in a 'comprehensive' school are certainly absent in the Soviet (and for that matter the American) system. On the other hand, repeating the year may obviously shake pupils' self-confidence and the mixing of older with younger pupils may have other undesirable social features.

In Soviet administrative theory, education is a responsibility of the individual Union Republics which have their own educational ministries. Despite this superficial devolution, the Soviet educational system is highly centralised. Policy statements issued jointly by the Council of Ministers on behalf of the Supreme Soviet and the Central Committee are followed in the Union

[1] Cited by N. Grant, *Soviet Education* (1964), p. 44.
[2] 'Eto kasaetsya vsekh', 24 April 1965.
[3] For further details see N. Grant, *Soviet Education* (1964), pp. 90-4.

Republics whose laws and practice are in conformity one with another.[1] As the economy (involving manpower needs) is centrally planned, it requires a high degree of centralisation and co-ordination of the supply of trained manpower. This does not mean that no variation exists from one area to another. Tuition (particularly at school level) is carried out in the vernacular languages of the Union and Autonomous Republics.[2] Variations in local culture – folklore, history, dancing and art – are also reflected in school syllabuses. Significant differences in educational standards exist between Republics: Georgia in 1959 had proportionally twice as many persons with higher education than the all-union average (38 per thousand against 18 per thousand) whereas Tadzhikistan had just over half (10 per thousand) (see Table 52). This represents a great achievement by the Soviet authorities. In 1917, Tadzhikistan had no institutions of higher learning; now there is an Academy of Science, and eight higher educational institutions.

Table 52. Higher Education 1939 and 1959 by Union Republic

Republic	Total (000s)		Per 1,000 of the population	
	1939	1959	1939	1959
RSFSR	709	2,266	7	19
Ukraine	272	715	7	17
White Russia	33	96	4	12
Uzbekistan	20	105	3	13
Kazakhstan	27	114	5	12
Georgia	40	153	11	38
Azerbaidzhan	22	77	7	21
Lithuania	6	35	2	13
Moldavia	7	30	3	10
Latvia	14	44	7	21
Kirgizia	3	27	2	13
Tadzhikistan	3	21	2	10
Armenia	8	49	6	28
Turkmenistan	4	20	3	13
Estonia	9	25	8	21
Total USSR	1,177	3,778	6	18

Source: *Itogi vsesoyuznoy perepisi naseleniya 1959g. SSSR (Svodny tom)* (Moscow, 1962), Table 23 (Adapted).

Not only are syllabuses completely laid down by the Ministries of Education, but teaching methods and techniques are also prescribed. In contrast to 'projects' and other methods employed in the early years of Soviet power, the present techniques are based on formal class teaching.[3] Here again, one may

[1] G. S. Dorokhova, *Upravlenie narodnym obrazovaniem v SSSR* (Moscow, 1965), p. 14.
[2] In non-Russian speaking areas, Russian is the compulsory second language.
[3] See N. Grant, *Soviet Education* (1964), pp. 102-7.

find variations between schools and republics. In Georgia, for example, to increase motivation in certain schools, class marks have been abolished.[1]

The inculcation of moral attitudes and the learning of mores is an important aspect of the general process of socialisation carried out by the school. Though the indoctrination of communist political principles is often stressed by western writers, Soviet schools are charged with much general character training impressing on the child elementary ideas of good and bad, love of the motherland, industriousness and frugality, truthfulness, honesty, modesty and kindness, friendship and comradeship, discipline, love of studies and conscientiousness, good social conduct – in the school, at home, in the streets and in public places.

The code,[2] in some respects, presents a set of values not unlike that of the 'protestant ethic': it stresses discipline, industriousness and frugality; honesty and modesty, it seeks to develop attitudes to work based on punctuality and conscientiousness. It would be interesting to compare this code with the rules of missionary schools in the nineteenth century British Empire. Possibly both had the function of providing a moral code to people uprooted from a rural background.

The emphasis on character and manners follows rather more closely the British than the continental educational tradition: 'Manners maketh man' is not only written over the gates of an English public school to impress its young gentlemen in the making, it is behoven to all Soviet children.

The political values taught are peculiarly Soviet: loyalty to the theories of Marxism-Leninism, the Communist Party of the Soviet Union, the Soviet government and its people, the Soviet motherland. Teaching inculcates a strong Soviet patriotism. As a Soviet report on education puts it: the students in the final year are taught about:

the inevitability of the end of capitalism and victory of socialism and communism and the leading and organising role of the Communist Party of the Soviet Union in building communism in our country.

History and society study are important means of bringing the pupils up in a spirit of selfless love for, and devotion to, their socialist motherland, in a spirit of peace and friendship among the nations in the spirit of proletarian internationalism.[3]

Soviet children generally are exposed to more explicit political indoctrination than those in Britain. In addition to the school, other media perform a political socialisation role. For instance, a study of the children's monthly Magazine *Barvinok* (circulation 145,000) in 1965, shows stories about the Civil

[1] *Soviet News*, no. 5398, 8 August 1967, p. 69.

[2] The code of moral education prepared by the Academy of Pedagogic Sciences for the first five years of school (see Reading no. 19).

[3] International Conference on Public Education, Session 27, General 1964, *Public Education in the Soviet Union* (Moscow, 1964), p. 54.

War and the great hero fighting for the Bolshevik cause, about the activity of
Red Partisans in the Civil War, about the revolutionaries' battles with the
Tsar who did 'not want the people to build a new bright happy life for them-
selves', and about the little boy who helps Russian partisans against the
German fascists.

Inter-personal relations play an important part in character formation.
Teachers are encouraged to use 'positive' methods: to point out the bad effects
of hooliganism and to glorify Soviet achievements. Persuasion and personal
example are the chief disciplinary methods advocated. Corporal punishment
is illegal and, by all accounts, very rarely resorted to. Oral reprimands, being
kept behind at school, a bad mark in the pupil's record book, pressure on
parents and, in the last resort, expulsion are the sanctions open to the head
teacher. Responsibility for behaviour and discipline is shared more widely
in Soviet schools than in the West. The pupils' organisation, *The Pioneers*,
will attempt to bring bad boys to heel – by offering advice, by socially isolating
the individuals or by public ridicule. Other organisations, such as the Communist Party, parent-teacher associations and trade-union branches may help
or publicly condemn the parents of badly-behaved children. The boundaries
between the school and other institutions are not as closely defined or maintained as in the West: the school is closely related and responsible to the
Soviet state and other groups. This closer link reflects the greater fusion of
state and society in the USSR than in liberal societies.

Higher Education

The chief function of higher education is to train specialist manpower to meet
the needs of the Soviet economy and society at large. With the immense
economic expansion a severe burden has been put on the higher educational
system. In the fifty years after the revolution, the growth in numbers engaged
in higher education has been one of the most spectacular advances claimed by
the Soviet government. From only 127,400 students in 1914, the number of
enrolments has climbed to over three and a half million in 1964–5,[1] and the
number of universities from eight to forty. Comprehensive statistics of the
educational stock are shown on Table 53.

Higher education takes place in universities and institutes. Generally,
university education has a higher prestige than that of an institute. But some
institutes have higher status than equivalent university departments, being in
an analogous position to MIT in the United States. Institutes tend to concentrate on specialised aspects of higher education or research, usually in the
fields of engineering, agriculture, medicine or teacher training. Universities
teach more of the theoretical and less of the applied fields; they also offer the

[1] *Narodnoe obrazovanie v Sovetskom Soyuze* (Moscow, 1964), p. 11.

Table 53: Secondary and Higher Education in the USSR

	1959 (Millions)	1967 (Estimate on Jan. 1st) (millions)
Higher Education (completed)	3.8	6.4
Higher Education (not yet completed)	1.7	2.8
Secondary specialised Education (i.e. having completed a course in a technicum or similar institution)	7.9	11.9
Secondary general (having completed a secondary school course)	9.9	14.5
Incomplete Secondary (having finished 7 years school but not completing the whole of Secondary school)	35.4	48.9
Total (Primary and Secondary whether completed or not)	58.7	84.5

Source: Narodnoe Khozyaystvo SSSR v 1967g. (Moscow 1968) p. 34.

whole range of academic subjects, unlike institutes which usually only cater for specialities. The distinction between institute and university is not unlike that between *Technische Hochschule* and university in Germany.

The respective emphasis on arts and sciences between universities and institutes is illustrated by the following table.

Table 54. The Number of Professors and Doctors of Science in Soviet Higher Educational Institutions, by Speciality

	Numbers of Professors and Doctors of Science		Proportion at Universities
Arts Subjects	History	117	63%
	Philology	176	65.5%
Science Subjects	Biology	429	43%
	Chemistry	315	36%
	Physics and Mathematics	543	43%

Source: V. M. Remenikov and G. I. Ushakov, *Universitetskoe obrazovanie v SSSR* (Moscow, 1960), p. 57.

The table not only shows the preponderance of scientists but also their concentration in institutes. The universities cater more for the advanced work done in history and language.

The standard of all diplomas of Soviet higher educational institutions are roughly equal to the level of British University degrees. On this basis, Soviet

R*

educational achievement, in the last half century, is remarkable and is illustrated by Table 55 below. The numbers of students in higher education up to British first degree level surpass as a proportion of the population those of advanced European countries.

Table 55. Total number of students receiving full-time higher education in selected countries
1959/60

	Total British degree level (1)	All levels (2)	Per 10,000 population British degree level (3)	All levels (4)
Great Britain	105,700	154,800	21	31
Australia	29,700	44,700	29	44
Canada	95,500	125,500	52	69
France	205,700	223,100	46	49
Germany (F.R.)	172,700	246,000	31	45
Netherlands	35,900	53,400	32	47
New Zealand	6,300	11,400	27	48
Sweden	31,900	52,500	43	71
Switzerland	34,400	—	26	—
USA	—	2,307,700	—	129
USSR	1,164,600	1,164,600	55	55

Note: In this Table the full-time courses included under the heading 'British degree level' comprise all full-time study at and above the level of first degrees or equivalent qualifications. (Students enrolled for university courses and technical high schools in Europe, first diplomas in all higher educational institutions in USSR, in the USA entry to the 3rd year. See *Higher Education*, p. 8.)

Source: *Higher Education* (Appendix Five), Cmnd. 2154 – V (HMSO, London, 1964). p. 16.

The emphasis put on technological education may be judged by the 'specialities' of all occupied graduates in 1960: engineers 31.5 per cent; agronomists, vets and other agricultural and animal specialists 6.8 per cent; economists and *tovaroveds* (commodity experts) 6.1 per cent; lawyers 2.0 per cent; doctors (excluding dentists) 11.3 per cent; teachers, librarians and occupations in fine arts 38.9 per cent.[1]

These figures are not very detailed and do not show the proportions of students studying arts and science subjects: many 'teachers' are in science and technology. DeWitt has estimated that in 1955–56, 55.5 per cent of university students were studying science (mathematics, physics, and engineering: 27.4 per cent, chemistry and biology: 19.3 per cent), social sciences (including geography and law) 16.1 per cent and humanities (history, languages and literature) 27.8 per cent.[2]

[1] *Vysshee obrazovanie v SSSR* (Moscow, 1961), Table 12.
[2] N. DeWitt, *Education and Professional Employment in the USSR*, p. 213.

The main differences in the structure of education compared to the USA are the absence of liberal arts and business schools. The lack of the former is perhaps to be expected, as the educational system is most closely geared to the needs of the economy. In the West it is sometimes argued that a degree in Greats helps to sell oil; in the USSR the approach has been to educate specialists who can produce it. The deficiency in business training is due to the low prestige of administration and is also conditioned by the needs of the economy in which until recently the production of a commodity guaranteed its sale.

A large proportion of Soviet students are not in full-time attendance at the university or college. Of the 4,311,000 higher education students in 1967–8, 43.8 per cent were full-time, 15.1 per cent were evening (or part-time) and 41.1 per cent were taking correspondence courses.[1] (The proportions for 1959 were: full-time 55 per cent, evening 7 per cent, correspondence 38 per cent.) Correspondence students are attached to institutes or university departments and are required to attend for 'consultation' with their supervisors; short courses at the institution are also arranged. Part-time and correspondence students share scarce buildings and teachers, they require less subsidy by the state and, by continuing with their work, they also contribute to production. The increase in part-time students has been the most spectacular between 1950 and 1965 and has accounted for more than two-thirds of the total increase of students.[2]

These figures show the intensive use made of facilities and indicate the way education costs have been kept down while the number of students has been increased. Estimates of Soviet expenditure on education range from 4.4 per cent to 8.0 per cent of the Gross National Product. The lower figure (for 1959–60) is estimated in *Higher Education*.[3] DeWitt's estimate (for the late 1950s) is 5.0 per cent and an American government estimate, 8.0 per cent.[4]

The usual period of full-time higher education is from four to five and a half years; medicine being five and a half; engineering five; law, history, journalism and art four years; agriculture, four and a half. Before June, 1964, the courses were on average six months longer.

Though Soviet education involves specialised study, it also calls for considerable effort on subjects outside the speciality. Excluding courses on civics

[1] *Narodnoe khozyasystvo SSSR v 1967g* (Moscow, 1968), p. 788. But of the 1968 intake of higher education students, just over half were full-time. *Narkhoz SSSR v 1968g* (Moscow, 1969), p. 687.

[2] *Narodnoe khozyaystvo SSSR v 1964g* (Moscow, 1965), p. 678.

[3] HMSO Appendix Five, Cmnd. 2154-V (London, 1963), p. 17. The same source estimates that British education expenditure (in 1959) was 4.0 per cent, West German 3.0 per cent, and French 3.4 per cent.

[4] DeWitt, *Education and Professional Employment in the USSR*, p. 63, and 'US versus Soviet Spending for Major GNP Categories', *Intelligence Information Brief*, no. 87, Feb. 24 1959 (p. 3), cited by DeWitt, *ibid.*

(party history, economics, dialectical and historical materialism) other subjects constitute about 10.0 per cent of the total time; a foreign language 3.0 per cent and physical education 3.0 per cent. Though Soviet university education is more specialised than the American, it is much wider than the British – at both school and university.

At the undergraduate level, students have to carry out a piece of research work which forms part of their diploma examination. But the chief research role of the university lies with the training of postgraduates. Postgraduate study is usually undertaken after a period of work (at least two years) when students register for the Candidate of Science degree (*Kandidat Nauk*) which is roughly equivalent to an American PhD; it involves course work, examinations and the submission of a dissertation. The Doctor of Science is awarded on the basis of a major piece of research; its standard is higher than the typical British PhD. University teachers are supposed to carry out an average three hours' individual research a day.

Selection for Higher Education

The process of educational selection is instrumental in assigning to individuals their occupation in society and the roles and status that go with it. In the absence of family property the educational process is the major determinant of the life chances of the Soviet citizen. Selection for higher education, therefore, is a crucial social and political process.

In the 1920s and early 1930s selection was strongly politically biased: priority was given to applicants of proletarian origin and restrictions were placed on groups of other social origins, such as the aristocracy or bourgeoisie. But according to data summarised by DeWitt, the intake of higher education students between 1927 and 1938 included only 39.7 per cent of worker origin; 19.3 per cent of peasant and 41.0 per cent of 'other' (white collar and intelligentsia).[1] Jews (largely of the intelligentsia and non-manual groups) accounted for 12.4 per cent of the students between 1929 and 1935 compared with their 1.8 per cent share of the population.[2] These figures suggest that the 'proletarianisation' of higher educational institutions was only partially successful. Inkeles and Bauer's survey of post-1945 Russian émigrés found that of those aged between 21 and 35 in 1940:

> . . . the great majority of the children of the intelligentsia got to college. Most of the rest got at least to high school and very few 'disgraced' their families by failing to get past the primary school. By contrast the overwhelming majority of the peasants got just this minimum although about one in ten did attain the exalted college level. Between these poles the proportion with only elementary schooling

[1] N. DeWitt, *op. cit.*, Table IV-A-6, page 655.
[2] N. DeWitt, *op. cit.*, Table IV-A-7, p. 656.

falls and with college training rises as one ascends the occupational ladder. The sharpest point of division comes, however, when we pass over the line from manual labour to white-collar jobs. The poor showing of the peasants cannot be attributed to the high proportion of the dekulakised among them, since they fared about as well as those not discriminated against by the government.[1]

Differential access by various social groups to higher education is an established fact in both the United States and Great Britain. An interesting table (see Table 56 below) has been devised by Robert A. Feldmesser comparing the proportion of college students of certain status groups with the percentage of the status group in the population as a whole. The 'index of representation' shows the relative educational opportunity of different groups: numbers over a hundred show that in a certain status group the proportion of students is more than in the population as a whole and is therefore relatively privileged, a score of under one hundred indicates relative deprivation.

Table 56. Representation of Status Groups Among College Students in the United States and the Soviet Union

Status Group	Population (%)	College Students (%)	Index of Representation
United States			
Non-manual	24.4	54.7	224
Manual	60.1	30.5	51
Farmers	14.0	9.4	67
Others, Unknown	1.2	5.4	—
Soviet Union			
Non-manual	17.5	42.2	241
Manual	32.3	33.9	105
Peasants	46.4	21.7	47
Others	3.9	2.2	—

Source: Robert A. Feldmesser, 'Social Status and Access to Higher Education', *Harvard Educational Review*, Vol. 27(2) (1957), p. 94.
US data refer to Indiana State University and Indiana State, collected in 1946-7. Soviet data refer to 1937-8. The American data ignore teacher training colleges while the Soviet include them.

The tables show a predominance of the non-manual strata in higher education in both societies. In the USSR, however, the 'manual' students category is more than the population as a whole, whereas in the USA it is only half. In both societies the agricultural sector is under-represented – but rather more so in the USSR. Despite the difficulties involved in making a comparison on the basis of the data, Feldmesser concludes: '. . . one's status makes more of a

[1] Alex Inkeles and Raymond A. Bauer, *The Soviet Citizen* (Cambridge, Mass., 1959), p. 141.

difference to one's chances of getting a college education in the United States than in the Soviet Union.'[1] Again, the Soviet data refer to the pre-World War II period.

At present, merit is the main official criterion for admission. Rules are laid down by decree of the Ministry of Higher Education. Selection is on the basis of competitive examination conducted by the institute or university. Examinations, both oral and written, take place in the student's speciality together with Russian and a foreign language. Differences in the standards required based on supply and demand exist between institutions. The older or better-known urban centres, such as Moscow and Leningrad, attract more better-qualified applicants and, therefore, higher marks may be necessary. Specialist courses, for instance on computer technology, are also in great demand. No centralised 'clearing house' system exists and, unless students may persuade some other institutions to take them (they receive their entrance examination marks), they have either to start work or wait to compete again the next year. For those who are admitted, education is provided free and a system of grants is operated to help students meet their living expenses. Grants are awarded on the criteria of parental income, year of study (senior students get more than junior), field of study (scientists receive more than those in humanities), and performance (good students get more than bad ones). Though students complain, the awards provide a basic minimum.[2]

Academic standards are not the only criteria for admission to higher education, As at British universities, 'character' is taken into account; students have to produce a reference from their place of work or from Party or *Komsomol* organisation. Much is made of this condition by western writers but in fact no concrete statistics of exclusion on political grounds are available. It seems likely that in some cases party activists may be favoured and known Christians excluded, although much may depend on the subject and institution; political considerations being more important in history or philosophy than in physics or ballet. The main criterion for admission is academic achievement.

From 1958 until 1965 experience of practical work was also a requirement – only 20 per cent of new entrants being admitted straight from school. This experiment was justified by Khrushchev to bring manual and intellectual work closer together. It has been argued that other political factors were involved: such measures would reduce 'demand' for places which could not be met by the existing facilities; non-academic factors were being strengthened to permit greater party influence and to maintain the Soviet elite's grip over educational facilities.[3] Again there is no empirical data to support such views which

---

[1] R. A. Feldmesser, *loc. cit*, p. 95.
[2] See N. Grant, *Soviet Education* (1964), pp. 119-20.
[3] See DeWitt, p. 255.

are based on *a priori* reasoning. Since Khrushchev's departure from the political scene, the regulations have been dropped.

Family influence can also lead to admission: '. . . a person is admitted to a higher educational establishment not because he is well prepared, but because he has an influential papa and mama who can help to get him in'.[1] Again, in September 1958, Khrushchev said, '. . . frequently, it is not enough to pass the examinations to enter college. Great influence of the parents also plays a part here. With good reason, one rather widely hears youth entering college saying that after they themselves pass the contest, a contest among the parents begins – and it often decides the whole matter'.[2] It is doubtful whether such practices are wide-spread: examination committees are frequently changed and examinees must submit written scripts under pseudonym. In marginal cases, however, selection boards may be swayed by parents' pressures.[3] Probably more important is the greater 'know-how' of executives and professional workers, who are more able to place their children for admission to higher education.

The proportion of students from peasant and lower working strata has nowhere been comprehensively and accurately collected.[4] DeWitt reports that American exchange students at Moscow and Leningrad universities have estimated that only between 10 and 20 per cent of Soviet students at these universities are of peasant or worker stock.[5] Khrushchev himself said that only 30 to 40 per cent of all students at Moscow higher educational establishments were of worker or peasant origin.[6] Clearly, these sources are insufficient and more precise information is required.

Soviet research conducted on students at various institutes of higher education confirms the higher representation of non-manual strata. This is illustrated by Table 57 (page 508), which shows the social origin and social position of entrants to the Urals Politechnic in 1958, 1962 and 1967.

Not only do the figures show the predominance of the non-manual worker, but also give some indication of the effects of Khrushchev's reforms by which preference was given to entrants with work experience. In the period 1962–3, 61.6 per cent of the intake hailed from manual worker and collective farmer background while only 19.1 per cent were recruited from school. In 1967/8, while the proportion of school leavers rose to 67.8 per cent, the number of students of working class and peasant background fell to 43.7 per cent.

---

[1] N. Khrushchev, *Pravda*, 19 April 1958, cited by De Witt, p. 247.

[2] N. S. Khrushchev, 'Ob ukreplenii svyazi s zhiznyu i o dalneyshem razvitii sistemy narodnogo obrazovaniya v strane,' *Pravda*, 21 September 1958, cited in Bereday, Brickman and Read, p. 427.

[3] Examples are known of parents bribing lecturers to secure their children's admission. See account in *The Times* 23 Sept. 1969.

[4] See also above, pp. 360-2, 411-16.

[5] DeWitt, note 40, p. 246.

[6] N. Khrushchev, *Pravda*, 21 September 1958.

Table 57. The Changing Social Composition of Entrants to the Urals Polytechnic 1958-1968

School Year	Social origins (%)			Social position (%)			
			Collective		Collective		
	Manual Workers	Non- Manuals	Farm Peasants	Manual Workers	Farm Peasants	Non- Manuals	School Pupils
1958/59	34.2	52.9	12.9	38	4.2	28	29.8
1962/63	46.8	38.4	14.8	40	0.3	32.6	19.1
1967/68	42.1	56.3	1.6*	19.1	0.2	12.9	67.8

* Mainly accounted for by the transfer into state farms of the majority of collective farms in the area. 'Collective' farmers thereby lose their status and are reclassified as agricultural workers.
Source: Klassy, sotsial'nye sloi i gruppy v SSSR (Moscow, 1968), p. 158.

It seems likely, therefore, that where 'open competition' for higher education takes place, the most successful and most highly qualified candidates come from the higher social strata. In this respect Soviet experience is similar to that of the West. In order to combat this tendency, special departments in higher educational establishments are to be set up to arrange eight to ten month courses for workers and collective farmers lacking formal qualifications.[1] While this is laudable, experience of the workers' faculties in the early 1930s would suggest that this is not a complete remedy.

Our study of Soviet education confirms Durkheim's view that education is a 'methodological socialisation of the young'. It not only transmits the culture of a society to the young but inculcates values and attitudes usually determined by the society's political elites. In the USSR, the educational system has been an agency for the indoctrination of Bolshevik social and political norms. As in other advanced industrial societies, the teaching of skills has become institutionalised in schools and higher educational institutions. These have become important levers in economic change; Soviet technological development has depended on the supply of trained manpower from the educational sector. Education has become universal, ensuring widespread literacy and Soviet education has emphasised technological competence. In all societies, education is a major determinant of the individual's life chances. This is particularly so in the USSR where the family has no legal rights over property. Access to higher education has been determined by a combination of merit and ascription. In the early days of Bolshevik power, the previously deprived proletarian and peasant strata were given priority, though other social factors, particularly the higher educability of the professional and white collar strata, gave some weight to 'merit'. While Soviet education has attempted to bring

[1] See 'New Developments in Soviet Education', Soviet News, 28 October 1969, p. 46.

down the barriers which barred deprived social and national groups from higher education, the cultural forces generated by family and parental occupation have asserted themselves. As in western societies, though perhaps to a lesser extent, professional strata pass on the advantages of their own education to their children thereby making them more educable, more worthy of 'merit'. Khrushchev's attempts to mitigate this tendency by placing greater influence on boarding schools and by stipulating recruitment from the bench rather than from the school desk were egalitarian, but they were short-lasting. The main characteristics of Soviet education are its manifest connexion with economic and political institutions, and its emphasis on technological training and political socialisation. It is meritocratic, and now largely determines the life chances of the Soviet citizen.

Reading No. 19
Code of moral education recommended by Soviet Academy of Pedagogic Sciences
Source: G. Z. F. Bereday, W. W. Brickman, G. H. Read, *The Changing Soviet School* (Constable, London, 1960), pp. 428-30.

I. Elementary ideas of good and bad.
   A. To differentiate between good and bad actions.
   B. To behave well.
      1. To love all useful work, especially manual work.
      2. To carry out properly all duties.
      3. To study diligently.
      4. To be orderly and obey all rules.
      5. To help fellow comrades and younger children.
      6. To be truthful, brave and kind.
      7. To take good care of one's health.
      8. To know that breaking rules is bad.
      9. To obey the teacher and parents.
      10. To follow the example of the best pupils.
      11. To follow the rules of the Octobrists and the laws of the Young Pioneers.
II. Love of Motherland.
   A. To respect the work of adults for the common good and the welfare of the family.
      1. To bring adults joy through one's success in study and in behaviour.
   B. To love one's school.
      1. To develop the ability to study well.
      2. To respect the teacher.
   C. To love one's native locale.
   D. To take an interest in the heroic past and present of our Motherland.
      1. To have a warm love for V. I. Lenin.
      2. To have a feeling of gratitude to the Communist Party and the Soviet Government.
   E. To have a feeling of friendship for the children of all nations.
   F. To hate instigators of wars.
   G. To have a desire to be good Octobrists or Pioneers.
III. Industriousness and frugality.
   A. To respect all socially useful labour, especially manual labour.
   B. To have habits of self-service and assistance to the family.
   C. To desire to work for the social good.
      1. To make useful things.
      2. To take care of 'green friends', birds, and animals.

    D. To have good work habits.

    E. To respect property.

IV. Truthfulness, honesty, modesty, and kindness.

    A. To speak the truth.

    B. To carry out promises.

    C. To avoid boasting about successes.

    D. To recognise mistakes and to avoid them in the future.

    E. To apologise if you are wrong.

    F. To fulfill honourable duties.

V. Friendship and comradeship.

    A. To have friends and comrades among the students.

    B. To give help to a comrade.

    C. To be able to plan work together.

    D. To respect the monitors and to obey their orders.

    E. To obey the decisions of the collectives.

VI. Discipline.

    A. To carry out assignments.

    B. To obey 'The Rules for Pupils' and to understand the reasons for them.

    C. To obey these rules without being reminded of them.

VII. Love of studies and conscientiousness.

    A. To be curious, listen attentively, read, observe, work, study, and create.

    B. To carry out all requirements and teachers' instructions with a degree of independence.

    C. To apply the acquired knowledge to life and to share it with others.

VIII. Good social conduct in the school, at home, in the streets, and in public places.

    A. To be orderly, neat, and well-groomed.

    B. To be polite.

       1. To use common forms of politeness, such as 'Good morning', 'Please', 'Thank you', and so forth.

       2. To look affable during conversations and not interrupt each other.

    C. To behave properly at home.

       1. To leave and to enter the home quietly and without banging doors.

       2. To ask permission to take something or permission to leave the house.

    D. To conduct oneself properly in the streets and in public places.

       1. To obey the rules of conduct in movies, dining rooms, libraries, and so forth.

         a. To be on time.

         b. To wipe footwear at the entrance.

         c. Not to turn around.

         d. Not to break in line.

         e. Not to speak loudly.

       2. To prevent comrades from committing bad actions.

INTRODUCTORY

Bereday, G. Z. F., W. W. Brickman and G. H. Read (eds.). *The Changing Soviet School. The Comparative Education Society Field Study in the USSR.* London: Constable, 1961.

Floud, J. and A. H. Halsey. 'The Sociology of Education', in *Current Sociology*, Vol. 7, No. 3, 1958.

Grant, N. *Soviet Education.* London: Penguin, 1964.

Shore, M. *Soviet Education.* New York: Philosophical Library, 1947.

BASIC

Banks, O. *The Sociology of Education.* London: Batsford, 1968.

Charlton, Kenneth. 'Polytechnical Education: An Idea in Motion', in *International Review of Education*, Vol. 14, No. 1, 1968, pp. 43-61.

DeWitt, N. *Education and Professional Employment in the USSR.* Washington: National Science Foundation, 1961.

Feldmesser, R. A. 'Social Status and Access to Higher Education', *Harvard Educational Review*, Vol. 27, No. 2, 1957.

Hans, N. *The Russian Tradition in Education.* London: Routledge, 1963.

Inkeles, A. and R. A. Bauer. *The Soviet Citizen.* Cambridge, Mass.: Harvard University Press, 1959.

Lenin, V. I. 'On Proletarian Culture', in *Collected Works*, Vol. 31. Moscow, 1966.

Matthews, M. in *New Society*, 19 December 1968.

Narodnoe obrazovanie v Sovetskom Soyuze. Moscow, 1964.

Remenikov, B. M. and G. I. Ushakov. *Universitetskoe obrazovanie v SSSR, ekonomiko-statisticheski obzor.* Moscow, 1960.

Rosen, S. M. *Significant Aspects of Soviet Education.* Washington: Department of Health, Education, and Welfare, 1965.

Rutkevich, M. N. 'Intelligentsiya kak sotsial'naya gruppa i ee sblizhenie s rabochim klassom', *Klassy sotsial'nye sloi i gruppy v SSSR.* Moscow, 1968, pp. 136-61.

SPECIALISED

Aitov, N. in *Molodoy Kommunist*, No. 7, 1966, pp. 77-85.

Basov, V. 'Nekotorye voprosy ekonomiki narodnogo obrazovaniya', *Finansy SSSR*, No. 5, 1967, pp. 15-19.

Brookover, W. B. and D. Gottlieb. *A Sociology of Education.* 2nd Edition. New York: American Book Co., 1964.

'US versus Soviet Spending for Major G.N.P. categories', *Intelligence Information Brief*, No. 87, 24 Feb. 1959.

Dorokhova, G. A. *Upravlenie narodnym obrazovaniem v SSSR.* Moscow, 1965.

Durkheim, E. *Education and Society.* Glencoe, Ill.: Free Press, 1956.

Engels, F. 'Letter to J. Bloch', 21 September 1890, in K. Marx and F. Engels. *Selected Works*, Vol. 2, Moscow, 1951.

'Eto kasaetsya vsekh'. *Literaturnaya gazeta*, 24 April 1965, p. 2.

Goncharov, N. K. 'Sovetskaya pedagogicheskaya nauka', *Narodnoe obrazovanie*, No. 11, Nov. 1957, pp. 65-70.

Higher Education. Cmnd 2154-V. London: HMSO, 1964.

International Conference on Public Education, Session 27, General, 1964. *Public Education in the Soviet Union.* Moscow, 1964.

Khrushchev, N. S. 'Ob ukreplenii svyazi s zhizn'yu i o dalneyshem razvitii sistemy narodnogo obrazovaniya v strane', *Pravda*, 21 September 1958. (No. 264).

Khrushchev, N. S. Final Speech at 13th Congress of the VLKSM, *Pravda*, 19 April 1958, pp. 1-3.

Marx, K. and F. Engels. *The German Ideology.* London: Lawrence and Wishart, 1965.

Narodnoe obrazovanie v SSSR. Moscow, 1957.

Osipov, G. *Rabochi klass i tekhnicheski progress.* Moscow, 1965.

Pyatdesyat'. 50 let Sovetskogo zdravookhraneniya, 1917–1967. Moscow, 1967.

Rashin, A. G. *Formirovanie rabochego klassa.* Moscow, 1958.

The Times, 23 September 1969. (On University Admissions).

Tsentral'noe statisticheskoe upravlenie. *SSSR v tsifrakh v 1963g.* Moscow, 1964.

Tsentral'noe statisticheskoe upravlenie. *Narodnoe khozyaystvo SSSR v 1964g.* Moscow, 1965.

Tsentral'noe statisticheskoe upravlenie. *Narodnoe khozyaystvo SSSR v 1968g.* Moscow, 1969.

Tsentral'noe statisticheskoe upravlenie, *Zhenshchiny i deti v SSSR.* Moscow, 1963.

Vysshee obrazovanie v SSSR. Moscow, 1961.

APPENDIX A

Membership of the CPSU 1917–1969

January 1	Members	Candidates	Total
1917	23,600	—	23,600
1918	390,000	—	390,000
1919	350,000	—	350,000
1920	611,978	—	611,978
1921	732,521	—	732,521
1922	410,430	117,924	528,354
1923	381,400	117,700	499,100
1924	350,000	122,000	472,000
1925	440,365	361,439	801,804
1926	639,652	440,162	1,079,814
1927	786,288	426,217	1,212,505
1928	914,307	391,547	1,305,854
1929	1,090,508	444,854	1,535,362
1930	1,184,651	493,259	1,677,910
1931	1,369,406	842,819	2,212,225
1932	1,769,773	1,347,477	3,117,250
1933	2,203,951	1,351,387	3,555,338
1934	1,826,756	874,252	2,701,008
1935	1,659,104	699,610	2,358,714
1936	1,489,907	586,935	2,076,842
1937	1,453,828	527,869	1,981,697
1938	1,405,879	514,123	1,920,002
1939	1,514,181	792,792	2,306,973
1940	1,982,743	1,417,232	3,399,975
1941	2,490,479	1,381,986	3,872,465
1942	2,155,336	908,540	3,063,876
1943	2,451,511	1,403,190	3,854,701
1944	3,126,627	1,791,934	4,918,561
1945	3,965,530	1,794,839	5,760,369
1946	4,127,689	1,383,173	5,510,862
1947	4,774,886	1,277,015	6,051,901
1948	5,181,199	1,209,082	6,390,281
1949	5,334,811	1,017,761	6,352,572
1950	5,510,787	829,396	6,340,183
1951	5,658,577	804,398	6,462,975

January 1	Members	Candidates	Total
1952	5,853,200	854,339	6,707,539
1953	6,067,027	830,197	6,897,224
1954	6,402,284	462,579	6,864.863
1955	6,610,238	346,867	6,957,105
1956	6,767,644	405,877	7,173,521
1957	7,001,114	493,459	7,494,573
1958	7,296,559	546,637	7,843,196
1959	7,622,356	616,775	8,239,131
1960	8,017,249	691,418	8,708,667
1961	8,472,396	803,430	9,275,826
1962	9,051,934	839,134	9,891,068
1963	9,581,149	806,047	10,387,196
1964	10,182,916	839,453	11,022,369
1965	10,811,443	946,726	11,758,169
1966	11,548,287	809,021	12,357,308
1967	12,135,103	549,030	12,684,133
1968	12,484,836	695,389	13,180,225
1969	—	—	13,755,000

Sources. Figures for 1917: cited by Merle Fainsod, *How Russia is Ruled* (Cambridge, Mass. 1963), p. 249. For 1918–1967: *Kommunist* no. 15, 1967, pp. 90–91. For 1968: *Ezhegodnik bol'shoy Sovetskoy entsiklopedii, 1968* (M. 1968). In 1968, there were 349,000 basic Party units. For 1969 (June): *Partiynaya zhizn'*, no. 11 (June), 1969, p. 8.

APPENDIX B

Rules of the Communist Party of the Soviet Union[1]

The Communist Party of the Soviet Union is the tried and tested militant vanguard of the Soviet people, which unites, on a voluntary basis, the more advanced, politically more conscious section of the working class, collective-farm peasantry and intelligentsia of the USSR.

Founded by V. I. Lenin as the vanguard of the working class, the Communist Party has travelled a glorious road of struggle, and brought the working class and the working peasantry to the victory of the Great October Socialist Revolution and to the establishment of the dictatorship of the proletariat in the USSR. Under the leadership of the Communist Party, the exploiting classes were abolished in the Soviet Union, and the moral and political unity of Soviet society has taken shape and grown in strength. Socialism has triumphed completely and finally. The Communist Party, the party of the working class, has today become the party of the Soviet people as a whole.

The Party exists for, and serves, the people. It is the highest form of social and political organisation, and is the leading and guiding force of Soviet society. It directs the great activity of the Soviet people, and imparts an organised, planned, and scientifically-based character to their struggle to achieve the ultimate goal, the victory of communism.

The CPSU bases its work on unswerving adherence to the Leninist standards of Party life—the principle of collective leadership, the promotion, in every possible way, of inner-Party democracy, the activity and initiative of the Communists, criticism and self-criticism.

Ideological and organisational unity, monolithic cohesion of its ranks, and a high degree of conscious discipline on the part of all Communists are an inviolable law of the CPSU. All manifestations of factionalism and group activity are incompatible with Marxist-Leninist Party principles, and with Party membership.

In all its activities, the CPSU takes guidance from Marxist-Leninist theory and the Programme based on it, which defines the fundamental tasks of the Party for the period of the construction of communist society.

In creatively developing Marxism-Leninism, the CPSU vigorously combats all manifestations of revisionism and dogmatism, which are utterly alien to revolutionary theory.

The Communist Party of the Soviet Union is an integral part of the international Communist and working class movement. It firmly adheres to the tried and tested

[1] Adopted at *22nd Congress of CPSU*, 31 Oct. 1961. Source: *Soviet Booklet*, no. 82 (1961).

Marxist-Leninist principles of proletarian internationalism; it actively promotes the unity of the international Communist and working-class movement as a whole, and fraternal ties with the great army of the Communists of all countries.

1.PARTY MEMBERS, THEIR DUTIES AND RIGHTS

1. Membership of the CPSU is open to any citizen of the Soviet Union who accepts the Programme and the Rules of the Party, takes an active part in communist construction, works in one of the Party organisations, carries out all Party decisions, and pays membership dues.

2. It is the duty of a Party member:

(a) to work for the creation of the material and technical basis of communism; to serve as an example of the communist attitude towards labour: to raise labour productivity; to display the initiative in all that is new and progressive; to support and propagate advanced methods, to master techniques, to improve his skill; to protect and increase public socialist property, the mainstay of the might and prosperity of the Soviet country;

(b) to put Party decisions firmly and steadfastly into effect; to explain the policy of the Party to the masses; to help strengthen and multiply the Party's bonds with the people; to be considerate and attentive to people; to respond promptly to the needs and requirements of the working people;

(c) to take an active part in the political life of the country, in the administration of state affairs, and in economic and cultural development; to set an example in the fulfilment of his public duty; to assist in developing and strengthening communist social relations;

(d) to master Marxist-Leninist theory, to improve his ideological knowledge, and to contribute to the moulding and education of the man of communist society. To combat vigorously all manifestations of bourgeois ideology, remnants of a private-property psychology, religious prejudices, and other survivals of the past; to observe the principles of communist morality, and place public interests above his own;

(e) to be an active proponent of the ideas of socialist internationalism and Soviet patriotism among the masses of the working people; to combat survivals of nationalism and chauvinism; to contribute by word and by deed to the consolidation of the friendship of the peoples of the USSR and the fraternal bonds linking the Soviet people with the peoples of the countries of the socialist camp, with the proletarians and other working people in all countries;

(f) to strengthen to the utmost the ideological and organisational unity of the Party; to safeguard the Party against the infiltration of people unworthy of the lofty name of Communist; to be truthful and honest with the Party and the people; to display vigilance, to guard Party and state secrets;

(g) to develop criticism and self-criticism, boldly lay bare shortcomings and strive for their removal; to combat ostentation, conceit, complacency, and parochial tendencies; to rebuff firmly all attempts at suppressing criticism; to resist all actions injurious to the Party and the state, and to give information of them to Party bodies, up to and including the Central Committee of the CPSU;

(h) to implement undeviatingly the Party's policy with regard to the proper selection of personnel according to their political qualifications and personal qualities. To be uncompromising whenever the Leninist principles of the selection and education of personnel are infringed;

(i) to observe Party and state discipline, which is equally binding on all Party members. The Party has one discipline, one law, for all Communists, irrespective of their past services or the positions they occupy;

(j) to help, in every possible way, to strengthen the defence potential of the USSR; to wage an unflagging struggle for peace and friendship among nations.

3. A Party member has the right:

(a) to elect and be elected to Party bodies;

(b) to discuss freely questions of the Party's policies and practical activities at Party meetings, conferences and congresses, at the meetings of Party committees and in the Party press; to table motions; openly to express and uphold his opinion as long as the Party organisation concerned has not adopted a decision;

(c) to criticise any Communist, irrespective of the position he holds, at Party meetings, conferences and congresses, and at the full meetings of Party committees. Those who commit the offence of suppressing criticism or victimising anyone for criticism are responsible to and will be penalised by the Party, to the point of expulsion from the CPSU;

(d) to attend in person all Party meetings and all bureau and committee meetings that discuss his activities or conduct;

(e) to address any question, statement or proposal to any Party body, up to and including the Central Committee of the CPSU, and to demand an answer on the substance of his address.

4. *Applicants are admitted to Party membership only individually. Membership of the Party is open to politically conscious and active workers, peasants and representatives of the intelligentsia, devoted to the communist cause. New members are admitted from among the candidate members who have passed through the established probationary period.

Persons may join the Party on attaining the age of eighteen. Young people up to the age of twenty may join the Party only through the Leninist Young Communist League of the Soviet Union (YCL).

The procedure for the admission of candidate members to full Party membership is as follows:

(a) Applicants for Party membership must submit recommendations from three members of the CPSU who have a Party standing of not less than three years and who know the applicants from having worked with them, professionally and socially, for not less than one year.

Note 1.—In the case of members of the YCL applying for membership of the Party, the recommendation of a district or city committee of the YCL is equivalent to the recommendation of one Party member.

Note 2.—Members and alternate members of the Central Committee of the CPSU shall refrain from giving recommendations.

* See Amendment No. 1, below.

(b) Applications for Party membership are discussed and a decision is taken by the general meeting of the basic Party organisation; the decision of the latter takes effect after endorsement by the district Party committee, or by the city Party committee in cities with no district divisions.

The presence of those who have recommended an applicant for Party membership at the discussion of the application concerned is optional;

(c) citizens of the USSR who formerly belonged to the Communist or Workers' Party of another country are admitted to membership of the Communist Party of the Soviet Union in conformity with the rules established by the Central Committee of the CPSU.

Former members of other parties are admitted to membership of the CPSU in conformity with the regular procedure, except that their admission must be endorsed by a regional or territorial committee or the Central Committee of the Communist Party of a Union Republic.

5. Communists recommending applicants for Party membership are responsible to Party organisations for the impartiality of their description of the moral qualities and professional and political qualifications of those they recommend.

6. The Party standing of those admitted to membership dates from the day when the general meeting of the basic Party organisation decides to accept them as full members.

7. The procedure of registering members and candidate members of the Party, and their transfer from one organisation to another is determined by the appropriate instructions of the Central Committee of the CPSU.

8. If a Party member or candidate member fails to pay membership dues for three months in succession without sufficient reason, the matter shall be discussed by the basic Party organisation. If it is revealed as a result that the Party member or candidate member in question has virtually lost contact with the Party organisation, he shall be regarded as having ceased to be a member of the Party; the basic Party organisation shall pass a decision thereon and submit it to the district or city committee of the Party for endorsement.

9.* A Party member or candidate member who fails to fulfil his duties as laid down in the Rules, or commits other offences, shall be called to account, and may be subjected to the penalty of admonition, reprimand (severe reprimand), or reprimand (severe reprimand) with entry in the registration card. The highest Party penalty is expulsion from the Party.

Should the necessity arise, a Party organisation may, as a Party penalty, reduce a Party member to the status of candidate member for a period of up to one year. The decision of the basic Party organisation reducing a Party member to candidate membership is subject to endorsement by the district or city Party committee. On the expiration of his period of reduction to candidate membership his readmission to full membership of the Party will follow regular procedure, with retention of his former Party standing. In the case of insignificant offences, measures of Party education and influence should be applied—in the form of comradely criticism, Party censure, warning, or reproof. When the question of expelling a member from

* See Amendment No. 2 below.

the Party is discussed, the maximum attention must be shown, and the grounds for the charges preferred against him must be thoroughly investigated.

10. *The decision to expel a Communist from the Party is made by the general meeting of a basic Party organisation. The decision of the basic Party organisation expelling a member is regarded as adopted if not less than two-thirds of the Party members attending the meeting have voted for it, and is subject to endorsement by the district or city Party committee. The decision of the district or city committee expelling a member takes effect after endorsement by a regional or territorial committee or the Central Committee of the Communist Party of a Union Republic.

Until such time as the decision to expel him is endorsed by a regional or territorial Party committee or the Central Committee of the Communist Party of a Union Republic, the Party member or candidate member retains his membership card and is entitled to attend closed Party meetings.

An expelled Party member retains the right to appeal, within the period of two months, to the higher Party bodies, up to and including the Central Committee of the CPSU.

11. The question of calling a member or alternate member of the Central Committee of the Communist Party of a Union Republic, of a territorial, regional, area, city or district Party committee, as well as a member of an auditing commission, to account before the Party is discussed by basic Party organisations.

Party organisations pass decisions imposing penalties on members or alternate members of the said Party committees, or on members of auditing commissions, in conformity with the regular procedure.

A Party organisation which proposes expelling a Communist from the CPSU communicates its proposal to the Party committee of which he is a member. A decision expelling from the Party a member or alternate member of the Central Committee of the Communist Party of a Union Republic or a territorial, regional, area, city or district Party committee, or a member of an auditing commission, is taken at the full meeting of the committee concerned by a majority of two-thirds of the membership.

The decision to expel from the Party a member or alternate member of the Central Committee of the CPSU, or a member of the Central Auditing Commission, is made by the Party congress, and in the interval between two congresses, by a full meeting of the Central Committee, by a majority of two-thirds of its members.

12. Should a Party member commit an indictable offence, he shall be expelled from the Party and prosecuted in conformity with the law.

13. Appeals against expulsion from the Party or against the imposition of a penalty, as well as the decisions of Party organisations on expulsion from the Party shall be examined by the appropriate Party bodies within not more than one month from the date of their receipt.

II. CANDIDATE MEMBERS

14. All persons joining the Party must pass through a probationary period as

* See Amendment No. 2 below.

candidate members in order to familiarise themselves more thoroughly with the Programme and the Rules of the CPSU and prepare for admission to full membership of the Party. Party organisations must assist candidates to prepare for admission to full membership of the Party, and test their personal qualities.

The period of probationary membership shall be one year.

15. The procedure for the admission of candidate members (individual admission, submission of recommendations, decision of the primary organisation as to admission, and its endorsement) is identical with the procedure for the admission of Party members.

16. On the expiration of a candidate member's probationary period the basic Party organisation discusses and passes a decision on his admission to full membership. Should a candidate member fail, in the course of his probationary period, to prove his worthiness, and should his personal traits make it evident that he cannot be admitted to membership of the CPSU, the Party organisation shall pass a decision rejecting his admission to membership of the Party; after endorsement of that decision by the district or city Party committee, he shall cease to be considered a candidate member of the CPSU.

17. Candidate members of the Party participate in all the activities of their Party organisations; they shall have a consultative voice at Party meetings. They may not be elected to any leading Party body, nor may they be elected delegates to a Party conference or congress.

18. Candidate members of the CPSU pay membership dues at the same rate as full members.

III. ORGANISATIONAL STRUCTURE OF THE PARTY. INNER-PARTY DEMOCRACY

19. The guiding principle of the organisational structure of the Party is democratic centralism, which signifies:

(a) election of all leading Party bodies, from the lowest to the highest;

(b) periodical reports of Party bodies to their Party organisations and to higher bodies;

(c) strict Party discipline and subordination of the minority to the majority;

(d) the decisions of higher bodies are obligatory for lower bodies.

20. The Party is built on the territorial-and-production principle: basic organisations are established wherever Communists are employed, and are associated territorially in district, city, etc., organisations. An organisation serving a given area is higher than any Party organisation serving part of that area.

21. All Party organisations are autonomous in the decision of local questions, unless their decisions conflict with Party policy.

22. The highest leading body of a Party organisation is the general meeting (in the case of basic organisations), conference (in the case of district, city, area, regional or territorial organisations), or congress (in the case of the Communist Parties of the Union Republics and the Communist Party of the Soviet Union).

23. The general meeting, conference or congress, elects a bureau or committee

which acts as its executive body and directs all the current work of the Party organisation.

24. *The election of Party bodies shall be effected by secret ballot. In an election, all Party members have the unlimited right to challenge candidates and to criticise them. Each candidate shall be voted upon separately. A candidate is considered elected if more than one-half of those attending the meeting, conference or congress have voted for him.

25. *The principle of a systematic renewal of the composition of Party bodies and of continuity of leadership shall be observed in the election of those bodies.

At each regular election, not less than one-quarter of the composition of the Central Committee of the CPSU and its Presidium shall be renewed. Members of the Presidium shall not, as a rule, be elected for more than three successive terms. Particular Party officials may, by virtue of their generally recognised prestige and high political, organisational and other qualities be successively elected to leading bodies for a longer period. In that case, a candidate is considered elected if not less than three-quarters of the votes are cast for him by secret ballot.

The composition of the Central Committees of the Communist Parties of the Union Republics, and of the territorial and regional Party committees shall be renewed by not less than one-third at each regular election; the composition of the area, city and district Party committees and of the committees or bureaus of basic Party organisations, by one-half. Furthermore, members of these leading Party bodies may be elected successively for not more than three terms, and the secretaries of basic Party organisations, for not more than two terms.

A Party meeting, conference or congress may, in consideration of the political and professional qualities of an individual, elect him to a leading body for a longer period. In such cases a candidate is considered elected if not less than three-quarters of the Communists attending vote for him.

Party members not re-elected to a leading Party body due to the expiration of their term may be re-elected at subsequent elections.

26. A member or alternate member of the Central Committee of the CPSU must by his entire activity justify the great trust placed in him by the Party. A member or alternate member of the Central Committee of the CPSU who degrades his honour and dignity may not remain on the Central Committee. The question of the removal of a member or alternate member of the Central Committee of the CPSU from that body shall be decided by a full meeting of the Central Committee by secret ballot. The decision is regarded as adopted if not less than two-thirds of the membership of the Central Committee of the CPSU vote for it.

The question of the removal of a member or alternate member of the Central Committee of the Communist Party of a Union Republic, or of a territorial, regional, area, city or district Party committee from the Party body concerned is decided by a full meeting of that body. The decision is regarded as adopted if not less than two-thirds of the membership of the committee in question vote for it by secret ballot.

A member of the Central Auditing Commission who does not justify the great trust placed in him by the Party shall be removed from that body. This question shall be

* See Amendment No. 3 below.

decided by a meeting of the Central Auditing Commission. The decision is regarded as adopted if not less than two-thirds of the membership of the Central Auditing Commission vote by secret ballot for the removal of the member concerned from that body.

The question of the removal of a member from the auditing commission of a republican, territorial, regional, area, city or district Party organisation shall be decided by a meeting of the appropriate commission according to the procedure established for members and alternate members of Party committees.

27. The free and business-like discussion of questions of Party policy in individual Party organisations or in the Party as a whole is the inalienable right of every Party member and an important principle of inner-Party democracy. Only on the basis of inner-party democracy is it possible to develop criticism and self-criticism and to strengthen Party discipline, which must be conscious and not mechanical.

Discussion of controversial or insufficiently clear issues may be held within the framework of individual organisations or the Party as a whole.

Party-wide discussion is necessary:

(a) if the necessity is recognised by several Party organisations at regional or republican level;

(b) if there is not a sufficiently solid majority in the Central Committee on major questions of Party policy;

(c) if the Central Committee of the CPSU considers it necessary to consult the Party as a whole on any particular question of policy.

Wide discussion, especially discussion on a country-wide scale, of questions of Party policy must be so held as to ensure for Party members the free expression of their views and preclude attempts to form factional groupings destroying Party unity, attempts to split the Party.

28. The supreme principle of Party leadership is collective leadership, which is an absolute requisite for the normal functioning of Party organisations, the proper education of cadres, and the promotion of the activity and initiative of Communists. The cult of the individual and the violations of inner-Party democracy resulting from it must not be tolerated in the Party; they are incompatible with the Leninist principles of Party life.

Collective leadership does not exempt individuals in office from personal responsibility for the job entrusted to them.

29. The Central Committees of the Communist Parties of the Union Republics, and territorial, regional, area, city and district Party committees shall systematically inform Party organisations of their work in the interim between congresses and conferences.

30. Meetings of the *aktiv* of district, city, area, regional, and territorial Party organisations and of the Communist Parties of the Union Republics shall be held to discuss major decisions of the Party and to work out measures for their execution, as well as to examine questions of local significance.

IV. HIGHER PARTY ORGANS

31. The supreme organ of the Communist Party of the Soviet Union is the Party

Congress. Congresses are convened by the Central Committee at least once in four years. The convocation of a Party Congress and its agenda shall be announced at least six weeks before the Congress. Extraordinary congresses are convened by the Central Committee of the Party on its own initiative or on the demand of not less than one-third of the total membership represented at the preceding Party congress. Extraordinary congresses shall be convened within two months. A congress is considered properly constituted if not less than one-half of the total Party membership is represented at it.

The scale of representation at a Party Congress is determined by the Central Committee.

32. Should the Central Committee of the Party fail to convene an extraordinary congress within the period specified in Article 31, the organisations which demanded it have the right to form an Organising Committee which shall enjoy the powers of the Central Committee of the Party in respect of the convocation of the extraordinary congress.

33. The Congress:

(a) hears and approves the reports of the Central Committee, of the Central Auditing Commission, and of the other central organisations;

(b) reviews, amends and endorses the Programme and the Rules of the Party;

(c) determines the line of the Party in matters of home and foreign policy, and examines and decides the most important questions of communist construction;

(d) elects the Central Committee and the Central Auditing Commission.

34. The number of members to be elected to the Central Committee and to the Central Auditing Commission is determined by the Congress. In the event of vacancies occurring in the Central Committee, they are filled from among the alternate members of the Central Committee of the CPSU elected by the Congress.

35. Between congresses, the Central Committee of the Communist Party of the Soviet Union directs the activities of the Party, the local Party bodies, selects and appoints leading officials, directs the work of central government bodies and public organisations of working people through the Party groups in them, sets up various Party organs, institutions and enterprises and directs their activities, appoints the editors of the central newspapers and journals operating under its control, and distributes the funds of the Party budget and controls its execution.

The Central Committee represents the CPSU in its relations with other parties.

36. The Central Committee of the CPSU shall keep the Party organisations regularly informed of its work.

37. The Central Auditing Commission of the CPSU supervises the expeditious and proper handling of affairs by the central bodies of the Party, and audits the accounts of the treasury and the enterprises of the Central Committee of the CPSU.

38. The Central Committee of the CPSU shall hold not less than one full meeting every six months. Alternate members of the Central Committee shall attend its full meetings with consultative voice.

39. *The Central Committee of the Communist Party of the Soviet Union elects a Presidium to direct the work of the Central Committee between full meetings and a

* See Amendment No. 9 below.

S

Secretariat to direct current work, chiefly the selection of cadres and the verification of the fulfilment of Party decisions, and sets up a Bureau of the Central Committee of the CPSU for the RSFSR.

40. The Central Committee of the Communist Party of the Soviet Union sets up the Party Control Committee of the Central Committee.

The Party Control Committee of the Central Committee of the CPSU:

(a) verifies the observance of Party discipline by members and candidate members of the CPSU, and takes action against Communists who violate the Programme and the Rules of the Party or state discipline, and against violators of Party ethics;

(b) considers appeals against decisions of Central Committees of the Communist Parties of the Union Republics or of territorial and regional Party committees to expel members from the Party or impose Party penalties upon them.

V. REPUBLICAN, TERRITORIAL, REGIONAL, AREA, CITY AND DISTRICT ORGANISATIONS OF THE PARTY

41. The republican, territorial, regional, area, city and district Party organisations and their committees take guidance in their activities from the Programme and the Rules of the CPSU, conduct all work for the implementation of Party policy and organise the fulfilment of the directives of the Central Committee of the CPSU within the republics, territories, regions, areas, cities and districts concerned.

42. The basic duties of republican, territorial, regional, area, city and district Party organisations, and of their leading bodies, are:

(a) political and organisational work among the masses, mobilisation of the masses for the fulfilment of the tasks of communist construction, for the maximum development of industrial and agricultural production, for the fulfilment and over-fulfilment of state plans; solicitude for the steady improvement of the material and cultural standards of the working people;

(b) organisation of ideological work, propaganda of Marxism-Leninism, promotion of the communist awareness of the working people, guidance of the local press, radio and television, and supervision over the activities of cultural and educational institutions;

(c) guidance of Soviets, trade unions, the YCL, the co-operatives and other public organisations through the Party groups in them, and increasingly broader enlistment of working people in the activities of these organisations, development of the initiative and activity of the masses as an essential condition for the gradual transition from socialist statehood to public self-government under communism.

Party organisations must not act in place of government, trade union, co-operative or other public organisations of the working people; they must not allow either the merging of the functions of Party and other bodies or undue parallelism in work;

(d) selection and appointment of leading personnel, their education in the spirit of communist ideas, honesty and truthfulness, and high sense of responsibility to the Party and the people for the work entrusted to them;

(e) large-scale enlistment of Communists in the conduct of Party activities as voluntary workers, as a form of social work;

(f) organisation of various institutions and enterprises of the Party within the bounds of their republic, territory, region, area, city or district and guidance of their activities; distribution of Party funds within the given organisation; the provision of systematic information to the higher Party body and accountability to it for their work.

Leading Bodies of Republican, Territorial and Regional Party Organisations

43. The highest body of regional, territorial and republican Party organisations is the respective regional or territorial Party conference or the congress of the Communist Party of the Union Republic, and in the interim between them the regional committee, territorial committee or the Central Committee of the Communist Party of the Union Republic.

44. Regular regional and territorial Party conferences, and congresses of the Communist Parties of the Union Republics, are convened by the respective regional or territorial committees or the Central Committee of the Communist Parties of the Union Republics once every two years, and extraordinary conferences and congresses are convened by decision of regional or territorial committees, or the Central Committee of the Communist Parties of the Union Republics, or on the demand of one-third of the total membership of the organisations belonging to the regional, territorial or republican Party organisation. Congresses of Communist Parties of the Union Republics divided into regions (the Ukraine, Byelorussia, Kazakhstan and Uzbekistan) may be convened once in four years.

The scale of representation at regional and territorial conferences and at congresses of the Communist Parties of the Union Republics is determined by the respective Party committees,

Regional and territorial conferences and congresses of the Communist Parties of the Union Republics hear the reports of the respective regional or territorial committees, or the Central Committee of the Communist Party of the Union Republic, and of the auditing commission; discuss at their own discretion other matters of Party, economic and cultural development, and elect the regional or territorial committee, the Central Committee of the Union Republic, the auditing commission and the delegates to the Congress of the CPSU.

45. The regional and territorial committees and the Central Committees of the Communist Parties of the Union Republics elect bureaus, which also include secretaries of the committees. The secretaries must have a Party standing of not less than five years. The full meetings of the committees also confirm the chairmen of Party commissions, heads of departments of these committees, editors of Party newspapers and journals.

Regional and territorial committees and the Central Committees of the Communist Parties of the Union Republics may set up secretariats to examine current business and verify the execution of decisions.

46. The full meetings of regional and territorial committees and the Central Committees of the Communist Parties of the Union Republics shall be convened at least once every four months.

47. The regional and territorial committees and the Central Committees of the

Communist Parties of the Union Republics direct the area, city and district Party organisations, inspect their work and regularly hear reports of area, city and district Party committees.

Party organisations in Autonomous Republics, and in autonomous and other regions forming part of a territory or a Union Republic, function under the guidance of the respective territorial committees or Central Committees of the Communist Parties of the Union Republics.

Leading Bodies of Area, City and District (Urban and Rural) Party Organisations

48. The highest body of an area, city or district Party organisation is the area, city and district Party conference or the general meeting of Communists convened by the area, city or district committee at least once in two years, and the extraordinary conference convened by decision of the respective committee or on the demand of one-third of the total membership of the Party organisation concerned.

The area, city or district conference (general meeting) hears reports of the committee and auditing commission, discusses at its own discretion other questions of Party, economic and cultural development, and elects the area, city and district committee, the auditing commission and delegates to the regional and territorial conference or the congress of the Communist Party of the Union Republic.

The scale of representation to the area, city or district conference is established by the respective Party committee.

49. The area, city or district committee elects a bureau, including the committee secretaries, and confirms the appointment of heads of committee departments and newspaper editors. The secretaries of the area, city and district committees must have a Party standing of at least three years. The committee secretaries are confirmed by the respective regional or territorial committee, or the Central Committee of the Communist Party of the Union Republic.

50. The area, city and district committee organises and confirms the basic Party organisations, directs their work, regularly hears reports concerning the work of Party organisations, and keeps a register of Communists.

51. The full meeting of the area, city and district committee is convened at least once in three months.

52. The area city and district committee has voluntary officials, sets up standing or *ad hoc* commissions on various aspects of Party work and uses other ways to draw Communists into the activities of the Party committee on a voluntary basis.

VI. BASIC PARTY ORGANISATIONS

53. The basic Party organisations are the basis of the Party.

Basic Party organisations are formed at the places of work of Party members – in factories, state farms and other enterprises, collective farms, units of the Soviet Army, offices, educational establishments, etc., wherever there are not less than three Party members. Basic Party organisations may also be organised on the residential principle in villages and in blocks of flats.

54. At enterprises, collective farms and institutions with over fifty Party members and candidate members, shop, sectional, farm, team, departmental, etc., Party organisations may be formed as units of the general basic Party organisation with the sanction of the district, city or area committee.

Within shop, sectional, etc., organisations, and also within basic Party organisations having less than fifty members and candidate members, Party groups may be formed in the teams and other production units.

55. The highest organ of the basic Party organisation is the Party meeting, which is convened at least once a month.

In large Party organisations with a membership of more than 300 Communists, a general Party meeting is convened when necessary at times fixed by the Party committee or on the demand of a number of shop or departmental Party organisations.

56. For the conduct of current business the branch, shop or departmental Party organisation elects a bureau for the term of one year. The number of its members is fixed by the Party meeting. Branch, shop and departmental Party organisations with less than fifteen Party members do not elect a bureau. Instead, they elect a secretary and deputy secretary of the Party organisation.

Secretaries of branch, shop and departmental Party organisations must have a Party standing of at least one year.

Basic Party organisations with less than 150 Party members shall have, as a rule, no salaried officials released from their regular work.

57. *In large factories and offices with more than 300 members and candidate members of the Party, and in exceptional cases in factories and offices with over 100 Communists by virtue of special production conditions and territorial dispersion, subject to the approval of the regional committee, territorial committee or Central Committee of the Communist Party of the Union Republic, Party committees may be formed, the shop and departmental Party organisations at these factories and offices being granted the status of basic Party organisations.

The Party organisations of collective farms may set up Party committees if they have a minimum of fifty Communists.

The Party committees are elected for the term of one year. Their numerical composition is fixed by the general Party meeting or conference.

58. In its activities the basic Party organisation takes guidance from the Programme and the Rules of the CPSU. It conducts its work directly among the working people, rallies them round the Communist Party of the Soviet Union, organises the masses to carry out the Party policy and to work for the building of communism.

The basic Party organisation:

(a) admits new members to the CPSU;

(b) educates Communists in a spirit of loyalty to the Party cause, ideological staunchness and communist ethics;

(c) organises the study by Communists of Marxist-Leninist theory in close connection with the practice of communist construction and opposes all attempts to introduce revisionist distortions of Marxism-Leninism or a dogmatic interpretation of Marxism-Leninism;

* See Amendment No. 5 below.

(d) ensures the vanguard role of Communists in the sphere of labour and in the social and political and economic activities of enterprises, collective farms, institutions, educational establishments, etc.;

(e) acts as the organiser of the working people for the performance of the current tasks of communist construction, heads the socialist emulation movement for the fulfilment of state plans and undertakings of the working people, rallies the masses to disclose and make the best use of untapped resources at enterprises and collective farms, and to apply in production on a broad scale the achievements of science, engineering and the experience of front-rankers; works for the strengthening of labour discipline, the steady increase of labour productivity and improvement of the quality of production, and shows concern for the protection and increase of social wealth at enterprises, state farms and collective farms;

(f) conducts agitational and propaganda work among the masses, educates them in the communist spirit, helps the working people to acquire proficiency in administering state and social affairs;

(g) on the basis of extensive criticism and self-criticism, combats cases of bureaucracy, parochialism, and violations of state discipline, thwarts attempts to deceive the state, acts against negligence, waste and extravagance at enterprises, collective farms and offices;

(h) assists the area, city and district committees in their activities and is accountable to them for its work.

The Party organisation must see to it that every Communist should observe in his own life and cultivate among working people the moral principles set forth in the Programme of the CPSU, in the moral code of the builder of communism:

loyalty to the communist cause, love of his own socialist country, and of other socialist countries;

conscientious labour for the benefit of society, for he who does not work, neither shall he eat;

concern on everyone's part for the protection and increase of social wealth;

lofty sense of public duty, intolerance of violations of public interests;

collectivism and comradely mutual assistance: one for all, and all for one;

humane relations and mutual respect among people: man is to man a friend, comrade and brother;

honesty and truthfulness, moral purity, unpretentiousness and modesty in public and personal life;

mutual respect in the family circle and concern for the upbringing of children;

intolerance of injustice, parasitism, dishonesty, careerism and money-grubbing;

friendship and fraternity among all peoples of the USSR, intolerance of national and racial hostility;

intolerance of the enemies of communism, the enemies of peace and those who oppose the freedom of the peoples;

fraternal solidarity with the working peoples of all countries, with all peoples.

59. *Basic Party organisations of industrial enterprises and trading establishments, state farms, collective farms and designing organisations, drafting offices and research

* See Amendment No. 10 below.

institutes directly related to production, enjoy the right to control the work of the administration.

The Party organisations at Ministries, State Committees, economic councils and other central and local government or economic agencies and departments which do not have the function of controlling the administration, must actively promote improvement of the apparatus, cultivate among the personnel a high sense of responsibility for work entrusted to them, promote state discipline and the better servicing of the population, firmly combat bureaucracy and red tape, inform the appropriate Party bodies in good time of shortcomings in the work of the respective offices and individuals, regardless of what posts the latter may occupy.

VII. THE PARTY AND THE YCL

60. The Leninist Young Communist League of the Soviet Union is an independently acting social organisation of young people, an active helper and reserve of the Party. The YCL helps the Party educate the youth in a communist spirit, to draw it into the work of building a new society, to train a rising generation of harmoniously developed people who will live and work and administer public affairs under communism.

61. YCL organisations enjoy the right of broad initiative in discussing and submitting to the appropriate Party organisations questions relating to the work of enterprises, collective farms and offices. They must be active levers in the implementation of Party directives in all spheres of communist construction, especially where there are no basic Party organisations.

62. The YCL conducts its activities under the guidance of the Communist Party of the Soviet Union. The work of the local YCL organisations is directed and controlled by the appropriate republican, territorial, regional, area, city and district Party organisations.

In their communist educational work among the youth, local Party bodies and primary Party organisations rely on the support of the YCL organisations, and uphold and promote their useful undertakings.

63. Members of the YCL who have been admitted into the CPSU cease to belong to the YCL the moment they join the Party, provided they do not hold leading posts in YCL organisations.

VIII. PARTY ORGANISATIONS IN THE SOVIET ARMY

64. Party organisations in the Soviet Army are guided in their work by the Programme and the Rules of the CPSU and operate on the basis of instructions issued by the Central Committee.

The Party organisations of the Soviet Army carry out the policy of the Party in the Armed Forces, rally servicemen round the Communist Party, educate them in the spirit of Marxism-Leninism and boundless loyalty to the socialist homeland, actively further the unity of the army and the people, work for the strengthening of military discipline, rally servicemen to carry out the tasks of military and political training and acquire skill in the use of new technique and weapons, and to carry out irreproachably their military duty and the orders and instructions of the command.

65. The guidance of Party work in the Armed Forces is exercised by the Central Committee of the CPSU through the Chief Political Administration of the Soviet Army and Navy, which functions as a department of the Central Committee of the CPSU.

The heads of the political administrations of military areas and fleets and heads of the political administrations of armies must be Party members of five years' standing, and the heads of political departments of military formations must be Party members of three years' standing.

66. The Party organisations and political bodies of the Soviet Army maintain close contact with local Party committees, and keep them informed about political work in the military units. The secretaries of military Party organisations and heads of political bodies participate in the work of local Party committees.

IX. PARTY GROUPS IN NON-PARTY ORGANISATIONS

67. At congresses, conferences and meetings and in the elective bodies of Soviets, trade unions, co-operatives and other mass organisations of the working people, having at least three Party members, Party groups are formed for the purpose of strengthening the influence of the Party in every way and carrying out Party policy among non-Party people, strengthening Party and state discipline, combating bureaucracy, and verifying the fulfilment of Party and government directives.

68. The Party groups are subordinate to the appropriate Party bodies: the Central Committee of the Communist Party of the Soviet Union, the Central Committees of the Communist Parties of the Union Republics, territorial, regional, area, city or district Party committees.

In all matters the groups must strictly and unswervingly abide by decisions of the leading Party bodies.

X. PARTY FUNDS

69. The funds of the Party and its organisations are derived from membership dues, incomes from Party enterprises and other revenue.

70. The monthly membership dues for Party members and candidate members are as follows:

Monthly earnings	Dues	
up to 50 roubles	10 kopeks	
from 51 to 100 roubles	0.5 per cent	
from 101 to 150 roubles	1.0 per cent	
from 151 to 200 roubles	1.5 per cent	of monthly
from 201 to 250 roubles	2.0 per cent	earnings
from 251 to 300 roubles	2.5 per cent	
over 300 roubles	3.0 per cent	

71. An entrance fee of 2 per cent of monthly earnings is paid on admission to the Party as a candidate member.

RESOLUTION OF THE 23RD CONGRESS OF THE COMMUNIST PARTY OF THE SOVIET UNION ON PARTIAL CHANGES IN THE CPSU RULES

The 23rd Congress of the Communist Party of the Soviet Union resolves to introduce the following changes in the CPSU Rules:

1. In order to further improve the qualitative composition of the new membership of the CPSU and to raise the responsibility of Party organisations for the admission into the Party of new members, to establish that:

(a) young people, up to the age of 23 inclusive, join the Party only through the Leninist Young Communist League, Members of the YCL joining the CPSU submit a recommendation of a District Committee or a City Committee of the YCL which is equivalent to the recommendation of one Party member;

(b) those recommending to the Party must have a Party standing of not less than five years;

(c) a decision of the primary Party organisation on admission to the Party is regarded adopted if not less than two-thirds of the Party members attending the meeting have voted for it.

2. Proceeding from the tasks of further strengthening Party discipline and raising the responsibility of Communists for the fulfilment of the duties prescribed by the Rules:

(a) to add to the introductory section of the Rules a clause to the effect that the Party purges itself of individuals who violate the CPSU Programme, the Rules, or by their behaviour compromise the lofty title of Communist;

(b) to establish that a decision of a primary Party organisation on the expulsion of a Communist from the Party takes effect after endorsement by a District Committee or by a City Committee of the Party;

(c) to abolish the transfer of a Party member to the status of candidate member as a Party penalty.

3. Bearing in mind the proposals of many Party bodies and Communists, and taking into account the fact that during elections the composition of Party Committees is regularly renewed with due regard for concrete local conditions and businesslike and political qualities of members, and that the regulations on these questions did not justify themselves in practice, to regard as inexpedient the further retention in the Rules of the CPSU the principles which determine the norms of renewing and changeability of the composition of Party bodies and secretaries of Party organisations. In this connection paragraph 25 should be deleted from the Rules. An addition should be made to paragraph 24 that during elections of all Party bodies, from the primary organisations to the Central Committee of the CPSU, the principle be observed of the systematic renewal of their composition and continuity of leadership.

4. To supplement the section of the Rules concerning primary Party organisations with a new paragraph which should establish that the Party Committees of primary

organisations numbering more than 1,000 Communists may, with the permission of the Central Committee of the Communist Party of a Union Republic, be granted the rights of a district Party Committee in issues concerning the admission to the CPSU, registration of Party members and candidates, and examination of cases of violating Party discipline by Communists. Inside these organisations, if necessary, Party Committees may be organised in shops, while the Party organisations of production sections may be granted the rights of a primary Party organisation. The Party Committees which enjoy the rights of a district Party Committee are elected for a term of two years.

5. To supplement paragraph 57 of the Rules with a clause that in state farms Party Committees may be established if there are 50 Communists.

6. Bearing in mind the Party organisations' suggestion to the effect that the CPSU Rules should determine in a more differentiated way the terms for the convocation of meetings in primary Party organisations, depending on the conditions of their work, structure and membership, to establish that in the primary Party Organisations which have up to 300 members and where there are shop organisations, general Party meetings should be held at least once every two months.

7. To establish in the Rules that Communist Party Congresses in all Union Republics should be held at least once every four years.

8. To make provisions in the Rules that in the period between Party Congresses the Central Committee may, when it deems necessary, convoke an All-Union Party Conference to discuss urgent issues of the Party's policy, while the Central Committees of the Communist Parties in the Union Republics may convoke republican Party conferences.

The order of conducting an All-Union Party Conference is fixed by the CPSU Central Committee, while that of republican Party conferences, by the Central Committees of the Communist Parties of the Union Republics.

9. To make provisions in the Rules that the Central Committee of the Communist Party of the Soviet Union elects: a Politbureau for guiding the work of the Party between Plenums of the Central Committee; a Secretariat for supervising the current work, mainly in the field of personnel and organising check-ups on the carrying out of Party resolutions. The Central Committee elects the General Secretary of the CPSU Central Committee.

The clause stipulating that the Central Committee establishes a CPSU Central Committee Bureau for the RSFSR, in paragraph 39 of the Rules, should be omitted.

10. Mention about economic councils in paragraph 59 of the Rules should be omitted.

APPENDIX C

The Constitution of the USSR
(*As Amended by the Sixth Session of the Seventh Supreme Soviet of the USSR*)

'Workers of All Countries, Unite!'

The Social Structure

ARTICLE I

The Union of Soviet Socialist Republics is a socialist state of workers and peasants.

ARTICLE II

The political foundation of the USSR is the Soviets of Working People's Deputies, which grew and became strong as a result of the overthrow of the power of the landowners and capitalists and the attainment of the dictatorship of the proletariat.

ARTICLE III

All power in the USSR is vested in the working people of town and country as represented by the Soviets of Working People's Deputies.

ARTICLE IV

The economic foundation of the USSR is the socialist system of economy and the socialist ownership of the instruments and means of production, firmly established as a result of abolishing the capitalist system of economy, the private ownership of the instruments and means of production, and the exploitation of man by man.

ARTICLE V

Socialist property in the USSR exists either in the form of state property (belonging to the whole people) or in the form of co-operative and collective-farm property (the property of collective farms or co-operative societies).

ARTICLE VI

The land, its mineral wealth, waters, forests, the factories and mines, rail, water and air transport facilities, the banks, means of communication, large state-organised agricultural enterprises (state farms, machine and tractor stations, etc.), as well as municipal enterprises and the bulk of the dwelling houses in the cities and industrial localities, are state property, that is, belong to the whole people.

ARTICLE VII

The enterprises of the collective farms and co-operative organisations, with their livestock, buildings, implements, and output, are the common, socialist property of the collective farms and co-operative organisations.

Every collective-farm household, in addition to its basic income from the collective farm, has for its own use a small plot of land attached to the house and, as its own property, a dwelling-house, livestock, poultry, and minor agricultural implements – in conformity with the Rules of the Agricultural Artel.

ARTICLE VIII
The land occupied by the collective farms is made over to them for their free use for an unlimited time, that is, in perpetuity.

ARTICLE IX
In addition to the socialist system of economy, which is the predominant form of economy in the USSR, the law permits the small private undertakings of individual peasants and handicraftsmen based on their own labour and precluding the exploitation of the labour of others.

ARTICLE X
The right of citizens to own, as their personal property, income and savings derived from work, to own a dwelling-house and a supplementary husbandry, articles of household and articles of personal use and convenience, is protected by law, as is also the right of citizens to inherit personal property.

ARTICLE XI
The economic life of the USSR is determined and guided by the state economic plan for the purpose of increasing the wealth of society, steadily raising the material and cultural standards of the working people and strengthening the independence of the USSR and its defence potential.

ARTICLE XII
Work in the USSR is a duty and a matter of honour for every able-bodied citizen, in accordance with the principle: 'He who does not work, neither shall he eat.'

The principle applied in the USSR is that of socialism: 'From each according to his ability, to each according to his work.'

The State Structure

ARTICLE XIII
The Union of Soviet Socialist Republics is a federal state, formed on the basis of a voluntary union of equal Soviet Socialist Republics, namely:

Russian Soviet Federative Socialist Republic,
Ukrainian Soviet Socialist Republic,
Byelorussian Soviet Socialist Republic,
Uzbek Soviet Socialist Republic,
Kazakh Soviet Socialist Republic,
Georgian Soviet Socialist Republic,
Azerbaijan Soviet Socialist Republic,
Lithuanian Soviet Socialist Republic,
Moldavian Soviet Socialist Republic,
Latvian Soviet Socialist Republic,
Kirghiz Soviet Socialist Republic,

Tajik Soviet Socialist Republic,
Armenian Soviet Socialist Republic,
Turkmen Soviet Socialist Republic,
Estonian Soviet Socialist Republic.

ARTICLE XIV

The jurisdiction of the Union of Soviet Socialist Republics, as represented by its higher organs of state power and organs of state administration, covers:

(a) Representation of the USSR in international relations, conclusion, ratification and denunciation of treaties of the USSR with other states, establishment of general procedure governing the relations of the Union Republics with foreign states;

(b) Questions of war and peace;

(c) Admission of new republics into the USSR;

(d) Control over the observance of the Constitution of the USSR, and ensuring conformity of the Constitutions of the Union Republics with the Constitution of the USSR;

(e) Approval of changes to boundaries between Union Republics;

(f) Approval of the formation of new Autonomous Republics and Autonomous Regions within Union Republics;

(g) Organisation of the defence of the USSR, direction of all the Armed Forces of the USSR, formulation of principles guiding the organisation of the military formations of the Union Republics;

(h) Foreign trade on the basis of state monopoly;

(i) State security;

(j) Approval of the economic plans of the USSR;

(k) Approval of the consolidated state budget of the USSR and of the report on its implementation; fixing taxes and revenues that go to the Union, Republican and local budgets;

(l) Administration of banks and industrial, agricultural and trading enterprises and institutions under Union jurisdiction; general direction of industry and building under Union-Republican jurisdiction;

(m) Administration of transport and communications of all-Union importance;

(n) Direction of the monetary and credit system;

(o) Organisation of state insurance;

(p) Contracting and granting of loans;

(q) Definition of the basic principles of land tenure and of the use of mineral wealth, forests and waters;

(r) Definition of the basic principles in the spheres of education and public health;

(s) Organisation of a uniform system of economic statistics;

(t) Definition of the fundamentals of labour legislation;

(u) Definition of the fundamentals of legislation on the judicial system and judicial procedure and the fundamentals of civil criminal and corrective labour legislation;

(v) Legislation on Union citizenship; legislation on rights of foreigners;

(w) Definition of the fundamentals of legislation on marriage and the family;

(x) Promulgation of all-Union acts of amnesty.

ARTICLE XV

The sovereignty of the Union Republics is limited only in the spheres defined in Article XIV of the Constitution of the USSR. Outside of these spheres each Union Republic exercises state authority independently. The USSR protects the sovereign rights of the Union Republics.

ARTICLE XVI

Each Union Republic has it own Constitution, which takes account of the specific features of the Republic and is drawn up in full conformity with the Constitution of the USSR.

ARTICLE XVII

The right freely to secede from the USSR is reserved to every Union Republic.

ARTICLE XVIII

The territory of a Union Republic may not be altered without its consent.

ARTICLE XVIII A

Each Union Republic has the right to enter into direct relations with foreign states and to conclude agreements and exchange diplomatic and consular representatives with them.

ARTICLE XVIII B

Each Union Republic has its own Republican military formations.

ARTICLE XIX

The laws of the USSR have the same force within the territory of every Union Republic.

ARTICLE XX

In the event of divergence between a law of a Union Republic and a law of the Union, the Union law shall prevail.

ARTICLE XXI

Uniform Union citizenship is established for citizens of the USSR.
Every citizen of a Union Republic is a citizen of the USSR.

ARTICLE XXII

The Russian Soviet Federative Socialist Republic includes the Bashkirian, Buryat, Checheno-Ingush, Chuvash, Daghestan, Kabardinian-Balkar, Kalmyk, Karelian, Komi, Mari, Mordovian, North Ossetian, Tatar, Tuva, Udmurt and Yakut Autonomous Soviet Socialist Republics; and the Adygei, Gorny Altai, Jewish, Karachai-Cherkess and Khakass Autonomous Regions.

ARTICLE XXIII

Repealed.

ARTICLE XXIV

The Azerbaijan Soviet Socialist Republic includes the Nakhichevan Autonomous Soviet Socialist Republic and the Nagorny Karabakh Autonomous Region.

ARTICLE XXV

The Georgian Soviet Socialist Republic includes the Abkhazian and Ajarian Autonomous Soviet Socialist Republics and the South Ossetian Autonomous Region.

ARTICLE XXVI

The Uzbek Soviet Socialist Republic includes the Kara-Kalpak Autonomous Soviet Socialist Republic.

ARTICLE XXVII

The Tajik Soviet Socialist Republic includes the Gorny Badakhshan Autonomous Region.

ARTICLE XXVIII

The Settlement of questions pertaining to the regional or territorial administrative division of the Union Republics comes within the jurisdiction of the Union Republics.

ARTICLE XXIX

Repealed.

The Higher Organs of State Power in the Union of Soviet Socialist Republics

ARTICLE XXX

The highest organ of state power in the USSR is the Supreme Soviet of the USSR.

ARTICLE XXXI

The Supreme Soviet of the USSR exercises all rights vested in the Union of Soviet Socialist Republics in accordance with Article XIV of the Constitution, in so far as they do not, by virtue of the Constitution, come within the jurisdiction of organs of the USSR that are accountable to the Supreme Soviet of the USSR, that is, the Presidium of the Supreme Soviet of the USSR, the Council of Ministers of the USSR, and the Ministries of the USSR.

ARTICLE XXXII

The legislative power of the USSR is exercised exclusively by the Supreme Soviet of the USSR.

ARTICLE XXXIII

The Supreme Soviet of the USSR consists of two Chambers: the Soviet of the Union and the Soviet of Nationalities.

ARTICLE XXXIV

The Soviet of the Union is elected by the citizens of the USSR voting by election districts on the basis of one deputy for every 300,000 of the population.

ARTICLE XXXV

The Soviet of Nationalities is elected by the citizens of the USSR voting by Union Republics, Autonomous Republics, Autonomous Regions, and National Areas on the basis of 32 deputies from each Union Republic, 11 deputies from each Autonomous Region, and one deputy from each National Area.

ARTICLE XXXVI

The Supreme Soviet of the USSR is elected for a term of four years.

ARTICLE XXXVII

The two Chambers of the Supreme Soviet of the USSR, the Soviet of the Union and the Soviet of Nationalities, have equal rights.

ARTICLE XXXVIII

The Soviet of the Union and the Soviet of Nationalities have equal powers to initiate legislation.

ARTICLE XXXIX

A law is considered adopted if passed by both Chambers of the Supreme Soviet of the USSR by a simple majority vote in each.

ARTICLE XL

Laws passed by the Supreme Soviet of the USSR are published in the languages of the Union Republics over the signatures of the President and Secretary of the Presidium of the Supreme Soviet of the USSR.

ARTICLE XLI

Sessions of the Soviet of the Union and of the Soviet of Nationalities begin and terminate simultaneously.

ARTICLE XLII

The Soviet of the Union elects a Chairman of the Soviet of the Union and four Vice-Chairmen.

ARTICLE XLIII

The Soviet of Nationalities elects a Chairman of the Soviet of Nationalities and four Vice-Chairmen.

ARTICLE XLIV

The Chairmen of the Soviet of the Union and the Soviet of Nationalities preside at the sittings of the respective Chambers and have charge of the conduct of their business and proceedings.

ARTICLE XLV

Joint sittings of the two Chambers of the Supreme Soviet of the USSR are presided over alternately by the Chairman of the Soviet of the Union and the Chairman of the Soviet of Nationalities.

ARTICLE XLVI

Sessions of the Supreme Soviet of the USSR are convened by the Presidium of the Supreme Soviet of the USSR twice a year.

Extraordinary sessions are convened by the Presidium of the Supreme Soviet of the USSR at its discretion or on the demand of one of the Union Republics.

ARTICLE XLVII

In the event of disagreement between the Soviet of the Union and the Soviet of Nationalities, the question is referred for settlement to a conciliation commission formed by the Chambers on a parity basis. If the conciliation commission fails to arrive at an agreement or if its decision fails to satisfy one of the Chambers, the the question is considered for a second time by the Chambers. Failing agreement between the two Chambers, the Presidium of the Supreme Soviet of the USSR dissolves the Supreme Soviet of the USSR and orders new elections.

ARTICLE XLVIII

The Supreme Soviet of the USSR at a joint sitting of the two Chambers elects the Presidium of the Supreme Soviet of the USSR consisting of a President of the Presidium of the Supreme Soviet of the USSR, fifteen Vice-Presidents—one from each Union Republic, a Secretary of the Presidium and twenty members of the Presidium of the Supreme Soviet of the USSR.

The Presidium of the Supreme Soviet of the USSR is accountable to the Supreme Soviet of the USSR for all its activities.

ARTICLE XLIX

The Presidium of the Supreme Soviet of the USSR:

(a) Convenes the sessions of the Supreme Soviet of the USSR;

(b) Issues ordinances;

(c) Interprets the laws of the USSR in operation;

(d) Dissolves the Supreme Soviet of the USSR in conformity with Article XLVII of the Constitution of the USSR and orders new elections;

(e) Conducts nation-wide polls (referendums) on its own initiative or on the demand of one of the Union Republics;

(f) Annuls decisions and orders of the Council of Ministers of the USSR and of the Councils of Ministers of the Union Republics if they do not conform to law;

(g) In the intervals between sessions of the Supreme Soviet of the USSR, appoints or removes Ministers of the USSR on the recommendation of the Chairman of the Council of Ministers of the USSR, subject to subsequent confirmation by the Supreme Soviet of the USSR;

(h) Institutes decorations (Orders and Medals) and titles of honour of the USSR;

(i) Awards Orders and Medals and confers titles of honour of the USSR;

(j) Exercises the right of pardon;

(k) Institutes military titles, diplomatic ranks and other special titles;

(l) Appoints and removes the high command of the Armed Forces of the USSR;

(m) In the intervals between sessions of the Supreme Soviet of the USSR, proclaims a state of war in the event of an armed attack on the USSR, or when necessary to fulfil international treaty obligations providing for mutual defence against aggression;

(n) Orders general or partial mobilisation;

(o) Ratifies and denounces international treaties of the USSR;

(p) Appoints and recalls plenipotentiary representatives of the USSR to foreign states;

(q) Receives the letters of credence and recall of diplomatic representatives accredited to it by foreign states;

(r) Proclaims martial law in separate localities or throughout the USSR in the interests of the defence of the USSR or of the maintenance of law and order and the security of the state.

ARTICLE L

The Soviet of the Union and the Soviet of Nationalities elect Credentials Committees to verify the credentials of the members of the respective Chambers.

On the report of the Credentials Committees, the Chambers decide whether to recognise the credentials of deputies or to annul their election.

ARTICLE LI

The Supreme Soviet of the USSR, when it deems necessary, appoints commissions of inquiry and audit on any matter.

It is the duty of all institutions and officials to comply with the demands of such commissions and to submit to them all necessary materials and documents.

ARTICLE LII

No Member of the Supreme Soviet of the USSR shall be prosecuted or arrested without the consent of the Supreme Soviet of the USSR, or, when the Supreme Soviet of the USSR is not in session, without the consent of the Presidium of the Supreme Soviet of the USSR.

ARTICLE LIII

On the expiry of the term of office of the Supreme Soviet of the USSR, or on its dissolution prior to the expiry of its term of office, the Presidium of the Supreme Soviet of the USSR retains its powers until the newly-elected Supreme Soviet of the USSR shall have formed a new Presidium of the Supreme Soviet of the USSR.

ARTICLE LIV

On the expiry of the term of office of the Supreme Soviet of the USSR, or in the event of its dissolution prior to the expiry of its term of office, the Presidium of the Supreme Soviet of the USSR orders new elections to be held within a period not exceeding two months from the date of expiry of the term of office or dissolution of the Supreme Soviet of the USSR.

ARTICLE LV

The newly-elected Supreme Soviet of the USSR is convened by the outgoing Presidium of the Supreme Soviet of the USSR not later than three months after the elections.

ARTICLE LVI

The Supreme Soviet of the USSR, at a joint sitting of the two Chambers, appoints the Government of the USSR, namely, the Council of Ministers of the USSR.

The Higher Organs of State Power in the Union Republics

ARTICLE LVII

The highest organ of state power in a Union Republic is the Supreme Soviet of the Union Republic.

ARTICLE LVIII
The Supreme Soviet of a Union Republic is elected by the citizens of the Republic for a term of four years.

The basis of representation is established by the Constitution of the Union Republic.

ARTICLE LIX
The Supreme Soviet of a Union Republic is the sole legislative organ of the Republic.

ARTICLE LX
The Supreme Soviet of a Union Republic:

(a) Adopts the Constitution of the Republic and amends it in conformity with Article XVI of the Constitution of the USSR;

(b) Confirms the Constitutions of the Autonomous Republics forming part of it and defines the boundaries of their territory;

(c) Approves the economic plan and the budget of the Republic;

(d) Exercises the right of amnesty and pardon of citizens sentenced by the judicial bodies of the Union Republic;

(e) Decides upon the representation of the Union Republic in its international relations;

(f) Determines the manner of organising the Republic's military formations.

ARTICLE LXI
The Supreme Soviet of a Union Republic elects the Presidium of the Supreme Soviet of the Union Republic, consisting of the President of the Presidium of the Supreme Soviet of the Union Republic, Vice-Presidents, a Secretary of the Presidium and members of the Presidium of the Supreme Soviet of the Union Republic.

The powers of the Presidium of the Supreme Soviet of a Union Republic are defined by the Constitution of the Union Republic.

ARTICLE LXII
The Supreme Soviet of a Union Republic elects a Chairman and Vice-Chairmen to conduct its sittings.

ARTICLE LXIII
The Supreme Soviet of a Union Republic appoints the Government of the Union Republic, namely, the Council of Ministers of the Union Republic.

The Organs of State Administration of the Union of Soviet Socialist Republics

ARTICLE LXIV
The highest executive and administrative organ of the state power of the Union of Soviet Socialist Republics is the Council of Ministers of the USSR.

ARTICLE LXV
The Council of Ministers of the USSR is responsible and accountable to the Supreme Soviet of the USSR, or, in the intervals between sessions of the Supreme Soviet, to the Presidium of the Supreme Soviet of the USSR.

ARTICLE LXVI

The Council of Ministers of the USSR issues decisions and orders on the basis and in pursuance of the laws in operation, and verifies their execution.

ARTICLE LXVII

Decisions and orders of the Council of Ministers of the USSR are binding throughout the territory of the USSR.

ARTICLE LXVIII

The Council of Ministers of the USSR:

(a) Co-ordinates and directs the work of the all-Union and Union-Republican Ministries of the USSR, the state Committees of the Council of Ministers of the USSR and of other bodies under its jurisdiction;

(b) Adopts measures to carry out the economic plan and the state budget, and to strengthen the credit and monetary system;

(c) Adopts measures for the maintenance of law and order, for the protection of the interests of the state, and for the safeguarding of the rights of citizens;

(d) Exercises general guidance in the sphere of relations with foreign states;

(e) Fixes the annual contingent of citizens to be called up for military service and direct the general organisation of the Armed Forces of the country;

(f) Sets up State Committees of the USSR, and, whenever necessary, special Committees and Central Boards under the Council of Ministers of the USSR for economic and cultural affairs and defence.

ARTICLE LXIX

The Council of Ministers of the USSR has the right, in respect of those branches of the administration and economy which come within the jurisdiction of the USSR, to suspend decisions and orders of the Councils of Ministers of the Union Republics and to annul orders and instructions of Ministers of the USSR and also statutory acts of other bodies under its jurisdiction.

ARTICLE LXX

The Council of Ministers of the USSR is appointed by the Supreme Soviet of the USSR and consists of:

Chairman of the Council of Ministers of the USSR;

First Vice-Chairmen of the Council of Ministers of the USSR;

Vice-Chairmen of the Council of Ministers of the USSR;

Ministers of the USSR;

Chairman of the State Planning Committee of the Council of Ministers of the USSR;

Chairman of the State Building Committee of the Council of Ministers of the USSR;

Chairman of the State Committee of the Council of Ministers of the USSR for Material and Technical Supply;

Chairman of the People's Control Committee of the USSR;

Chairman of the State Labour and Wages Committee of the Council of Ministers of the USSR;

Chairman of the State Committee of the Council of Ministers of the USSR for Science and Technology;

Chairman of the State Committee of the Council of Ministers of the USSR for Vocational Training;

Chairman of the State Committee of the Council of Ministers of the USSR for Farm Produce Purchases;

Chairman of the State Forestry Committee of the Council of Ministers of the USSR;

Chairman of the State Foreign Economic Relations Committee of the Council of Ministers of the USSR;

Chairman of the State Security Committee under the Council of Ministers of the USSR;

Chairman of the All-Union Board of the Council of Ministers of the USSR for the Supply of Farm Machinery, Fuel and Fertilisers;

Chairman of the Administrative Board of the State Bank of the USSR;

Chief of the Central Statistical Board under the Council of Ministers of the USSR.

The Council of Ministers of the USSR includes the Chairmen of the Councils of Ministers of the Union Republics by virtue of their office.

ARTICLE LXXI

The Government of the USSR or a Minister of the USSR to whom a question of a member of the Supreme Soviet of the USSR is addressed must give a verbal or written reply in the respective Chamber within a period not exceeding three days.

ARTICLE LXXII

The Ministers of the USSR direct the branches of state administration which come within the jurisdiction of the USSR.

ARTICLE LXXIII

The Ministers of the USSR, within the limits of the jurisdiction of their respective Ministries, issue orders and instructions on the basis and in pursuance of the laws in operation, and also of decisions and orders of the Council of Ministers of the USSR, and verify their execution.

ARTICLE LXXIV

The Ministries of the USSR are either all-Union or Union-Republican Ministries.

ARTICLE LXXV

The all-Union Ministries direct the branch of state administration entrusted to them throughout the territory of the USSR either directly or through bodies appointed by them.

ARTICLE LXXVI

The Union-Republican Ministries, as a rule, direct the branches of state administration entrusted to them through the relevant Ministries of the Union Republics; they administer directly only a certain limited number of enterprises according to a list approved by the Presidium of the Supreme Soviet of the USSR.

ARTICLE LXXVII

The following are all-Union Ministries:
  Ministry of the Aircraft Industry;
  Ministry of the Automobile Industry;
  Ministry of Foreign Trade;
  Ministry of the Gas Industry;
  Ministry of Civil Aviation;
  Ministry of Engineering;
  Ministry of Machine-Building for the Light and Food Industries and Household
    Appliances;
  Ministry of the Medical Industry;
  Ministry of the Merchant Marine;
  Ministry of the Defence Industry;
  Ministry of General Engineering;
  Ministry of Instrument-Making, Means of Automation and Control Systems;
  Ministry of Railways;
  Ministry of the Radio Industry;
  Ministry of Medium Machine-Building;
  Ministry of the Tool-Making Industry;
  Ministry of Building, Road and Communal Machinery;
  Ministry of Shipbuilding;
  Ministry of Tractor and Agricultural Machinery Building;
  Ministry of Transport Building;
  Ministry of Heavy, Power and Transport Engineering;
  Ministry of Chemical and Oil Machine-Building;
  Ministry of Pulp and Paper Industry;
  Ministry of the Electronic Industry;
  Ministry of Electrical Engineering;

ARTICLE LXXVIII

The following are Union-Republican Ministries:
  Ministry of Higher and Secondary Specialised Education;
  Ministry of Geological Survey;
  Ministry of Public Health;
  Ministry of Foreign Affairs;
  Ministry of Culture;
  Ministry of the Light Industry;
  Ministry of the Timber and Woodworking Industry;
  Ministry of Melioration and Water Conservancy;
  Ministry of Assembly and Specialised Building Work;
  Ministry of the Meat-Packing and Dairy Industry;
  Ministry of the Oil Extracting Industry;
  Ministry of the Oil Refining and Petro-chemical Industry;
  Ministry of Defence;
  Ministry of Internal Affairs;
  Ministry of the Food Industry;

Ministry of Industrial Construction;
Ministry of the Building Materials Industry;
Ministry of Public Education;
Ministry of Fisheries;
Ministry of Communications;
Ministry of Rural Construction;
Ministry of Agriculture;
Ministry of Construction;
Ministry of Heavy Industry Construction;
Ministry of Trade;
Ministry of the Coal Industry;
Ministry of Finance;
Ministry of the Chemical Industry;
Ministry of Non-ferrous Metallurgy;
Ministry of Ferrous Metallurgy;
Ministry of Electric Power Development and Electrification.

The Organs of State Administration of the Union Republics

ARTICLE LXXIX

The highest executive and administrative organ of the state power of a Union Republic is the Council of Ministers of the Union Republic.

ARTICLE LXXX

The Council of Ministers of a Union Republic is responsible and accountable to the Supreme Soviet of the Union Republic, or, in the intervals between sessions of the Supreme Soviet of the Union Republic, to the Presidium of the Supreme Soviet of the Union Republic.

ARTICLE LXXXI

The Council of Ministers of a Union Republic issues decisions and orders on the basis and in pursuance of the laws of the USSR and of the Union Republic, and of the decisions and orders of the Council of Ministers of the USSR, and verifies their execution.

ARTICLE LXXXII

The Council of Ministers of a Union Republic has the right to suspend decisions and orders of the Councils of Ministers of its Autonomous Republics, and to annul decisions and orders of the Executive Committees of the Soviets of Working People's Deputies of its Territories, Regions and Autonomous Regions.

ARTICLE LXXXIII

The Council of Ministers of a Union Republic is appointed by the Supreme Soviet of the Union Republic and consists of:
  The Chairman of the Council of Ministers of the Union Republic;
  The Vice-Chairmen of the Council of Ministers;
  The Ministers;

The Chairmen of State Committees, Commissions, and the heads of other departments of the Council of Ministers set up by the Supreme Soviet of the Union Republic in conformity with the Constitution of the Union Republic.

ARTICLE LXXXIV

The Ministers of a Union Republic direct the branches of state administration which come within the jurisdiction of the Union Republic.

ARTICLE LXXXV

The Ministers of a Union Republic, within the limits of the jurisdiction of their respective Ministries, issue orders and instructions on the basis and in pursuance of the laws of the USSR and of the Union Republic, of the decisions and orders of the Council of Ministers of the USSR and the Council of Ministers of the Union Republic, and of the orders and instructions of the Union-Republican Ministries of the USSR.

ARTICLE LXXXVI

The Ministries of a Union Republic are either Union-Republican or Republican Ministries.

ARTICLE LXXXVII

Each Union-Republican Ministry directs the branch of state administration entrusted to it, and is subordinate both to the Council of Ministers of the Union Republic and to the corresponding Union-Republican Ministry of the USSR.

ARTICLE LXXXVIII

Each Republican Ministry directs the branch of state administration entrusted to it, and is directly subordinate to the Council of Ministers of the Union Republic.

The Higher Organs of State Power in the Autonomous Soviet Socialist Republics

ARTICLE LXXXIX

The highest organ of state power in an Autonomous Repubic is the Supreme Soviet of the Autonomous Republic.

ARTICLE XC

The Supreme Soviet of an Autonomous Republic is elected by the citizens of the Republic for a term of four years on a basis of representation established by the Constitution of the Autonomous Republic.

ARTICLE XCI

The Supreme Soviet of an Autonomous Republic is the sole legislative organ of the Autonomous Republic.

ARTICLE XCII

Each Autonomous Republic has its own Constitution, which takes account of the specific features of the Autonomous Republic and is drawn up in full conformity with the Constitution of the Union Republic.

The Supreme Soviet of an Autonomous Republic elects the Presidium of the Supreme Soviet of the Autonomous Republic and appoints the Council of Ministers of the Autonomous Republic, in accordance with its Constitution.

The Local Organs of State Power

ARTICLE XCIV
The organs of state power in Territories, Regions, Autonomous Regions, Areas, Districts, cities and rural localities (stanitsas, villages, hamlets, kishlaks, auls) are the Soviets of Working People's Deputies.

ARTICLE XCV
The Soviets of Working People's Deputies of Territories, Regions, Autonomous Regions, Areas, Districts, cities and rural localities (stanitsas, villages, hamlets, kishlaks, auls) are elected by the working people of the respective Territories, Regions, Autonomous Regions, Areas, Districts, cities and rural localities for a term of two years.

ARTICLE XCVI
The basis of representation for Soviets of Working People's Deputies is determined by the Constitutions of the Union Republics.

ARTICLE XCVII
The Soviets of Working People's Deputies direct the work of the organs of administration subordinate to them, ensure the maintenance of public order, the observance of the laws, protect the rights of citizens, direct local economic and cultural affairs and draw up and approve local budgets.

ARTICLE XCVIII
The Soviets of Working People's Deputies adopt decisions and issue orders within the limits of the powers vested in them by the laws of the USSR and of the Union Republic.

ARTICLE XCIX
The executive and administrative organ of the Soviet of Working People's Deputies of a Territory, Region, Autonomous Region, Area, District, city or rural locality is the Executive Committee elected by it, consisting of a Chairman, Vice-Chairmen, a Secretary and members.

ARTICLE C
The executive and administrative organ of the Soviet of Working People's Deputies in a small locality, in accordance with the Constitution of the Union Republic, is the Chairman, the Vice-Chairman and the Secretary elected by the Soviet of Working People's Deputies.

ARTICLE CI
The executive organs of the Soviets of Working People's Deputies are directly accountable both to the Soviets of Working People's Deputies which elected them and to the executive organ of the superior Soviet of Working People's Deputies.

The Courts and the Procurator's Office

ARTICLE CII

In the USSR justice is administered by the Supreme Court of the USSR, the Supreme Courts of the Union Republics, the Courts of the Territories, Regions, Autonomous Republics, Autonomous Regions and Areas, the Special Courts of the USSR, established by decision of the Supreme Soviet of the USSR, and the People's Courts.

ARTICLE CIII

In all Courts cases are tried with the participation of people's assessors, except in cases specially provided for by law.

ARTICLE CIV

The Supreme Court of the USSR is the highest judicial organ. The Supreme Court of the USSR is charged with the supervision of the judicial activities of all the judicial bodies of the USSR and of the Union Republics within the limits established by law.

ARTICLE CV

The Supreme Court of the USSR is elected by the Supreme Soviet of the USSR for a term of five years.

The Supreme Court of the USSR includes the Chairmen of the Supreme Courts of the Union Republics by virtue of their office.

ARTICLE CVI

The Supreme Courts of the Union Republics are elected by the Supreme Soviets of the Union Republics for a term of five years.

ARTICLE CVII

The Supreme Courts of the Autonomous Republics are elected by the Supreme Soviets of the Autonomous Republics for a term of five years.

ARTICLE CVIII

The Courts of Territories, Regions, Autonomous Regions and Areas are elected by the Soviets of Working People's Deputies of the respective Territories, Regions, Autonomous Regions or Areas for a term of five years.

ARTICLE CIX

People's Judges of District (City) People's Courts are elected by the citizens of the districts (cities) on the basis of universal, equal, and direct suffrage by secret ballot for a term of five years.

People's Assessors of District (City) People's Courts are elected at general meetings of industrial, office and professional workers, and peasants in the place of their work or residence, and of servicemen in military units, for a term of two years.

ARTICLE CX

Judicial proceedings are conducted in the language of the Union Republic, Autonomous Republic or Autonomous Region, persons not knowing this language being guaranteed the opportunity of fully acquainting themselves with the material of the case through an interpreter and likewise the right to use their own language in court.

ARTICLE CXI

In all Courts of the USSR cases are heard in public, unless otherwise provided for by law, and the accused is guaranteed the right to defence.

ARTICLE CXII

Judges are independent and subject only to the law.

ARTICLE CXIII

Supreme supervisory power to ensure the strict observance of the law by all Ministries and institutions subordinated to them, as well as by people in office and citizens of the USSR generally, is vested in the Procurator-General of the USSR.

ARTICLE CXIV

The Procurator-General of the USSR is appointed by the Supreme Soviet of the USSR for a term of seven years.

ARTICLE CXV

Procurators of Republics, Territories, Regions, Autonomous Republics and Autonomous Regions are appointed by the Procurator-General of the USSR for a term of five years.

ARTICLE CXVI

Area, district and city procurators are appointed by the Procurators of the Union Republics, subject to the approval of the Procurator-General of the USSR, for a term of five years.

ARTICLE CXVII

The organs of the Procurator's Office perform their functions independently of all local bodies, being subordinate solely to the Procurator-General of the USSR.

Fundamental Rights and Duties of Citizens

ARTICLE CXVIII

Citizens of the USSR have the right to work, that is, the right to guaranteed employment and payment for their work in accordance with its quantity and quality.

The right to work is ensured by the socialist organisation of the national economy, the steady growth of the productive forces of Soviet society, the elimination of the possibility of economic crises, and the abolition of unemployment.

ARTICLE CXIX

Citizens of the USSR have the right to rest and leisure.

The right to rest and leisure is ensured by the establishment of a seven-hour day for industrial, office, and professional workers, the reduction of the working day to six hours for arduous trades and to four hours in shops where conditions of work are particularly arduous; by the institution of annual vacations with full pay for industrial, office, and professional workers, and by placing a wide network of sanatoriums, holiday homes and clubs at the disposal of the working people.

ARTICLE CXX

Citizens of the USSR have the right to maintenance in old age and also in case of sickness or disability.

ARTICLE CXXI

Citizens of the USSR have the right to education.

This right is ensured by universal compulsory eight-year education; by extensive development of secondary polytechnical education, vocational-technical education, and secondary specialised and higher education based on close ties between the school, real life and production activities; by the utmost development of evening and extramural education; by free education in all schools; by a system of state scholarship grants; by instruction in schools in the native language, and by the organisation of free vocational, technical and agronomic training for the working people in the factories, state farms, and collective farms.

ARTICLE CXXII

Women in the USSR are accorded all rights on an equal footing with men in all spheres of economic, government, cultural, political, and other social activity.

The possibility of exercising these rights is ensured by women being accorded the same rights as men to work, payment for work, rest and leisure, social insurance and education, and also by state protection of the interests of mother and child, state aid to mothers of large families and to unmarried mothers, maternity leave with full pay, and the provision of a wide network of maternity homes, nurseries and kindergartens.

ARTICLE CXXIII

Equality of rights of citizens of the USSR, irrespective of their nationality or race, in all spheres of economic, government, cultural, political and other social activity, is an indefeasible law.

Any direct or indirect restriction of the rights of, or, conversely, the establishment of any direct or indirect privileges for, citizens on account of their race or nationality, as well as any advocacy of racial or national exclusiveness or hatred and contempt, are punishable by law.

ARTICLE CXXIV

In order to ensure to citizens freedom of conscience, the church in the USSR is separated from the state, and the school from the church. Freedom of religious worship and freedom of anti-religious propaganda is recognised for all citizens.

ARTICLE CXXV

In conformity with the interests of the working people, and in order to strengthen the socialist system, the citizens of the USSR are guaranteed by law:

(a) freedom of speech;
(b) freedom of the press;
(c) freedom of assembly, including the holding of mass meetings;
(d) freedom of street processions and demonstrations.

These civil rights are ensured by placing at the disposal of the working people and their organisations printing presses, stocks of paper, public buildings, the streets, communications facilities and other material requisites for the exercise of these rights.

ARTICLE CXXVI

In conformity with the interests of the working people, and in order to develop the initiative and political activity of the masses of the people, citizens of the USSR are guaranteed the right to unite in mass organisations – trade unions, co-operative societies, youth organisations, sport and defence organisations, cultural, technical and scientific societies; and the most active and politically-conscious citizens in the ranks of the working class, working peasants and working intelligentsia voluntarily unite in the Communist Party of the Soviet Union, which is the vanguard of the working people in their struggle to build communist society and is the leading core of all organisations of the working people, both government and non-government.

ARTICLE CXXVII

Citizens of the USSR are guaranteed inviolability of the person. No person shall be placed under arrest except by decision of a court of law or with the sanction of a procurator.

ARTICLE CXXVIII

The inviolability of the homes of citizens and privacy of correspondence are protected by law.

ARTICLE CXXIX

The USSR affords the right of asylum to foreign citizens persecuted for defending the interests of the working people, or for scientific activities, or for struggling for national liberation.

ARTICLE CXXX

It is the duty of every citizen of the USSR to abide by the Constitution of the Union of Soviet Socialist Republics, to observe the laws, to maintain labour discipline, honestly to perform public duties, and to respect the rules of socialist society.

ARTICLE CXXXI

It is the duty of every citizen of the USSR to safeguard and fortify public, socialist property as the sacred and inviolable foundation of the Soviet system, as the source of the wealth and might of the country, as the source of the prosperity and culture of all the working people.

Persons committing crimes in respect of public, socialist property are enemies of the people.

ARTICLE CXXXII

Universal military service is law.

Military service in the Armed Forces of the USSR is the honourable duty of citizens of the USSR.

ARTICLE CXXXIII

To defend the country is the sacred duty of every citizen of the USSR. Treason to the Motherland – violation of the oath of allegiance, desertion to the enemy, impairing the military power of the state, espionage – is punishable with all the severity of the law as the most heinous of crimes.

The Electoral System

ARTICLE CXXXIV
Members of all Soviets of Working People's Deputies – of the Supreme Soviet of the USSR, the Supreme Soviets of the Union Republics, the Soviets of Working People's Deputies of the Territories and Regions, the Supreme Soviets of the Autonomous Republics, the Soviets of Working People's Deputies of the Autonomous Regions, and the Area, District, city and rural (stanitsa, village, hamlet, kishlak, aul) Soviets of Working People's Deputies – are elected on the basis of universal, equal and direct suffrage by secret ballot.

ARTICLE CXXXV
Elections of deputies are universal: all citizens of the USSR who have reached the age of eighteen, irrespective of race or nationality, sex, religion, education, domicile, social origin, property status or past activities, have the right to vote in the election of deputies, with the exception of persons who have been legally-certified insane.

Every citizen of the USSR who has reached the age of twenty-three is eligible for election to the Supreme Soviet of the USSR, irrespective of race or nationality, sex, religion, education, domicile, social origin, property status or past activities.

ARITICLE CXXXVI
Elections of deputies are equal: each citizen has one vote; all citizens participate in elections on an equal footing.

ARTICLE CXXXVII
Women have the right to elect and be elected on equal terms with men.

ARTICLE CXXXVIII
Citizens serving in the Armed Forces of the USSR have the right to elect and be elected on equal terms with all other citizens.

ARTICLE CXXXIX
Elections of deputies are direct: all Soviets of Working People's Deputies, from rural and city Soviets of Working People's Deputies to the Supreme Soviet of the USSR, are elected by the citizens by direct vote.

ARTICLE CXL
Voting at elections of deputies is secret.

ARTICLE CXLI
Candidates are nominated for each constituency.

The right to nominate candidates is secured to mass organisations and societies of the working people: Communist Party organisations, trade unions, co-operatives, youth organisations and cultural societies.

ARTICLE CXLII

It is the duty of every deputy to report to his electorate on his work and on the work of his Soviet of Working People's Deputies, and he may be recalled at any time upon decision of the electors in the manner established by law.

Arms, Flag, Capital

ARTICLE CXLIII

The arms of the Union of Soviet Socialist Republics are a sickle and hammer against a globe depicted in the rays of the sun and surrounded by ears of grain, with the inscription 'Workers of All Countries, Unite!' in the languages of the Union Republics. At the top of the arms is a five-pointed star.

ARTICLE CXLIV

The state flag of the Union of Soviet Socialist Republics is of red cloth with the sickle and hammer depicted in gold in the upper corner near the staff and above them a five-pointed red star bordered in gold. The ratio of width to length is 1:2.

ARTICLE CXLV

The capital of the Union of Soviet Socialist Republics is the City of Moscow.

Procedure for Amending the Constitution

ARTICLE CXLVI

Amendments to the Constitution of the USSR shall be adopted by a majority of not less than two-thirds of the votes in each of the Chambers of the Supreme Soviet of the USSR.

APPENDIX D

The Soviet Government

The USSR Council of Ministers – the Soviet government – consists of the following members:

CHAIRMAN

FIRST VICE-CHAIRMEN (2)

VICE-CHAIRMEN (9)

MINISTERS OF THE USSR
*All-Union Ministries:**
Aircraft Industry
Apparatus, Automation, and Control Systems Manufacture
Automobile Industry
Chemical and Oil Engineering
Civil Engineering
Defence Industry
Electrical Engineering
Electronics Industry
Gas Industry
Heavy, Power and Transport Engineering
Machine Building
Machine Building for Construction, Road - Building and Municipal Services
Machine Building for Light and Food Industries and Household Appliances
Machine Building, General
Machine Building, Medium
Machine-Tool and Instrument Making
Merchant Marine
Radio Engineering
Railways
Shipbuilding
Tractor and Agricultural Machinery
Trade, Foreign
Transport Construction

Union-Republican Ministries:
Agriculture
Assembly and Special Construction Work
Building Materials
Chemical Industry
Coal Industry
Communications
Culture
Defence
Finance
Fisheries
Food Industry
Foreign Affairs

Geology
Health
Higher and Specialised Secondary Education
Iron and Steel Industry
Land Reclamation and Water Conservancy
Light Industry
Meat and Dairy Industry
Non-Ferrous Metallurgy
Oil-Extraction Industry
Oil-Refining and Petrochemical Industry
Power and Electrification
Timber and Woodworking Industry
Pulp and Paper Industry
Ministry of Interior
Education
Trade, Home

CHAIRMEN OF STATE
COMMITTEES OF USSR
COUNCIL OF MINISTERS

Agricultural Products, Procurement of
Construction
Economic Relations with Foreign Countries

---

* All-Union ministries operate directly for the country as a whole, while Union-republican ministries operate through corresponding ministries in the Union republics. Industrial enterprises which come under the all-Union ministries are directly subordinate to those ministries, whereas the Union-republican ministries supervise the appropriate enterprises through similar ministries or agencies in the republics.

CHAIRMEN OF STATE
COMMITTEES OF USSR
COUNCIL OF MINISTERS
cont.—

Labour and Wages
Material and Technical
Supplies
Planning
Timber Industry
Science and Technology
Vocational and Technical
Education

and the Chairmen of:
The People's Control
Committee of the USSR

The Board of the USSR
State Bank
The Central Statistical
Board under the USSR
Council of Ministers
The State Security Com-
mittee under the USSR
Council of Ministers
Association for Supply
of Agricultural
Machinery
(Soyuzselkhoztekhnika)
Physical Culture and
Sport

CHAIRMEN OF
COUNCILS OF
MINISTERS OF
UNION REPUBLICS

Armenian SSR
Azerbaijan SSR
Byelorussian SSR
Estonian SSR
Georgian SSR
Kazakh SSR
Kirghiz SSR
Latvian SSR
Lithuanian SSR
Moldavian SSR
Russian SFSR
Tajik SSR
Turkmenian SSR
Ukrainian SSR
Uzbek SSR

Source: For names of Ministers see *Ezhegodnik bol'shoy Sovetskoy entsiklopedii 1968*
(Moscow 1968), pp. 30–1.

APPENDIX E

CPSU Politbureau and Secretariat 1969

Politbureau	*Secretariat*
MEMBERS:	
Brezhnev ——————————	Brezhnev (Gen-Sec)
Kosygin	
Podgorny	
Suslov ——————————	Suslov
Voronov	
Kirilenko——————————	Kirilenko
Shelepin	
Mazurov	
Polyanski	
Shelest	
Pel'she	
CANDIDATE MEMBERS:	
Demichev——————————	Demichev
Grishin	
Mzhavanadze	
Rashidov	
Ustinov ——————————	Ustinov
Shcherbitski	
Kunaev	
Masherov	
Andropov	
	Ponomarev
	Kapitonov
	Kulakov
	Solomentsev, M. S.
	Katushev, K. F.

Politbureau and Secretariat of the Central Committee of the CPSU: Social Origin and Education (All members, 1966–March 1969)

Name	Social origin	Education
Brezhnev	working class	higher/technical
Kosygin	working class	higher/technical
Podgorny	working class	higher/technical
Suslov	poor peasant	higher/economic
Voronov	rural intelligentsia	higher/technical/political
Kirilenko	petty bourgeois [?]	higher/technical
Shelepin	working class	higher/humanities [?]
Mazurov	peasant	higher/technical/Party
Polyanski	poor peasant	higher/agric-tech/Party
Shelest	poor peasant	higher/technical
Pel'she	peasant	higher[1]
Demichev	working class	higher/military/technical/Party
Grishin	working class	incomplete higher
Mzhavanadze	working class	higher/military-political
Rashidov	poor peasant	higher/humanities/Party
Ustinov	working class	higher/military-technical
Shcherbitski	working class	higher/technical
Kunaev	employee	higher/technical
Masherov	peasant	higher/pedagogical
Andropov	employee	incomplete higher
Ponomarev	employee	higher[2]
Kapitonov	peasant	higher/technical
Kulakov	peasant	higher/agricultural
Rudakov		
Solomentsev	peasant	higher/technical
Katushev		higher/technical

[1]Graduate, Institute of Red Professors.
[2]Graduate, Moscow State University and Institute of Red Professors.
I would like to thank Mr. Peter Frank for putting the above data at my disposal.

APPENDIX F

Population Statistics

Basic Population Data of USSR 1897–1969

Total Population

	Total (Mills)	Urban (Mills)	Rural (Mills)	Percentage of Total Urban %	Rural %
1897	124.6	18.4	106.2	15	85
1913	159.2	28.5	130.7	18	82
*1926	147.0	26.3	120.7	18	82
*1929	153.0	28.7	124.7	19	81
1940	194.1	63.1	131.0	33	67
1950	178.5	69.4	109.1	39	61
1960	212.3	103.8	108.5	49	51
1969	238.9	134.2	104.7	56	44

Source: *Narodnoe khozyaystvo SSSR v 1968 g.* (Moscow 1969), p. 7.
Narodnoe khozyaystvo SSSR v 1962 g. (Moscow 1963), p. 7. Figures for 1926 and 1929 refer to borders of USSR before 17 September 1939. All other dates refer to area encompassed by present borders.

Changes in the Sex-Ratio in the USSR 1926–1969

	Total (Mills)	Male (Mills)	Female (Mills)	Percentage of Total Male %	Female %
1926	147.0	71.0	76.0	48.3	51.7
1939	170.6	81.7	88.9	47.9	52.1
1959	208.8	94.0	114.8	45.0	55.0
*1969	238.9	109.8	129.1	46.0	54.0

*Estimate of Jan. 1.
Source: *Narodnoe khozyaystvo SSSR v 1965 g.* (Moscow 1966), p. 8 and *Narodnoe khozyaystvo SSSR v 1968 g.* (Moscow 1969), p. 8.

Birth and Death Rates and Natural Increase in Population of the USSR

Year	Per 1,000 of the Population			No. of deaths, per 1,000 of population, of children under 1 year
	No. born	No. of deaths	Natural Increase	
1913 (within frontiers of USSR up to 17/9/39)	47.0	30.2	16.8	273
(within contemporary frontiers of USSR)	45.5	29.1	16.4	269
1926	44.0	20.3	23.7	174
1928	44.3	23.3	21.0	182
1938	37.5	17.5	20.0	161
1940	31.2	18.0	13.2	182
1950	26.7	9.7	17.0	81
1960	24.9	7.1	17.8	35
1968	17.3	7.7	9.6	26

Source: Narodnoe khozyaystvo SSSR v 1968 g. (Moscow 1969), p. 36.

Population distribution in the Republics of the USSR (thousands)

	1913	1940 (1 Jan)	1959 (1 Jan)	1969 (1 Jan)
USSR (Total)	159,153	194,077	208,827	238,943
RSFSR (Russian Federation)	89,902	110,098	117,534	128,526
Ukraine	35,210	41,340	41,869	46,752
Byelorussia	6,899	9,046	8,055	8,897
Uzbekistan	4,366	6,645	8,261	11,669
Kazakhstan	5,565	6,054	9,154	12,877
Georgia	2,601	3,612	4,044	4,710
Azerbaidzhan	2,339	3,274	3,698	5,042
Lithuania	2,828	2,925	2,711	3,103
Moldavia	2,056	2,468	2,885	3,531
Latvia	2,473	1,886	2,093	2,323
Kirghizistan	864	1,528	2,066	2,926
Tadzhikistan	1,034	1,525	1,981	2,823
Armenia	1,000	1,320	1,763	2,363
Turkmenia	1,042	1,302	1,516	2,085
Estonia	954	1,054	1,197	1,316

Source: Narodnoe khozyaystvo SSSR v 1968 g. (Moscow 1969), p. 9.

*Size of Family by Nationality**

	Average size of Family
Tadzhiks	5.2
Turkmens	5.0
Uzbeks	5.0
Azerbaidzhanies	4.8
Armenians	4.7
Kazakhs	4.6
Kirgiz	4.5
Georgians	4.0
Moldavians	3.9
White Russians	3.7
Lithuanians	3.6
Russians	3.6
Ukrainians	3.5
Latvians	3.1
Estonians	3.0

* *Itgi vsesoyuznoy perepisi naseleniya 1959 g. SSSR (svodny Tom).* (Moscow 1962). Table 64a, p. 252.

APPENDIX G

The Kosygin Reforms

A. N. Kosygin, 'On Improving Management of Industry, Perfecting Planning and Economic Stimulation of Industrial Production,' *Pravda*, 28 Sept. 1965. Translated in: *New Directions in the Soviet Economy*, Joint Economic Committee of Congress (Washington, 1966), pp. 1042–63.

Improving industrial planning and increasing the economic independence of enterprises

In order to increase the economic independence of enterprises it is proposed to reduce the number of indexes assigned from above. At the same time the indexes retained in the plan should be aimed at raising production efficiency.

Experience shows that the index of overall volume of output does not stimulate the enterprises to produce goods really needed by the national economy and the population, and in many cases holds up the improvement of assortment and quality. Not infrequently our enterprises produce low-quality goods which the consumer does not want and which therefore do not sell.

Instead of an overall volume of production index, it is proposed that the plans of enterprises should incorporate assignments for the volume of goods actually sold. This will make enterprises pay greater attention to quality in order to be able to fulfill their assignments for marketed products. An enterprise that produces low-quality goods will experience difficulties in selling them and, consequently, will be unable to fulfill its plan. Under the existing system of evaluating the activities of an enterprise on the basis of overall volume of output, such an enterprise would have been considered as having fulfilled its plan.

However, it would not be sufficient to appraise the work done by an enterprise only on the basis of the volume of goods sold. The national economy requires definite products to satisfy the needs of society.

For this reason assignments for the more important items must be retained as plan indexes.

When economic ties between enterprises have been well organised and the contract system well developed, it will be possible steadily to reduce the assortment of goods produced according to the state plan, and to substitute for it a classified, or enlarged, list of commodities.

If the assignment for goods sold is aimed at establishing closer ties between production and consumption, to orientate the enterprise toward raising efficiency, it would appear better to use the profit index, the index of profitability. The size of obtained profits characterises, to a considerable extent, the contribution made by an enterprise to the net national income which is used to expand production and raise the people's standard of living.

It goes without saying that profit assignments do not make the need to lower production costs less important but, on the contrary, increases its importance. One of the most important tasks of economic managers is to lower production costs. The production cost index should command special attention in the technical, production and financial plan of the enterprise.

The state is interested in constantly increasing accumulations not only by lowering the cost of production of each item, but also by producing more, and by expanding and modernising the range of manufactured goods and raising their quality. Profit reflects all these aspects of the production activities of an enterprise in a much more complete way than the production cost index. What is important in this case is to take into account not only the amount and increment of profit obtained, but also the level of profitability, i.e., the amount of profit per ruble of fixed assets.

Substantial changes are also envisaged in the planning of labour at enterprises.

At present the enterprises receive four labour indexes from above – productivity of labour, number of workers, average wages, and wage fund. From now on it is proposed to hand down only one of these indexes – the wage fund. This, of course, does not mean that the other indexes have lost their significance. The indexes of labour productivity, number of employees, and average wages will remain important elements of the national economic plan and the production plan of the enterprise. But is it really necessary to hand down all these assignments to the enterprise from above? Experience has shown that such planning fetters the initiative of the enterprise in the search for means and ways of increasing labour productivity.

There have been proposals that the wage fund of the enterprise be not assigned from above, either. But to discard the planning of the wage fund would be premature. There must be a proper balance between the quantity of consumer goods manufactured and the population's purchasing power. And the purchasing power is determined in large measure by the wage fund.

In the future, when we have succeeded in considerably expanding the production of consumer goods and accumulating adequate stocks of these goods, we will be able to discontinue the wage fund of the enterprise from above. We plan to do this, first of all, in the industries producing consumer goods.

Thus the enterprise will have the following indexes passed down from above:

The volume of goods to be sold;

The main assortment of goods;

The wage fund;

The amount of profit and level of profitability; and

Contributions to the budget and allocations from the budget.

Besides, they will be assigned:

The volume of centralised investment and the putting into operation of production capacities and fixed assets;

The main assignments for introducing new techniques; and

The indexes of material and technical supply.

All other indexes of economic activity will be planned by the enterprises themselves, without endorsement from above. This will relieve the enterprise of uncalled-for tutelage, and will enable it to adopt the most economical decisions according to the actual conditions of production.

While extending the economic independence of the enterprises, the state will continue to conduct a unified policy in the sphere of technical progress, investment, labour remuneration, prices and financing, and will insure the compilation of accounts and statistical returns according to a unified system.

Improving the quality of goods in conformity with the demands of consumers and modern technical standards is one of the main tasks facing the planning and economic organisations.

The plans must incorporate the most important indexes relating to technical standards and the quality of goods, and all the financial, manpower, and material resources necessary to achieve them.

It is necessary to raise the role of state standards as an effective means of raising the quality of output. State standards should be steadily improved in the light of the latest achievements of science and technology. A system of state certification of the quality of goods should be introduced.

The normal economic activity of an enterprise is frequently upset by the fact that the plans assigned them from above are not supported with the necessary technical and economic calculations and that the different sections of the plans are not correlated. Little attention has been given so far to the working out of the technical and economic management. Plans are frequently changed, which upsets the work of the enterprise and lowers production efficiency. One of the main tasks in improving planning is to work out stable plans for enterprises on the basis of scientifically sound standards and technical and economic calculations taking into account the peculiarities of the industries and groups of enterprises concerned.

The need to raise the scientific standards of planning confronts our professional economists with the task of analysing modern processes of the technical and economic development of the country, and of ascertaining the trends and prospects that are emerging. A special effort should be made to increase the economic effectiveness of new machinery and equipment, readjust the patterns of both production and consumption, and study economic ties, the comprehensive development of regional economies and the territorial division of labour throughout the country.

Now that raising the technical standards of production and its efficiency has become a most important task, planned management of the economic activity of enterprises cannot be restricted to annual plans. As to long-term plans, their importance has been under-rated. Many enterprises did not take the trouble to compile them at all, and those that did usually failed to correlate them with plans for the development of the national economy. Another major drawback of the existing system of long-term planning was that the assignments included in long-term plans and, in particular, the target figures of the 7-year plan, were not broken down into annual figures.

As a result, enterprises do not know their production prospects and so cannot make preparations in time nor establish links with suppliers and consumers on a permanent basis.

It is proposed to make the 5-year plan the basic form of planning, distributing the

T*

more important assignments by years, so that the enterprises may carry out their production and economic activities on the basis of this plan.

Lately national economic plans have envisaged few measures aimed at increasing production efficiency by industries, which is due to violation of the branch principle of management. In industrial management and in national economic plans, the task is to increase the significance of each branch of industrial production and to guarantee a correct combination of planning by branches and planning at republic and economic-area level.

In this connection we must mention the tasks facing the state planning committee of the USSR. The committee must concentrate on guaranteeing proper balances and relationships within the national economy, raising the efficiency of social production, and searching for means of hastening the growth of the national income and the improvement of the people's standard of living. Of special importance in this respect will be a more profound and thorough elaboration of national income and its utilisation, of the manpower supply and its utilisation, both in the country as a whole and in individual areas, the balance of money incomes and expenditures of the population, the balance of financial resource, and the more important material balances.

Increasing economic stimuli for enterprises and promoting cost accounting

Improvement of the forms and methods of planning will make it possible to tackle the problem of strengthening and developing cost accounting in a new way. Lenin stressed that each enterprise must work at a profit, i.e., completely cover its expenditures from its incomes and make a profit.

The enterprises operating on a cost-accounting basis, and their managers, must bear full responsibility for the economic results of the work they do. Lenin's ideas of cost accounting should underline our economic activities. We see their consistent implementation and further development as the way to solve urgent problems of Communist construction at the present stage.

What must we do to strengthen and develop cost accounting in the new conditions?

First, we must create conditions in which the enterprises will be able to solve problems of improving production independently, and will be interested in making better use of the fixed assets assigned to them to increase output and profit. It is therefore necessary to leave to the enterprises more of the profit they derive, so that they can develop production, improve techniques, materially encourage the staff and improve its working and living conditions. The proportion of funds to be left to the enterprise should be made directly conditional on how effectively it uses its fixed assets, increases the volume of goods sold, improves the quality of its goods and increases profitability. At the same time the state should restrict the gratuitous financing of investment and extend the use of credits.

Secondly, it is necessary to strengthen the principle of cost accounting in the relations between enterprises, guarantee strict fulfilment of delivery commitments and increase material responsibility for their fulfilment.

Thirdly, on the basis of cost accounting, it is necessary to provide material incentives for the entire personnel and every shop and section of the enterprise, so that they will not only fulfil their own assignments but also improve the overall results of the enterprise. The system of incentives should be so devised that the enterprise will be interested in working out and fulfilling higher plan assignments and in making better use of its internal resources.

In short, it is necessary to direct the entire activity of the enterprise toward finding ways of improving the economics of production, increasing the incomes of the enterprise and thereby increasing the overall national income.

Under the existing system, investments are almost exclusively allocated according to the central plan, and a considerable proportion of them is spent on new construction. Many of the operating enterprises lack adequate means and so cannot replace obsolete plant in time. This holds up the growth of labour productivity, improvement of the quality of goods produced and the growth of the profitability.

It is proposed that every enterprise establish a production development fund which would include deductions from its profit. Part of the depreciation money intended for the complete restoration of fixed assets would also be contributed to the fund. At present this part of the depreciation money is allocated on a centralised basis for financing capital construction, and the enterprises cannot use it as they see fit.

When these measures have been implemented, the production development fund – which the enterprises will be free to use for technical improvements in production – will constitute a much larger sum than is the case now. This can be seen from the following data.

In 1964 expenditures from enterprises' funds for the introduction of new techniques and development of production in industry totalled 120 m. rubles, and 600 m. rubles in bank credits was spent for the same purposes; the total figure was therefore 720 m. rubles. Under the new conditions, the development funds will approximate to 4,000 m. rubles in 1967, including 2,700 m. rubles from the depreciation fund.

The promotion of cost accounting and the economic stimulation of production depend on the basis on which the state grants means to the enterprise, and on the way in which the enterprise transfers part of its income to the budget.

Investment at present is financed gratis from the budget. Enterprise managers show little concern as to the cost of the reconstruction of the enterprise or the effect that original investment will produce, because their enterprises are not obliged to refund the sums granted them. Hence we need a system that will induce our economic managers to strive for the most judicious use of investment funds, so that new shops and units can be built with a minimum of investment and put into operation in time and that their rated capacities are put to use as early as possible.

One way of solving this problem is to switch from the free allocation of means for capital construction to long-term credits. The idea is that credits will be introduced, first of all, for investment in operating enterprises. As for new construction, it would apparently be expedient to introduce long-term credit for projects with a comparatively short period of recoupment.

Of great importance in making production more efficient is correct and economical use of the working capital allocated to the enterprise. At present, any shortage in the working capital of the enterprise is made up from the budget. We cannot, therefore, speak of genuine cost accounting if the enterprise does not, in effect, bear any economic responsibility for the utilisation of the working capital allocated to it. It is proposed to abolish the practice of providing free supplements to the working capital of enterprises from the budget and to grant them credits if necessary. Such a system will induce enterprises to use the working capital allocated to them more thriftily.

A change in the system by which enterprises make payments to the state budget from their incomes is also envisaged. At present the amount of the deductions made from profits of enterprises in favour of the budget does not depend on the value of the fixed assets assigned to them. That is one of the reasons why enterprises attempt to obtain more money from the state for investment and for supplementing their working capital, without taking the necessary measures for their rational use. Sometimes an enterprise purchases equipment it does not need just to spend the funds allocated to it.

As has been said, the effectiveness of fixed assets has recently declined in a number of industries. It is most important, therefore, to interest enterprises in increasing their output and raising not only the sum total of their profits but also the amount of profit made per ruble of fixed assets assigned to them. To this end it is necessary to introduce deductions in favour of the budget from the profits of enterprises in proportion to the value of fixed assets and working capital allocated to them, as payment for the fixed assets.

Rates of payment for fixed assets and working capital will be established for a long period – over several years – so that after each payment a normally functioning enterprise will have profits left for setting up incentive funds and for covering its planned expenses. Those enterprises which make better use of their fixed assets and working capital will retain more profit for setting up incentive funds, which will provide adequate material encouragement for better use of the public funds allocated to the enterprises.

New machines, newly installed equipment, and shops and enterprises just put into operation cannot in every case produce their full economic effect immediately, and enterprises may therefore experience temporary financial difficulties. Therefore it is proposed that deductions for fixed assets and working capital be made only when the planned time limit for mastering new capacities has passed.

It must be stressed that these payments are not proposed as additional contributions to the budget over and above payments which enterprises make now; the idea is to divert a considerable proportion of the payments to the budget through a new channel. Eventually payments for fixed assets and working capital will become a most important part of the budget income, and the importance of other payments, including the turnover tax, will decrease accordingly.

It is also planned to use cost accounting more freely between enterprises. At present the mutual economic responsibility of enterprises is most inadequate Contracting has not as yet acquired the importance it deserves in relations between enterprises.

It is proposed to increase the material responsibility of enterprises and organisations in cases of nonfulfilment of contract obligations for deliveries of goods so that, as a rule, losses will be made good by the faulty enterprise. The responsibility of rail, water, road and other transport organisations for delays in moving goods from enterprises and retarding their delivery to the customer will also be increased. It is necessary that design organisations should also be responsible for errors made in projects, technical drawings and designs, if these errors lead to material losses and additional expenditures during the building of a project or while production at new-built plants is being organised.

The introduction of the sales index makes the position of the producing enterprises and the size of their funds dependent on payments by customers. It goes without saying that every enterprise must itself bear full responsibility for making payments and for clearing accounts with suppliers in time. A cost-accounting relationship between enterprises demands that payment discipline be tightened. Simultaneously the role of State credit in economic turnover must be intensified with the aim of guaranteeing unhindered clearance of accounts between suppliers and their clients.

Increasing material incentives for workers to improve the work of enterprises
At present the material incentives provided for production collectives and for individual workers to improve the overall results of the work of their enterprises are quite inadequate. Enterprises have very limited opportunities of raising the pay of their staffs out of sources of income created by the enterprises themselves.

About 50 per cent of the industrial enterprises have no funds created from their own profits, and where these funds do exist they are very small and the sums paid out of them by way of encouragement are insignificant. Nearly every kind of bonus and other stimuli are paid, not out of profits, but out of the wage fund. The achievements of the enterprise in increasing profits and raising profitability have no direct effect on the wages and salaries of the staff.

We must change this practice in order to provide staffs with greater material incentives. We must establish a system under which the enterprise's opportunities for increasing the remuneration of its staff would be determined, above all, by the growth of production, improved quality, increased profits and greater profitability. Basic wages and salaries will be raised on a centralised basis as before. At the same time enterprises should have – in addition to the wage fund – a special fund to stimulate their employees for individual achievements and for a good performance of the enterprise as a whole.

This fund should consist of a part of the profit obtained by the enterprise, which would use it not only to pay the staff bonuses for high efficiency in the course of the year, but also an extraordinary allowance at the end of the year. In doing this, account will be taken of the length of uninterrupted service at the enterprise, which will help to check the outflow of skilled manpower.

Under the existing system of material incentives, enterprises are not interested in providing in their plans for the fullest utilisation of their internal resources, because the performance of the enterprise is appraised and its staff offered inducements according primarily to the extent that plan targets are exceeded. This system encourages enterprises to strive for lower plan assignments in terms of volume of output, growth of labour productivity, and lower costs, and for larger wage funds, staffs, investments and material funds, so that it will be easier for them to exceed plans. This makes it difficult to draft realistic plans. How is this system to be changed?

A fund for the material stimulation of the staff will be set up at each enterprise. It will be derived from the profits obtained by the enterprise. Allocations for the material stimulation fund should be made according to stable quotas established for a number of years and in such a manner as to insure that the amount of the material incentive fund is determined by increases in the sale of products or in profit and by the level of profitability envisaged by the plan. Those who exceed the plan will be paid relatively less by way of incentive than those who achieve plan indices. This will induce enterprises to find reserves in time and to accept larger plan assignments.

The material stimulation fund will also increase depending on the proportion of new products and on additional returns derived by the enterprise from higher prices for goods of high quality. Enterprises will be interested in mastering the production of new items and in improving their quality as soon as possible.

Since the pattern and cost of production and the ratio between profit and wages vary from industry to industry, we propose to differentiate the rates of allocation for the stimulation fund according to groups of enterprises, taking the amount of the wage fund into account.

A fund for financing social and cultural development and housing construction must also be set up at enterprises. Allocations from this fund will be spent for housing construction (over and above the sums allocated for this purpose on a centralised basis), the construction and upkeep of children's institutions, Young Pioneer camps, holiday and health homes, and other social and cultural purposes.

Consequently, the better an enterprise functions, the more opportunities it will have, not only to raise wages and salaries, but also to improve the living conditions of its staff and carry out cultural and health protection measures.

The proposed changes in the methods of planning and economic stimulation are not based on theoretical conclusions alone but also on experience.

In 1964 and 1965, new methods of planning and economic stimulation were introduced at a number of enterprises of the sewing, footwear, and textile industries. The performance of these enterprises is evaluated according to output and profit under the plan.

Recently a new bonus system for managers, engineers, technicians, and office workers has been introduced at enterprises in a number of industries to afford the personnel greater incentives to increase output and improve quality. The first results show that we are on the right track. I would like to dwell in some detail on a practical experiment involving the use of the new system. It has to do with motor transport.

These are some major shortcomings in motor transport. About half of the runs are empty ones. Of course, plans every year envisage a reduction of empty runs, a lowering of maintenance costs, an increase in loads, etc. But they yield scant results. Motor transport organisations put forward any number of arguments to prove that the plan quotas assigned to them are unrealistic.

Five months ago the Council of Ministers of the USSR instructed the Labour and Wages Committee and the Moscow and Leningrad City Soviets to introduce the new system of planning and economic stimulation in some motor transport organisa-

tions. The system was introduced in three Moscow and two Leningrad organisations. They are large organisations servicing construction, the trading network,
industry and inter-urban transport.

The economic independence of these organisations wased extend: they had fewer
plan indexes assigned from above and were allowed greater freedom in using above
plan profit and savings on the wage fund to encourage their personnel in material
terms, improve social and cultural conditions and expand production facilities.

The Presidium of the Council of Ministers of the USSR recently examined the
first results of their work and heard the reports of the directors of two of the Moscow
motor transport organisations. The very first results showed that the introduction
of the new system of planning and economic stimulation produces a considerable
effect. Having received ample powers and opportunities, the collectives found ways
and means to improve their work and to transport more, above all by reducing
empty runs. They extended the range of enterprises and organisations using their
services, considerably improved the quality of service, encouraged their clients
to shorten loading and unloading time, improved the organisation of repairs and
maintenance, sold the lorries and equipment they did not need, and reduced their
staffs.

The new system of planning and economic stimulation increased the employees'
interest in the results of their work. In 4 months of work under the new conditions
(May–August 1965) empty runs were reduced by 15 per cent, with the result that
haulage increased by 34 per cent. Labour productivity went up by 31 per cent and
profits more than doubled, making it possible to raise wages. Above-plan profit
in the five organisations totalled 969,000 rubles in 4 months. As before 40 per cent
of the profit was transferred to the budget, and the balance – over 550,000 rubles –
was used for improving facilities, accumulating reserves, meeting social and cultural
requirements and stimulating the staffs materially.

Of course, one can hardly expect that the work of all the motor transport organisations would improve in the same way. Nevertheless, the results of the experiment
speak for themselves. We see in them something new that will also yield important
results in other branches of the national economy.

The transition to new forms and methods of economic stimulation of industrial
production demands improvements in the pricing system. Prices should increasingly
reflect the expenditures of socially necessary labour, cover production and circulation outlays and insure that each normally functioning enterprise makes profit.

The existing under-estimation of economic methods in planning and managing
the national economy, and neglect of cost accounting, are connected to a considerable
extent with the serious shortcomings in price formation. If prices are not well-
grounded, economic calculations become less reliable, which, in turn, leads to the
adoption of subjectivist decisions.

From now on, in fixing wholesale prices for industrial goods, it will be necessary
to calculate the level of profitability of the various industries on the strength of
scientific evidence. Normally functioning enterprises should make profit from the
sale of their products at wholesale prices and so be able to form a corresponding
stimulation fund, and also have the necessary means for expanding their activities,
paying for their fixed assets and making other contributions to the budget.

Prices must also play a major role in solving problems of quality and in extending the reasonable length of service and dependability of products. This is why, in pricing new, improved articles, the additional expenditures made by the manufacturers and the economic effect which customers will derive from improved products should be taken into consideration. This will encourage manufacturers to improve their products, and will make it economically more advantageous for customers to use these products.

In preparing for this plenary meeting, the Presidium of the CC, CPSU and the Council of Ministers of the USSR decided to set up a State Committee for Prices under the State Planning Committee of the USSR. This committee is entrusted with working out and presenting by 1 January 1966, guidelines for fixing wholesale prices for industrial goods with a view to bringing prices as near as possible to the value of socially necessary labour expended. These prices must guarantee the implementation of the contemplated measures for the improvement of planning and economic stimulation of enterprises.

A better pricing system and the fixing of wholesale prices will help in improving the economic indexes of the work of industry, in finding additional reserves and in insuring steady reduction of production costs. Needless to say retail prices may be revised only with the aim of reducing them.

Experience shows that establishing wholesale price levels for every product, and preparing new price lists for every industry will take considerable time. It will probably be possible to introduce new prices in 1967 or 1968.

However, the State Planning Committee, the Ministry of Finance, and the Committee for Prices will have to introduce the necessary amendments into current prices in all those industries where the new forms of economic stimulation will be adopted at an earlier date, in order to eliminate unjustified differences in profitability.

Such are roughly the main proposals for improving planning and stimulation in industry. The proposed system of planning and stimulation is also applicable, in its main features, to the building industry, railway transport and certain other branches of the national economy. But it must not be extended to these branches mechanically, without taking into account their special economic features and the tasks facing them. Work in this direction will be gradually carried on.

IMPROVING THE ORGANISATION OF INDUSTRIAL MANAGEMENT

Improving the organisational forms of economic management on the Leninist principle of democratic centralism and through the timely elimination of outdated forms of management is objectively necessitated by the development of the productive forces and of socialist relations of production.

It goes without saying that genuine improvement of economic management has nothing in common with rash, ill-advised changes divorced from economic reality and running counter to objective economic laws.

Recent years have seen a large-scale reorganisation of economic management in our country. Ever since 1957 industry has been managed through economic councils. Industrial ministries were abolished, and the enterprises operating under them were subordinated to economic councils.

The organisation of industrial management through economic councils had a number of positive aspects. In some cases it resulted in the useful amalgamation of kindred enterprises, in the setting up of plants for equipment repairs and for the production of semi-manufactured parts and tools for a wide range of industries.

But in time major shortcomings began to make themselves felt. Division of managerial functions in industries constituting a single production and technical entity among numerous economic regions disrupted management. The various industries were dissolved, so to speak, in the economy of the economic regions. Heterogeneous industries are often managed by economic councils not through specialised, but through multisector boards. The councils lack competent personnel for some of the industrial branches.

This state of affairs prompted us to look for remedies. In 1960 republic economic councils were set up in the Russian Federation, Ukrainian SSR and Kazakh SSR, and in 1962 some economic councils were amalgamated. The national economic councils and Supreme Economic Council of the USSR and state committees for branches of industry were established. However, these additional measures could not eliminate basic defects.

The branch committees had no decisive effect on the technical standards of industrial production. Lacking adequate rights as they did, they became in fact, consultative bodies dissociated from the enterprises concerned and the entire range of production problems.

As matters stand today, plans for new plants are examined and decided upon by one agency, plans for production and capital construction by another, and supply problems by a third. There is virtually no single agency that could examine and decide upon every aspect of the development of an industry.

All this has produced an adverse effect on technical progress, growth of output, specialisation, and the production ties between enterprises located in different economic regions.

Departures from the industrial branch principle have told on management. They have led to infringements of the uniform technical policy and to the dispersion of competent personnel and given rise to a multistage system of management. Numerous agencies bearing no direct responsibility for the development of the particular branch have appeared. The overall result is irresponsibility, endless co-ordination of decisions, and managerial inefficiency.

Thus the problem of seriously improving industrial management has become urgent. To develop industry successfully, it is essential to integrate the management of production, technology, economics and research in every particular industry. Under the socialist system the managerial forces of industry can be proprely concentrated and centralised only by following the branch principle of management.

Characteristically, industrial progress has necessitated a new form of organisation – branch amalgamations operating on the cost-accounting principle. The rise of branch amalgamation based on cost accounting within the framework of economic councils proves that the branch form of management is gaining ground because it is more effective. This form promotes the specialisation, co-ordination and concentration of production, makes for a more judicious use of competent personnel, and creates favourable conditions for improving technical and economic management.

To improve management, we must set up managerial bodies on the branch principle, that is, industrial ministries fully empowered to manage production branches and fully responsible for the development of these branches.

The ministries are to plan and control production and handle technical policy, supplies, financing, labour and wages, They will run branch research institutions. This will facilitate production and economic activity of the enterprises, since all the important problems of this activity will be settled by a single body, the ministry.

The ministries will be responsible for satisfying the demands of the national economy and the population. They will have to take the initiative in manufacturing new, more up-to-date items and see to it that the output of these items keeps pace with demand.

It is clear that centralised planned management of the economy should be combined with measures to encourage the initiative of the union republics, of local bodies and enterprises.

We propose to establish all-union, union-republic and republic industrial ministries, with due regard to the production and technical peculiarities of each industry.

We plan to set up all-union ministries by branches of the engineering industry, which is particularly in need of integrated technical management on a countrywide scale, such as would enable it to carry out standardisation and unification of articles, units, and parts and to guarantee that they are up to the present high standard of world science and technology. These problems can be dealt with provided the engineering industry is managed on a country-wide scale.

We propose to establish the following all-union ministries for the management of branches of engineering:

Ministry of Heavy, Power, and Transport Machine Building;

Ministry of the Building, Road Building, and Municipal Machinery Industry;

Ministry of the Tractor and Farm Machinery Industry;

Ministry of the Automobile Industry;

Ministry of Power Engineering;

Ministry of the Instrument Making, Automation Facilities, and Control Systems Industry;

Ministry of Chemical and Oil Machine Building;

Ministry of the Machine-Tool and Tool Industry;

Ministry for the Manufacture of Machinery for the Light and Food Industries and of Household Machines.

Other industries are to be put under union-republic jurisdiction. This will enable the union republics to take part in the management of these industries. Both union-republic ministries of the USSR and ministries of the same name in the union republics will be set up, and the republics themselves will decide, by agreement with the corresponding ministry of the USSR, whether to set up a ministry or a board (economic association) for the industry concerned in the republic.

We propose to set up the following union-republic ministries of the USSR:

Ministry of the Iron and Steel Industry;

Ministry of the Nonferrous Metals Industry;
Ministry of the Coal Industry;
Ministry of the Chemical Industry;
Ministry of the Oil-Extracting Industry;
Ministry of the Oil-Refining and Petrochemical Industry;
Ministry of the Timber, Cellulose and Paper, and Woodworking Industry;
Ministry of the Building Materials Industry;
Ministry of Light Industry;
Ministry of the Food Industry;
Ministry of the Meat and Dairy Industry.

The union-republic industrial ministries or boards (associations) in the union republics will be subordinated to the councils of ministries of the union republics and the corresponding union-republic ministry of the USSR, and in their management of enterprises will follow the guidelines elaborated by the union-republic ministries of the USSR.

As regards industry under republic jurisdiction, the republics will decide themselves whether to set up this or that ministry or economic association. A vital function of the republic bodies will be to develop local industry, which is very important for the population.

The central committee of the CPSU and the Council of Ministers of the USSR have upon discussion decided to grant new powers to the union republics in the field of planning, capital constructions, financing, labour and wages. In the future as well, we will have to promote the initiative of the union republics in the sphere of economic and cultural development.

The setting up of ministries should by no means lead to increases in managerial staffs. On the contrary, they must be reduced. We must devise a simple pattern for the ministries and assign them small staffs since the enterprises and economic associations are to be granted extensive rights and hence there is no need for a machinery exercising petty tutelage over enterprises.

The setting up of branch ministries will call for enhancing the role of the State Planning Committee. The existence of centralised branch management bodies will increase the importance of co-ordinated development of the various branches of the economy and economic areas of the country.

The State Planning Committee of the USSR is at present subordinated to the Supreme Economic Council. But as Lenin stressed, the task of the State Planning Committee is to plan the entire national economy along scientific lines. We therefore propose to subordinate the State Planning Committee, a union-republic agency, directly to the Council of Ministers of the USSR.

To insure proper territorial planning and comprehensive exploitation of the natural, labour, power and other resources of the economic areas, the state planning committees of the republics will draft economic development plans of the republics, including industries under union-republic and republic jurisdiction. The state planning committees of the republics will also have to draw up proposals for the draft plans of the enterprises under union jurisdiction, situated on the territory of the republics in question.

Thus, the state planning committees of the union republics will become agencies dealing with problems of the industrial development of the republics as a whole, bearing in mind the interests of the entire national economy. This will enable the union republics to rule out parochialism.

The State Committee for the Co-ordination of Scientific Research of the USSR is to be reorganised into an all-union State Committee of the Council of Ministers of the USSR for Science and Technology. It is expedient to reorganise the State Committee for Construction of the USSR, now under the Supreme Economic Council, into the State Committee of the Council of Ministers of the USSR for Construction, preserving it as a union-republic agency.

We plan to abolish the Supreme Economic Council and the Economic Council of the USSR as well as economic councils of the republics and economic areas.

The organisation of material and technical supply is an important field of economic management. On it depend in large measure the proper utilisation of material resources, labour productivity, profitability and quality. Material and technical supply must be planned and managed as a single whole if it is to meet the needs of the national economy.

A departmental system of material and technical supply, with numerous over-lapping small offices, depots and warehouses, existed till 1957. It was a costly system under which economic resources could not be handled flexibly.

The measures taken in recent years to organise supply and sales along territorial lines have resulted in improving this system somewhat. The vast number of small supply-and-sale organisations has been cut. Larger and better equipped specialised depots, general (inter-branch) offices and warehouses have been set up. Fuller use is being made of local resources.

In the future the State Planning Committee of the USSR will place material and technical resources at the disposal of the Union ministries, which will control these resources and distribute them among the consumers subordinated to them.

The resources will be used by the central supply-and-sales boards and territorial material and technical supply bodies operating at the present time.

It is intended to retain the existing territorial material and technical supply bodies with their network of offices and specialised and general depots and warehouses for the utilisation of raw and other materials and equipment according to plan. They will be responsible for the utilisation of material resources supplied by the enterprises situated in the areas concerned and for the control over delivery of the products of these enterprises to consumers in other areas.

We should encourage more extensive direct contacts between manufacturing and consuming enterprises in the sphere of material and technical supply. We should gradually go over to wholesale trade in certain materials and items of equipment through territorial supply-and-sales centres in the areas of consumption.

We plan to entrust the guidance of material and technical supply in the country to a Union-republic State Committee of the Council of Ministers of the USSR for Material and Technical Supply. It will be responsible for the realisation of supply plans, co-ordinated inter-branch deliveries, and control over the timely fulfilment of delivery plans. It is intended to subordinate to this committee the central boards of inter-republican deliveries now under the Economic Council of the USSR.

However, no supply system will meet the interests of the national economy unless enterprises and organisations are really made responsible for the fulfilment of economic contracts and unless they are afforded adequate material incentives.

This, in the main, is how the economic management of industry is to be reorganised.

It may seem at first glance that what is suggested is a mere return to the ministries of the past. To think so, however, would mean disregarding a number of new factors and making a mistake. The new ministries will work in entirely different conditions. The administrative management of industry will be combined with a considerably greater application of cost-accounting methods and economic incentives. The economic powers of enterprises will be substantially extended and their initiative stimulated.

A network of cost-accounting organisations is to be set up in the various industries to exercise direct management of their respective enterprises. Management will be increasingly built on the principle of cost accounting, with strict adherance to state planning discipline. The ministries will enlist the assistance of cost-accounting organisations by handing over many of their own routine functions to them. Moreover, within the ministries themselves, particularly those of the light and food industries, many departments will operate on the principle of cost accounting. The ministries will concentrate on the main progressive trends of development of the industries they manage. Emphasis will be laid on economic levers, on rendering enterprises practical assistance to improve their operation and steadily to introduce complete self-sufficiency.

The development of economic methods of industrial management changes the very character of relations between enterprises and higher bodies. The old notion that the leading economic bodies have only rights and the enterprises only duties must be given up. The development of economic methods of management, the extensive introduction of cost accounting in industry, calls for the establishment of mutual rights and duties between enterprises and industrial management bodies, and for greater responsibility on the part of both.

The draft statute of the Socialist state-owned industrial enterprise was discussed for a long time with broad participation of factory workers. It was studied by the presidium of the Central Committee of the CPSU and the Council of Ministers of the USSR and will be introduced after this plenary meeting. The statute settles pressing questions of the economic activity of enterprises not only in industry, but also in construction, agriculture, transport, and communications.

The enterprise will enjoy wider powers in the use of its working capital, depreciation funds, and also the receipts from the sale of surplus equipment and other material values. The housing built by it will be distributed only among its workers. The enterprise will enjoy wider powers in the use of the money saved on the wage fund during the year. It will decide independently, without registering in financial bodies, on its structure and staff and on administrative expenses. It will be allowed greater economic initiative and independence in solving other production problems. The statute will no doubt promote cost accounting.

The proposed measures for improving the organisation and the economic methods of industrial management combine centralised planning by the state with complete self-sufficiency of the enterprise, centralised management of industry with far-reaching local economic initiative, the principle of one-man management with greater say for the personnel. This system will meet present-day requirements and will help to use the advantages of the socialist system more effectively.

The rapid growth of our socialist economy will continue to call for improvements in economic management. This is why we must overcome the lag in research in this field and carefully elaborate the scientific principles of managing social production.

IMPLEMENTING THE NEW PLANNED INDUSTRIAL MANAGEMENT SYSTEM IN ORGANISED FASHION

Comrades, the decisions of this plenary meeting will bring big changes into the planned management of industry. It is, in fact, an important economic reform covering the production activities of the millions of factory and office workers, technicians, economists, and industrial executives.

The adoption of new economic and organisational methods in industry will no doubt benefit the entire national economy. It will enable us to raise the entire economic system to a qualitatively new stage, to draw on additional sources in increasing the wealth of our country and improving the people's living standard.

But success will not come of itself. To use the opportunities being provided, we must make careful organisational preparations for the transition of the economic management of industry to new working conditions, raise the standard of the economic activity of industrial personnel in keeping with new tasks and requirements, and allow proper scope for the creative activity of the workers, individually and collectively.

The measures planned to improve industrial management must be implemented in an organised manner, by stages and in strict accordance with the plan. The organisation of ministries will take time. The transition to the new managerial system must be so effected as to insure that state plans are fulfilled and that industry operates normally.

Until every production unit has been placed under the control of the relevant ministry, the economic councils must continue to work and bear full responsibility for the uninterrupted operation of the production units under their jurisdiction. This applies also to the state production committee and their duties.

The drawing up of the economic development plan and the state budget for 1966 is nearing completion. The plan and the budget have been suited to the present structure of industrial management.

The Councils of Ministers of the Union Republics, the economic councils and the appropriate state committees must therefore hand the plans down to production units in time.

In view of the establishment of new ministries, the list of production units to be assigned to each ministry should be specified as early as possible and, accordingly, the economic plan and budget targets determined for every industry, in line with the new managerial structure. The State Planning Committee should carefully organise and supervise this work. The Finance Ministry should carry out appropriate work to draw up the state budget for 1966 with due regard to the new structure of industrial management.

On the basis of decisions to be adopted, the State Planning Committee, Finance Ministry, State Labour and Wages Committee, State Prices Committee, State Bank and the industrial ministries must carry out this year, and especially in 1966 and 1967, a great deal of work to prepare regulations, methodological instructions and directives taking into account the specific features of each industry and each group of production units. This work must be conducted with the participation of industrial executives, leading specialists and research workers.

The transition to the new industrial management system will necessitate a redistribution of executive personnel. This important problem should receive serious attention from the central committees of the Communist parties of the Union Republics, the councils of ministers of the Union Republics, ministries and local party, government and economic organisations.

We must do our utmost to provide production units with highly qualified personnel. After all, it is on them that success hinges. We must also carefully select competent people for the new ministries, for the efficiency of industrial management will largely depend on this. We must give maximum attention to executive personnel and use every worker properly.

Many thousands of able and competent organisers of socialist production have been trained in our country in Soviet years. At the present time more than two million experts with a higher or secondary education are employed in industrial establishments. There are more than four million Communists working in industry. This is a large force with which we can accomplish very complicated tasks. The party and the people value the country's experts and executives whom they fully trust and support in their difficult work for the good of society.

The demands on our industrial and managerial personnel are growing due to changing conditions. Managers are expected to display initiative based on competence, an ability to make prompt decisions, a business-like approach to problems, a sense of the new, an ability to make the maximum use of production resources in the given situation.

As their powers are extended, economic executives must show an increasing sense of responsibility to the party and the state. They will have to solve, together with their staffs, problems which formerly were solved for them higher up.

The training of specialists for industry in the new conditions will be much more important. There are serious shortcomings in this sphere for many of which the Ministry of Higher and Specialised Secondary Education and the State Planning Committee are to blame. Major imbalances have been allowed to develop in the training of technicians and engineers, with the result that we have a shortage of specialists in some industries and a surplus in others.

The economic training of engineers and technicians is poorly organised. It is impermissible for an engineer or designer to have a superficial understanding of production economics today.

The training of economists will be of paramount importance. We must give greater attention to this matter since there is a serious shortage of trained economists. At the beginning of 1965 specialists with a higher economic education constituted only 6 per cent of the total number of specialists in the USSR, somewhat less even than the figure at the end of 1940.

The earlier system of raising the qualifications of key executives, which proved its worth, should be restored. It was a big mistake to abolish it.

Many establishments use engineers and technicians wrongly. Heads of factories and building projects, engineers and technicians are often obliged to participate in useless conferences instead of attending to their direct functions. Some of the specialists are compelled to draw up all kinds of performance and statistical reports, which are not really their duty.

These shortcomings in the training and utilisation of personnel must be eliminated.

The industrial manager is personally responsible for the job assigned him by the state. This responsibility, and one-man leadership in industry, is of especial importance now. But one-man management should go hand in hand with the broadest participation of the staffs in discussing every important economic problem of the enterprise and its management. The success of a manager's work depends on the support he receives from his staff and on the authority he wins by his competence and integrity.

Better management is impossible without carrying forward its democratic principles and considerably extending the participation of the masses in it. The role of the workers and their organisations in the solution of planning problems, the mustering of internal production reserves, the assessment of the results of work, and the provision of incentives must be substantially enhanced. As the funds of the enterprises are to be increased, factory organisations will have to play a much greater role in the use of these funds. Every worker should be made to feel that he is one of the owners of the factory. No factory can operate efficiently without strict labour and production discipline, and unless every executive, engineer, office employee, or worker is properly fulfilling his duties and tasks.

The collective agreement is an important means of enlisting the participation of the personnel in the effort for more efficient operation of the factories. Its role will be greatly enhanced. Collective agreements should be extensively and carefully discussed by the workers, for they are going to have a much greater stake in improving overall results. Every employee should know of the specific measures that will be taken to operate the factory better and more profitably, of how improved operation of the factory will effect his working and living conditions and pay, and of the responsibility the collective agreement places on every employee. Managers and trade union organisations must improve the negotiation of collective agreements and see to it that the commitments contained in the agreements are fulfilled.

To improve management, the party and trade union organisations and heads of enterprises must radically improve the organisation of the Socialist emulation movement. The new methods of economic management provide a solid economic foundation for this movement, organising labour on scientific lines, achieving greater profitability, improving the quality of output, and raising labour productivity. Every new departure at an enterprise should be popularised through the Socialist emulation movement. This is an important condition for raising the standard of Socialist management at every enterprise.

The party, the trade unions, the Government and economic agencies must organise the extensive popularisation of the measures to improve planning and management, and to provide greater economic stimuli for industrial production with a view to rallying the efforts of all the working people and insuring that every enterprise, and industry as a whole, works efficiently.

Comrades, our Leninist Communist Party is the leading and guiding force in the advance of the Socialist economy to communism. It always strives to find the most effective ways and means of solving our country's major economic problems. This meeting of the central committee of our party will discuss and adopt decisions of fundamental importance. Their implementation and, consequently, the progress of our economy will depend in decisive measure on the political and organising work of our party, of its organisations and members.

The very nature of the proposed measures points to the growing role of party guidance of the economy. The responsibility of the central committees of the Communist parties of the union, republics and the territorial and regional party committees for insuring truly scientific management of industry, management free from any influence of parochialism and departmentalism, for the full use, in the interests of Communist construction, of the opportunities which will be afforded by the new methods of management, will increase steadily. The responsibility of the territorial and regional party committees for the management of industry will now be greater than ever before.

Without doing the job of the economic management agencies, and without exercising petty patronage over them, party committees at all levels should work, in their own specific way, first of all, among the people, among the workers and specialists. The important thing is to encourage their initiative and activity, to pool their experience and creative energy.

The increased rights and independence of the enterprise will be accompanied by the growth of the role of its party organisation. One of the important tasks of the latter will be to find reserves for increasing output, improving quality, and making proper use of economic stimuli. It is the party organisation that must provide moral stimuli for work, and promote the Communist consciousness of the working people.

There can be no doubt that, given a steady effort by all our party organisations, the measures proposed for improving production management will yield favourable results and their success will contribute to the construction of Communist society in our country.

Comrades, the work of this plenary meeting is bound to evoke widespread comment abroad. We are sure that our friends in the Socialist countries, who are following Soviet life and economic progress with keen interest, will be gratified by the decisions of this meeting. But our enemies will certainly try to misrepresent these decisions. Bourgeois ideologists, who have heard about the economic reform being prepared in the USSR are already trying to present it as evidence of the weakness of Socialist economic planning. The bourgeois press, emphasising some real but mostly imaginary shortcomings of our economic development, talks of 'chaos' and 'crisis' in the Soviet economy. Apparently that is the distorted way in which the discussions we had on improving economic planning and management were reflected in the minds of some bourgeois 'Sovietologists'. While we think of how to make our work still more effective and how to use the opportunities of socialism to still greater advantage, they keep talking, as in times past, about the 'failure' of our system of social production, about the Soviet Union 'reverting' to capitalist economic management and replacing the principles of planning by the chaotic machinery of market regulation.

Vain hope. The character of an economic system depends on who wields state power and owns the means and instruments of production, in whose class interests production is developed and profit distributed. This is a fundamental issue, and in this issue we have always adhered, and will continue to adhere, to an unshakable Marxist-Leninist position. The Soviet Union stands firm as a country of victorious socialism, a country confidently building the material and technical base for communism. Socialist property in the USSR is developing into Communist property. And the bourgeois economists' talk about the gradual 'return' of the Soviet economy to the capitalist track is merely wishful thinking.

We realise that the propaganda fuss about 'difficulties' in the Soviet economy and about its 'bourgeois transformation' has yet another air. Our enemies are alarmed because many independent Afro-Asian countries choose the Socialist road of development, study the experience of the Soviet Union and other Socialist countries, and develop economic and political relations with them.

Their tale about 'crisis' in the Soviet economy is designed to discredit socialism, its economic methods, its economic efficiency, and so to defame our country's economic policy. It will not help them. Decisions which this plenary meeting will make open opportunities of making still better use of the advantages of the Socialist economic system.

An important international feature of the proposed economic reform is that it will strengthen socialism in the economic competition between the two different social systems.

Economic management is being improved in almost every European Socialist country. The distinctions in the approach to the solution of specific problems reflect peculiarities of the national economies concerned. The changes that are taking place are aimed at raising the scientific standard of planning, providing stronger economic stimuli for production, promoting cost accounting and increasing the independence of enterprises.

It is typical of all the European Socialist countries that they are developing the branch principle of management, with branch amalgamations working on the cost-accounting basis and playing a growing role.

The adoption of new methods of Socialist economic management in our country and in other Socialist countries of Europe will contribute to the development of the international Socialist division of labour and to the close and mutually profitable co-ordination of economic development plans. This also shows the great international significance of the decisions to be taken by this meeting.

The Presidium of the Central Committee of the CPSU and the Council of Ministers of the USSR consider that the adoption of the new methods and forms of planning and management of industry will strengthen the economic foundations of the Soviet policy of co-operation between countries. The proposed reform meets the basic interests of the Soviet people, who want to see their country prosper. Its implementation will help improve the life of the Soviet people, increase the might and defence capacity of our country, and hasten our advance to communism.

Allow me to express confidence that the measures worked out by the Presidium of the Central Committee of the CPSU and the Council of Ministers of the USSR for improvements in industrial management will be fully supported by the members of the central committee and receive the unanimous approval of the party and the people.

APPENDIX H

Comparative Statistics

	USSR	USA	UK
Infant Mortality Rate 1964			
(Deaths under 1 year: per 1,000 live births)	30.0	24.2	21.7*
Births per 1,000 women aged 15–44 years, 1964	7.0	9.2	11.3*

* 1963

Civilian Labour Force

	Year	Men	Thousands Women	Total	% of total population Men	Women	Total %
UK	1964	16,579	8,777	25,356	63	32	47
USSR	1964	50,200	53,800	104,000	49	44	46
USA	1964	48,410	25,823	74,233	51	27	39

Civilian Labour Force by Main Sectors of Economic Activity

	Year	Agriculture 000	%	Industry 000	%	Services 000	%	Unemployed 000	%	Total 000	%
UK	1964	948	4	11,887	47	12,171	48	349	1	25,356	100
USSR	1964	39,710	38	31,250	30	33,040	32	—	—	104,000	100
USA	1963	5,559	8	22,356	31	40,194	55	4,166	6	72,275	100

General Indices of Industrial Production. 1958 = 100

	1954	1958	1960	1962	1964
UK	—	100	113	114	127
USSR	66	100	122	147	169
USA	92	100	116	126	141

Motor Vehicles: Production 1964 and in use

| | Production | | In Use (1.1.1965) |
	Passenger Cars 000's	Commercial Vehicles 000's	Passenger Cars per 1,000 of population
UK	1,867.6	464.7	158
USSR	185.2	417.9	4
USA	7,745.5	1,562.4	360
Germany (FR)	2,650.2	253.8	146

Building: Number of Dwellings Completed 1964

	Dwellings Completed	Dwellings Completed per 1,000 inhabitants
Germany (FR)	623.8	10.7
UK	392.4	7.2
USSR	2,314.0*	10.2
USA	1,591.0†	8.1

*1963   †Dwellings begun in 1964.

External Trade 1964

	Imports $ per head	Exports $ per head
Germany (FR)	251	278
UK	285	228
USSR	34	34

Total Imports by area of origin and Exports by area of destination 1964 (%)

	EEC	EFTA	USA	Rest of World
USSR Imports origin:	5.4	4.1	2.1	88.4 (E. Europe 57.5)
USSR Exports destination	6.2	5.0	0.3	88.5 (E. Europe 58.6)

Housing

	Year	No. of Dwellings Occupied	Average No. of Rooms per Dwelling	Persons per Room
UK	1961	15,834	4.7	0.7
Germany (FR)	1961	15,564	4.1	0.9
USSR	1960	50,900	2.8	1.5
USA	1960	53,024	5.0	0.7

Radio, TV sets and Telephones in Use 1 Jan. 1965 (Per 1,000 of population)

	Radios*	TV's	Telephones (1963)
Germany (FR)	297	170	131
UK	294	242	171
USSR	313	52	29
USA	1,143	334	443

*Either number of licences or number of receivers. Receivers sometimes include rediffusion apparatus.

Health Services (1963) (Per 100,000 population)

	Doctors	Pharmacists	Hospital beds†
Germany	144	32	1,064
UK	107	40	1,022
USSR	205	—	903
USA	149	—	900

†Including clinics, mental hospitals, sanatoria, rest and convalescent homes.

Source: *Basic Statistics of the Community*, Statistical Office of the European Communities (Brussels 1965).

Newsprint consumption (per capita, kilogrammes)

	Average 1955–59	1961	1964
UK	19.7	24.0	26.0
USA	35.7	36.3	37.9
USSR	1.6	2.0	2.7

Source: *Statistical Yearbook 1965* (New York, UN 1966), p. 724.

Radio Broadcasting (radios) and television receivers (thousands)

L = licences; R = receivers in use.

		Radios 1948	Radios 1964	Radios 1966		Televisions 1964	Televisions 1966
UK	L	11,460	16,015	16,432	L	13,155	13,919
USA	R	74,000	225,000	262,700	R	67,100	74,100
USSR	L	11,452	72,300	76,800	L	12,900	19,000

Source: *Statistical Yearbook 1965 and 1967* (NY, UN 1966, 1968), , pp. 733–735 (1965) and pp. 769–773 (1968).

Books: First Editions

	1966
USSR	65,609
UK	22,902
USA	50,286

Source: *Statistical Yearbook 1967* (New York, UN 1968), p. 760.

Annual attendance at cinemas

	Year	Per inhabitant
UK	1966	5
USA	1965	12
USSR	1966	18

Source: *Statistical Yearbook 1967* (New York, UN 1968), p. 769.

Production of long films

	Minimum length (metres)	1959	1961	1963	1965
UK	900	122	117	113	93
	1,980	79	77	72	69
USA	2,400	223	254	155	191
USSR	—	145	137	133	167

Source: *Statistical Yearbook 1967* (New York, UN 1968), p. 766.

Physicians, dentists, midwives and pharmacists

	Year	Physicians	Dentists	Midwives	Pharmacists	Inhabitants per Physician
England, Wales	1965	47,000*	12,400*	22,600*	1,420*	840†
USA	1965	288,671	93,400	600	118,284	670
USSR	1965	485,000	25,500	250,700	85,231‡	480

Source: *Statistical Yearbook 1965 and 1967* (New York, UN 1966, 1968), p. 667 (1966) and p. 698 (1968).

*National Health Service Personnel only.

†1963 (All Physicians).

‡1963.

APPENDIX I

Basic Principles of Legislation in the USSR and Union Republics on Marriage and the Family effective from 1 October 1968

Sources: Soviet News, 2 July 1968 and 24 Sept. 1968. See also *Izvestiya*, 28 June 1968.

Concern for the Soviet family, in which the social and personal interests of citizens are harmoniously blended, is one of the most important tasks of the Soviet state.

The most favourable conditions for the consolidation and flourishing of the family have been created in the Soviet Union. The material welfare of citizens is constantly rising and the housing, everyday and cultural conditions of family life are improving. Our socialist society pays great attention to the welfare conditions and encouragement of motherhood and to ensuring a happy childhood.

The communist education of the rising generation and the development of its physical and spiritual forces is a major duty of the family. The state and society render all-round help to the family in the bringing up of children; the network of nursery schools, creches, boarding schools and other children's institutions is expanding.

Soviet women are assured all the necessary social and everyday conditions for the blending of happy motherhood with an ever more active and creative participation in industrial and social and political life.

Soviet legislation on marriage and the family is designed actively to encourage the final liberation of family relations from materialistic calculations and the elimination of survivals of woman's unequal position in everyday life, and to create the communist family in which people's most profound personal feelings will find full satisfaction.

Section 1. General Propositions

ARTICLE I

The tasks of Soviet legislation on marriage and the family.

The tasks of Soviet legislation on marriage and the family are as follows:

The further consolidation of the Soviet family, which is based on the principles of communist morality;

The basing of family relations on a voluntary marital union of man and woman and on a sentiment – free of materialist calculations – of mutual love, friendship and respect among all members of the family.

The family education of children in organic unity with their social education in a spirit of devotion to the motherland, a communist attitude towards work and the preparation of children for active participation in the construction of a communist society;

Full protection of the welfare of mother and child and the ensuring of a happy childhood for every child;

The final eradication of the harmful survivals and customs of the past in family relations;

The education of a sense of responsibility to the family.

ARTICLE II
Relations regulated by legislation on marriage and the family.

Legislation on marriage and the family establishes the procedure and conditions of entry into marriage, regulates personal and property relations arising in the family between man and wife, parents and children and between other members of a family, relations arising in connection with the adoption of children, guardianship and trusteeship*, the procedure and conditions of dissolution of marriage and the procedure of registration of births, marriages and deaths.

ARTICLE III
Equality of the man and woman in family relations.

In their family relations the woman and the man enjoy equal personal and property rights.

The equality of family rights is based on the equal rights of the woman and the man, as laid down in the Constitution of the USSR, in all spheres of the state, social, political, economic and cultural life of the country.

ARTICLE IV
Equality of citizens in their family relations, irrespective of nationality, race and religion.

All citizens, irrespective of nationality, race and religion, enjoy equal rights in family relations.

No direct or indirect restriction of rights, nor the establishment of direct or indirect advantages on entry into marriage and in family relations based on nationality, race or religion, are allowed.

ARTICLE V
Protection and encouragement of motherhood.

In the USSR motherhood is held in nation-wide respect and esteem and is protected and encouraged by the state.

Protection of the interests of mother and child is ensured by the organisation of an extensive network of maternity hospitals, creches and nursery schools, boarding schools and other children's institutions, by the granting to women of pregnancy and maternity leave with full pay, by the granting of privileges to pregnant women and to mothers, by labour protection measures in industry, by the payment of

---

* Soviet law makes a distinction between a guardian, who is responsible for a child up to the age of 14, and a trustee, who is responsible for a child between the ages of 14 and 18; there are certain differences in responsibility. In practice, of course, the guardian normally becomes the trustee of the same child in due course.

V

state grants to unmarried mothers and to mothers of large families, as well as other forms of State and social aid to the family.

ARTICLE VI

Legal regulation of marriage and family relations by the state.

Legal regulations of marriage and family relations in the USSR is effected by the state alone.

Only civil marriage is recognised. The religious ceremony of marriage, as well as other religious ceremonies, have no significance in law.

This rule does not apply to religious ceremonies and the appropriate documents of the registration of birth, marriage, dissolution of marriage or death effected prior to the establishment or restoration of Soviet registry offices for births, marriages or deaths.

ARTICLE VII

Legislation by the Union of Soviet Socialist Republics and by the Union republics on marriage and the family.

Legislation on marriage and the family consists of the present Basic Principles and other legislative acts of the USSR and the codes of marriage and the family and other legislative acts of the Union republics as enacted in keeping with the present Basic Principles.

Legislation by the Union republics deals with questions referred to their competence by the present Basic Principles, as well as questions of marriage and family relations that are not directly provided for by the Basic Principles.

ARTICLE VIII

Application of legislation by the Union republics on marriage and the family.

Entry into marriage, relations between husband and wife and between parents and children, adoption, the establishment of paternity, the exaction of maintenance, guardianship and trusteeship, dissolution of marriage, and registration of births, marriages and deaths are regulated by the legislation of the given Union republics, whose appropriate body carries out or registers the civil act in question, or resolves any dispute that has arisen.

The validity of marriage, adoption, guardianship and trusteeship as well as of registration of births, marriages or deaths is determined by the legislation of the Union republic on whose territory the marriage has been concluded, adoption has been made, guardianship or trusteeship has been established, or a given birth, marriage or death has been registered.

Section 2. Marriage

ARTICLE IX

Entry into marriage.

Marriage is entered into at state registry offices for the civil registration of births, marriages and deaths.

Registration of marriage is established both in the interests of the state and society and with the aim of protecting the personal and property rights and interests of the partners and their children.

The rights and duties of the partners to a marriage are engendered only by marriage entered into at state registry offices for the registration of births, marriages and deaths.

A marriage is registered at least one month after the couple desirous of entering into marriage submit a form of application to a state registry office. In individual cases the legislation of union republics may provide for a reduction of this period.

Marriage is registered in a ceremonial atmosphere. The Registry Office ensures a festive atmosphere for the registration of marriages with the consent of the partners to the marriage.

ARTICLE X

Conditions of entry into marriage.

Entry into marriage demands the mutual consent of the persons entering into it and their achievement of the age of marriage.

The age of marriage is established at 18 years. The legislation of the Union republics may provide for a lowering of the age of marriage, but by not more than two years.

Marriage may not be entered into:

If either of the persons concerned is married;

Or between relatives in the line of ascent or descent, between full- or half-sisters and brothers, and also between adoptive parents and adoptive children;

Between persons either of whom has been recognised as incapable in law in consequence of mental disease or imbecility.

ARTICLE XI

Personal rights of partners to a marriage.

On entering into marriage, husband and wife are entitled to choose the surname of either of them as their joint surname or else either of the partners may keep his or her pre-marriage surname. Either may also add to his or her surname the surname of the other partner.

Questions of the education of children and other questions of family life are jointly resolved by husband and wife.

Each of the partners to a marriage is free in the choice of occupation, profession and place of residence.

ARTICLE XII

Property of husband and wife.

Property acquired by husband and wife during their marriage is their joint property. Husband and wife enjoy an equal right to possess, use and dispose of this property.

Husband and wife also enjoy equal rights to property if one of them has been engaged in running the household, taking care of the children, or has no independent earnings for valid reasons.

In the case of the division of jointly owned property, the share of each of the partners is recognised as equal to the other's share. In individual cases the court may depart from the principle of equality of shares of husband and wife on account of the interests of the children under age or the reasonable interests of either of the partners to the marriage.

Property belonging to either of the partners prior to their marriage or received by him or her during the marriage either as a gift or by inheritance is the property of the partner concerned.

The provisions of the present article extend only to that property of husband and wife who are members of a collective farm which comprises their personal property.

The right of husband and wife to own, use and dispose of the property of a collective farm is established by the legislation of the Union republics.

ARTICLE XIII
The duties of husband and wife in respect of mutual maintenance.

Husband and wife are obliged to maintain each other materially. In case of refusal to provide such maintenance, the disabled partner in need of material aid or the wife during pregnancy and in the course of one year after the birth of the child is entitled to receive maintenance from the other partner, this through a court, if that partner is in a position to provide that maintenance. This right is also preserved after dissolution of marriage.

A divorced husband or wife is also entitled to maintenance if he or she becomes disabled in the course of one year after dissolution of marriage. If a husband or wife have been in lengthy wedlock, a court is also entitled to award maintenance in favour of the divorced partner if the latter reaches the pensionable age not later than five years following the dissolution of marriage.

In individual cases, a husband or wife may be exempted from the duty of maintaining the other partner or that duty may be limited in time. The conditions in which a court may exempt a partner to a marriage from the duty of maintaining the other partner or to limit that obligation to a definite period is established by the legislation of the Union republics.

ARTICLE XIV
Termination of marriage.

A marriage is terminated in consequence of the death, or a court decision on the recognition of the death, of either of the partners to the marriage.

In the lifetime of the two partners, a marriage may be dissolved through divorce, by application of either or both of the partners.

A marriage is dissolved by a court. The court takes steps to reconcile the partners to a marriage.

A marriage is dissolved if it is established by a court of law that the further joint life of the partners and the preservation of their family have become impossible.

A husband is not entitled, without the consent of his wife, to apply for dissolution of their marriage during the pregnancy of the wife or in the course of one year after the birth of a child.

When dissolving a marriage, the court, when necessary, takes measures to protect the interests of children under age and of a disabled wife.

A husband and wife who do not have children under age may dissolve a marriage, by mutual consent, at a Registry Office. In these cases the divorce is registered and certificates on the dissolution of the marriage are handed out three months after the husband and wife have applied for a divorce.

The Registry Office also dissolves marriages in the case of persons:

Whose whereabouts are unknown, according to the rules established by law;

Who are incapacitated as a result of disease or imbecility, according to the rules established by law;

Who are sentenced for crimes with terms of imprisonment not less than three years;

Where disagreements arise over the dissolution of a marriage, these are settled by a court.

A spouse who takes the surname of the other spouse when entering into marriage has the right, after the dissolution of the marriage, to retain this surname or, on request, to revert to the pre-marriage surname.

ARTICLE XV
Non-validity of marriage.

A marriage may be recognised as non-valid in cases of infringement of the conditions set out in Article X of the present Basic Principles and also in cases of registration of marriage without the intention of creating a family (fictitious marriage). The recognition of the non-validity of a marriage is established by a court of law.

Recognition of non-validity of a marriage does not affect the rights of children born of such marriage. Other consequences of the recognition of the non-validity of a marriage are established by the legislation of the Union republics.

Section 3.The family

ARTICLE XVI
Basis of parents' and children's rights and duties.

Mutual rights and duties of parents and children are based on the origin of children certified according to procedures established by law.

The origin of a child from parents who are in wedlock is certified by the parents' marriage registration. The origin of a child of parents who are not in wedlock is established by the submission of a joint statement by the father and the mother of the child to state registry offices.

If a child is born to parents who are not in wedlock and in the absence of a joint statement from the parents, paternity may be established by a court of law.

In establishing paternity the court takes into consideration the fact of the mother of the child and the defendant having lived together and having conducted a joint household prior to the birth of the child, and also the joint upbringing or maintenance of the child by them both, or evidence authentically proving recognition of paternity.

ARTICLE XVII
Registration of parents in birth registers.

The mother and the father of a child who are in wedlock are registered as the child's parents in the register of births, following a statement of either of the two.

If the parents are not in wedlock, registration of the mother's child is carried out by statement of the mother, and registration of the child's father by a joint statement of the child's father and mother, or else the father is registered in accordance with a decision by a court of law.

In the case of a mother dying, or in the event of it being impossible to establish her place of residence, registration of the child's father is carried out on the basis of the father's statement.

If a child is born to an unmarried mother and if there is no joint statement by the parents or a court decision on the establishment of paternity, registration of the father of the child in the register of births is made in the mother's surname; the name and patronymic of the child's father are registered according to her instructions.

ARTICLE XVIII

Rights and duties of parents.

The father and the mother have equal rights and duties in respect of their children.

Parents must educate their children in the spirit of the moral code of a builder of communism, attend to their physical development, schooling and preparation for socially useful activities.

Parents are in duty bound to maintain their under-age children, and disabled children after their majority who are in need of their help.

The defence of the rights and interests of minors rests on their parents.

Parents are entitled to demand the return of their children from any person who has taken custody of the children without legal grounds or decision of a court.

Parents' rights cannot be given effect in contradiction of the interests of the children.

Parents also enjoy equal rights and bear equal duties in relation to their children in cases where the marriage has been dissolved. Disagreements between parents on questions relating to where the children are to live and be brought up are settled according to the legislation of the Union republics.

ARTICLE XIX

Deprivation of parental rights.

Both parents or either can be deprived of parental rights if it is established that they do not carry out their duties in bringing up their children, or abuse their parental rights, maltreat the children, exert a harmful influence on the children by their amoral and anti-social behaviour, and also if the parents are chronic alcoholics or drug addicts.

Court proceedings on the deprivation of parents of their rights are considered following an appropriate statement by state or social bodies, by either of the parents or by the guardian (or trustee) of the child, and also by action brought by a prosecutor.

If both parents are deprived of parental rights the child is placed in the care of guardianship and trusteeship institutions. A court may decide that a child be taken away and placed in the care of the above-named institutions, irrespective of the parents being deprived of their parental rights, if the child's remaining with the persons in whose care it is constitutes a danger to it.

Restoration of parental rights is permissible if the interest of the child requires it, or if the child has not been adopted.

Deprivation of parental rights and restoration of such rights can be effected only by a court of law.

Deprivation of parental rights does not exempt parents from their duties in maintaining their children.

ARTICLE XX
Children's duties in maintaining their parents.

Children who are majors are in duty bound to maintain their invalid parents who are in need of assistance.

Children may be exempted from their duties in maintaining their parents if the court establishes that the parents have disregarded their parental duties.

ARTICLE XXI
Duties of other members of a family in respect of maintenance.

If children who are minors are parentless, the duty of maintaining such children may be placed on other relatives – grandfather, grandmother, brother or sister, and also on the child's stepfather or stepmother.

The obligation of maintaining minors can also be placed on persons who have undertaken the regular education and maintenance of such children and later have refused to maintain them.

The obligation to maintain invalid members of a family who are majors but need assistance – should they be unmarried, or have neither parents nor children who are majors – can be placed on their grandchildren and also on stepsons and stepdaughters.

The obligation of maintaining majors who are invalids and need assistance can also be placed on persons who were previously regularly educated and maintained by the former.

The legislation of the Union republics may establish different conditions for obligations that arise in respect of maintenance than provided for by the present Article.

ARTICLE XXII
Amount of maintenance.

Maintenance for minors is paid by their parents in the following amounts: for one child, one-quarter; for two children, one-third, and for three or more children, one-half of the earnings (income) of the parents.

The size of these shares may be reduced by a court if a parent who is obliged to pay maintenance has other children who are minors and who, if maintenance is awarded in the proportion established by the present Article, will be placed in a worse material position than the children in receipt of maintenance, and also in the cases of the parent who pays the maintenance being an invalid of the first or second group, and also if the children are working and have sufficient earnings.

A court of law is entitled to reduce the amount of maintenance or exempt from payment of maintenance if the children are being fully maintained by a state or by a social body. Charges for the maintenance of children placed in children's institutions may be extracted from the parents of the children in favour of such institutions within the limits established in the present Article.

In individual cases, when exaction of maintenance as a share of the parents' earnings is impossible or difficult, the legislation of the Union republics may provide for the size of maintenance for minors to be established as a definite sum of money. The size of this sum is established on the basis of the parents' presumed earnings (income), proceeding from the principles set out above.

Parents paying maintenance for children under age may be made to bear additional expenditures due to exceptional circumstances (serious illness, crippling of a child, etc.).

The earnings (incomes) taken into account when deducting maintenance are fixed according to the rules established by the USSR Council of Ministers.

When parents pay maintenance for children who are majors but invalid and in need of help, and also in all other cases of funds being exacted for the purpose of maintenance, the amount of maintenance is established as a definite sum of money, on the basis of the material and family status of the person who pays maintenance and the person receiving it.

ARTICLE XXIII
Procedure for payment or exaction of maintenance.

Maintenance is paid in person voluntarily by the person obligated to pay maintenance or through the administration of his or her place of employment or where the pension or allowance is received.

Voluntary payment of maintenance does not preclude the right of the person in receipt of maintenance to go to court with a suit on the award of maintenance.

The administration of the enterprise, institution or organisation deducts maintenance monthly from the wages (pension, grant, stipend, etc.) of the payer of maintenance on the basis of a written statement from him or her, and pays out or remits the sum concerned to the person indicated in the statement.

ARTICLE XXIV
Adoption.

Adoption is permitted only in respect of children who are minor and in their interests.

Adoption is effected by decision of the executive committee of a district or city Soviet of Working People's Deputies, at the request of the person who desires to adopt a child.

For adoption the consent is required of parents who have not been deprived of parental rights, and also the consent of the adoptee, should the latter have reached the age of 10. The procedure for ascertaining a child's consent is established by the legislation of the Union republics.

If parents do not take part in the upbringing of a child, adoption may, as an exception, be effected without their consent. The procedure of adoption and the conditions required for it to be effected without the consent of the parents are established by the legislation of the Union republics.

If a child is adopted by a person who is married, and if the child is not adopted by both partners to a marriage, the consent of the other partner is required for adoption. The legislation of the Union republics establishes the conditions in which adoption, as an exception, may be effected without the consent of the other partner to a marriage.

Recognition of non-validity of adoption and cancellation of adoption are allowed only through a court of law.

The rules of adoption, the conditions for adoption to be recognised as non-valid, and the conditions for the cancellation of adoption, as well as the consequences of such cancellation, are established by the legislation of the Union republics.

The legislation of the Union republic establishes conditions to ensure adoption being kept secret.

ARTICLE XXV

The rights and duties of adopters, adoptees and their relatives.

Adoptees and their issue – this with regard to adopters and their relatives – and adopters and their relatives – this with regard to adoptees and their issue – have the same personal and property rights and obligations as relatives by birth.

Adoptees lose their personal and property rights and are exempt from their duties with regard to their parents and their relatives. In cases of the adoption of a child by one person these rights and duties may be preserved at the desire of the mother, if the adopter is a man, or at the desire of the father, if the adopter is a woman. Minors, who at the moment of adoption are entitled to a pension or grant from state or social bodies, this in connection with the loss of a breadwinner, preserve this right in the case of their being adopted.

At the request of adopters, the latter may be registered in the register of births as parents of the adoptees.

ARTICLE XXVI

Guardianship and trusteeship.

Guardianship and trusteeship are established for the upbringing of minors who, in consequence of the death of their parents, deprivation of parents of their parental rights, illness of the parents or other reasons, have remained without parental care, and also for the protection of the personal and property rights and interests of such children.

Guardianship and trusteeship are also established for the protection of the personal and property rights and interests of majors who, because of the condition of their health, cannot independently perform their rights and duties.

Guardianship and trusteeship are established by the executive committee of a district, city, settlement or village Soviet of Working People's Deputies.

The rights and duties of guardians and trustees and also the rules governing guardianship and trusteeship are established by the legislation of the Union republics.

Section 4. Acts of civil state

ARTICLE XXVII

Registration of births, deaths, marriage, dissolution of marriage, adoption, the establishment of paternity and changes of names, patronymics and surnames.

V*

Births, deaths, entry into marriage, dissolution of marriage, adoption, the establishments of paternity, and changes of names, patronymics and surnames must be registered at a state registry office.

ARTICLE XXVIII
Procedure for such registration to be disputed.

Rectification of errors and entries and changes in such registration – if given sufficient grounds exist and in the absence of dispute between the persons concerned – is effected by state registry offices.

The refusal of a state registry office to rectify or change an entry can be taken to court.

In the case of dispute between the persons concerned, rectification of entries is carried out on the basis of a court decision. Annulment of entries is allowed only by decision of a court.

ARTICLE XXIX
Registry books, Rules of registration.

The basic rules determining the procedure for modifying or restoring entries concerning civil status, as well as the make-up of registry books and the make-up of certificates issued on the basis of entries in such books and the procedure and terms of preservation of registry books are established by the Council of Ministers of the USSR.

The rules of registration of civil status, including ceremonial registration of marriages and births, as well as the rules of those entering into marriage informing each other about their state of health and family position, and on an explanation being given of their rights and duties as a future husband or wife and as parents, are established by the legislation of the Union republics.

Section 5. Application of Soviet legislation on marriages and the family in respect of foreigners and stateless persons resident in the USSR. Application of laws of foreign states governing marriage and the family, and also of international treaties and agreements.

ARTICLE XXX
Citizenship of children.

A child both of whose parents are citizens of the USSR at the moment of its birth is recognised as a citizen of the USSR, irrespective of the place of birth.

If the parents hold different citizenship and one of them is a citizen of the USSR at the moment of the child's birth, the child is recognised as a citizen of the USSR if at least one of the parents was resident on USSR territory at the time. If, however, both parents were resident outside the USSR at the moment of birth, the child's citizenship is established by agreement between the parents.

ARTICLE XXXI
Marriage between Soviet citizens and foreigners, and marriage between foreigners in the USSR.

Marriages between Soviet citizens and foreigners and also marriages between foreigners are concluded in the USSR in accordance with the general rules.

Entry of Soviet citizens into marriage with foreigners does not lead to any change of citizenship.

Marriages between foreigners entered into at embassies or consulates of foreign states in the USSR are recognised as valid in the USSR, given the condition of reciprocity, if, at the moment of marriage these persons are citizens of the state which has appointed the ambassador or consul.

ARTICLE XXXII

Marriages between Soviet citizens at USSR embassies or consulates, recognition of marriages entered into outside the USSR.

Marriages between Soviet citizens resident outside the USSR are concluded at embassies or consulates of the USSR.

In respect of a marriage or registration of other civil acts at USSR embassies and consulates abroad, the laws of the Union republic of whom the persons concerned are citizens are operative. If the persons concerned are citizens of different Union republics, or if it has not been established which republic they are citizens of, the laws of one of the Union republics, given consent between the partners, are applied; should any differences arise, the matter is decided by the official registering the event.

When marriages between Soviet citizens and marriages between Soviet citizens and foreigners are entered into outside the USSR, with due observance of the form of marriage established by the law of the place of its solemnisation, such marriages are recognised as valid in the USSR, if there are no obstacles to that marriage arising from Article X and XV of the present Basic Principles.

Marriages between foreigners performed outside the USSR according to the laws of the state concerned are recognised in the USSR.

ARTICLE XXXIII

Dissolution of marriages between Soviet citizens and foreigners and of marriage between foreigners in the USSR. Recognition of the dissolution of marriages performed outside the USSR.

Dissolution of marriages between Soviet citizens and foreigners and also between foreigners in the USSR is effected in accordance with the general rules.

Dissolution of marriages between Soviet citizens and foreigners performed outside the USSR in accordance with the laws of the states in question are recognised as valid in the USSR, if at the moment of dissolution of marriage at least one of the two partners was resident outside the USSR.

Dissolution of marriages between Soviet citizens performed outside the USSR in accordance with the laws of the states in question is recognised as valid in the USSR, if both partners were resident outside the USSR at the moment of dissolution of marriage.

Dissolution of marriage between foreigners effected outside the USSR and in accordance with the laws of the states in question is recognised as valid in the USSR. Soviet citizens permanently residing abroad have the right to dissolve their marriage in a USSR court.

ARTICLE XXXIV

Adoption of children of Soviet citizenship resident outside the USSR. Procedure of adoption of children by foreigners in the USSR.

Adoption of a child of Soviet citizenship and resident outside the USSR is effected at an embassy or a consulate of the USSR. If the adopter is not a Soviet citizen, the permission of the duly authorised body of the Union republic is required for adoption.

The adoption of a child of Soviet citizenship effected by bodies of the state on whose territory the child is resident, on condition of previous consent to such adoption being received from the duly authorised body of the Union republic, is also recognised as valid.

The regulations governing the adoption of children of Soviet citizenship by foreigners on the territory of the USSR are established by the legislation of the Union republics.

ARTICLE XXXV

Application of legislation of the USSR and of legislation of the Union republics governing marriage and the family, with reference to stateless persons.

Stateless persons resident in the USSR enter into marriage, dissolve marriages, enjoy the rights stemming from the legislation on marriage and the family, and bear the obligations provided for by such legislation on the same grounds as Soviet citizens.

ARTICLE XXXVI

Application of foreign laws and of international treaties and agreements.

Foreign laws on marriage and the family or recognition of registration of civil status based on such laws cannot take place if that application or recognition conflicts with the Basic Principles of the Soviet system.

If an international treaty or international agreement to which the USSR is a signatory establishes rules other than those contained in Soviet legislation on marriage and the family, the rules in that international treaty or international agreement shall be given effect.

The same principle is applied on the territory of a Union republic if the international treaty or international agreement to which the given Union republic is a signatory has established rules differing from those provided for by that Union republic's legislation on marriage and the family.

GLOSSARY

Anti-Party Group Applied to those who in 1957, tried to unseat Khrushchev. Molotov, Kaganovich, Malenkov, and Shepilov are among the best known individuals identified with it.

Apparat Apparatus, staff. The top officials of the CPSU or of the state.

Apparatchik A member of the apparatus: a Party functionary.

ASSR Autonomous Soviet Socialist Republic.

AUCCTU All-Union Central Committee of Trade Unions.

AUCECB All-Union Council of the Evangelical Christians and Baptists.

Bolsheviks Faction of Russian Social-Democratic Labour Party led by Lenin. In 1918 formed into Communist Party (Bolsheviks).

CCTU Central Council of Trade Unions.

COMECON Council of Economic Mutual Assistance. Formed in 1949 with the purpose of improving socialist economic co-operation. Membership includes the USSR, the socialist states of East Europe and Mongolia.

Cominform Communist Information Bureau. Established September 1947, abolished April 1956.

Comintern Communist International. 1919-43.

CPSU Communist Party of the Soviet Union (in Russian, KPSS).

Desyatina Measure of area: one desyatina equals 2.7 acres.

Duma Name of advisory assembly in Tsarist Russia. There were Town Dumas and the State Duma.

Edinonachalie One-man management.

Gorispolkom Executive Committee of a City (Town) Soviet.

Gorkom City Party Committee.

Gosbank State Bank.

Gosplan	State Planning Committee (Commission).
Hectare	Area equal to 10,000 square metres or 2.471 acres.
Ispolkom	Executive Committee.
KGB	Commitee of State Security.
Kolkhoz	Collective Farm. Co-operative form of agricultural production.
Komsomol	YCL. Young Communist League. (Full title – All-Union Communist League of Youth).
Kray	Territory. A large sparsely populated, administrative region.
Kraykom	Territorial Party Committee.
Kremlinology	A process of forecasting based on indexes of Soviet protocol (e.g. order of appearance of names).
Kulak	Rich Peasant.
Mensheviks	Non-Leninist faction of Russian Socialist Democratic Labour Party. Favoured trade-union type and de-centralised form of party.
Mestnichestvo	Localism, regionalism. Pursuit of local interests at the expense of national interests.
Mir	See Obshchina
MTS	Machine-Tractor Station. Until 1958 the government owned and operated MTS's which supplied the col-lectives with agricultural equipment.
MVD	Ministry of Internal Affairs.
Narodniki	Populists. Nineteenth century revolutionaries.
NEP	New Economic Policy. Practised by Bolsheviks between 1921 and 1928. Allowed limited private enterprise and trade.
NKGB	People's Commissariat of State Security.
NKVD	People's Commissariat of Internal Affairs.
Nomenklatura	Appointment list controlled directly or indirectly by the Party.
Oblast	Province, region.
Oblispolkom	Executive Committee of Province Soviet.
Obkom	Region or Province Party Committee.

Obshchenarodnoe gosudarstvo	State of the whole people. (Official description of the Soviet State since 1961).
Obshchina	A village community, a commune. (In Tsarist Russia).
Okrug	Area, district.
Politbureau	Supreme body of CPSU. Called Presidium between 1952 and 1966.
Partiynost	Party allegiance; party spirit.
Plenum	Full assembly of all members (e.g. of the Central Committee of the Communist Party).
Provisional Government	Established after abdication of Nicholas II and his brother in February 1917. Overthrown by Bolsheviks in October 1917.
Pud	Measure of weight equalling 36.1 British pounds.
Rayon	District; an administrative division of a region, territory, republic, or of a large city.
Rayispolkom	Executive Committee of District Soviet.
Raykom	District Party Committee.
RSFSR	Russian Soviet Federative Socialist Republic.
RTS	Tractor Repair Station.
Ruble	Official currency of the Soviet Union. In January, 1961, under a currency reform, ten of the 'old' rubles were exchanged for one of the 'new' rubles. At the current rate of exchange 1 ruble equals $1.11; and £1 equals 2.16 rubles. 1969.
Sovkhoz	State Farm. Organised on same principles as industrial enterprise.
Sovnarkom	Council of People's Commissars.
Sovnarkhoz	Council of National Economy. Established on a regional basis in May 1957.
USSR	Union of Soviet Socialist Republics.
USSR Council of Ministers	Highest executive and administrative branch in the Soviet Union. Has power to issue decrees and is subject to ratification by the Supreme Soviet.
USSR Presidium of the Supreme Soviet	Elected by the Supreme Soviet, the Presidium of the Supreme Soviet is in full power while the Supreme Soviet is not in session.

USSR Supreme
Soviet

The highest legislative body in the USSR. It consists
of two Houses, the Council (or Soviet) of the Union
and the Council (or Soviet) of Nationalities.

VSNKH
(Vesenkha)

Supreme Economic Council.

Zemstvo

Elected district council in pre-revolutionary Russia.

Index

Tsarism

1905–14 ; Duma, enterprise time
WWI →1918
1917 Revs
1918–22 CW War Comm
1924 : Trotsky, Stalin et. al.
1926 : Stalin
1930s Purges
WWII →1945
1945–53 late Stalin
1953–6 Troika ; Khrushchev, Molotov
           Malenkov
1956–64 Khrushchev
1964–6 Brezhnev, Kosygin
1966–82 Brezhnev
1982–84 Andropov
1984 – Chernenko